In appreciati   he

Alumni a.

D1098131

The
Sons of
Brigham

Front view of the Education Building (*1895*)

The Sons of Brigham

By T. Earl Pardoe

Published by
Brigham Young University
Alumni Association

Lithographed by

DESERET NEWS PRESS

in the United States of America

Dedication

This book is affectionately dedicated to the more than a hundred thousand Alumni who supported a struggling academy to the present affluent university.

Their devotion to the ideals taught and practiced on the campus has carried into their lives, giving to the country and church men and women who have become national and international leaders.

The first two principals and the five subsequent presidents have each contributed to the growth and strength of the institution adding their own individual abilities to the spiritual foundation early inculcated in the faculty and student body.

The tributes paid in this volume are similar to others which could be written, of equal importance in many ways. To them we pay honor and praise.

To all who will strive to keep the standards of BYU and share them with the world, we pay special homage.

Foreword

This book is written to express gratitude for the many men who planned, initiated and stayed with an embryo university to its promising maturity. To answer all the questions involved in its evolution would require several volumes.

As I asked the question "Who were the men who contributed to its inception and growth from a training school and academy to a university?" I first gleaned some two hundred names worthy of attention. It became evident that more than one volume would be necessary to do justice to these men and the subject.

The division of material was not a difficult problem. The very short period of principalship by Warren N. Dusenberry which was soon terminated by the advent of Principal Karl G. Maeser easily started my first section. The other divisions fall under the presidencies of Benjamin Cluff, Jr., George H. Brimhall, Franklin S. Harris and Howard S. McDonald. The students and faculty who have come under the leadership of President Ernest L. Wilkinson open up another remarkable era and should be ready for print at the first opportunity. President Wilkinson himself is written up as a student under George H. Brimhall.

I have had the pleasure of intimately knowing all the men selected except Karl G. Maeser and Benjamin Cluff, whom I met several times but not to become as closely associated as the others. The difficult part of the book is the genealogical portion. I have long believed that ancestry is a vital part of a man's life and should be shown as a background for any biographer. It has been easier to obtain genealogy of the deceased than for many of the living and I have had to do considerable research to acquire some portions of this information. When incomplete, it is not the desire or lack of effort on the part of the author. Some of the living men selected for this volume did not furnish family data and accordingly are not presented.

Most of the material used has been approved by the individual biographer or by a close relative and has been of immeasurable assistance.

A Brigham Young University "Who's Who" would show many men not here written up. The struggle to keep the school operative is a heroic tale and only the revealed lives of some of these educational pioneers could adequately tell this story. As stated in my brochure "Events and buildings are chiefly the products of men; the evolution of the B.Y. Academy to a world-renowned University relates stories of sacrifice and loyalty seldom matched by any similar institution."

When the university was taken over by the General Authorities of the Church it immediately assumed the stature of an important institution of national promise. It has become world renowned. "A university is as great as its Alumni" is a challenge which has been met by the former students and faculty of the Brigham Young University.

The biographies have been presented in alphabetical order for easy reference, divided by time of attendance and association with the respective principals and presidents.

Emphasis of selection adhered to this time period: all alumni who studied and/or taught with Doctor Maeser are presented in the first section and the other subjects follow this pattern.

The index covers both names and subject matter for further use of reference.

The different formats used in a few instances reflects the material from which each biography is fashioned. My biggest regret in writing the book is the result of being limited to a reasonable space in order to accommodate a greater number in this first volume.

Cornerstone ceremony for the Maeser building (*probably 1909*)

Acknowledgments

Most of the biographies in this volume are presented from materials furnished by living Alumni of Brigham Young University. When the subject is deceased, the next of kin has been approached for genealogical assistance. Some deceased members have excellent references in the following books: "Pioneers and Prominent Men of Utah" by Frank Esshom, covering a period of those pioneers who came to Utah before the railroad and of prominent men after the coming of the railroad to 1913. Pictures in this book of each man are excellent. "History of Utah" by Orson F. Whitney in four volumes, illustrated, published in 1904, presented in convenient groups, such as pioneers, congressmen, journalists, lawyers, etc. A stupendous work of fourteen years research. "Church Chronology" and "Historical Record" by Andrew Jenson, the former a series of brief notes of people and events and the latter with detailed articles of various historical, biographical and chronological matter. "History of Utah Since Statehood" by Noble Warrum in four volumes, 1920; "L.D.S. Biographical Encyclopedia," four volumes, also by Andrew Jenson, 1920-1936; "Provo, Pioneer Mormon City" a compilation of 1942; various brochures and books of individual biography as noted in the respective writeups. The L.D.S. Church Historian's Office in Salt Lake City has been most helpful in supplying specific genealogical dates. The Archives of the J. Reuben Clark Library at BYU and the film library have been visited the past five years. Newbern I. Butt and Hollis Scott have given especial interest and service.

Diaries of the various persons selected have been invaluable and noted in their biographies.

"History of Brigham Young University" is a compilation of historic materials by J. Marinus Jensen, N. I. Butt, Elsie C. Carroll and Bertha Roberts, as a committee appointed by President F. S. Harris, 1942, is most helpful for reference. "Tullidge's Quarterly Magazine" in the 1880's presented several BYU personalities.

Personal interviews supply most of the material for the book and several who shared information regretfully are not presented in this first volume.

The Alumni Association has been the driving force back of the project, especially the executive directors, Ray E. Beckham and Ronald G. Hyde and past Emeritus President George H. Higgs. Jack D.

Blodgett of the Deseret News Press offered valuable help in the printing of this volume. Ernest L. Olson, chairman of University publications gave special help in reading the manuscript, as did Earl E. Olson of the Church Historian's office. Valuable material was also taken from the *Deseret News, Tribune,* and *Provo Daily Herald.*

CONTENTS

Fletcher, Harvey
Fletcher, James Chipman
Glade, Earl J.
Gourley, David
Hafen, Leroy Reuben
Hafen, Orval
Hales, Wayne Brockbank
Harris, Franklin Stewart
Higgs, Brigham Thomas
Higgs, Geoge Henry
Hill, George Richard, Jr.
Hinckley, Robert Henry
Hoyt, Harrison Val
Jensen, Christen
Johnson, J. Edward
Kirkham, Oscar Ammon
Kirkham, Francis Washington
Knudsen, Vern Oliver
Larsen, Bent F.
Lund, Anthony C.
Madsen, Arch Leonard
Markham, Fred L.
Marshall, Milton
Martin, Thomas Lysons
Maw, Charles E.
Merrill, Amos N.
Miller, Albert
Nicholes, Joseph Kelly
Nuttall, Leonard John II
Osmond, Alfred
Partridge, E. De Alton
Rasmussen, Andrew Theodore
Richards, Alma Wilford
Roberts, Eugne Lusk
Robertson, Leroy Jasper
Robinson, James William
Rowe, Edward Morris
Russell, G. Oscar
Sauer, Robert
Snow, William James
Swenson, Lyman Knut

Tanner, Vasco Myron
Taylor, Harvey L.
Taylor, Henry D.
Tietjen, Henry Roland
Wahlquist, John T.
Watkins, Arthur Vivien
Widtsoe, John Andreas
Wilkinson, Ernest L.
Wilson, David J.

Franklin Steward Harris (1921-1945)
Ballif, Ariel Smith, Sr.
Beckham, Raymond Earle
Booth, Wayne Clayson, Jr.
Bradford, Reed Howard
Butt, Newbern Isaac
Christensen, A. Sherman
De Jong, Gerrit, Jr.
Evans, Oakley Spencer
Garrett, Joseph Earl
Hutchings, Imri Joseph
Lewis, BEn Elden
Lloyd, Wesley Parkinson
Merrill, Harrison Reuben
Moffitt, John Clifton
Mortimer, George Harding
Nelson, Lowry
Nibley, Hugh W.
Olpin, Albert Ray
Peterson, Chesley Gordon
Richards, Lynn Stephen
Robinson, Oliver Preston
Romney, Marion George
Sauls, Kiefer B.
Thorn, Grant S.
Thorn, Paul A.
Wilson, Owen Meredity

Howard S. McDonald (1945-1949)
McDonald, Howard S.

Warren N. Dusenberry

(1875-1876)

Principal Warren N. Dusenberry (*Nov. 22, 1875—April 15, 1876*)

ORIGINAL TWENTY-NINE STUDENTS OF 1876 who registered on the first day.

Olive Smoot Bean
Hannah Billings Booth
Mary Jane John Cluff
Sarah Eggertsen Cluff
Minerva Jones Dailey
S. P. Eggertsen
Mary Roberts Farret
Alma Greenwood
Mary Nielson Hansen
Jonathan L. Harvey
Rose McEwan Haws
Hannah Stubbs Jones—the
    last survivor
Joseph B. Keeler
Marietta Riggs Beesley Kehl
Rachel Ferre McEwan
Caddie Daniels Mills
Alice Smoot Newell
Fannie Rogers
Rose Moore Searle
Electa Bullock Smoot
Reed Smoot—the first to register
Thomas Stradling
Emma Stubbs Taylor
Louisa Bean Thompson
John J. Walton
Andrew Watson
Zina Smoot Whitney
Martha John Williams
Diantha Billings Worsley

I
II

Men who studied with or under

Karl G. Maeser

(1876-1892)

Principal Karl G. Maeser (*April 24, 1876—Jan. 4, 1892*)

LEWIS ROBERT ANDERSON

(Class, 1891-2)

Born: March 26, 1872 **Place:** Fountain Green, Utah

Father: Lewis Anderson; born October 24, 1850, at Hackeberga, near Malmo, Sweden; son of Andrew and Anna Christina Olson. The family moved to Utah Aug. 29, 1859, in the James S. Brown Co. Took family to Fountain Green. Served two missions after marriage. Member of the Constitutional Convention. Managed the successful Central Utah Wool Co., organized the Manti Live Stock Co., and engaged in sheep and cattle business with his sons, L. R., and T. J., and R. E. L. Kenner. President of Manti City Savings Bank. With Anthon K. Lund he organized the first Republican Party in Sanpete County. President of the Manti Temple for twenty-seven years and President of the South Sanpete Stake for nineteen years to be succeeded by his son, L. R.

Mother: Mary Ann Crowther; married November 14, 1870. Born May 7, 1851, in Tipton Shropshire, England, the daughter of Thomas and Sarah Thompson. With parents came to America when three and a half years old. Mother died in St. Louis, leaving Mary Ann motherless. Thomas drove ox team across the plains to Salt Lake City, September, 1855. After marriage, Mary Ann served in Manti Temple for twenty-seven years.

Brothers and Sisters: (Lewis R.); Thomas Jefferson, born April 4, 1874, married Eliza Westenskow; Etta, born August 18, 1880, married Peter A. Poulson; Sarah Jane, born January 14, 1883, married Erastus Westenskow; Mary Mabel, born March 3, 1887, married George R. Taylor; Joseph Franklin, born May 17, 1890.

Marriage: Clara Maria Munk, December 11, 1895. Daughter of Peter Mikkel Munk of Bornholm, (an island) who came to Utah in 1853 when nine years of age with the first company from Scandanavia. Peter lived to be 101 and married Eunice Ann Brown March 13, 1851.
Clara taught school before marriage and became President of the local Daughters of the Utah Pioneers.

Children: R. Clair, L. Glen, Elliot A., Lucile, married Clark Keller, Eunice married Waldo Garbe, Mary married Earl Sorenson.

Died: Oct. 19, 1968.

1

To know Lewis R. Anderson is to know his illustrious father and pioneer grandfather. I know of no son who built better on his paternal foundation than Lewis R. Each served successful LDS Missions in tumultuous territories, each was President of the South Sanpete Stake for many years, each rounded out a life of Church devotion by becoming President of the Manti Temple.

The son carried on the several business ventures of his energetic father, extending their territories and values. The father had six children. Lewis R. was the eldest and had seven children, six of whom are living.

Lewis R. served a two-year mission in the Southern States, being a Counselor to President Ben E. Rich for twenty months. He wrote several of the letters sent by President Rich to his good friend, President Theodore Roosevelt, which led the Nation's President to request U.S. attorneys to prosecute the mobocrats who threatened the civil liberties of the Mormons. He has served his adult life in various services of his Church, being one of the State's first supporters and promoters of the Boy Scout program. He was President of the Bryce Canyon Council and was awarded the Silver Beaver in 1933, the second man to be so honored by the Utah National Parks Council. For fifteen years he was President of the South Sanpete Stake and President of the Manti Temple for sixteen years.

Elected Mayor of Manti for three terms, he was also Speaker of the House in the Utah Legislature, past President of the Snow College Board of Directors and member of the Board of Regents of the University of Utah, on the State Sheep Commission for eight years, ten years on the State Land Board, and Food Administrator for Sanpete County during World War I. In 1920 he was a delegate to the Republican National Convention.

In business he has expanded in many interests. For fifty years he was representative of the great Boston Wool Pools in Utah and other Western States. He has been a director in the Anderson-Taylor Co. Wholesale Grocers, Anderson-Dyreng Furniture and Hardware Co., and Director and Vice President of the Manti City Bank. During the depression eastern credit was extended to his wool holdings on his own name and established character. He was a moderate man of great power, basing all his acts upon consideration of others.

Now, at age ninety-five, he still acts as adviser in his son's business and his own holdings, keeps abreast of world events, and serves his State and Church as occasion demands. He believes that the United States will survive the present world unrest as the people revalue their liberties and return to the fundamental principles and rights which framed and shaped the foundation of our republic.

ALFRED LEWIS BOOTH

Born: June 17, 1864   **Place:** Alpine, Utah

Father: Richard Thornton Booth
b. August 21, 1822 of Welsh origin, at Gurton, Lancashire, England
Came to Utah with Jessie B. Martin Co., September 12, 1857.
Known as a good singer.

Mother: Elsie Edge
b. Dec. 21, 1826 at Bedford, Lancashire, England
daughter of John and Sara Davis
m. August 13, 1846 in Bedford
First Primary teacher and president in Alpine, Utah until death
One of her songs used at dedication of Salt Lake Temple
d. July 10, 1893

Brothers and Sisters: See John E. Booth biography
Alfred Lewis was the 8th child in a family of six sons and four daughters.

Marriage: (1) May Ashworth of Beaver, Utah, on May 12, 1900 daughter of William Booth Ashworth of Lancashire, England
d. Oct. 10, 1913. Her children, Editha and Leona (Mrs Lowell White)

(2) Edith Young, daughter of Oscar B. Young and granddaughter of Brigham Young, on June 23, 1915. Sister of Dr. Kimball Young.

Children: Edith had one son, Thornton Young Booth, Ph.D. Daughters, Virginia, m. Wendell Allred, Margery m. Donald Neville, and Phyllis Elsie m. Carlos Phillips.

Death: June 3, 1947

Alfred was born just eight years after the settlement of Alpine, where the Booth's had pioneered. The parents were staunch members of the Weslyan Methodist Church in England, but the father accepted the Gospel soon after it had been preached to him. The mother took months of study and prayer before acceptance. The father was not a graduate physician but served for thirty years as an Alpine family doctor with no set fees or regular charges. "Just what you want to pay or what is right." It was usually two dollars for bringing a baby into the world, in which he was most successful. The mother taught a ten week's summer school for children, taking produce for pay for the most part. The best books available were bought for the Booth home even at the expense of clothing, and the contents were discussed in family groups. When the Booths sailed from Liverpool, England, they had four small children and crossed the plains in two wagons pulled by two yoke of oxen.

Alfred L. had his first ride on a railroad when he went to Provo to attend the Brigham Young Academy in 1879. The school was occupying the remodeled Lewis Building on Center Street. He saw the building enlarged in 1882 and was a student when the building burned to the ground in a cold winter in 1884; he helped to move books and furniture to the old ZCMI building near the railroad tracks. The train whistle was very disconcerting to the students from out in the country who saw and heard their first train after they had arrived in Provo. If a person were praying at devotional and the whistle blew the train's approach to the depot, as it frequently did, the prayer was delayed for the interim and resumed when attention was possible, all keeping their heads bowed. President Maeser had his office on the balcony and could look down on most of the activity of the building, helping to improve the deportment of the steadily growing studentbody. With the moving of the school to the foot of First Street, the thoroughfare was soon named "Academy Avenue."

By 1886, Alfred graduated with a Normal Certificate and pre-pared for school teaching. He taught a summer term over at Alpine with eight grades and thirty pupils, receiving $30.00 a month salary. "I learned about life from them," he said. He then taught mathematics at BYA for six years under Dr. Maeser and was very proud when four of his children received degrees at the institution and the other two had one year of instruction each.

He was a charter member and president of the Polysophical Society at BYA, where the best literature, lives of great men, and significant events were presented and discussed. He stated that it was the best part of his education, as Dr. Maeser, James E. Talmage, Benjamin Cluff Jr., George H. Brimhall, Susa Y. Gates, Ed S. Hinckley and other leaders presented subjects after months of study and followed the presentation with a free and open discussion by all present.

In Alfred's diary he writes that he taught trigonometry, surveying, rhetoric and logic. For the year 1889-91, he was registrar at BYA and in 1898-99 he was president of the Alumni Association. He was assistant superintendent of the Model Sunday School in the Academy for 1893-94. Techniques developed there were given to the Church.

In May of 1890 he was made Provo City surveyor when the young city was expanding and the streets were being laid out and roads extended. Many of the streets were but cow trails which Alfred had so enthusiastically criticized that he accepted the proffered position as a challenge. He found many pieces of land improperly filed, some of the tenants encroaching on the street properties. Much of the land was subject to legal challenge. He voluntarily advised the owners what to do to protect their rights and property. He knew from memory the owners of almost all land within the Provo municipal boundaries. He strove to get the city to buy and own strategic land for recreation purposes and insisted on wide streets for the traffic that would some day come.

He was made Deputy County School Superintendent and assistant in the Utah Stake Sunday School, which encompassed all of Utah County. Travel was done in a buggy, surrey or on horseback in all kinds of weather.

In 1893, Alfred L. passed the bar examinations and was admitted to the bar in Provo. His colleagues in court said of him that he was one of the most logical thinkers they had ever met and his cases were presented so systematically that the court or opposing attorneys had no occasion to challenge his statements for clarity. He was an omnivorous reader, scanning rapidly with excellent recall. No man was ever turned away from his legal office for lack of funds, but Alfred had to have confidence in his client before he agreed to take his case. He avoided defending a criminal unless appointed by the Court to do so. He was a natural peace maker and settled many disputes out of court.

In 1894, he went to Great Britain for an LDS mission. The fare to England, he notes, was $63.50. He was set apart by Apostle Heber J. Grant and was soon associate editor of the British *Millennial Star*. (His son Thornton had the same privilege in 1937.) When he returned to Provo, he became a partner with his brother, Judge John Edge Booth. He was Provo's Justice of the Peace in 1896-98, member of Provo's Board of Education in 1897-1900, City Attorney 1902-04, City Councilman 1904-08, and in the State Senate 1911-1914. He was interim Provo City Judge until his death. He formed a partnership with Attorney Isaac E. Brockbank, who had married his niece, Elsie. Isaac said of him, "A. L. Booth built stepping stones not stumbling blocks." He was assistant County Attorney 1926-28, Deputy County Attorney, 1930-33.

Church work and civic affairs consumed his time up to his death on June 3, 1947. His Alumni Distinguished Service citation stated, "a wise teacher, an honest lawyer, a model citizen, a man who sees through clear eyes and always with a saving sense of humor." President Franklin D. Roosevelt awarded him for his patriotic service the Certificate of Appreciation on January 19, 1943.

The Utah Bar Association eulogized him as few of their colleagues have ever been so honored and cited traits of his character such as "A man of unimpeachable integrity, certain of his divine destiny and convinced of the immortality of his soul . . . a friend, wholesome counselor and a good servant."

He resembled Abraham Lincoln more in character than in physique, but on one occasion when I made him up for a patriotic program, his tall, gangling frame, bushy eyebrows and dark steady eyes needed no plug hat to complete the illusion; his fund of humorous stories kept his eyes atwinkle, honesty beamed from his kindly face, and quotes from Lincoln revealed his intimate acquaintance with the man who was his political ideal.

He was one of Brigham's great sons and sincere patriots.

JOHN EDGE BOOTH

Born: June 29, 1847   **Place:** Bedford Leigh, Lancashire, England

Father: Richard Thornton Booth
d. May 27, 1888 in Alpine, Utah, after residence of 30 years
Came to Utah in an old time sailing vessel "George Washington" to Boston in 22 days
Crippled as a boy in a mill—Self educated, learned French and Hebrew

Mother: Elsie Edge (See biography of Alfred Lewis Booth)

Brothers and Sisters: Father and Mother sailed with 4 children
1. (John Edge)
2. James Davis—at 27 unmarried
3. Martha Hannah, m. Ebenezer Hunter
4. Sarah Jane "Jennie," m. James R. Lane
5. Robert Ebenezer, born on the way to Utah, m. Lorinia Chipman
   In 1858, with threat of Johnston's Army, moved to Alpine (called Mountainville). Sold wagon to Porter Rockwell for $50.00 and bought land
6. Margaret, m. Christopher Charles Hackett b. 1859 in Alpine
7. Richard Thornton Jr.
8. Alfred Lewis (see his biography)
9. Joseph Wilford, m. Rebecca Moyle
10. Merry May, m. James E. Talmage

Marriage:
(1) Maria Josephine Harvey, Oct. 11, 1873
daughter of Lewis and Lucinda, pioneers of 1851
Children: Josephine, m. Lloyd J. Woodruff
Vienna H., m. Ernest Kimball
Hannah Rowena, m. H. A. Cowans
Richard H. (born while John Edge was on mission and his wife died)
(2) Hannah Billings, 1876—died without issue
(3) Delia I. Winters
Children: James Milton, m. Cora Lewis
Delilah M. m. S. C. Adams
Elsie V., m. I. E. Brockbank
Edwin Winters, m. Matilda Ellis

Died: March 28, 1920

John E. Booth attended school in England to his ninth year. He was a tall thin boy with black eyes and "a mop of black hair," quick of action and very strong for one so young. He was ten years of age when his parents and the small family braved the watery journey over a stormy Atlantic and the unknown dangers on the plains of the West. Being the eldest child and having a handicapped father, John E. took over much of the heavy work.

No sooner had the Booths reached Salt Lake than the Saints were threatened by a United States Army. Its coming and purpose was not certain, and the Booths had heard gruesome tales of Missouri and Nauvoo. Orders for the move South were given and the impecunious family again packed their meager belongings and joined the Salt Lake exodus, going to a little valley north and east of American Fork. There they dug out an open cave in the hillside, felled the trees from the nearby canyon, framed a house and lean-to, put sand on the floors, built tables and chairs, and began to till the nearby soil. While others returned to Salt Lake Valley, the Booths remained in Alpine, then known as Mountainville. The neighbors called them "Mountain-villians," so they selected a name more to their liking.

John E. herded sheep until 1860 for $8.00 a month with board. Half of the pay in wheat at $2.00 a bushel went to his father. With the rest he bought clothes, his first pair of boots, a fiddle and a lamb. "The boots wore out, I sold the fiddle, and the lamb died," he said. The Booth children went to their parents' Alpine School and evening Mutual Improvement classes until 1866. At this time John E. was a volunteer in the Black Hawk War on the Sevier River for 75 days. With Indian attacks breaking out in unprotected places, the inhabitants of Alpine were ordered to Salt Lake. But the residents of Alpine built a barricade that they might remain in their homes.

It was but a few miles down Alpine canyon to Draper in Salt Lake County, and in 1868 John E. was a student of John R. Park, one of the west's best educators. In 1869-70 he enrolled as a student of the University of Deseret in Salt Lake. In 1870-71 he taught a full course of subjects in the Bountiful High School. But he craved a deeper insight into mathematics, so he moved to Provo, teaching and studying in the Timpanogos University, a branch of the University of Deseret with Warren H. Dusenberry. It was not long until he was studying law at night under John B. Milner and in 1875 was admitted to practice law before the Utah bar. Wherever he went he was accepted as a leader. As a lawyer he believed a man very much innocent until proved guilty. Money was not a criterion for his accepting a case for the court. His colleagues stated that he enthusiastically enjoyed defending the innocent. He was appointed city attorney for Provo in 1875 and was a city counselor from 1876-1882.

Judge Booth took great pride in the fact that he was a prime mover in getting a university in Provo and was most happy when Karl G. Maeser assigned him the chair of mathematics at the new Brigham Young Academy. He taught civil government and law at the Academy for many years without pay—(1886-1920). Some of the best legal minds of the state got their inspiration and start from Judge John E. Booth.

In 1876 he joined W. B. Pace in revising the Provo City ordinances and supervised their publication. In 1877 he joined E. A. Wilson, working with him for four years. In 1880 he was appointed court commissioner by the Utah Legislature for auditing the accounts of jurors and witnesses for the First Judicial Court. By 1881 he was District Prosecuting Attorney for this district and in August was elected to the House of Representatives on the Peoples Party. He also became a director of the First National Bank of Provo. In April of 1882 he assisted in forming the State Constitution for the proposed State of Deseret. He almost memorized the United States Constitution before working on this assignment. "The world must know that the Constitution governs the Mormon social and political life," he stated.

The Church used most of his time in the 1880's, and he was released from a mission to become the mayor of Provo (2 years) and also the president of the school board (4 years). For the State he was a member of the Territorial Board of Equalization and Taxes and in 1892 was appointed for a four year term. In the year 1899, he was appointed as Judge of the Fourth District Court to fill the unexpired term of Warren H. Dusenberry and was re-elected in 1900.

We learn from the family and some of his intimate friends that the Judge kept many college students in school, letting them work for their board and for some paying their tuition. He accepted no student notes, but if they borrowed he expected them to pay when they could, telling them, "Your word is better than your note."

He drew up the papers of many of the young Utah County enterprises and was president of the Western Union and Blue Cliff Canal Company; a director of the Provo Woolen Mills, and the Provo Lumber and Building Co.; vice-president of the Provo Building and Loan, one of the most helpful builders of homes in the West; vice-president of the Taylor Paper Company, now discontinued.

As time advanced he spent most of his life for the Church and his family and was a very popular political and funeral speaker. He spoke many times to BYU audiences and was one of the first to talk to an assembly in "Room D" in the Education Building. He was a frequent visitor with Karl G. Maeser who honored his judgment.

Of the many anecdotes we could relate of his life the following is typical: George Sutherland and Judge John E. were political rivals for the mayoralty of Provo. At a political rally in the old Opera House on First West Street, a heckler yelled out "How can you be a mayor living in a little dobey house?" The next night the same heckler asked again "Ain't you gonna answer about that house?" Black eyes flashed and sharp words flew, "If a bed bug bites you, you don't bite it back, do you?" The answer spread over the town and John E. was elected by a good majority.

He served the Fourth Ward as its bishop for eighteen years, 1878-95. He was twice mission president to the Northern States, 1883-84 and 1889-90. His partnership with his brother, A. L., "Booth and Booth" lasted until his death.

When I first saw Judge Booth, I thought he must be a Kentucky colonel, with his black hair, heavy moustache and sharp goatee which started from his lip. He walked with a long stride as if he must get somewhere soon; his smile flashed over his face and was quickly gone. His sister-in-law, Edith Young Booth, wrote of his life a revelatory tribute, "The Pioneer Attorney," which gives many facts gleaned for this biography. Noble Warrum in his "Utah Since Statehood" calls him "Honorable John Edge Booth" and concludes his biography, "In the practice of his profession he has ever recognized the fact that the lawyer and Judge not only mete out justice but also have it within their power to extend the higher attributes of mercy and call to life the good that lies dormant in every individual."

Many B.Y.U. students and Provo citizens call him Blessed.

WILLIAM HENRY BOYLE, JR.

Born: October 19, 1874, Santaquin, Utah

Father: Wm. Henry Boyle, son of Henry Green Boyle of West Virginia and Keziah D. Holliday, b. February 19, 1851, Ogden, Utah Family home in Santaquin, Utah
Member Board of Education 9 years and City Council

Mother: Mary Jane Ewell, m. December 24, 1869, Santaquin, Utah daughter of Wm. Thos. Ewell and Polly Lea
b. February 5, 1849
Father died at Council Bluffs, Iowa and Mary Jane's mother walked across the plains with a family of six, the youngest being Mary Jane, six weeks of age

Brother and Sisters: Mary Keziah, b. Dec. 13, 1870, m. B. D. Harper
Sousa Louisa, b. Jan. 30, 1873, m. W. B. Thurman (Wm. H.)
Lydia Ann, b. Aug. 11, 1876 m. John F. Harris
Emma Jane, b. July 18, 1878 m. George H. Chatwin
James Hollis, b. Mar. 5, 1883, d. April 15, 1883
Leona Pearl, b. Mar. 6, 1893, m. Flint C. Dixon

Marriage: Minnie Wright, b. in Nephi, Utah, September 10, 1880 m. September 3, 1902, daughter of John Sydney Wright and Ida Ann Norton of Nephi, Utah (Wright from England)

Children: Melva B. m. Laurence S. Hutchings; resides in Salt Lake City
Wilma S. m. Bertell Bunker; resides in Salt Lake City
Dr. William Sidney Boyle, m. Rowena Christensen, Logan, Utah

Died: Thurs. March 18, 1965 at age 90 in Provo

William Henry Boyle was schooled at Santaquin and went to BYA when he was seventeen years of age with money he had saved by working in the mines and hauling lumber. "The work gave me muscles and a big appetite," he said. He studied under Karl G. Maeser for the last three months at the old Z.C.M.I. Building and marched to the new grounds, cleared by faculty and students.

He mustered up courage and told the new principal, Benjamin Cluff, Jr. of his financial troubles. Mr. Cluff had him take care of cows and chickens, chop wood and keep lawn cut, telling him, "You can board with us, but we have no place to sleep." Prof. McKendric loaned him a bed out of his loft, and he slept in a small room in the academy. He studied in Room D. Later he batched with other boys going to school.

1893—took position of teaching at Scipio, Utah, on a temporary certificate.

1894—taught at Juab, Utah, a place which was also a rail terminal, with better salary, Taught 8 grades in a one room house and had two 8th grade graduates in spring.

1895—principal, school at Levan

1898—mission to Southern States, where his grandfather, Henry G. Boyle, had filled 13 missions and was first president of the mission.

1900—August, entered BYA for one year

1901—teacher of 8th grade in Nephi, Utah, 2 years

1903—given job as principal of the sub High School at BYA.

1910—principal secondary training school BYU to 1926

1926—on staff in College of Education as assistant professor

1933—associate professor

1933—appointed to State Board of Insanity for 1 year, and appointed for seven years more by Governor Blood

On committee for formulating State Liquor Law (12 members) at 71—joined staff at State Mental Hospital as Family Counselor and psychiatric social worker—felt he gave greatest service here.

1936—Professor of Education, carried full load in college until 71 years of age

1945—Professor Emeritus—taught part time

25 years Chairman of Counseling Committee and a member 35 years

At Nephi he met, loved and married vivacious Minnie Alice Wright. When they moved to Provo, they rented a place for $6.00 per month. Later they bought a home on 7th North and 2nd East. They lived for six years in that home then bought a home on North University which was his home until death. In this home they reared their family. All the children went through BYU from kindergarten to college graduation.

William received his A.B. (1913) and M.A. (1923) at BYU and continued a year of graduate work at USC and two summer schools at Berkeley. He taught at Juarez Academy in summer school, and was under five BYU presidents, Cluff, Brimhall, Harris, McDonald and Wilkinson.

William was an omnivorous reader in early and middle age. Students and friends came to him for advice which he gave gratuitously. He had many speaking engagements and wrote many 30 minute sermonettes. He was on the stake high council for many years and for twelve years he was advanced Gospel teacher in his own ward.

A devotee of good drama, he played "David Garrick" with Miriam Nelke, teacher of dramatic arts, while at BYU.

At 90 years of age, he wrote as health permitted, wrote a daily diary, and kept abreast of the times by conversation with his vivacious wife, Minnie. He received friends for short visits. His active mind embraced the major part of BYU's history, as he was connected with the school for more than sixty years and served on most of the major committees. Students with problems of deportment, homesickness, companion difficulties, poor attendance were sent to Prof. Boyle for advice and counsel, often going to his office in tears, but usually leaving with smiles and renewed determination. He will long be remembered as Counselor Boyle.

13

GEORGE HENRY BRIMHALL

Born: December 9, 1852   **Place:** Salt Lake City, Utah

Father: George Washington Brimhall; son of Sylvanus, born November 14, 1814 in South Fremont, Oneida County, New York. He came to Utah in 1849. He assisted in the erection of the Nauvoo Temple and in locating the settlement of Parowan. He was one of the pioneer musicians in Utah. He first settled in Ogden, Utah, then later moved to Spanish Fork in 1865, as builder, farmer and musician. He first married Lucretia Metcalf, who remained in the East, their home being in Galesburg, Illinois. Children: Rufus, Mary and Sylvanus.

Mother: Rachel Ann Mayer (second wife), born February 9, 1829, daughter of George Mayer and Ann Yost of Nauvoo. Married February 2, 1852 in Salt Lake City, Utah.

Brothers and Sisters: (George H.), Rachel Emma (Robertson), Emer M., Orilla M. (Boyack), Omer M., Ruth R., Prudence M., Ether Record, Tryphena M. (Garff), Grace M. (Calderwood).

Marriage: (1) Alsina Elizabeth Wilkins of Spanish Fork, Utah; married December 28, 1874; children: Lucy Jane, m. J. Will Knight; Alsina Elizabeth m. Lafayette Hinckley Holbrook; George W., Mark Henry; Wells L., Milton A. (Died 1884).

(2) Flora Robertson of Spanish Fork, Utah; married September 11, 1885; children: Dean R., Fay R., m. Julian M. Cummings, Faun R. m. Thomas E. Mckay (Fay and Fawn were twins), Burns R., Ruth Afton, Paul R., Alta R., Golden H., Areo R. The family lived in Provo, Utah.

Death: July 21, 1932 at 80 years of age.

In an interview appearing in the *Deseret News* of March 2, 1922, President Brimhall tells "How I Began Life." When I discussed this article with him, he added several other facts which I share with you.

He was born in a log cabin in the Ninth Ward in Salt Lake City. When he was six years of age, his father, George W., was called out to defend Echo Canyon during the Johnston Army episode. Young George wanted to go with his father and his black eyes filled with tears when he was told he could do more good at home. He was partly appeased when he was allowed to feed the oxen.

His patient, versatile mother not only made his clothes, but made his shoes as well. At an early age he showed his love of drama and oratory. He made his first public speech when seven years old, and several of the presiding brethren said, "he is a comer."

When going around the Ogden bench in search of stray cows, he stumbled onto a school house, cautiously surveying the building, went in and sat down. "Old Lady Shurtliff" was teaching as the eager-faced boy listened. He forgot about his cows and everything else except the teacher, her questions, the books, and the use of the slate board. When his anxious mother finally found him, George was amazed that she should weep to see him. As he talked on the way home, his mother foresaw his becoming a teacher. He said "Out of my own family of thirteen, five daughters and one son are teachers. Four of my sisters are teachers."

Living in Cedar Fort, young George went to school under Zerubbabel Snow, whom he called a great educator and who was the first Mormon to be appointed to a Federal position in Deseret Territory. When the family moved to Dixie, George H. met Henry Y. Young, another great teacher. "I was fortunate in having excellent teachers all through life," he said.

"My mother used to set George upon a tall, hard box and made him digest a page or two of some book before he could get down. Many of the bits I learned in these lessons have gone through life with me. They recall easily."

At twelve, he attended a spelling bee at Virgin City in Dixie and "spelled them all down but one man." Each new word fascinated George and he studied it until he could use it properly. He was an earnest student of grammar and rhetoric and was known to be very severe with stupid errors in orthography or punctuation on the part of his stenographers. He wrote out his short speeches as he grew older, wrote them with a pencil and kept on his person until he was satisfied with their thought and composition. Early in life, he wrote down thoughtful phrases of good titles which he could develop later.

During the grasshopper war of 1865, he picked up wheat, kernel by kernel, until he had a full peck. If he gave his word or accepted an obligation, he stayed with it at whatever cost of time or patience.

The family pride in education is related by him in this manner:

"They started a high school at Provo called Timpanogos University. (This was the Dusenberry school on 2nd East Street.) And I attended, doing chores for my board. Second year, I couldn't find any work and I walked twelve miles to Spanish Fork every Friday in order to get out wood on Saturday. Outside of that I didn't have anything to do.

"Just about despaired getting back to Provo when one day my Dad killed an ox. He hung one quarter up in the store room and put three quarters in the wagon under a sheet of canvas. I got to peering around and discovered most of this ox and inquired what it was for. 'Well, you've got to go to school, haven't you?' and I said 'Not while the family goes hungry.' 'Well, go talk to your mother about it.'

"That blessed woman looked me right in the eye and said: 'Son, if you don't get up there to that school mighty pronto, I'll take you across my knee like I used to' or words to that effect. She said I might amount to something if I went out and learned something.

"So, I shucked corn and hauled wood and made the grade. Then, 42 of us young fellows decided it would be a good idea to have a high school in Spanish Fork and we contributed $15 each in work and money. We brought the logs down from Santaquin Canyon. In 40 days we had a big house-raising with the whole community present. We called it the Young Men's academy but women came too. My wife attended, Tom Beesley taught the first and I taught the next two or three years, Algebra, Bookkeeping, Grammar, History, and Elocution."

Dr. Dean R. Brimhall, a distinguished son, wrote of his father 'in the *Wye Magazine* (Vol 8, No. I):

"His life, like that of the group in which he lived, began under the most primitive conditions and ended in a state of extremely high cultural development. He and his parents had savages to fight, hunger to stave off by hunting, shelter only in mud houses or tents, transportation by walking or ox teams, and later horses—yet within the space of his life there evolved conditions equal to the best in the world. . . . He and his people were isolated not only by distance, but by lack of intellectual contacts with the rest of the world. It was not unusual in early days to have news six months old arrive in Salt Lake from New York City. Libraries were at best a few dog-eared readers. Artists, musicians, lecturers and the like could not feed the Latter-day Saints because they could not get to Utah. Ideas were therefore naturally primitive and actions in many cases quite in accordance. . . . He frequently ridiculed those who thought the young people of his time were going to the dogs. His clear and fearless insight saw the changes that had come in intellectual and cultural values to the great benefit of young and old. His early library was practically nothing. In his later life, he had the best of all the world at his 'immediate call.' He associated with the outstanding educators, philosophers, men of science, artists, statesmen and the like.

"What a genius he was when it came to accepting the new. He not only accepted such changes, he sought them out. His intellectual curiosity was insatiable. As a young man, he lifted every community and person who was fortunate enough to come under his influence. . . . He has stamped a state with his integrity and unyielding purpose. Lucky are those who came under his influence."

What a wonderful tribute from a talented son! Such a tribute in different words has been paid to him by many of his associates and students.

Of the many facets of his character, the desire for education and understanding was almost a passion. He borrowed books from miles about him to learn more of great men or a challenging subject. When he took a trip to the canyon for wood, rode hills with cattle, or followed sheep, somewhere on his saddle blanket was a new and often borrowed book. He read thousands of pages by camp fire and tallow candle.

He worked his way through school as a janitor, a supervisor, an assistant, and ultimately as a teacher. He often stated that each student was a new challenge. He early learned not to evaluate intelligence by the age of the person. He valued heritage very highly, but knew that each individual was an independent entity, often with great variations from a family norm.

He was one of the first graduates of the BYA, serving in the Academy in many capacities. He earnestly encouraged adult education as well as training for all members of a family. He worked hard for free schooling under state supervision. The burden of education had rested upon the LDS church and the railroad brought many non-Mormon families to Utah communities, especially mining communities. In 1888, George H. introduced the hiring of male teachers on a basis of teaching being their life's profession. Most teachers taught until they found something with more financial promise. Professor Brimhall saw dignity in teaching and was one of the first in the territory to realize that promotion of education must become a permanent profession. In 1890 a law was passed to establish free public schools in Utah.

He was made superintendent of the Spanish Fork schools for two terms and induced to come to Provo as Superintendent for another two years, hiring only teachers who thought of teaching for more than one year. He visited heads of families, inquiring as to why all their children were not in school. He strove to break down the child-apprentice system which carried over, with the first European converts and to get the child into school that he may better be prepared to meet competitive life and choose his own profession.

When Pres. Benjamin Cluff took his expedition to South America in 1900, George H. Brimhall was advised to accept the position, of acting president, which he did. President Abraham O. Smoot first induced George H. to come to BYA to work in the Preparatory Department at a salary of $20 a month. This was acceptable, as most of the teaching professors had their own farms and necessary livestock. Produce from the farm kept Brother Brimhall's family and was shared with needy students who came for an education with little or no financial aid.

During the absence of President Cluff, George H. asked the authorities for a Church Normal Training School Building with a gymnasium on the top floor. The munificence of Uncle Jesse Knight and his gift of $15,000 gave impetus to and immediate authorization of the project. The building was dedicated on February 17, 1902 and was the pride of the entire county. Champion basketball teams soon followed its erection, and many nights crowds over-jammed the Gym and literally hung on the rafters to see the games. Spectators' legs spread onto the playing floor.

It was not long after President Cluff's return from South America that he expressed a desire to resign from the school's presidency and by unanimous approval George H. Brimhall was appointed president on April 16, 1904. The school became the Brigham Young University in 1903. President Brimhall introduced the conferring of the B.S. degree in 1904 and the B.A. in 1907. The first M.A. was given in 1919. Following the plan of Dr. Maeser, President Brimhall and his faculty visited the several neighboring states and all of Southern Utah to enlist students. As a result, the young university grew rapidly and the square block between Academy (University) Avenue and First East was soon recognized as being inadequate for ultimate expansion. President Brimhall selected two excellent teachers and astute business men to be his first and second counselors, Joseph B. Keeler and Edwin S. Hinckley. This committee immediately set about to buy land on the Old Lake Bonneville alluvial fan which projected into the city, a point known as Temple Hill, the present area of the upper enlarged campus. Faculty and students purchased 17 acres to provide land for a proposed memorial building, concluding arrangements by 1907. For the actual point of the hill which runs to the Provo street level, a parcel of some $1^1/_2$ acres. This hill point provided space for the Maeser Memorial in 1909. The cornerstone of the beautiful, classic building was laid October 26, 1909 and the building occupied in 1911. It cost some $130,000, of which the Knight family provided $65,000 and the Alumni contributed $50,000. The sale of Blue Bench Irrigation Co. bonds owned by the school paid the balance.

The Missionary and Preparatory Building was dedicated October 26, 1904, to be called The Art Building. This building cost $13,000, and $9,000 was allotted to the four stakes, Utah, Alpine, Nebo and Wasatch.

Many pages could be written of President Brimhall's interest in women's suffrage, and this was the period of greatest activity for suffrage in the nation's history. One of the nation's few gymnasiums devoted exclusively to physical education for women was erected in 1913 on the west side of University Avenue. This building was soon used for the growing crowds attending basketball games.

Another facet of President Brimhall's educational program was based upon a desire that each student should have a trade dependent upon manual dexterity. Girls should know all about the care and keeping of a home; boys should be carpenters, painters, plumbers, leathermen and draftsmen, and mechanics. For such purposes a Mechanic Arts Building was erected in 1919. The school was, for a long period of time, subject to the personal desires of the heirs of Brigham Young, though he left no provision to endow or support the young college. A gradual transition from the heirs' control to the Utah County four stakes and ultimately to the three Utah County stakes of the period left much of the financing up to local committees as far as buildings were concerned. Adequate salaries remained a neglected problem up until the time of President Howard S. McDonald. The BYA Presidency and faculty were obliged to acquire funds from every available source to keep the institution alive. Acquiring of land and building a campus were paramount issues under George H. Brimhall and his assistants, as it was the driving concern of his successor, Franklin S. Harris.

Under George H. Brimhall five buildings were erected: the Training School, 1902; Art Building, 1904; Maeser Memorial, 1911; Women's Gymnasium, 1913; and Mechanic Arts Building 1919. He acquired 37 acres on Temple hill, making 75 acres in all. Dr. Brimhall's term was as long as President Karl G. Maeser's and Benjamin Cluff's combined.

Alice Louise Reynolds records a very pertinent note that we should understand of President Brimhall: "Three years prior to becoming President (1898) the responsibility of the office fell to him, owing to President Cluff's absence in South America. Heavily loaded with class work, and in constant demand on the platform, his strong physique gave way. The doctor who examined and cared for him during his illness gave no hope of recovery, but the prayers of his friends prevailed. When he returned to the institution as President he was so frail that he had to be assisted up the stairs to the rostrum. When we think of the vigor he has put into his work, and the spirit with which he lays it down, we can but exclaim: 'See what God hath wrought!' "

Many of his friends thought he lived to the very limit of his strength most of the time while he was President of the University.

The additional duties that came to President Brimhall were of themselves sufficient for a full time job. He took an active part in the newly organized Boy Scout Council (1920) in Utah County, being its first chairman of the Court of Honor. President Brimhall zealously worked with the new Council and in 1932 was the recipient of the first Silver Beaver to be awarded by the Utah National Parks Council.

The stress of duty outside of BYU, the raising of funds and promoting of university expansion caused President Brimhall's health to give the Executive Committee and the Board grave concern and a search for a successor was quietly begun. With reluctance upon the part of his employers and Church Authorities, but with the full cooperation of President Brimhall himself, he was made President Emeritus in 1921 and Dr. Franklin S. Harris of Logan was named his successor.

President Brimhall had two doctor's degrees conferred upon him, one by the General Board of Education of the LDS Church and the other by the University itself, the latter a Doctor of Laws.

On the occassion of his receiving the President Emeritus status, President Heber J. Grant said: "I appreciate more than tongue can tell the very wonderful force and power and spirit of the Gospel of Jesus Christ that has been in this school under the administration of President Brimhall. I feel in my heart that from the time Brother Brimhall took charge of this school the spirituality in it—the spirit that should characterize our Church school system, namely that of making Latter-day Saints—this spirit has been in the school as perfectly as it is given mortal man to make it."

At the first Alumni banquet held after President Brimhall's retirement, President Bryant S. Hinckley remarked: "He had in a high degree that quality of arousing students to learn and do their best, and he won an immortal place among the teachers of his day."

As a short speech expert he excelled. Few men I ever heard or knew could match his ability in this art. He could hold a Boy Scout troop in wrapt attention, under the stars or in a small church room. His stories were filled with personal observations or examples from mythology or great literature. His Indian tales were heroic, even epic in spirit as occasion permitted. He was an outstanding patriotic speaker and the most celebrated days in his time were July 4th and 24th, Lincoln and Washington's birthdays. He was sought as a speaker over the state and these dates he filled when the saddle or buck-board were the only available means of transportation. "Decoration" or Memorial Day gave him occasion to extoll the deeds of the dead as a challenge to the living; under a pine tree with pioneer headstones all about him, great characters would seem to arise and walk in friendship among the living. His funeral sermons, always brief, were the essence of spirituality and comfort. One of his most inspiring statements was given in many different forms in these sermons: "Keep up your correspondence with your Father in Heaven." Another favorite theme was: "If there be eternal progress there must be perpetual change."

He found joy in the success of his friends. "When the BYA conferred the degree of Doctor of Laws upon President Charles A. Penrose, it reflected honor to itself. . . . Our illustrious alumnus, Dr. Penrose should be honored . . . as the author of 'Oh Ye Mountains High', 'School Thy Feelings, Oh My Brother', 'Up Awake, Ye Defenders of Zion', etc. Let us each pledge to give one dollar each to found the Charles W. Penrose Library of Poetry, to his Alma Mater, the BYA. Let us plan to give him this gift at Commencement, June 12, 1922." In most of his personal gifts he desired and planned to honor others with little or no credit to himself.

On May 26, 1922, the Salt Lake Telegram reported that President George H. Brimhall urged a Bird Sanctuary in Provo Canyon, which was eventually provided. He also advocated the placing of elk, caribou and mountain sheep in the Timpanogos country and the area of both forks of the Provo River.

At 70 years of age a gala celebration was given to honor him and to establish a Theology Library that would bear his name. Each year thereafter a school celebration was held on his birthday and some donation made to his beloved University.

When a noted visitor came up to him to thank him for his great and inspiring speech at a devotional in College Hall, Dr. Brimhall turned to him and said, "I would be remiss indeed if I could not respond to the inspiring music. I wish I could measure up to Professor Lund and his chorus." It did make a superb combination in the intimate auditorium—a glorious choir and a great speaker. He was willing to share his inspiration with others.

May a life be summed up in a few words? Perhaps, but I do not have the ability to give even an outline of the achievements when George H. Brimhall stood before his audience in beloved College Hall, he raised his glasses over his eyebrows and swept the crowd with his burning, black eyes, often resting his glance upon one person and speaking directly to that person for an entire speech. One morning as he walked down the aisle to the platform on the stage, he paused a moment, looked at the floor, sunk his head and slowly mounted the steps to get to his central seat. He remained in deep meditation as the choir sang and invocation was pronounced. He rose slowly, took a longer time than usual as he looked over the congregation, and finally rested his eyes on a pretty blue-eyed, blonde girl about six rows in the center in front of him. Pointing his finger directly at her, he said: "If you expectorate on the floor, you can't expect to rate high in life. No thinking person would ever wish to share his scum with the public. There are certain amenities of decorum which all ladies and gentlemen observe; certain protections of health which all of us must observe." Before he was finished the little girl was deep in her seat and tears filled her eyes. The Doctor had talked almost exclusively to her and she had taken every word personally. As the devotional dispersed, the blonde girl sat crying in her seat and some of her friends were trying to console her: "He didn't mean you," "He was talking to all of us," etc. The President came down and asked the cause of the gathering. When apprised of the real reason the earnest teacher was most embarrassed. He came to her and raised her gently by the hands: "Why, my dear, if I talked to none but you it was because yours was the most interesting face in the audience and your beautiful hair and happy face bespoke attention. I like to talk to people who listen to me. I wouldn't hurt so sensitive a soul as yours, not for a kingdom. May I confess to you a personal secret? When I come from the light into a darkened room, my eyes don't focus as well as they used to, and distant faces appear as a blur for some time. So I talked to you as I saw you plainly. Will you forgive me?" There were handshakes, forgiveness and smiles all around, as the Doctor started away, stopped and looked toward them. "None of us must ever spit on a floor or sidewalk." Then he walked to the doorway, already absorbed in other thoughts.

Another example of his teaching is shown by the following: There was a big abutment of brick walls that projected into the College Hall "stage" which divided the space to permit the orchestra to play on one side and the choir to sing on the other. The faculty had about four rows of chairs in front of this brick abutment. The drama department needed the entire space of the platform for a stage, but the projection of the bricks into the center robbed us of some 200 square feet. A popular student and I conceived of a plan. Removing several bricks on each side of this projection near the floor made the winter air on all faculty feet very uncomfortable. Two weeks of this discomfort brought no action though we called these holes to the attention of our efficient custodian, B. T. Higgs. "I know the building is bad near the floor, but we have no money to make repairs until next year, and maybe not then." Next week more bricks had disappeared and feet became colder. As President Brimhall came up the back stairway I called his attention to the large holes and the cold which poured in and suggested that perhaps we should remove all the abutment and avoid the discomfort by building the east brick wall straight across. President Brimhall looked almost through me. "Professor Pardoe, you want that stage very much, don't you? Well, don't take any more bricks away until you hear from me. Health is an important factor in all our lives." He knew all the time what we were doing and had smiled at our audacity. The east wall was straightened within two weeks! And we started to erect our stage under the smiling approval of the president, who had a great love for the drama.

George H. Brimhall had many honors bestowed upon him. He was President of the Utah Educational Association (1897-1898) in its formative period; he became a life member in the National Educational Association and was frequently programmed in their important policy making sessions. He was Principal of the LDS Seminaries and planned for their expansion. The Red Cross called upon him through the years and made him a director. A building on the campus was named in his honor in 1935 by President Heber J. Grant. A beautiful bust was made by sculptor Knaphus and placed in the building corridor. When he died he was the Senior member of the YMMIA Board. When he accepted a Life Membership as an Honorary Kiwanian he gave a speech on service and building that aroused the Club to give him a standing ovation. His editorials, short articles on timely subjects and articles for the *Relief Society Magazine* and *Improvement Era* would make several volumes. One of his progeny should collect these pithy and illuminating writings along with his recorded speeches.

His book *Long and Short Arrows,* a collection of his sayings and speeches, has been out of print for some time. His song, "I Love Thee Utah Valley," put to music by William F. Hanson, was sung on almost every school occasion for years. He knew the power of a well directed Alumni Association and took an active part in the BYU Alumni up to his last years. "Build, Alumni, build!" was a challenge to arouse any loyal group. I watched him write it on scratch paper and heard him read it a few minutes later.

He is known in so many aspects of his character. The careful, meticulous artist Aretta Young said of him: "No other man of my acquaintance has done so much to give dignity to the professional woman as has President George H. Brimhall." Lowry Nelson, nationally known sociologist spoke of him: "As a teacher of moral principals and of those things that build character, Pres. Brimhall is almost without a peer." President F. S. Harris frequently referred to him in some manner as counselor, spiritual advisor, incomparable teacher, a man of great vision, scholar and searcher for truth, a scientist with spiritual eyes, a gentleman—all of his references to his former teacher and President were factually complimentary and expressions of gratitude.

As a Son of Brigham Young University, none will surpass the faith and hope that President Brimhall had in the destiny of the Church University.

It was President Brimhall who asked me to consider appointment to the BYU. He was a member of the YMMIA Board who came to Ogden and held a two-day conference of Weber Stake Mutuals. I had been assigned public speaking and dramatic art. In the midst of a lesson, this slender, dark-eyed gentleman entered the room. I immediately asked if he cared to take over or if he had a message for us. He told me to carry on, which I did. A period of questioning followed, and then he took charge. He asked the class if they had learned anything? Would it carry over? Does your teacher honor time? Do you have definite subject assignments? If they merely said: "Yes," he asked in what manner and how effectively? Have you all participated or have two or three of you commanded most of the time? Do you understand him? Can you hear in the back of the room? Do you believe he is a sincere teacher? Has he developed the subject for which you came? At the end of his questions, he turned to one young lady who had not responded: "Young woman, will you kindly arise and tell me what you have learned in this class the past two days?" She hesitatingly arose and said: "Well, Brother Brimhall, I'm one of the worst in the class, but I do remember something," and she haltingly told what she had remembered. He looked at the class in a manner I was soon going to see very often and smiled before he spoke: "You have just hired a teacher for the Brigham Young University. If he qualifies as his grandfather's grandson (He knew Lorin Farr very well) and he is interested, we may come to terms. May I see you for a few minutes?" In direct manner I was quickly and thoroughly interviewed with such leading questions as: "Do you have a testimony of the Gospel? Whom did you marry? Would your wife enjoy living in Provo? Any money saved up? Is salary the biggest item of your interest? Could you build a department from scratch, I mean *scratch?* Do you enjoy hard work? What is your idea of a speech department for a Church school?" The interview lasted for about fifteen minutes. A last thought, "Of course, you keep the Word of Wisdom? I expect to hear from you next week. You'll be hearing from President Taylor."

I soon learned the power of the great teacher. Each assembly day we heard precious gems of character. Some of his speeches I can almost repeat verbatim to this day. Who will ever forget his master-piece on "Driftwood"? I learned that he kept most of his speeches, usually in pencil script. When we made trips together he sometimes would "leave me" for a period of fifteen minutes or more without a word and then pick up our conversation just where we had left off. He had left me in silence while he finished some paragraph, or a quatrain, or even a part of a plan for better teaching before he wrote it out or discussed it with his friends.

He was the product of a great pioneer dynasty in whom sacrifice, tribulation and hard work were stepping stones to character progress. He craved knowledge, recognized wisdom, fitted his actions to some part of eternal growth. Although he was serious and absorbed, he was also considerate.

His great spirit hovers benignly over the destinies of the Brigham Young University.

STEPHEN L. CHIPMAN

Born: March 18, 1864   **Place:** American Fork, Utah

Father: James Chipman; born in Far West, Missouri, April 9, 1839; son of Stephen Chipman and Betsy Murdock who came to Utah in September, 1847; moved to Utah County among the first six families; Mayor of American Fork; first treasurer of the State of Utah, 1896.

Mother:
1) Sarah A. Green of Nauvoo, Illinois; died when Stephen L. was 8 months old.
2) Salina Huntsman—the mother he knew

Brothers and Sisters: James, Alphonso G., Betsy, Richard Preston, (Stephen L. the youngest child of Sarah A. Green)

Marriage:
1) Sina Neilsen at Logan, Utah, daughter of Niels Nielsen and Karen Jensen Peterson, December 13, 1885.
2) after Sina's death, m. Annie Maddick Jamison of Manchester, England and Salt Lake City; married Feb. 15, 1940; born Feb. 15, 1875; died December, 1960.

Children: Zina Annabella (Virginia), m. Royal J. Murdock; Karen Lorena, m. Harvey Fletcher; Bessie Fern, m. Carl F. Eyring; Stephen Howell, m. 1) Pearl Romney, 2) Virginia Pendleton; Elva, m. A. Ray Olpin; and Leah, m. Rulon Van Wagenen; Alfred Stanley died in infancy.

Death: March 31, 1945, in Salt Lake Hospital. Funeral in Alpine Stake Tabernacle, with capacity crowd; President J. Reuben Clark the chief speaker.

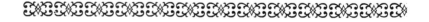

Stephen L. Chipman was a lively boy, knowing all the adventures and fun of Utah Lake, the canyons and mountains, fishing and hunting. He early learned the meaning of hard work and long hours. A high wheel bicycle, horseback, and buggy and the buckboard were his aids in transportation. The Big Red Cars (Orem Railroad) were a part of his cooperative efforts, and the car ran down American Fork main street, stopping at a depot only a few feet from Chipman Mercantile.

His early schooling was obtained in American Fork, and he was graduated from Brigham Young Academy in Bookkeeping and Business in 1883, having the guidance of Dr. Karl G. Maeser from 1880 to 1884, and going only in the winter months.

He married Sina Neilsen of American Fork in 1885 and was soon sent on a mission to the Southern States, North Carolina, Virgina, and Tennessee, to encounter unusual animosity and clergical opposition. However, his kind disposition and controlled deportment won him many friends. Upon his release in November, 1887, he was made Superintendant of the American Fork YMMIA and soon thereafter, a member of the School Board.

He moved to Provo in 1889 for better family schooling opportunities and became Superintendant of the Provo East Co-op. He was also made a member of the Utah Stake High Council and Assistant Superintendant of the 4th Ward Sunday School. After three years he was recalled to American Fork in June, 1892, to take over the management of the Chipman Mercantile Company, the largest department store (10 departments) south of Salt Lake. He built a comfortable house across the street from the big store. His civic duties called him to a Utah County Commissionership and many trips were made to Provo, the county seat.

In 1901, he succeeded Reed Smoot as Second Counselor to Edward Partridge in Utah Stake. Later, Utah Stake was made into three stakes, with Alpine Stake including American Fork, Lehi, Pleasant Grove, Lincoln, Manila, Alpine, and Cedar. Stephen L. Chipman was President of Alpine Stake with James H. Clark and Abel John Evans as counselors. He was also elected a director and member of the executive committee of Beneficial Life Insurance Company and a member of the Board of Trustees for Brigham Young Academy, a position he held for over forty years.

In 1903 he was elected to the State Legislature where he was an active Republican on several of the more important committees.

Under his stake presidency, a new tithing office and ten new Ward churches were built (4 churches in American Fork), and a new Tabernacle. He was manager of the Chipman Mercantile Company for some thirty-four years. As his Church duties increased he relinquished more of his business interests.

Among his many positions, he was President and Director of the Salt Lake and Utah Railroad Company; the Utah County Light and Power Company; Director of the Provo Reservoir Company; Utah Lake Irrigation Company; and the Bank of American Fork. He was also Vice-Chairman of Utah County Council, Boy Scouts of America. He was one of a small committee who opened up Timpanogos Cave in American Fork Canyon and was also a motivating power in establishing the Mutual Dell Home in American Fork Canyon. He was one of ten who gave $1,000 each to build College Hall for B.Y.U. The Stephen L. Chipman Hall on the BYU Campus was named in his honor.

In 1926 he went to California on another mission and was assigned to San Francisco. He had twenty missionaries from Alpine Stake sent out to him. After a period he was sent down to San Jose, California, and this became one of the joyous periods of his life. On Thanksgiving Day, a group of missionaries stood in a safety zone awaiting the traffic light signals when they were crashed into by a drunken driver. Among them was President Chipman, who was dangerously hurt. He recovered, but was retarded in action for the remaining years of his life. On January 10, 1935, he was appointed counselor to President George F. Richards of the Salt Lake Temple and later became president of all Church Temples. His genial smile and radiant spirituality fitted him admirably for this position.

The companion of his life, Sina, died November 11, 1936, having seen their children all successfully married—some of the sons-in-law world acclaimed. On February 15, 1940, President Chipman married a widow and Temple ordinance worker, Annie Maddick Jamison, who died in December of 1960.

He served on the BYU Board from 1896 to 1939, twenty years of which were on the executive committee.

President Chipman died Mar. 31, 1945. He will be long remembered for his beautiful family life, his friendly disposition, his willingness to aid the needy, sick and afflicted, his support of all character building projects, his business integrity, and his loyalty to Church and community.

AMASA L. CLARK

Born: June 6, 1865 in Farmington, Utah, just after Abraham Lincoln's assassination.

Father: Ezra T. Clark
b. Nov. 23, 1823 in Illinois
son of Timothy B. and Polly Keeler
d. Oct. 17, 1901 at Farmington, Utah

Mother: Mary Stevenson
b. Aug. 29, 1825 at Gibraltar, Spain
m. June 1845

Brothers and Sisters: Ezra James
Timothy B., m. Lucy A. Rice
Margaret Elizabeth, m. Joseph E. Robinson
William H., died as infant
Joseph S., m. Lucy Maria Robinson (lived to be 103)
Hyrum D. C., m. Eliza Porter
Edward R., m. (1) Wealthea Richards, (2) Alice Randall (he lived to be 96)
Charles R., m. (1) Mary Emma Woolley, (2) Annie Waldron
Wilford W., m. Pamelia Dunn (he lived to be 93)
Amasa L., m. (1) Alice Steed, (2) Susie Duncan

Marriage: (1) Alice Steed, m. Dec. 16, 1885 in Logan Temple
d. 1895
she had three sons and a daughter
(2) Susie Duncan, m. March 31, 1897 in Salt Lake Temple
mother of four sons and one daughter

Children: (of Alice)
Alice Maude, died as infant
A. Sterling
Herald R., late Dean Emeritus, College of Commerce, B. Y. U.
Grant S.

(of Susie)
Julian D.
Phyllis Clark Lewis—deceased
Nell C. (DeAlton) Partridge
Dale G.
Lewis D.—deceased

Died: May 25, 1968, after this biography was written.

His life as unfolded in his activities:

Education:
>Early schooling in Farmington, in a one-room school house
>Came to B.Y.A. in 1883 for two years
>To University of Utah for one year
>One of Utah's earliest and oldest bicyclists, riding to school and later to his bank is all the same to him

Occupational Activity:
>Began banking in 1892 in father's bank in Farmington
>Elected president year after year conducting the business in prosperous solvency

Church Activity:
>The only surviving member of the first L.D.S. Primary class, organized in Farmington by Mrs. Aurelia Spencer Rogers
>Master M-Man Award—honorary
>Davis Stake Sunday School Superintendent over 15 years
>Bishop of Farmington Ward for 15 years.

Civic and Social honorary affiliations:
>Two terms as Mayor of Farmington; established first electrical system in Farmington in his administration
>Treasurer Davis County School board for 16 years
>Committee member Utah Bankers Association
>Committee member American Bankers Association
>Silver Beaver in Scouting
>Chairman and director of numerous Red Cross, government bond and civic drives
>Vice-president B.Y.U. Emeritus Club 1960-68
>District Chairman B.Y.U. Alumni Fund drive and a yearly contributor

An ardent advocate of the Word of Wisdom; has eaten whole wheat most of his life.

He is a most generous benefactor of approved charities. He prepared a suggested epitaph—"He paid his taxes willingly, his contributions wih pleasure, and displayed the flag at his home on holidays."

His keen judgment and direct honesty has made him a leader all through his adult life. The Salt Lake Tribune of July 5, 1964, featured him as an enthusiastic bicycle rider, successful banker and civic worker.

On his hundredth birthday the State, the Church, men and women across the nation, relatives and countless friends paid him tribute. He was present on the campus a few days before his hundredth birthday as vice president of the B.Y.U. Emeritus Club and shared in executive counsel. He dignifies every group by his presence.

To summarize a life of a hundred years of service is more difficult than trying to put a bushel of peaches in a quart bottle. To relate all the deeds of merit which relate to Amasa Clark would require a full volume.

Being a successful banker for seventy-six years has given him an unusual opportunity to observe the struggles of a Territory to become a State, of small business ventures to develop into huge corporations, to see a great rural area relinquish its importance to growing urban concentration and manufacturing centers. He has seen the candle and kerosene lamp give way to gas and electricity, narrow dirt roads develop into broad, paved highways. Produce from a farm which filled kitchen cellar shelves and cellar storage, all raised and prepared by hands of the family, are now supplanted by sacks of food bought at a super-chain store. The friendly corner grocery with free delivery has disappeared and been absorbed by giants of interstate commerce. The coal bin no longer exists, victim of a gas or electric register. These transitions have been the cause of failure of many financial institutions but the sagacity of the Clark bank adjusted with the progress of time, weathered all depressions, paid consistent dividends and is one of the strong firms of the state to remain a family institution.

"To accept, care for and invest another person's money is a sacred trust. If I cannot honor that trust I could not be a banker" is the philosophy of Amasa Clark. "Character is a safer commodity to trust than any storage vault for money." "Money is like a person, you have to keep it working to keep it healthy." "Wealth may make a man selfish unless he learns how to share it." To sit in counsel with the venerable patriarch is to learn of his quiet power, his adherence to truth, his concern for the other fellow.

His health and longevity is no accident, as he is a sincere advocate of the Word of Wisdom and the practice of moderation in all of his personal activities. Exercise, proper eating and adequate rest have given him strength of body; adhering to truth, the avoiding of worry and a friendly concern for others have enriched his social life.

His life is his greatest monument.

BENJAMIN CLUFF, JR.

Born: February 7, 1858   **Place:** Provo, Utah

Father: Benjamin Cluff, Sr.; son of David Cluff and Betsy Hall who came to Utah on October 13, 1850, with the Edward Hunter Company; Missionary to Hawaii 1864-70; mechanic and carpenter; died 1910 in Tobasco, Mexico.

Mother: Mary Ellen Foster; pioneer of 1852, whose mother, Jane McCullough, died on the plains.

Brothers and Sisters: Mary, (Benjamin Jr.), George, Walter

Marriage:
1) Mary Jane John, daughter of David John of the Utah Stake Presidency; married August 16, 1883.
2) Harriet Cullimore, married December 17, 1886.
3) Florence Reynolds, in Mexico

Children: (of Mary Jane John) Fern C. Ingram, Ethel C. Crowther, Benjamin, Harriet L. Talbot, David T., Goldwin W., Wilford O., Aaron and Dawson.
(of Harriet Cullimore) Vida C. Gardner, Cyril B. Waldo, Harvey C., Delores C. Fife, and George H.
(of Florence Reynolds) Alice C. Wilson, Esther D. Laird, Joseph B., Margaret C. Parson, Elda C. Rippy, and Benito R.

Death: June 16, 1948, in California; at 90 years of age.

Benjamin Cluff was a boy with a restless soul. Born in Provo, of pioneer parentage, he spent his youth in Logan. At the age of seven he went to the Sandwich Islands (Hawaii) to join his father, then on a mission, and remained at Laie for five years. He readily learned the native language and helped to pick the first cotton grown on the island, assisting in the building of the first sugar mill and the manufacturing of sugar.

When twelve years of age, he returned to Logan to help his father as a carpenter. He didn't like school until, at the age of fifteen, a sudden change in attitude set him feverishly in search of knowledge and an education. In 1875 his Uncle, William W. Cluff, President of Summit Stake, had "Benny" come to Coalville, Utah, where the young man worked in the tithing and post offices for two years.

Just over the hill was a growing center of education, and in May, 1877, the nineteen year old lad set out on foot for the sixty-five mile hike, with an umbrella and a small bundle of clothing. In Provo, Harvey H. Cluff, a director of the Academy introduced Benny to Karl G. Maeser. Though the school year was but three weeks from closing, the lad got "school fever" and began to plan for the coming school year. During the summer he hauled coal and supplies between Coalville and Provo. His father offered him a third interest in a good farm in Wasatch County, but Benny told his father, "If you release me to go to school, I will never ask you for assistance." The next morning he was in school in Provo and was hired as a part-time janitor to aid with his expenses. He was chosen a member of the Normal Class and soon became a teacher in the primary department. He early started to study school organization and was enthusiastically proceding with his schooling when President Maeser told him they needed missionaries for the Islands and that his schooling was primarily intended to prepare him for a mission and life. Though the call was entirely unexpected and school was just starting, he left in October of 1878, had a most successful mission, and returned to Utah in 1882. The islanders and the Indians provided subject matter for Book of Mormon research as he early formed a theory of emigration from the mainland to the islands of the Pacific. Ethnology and archeology took on new meaning to the young scholar.

The Academy welcomed his return and engaged him as an instructor in mathematics, with James E. Talmage, Joseph M. Tanner, Joseph B. Keeler, who had been his fellow students.

In August, 1884, he married Mary Jane John, the daughter of President David John, and was appointed Stake Superintendent of the YMMIA. A yearning for more education motivated him to matriculate at Michigan University in 1886, and while there he debated before the student body a question of national interest, "Resolved, that Utah is ready for Statehood." (Utah did not become a state until ten years later.) That experience made him a marked man, and many challenges were literally hurled at him as long as he was on the campus. He accepted as many debates and conferences as his schooling permitted. He graduated in the upper brackets with a B.S. in 1890, one of the first Utahns to procure an eastern university degree.

When the upper story of the ZCMI Warehouse was rented for the Academy in 1885, a block on North Academy Avenue was purchased and a large foundation laid, only to lie dormant for seven years. When Benjamin Cluff returned from Ann Arbor, he became a vigorous leader in plans and work to complete the building. By the second semester in 1892 the second and third stories were completed. Members of the Board mortgaged their private property to aid in financing it. Regular courses for a four year Academy were laid out, and the school moved to its long-awaited quarters. A sincere effort was made to organize the school as a leading normal training institution, with full courses in kindergarten, primary, commerce and missionary divisions. Much of the academic planning came from Benny Cluff. The Church became very aware that they needed acceptable, trained leaders, and Professor Cluff readily accepted the opportunity to return to Michigan in 1893 to obtain his Master's Degree and then visit the leading schools in the northern U.S. and parts of Canada, better to aid in building the Provo curriculum. He had introduced psychology in the school, a subject new to this area.

Under Principal Cluff, white and blue were selected as the school colors. Class organizations were inaugurated and the first class organized with Richard R. Lyman as president (1891). Also at Benny's suggestion, Founder's Day was instituted on October 16, 1891. In the same year a student Loan Association was organized. On January 4, 1892, he put all classes on the hour basis. They had been on the half-hour before. In the summer of this year he established the first Summer School in the State of Utah and brought Col. Francis W. Parker of Chicago as educational psychologist and lecturer, who attracted many students from all over the state. The popular Parker School in Provo (now torn down) was named in his honor.

The Alumni Association was founded during Commencement exercises, June, 1893, and George H. Brimhall was installed as acting President, serving in this capacity to 1894. Principal Cluff was given leave of absence and returned with a Masters degree. While away, he met and employed a very charming teacher, Miss Abby Celestia Hale, niece of Edward Everett Hale, U. S. Senate Chaplain and author of "Man Without a Country." She was the first non-Mormon to be employed on the regular faculty, remaining three years as director of the training school. Her work was adjudged of the highest standards.

On July 20, 1895, the Board of Trustees had the term "principal" apply to heads of departments and "president" to former principal Cluff. In July, 1896, the year of Utah's statehood, registration was opened to non-Mormons for the first time. To further dignify the leadership of President Cluff, in 1898 the Board conferred upon him the degree Doctor of Didactics.

President Cluff asked for the erection of College Building and appointed Reed Smoot as Chairman. The building was dedicated at Commencement of 1898. Opera seats were donated for College Hall and brass name plates were placed on the respective seats, which gave the donor certain seating privileges.

The desire to do archeological research was consummated for President Cluff when he was given a leave of absence to take a South American Expedition in 1900. On the 17th of April a group of well equipped men left the College Building, led by a band and followed by most of the studenbody marching to Spanish Fork. There a grand reception was held, food served, final speeches were made, and the little group started its trek to Mexico and South America. The full story of this expedition would require a small book and I leave its telling to others. President Cluff returned on February 7, 1902, without success, although Chester Van Buren, a naturalist, went on to Columbia, S. A., and remained in the jungles until 1903, bringing upon his return some 1200 birds, snakes, mammals, Indian patterns, etc., for a pretentious museum which was established by Professor Van Buren, Professor Edwin H. Smart, and a student, George Talmage. For many years College Hall had a very lifelike exhibition of the Amazon jungle.

Plans had been set afoot for a campus block of new buildings, and under acting President Brimhall the Training School and Gymnasium were dedicated on February 17, 1902, at a cost of $35,000. Most of the funds were furnished by Jesse Knight.

At the request of President Cluff the school was designated as Brigham Young University on October 3, 1903. In this year the Board accepted the resignation of President Benjamin Cluff, Jr. and he was formally released on December 23, having served the University since 1882 in various executive positions, and as President since 1892. During his tenure he stressed an expanded, trained faculty. He led the way in personally procuring two degrees and more buildings and equipment. He encouraged school spirit, recreation and competitive games, organized classes, established the Alumni Association, started the first two school papers, systematized department organization, started the Summer School, hired the first non-Mormon, and particularly got the school prepared for a University service without sacrificing the teacher training and missionary work. During all the promotional school work, he felt he had been deprived of a life's ambition, to find proof for Book of Mormon evidences and strata in Lamanite history. Soon after his release from the University he paid all his debts, gave homage to his colleagues and moved hopefully to Mexico. Another book could be written of his hardships, misplaced confidences, the failure of his rubber plantation, and the losses he suffered from theft and deception. He left Mexico for California, where he engaged in the grocery business and helped in the Church as occasion presented itself.

For distinguished service to the University, the Church, and his state, the Alumni Association conferred him the Distinguished Service Award in 1946. The University further honored him by naming a new botanical building the "Benjamin Cluff Jr. Plant Science Laboratory," a nursery for the University's expanded landscaping and beautification program and for the scientific research of three departments: Agronomy, Botany, and Horticulture.

Under him a training school evolved to a University. He gained the admiration, confidence, and respect of the leading men of the pioneer state, and of the scholastic world. If he had a challenging weakness it was inability to "stay put." He looked out upon so many vistas that he had to leave one venture to explore another. He went to many supporting friends of the University, explained the needs of the school, and got families to establish laboratories and libraries; to list them is almost a summary of his vast interests:

The Laboratory of Physics, established by the Holt Family.

The Laboratory of Chemistry, established by the Magelby Family.

The Laboratory of General Mechanics, by the Beckstead Family.

The Laboratory of Natural Sciences, by the Hindley Family.

The Library of General Scientific Works, by F. Warren Smith of California.

The Library of Philosophy, by the class of 1897.

The Library of Theology, by the class of 1898.

The Library of General Literature, by the class of 1900.

In the sunset of his life he turned his thoughts longingly beyond the shadows of Chapultepec and Oaxaca and smiled benignly upon the progress of the BYU, culminating ninty years of service and restless research.

HARVEY H. CLUFF

Born: Oct. 24, 1872 in Provo, Utah, Cousin of President Benjamin Cluff, Jr.

Father: Samuel Sampson Cluff of Durham, New Hampshire, son of David Cluff and Betsy Hall.
To Utah Oct. 13, 1850.
Born: Sept. 27, 1837 in Kirtland, Ohio.

Mother: Frances A. Worsley, daughter of John Worsley and Sarah Hamer, pioneers of Sept. 17, 1853.
Born: Nov. 8, 1841,

**Brothers
and Sisters:**   Henry, b. Mar. 17, 1862, d. April, 1863.
Fannie, b. Mar. 21, 1865, m. Dave Bonnett.
Sarah Jane, b. Apr. 6, 1867, d. Feb., 1868.
Bessie, b. July 10, 1870, d. Nov. 6, 1879.
(Harvey)
Samuel, b. May 15, 1878, m. Minnie Moyle.
Elmo, b. Sept. 20, 1880, m. Mamie Grain.
Sidney, b. May 1, 1882, m. Kadie Colvin.

Marriage: Freda Barnum, daughter of Guy C. and Amelia Barnum of Provo.
Born: Mar. 14, 1876.
Married: Oct. 11, 1900.

Children: Bernice, b. Feb. 23, 1903, m. I. J. Bishop.
Frances, b. Mar. 30, 1907.

Death: Jan. 1, 1949.

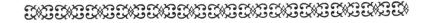

Harvey H. Cluff, Provo's eminent lawyer and jurist, is not to be confused with Harvey Harris Cluff, born in 1836, his namesake, who helped to build Provo's New Fort and was a long-time member of the Board of Trustees for BY Academy. He was the fifth child of eight children with a name of prestige in Provo, coming from a family of builders, cabinet-makers, and successful farmers who were active in the LDS Church.

Harvey was one of the students in old ZCMI Building and held a flag when he marched up Academy Avenue to the newly completed Education Building in 1892. He was given a diploma in education and certificate of accounting at BY Academy in 1895 when he was twenty-three years of age. An LDS mission took him to the Southern States in the turbulent days of 1895-98, and he returned with a firm resolve to study law. He had worked his way through the Academy when work was there for the asking and had no doubt as to his ability to "make it go" in a college of law.

Harvey had seen his namesake, Harvey Harris Cluff, in plays in "The Cluff Hall," a building erected with his four uncles to accommodate furniture, dancing, and the theatre. His portrayals of "Claud Melnot" and "Don Caesar de Bezar" were especially well received by the Provo public, and other members of the Cluff family took parts in these plays which gave young Harvey a heritage to honor and support. He became an excellent speaker, created a convincing character, and used the stage to improve his speech and carriage.

He went to the Highland Park College in Des Moines, Iowa, and obtained his L.L.B. He looked confidently to a career in Utah, being admitted to the Utah Bar in 1902 and to a partnership in Booth & Cluff (Alfred Booth). He remained in this firm until 1909. He was appointed secretary to the State Board of Insanity 1904-08, 1912-1916. He was District Attorney for the 4th Judicial District, 1908-1912. Harvey was active in politics, being chairman of the Republican Utah County Committee for 1917-1920. He was one of Utah's most successful Attorney Generals in 1921-1929, and in 1929 formed the firm of Cluff and Cluff in Salt Lake City.

Harvey Cluff was an active member of the Utah Bar Association, the American Bar, and the National Association of Attorney's General, being president of the latter in 1924-25 and chairman of its executive committee in 1925-1929.

The underpriveleged and socially unfortunate became a concern for him early in life, and he was appointed a trustee for the State Industrial School in Ogden, as well as the State School for the Deaf and Blind.

The Chambers of Commerce in Provo and Salt Lake received a share of his time and talents. Two social organizations designed for community service received his membership: International Order of

Odd Fellows and the Benevolent and Protective Order of Elks. He became counsel for both organizations.

When Harvey wed Frieda Barnum, he married one of the most talented readers in the State. She possessed great dramatic ability and leadership qualities.

The Utah and National Bar Associations joined the state in paying him especial homage at the time of his death.

DON BYRON COLTON

Born: September 15, 1876   **Place:** Mona, Utah

Father: Sterling Driggs Colton; born May 22, 1851 in Provo, Utah; one of the first discoverers of gilsonite; son of Philander and Matilda Merrill Colton (see notes on Warren A. Colton).

Mother: Nancy Adelaide Wilkins; born July 14, 1853; married March 21, 1870; died March 28, 1934.

Brothers and Sisters: Flora Elsie C. Collete; Sterling LeRoy; (Don Byron); Frank Edwin; Warren Alfred; Charles Henry; Louis L. Lycurgus; Nancy Fern (died 1892); Zora Maria; Hugh Wilkins.

Marriage: (1) Mary Marion Hall on August 23, 1900; died July 9, 1905. (2) Grace Stringham of Vernal, on June 17, 1908; daughter of Phillip Stringham and Caroline Crouch.

Children: Mera, born March 20, 1900
Alice, born January 1, 1912
Glade Byron, born March 24, 1916; married Alice Mae Anderson
Gwen Mary, born April, 1919; married Joseph M. Anderson

Death: August 1, 1952, in Salt Lake City, Utah.

Don B. Colton was a stalky young boy, fast of foot, a good horseman who loved the sage brush hills of mountainous Utah. His father believed a farm to be the proper place to rear a family of boys, and each of his sons had his own sheep and colt to tend and shared chores with each other. Family prayers and evening reading sessions were parts of a family program. Both his father and mother taught organization, parental obedience and respect, giving the group a lifetime love for each other.

One-room school houses were the rule, and several members of the Colton family would be seen studying in one room with the same teacher of different grades. Don received his schooling in the country schools until he could afford to go down the valley from Vernal to Provo. He graduated from the B.Y.A. commerce department and became principal of the preparatory department. His mission to England for the Church in 1896-98 gave him a maturity and assurance which accompanied him all his life. Most of his later experiences were judged from a moral viewpoint and their effects on his fellow men. With a degree to his credit, he went to Vernal and was principal in the Uintah Stake Academy (1902-03).

His going to Ann Arbor (1903-05) and procuring a L.L.B. in 1905 determined the course of his professional life. He had been elected to the House of Representatives when he was in his twenties. Returning from the east, he started to practice law and extended his ranching interests. He was recorder for the U. S. Land Office at Vernal from 1905-1914 and in 1920-32 was a member of U. S. Congress, one of the longest Utah tenures. His major committee work was in agriculture, livestock, mining, reclamation, Indian affairs, and better administration of the public domain. He worked in close harmony with Reed Smoot of the Senate in all these vital Western issues. His vote was chiefly concerned with the proper study of the issue at hand and its value and cost to the public, regardless of the part of the nation most benefited.

The Colton-Oddie law passed by Congress made available more and better construction of roads over the public domain. With the advent of Franklin D. Roosevelt and the Democratic victory, Congressman Colton returned to Utah and opened law offices in Salt Lake City. After a few months at home, he was sent to the Eastern States to become President of the Mission, 1933-37. While here, he initiated and sought writers for the Palmyra Pageant. At his request BYU Art and Speech Departments sent to him all their available costumes which could be used in portrayal of Hebrew and Indian characters from the Book of Mormon.

In 1938 he left New York and returned to Salt Lake, being soon appointed director of the Missionary Home on north State Street.

He and his wife, Grace, made a real home for hundreds of young men and women, many of whom made them their confidants even after marriage.

Don B. Colton was President of the Utah Society Sons of the American Revolution in 1942 and an officer until his death. His business affiliations were varied. He was President of the Vernal Express, a publishing company; President of the Uinta Telephone Co., which he extended over the valley; rancher and stockman of note as an executive member of Colton Brothers; and President of the Vernal Investment Co. He was one of the first to exploit the beauties of the nearby Green River Narrows. He envisioned a park of world importance near Jenson, Utah, where dinosaur skeletons were being uncovered.

Along with his law and business activities, he paralleled his work in the Latter-day Saint Church. He was Stake Superintendent of Religion Classes in 1901-02; a Bishop of the Maeser Ward in Vernal 1905-06; President of the Uintah Stake for eleven years; filled two missions, one to England for two years and another in the Eastern States for four years; and was president of the mission training home while he was a member of the General Sunday School Board.

The Brigham Young University Alumni Association bestowed upon him the Distinguished Service Award in 1948 for outstanding service to his state, the nation, his Church, his Alma Mater, and the youth of America. A friend said of him, "He was happiest when he had a dozen jobs to attend to at one time." He had a great capacity for service, proper organization, and for getting others to work.

His last home was at 607 First Avenue in Salt Lake City. In the presence of his faithful companion, his heroic soul came to rest on August the first, 1952, at the age of 76. That which was pioneer seems to linger about him whenever his deeds are recalled. He will be best remembered as the originator of the Palmyra pageant.

WARREN ALFRED COLTON

Born: March 29, 1883 **Place:** Vernal, Utah

Father: Sterling Driggs Colton; son of Philander Colton and Polly Merrill; born in Provo, Utah, March 22, 1851; died Oct. 20, 1933; first lived in Provo, then moved to Mona, Utah where Sterling Leroy, Don Byron, and Frank Edwin were born; Bishop of old "Mill Ward" now Maeser Ward.

Mother: Nancy Adeline Wilkins; daughter of John G. and Nancy Wilkins; born in Provo July 14, 1853; married March 21, 1870; died March 28, 1934.

Brothers and Sisters: Flora C. Collett (R.S.); d. in San Francisco, Calif. Jan. 25, 1954; Sterling Leroy, d. July 11, 1914; Don Byron, d. Aug. 1952; Frank Edwin Charles Henry, b. Dec. 18, 1884; Lewis Lycurgus, b. Nov. 30, 1886; Nancy F., b. Feb. 25, 1890; Zora C. Paulsen, b. Oct. 21, 1892; Hugh Wilkins, b. Jan. 11, 1901.

Marriage: Merle Crandall, daughter of Lucian D. Crandall, son of Myron Crandall and Tryphena Bisbee; her mother was Elizabeth Cook Crandall, daughter of Joseph Cook and Martha Barlow; both parents native of Springville, Utah. Married Oct. 26, 1906; died Dec. 13, 1962.

Children: Helen Merle Lockhead (H.B.); Dr. Warren A. Jr.; Beth Duncan (Robert L.)

Death: Tuesday, October 8, 1963 in Ossing, New York hospital while visiting his daughter Beth; buried in Salt Lake Wasatch Lawn Memorial.

Warren Alfred Colton lived in the primitive area of Ashley Valley where Indians lived throughout the year. There were bears, wolves, coyotes, rabbits, wild horses, deer, and buffalo, wild sheep and goats, in the mountains, bob cats, lynx and cougars near the forests, eagles and hawks circling in the air and sage hens, grouse, prairie dogs and snakes living in the open plains. Fish were in the waters for the catching. A boy was given a gun early in life and learned the traits of the predator and the habitats of edible animals. He herded sheep, grazed the cattle and pastured horses, built corrals and long wooden fences, cleared the fields of rocks and sage. It was boyish sport to chase a jack rabbit, to jump over sagebrush in hot pursuit, leap a gurgling creek and flush a partridge or covey of quail. This early training in running and jumping laid the foundation for Warren's athletic prowess while at the Brigham Young Academy. He would spend the summers on the range and distant pastures, then drive the stock back to the farm to feed them hay raised in the upper Ashley during the summer and stored for winter feed.

Warren's father was the first sheriff of Uintah County, and outlaws with national reputations would appear in the valley, shoot up isolated camps, slaughter a young calf or help themselves to a small store's supplies. The boys got so they recognized the molesters by sight and Butch Cassidy was especially friendly to youngsters. The young campers were taught to share their victuals without protest and avoid trouble.

The Colton boys attended the Uintah Stake Academy, one school room with eight to twelve grades, for two years. The High School teacher for Warren was A. B. Anderson of Lehi. When Warren went to BYA his physical agility attracted considerable attention and Professor John C. Swenson was head of the physical education, then a small department of uncertain value. I quote from Dr. Colton's biography:

"During my early student days at BYA. . . . I was approached by Professor John C. Swenson early in 1900 to see if I would like to go to Stanford University to study Physical Education with the view of teaching it at BYA. After consulting my parents and my "best girl" I told President Brimhall that I would like to go and proceeded to make preparations to leave for Palo Alto the first of the year (1901). The school advanced me some money and with my father's help I was able to spend a year at Stanford and the summer at Cooper Medical College in San Francisco, where I studied anatomy.

On the advice of Dr. Tom Storey and Ray Lyman Wilbur, I registered at Stanford as a physiology major and spread myself considerably to get all they had to offer. I knew it would not be possible for me to stay more than one year. . . . I passed all my examinations and came back to Provo in January, 1902, enthusiastic and ready to go. . . . My main assignment at the school BYA was physical education and coaching of the athletic teams in basketball, baseball, and track. The new gymnasium had been finished and the usual setting up exercises and apparatus work were taught personally. . . . Our motto was "a strong mind in a strong body."

In the Spring we moved to the athletic field on Temple Hill where the Joseph Smith Building now stands. . . . I stayed at the BY for two and a half years; then I resigned to work with my father to earn enough money to study medicine. . . . I have always been proud of the assignment as first athletic coach of the BYA."

In him, the University had its first athletic coach and fixes the date when the school first used the athletic field on the hill. He led the men in building a large wooden pavilion, facing north, to seat spectators, which lasted until 1920 when it was mysteriously burned down.

During his first year at BYA, Warren was invited to go to Beaver, Utah, to help set up an athletic program for the Church Academy there. This program advanced their school to a real competetive institution. In his classes at the BY he had John C. Swenson, E. S. and B. S. Hinckley, E. H. Holt, Calvin and Harvey Fletcher, Earl J. Glade, Arthur V. Watkins, and men of such calibre who became well known in their professional years. Clayton Teetzel succeeded Warren as coach and physical education leader at Warren's invitation.

Graduation at Columbia University (M.D. in 1913) was followed by internship at Bellevue Hospital in New York City and the LDS Hospital in Salt Lake City. He was engaged in the practice of medicine and surgery in Salt Lake City from 1914 to 1923, when he joined the Veterans Administration and was assigned to a hospital in Dawson Springs, Kentucky for two years. He then spent seven and a half years at Castle Point, New York, and another seven and a half years at the hospital at Minneapolis, Minnesota as clinical director and manager. Another V.A. assignment took him and his family to Kecoughton, Virginia and Hines, Illinois. He asked for and got assignment to Salt Lake where he was manager for another seven and one half years, then retired from Veteran's Administration on April 1, 1953. At Kecoughton, Virginia he was given the commission of Lt. Commander in the Naval Reserve and was ordered to Chicago Hines Hospital and given the rank of Colonel in the U. S. Army. He remained in this grade until the end of World War II.

His later life was lived in semi-retirement, visiting his children, writing articles, and going to the Temple, enjoying the fruits of his efforts in service to his fellow men. He died while on a visit to his daughter, Beth, in New York, following his beloved life companion, Merle Crandall, who died on Dec. 13, 1952 in Salt Lake City. Both were reared in Provo.

ASA LYMAN CURTIS

Born: February 13, 1877 **Place:** Salem, Utah

Father: Lyman, one of the original 143 Utah Pioneers of 1847; born January 12, 1812 at New Salem, Massachusetts; married July 27, 1862; lived in Salem, Utah; died August, 1898.

Mother: Sarah Hartley; born August 10, 1836 at Sheffield, Yorkshire, England; died July 13, 1921 in Salem, Utah.

Brothers and Sisters: Lucina, Elizabeth Jane, Millicent, Emma Cornelia, Josephine Matilda, (Asa Lyman).

Marriage: Annie Beatrice Littlewood; married January 4, 1905 in the Manti Temple; died March 6, 1958.

Children: Bretnall, Lucille, m. Horace Magleby, Evelyn, m. Grant Larson, Mildred, m. Max Warner, Nelva, m. Byron Darley, Helen, m. Frank Mumford, Dr. Emerson, m. Jacqueline Bardsley, Delbert

Death: October 5, 1961 of a heart attack at age 84. Buried in Payson, Utah.

Dr. Asa Lyman Curtis was of a quiet mien, stocky of build with observing eyes. He was a man who preferred to listen, but could talk eloquently. He chose one major subject at a time, and after a careful consideration carried the project to a successful fruition.

He was proud of his ancestry and honored his inheritance all his life. He was a direct descendant of Moses Curtis, Minute Man of Lexington, Massachusetts. His father, Lyman Curtis was one of the original 143 pioneers to see Salt Lake Valley.

Lyman Curtis was one of the nine explorers to precede the main company in 1847 to explore the land and find a place to plant seeds. Orson Pratt wrote on July 22. "This morning George A. Smith and myself accompanied by seven others, rode into the valley to explore, leaving the camp to follow on and work the road." The list of nine horsemen reads: Orson Pratt, George A. Smith, Erastus Snow, Joseph Mathews, John Brown, John Pack, Porter Rockwell, Lyman Curtis, and Jesse C. Little. An interesting bit of history under title of firsts indicates that Orson Pratt was the first to stand on the land later plotted as Salt Lake City, George A. Smith was first to plant potatoes, Wilford Woodruff was the first to climb Ensign Peak, and Lyman Curtis was the first to build a fire on the camp site which would be just east of Temple Square. Lyman Curtis lived to be the last of the nine horsemen and was especially honored in the 1897 celebration. Born in Salem, Massachusetts, he named the town he pioneered in Southern Utah County after his birthplace. Asa's father later took a fertile piece of land in Salem.

As a member of the Utah Society, Sons of the American Revolution, Asa attended state meetings for many years and was elected State President in 1944.

His schooling was taken in Salem and at twenty years, with an advanced vocabulary, he entered Brigham Young Academy, and graduated in 1898 with a two-year normal certificate. School teaching followed at Salem, Thatcher, Arizona and Payson. He enrolled in medicine at the University of Utah and graduated from Medical College at Northwestern University. In 1911 he started practice at Payson and immediately became an important citizen of the community. He served Uncle Sam in World War I as army medical director at Fort Riley, Kansas and revived his practice in Payson at the War's end.

Payson and Utah were important to Asa, and he became a member of the Payson City Council, 1926-1933. Water and streets were his major interests; he developed Payson's water system by building reservoirs in Payson Canyon. His foresight gave him expanded interests and he gained the sobriquet of "Father of the Central Utah Water Project," only now coming into its real significance. His pioneer ancestry aroused his attention and he became an officer in the Payson

Chapter, Sons of the Utah Pioneers. He was also an officer and active in civic programs of the Lion's Club.

Dr. Curtis served The Church of Jesus Christ of Latter-day Saints from his early boyhood. At twenty-three he served a mission to New Zealand, 1901-04, often attending Maori Conferences thereafter. He was a member of the Nebo Stake High Council presidency and of the High Priests Quorum.

In his practice he went where called and charged but moderate fees, many times taking farm produce for pay. He loved horses and trained good stock. His horse and buggy took him to distant farm homes in the dead of night and on cold winter days. In his early days a doctor had more visits to patients than calls at his office. He set up the first clinic in lower Utah County, the Curtis Hospital, but worked for years for a Payson City Hospital, acting as advisor and fund raising chairman. When he retired in 1960 the Utah State Medical Association named him honorary President.

A man of sterling character, he lived a life of service for his fellow men. He cherished his talented and cultured wife who died in 1958. You would usually see him with one of his three sons or five daughters; his neighbors knew him as a devoted family man. Any project fostered by Asa L. Curtis was made better by his association with it.

JOHN DeGREY DIXON

Born: July 16, 1869 in Salt Lake, Utah.

Father: Henry Aldous Dixon
b. March 14, 1835 in Pope Colony, South Africa
Son of H. A. Dixon who left England in 1820 for South Africa
To Salt Lake City in 1856—worked in tithing office
1860-65—served African Mission
1870 moved to Provo—Secretary Provo Woolen Mills
To England 1879
d. April 28, 1888

Mother: Sarah DeGrey
b. January 27, 1845 in Dudley, England
m. Jan. 27, 1865
When husband died left with 7 children
d. April 17, 1926

Brothers and Sisters: 9 children: John DeGrey was the first of the family
Arthur D., killed 1911, by electricity at Murdock Power Co.
Maria, m. Arthur N. Taylor
Ernest, m. May Painter
Charles Owen, m. Virginia Beckstead
Walker D., m. Louis Maiben
LeRoy, m. Electa Smoot
Arnold, m. May Banks

Marriage: Sarah Ann Lewis on Sept 18, 1889 in Manti Temple
d. of bp. John Wm. Lewis and Jane Davis of Wales
Pioneers of Daniel Jones Handcart Co.
b. April 23, 1868
d. October 30, 1951
"a mother to a neighborhood"

Children: Henry Aldous, June 29, 1890—m. Lucile Knowlden
John Wm., September 6, 1892—d. June 6, 1894
Stanley Lewis, March 3, 1895
Rulon Sterling, September 9, 1898
Maud, February 28, 1901—m. Fred L. Markham, Architect
Grant B.—died in infancy
Lucian—died in infancy

Death: October 4, 1923—died suddenly at his Provo home of heart trouble.

49

John DeGrey Dixon was a restless man, not so much in your presence as with himself. He would finish a job and immediately say "What must I do next?" instead of the usual "Now I can rest." He had great energy which he treated as inexhaustible, but died after a day's illness.

He had three driving passions, church, government and family. One of these occupied his time throughout his life. He came from a family of boys and was the father of six boys himself. He had but one sister, Marie, who married Arthur N. Taylor, another father of a dominantly boys' family, and one daughter, Maud, who married Utah's successful architect, Fred L. Markham. His philosophy in self and family, "Keep plenty of work on hand and thwart mischief before it begins." His large orchard provided the work for himself and growing boys, only three of whom reached maturity, and an ample garden with barn yard nearby supplied additional chores for all. I once heard him say, "Seems like I am always changing clothes."

John D. was one year old when his father moved from Salt Lake to Provo to become secretary of the Provo Woolen Mills. Later he became the treasurer of the new branch of Zion's Cooperative Mercantile Institution and councilman for Provo City. John D. was nineteen when his father died and left him virtually the head of the family.

Educated in the expanding Provo grade schools, he went to the B.Y. Academy and took a business course before taking employment with Samuel Lilliard, building contractor. He kept abreast of current affairs, especially legislation which encroached upon individual liberties.

His major activities are listed herewith:
Business: Bookkeeper for Lilliard Construction Co., 3 years
    Provo Lumber and Bldg. Co., 4 years
    Taylor Brothers—made secretary-treasurer at time of incorporation, a position he held until death.
    Cashier and Manager of Farmers Merchants Bank 1906 to death.
Government and Civic Activities:
    1900—State Treasurer on Republican Ticket.
    Author of bill to tax foreign corporation stock, which resulted in acquiring funds to build the Capital Building on upper State Street in Salt Lake City.
    Served Provo City Council two terms.
    Appointed secretary of State Land Board by Gov. John C. Cutler —2 year term.
    Served as Provo City Recorder
    Guiding member of City Council when city water works established—replaced the numerous flowing wells over the city.
    World War I—Liberty Loan Chairman.

Officer and promoter of Provo Bldg. and Loan Co.

Advocated the development of Utah Lake as a State recreation and sports center.

Member and officer in Provo Commercial Club.

Church: Active as teacher and officer in Sunday School and YMMIA work.

Served in L.D.S. mission to Virginia in 1896-97.

Bishop's Counselor in 30th Ward Salt Lake City.

Member of Utah Stake High Council when the Stake covered the present Utah County territory.

Sunday School Stake Superintendent

Before church welfare was installed John D. Dixon distributed produce from his orchards to the poor.

Paralleling his church and civic activities was his keen interest in the Brigham Young University. In all Provo City and commercial projects he invariably would ask, "Is it best for the city and how will it affect the school (B.Y.U.)?"

LEROY DIXON

Born: Oct. 16, 1881 **Place:** Provo, Utah

Father: Henry Aldous Dixon
(See notes under John DeGrey Dixon)

Mother: Sarah DeGrey
(See notes under John DeGrey Dixon)

Brothers and Sisters: (Same list as for John DeGrey Dixon) Henry Alfred, John DeGrey, Arthur DeGray, Maria Louise, Ernest DeGrey, Charles Owen, Walter DeGrey, Leroy, Arnold
Half brothers and sisters—
Albert Smith, m. Sena Rasmussen
Parley Smith, m. Etta Dangerfield
William Aldous, m. Harriet Hands
Alice, m. J. W. Dangerfield
Sarah, m. Alexander McConachie
Hattie Amelia m. Geo. W. West

Marriage: Electa Smoot, m. in 1903
daughter of A. O. Smoot II, half brother to Senator Reed Smoot, and Electa Bullock of Provo.
d. Jan. 6, 1905

Children: LeRoy, d. in infancy
Paul S., m. Ora Anderson d. Dec. 4, 1955
Allie, m. Reed S. Gardner
Sarah Vera m. Clyde J. Summerhays
Maurine, m. Myron Devere Childs
Helen, m. Ezrel Junius Payne
Arthur, died in early youth
Gladys, m. Ivan Wm. Nelson

Death: Dec. 28, 1926. Blood poisoning from defective teeth, to pneumonia

Each son of Henry Aldous Dixon Sr. was intimately affected by the example of his father. Sons John D. and LeRoy were especially close; each served in the State, the County and the City. Each man made honest work the absorbing plan of his life.

LeRoy was a young student in the Provo public schools and B.Y.A. He was a monitor in a section of the parade from the old Z.C.M.I. and enjoyed the new B.Y.A. Education building occupied in 1892, knowing its halls until 1898 when he was seventeen years of age and became efficient in business courses.

In 1898 he entered the employ of Taylor Brothers Company and learned the departmentizing of general merchandise. The only rival the store had south of Salt Lake City was the Chipman Mercantile in American Fork. But land and water were his major concern. "The wealth of the people rests upon ownership of land and water rights for the city," he said. Accordingly he entered the employ of W. H. Ray & Co., Real Estate & Loans.

In 1906 he accepted a mission call to England, centering his work around Birmingham, where considerable challenges to the Church had generated. His earnest manner and ready smile opened many doors, of the skeptical and quiet conversions were made. When his two years were finished, he returned to Provo and established the Dixon Real Estate Co. with J. Elmer Jacobsen. This company quickly became one of the states best real estate concerns. -

His business connections proved his versatility and organizing abilities:

1905—Organizer and president until his death of the Provo Ice & Cold Storage Co. Ice was a luxury in his day and the ice plant was near the Denver & Rio Grande tracks by the mill race on 12th North and 2nd West, where Barbizon Co. now operates. The Company shipped ice to Heber Valley and through Utah County and fruit was iced there until the Railroad built its ice plant. Electricity put the icebox out of business.

Within a period of ten years, he was president of the Blue Cliff Canal Co., the State Realty Assn., secretary for the Utah Land Owners Assn., the South Fork Cattle Company, and supervisor of the Skipper Bay Drainage District. He was one of the first appraisers of the Provo Building & Loan Assn., director of the American Building & Loan Assn., and the Dixon Ranch Co. If he had acted upon his own appraisal and judgment, his heirs would have owned most of the highly priced eastern bench. "Some day, that district will be the choice spot in the County," he said. But Roy Dixon was never money-mad.

In politics and civic work he early became a favored leader, a vigorous Republican, and a devoted public servant.

1912-17, Provo City Commissioner

1918-22, Mayor of Provo

1913—until near death, treasurer of the Provo Board of Education

1918—to end of World War I, chairman of the demanding Utah County Draft Board

Member of the Municipal League of Utah for 10 years

Member of the Utah Water Storage Commission to 1920

Chairman of the Utah County Taxpayers Association

Member of the Executive Committee of the Utah Public Health Assn., one of the first to challenge the contamination of Utah Lake

Member of Utah County Reclamation

12 years a member of Provo Public Library Board

An active member of the Provo Chamber of Commerce

As time permitted, he honored his Kiwanis membership

He was mindful of his own health and became an ardent tennis devotee in the Provo Tennis Club, playing on the Woolen Mills Tennis Courts, on the lots just south of the P. E. Ashton Auto Company of today.

LeRoy Dixon was a booster of B.Y.U. and town sports, encouraging his own family and all young people to go to college and assisting many with finances. The State mourned his sudden death and praised his active conservative and patriotic life.

FRANK MILTON DRIGGS

His forefathers developed New Netherlands in America
and were heroes in the American Revolution

Born: November 20, 1870   **Place:** Pleasant Grove, Utah

Father: Benjamin Woodbury Driggs

Mother: Rosalie Cox born in Nauvoo, Illinois. She was a Black
Hawk war bride.

Brothers and Sisters: Howard R., nationally known educator and pioneer historian
Barton W., former superintendent Idaho School for the Deaf
Wm. King Driggs, musician, artist, and director; father of the famous King Sisters and King Family
Leonore D. Dowd, Geneva D. Halverson, Alice D. Brown Maude D. Christensen, and Lucille D. Heller
An illustrious family of educators and civic workers

Marriage: Maude Elsie Short
married Jan. 10, 1898

Children: Mrs. Nell Clarice Reed of Los Angeles, California
Milton Short Driggs, deceased at early age

Death: February 5, 1959 in Los Angeles, California, where he and
family went after his 1945 retirement.

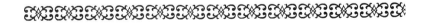

Frank M. Driggs, like his brothers, grew tall, and worked vigorously and intensely as if his time were limited. An illustrious son of an illustrious family, deeply religious and intensely patriotic, Frank pursued his religious duties in a quiet manner as he did most of his work.

At an early age he became interested in the problems of hearing, especially deploring deafness which he was told was hereditary. This he early disproved. He went through grade school with his brothers, took his share of the farm work, passed his home studies as well as his school assignments. He spent two years at the BY Academy and had the encouragement of Dr. Maeser and faculty to become an authority in teaching the deaf. He accordingly got approval from his parents to go the world's greatest school for teaching the deaf, the Gallaudet College in Washington, D. C., from which he graduated with honors for his Master's Degree. A few years later the College conferred on him an honorary doctorate.

He became a member of School for the Deaf operating in Salt Lake City in 1889 and accepted the superintendency of the School of Deaf and Blind located for the state in Ogden, Utah, near Five Points. A plan of expansion was immediately begun and Frank began to sell the school to legislators and county and city authorities. He invited groups to be first hand witnesses of the work accomplished and that to be done. Buildings and dormitories began to spring up, and fields were cultivated for self-support and training of students. The deaf outnumbered the blind for five, as much as ten to one. The school rapidly achieved a national and international reputation. Students were put into basketball leagues and baseball become popular. Trades were developed as fast as means were acquired to purchase equipment. The faculty was trained and increased to meet growing demands. Neighboring states sent their favored children to Utah's school.

As the school was growing, Frank Driggs was selling his product in Ogden, in Weber County, and in the State. He became president of Ogden's alert Chamber of Commerce, president of the Ogden Rotary Club and Rotary District Governor. Business men elected him secretary for People's Finance and Thrift Co. With differing lengths of terms he became President of the Utah Development League, the Utah Chatauqua Association, Utah Education Association, National President of Superintendents of Schools for Deaf in the United States and Canada, an active member in American Convention of Instructors of the Deaf. He enjoyed recreational activities at the Ogden Golf and Country Club. Most of his adult life he taught classes or was an officer in the LDS Sunday School.

He served the state as Superintendent of the Deaf and Blind School from 1906-1945, when he retired. Beautiful residence, dormitory, and school buildings were scattered over the ample campus, blooded Holsteins furnished their dairy products, hard wood trees and multicolored flowers graced the spacious walks and gardens.

Hard work had worn a willing body to the point where it needed rest and recuperation. The hundreds of students he had taught, helped, and advised came to his testimonial, a state and almost a national affair. With his devoted wife and daughter Nell, he moved to California, where he gave lectures and wrote articles. On February 5, 1959, his death was announced to the world. A great scholar who devoted so much of his life to the handicapped had left an imperishable record of servicable deeds.

HOWARD ROSCOE DRIGGS

Born: August 8, 1873   **Place:** Pleasant Grove, Utah

Father: Benjamin Woodbury Driggs, son of Shadrach Driggs; his forefathers developed New Netherlands in America: Joseph Driggs—founder of the family in America, born 1682 in Brooklyn, N.Y., under Dutch name of Josias, married Elizabeth Baarn, died 1748. Daniel his son, died 1748

Mother: Rosalia Ellen Cox; born in Nauvoo; a Black Hawk war bride, married in Manti, Utah.

Brothers and Sisters: Frank M., (Howard R.), Lenore D. Dowd, Maud D. Christensen, an infant, Lucille D. Heller, Geneva D. Halverson, Burton W. (See under Wm. King Driggs for children of first wife, Howard's half brothers and sisters.)

Marriage: (1) Eva Frampton, September 8, 1897, died 1947.
(2) Margaret Brazier Quarrier, September 26, 1948.

Children: Howard Wayne Driggs, Perry Driggs

Death: Sunday, February 17, 1963 of a heart attack at his home in Queens, New York.

The ancestry of the Driggs family is worthy of attention here. Joseph Driggs Jr. and Rachel Johnson had three sons who fought in the American Revolution: Joseph Driggs Jr. II, Israel, and Elisha. Daniel Driggs and Elizabeth Strickland had four sons: Daniel Jr., John, Bartholomew, and David. These seven Driggs heroes enlisted in 1775 and saw service throughout the war with records of various deeds of valor. Uriel Driggs and wife, Hannah Ford, joined the LDS Church and gathered at Nauvoo in 1838, along with their children, Sterling, Samuel and Ruth. Remaining loyal to Brigham Young, the Driggs family left Nauvoo in May, 1846. Uriel died in Lee County, a worn-out man. His sons, Shadrach, Lorenzo, and Sterling made his coffin. The father of Don B. Colton was Sterling Driggs Colton. Sterling was a pioneer of July 24, 1847, and one of the best explorers for the Church.

With this background there is little wonder that Howard R. spent much of his life searching for stories of the pioneers and Western colonizers, becoming a noted writer, outstanding educator, and nationally accredited historian. To list his publications would amply suffice to list him as a famous Son of Brigham.

He knew the joys of boyhood connected with farm life, mountain climbing, fishing and swimming, corn husking, and Indian association. As a young man he heard the story of Battle Creek (Utah County) and the killing of a white settler, the first to die by Indian arrows south of Salt Lake at a place later known as Pleasant Grove. Buffalo, Indian, and Pioneer stories fascinated him, and he early collected tales of the plains and mountains and gradually came to sympathize with the Indians for their losses of land, hunting grounds, and seasonal meanderings. He was reared with the pioneers and knew their struggles for land without conflict, worship without duress, and security from fickle elements such as drought, early frosts, and plague.

Howard R. was seventeen when he came to BYA. This was the last year it was held in the Z.C.M.I. warehouse. He came in contact frequently with Dr. Maeser, who both awed and inspired him. In 1892 Howard achieved a Normal Diploma and a firm resolve to be a teacher. He later recalled to our student body in College Hall the march of joy and anticipation he had with the entire school from the Z.C.M.I. building to the new Education Building on 5th North. His word pictures were so vivid we actually saw the parading band, the Grand Old Flag in front of an organized group waving flags and singing their way to new heights in education. The Board of Directors, the faculty, the college classes, high school, grades down to kindergarten and townspeople followed in buggies, surreys and wagons. A glorious rally followed in a large, high ceiling room, to be known as Room D, crowded to window sills with people filling the adjacent halls. A new home, a greater opportunity and challenge! "We left that room with religion in our souls."

School occupied most of Howard R.'s teen-age life. He graduated from the University of Utah in 1897 when David O. McKay was class President; Howard was class poet for their exercises. He took a B.A. from Utah in 1908, an M.A. from New York University in 1918, and a PhD in English Literature from the same school in 1926. In 1906 he had won a scholarship to the University of Chicago.

He began teaching at Pleasant Grove in an ungraded school at Manila, Utah in 1891, was principal at Lindon in 1894, instructor at Cedar City Branch Normal 1897-1900, assistant principal from 1904-06. The University of Utah engaged him as instructor from 1912-14, and he became Professor of English 1914-1923. New York University used him as a visiting Professor of English Education in 1923, then he became associate Professor in 1924-1926, and Professor from 1928-1942, when he was made Professor Emeritus until his death.

With his teaching he had an insatiable hobby, the collecting and writing of American pioneer stories. He wrote more than twenty books and co-authored twelve more. For his *This is the West* he won the Spier Award from the League of Western Writers. His stories were published in a series, *The Pioneer Life, Rise of the Lone Star,* and *Westward America.* His series of texts written for the teaching of English were nationally adopted in the early 1920's. His *Westward America,* 1942, was acclaimed as one of the nation's best books of history. *Money Rock—A Drama of the Pony Express* was his last book, published in 1960.

Howard Driggs was not a desk man only. Wherever he went he became a part of the institution or community. He was executive secretary of the Utah State Board of Education, in charge of libraries 1915-1916; President of Utah Educational Association 1916; Vice President of the National Education Association 1919-1920 and a life member; Vice President of the N.Y. Teachers Club 1931-32; Charter member of Utah Trails and Landmarks Association 1931; President of the Oregon Trail Memorial Association, 1930; director of the Covered Wagon Centennial, 1930; and organizer of the Pony Express Diamond Jubilee, 1935. He especially enjoyed being President of the American Pioneer Trails from 1942 until his death, retelling stories of some 4,000 pioneers who pushed handcarts across hostile plains and mountains into Utah.

He is credited as being one of the first educators to use radio in the class room and was constantly striving to devise means of vitalizing English to interest every person in the nation. He deplored poor spelling and bad speech as companions of ignorance. He stressed these subjects when he edited the *Utah Education Review* in 1917-1918.

Brigham Young University honored him with its Alumni Distinguished Service Award in 1955. He was elected to the Western Hall of Fame in 1952. The Utah Club of New York presented him with its first Achievement Award in 1941 at the Waldorf Astoria Hotel, a medal designed and cast by Mahonri Young.

Religious from an early age, Dr. Driggs taught in Mutual Improvement Association and Sunday School most of his mature life, becoming a member of the General Sunday School Board from 1910 until his death. He assisted Apostle Reed Smoot in organizing the first LDS Sunday School in Washington, D. C. in 1934 and was counselor and President of the N.Y. Branch from 1928-1930. He was set apart as a High Priest in 1934 by President J. Reuben Clark Jr.

His stories are a treasure house of Western history and pioneer life. He long stressed his belief that a country's greatest assets were not its material riches but its heritage of founding pioneers. The *Deseret News* eulogized: "His impressive personality, his eloquence, his flashes of humor, his warm humanity, his directness of thought—these are qualities in the life of this fine gentleman that will linger long in the memories of his myriads of friends, admirers and loved ones."

Descending from patriotic American Revolutionists and Mormon pioneers, he and his brothers are true Sons of Brigham.

WARREN N. DUSENBERRY

Born: November 1, 1836   **Place:** Whitehaven, Luzerne County
Pennsylvania.
In Provo from 1862 until early in the 1900's, when the
family moved to California.

Father: Mahlon Dusenberry; born March 1, 1808, in Frenchtown,
New Jersey; came to Utah in July 18, 1860; carpenter
and cabinet maker; died August 22, 1899, in Sacramento,
California.

Mother: Aurilla Coray; born May 21, 1831, at Easton, Pennsylvania;
daughter of Silas Coray and Mary Stephens of Danville,
New York; came to Utah in 1862, with children from
California; died December 6, 1884; buried in Dusenberry
plot in Provo Cemetery.

Brothers   John B., b. Aug. 2, 1832; Mary Ann, b. Feb 2, 1834; Warren
and Sisters: N., b. Nov. 1, 1836; Silas B., b. Dec. 11, 1838; William B.,
b. June 12, 1845; George, b. July 7, 1848; Albert, b. Dec.
30, 1850; (Silas, William, George and Albert all died in
early childhood).

Marriage: Adelaide Elizabeth Webb

Children: Clara D. Park, Jennie, Walter, Frank E., Arthur, Harvey,
and Grover survived father's death.

Death: March 30, 1915; died as a result of wounds from an ax,
San Francisco, Calif.

The Dusenberry brothers came to Utah in 1862, after Johnston's Army had passed through Salt Lake and had quartered some distance away from Camp Floyd. The Dusenberry mother and children, with the father, had gone on to California but returned to Utah, leaving the father in Sacramento still disinterested in the Mormon faith. Warren N. and Wilson H. were most companionable brothers and had many similar characteristics. Each excelled in school teaching, was active and successful in politics, and was prominent in church circles.

They came to Utah out of love for a mother and remained to teach. Warren was first engaged to teach in the First District of Provo, under the auspices of the City and the First Ward of the LDS Church.

Soon thereafter the brothers opened a school for all ages in the Cluff Hall at Second North and Second East, where at night shows were presented by the Provo Dramatic Club, of which Warren had become a member. They made progress for two years with a grade school but concluded that a school of higher grades would be more practical and profitable. At this time Warren was called and went on a church mission in 1865 of which he was proud the rest of his life. Returning in 1868, the brothers engaged the Kinsey Building on Center Street at First West, divided it into rooms, and Warren made some of the desks and school furniture which were later used at the BY Academy. The classes were scheduled for the third grade and up.

The pupils were so poorly supplied with books that Warren went to Salt Lake and purchased fifty dollars worth of books and made them available to the parents as well as the students. The brothers advocated less harshness in discipline, insisting on good manners and sound conduct. J. Marinus Jensen stated, "The two brothers did much to raise the social and cultural standards of the city."

By 1869-70 so many students had applied for enrollment that they rented the Lewis Building for $50.00 a month, located on Third West and Center Street where the Chamber of Commerce is now located. At this time another teacher, T. B. Lewis, was engaged. He later became Territorial Commissioner of Education.

In 1870, Territorial School Superintendent Robert L. Campbell came to Provo with other territorial officials, saw the success and efficiency of Dusenberry school, and proposed that it become the Timpanogos Branch of the University of Deseret in Salt Lake City. This arrangement was soon accepted and students were so enrolled. Several authorities of Utah praised the school, its teachers and management but later found the school "imperfect in organization because it provided no religious education."

In 1874-75 the Superintendent reported that the operation of the school was suspended because of its "imperfect organization," and lack of funds to pay teachers and to expand the school. On November 22nd a new organization was affected and the deed to the property was given by President Brigham Young, who had acquired all rights to the location and building, to seven chosen trustees to establish an academy. They elected Warren N. as first principal. He realized that the school had a better opportunity for success with Church support. He was already practicing law when he was made principal, and his brother Wilson had withdrawn from teaching. Warren stayed but one term, leaving with an enrollment of 97 students, one of whom was George H. Brimhall. His teachers were J. E. Booth and Frank E. Stone.

When he resigned his principalship he relinquished all teaching ties and was happy with the selection of his successor, Karl G. Maeser. In fact, he was on the committee with President Abraham O. Smoot which asked President Young for the services of Doctor Maeser. At the fire of the Lewis Building in 1884 Warren N. was a tireless worker and was one of the first to tell the disheartened crowd that the school "Must carry on" and to urge immediate rebuilding. He was then the Judge of the City Court and used all his influence in the school's rehabilitation.

A few more details of the Academy's founding prove interesting:

After several weeks of deliberation and study, President Young appointed a committee of three to wait upon Professor Maeser at his home to discuss the enlarging of the Provo school to meet academic standards. The meeting was successful and the committee; George Q. Cannon, George Reynolds, and Warren N. Dusenberry, attended a Board meeting at Savage's Art Gallery and arrangements were made for a preliminary session of the new school. Brother Maeser's salary was set at $1,200 for the first year, to be paid such in commodities as the treasurer might take in tuition. The new principal could chose his own faculty, and the B. Y. Academy officially opened on January 3, 1876.

Before we disassociate Warren N. from these school ties we quote from the "Ogden Junction," 1873, the year the Utah Southern Railroad reached Provo: "The Timpanogos University, two blocks southwest of the factory, is a great feature of this important city . . . The University is ably conducted by Professor W. N. Dusenberry, assisted by Messrs. J. E. Booth and Frank M. Stone."

Most of Warren's subsequent life was concerned with law and politics. In 1874 he was Prosecuting Attorney (City), and in 1880 he was Superintendent of the State Insane Asylum (Utah State Mental). This Institution was located in Provo largely because of the vigorous efforts of Warren N. In the 80's and 90's Warren was busy with land and water suits and often, with out of court arbitration. The need for the territory's entrance into the Union was paramount and was the core of political discussions. Eighteen-hundred-ninety-two, the year of the Academy's move into a long awaited building at 5th North, was a year of an intense mayorality campaign. Reed Smoot (Republican), Henry W. Davis (Liberal), and Warren N. Dusenberry (Democrat) came to the polls, each certain of victory. The next morning Warren N. Dusenberry was Mayor of Provo, a position he held for one term. He had been soundly beaten as a candidate for Mayor in 1890 when John E. Booth defeated a Reed Smoot candidate, George Sutherland. Warren N. was Probate Judge of Utah County for many years and judge of the 4th District Court in 1898 and 1899.

The Judge took part in all types of civic affairs and was especially active in the Commercial Club. A condensed newspaper report of the time reports: "At a Chamber of Commerce discussion it was proposed to erect a street railway in Provo. Judge Warren N. Dusenberry was appointed chairman to go to City Council and ask for a franchise; after a long discussion on the effect upon houses, the petition was granted. In February, 1889, the petition for a car line on University Avenue and Center St. was granted. It took a year to build and equip (The terminals were the BY University, not yet built but projected, and Utah Lake) the Depot at the foot of University. A motor engine was used and the road to the Provo Lake Resort was operated in the summer. The car was frequently out of repair and often jumped the track. It was not uncommon for a dozen volunteers to assist in putting the car on the rails.) Cows stopped it for minutes when crossing as they came from the outlying pastures. In 1892 the cars ceased to run and the franchise was forfeited on Jan. 9, 1893. The stockholders were sued and brunt of the burden fell on Warren N. Dusenberry.

Soon after this experience, he and his family moved to California and little was heard of him in Utah. His death was most tragic. The San Francisco report to his son, Frank E. Dusenberry, in Provo, gave only meager details. Told in brief: the youngest son, Grover, and father, Warren, were in the cellar chopping wood when apparently a quarrel developed and a demented boy seized the axe before the father could defend himself, inflicting several severe cuts. Taken to the hospital the Judge recuperated quickly and apparently was on the way to recovery. But due to a sudden relapse, and with no animosity toward his son, he died, survived by his wife and following children: Clara, Jennie, Walter, Arthur, and Grover in California, Frank E. in Provo, and Harvey in the East. His brother, Wilson, in Provo, and also Mrs. Glazier who lived in Salt Lake, also survived him.

The Dusenberrys, Warren and Wilson, were important contributors to the culture and educational atmosphere of Utah County and the State. They were proud of their parts in establishing the Brigham Young University.

WILSON HOWARD DUSENBERRY

Born: April 7, 1841   **Place:** Perry, Pike County, Illinois
Came to Utah with his mother and family in 1862.

Father: Mahlon Dusenberry, born March 1, 1808, Frenchtown, New Jersey; came through Utah in July of 1860 and settled in California; a carpenter and cabinet maker; died August 22, 1899, in Sacramento, California.

Mother: Aurilla Coray, m. May 21, 1831, at Easton, Pennsylvania; daughter of Silas Coray and Mary Stephens of Danville, New York; came to Utah July 18th, 1860, with Capt. Williams Company; died December 6, 1884; buried in the Dusenberry plot in Provo.

**Brothers
and Sisters:**   John, Mary Ann (Long), (Watson), (Ogden), Warren N., Silas*, Wilson Howard, Martha Jane (Glazier), William*, George*, Albert* (* died in infancy).

Marriage: 1) Harriet Virginia Coray, December 4, 1864, in Provo; daughter of Howard Coray and Martha Jane Knowlton of Danville, N.Y., pioneers of 1852; she was born August 13, 1848, died June 6, 1872.

              2) Margaret Thompson Smoot, Nov. 25, 1874, in Salt Lake City; daughter of Abraham O. Smoot and Emily Hill of Provo; she was born Aug. 27, 1854 in Sugar House.

Children: (of Harriet) Charles Wilson, b. June 2, 1866; May, b. Nov. 25, 1867; Blanche (Parker), b. April 20, 1870; Harriet Virginia, died as an infant.
(of Margaret) Abraham Owen, b. Dec. 5, 1875; Lorena, b. April 3, 1878; Ada (Nibley), b. April 6, 1881; Cora, b. Sept. 13, 1883; Eva, b. Jan. 23, 1887; Edith, b. May 16, 1891.

Death: March 20, 1925; buried in Provo Cemetery with his family.

The life of Wilson H. Dusenberry, for its greatest part, is linked with his elder brother, Warren N., only four and one half years separating their ages. Four of their brothers died in infancy or early childhood, bringing the two boys closer together.

The father, Mahlon, was an excellent carpenter and cabinet maker and found his best employment in larger cities rather than the unsettled west. (California was the objective of the father, with the mother, Aurilla, desiring a Utah home for Church affiliations. The family went with the father to California, but returned to Provo, Utah, without the father.)

Wilson married Harriet Virginia Coray, daughter of his mother's relative. With her he had four children. An infant named for her mother died in 1872 soon after birth, to be followed by the mother. A strong friendship had been established with President Abraham O. Smoot and his several families. In 1874 Wilson married Margaret Thompson Smoot, the daughter of Abraham O. and Emily Hill Smoot of Provo. They had one son, Abraham Owen Jr., and five daughters.

Adjusting to territorial conditions and needs, Wilson made teaching his major objective, but his ambitions as a teacher were greatly curtailed when the Dusenberry school was transferred to the Deseret University management. He was disillusioned with the teaching prospects the poorly financed schools offered. His family was growing and he needed means to assure their progress. He became Superintendent of Schools in Utah County from 1874 to 1880 and extended classroom teaching throughout his territory. He kept his interest in the new B. Y. Academy as a member of the Board of Trustees from 1883 to 1921, being secretary from 1887 to 1891 and secretary-treasurer from 1891 to 1915.

In September, 1876, Superintendant Wilson H. Dusenberry asked the County Court to visit Karl G. Maeser's Normal Class. On the recommendation of Superintendent Dusenberry, the Court agreed to provide tuition for twenty-six students to attend BYA. Three were from Provo, twenty-three from the rest of the County. This arrangement prevailed for a number of years.

Paralleling his other activities, he was a member of the Provo City Council from 1872-1888, a period of sixteen years, and Mayor of Provo from 1882-1889. During his councilship the Utah Southern Railroad came to Provo November 25, 1873, with a rollicking celebration in which Wilson H. was most active. In August of this year the *Provo Daily Times* began publication.

Being County Clerk added further to his duties and pay from 1875-1883. Encompassed in his busy schedule was his being a member of the State Legislature in 1880, 1882, and 1884, where he was chairman of the House Committee on Education.

With his capacity for diversity of work, he was appointed cashier of the First National Bank of Provo from 1882-1891, with Abraham O. Smoot as President. In 1891 further confidence was placed in him when he became cashier of the Utah County Savings Bank from 1891-1901. Politics called him once more when he was appointed assistant postmaster of Provo from 1901-1913, concluding his work when he was seventy-two years of age.

He also made time to work in the auxiliaries of the Church and was made a member of the High Council in 1878.

In 1883 the Provo Theatre Company was organized from two former rival companies, the Provo Amateur Dramatic Union and the Home Dramatic Company, who performed in Cluff's Hall. Harvey H. Cluff was President, John J. Graham was a director, and Wilson Dusenberry was secretary-treasurer. This group built the Provo Opera House located on the east side of First West, between Center and First North (now torn down and replaced with a parking lot), and presented its first play, "The Streets of New York." Most of the officers had been favorite amateur thespians.

On January 4, 1883, when the Academy burned down, Wilson H. was Mayor of Provo. On the next evening he called the City Council together and proposed a city fire department. As a result a committee soon reported that a hand-power fire engine could be obtained for $1,500. Authority was given to obtain the engine, but lack of funds and council cooperation put the matter off until 1890, when John E. Booth was Mayor. Proper action was taken and a $4,000 La France engine procured as had been advocated by Mayor Dusenberry. A hose cart drawn brigade manned by volunteer firemen was organized, and in the interim it was soon tried out.

Time lessened Wilson's working enthusiasm and his health began to fail in his later years. He spent more time with his growing family and less with politics and business. One of his last activities to keep his interest was being a member of the Executive Board of the Brigham Young University. He helped its growth with enthusiasm and praise and openly expressed his desires for its increase in a degreed faculty and expanding curriculum.

His picture and that of his brother, Warren N., may be seen in the long gallery in the City Building which displays the Mayors of Provo. They were the only two brothers to be Provo's executive heads, and, more important to our story, they were the nucleus of a school which became affiliated with the University of Deseret in Salt Lake. Their efforts further promoted the founding of Brigham Young Academy.

EPHRAIM G. GOWANS

Educator - Physician

Born: February 1, 1868 at Tooele, Utah

Father: Hugh Sibler Gowans b. Perthshire, Scotland, February 23, 1832. Son of Robert Gowans and Grace McKay Gowans. Came to Utah with his wife in 1855 from Scotland.

Mother: Betsey Ann Gowans, b. Arbroath, Scotland, February 22, 1832. Daughter of Andrew Gowans and Ann McLeish

Brothers and Sisters: Barbara, Hugh Jr., Robert, James, Annie, Andrew, Betsey Ann, Gowans Lyman, (Ephraim Gowans Gowans) Alonzo G., Charles Anthony

Marriage: Mary C. Lyman, sister of Dr. Richard R. Lyman
Daughter of President Francis M. Lyman and Rhoda Taylor. (Francis M. - President of the Council of the Twelve.)

Children: Louis Lyman, b. April 22, 1894, m. Helen Taylor, Oct. 5, 1918 Lois, b. December 20, 1895, m. Henry E. Beal May 15, 1918 Marjori b. June 7, 1889 m. Henry William Bennett July 19, 1928 Emerson Lyman b. January 19, 1905, d. May 25, 1951 Marion Lyman b. May 17, 1909 m. Rhoda Christine Hansen June 29, 1933 d. 1960.

Died: February 5, 1930

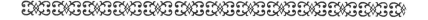

E. G. Gowans was not a tall man but "thick through the chest," a man of exceptional strength, especially with his hands.

His schooling proved him to be deeply religious, sincere of purpose and possessing a broad interest in life. He went to the Tooele public schools with well-trained, mature teachers; came to Brigham Young Academy to be grounded in mathematics, grammar, spelling, penmanship, chemistry and general science. With inadequate laboratories, the great outdoors very often became the class room for natural science. Most students were made conscious of soil products, water storage, strata of mountains, stock raising and reproduction. Aside from farming and livestock production a young man looked to teaching, medicine and law. E. G. qualified in all three and accumulated a magnificent library on these subjects.

His schooling was acquired at Brigham Young Academy, Brigham Young College (Logan), Baltimore Medical College, and after practice in Mt. Pleasant, Utah, he enrolled in Johns Hopkins University.

His mission called him to Scotland, home of his ancestors, in which he labored three years, and for several years he was active in the Deseret Sunday School Union and wrote lessons for class study.

He kept close to the state's educational program all of his adult life, sitting in policy-making committees. He never ceased being the physician and gave health talks wherever needed. Civic life took little of his time, though he enjoyed his association with the Bonneville, Exchange, and Ensign Clubs. He married the sister of his boyhood and lifetime friend, Dr. Richard R. Lyman. With her he had five children of whom they were justly proud. Lyman is a successful businessman of Honolulu, Hawaii.

E. G. Gowans, physician, educator, jurist and churchman, as he was eulogized at his funeral:

His expressions were usually crisp, in short sentences. His speech was clear, almost decisive but his voice revealed a kindly soul. A few words from one of his many essays will partly reveal the man, taken from "My Creed."

"I have one person to make good—myself. My duty to all others is to make them happy. If I would also be happy myself I must be healthy and must radiate cheerfulness and good will.

"When I am happy in body and mind the world in which we live is very beautiful, and I find the good in everything and everybody. Therefore I must live according to the simple laws of physical and mental health. This is the beginning of wisdom. . . .To radiate cheerfulnes and good will to others it is necessary to love them—not hate, judge or condemn them . . . As man is the crowning work of creation, so loyalty is his crowning characteristic. I must be loyal to the truth as I understand it."

In these few words taken from a full page essay, we see the friend, physician, jurist and teacher talking as one person. He constantly sought avenues for service—his change of vocation was not accidental; it revealed the spread of his interests in his fellow men. From the juvenile court in a city, to a state Industrial school, directorship of health in the public schools, and State Superintendent of Public Instruction—and practice of his medical profession as occasion demanded—he held no geographic boundary.

His later years were given to the University of Utah and his closing months to practice of his major interest, the care of the eye and the ear. He was a dynamic man seeking outlet of abilities that crowded for expression. Several professions claimed him as their very own.

FRED C. GRAHAM

Residence: 5657 Holladay Blvd., Salt Lake City, Utah

Born: October 18, 1874 in Salt Lake City, Utah

Father: Joseph Leland Graham; born September 28, 1843 in London, England; died January 30, 1909 in Provo, Utah; brother of John C. Graham, famed actor of old Salt Lake Theater and the Provo Opera House.

Mother: Sarah Ann Mitchell; born March 31, 1851 in St. Louis, Missouri; died December 6, 1928 in Salt Lake City; crossed the plains with oxen and wagon.

Brothers and Sisters: Joseph M. Graham, b. Salt Lake City Nov. 20, 1871, d. January 15, 1955; Rose Victoria Graham, b. Salt Lake City December 9, 1879, m. Neil C. Jensen, February 19, 1901; Sarah E. Graham, b. Salt Lake City on March 18, 1885, m. Lorenzo Price December 3, 1903;
William H. Graham, b. Salt Lake City on April 14, 1877, d. October 13, 1960;
Charles Henry Graham, b. Salt Lake City September 27, 1882.

Marriage: Allie Bishop; married in Salt Lake Temple, June 11, 1896; b. in Salt Lake City, November 4, 1873, the daughter of Captain F. M. Bishop, member of Powell's second expedition down the Colorado; grand-daughter of Orson Pratt, pioneer, scholar, and great missionary of the young Church; died in Salt Lake City on October 5, 1949.

Children: Frederick F. Graham, b. Salt Lake May 19, 1900, d. Salt Lake July 13, 1919;
Douglas I. Graham, b. Salt Lake City November 5, 1902, m. Manola Jorgensen in Salt Lake Temple August 10, 1934;
Edward W. Graham, b. Salt Lake City January 11, 1912, m. Helen Knudson on May 8, 1937.

When a complete history of music in Utah is written it must feature the life of Fred C. Graham who knew and worked with the state's musical pioneers and is intimate with the best in music of the present. His beautiful lyric voice was discovered when he was but 15; the transition from boyish soprano to a manly tenor was almost imperceptible. Ballads must have been written for him, for he rendered them so easily and with such audience empathy.

Fred was a "comic" from early childhood and could imitate most people who came within his observation. He was easily "the life of the party" and one of the most popular young men in the community. His pantomimic ability brought him before the public in every type of amateur productions, with or without music. Early in life he sang in testimonials, charity shows, and for countless funerals. "He puts soul into his song." In the days of minstrels, he was a favorite end man, supplying any dialect an interlocutor required.

One of his intimate friends said: "He takes happiness with him and has a good story for every occasion." Now over ninety you feel his happy disposition and kindly viewpoint toward life. Beauty fills his soul and will cause him to stop his work to better view a golden sunset or nature's brush on the autumn mountain.

"I love a quartette because we have to learn to work together and harmony fills my soul." In those words he revealed his inner self. One of his musical chums called him a peacemaker. "I never knew him in a quarrel."

He was a classmate of Maud Adams in the Salt Lake schools and shared her successes by letter and in frequent associations. Their meeting kindled nostalgic memories.

A brief of his interesting life:

Discovered at 15 in Provo for minstrels. Sang in operas at BYU.

1893—on tour with a company under Clomenia Pratt; comedy, villian, hero and character bit.

Mission to Colorado (Western States).

Worked for Oregon Short Line Railroad as disbursing officer. "If a man is worth anything to a corporation, he is worth just that much more to himself." He re-read this quotation and decided to quit.

Began teaching music; one of his earliest pupils, Sadie Rasband, wife of the late Mayor Earl J. Glade.

1906—Opened his Music Bureau. Booked George D. Pyper, Judith Anderson, Horace S. Ensign and Ed Midgley for a concert in Sandy Ward House; netted the sum of $1.50.

1907—Brought Chicago Symphony Orchestra to Salt Lake Tabernacle; the chorus and soloists were under Evan Stephens; performed Taylor's "Death of Minnehaha" and

"The Messiah"; the Tabernacle was filled for all three performances, and it made money.

1907-1914—Managed such artists as Emil Gorgorza, bairtone, Arthur Hartman, violinist; Johannah Gadski, Wagnerian soprano; Joseph Levine, pianist; Hellen Keller, etc.

Toured Orpheum Circuit with Imperial Male Quartette; sang in a mine shaft 2100 feet down, in Butte

1909—Tenor solist at the dedication of the Catholic Cathedral in Salt Lake.

1911—Toured as soloist with the Salt Lake Tabernacle Choir and sang McClellan's "Irrigation Ode"; was also soloist with the Choir in Madison Square Garden.

1917—Opened up schools of music at Cedar City, using well-known Utah teachers including the late Hugh Dougall, Edna Evans Johnson, Evangeline Thomas Beesley.

1918—Schools at Vernal and at Richfield; both successful.

Toured Utah with Minneapolis Symphony Orchestra.

1917-1929—Toured Utah and Idaho with the Tabernacle Choir to sing Stephen's "Vision", singing the tenor role of "Joseph." Toured with Charles Wakefield Cadman, singing Cadman's Indian Songs, featuring Tsianina Red Feather, Indian soprano.

For two years he toured Utah and Idaho with Babcock Varsity Players as manager and actor.

Served as Director of Music at Hotel Utah under George O. Relf.

Arranged tours for Emma Lucy Gates, Salt Lake Opera Quintette, etc.

Principal of Salt Lake Opera Co. from 1893 to October, 1928. Organized Lyceum Circuit 1935.

From 1893 a member of the Salt Lake Tabernacle Choir. Still manages his Bureau; member of the International Lyceum and Platform Association.

Soloist in last public appearance of former stars in the Salt Lake Theatre Festival given in College Hall in April, 1945 with John D. Spencer, George D. Pyper, Hugh Dougall Emma Lucy Gates Bowen, Jack Summerhays and Becky Almond, with BYU graduate players; scenes from their most beloved operas.

Member of the Chamber of Commerce in Salt Lake City and the select "Browser's Club" for nostalgic association; member of Sons of Utah Pioneers. Tends to his four acres of orchard and garden in beautiful Holladay.

Fred Graham is a man of most cheerful, happy disposition, loved by all who know him. He enjoys good company. A little bewildered by some trends in modern art, he sincerely believes that man is born that he might have joy.

Operas in which Fred has had leading parts, in the Salt Lake Theatre: "Madeline and the Magic Kiss," "The Mascot," "The Pirates of Penzance," "Martha," "The Girl and the Governor," "The Mandarin," "Tatinitza," "The Serenade," "Chimes of Normandy," "Trip to Africa," "The Wedding Day," and "Robin Hood."

To list his companions of the great pioneer theatre is to unfold the history of music and drama in the west, as Fred had a personal acquaintance with the early performers of the Salt Lake Theatre: David McKenzie, H. B. Clawson, J. B. Kelly, Phil Marggets, Heber M. Wells, W. C. Dunbar, Edith and Dollie Clawson, Luke Cosgrave, Bridie Cummings, B. S. Young, H. S. A. Culmer, Henry Maiben, and, of course, his uncle, John C. Graham and his close friend, John D. Spencer, in my opinion the greatest actor of them all. His personal acquaintance with the members of the early orchestra is, also a pleasure to remember: George Careless, C. J. Thomas, Henry Sadler, Thomas McIntyre, Horace K. Whitney, and Ebenezer Beesley.

His associates in the Salt Lake Theatre of the later years were: Lucy Gates, Lennie Savage, Lizzie Thomas Edwards, Nellie Bruce Pugsley, Bessie Dean, Viola Pratt, Arvilla Clark, Luella Ferrin, Sally Fisher, Lottye Levy, Hazel Taylor, Evangaline Thomas, Margaret Anderson, Bessie Browning, Agatha Berkhoel, Segred Pederson, Mabel Cooper, Edna Evans; and of the men: George D. Pyper, Bob Easton, Horace Ensign, John D. Spencer, Heber S. Goddard, Hugh W. Dougall, John D. Summerhayes, John Robinson, Melvin Peterson, Harry Shearman.

"I shall not soon forget the last performance in the Salt Lake Theatre, October 20, 1928, when the Salt Lake Opera Company presented the second act of 'Robin Hood,' and Lucy Gates Company presented the third act of 'La Traviata.' The theatre was packed from parquet to third circle, with the leading citizens of Utah paying honor and farewell to this great lovable and sacred edifice."

Fred C. Graham became President of the BYU Emeritus Club in 1951, and for twenty years brought talent from Salt Lake for their programs.

He is the last of the best to play the boards of the grand Salt Lake Theatre.

ALMA GREENWOOD

Born: October 18, 1854 in American Fork, Utah

Father: William Greenwood, son of Robison Greenwood and Elizabeth Cryer born August 7, 1822 in Burnley, Lancashire, England. Disowned by parents for accepting the gospel, but given $5,000 in father's will. First school master in American Fork and in first Bishopric, pioneer surveyor, excellent penman and conference clerk.

Died: January 26, 1891

Mother: Alice Houghton, daughter of Wm. Houghton and Alice Beardsworth
Born May 8, 1823
Married March 30, 1843 at Davenport, Iowa
Died November 13, 1886

Brothers and Sisters: Joseph Robison Greenwood b. March 10, 1844
Elizabeth Alice Greenwood b. March 8, 1845
Benjamin Young Greenwood b. February 9, 1856 m. Sarah Ann Julian
Margaret Ann Greenwood b. February 25, 1847 m. James C. Carter
Alice Greenwood b. February 14, 1849 m. Alfred Moyle
Wm. H. Greenwood b. April 13, 1850 m. Charlotte Wood
Samuel Greenwood b. March 3, 1852 m. Ellen Julian
Jacob Greenwood b. February 2, 1853 m. Melissa Snow
(Alma) Greenwood
Rachel Greenwood b. February 23, 1856 m. Wm. Hunter
Jededa Morgan Greenwood b. October 15, 1857 m. Barbra Edith Boley.
Mary Ellen Greenwood b. March 26, 1859 m. George F. Herbert
Joshua Greenwood b. July 29, 1860 m. Josephina Payne
Ruth Greenwood b. June 22, 1862 m. James Gardner

Marriage: (1) Florence Melissa Brown, daughter of A. Samuel Brown and Helen Vernera McBride.
Born May 12, 1857 in Fillmore, Utah. Her father killed by Indians near Chicken Creek.
A musician, teacher, and seamstress
Married June 12, 1879 in Endowment House, Salt Lake City
Died June 18, 1893 in Fillmore, Utah
(2) Evelyn Olsen, m. Jan. 19, 1894 died when 29
(3) Annena Sorensen five years after Evelyn's death

Children:	Samuel Alma Greenwood b. March 14, 1880 m. Josie Ray
	Alice Helen Greenwood b. August 25, 1885 m. Thales Mathew Derrick
	Wairoa Greenwood b. July 12, 1887 d. November 5, 1891
	Fern Greenwood b. May 13, 1889 m. Reno Wesley Vance
Death:	March 21, 1929 after one hour's illness. He was buried in the Fillmore family plot.

Alma Greenwood often said he was "raised on bread and molasses." During all his youth he herded cows and watched water run down ditches. He was one of the better students all through his boyhood and into college, going to the BY Academy as a strong, eager young man who was given the job of making the fires for Karl G. Maeser. Alma was especially commended as one of the more promising members of the first graduating class of the Academy and encouraged by Dr. Maeser to take up education as a profession.

In 1878 he went to Fillmore, Utah, as educator and teacher, where he founded and was principal of the Millard Stake Academy which was held in the lower floor in the old State House, pioneering in school methods and developing ideas projected at BYA. He became a vigorous protagonist for education of adults, stating that education was meant for all ages as he encouraged older people, most of them converts, to become conversant with the English language, spoken and written. "Every adult must know how to converse with knowledge on any subject important to a community. You live in America; learn its ways and language," was his advice.

In 1882, a mission took him and Ira N. Hinckley to New Zealand for three years, with a wife and child awaiting Alma's return.

When a call was given for him to go to Ephraim, Utah, in 1889 to start another academy, he moved his family of wife and three children to Sanpete County and became the first and organizing principal of Snow Academy. He spent uncounted hours arousing the valley to the value and need of a broad education. He fretted at an inability to move faster with his plans and hopes of reaching all the people as so many of the Scandinavians held tenaciously to their native speech and customs. His attempts for a quicker conversion became a frustration until he developed a nervous illness which prompted him to give up teaching, return to Fillmore and once again, take up farming.

The passing of his talented and devoted helpmate, Florence Melissa Brown at thirty-six, was his first severe challenge in adjusting to an increasing complex competitive life. With three children to rear, he employed house keepers until January 19, 1894, when he married Evelyn Olsen and at the birth of their son, Evan, Evelyn gave her life at age twenty-nine.

Over the years, Alma was called upon for many occasions as a pleasing, effective speaker, his dark eyes seeming to light up as he developed his subject. He was adept with groups in presenting a community need or a church assessment.

He was a brilliant and popular orator in the days when oratory and the longer speeches were in vogue, and he became a power in the State legislature, a member on the more important committees.

Entrusting the burden of the family to his young daughter, Helen, who was eleven, he shared time with his home, his church, and his business as a merchant. After five years, he wed Annena Sorensen, a patient, kind mother to the children and a wise companion to Alma. All his marriages had been Temple ordinances.

In 1908 the growing family moved from Fillmore to American Fork, but once more friends and a love of the soil took them back to Delta, where Alma died at seventy-five years, honored across the state as an educator, legislator, churchman, and devoted parent, with a family of outstanding merit and ability.

DANIEL HARRINGTON

Born: March 15, 1860   **Place:** American Fork, Utah
He was a twin (boy and girl). Mother died at their birth.

Father: Leonard E. Harrington of New Lisbon, Oswego County, New York. Born Jan. 7, 1816.
Came to Utah Oct. 1, 1847 with Edward Hunter Company. Established the first free public schools in Utah, in American Fork, Utah, 1866.
One of the Original trustees of BYA and frequent visitor. Bishop for 32 years; member of the Utah Legislature. Mayor of American Fork.

Mother: Mary Jones, born in Malvern Hills, England.
Married in 1855.
Died in American Fork, March 17, 1860.

Brothers and Sisters: (Daniel)
Mary H. Duncan

Marriage: Leonora Taylor, daughter of President John Taylor and Margaret Young.
Born March 25, 1864
Married March 17, 1886
Died July 26, 1935

Children: Jennie
Daniel T.
Florence, m. L. W. Hickey
John Taylor, m. Ione Lunt
Russell T.
Mary, m. John G. Strohm
Everett T., m. Genevieve Stringham

Death: Nov. 30, 1943.

Daniel Harrington is the son of two outstanding pioneer families. Leonard, the father, had a fair education when he came to Utah but the great number of colonists could not read, especially the younger people who had been reared in troublesome and place-moving times. In the beautiful Utah Valley he set out to remedy the literacy problem and he reputedly established the first free schools in Utah, in American Fork. He gave of his enthusiasm to his son, Daniel, whose mother died two days after his birth.

Young Daniel was an eager student and learned to be an omniverous reader. His father encouraged him in his desire to go to college when such an education was not too popular or well-known. He graduated from BYA in 1881, after a three-year attendance. His classmates were George Sutherland, John E. Booth, D. D. Houtz, J. L. Robison, Zina Y. Williams Card, William H. King, James E. Talmage and J. M. Tanner, to name but a few.

Daniel went to the Lewis School (Brigham Young Academy) on Center Street and visitors frequently attended the classes. Professor Milton Hardy would preside at the Wednesday conclaves while Professor Maeser would leave the platform to play the organ. Just about every time Leonard E. Harrington, BYA Trustee, visited the school, either for an assembly or in a class, Professor Hardy would gravely call upon son Daniel to give the opening or closing prayer. Daniel stated "All eyes fell on me as soon as father entered the room."

From 1881-86 he was principal and superintendent of County School at Richfield, Utah. He extended up-to-date schools throughout the county. "One non-educated person in any county is one too many," he said.

His youthful desire for a training in law was consumated by his graduation with a LLB from the University of Michigan in June of 1891. This determined his career and he was promptly appointed Assistant District Attorney in Utah's 3rd Judicial District which he served until 1893. Private practice in Salt Lake 1893-1928 led to appointment as Judge of the City Court in 1928-1937. A Progressive Republican, he was nominated for the Utah Legislature on the first state ticket of 1891.

His civic and commercial activities were extensive. From 1887-89 he was director and secretary in the Salt Lake and Fort Douglas Railroad and became secretary-director of the Salt Lake and Eastern Railroad (now the Denver and Rio Grande). He saw Utah as a great recreation center and became Director and President of the Scenic Resort Co.

His one major assignment in school teaching was his appointment as County Superintendent of Sevier County Schools, which preceded his law activity.

World War I saw him in numerous assignments; the one he enjoyed the most was being a Four Minute Man in Salt Lake City whose purpose was to sell War Bonds within an allotted time.

As Salt Lake became his residential center he accepted more church assignments, and for ten years he was a vigorous Home Missionary in the Salt Lake Stake.

He was attorney for quieting title to all waters of Mill Creek to Salt Lake County, suit having 400 defendants, largest number for any Utah suit up to that time. The case was before the district court for three years.

He was proud of his ancestry, becoming a charter-member of the Native Sons of Utah.

During his political career he drew heavily from the examples and teachings of two men, Karl G. Maeser and Abraham Lincoln. He was proud of the fact "that out of the first hundred men who fought at Lexington and Concord, seven were Harringtons. One of these, Jonathan Harrington, a distant cousin of Daniel's great-grandfather, was the first soldier killed in the Revolutionary War, and a statue at Lexington now marks the spot where he fell."

ALEXANDER HEDQUIST, JR.

Born: August 9, 1873   **Place:** Salt Lake City, Utah

Father: Alexander Hedquist, Sr.
Son of Nicholas Anderson, born September 15, 1838, in Goteborg, Gothenburg, Sweden. The second of a family of five; August, Alexander, Andrew, Swen, and Anna. Married his wife on shipboard enroute to America and Utah in June, 1866. Seven years old when his mother died and seven years later his father died, leaving the children orphans. An uncle was guardian for four years —family changed name to Hedquist. Alex Sr. used part of inheritance money to do missionary work in Eskilstuna for three years where he met Anna Hoagland. Alex Sr. started in Salt Lake as a shoemaker in the ZCMI, old Coop. Shoe Factory, for 17 years. Moved to Spanish Fork and opened shop in Provo, walking back to Spanish Fork on Saturday and returning on Monday; moved family to Provo and bought business property on Center Street. Built small home on 8th North and 2nd East. On August 25, 1903, a successful immigrant merchant died at 65, a devout Latter-day Saint.

Mother: Anna Louise Hoagland
Daughter of Andrew Ludwig Hoagland and Katheryn Dalquist. Born Nov. 5, 1841 in Eskilstuna, Torp Co., Sweden, 12 miles from Stockholm. Baptized into Church August 24, 1864. She took eight weeks to walk across the plains to Utah. Died November 2, 1922, at age 82. Anna's brothers and sisters: Sophie, Anna, Charlotte, Karl, Gustave, John, Fredrick, and Eric—Anna's mother, Katherine and sister, Charlotte, came to Utah to live in 1870, but returned to Sweden. Gustave settled in Milwaukee.

Brothers
and Sisters: Emily, b. May 24, 1868
Albert, b. May 16, 1870
Alex Jr., b. Aug. 9, 1872
Charles Axel, b. Jan 2, 1874; d. Aug 10, 1920
Louise, b. June 2, 1878; d. Aug., 1900
Francis Joseph, b. April 8, 1883; d. Mar. 4, 1927

Marriage: (1) Lavina Strong of Provo, January 8, 1897—died in 1908.
(2) Vivian Finlayson of Provo, January 2, 1916—Died Sept. 17, 1962.

Children: (of Lavina) Walter S.
Victor
Edith A., m. M. B. Kimberly
Helen, m. Stanley Innes
(of Vivian) Dorothy B., m. Owen Rowe
Junece, m. Donald Mackay

Death: Friday, February 5, 1965 at 91. Died in his home on 200 East and Center Street, Provo, Utah. Biography written prior to his death.

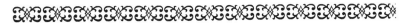

Education:

The Hedquist family moved to Provo in 1885 in order to receive a good education and improve opportunities for Alex Sr. to establish his shoe shop. Young Alex met Principal George H. Brimhall in the Provo Schools, where spelling was highly developed. In a popular spelling bee, Alex won a certificate as one of the two best spellers in the district. President Brimhall introduced young Alex to Karl G. Maeser, and he went to B.Y.U. for three years, obtaining a certificate in the Commercial Department in 1888. In a public address, Alex later gave Principal George H. Brimhall and Karl G. Maeser credit for inspiring him to achieve and honor the highest possible ethics in business and social life.

He worked at the town's largest drugstore while going to school and took some classes at Proctor Academy.

Occupational Activities:

Alex seemed destined to be a business man though the drug profession remained "a first love." In 1893 he was manager of a drug store and soon thereafter its owner, buying the store on installments. He expanded his business to four stores, using his sons, Walter and Victor, as managers as soon as they reached maturity. Honors came fast to him in his profession, even when the great depression swept the country causing failure and bankruptcy of many of the country's oldest firms and business centers. Among the firms in Provo obliged to close in 1932 was the Farmers and Merchant's Bank with Alex Hedquist as one of its biggest depositors. Fellow depositors met and asked Alex to help open the bank, which he did as organizing chairman within six months. To his surprise and against his judgment, they induced him to become president. Protesting that he was a druggist, not a banker, he opened the bank with revenues of $652,929 in 1932, and had $2,028,364 in 1944. He remained the bank's president until Walker Bank and Trust bought the controlling stock. Mr. Hedquist remained a director in the new affiliation.

A note of interest concerning him was written up in the *American Druggist*, a trade magazine. In his store No. 1, on Center Street, his soda clerk, Bill Sumner, upon request of some tennis players, mixed ice cream with milk and added chocolate flavoring, shook to a creamy flow and fountain trade skyrocketed. The new drink was known as a Tennis Special. With the "milk shake," which spread across the nation, he also encouraged and advertised a new candy concoction which was first introduced in the U.S. by Jack Pallas of Shupe-Williams Candy Company of Ogden, a chocolate covered three-flavored candy, given the name of Utahna Bar. It has since become known as an "Opera Bar." Alex was one of the first druggists in the West to arrange his goods and windows so that they sold. He gave his public information with salesmanship. His artistic and eye-appealing displays were noted in magazines across the country.

Occupational activities and affiliations;

Voted "The Most Outstanding Retail Druggist" by the American Druggist Association, 1939

President of Utah State Bankers Association, 1943, Utah County Bankers Association

Member of Utah State Board of Pharmacy and Independent Bankers Association

Director, Utah Wholesale Grocery Company and the American Wholesale Company of Seattle, Washington

Director, Utah Tax Payers' Association and the Utah Foundation

President of both Taylor Investment and Real Estate Company

Civic, Social, and Honorary Affiliations and Honors:

On committee to reopen Knight Woolen Mills after the disastrous fire in 1918

Charter Member and second President of Provo Kiwanis Club; Lt. Gov of Utah Idaho District, Kiwanis

Active member of Provo Chamber of Commerce since founding in 1922, and its 11th President, 1934; recipient of special recognition by the Chamber

A prime member of committee to locate Deer Creek Dam in Provo River

Member of Provo Metropolitan Water Board, Charter member and first President, Timpanogos Knife and Fork Club

Member of Board of Trustees directing the Utah State Training School;

On Governor's Committee for Distributing Relief Funds;

Member, Board of Directors, Utah Valley Hospital and a Director of Utah Health Association for ten years;

Director of Utah Tax Commission; a member of the Court of Honor of the Boy Scouts of America, and Chairman, Red Cross drives for many years.

Now, at 91, he cares for his beautiful rose garden, directs his business ventures and attends major public events. In his scrap book, I found these sentiments: "Together with my God, my country, and my family, my city is more entangled in my heart strings than is all else. Through boyhood, youth, manhood, old age, and even unto death, it is my one desire and wish to remain closely identified with my city."

In proof that he loves Provo and its environs, he states, "More magnificent mountains, beautiful lakes, health-giving atmosphere, superior drinking water, matchless kindness made beautiful by the splendid spirit of its people and its environs cannot be found. In fact, none can be found to equal those of my city."

Alex Hedquist, citizen and public servant.

BRYANT STRINGHAM HINCKLEY

Born:
July 9, 1867 at Coalville, Utah. He spent first years at Cove Fort, Utah, and thirteen years at Fillmore, Utah.

Father:
Ira Nathaniel Hinckley, a strong man of sterling character, born in Canada. Was a successful blacksmith, farmer and stockman. Moved to Rochester, New York; then to Utah in 1850 with the David Evans Company. He lived in Salt Lake City, Coalville, Cove Fort, Fillmore, and Provo.

Mother:
Angeline Wilcox Nobel, sister of Adlaide. Her parents were Michigan pioneers. They came to Utah in 1850. Angeline W. Nobel was born in 1832, four years before her husband.

Brothers and Sisters:
Angeline, m. Lafayette Holbrook
Laverne, m. James M. George
Ira N., m. Lillian King
Alonzo A., m. Rosa M. Robison
Elmer E., m. Angie Callister
Two children died in infancy.

Marriage:
Christina Johnson of Provo in June, 1893; died in July, 1908 Ada Bitner of Salt Lake in August, 1910; died in November, 1930 Mary Greene of Salt Lake in February, 1932; died in 1940 Lois Anderson of Salt Lake in June, 1944.

Children:
By Christina Johnson
Stanford, who died in France in World War I
Heber Grant, Lawyer
Lucile, m. Alfred Paxman
Carol, m. Tracy Y. Cannon
Christine, m. O. Preston Robinson
R. Waldo
By Ada Bitner
Gordon B., m. Marjorie Pay
Ruth B., m. Joseph Willis
Ramona B. m. Patrick Sullivan
Sylvia B., m. Don Wadsworth
Eleven of his fifteen children were living when he died.

Death:
June 5, 1961; when he was 94 years old, buried in Salt Lake City, Utah.

Bryant S. Hinckley was a recipient of one of the Special Awards presented by the Brigham Young University on June 5th, 1959. Dr. O. Preston Robinson said of his father-in-law, "Renowned author, inspirational and effective teacher, devoted churchman, builder of Christian character, beloved and loving parent and friend, Bryant Stringham Hinckley has given a life-time of dedicated and unselfish service to his God and his fellowmen."

That epitomizes a glorious life reaching near the century mark, a tribute to a son of a great pioneer, Ira Nathaniel Hinckley. While crossing the plains Ira's wife, Eliza Evans, died, leaving him a daughter, Eliza. With a sturdy body and a zealous determination, Ira brought the babe to the great Salt Lake Valley and married Adelaide C. Noble, on December 11, 1853. She, too, was a daughter of pioneer parents and also crossed the plains in 1850. They had nine children, Edwin S. being the sixth. Father Ira also married Adelaide's sister, Angeline Wilcox Noble, who had eight children; two died in infancy. Bryant S. was a fourth child of this marriage and was almost a full year older than his half-brother Edwin S.

Bryant S. Hinckley was born July 9, 1867. His father was directed by Brigham Young to go to Millard County, erect a fort for protection of the settlers against the Indians, and live there. This fort is one of only two old stone forts left in the mountain West; the other is at Pipe Springs, Arizona. The little families occupied neat, comfortable quarters within the stone block fort, which had a deep well in the center and a good size central yard for stock to be brought into in times of danger. Perpendicular deep slits which permitted rifle firing from advantageously protected positions punctuated the walls. Here part of a growing family was reared and taught, gleaning food from the hills, a little patch of corn, and seasonal hunting. The Fort was a wagon and coach station during different periods of its adaptability. The father was made a captain of a company to guard the U.S. mail from Indians and highwaymen. His young sons early learned horse-care and skill in riding in the saddle. The family was permitted to move from Cove Fort in 1871 and live in Fillmore, where the children could benefit from a one-roomed school. They often learned more from the church than they did from the school.

As a gangling youth, Bryant was sent to the Brigham Young Academy in Provo. While there the school was moved from the old Z.C.M.I. warehouse to the new Education Building on 5th North and Academy Avenue. He had the great privilege of studying and teaching under Karl G. Maeser and graduated from the Brigham Young Academy by 1889. He taught at Frisco, Beaver County, for two years before going to Provo. This adventurous man looked eastward for further education, graduating from the Eastman

National College at Poughkeepsie, New York, in 1892. He had received a B. Pd. from Brigham Young Academy in 1885 and the General Board of the Church Schools conferred upon him the B. D.

From 1893 to May 5, 1900 Bryant S. taught at Brigham Young Academy (to become a university) as head of the Commercial Department. Many older people with little formal education and with meager reading training came to the school. He took special delight in aiding them. The teachers and students who came to Brigham Young Academy became the county, state, church, and national leaders, most of them intimate friends of the Hinckleys. The Knights, Smoots, Kings, Driggs, Booths, Dixons, Christensens, Cluffs, Dusenberrys, Taylors, Jones, Sutherlands, Talmages, to name a few, were very close friends of the Hinckleys. Bryant outlived them all.

Pioneers lived in young communities, and Latter-day Saints frequently heard that their greatest glory was contingent upon a large family. Many married at an early age, but Bryant S. was twenty-six years of age when he married Christina Johnson of Provo in 1893. Their first son, C. Stanford, was killed in France in World War I. Most of their children married and lived near them in Salt Lake City. After fifteen years of marriage, Sister Christina, the mother and faithful companion, died in 1908.

In August of 1910, President Hinckley married Ada Bitner and their first son was Gordon B., now assistant apostle of the L.D.S. Church, which the father considered the highest honor that could come to any of his kin. Four other children followed. Each wife knew the rigors of pioneer life and the many lonely nights their husband was away on church and work duties.

Sister Ada died in November of 1930, and President Hinckley married Mary Greene of Salt Lake City on February 22, 1932. After the death of Mary, he married Lois Anderson in 1944. A man is known by his family; in this, Bryant S. Hinckley has found his greatest wealth and fullest joy.

To best present the character, scholarship, and leadership of B. S. Hinckley, we need only to list his positions for responsibility, all directly tied to youth and "just people."

President Hinckley left the Brigham Young Academy to become the Principal of the L.D.S. College at Salt Lake City from 1901 to 1910. Some of his richest experiences came with this assignment. He served on many church committees, both with speech and writing. Each year brought to him new responsibilities and a new coterie of friendships. He was ever a vigorous advocate of clean living and healthy bodies. He believed in healthy physical competition. Sports were in the ascendant and a grand gymnasium was conceived, planned and built where young men could compete in all indoor activities, and inter-ward competition became a church-wide development. In these plans and building, the central figure was Bryant H. Hinckley, and accordingly he was made General Secretary and manager of the Deseret Gymnasium in 1910. In this gymnasium basketball became world famed and was moved to the Brigham Young University field house because of the tournament's growth and importance. The swimming pool, hot baths and massaging techniques of this institution have prolonged the lives of our church leaders and vindicated every dollar spent in its up-keep.

With school activities he paralleled his interests in church and business. From 1900 to 1925 he was an active member of the General Board of the YMMIA and spoke to most of the church organizations, then chiefly confined to the Rocky Mountain States. He rose from Superintendent of Sunday School and Y.M.M.I.A. to Stake President of the Liberty Stake, where he served for some eighteen years.

Throughout his career he worked in Scouting, being one of the very first to take up Scouting in Utah. He was president of the Northern States Mission from 1935 through 1938. His speaking assignments on youth activities and pioneer achievements ocurred almost daily and he has written dozens of church pamphlets for the Priesthood and Y.M.M.I.A.

Biography and Genealogy were major interests during all his mature life; his writings and honors further accent his abilities.

Water preservation and its proper distribution has been one of his keenest concerns. He has been president of the Utah Reclamation Company, the Smart Water Company, and the president and director of the North Point Consolidated Canal Company.

For years the Faculty Assembly committee of Brigham Young University invited President Hinckley to be a featured speaker before the student body. His appearance always attracted a large audience. His life, more than many others, is a link between the pioneer past and the ever-changing present. Measured in terms of service and character he is a giant among men.

A bronze bust of Bryant S. Hinckley was donated by his wife and family for the Hinckley Hall on our campus.

HONORS

Brigham Young University Alumni Distinguished Service Award.
Lecture Hall named in his honor in the Jessie Knight Building on Campus.
Sons of the Utah Pioneers Special award, 1957.
Silver Beaver of the Salt Lake Council of Boy Scouts 1960 (His 90th Birthday)
Senior Member of the Sons of the American Revolution.
Descendant of the Mayflower Society.
Brigham Young University Special Award 1960.

POSITIONS

Professor of Commerce Brigham Young Academy, 1893-1900.
Principal of L.D.S. Business College, 1900-1908.
Manager and Secretary of Deseret Gymnasium, 1910-1936.
President Northern States Mission, 1936.
President of Liberty Stake for eighteen years.
Member of Y.M.M.I.A. Board for twenty-five years. (1900-1925)
Began first Stake missionary work.

AUTHOR

His complete works have been collected at our University as an additional memorial to his honored name.

Young Man and the Economical World

Religion and Achievement.

Some Essentials of Character (in three manuals.)

Mormonism In Daily Life.

Stones of the Plains.

Not By Bread Alone, (1956) when he was 89.

That Ye Might Have Joy, (1958) when he was 91.

Biographies of Daniel H. Wells, Melvin J. Ballard, and Heber J. Grant

Salient Features of Mormonism.

His life was his greatest book, an unblemished record.

EDWIN SMITH HINCKLEY

Born: July 21, 1868 in Cove Fort, Utah. The first white child born here.

Father: Ira Nathaniel Hinckley, born October 30, 1823. Died April 10, 1904 in Provo. He married the sisters Adelaide C. Noble and Angeline Wilcox Noble. President of Millard Stake 26 years; pioneer to Arizona and New Mexico; built Cove Fort in 1867 at request of Brigham Young; Mayor of Fillmore, a scientific farmer.

Mother: Adelaide Cameron Noble, married to Ira December 11, 1853. Daughter of Lucian Noble and Emily Wilcox of Livona, Michigan; pioneers of 1850 in William Snow Company. Adelaide born August 15, 1834.

Brothers: Minerva m. William A. Ray
and Sisters: Lois, m. James Frampton
Della, m. James H. Mace
Lucian N. m. Ada Robison
Frank, m. Helen Moody
Edwin S., m. Addie Henry
Nellie, m. Joseph H. Robison
Samuel Ernest, m. Ida Cheever
Sarah, m. Mosher F. Pack

Marriage: Adeline "Addie" Henry, in the Manti Temple, September 9, 1880. Born in Fillmore, Utah January 12, 1868. Died July 24, 1945.

Children: Robert Henry, b. June 8, 1891 m. Arbrelia Clarissa Seeley
Leonore Adelaide, b. April 17, 1894; m. Harold Chas. Walton
Edwin Carlisle, b. July 25, 1896; m. Emma Jacobs
Norma Elizabeth, b. October 12, 1897
Claudius Warren, b. May 30, 1899; m. Mildred Lewis
Paul Bryant, b. October 8, 1900
Frederick Russell, b. May 22, 1902; m. Lois B. Richards
John Noble, b. August 6, 1903; m. Elizabeth Skolfield
Evelyn Marguerite, b. March 9, 1905; m. Clarence H. Durrant
Gordon Holbrook, b. June 12, 1906
Muriel Aileen, b. September 4, 1907; died in infancy
G. Marion, b. March 1, 1909; m. Nita Johnson
Angela Ruth, b. May 30, 1910; m. Kenneth M. McKenzie
All the mature children attended Brigham Young Academy or University

91

Death: November 15, 1929, in Provo, Utah
        The E. S. Hinckley Fund founded by his family, reached
        over $250,000 in 1967.

Edwin Smith Hinckley was born during the Utah Indian uprisings, while United States soldiers were encamped at Cove Fort, there because of the frequent attacks made upon Millard County and nearby Sevier County. He was too young to participate in the Indian encounters but was exposed to adult discussions every day, and as soon as he could toddle, he watched through the peep holes. The family left the Fort and went to Fillmore when he was a small boy. The children of the two wives of Ira, Adelaide and Angeline, lived together, attended grammar school. Each child was welcome into either of the separate houses.

The two half brothers, Bryant and Edwin, were but a year apart in age and paralleled many events in their lives. However, when they came to Provo to school, Edwin married Addie Henry, 1890, and Bryant went on to school in the East and was not married until three years later. Each man remained a teacher and both taught at the Brigham Young Academy, Bryant from 1893 to 1900 and Edwin for twenty years. He was Dean of the Church Teacher College for seven years as well as being the school's first dean and was a second counselor to President George H. Brimhall until he resigned to take the position as Superintendent of the State Industrial School at Ogden, Utah.

While at Brigham Young University, he was Professor of Natural Science, teaching geology and physiography, and was one of the first scientists to explore the surrounding canyons and blaze the paths for future hikers. (He encouraged the late Eugene L. Roberts in his community hikes up Mt. Timpanogos.) Each new mountain was a challenge, and his rock hammer pounded many specimens of the great Wasatch range. He was one of the first to recognize the value of the gravel and sand laid down by the hundreds of years of the receding Lake Bonneville. He envisioned the dyking of Provo Bay in Utah Lake to reclaim hundreds of fertile acres and was one of the first to state that Utah's scenery would bring more wealth than her mines and that water was one of the greatest problems.

His four years at the University of Michigan prepared him to be one of the best teachers of science in the West. In all his teaching he regarded his students at Brigham Young as potential leaders of the nation and urged many young men to get their advanced degrees from the nation's best schools. He encouraged athletics for health and enjoyment more than for competition and personal aggrandizement. Under his guidance, athletics were fostered within the institution and pure amateur competition thrived.

President Benjamin Cluff organized the Alumni Association of the Brigham Young University in 1893 and put the responsibility for its promotion upon Dean E. S. Hinckley, who became its President in 1897 through 1898 and again in 1924 through 1925. He also served as a member of the Board of Trustees of the Alumni Association from 1925 through 1929 and long advocated the employment of a paid Alumni Secretary.

The Alumni Association, during the days of President T. N. Taylor of the old Utah Stake, had considerable to do with the policies and management of the Brigham Young Academy. The Association was the chief organ for fund raising and building programs and was very intimate with school affairs. Accordingly, E. S. Hinckley was on most fund drives for the school during all the days of his tenure (1891-1915).

On May 28, 1897, with fifty-nine Alumni members present, E. S. Hinckley was elected president and a motion was carried that they should build a memorial hall. Reed Smoot was appointed general agent for the Association, and each member was to be a soliciting agent and a donator. E. S. Hinckley gave fifty dollars, a very large sum in those days. They raised $615.00 at the meeting. It was also decided that three entertainments should be given on behalf of the new College Building. A concert under the direction of J. J. McClellan, a lecture by Dr. James E. Talmage, and a dance in the new building under the auspices of the Alumni Association were given. Obtaining Board approval, they spent a year raising funds, and the new College Building was dedicated May 26, 1898, while the Spanish-American War was in progress and a depression was slowly receding. President E. S. Hinckley gave a short address and the dedicatory prayer was given by President Joseph F. Smith. President Reed Smoot then represented the Alumni Association and presented the College Building to the Board. This is a typical program of acquiring buildings under the Brimhall, Keeler, Hinckley regime:

Sister Amanda Knight spoke for her family and stated that her two children were taught in the Academy, which prepared them for their British mission. Seats were to be obtained for the Hall by selling a chair, with donors' name plates costing $2.25 each. This would be his own seat thereafter. Karl G. Maeser was prevailed upon to speak. Comparing the Brigham Young Academy to a banyan tree whose branches extend from far North to far South, he drew vital parallels. Brother George H. Brimhall said, "We have passed through poverty, and I know the time will come when the cry will not be—shall we get the money?—but, how should we use the money that we have?" "Personal sacrifice is a part of a man's equipment."

The E. S. Hinckley home on the corner of Center and Seventh West was one of the beautiful homes of Utah Valley. Built to the square, it betokened the owner of the nature of direct honesty. The yard was resplendent with flowers and an ample garden. Not far from the stately home was the farm for milk cows, draft and saddle horses, swine and sheep. From an orchard and root cellar there was abundance which was often shared with less fortunate neighbors.

Ed Hinckley rode a horse as though he were born to the saddle. His young sons knew the chase after a strayed animal and followed deer tracks with their hunter father. The family went fishing on Provo River and Utah Lake, which abounded with trout and bass.

This valley had been the happy hunting grounds of the Ute Indians. They surrendered it with bitter reluctance and sometimes not without battle. The Hinckleys nursed the Indians when they were sick and treated them like brothers. Ed Hinckley said in many ways, "Some day the conscience of America will awake and make reparation to these simple souls, who will become a delightsome people."

To teach in Brigham Young Academy, one had to own and till a farm and be obliged to take watering turns between classes. The water flooded one city block after another until all the garden lots were watered. Tourists have marveled at the cold streams running in the present cement curbing, not knowing the story of pioneer necessity in a desert country. When Ed was Secretary of the Chamber of Commerce, he had occasion many times to protect this irrigation project and was instrumental in supplying drinking fountains on the downtown streets.

The Dean of the University followed Indian paths, picked up arrow heads and artifacts, searched the mountain slabs for pictographs. He predicted that these paths would induce the white man to ascend the great peaks by the hundreds. He urged the city cooperation with the university to make the great hike to Timpanogos a national event. In a pamphlet, "On the Trail to Timpanogos," E. S. Hinckley describes his beloved mountain as viewed from the summit:

"Fertile valleys, and fruitful fields, winding streams and the limpid waters of the lakes are all in the picture of the checkered handiwork of man, proclaiming his presence and his conquering mission. Range upon range of mountains rise in every direction and one's horizon is bounded with soft vanishing peaks of blued distances. This is indeed a holy moment in the life of mortal man." On such occasions he rose to oratorical excellence and carried his listeners to heights of inspirational appreciation.

A man's life is often divided into periods of activity. With President Hinckley it was boyhood, Brigham Young Academy, State Industrial School, and the Provo Chamber of Commerce. His marriage was a part of this, but his boyhood and his church were the sustaining framework of his life.

A book could be written of his brief stay at the old Territorial Reform School. The name was changed at his suggestion to the State Industrial School. When he was chosen to succeed Dr. E. G. Gowans for the Ogden position, he accepted with reluctance, but with no misgivings. It meant giving up his Deanship, his position in the university presidency, and a home which his beloved wife preferred over all others. The school was growing into a university and offered new challenges every day. All of his children had attended or were attending the Academy. When the family pulled up stakes, the oldest son, Robert H. was twenty-five years old and the baby, Angela Ruth, was six. Most of the children were moved to the residence of the Superintendent's home in Ogden, on the grounds of the Industrial School and looked upon new and strange faces and heard tales only of wayward boys and unfortunate girls. The family life was completely changed from its Provo environment and the father alone got the joy of challenge of his new work. "Aunt Addie" took the change with stoic adjustment and started to share a mother's love and care with another hundred children.

In an average year, 144 students were enrolled. There was one cottage for girls and three for boys.

The World War I period at the school came under Superintendent's directorship and E. S. Hinckley took some boys from the school, who had volunteered for war service, and had them help him in Liberty Bond Drives. He did everything he knew to dignify the boy at the school and to help him to be a better man in society.

Many touching stories could be related of the relationship which he shared with students. One little fellow had been released for good behavior but was soon returned. When he was brought to the office the superintendent asked, "Well, young man, what happened? Why are you here? I thought we. . .", but he was interrupted by the lad, who rushed up to the Superintendent saying, "I had to steal again so I could come back here and be with you. My pa and I. . ." A kind, strong arm went around the crying lad. "The damn parents. What can we do? Where can he go?" That night he wrote another article on parental delinquency.

During the devastating flu epidemic of 1916 through 1917, not one death occurred at the Industrial School. Love, care and diligence paid precious dividends.

The Hinckley management attracted national attention. "Have sensible rules, enforce them and trust each child on his merits. Healthful and helpful activity is the cure of delinquency. Start with the parents to save the child." He was one of the first to advocate a special school for the feeble-minded or mentally deficient. He went up and down the state telling the story of broken homes and their cost to society and innocent children. It was his "trust, not punish" policy that gave him his biggest concern. He did not get the support expected and needed to give his program a fair trial, and in September 1922 he resigned, giving no specific reasons but only "So I may enter my own business." Had he given all the reasons for his resignation, he would have been obliged to include personality problems which he preferred not to do.

While in Ogden he was elected president of the Rotary Club, took an active part in civic affairs and was appointed a member of the State Fair Board by Governor George Dern. He was also on the High Council of the Weber Stake and was recognized as a leader wherever he went.

He returned to Provo and was settled in his old home when he was asked to become the Secretary of the new Chamber of Commerce. This marked a new era for him, Provo, and Utah County. He fostered the Utah County Fair, for years a focus point of the County's bounteous crops and livestock. He started the Utah County's Holstein Association. He immediately began work on getting a steel plant in the valley and was secretary to the Provo Holding Company for the purpose of acquiring land and turning over the plant site to the Columbia Steel Company. Only the most persistent efforts of a dynamic leader and speaker was able to outbid Salt Lake interests. He convinced the eastern officials that the coal, iron, lime, water transportation and labor was here for assembling.

A return to Provo had brought him, his wife, and unmarried family back to most of their early associations, but his teaching at Brigham Young Academy was missing. He partially compensated for this by being a frequent and honored speaker.

In the seven years of his later Provo activities he had cooperation of one of Provo's most outstanding mayors, O. K. Hansen. This team worked as one, building the city and expanding its territory, water and sewer lines, paving streets, adding sidewalks, planting shade trees in curbing space, offering sites for manufacturers, holding public meetings for civic betterment. The coming of President F. S. Harris was another helpful factor in the life of E. S. Hinckley, as he frequently sat in and discussed many of the plans for building the Brigham Young University. In these later days he wrote many articles for the Era and the Y.M.M.I.A.

It was on a mission of civic improvement, going to the State Capitol in Salt Lake City, that he was injured in an automobile accident which further complicated his failing health, and on November 15, 1929 he died in his beloved home with his family about him. He personally arranged his funeral program, with B. H. Roberts, M. A. Tanner, President George H. Brimhall, Clayton Jenkins, and Alice Reynolds as speakers. The West joined Utah and Provo in mourning. There were numerous tributes from schoolmates, students, civic workers, church and governmental officials.

A man of strong pioneer breed had prematurely outrun his vigorous body in unrelenting service to his family, school, community and church. It is most fitting that his devoted family has established the E. S. Hinckley Fund at the University he so dearly loved and so faithfully served. Hinckley Hall, is one of the beautiful men's dormitories on the new campus. Hinckley is one of the great sons of Brigham.

JOSEPH BRIGHAM KEELER

Born: September 8, 1885   **Place:** Salt Lake City, Utah
Great grandson of Hannah Cox Keeler, prominent in New Jersey history. The Keelers originated in Holland—Samuel Keeler founded the family in America pre-Revolutionary War.

Father: Daniel Hutchinson Keeler, b. in Pemberton, New Jersey, Jan. 25, 1811
Assisted in building Girard College at Philadelphia
Helped to build Temple and Nauvoo House in Nauvoo
1852 came to Utah; to Provo in 1857
Built Roberts Hotel and Old Court House, with W. W. Allen
d. February 27, 1888

Mother: Ann Brown, b. Tildsley Banks, near Bolton, Lancashire, England
daughter of James Brown and Elizabeth Atkin
Ann was the widow of Benjamin Taylor, by whom she had the following children; James, Sarah, Ann, Mary Jane and Martha (who died early)

Brothers and Sisters: Amy, b. July 28, 1854, died early
(Joseph B.)
Theodosia, b. Aug. 31, 1858; m. Jacob Collier
Lucy, b. Oct 27, 1860.

Marriage: Martha Alice Fairbanks, b. June 29, 1860; m. May 17, 1883
Daughter of David Fairbanks, who came to Utah with parents, October, 1847
Jonathan Fairbanks, her paternal ancestor, native of England, came over in 1633
Brought own lumber and built house at Dedham, Mass., 1636
He and others signed covenant naming Dedham
David Fairbanks—one of the first justices of peace in Utah

Children: Major Joseph, b. Feb 19, 1884 (father of Jay J. Keeler of B.Y.U. faculty) m. Esther "Effie" Reese
Beulah May, b. Oct 25, 1885; m. Daniel H. McAllister
Karl Fairbanks, b. Jan. 1, 1887; m. Kitty Leatham
Eva Josephine b. Oct 15, 1894; m. Harry Greenall
David Hutchinson b. Apr. 1, 1896
Irving (deceased)
Ralph Budd, b. Dec 27, 1897; m. Gertrude Olson
Daniel Mandeville b. Oct 28, 1900; m. Virginia Christensen
Paul Fortescue, b. Feb 12, 1904; m. Bernice Barton

Death: December 23, 1935

Joseph B. Keeler was a man you visited for sound financial advice or for a helpful opinion affecting a choice in marriage. People of all ages went to President Keeler for counsel on innumerable family problems.

I first met "J. B." as he was affectionately known, just prior to his discontinuing service at B. Y. U. in 1920. He was a solidly built gentleman with a firm grip of the hand and an unflinching eye. Though he was serious in nature, his face was usually active in smiles. He was one of the most helpful listeners I ever knew and most of his conversations were questions to get you to talk. He came to welcome me to the University in early 1919 and we sat down in College Hall, a place which came to mean so much to me. It was already something special to him. "Do you know what this building is, and how it came to be?" In a few minutes I heard the story of its building, the donors and even the seats around us, most of them with small bronze plaques designating the persons who gave the chairs to furnish the room. In a few minutes I learned how the University was built, heard the names of many who had profited by its teaching, was told that character, devotion and sacrifice were traditional foundations. He asked about my parentage, education, family, my ambitions, what priesthood I held and where I lived. When we shook hands in separation I felt that I had a friend, realized I was in a great school with unlimited challenge, and he knew much more about me and why I came to Provo. Recollection revealed I knew little about President Keeler though we had been together half an hour. After he had "sold" the University to me, he asked well-pointed questions and listened.

Joseph B. started a diary at age 17, which has been useful to his daughter, Beulah K. McAllister in gleaning pertinent facts of her father's life. I am indebted to her for much of the information taken from this source.

Joseph B. Keeler was born September 8, 1855, in Salt Lake City, Utah. He moved to Provo, Utah, with his parents in the spring of 1858, when only two years of age. At the time when Johnston's Army came into Salt Lake Valley and Brigham Young had ordered all homes in the valley evacuated, Joseph's parents took him with their other children and all their possessions piled high on a single wagon, drawn by oxen, and drove southward.

Upon reaching Provo, the family located on a parcel of land, now in the vicinity of 3rd East and 4th North Streets, where Joseph grew into young manhood.

When seventeen years of age, Joseph records in his diary that he became vitally interested in his own education. He writes: "Early in the year of 1873, it seems I was impressed with the thought that I was sent to earth to perform a mission—. I began, therefore, to improve my mind by reading and studying good books. In the winter of 1873, I attended school and made rather rapid progress. Throughout the following summer I worked hard with the end in view of returning to school the coming winter, but on the first of October, 1874, I, with others from Provo, was called on a six-months work mission to the St. George Temple."

Following this work mission, J. B. returned to Provo determined to continue his education.

On April 24, 1876, a preliminary or first session of school was begun. Although short in duration it was the beginning term of Brigham Young Academy. Joseph B. Keeler was one of the original 29 students to enroll.

In 1880 he was appointed editor of the City newspaper, *The Provo Enquirer,* a position he held for only a few months, for in April of that year he received a call to serve on a Church mission in the Southern States. He served during many anti-Mormon demonstrations.

Released from this mission in March 1882, he returned to Provo and in June was appointed City Assessor to fill an unexpired term. A year later he became County Recorder, a position he held until January 1884, when he resigned to accept a teaching position at the Brigham Young Academy and to be head of the Intermediate Department.

Joseph's new work at the school was to begin on January 28th but, on the night of the 27th, the Lewis Building, in which the Academy was housed, caught fire and burned to the ground. However, within two days, classwork was commenced in temporary quarters, some classes being held in the basement of the old Tabernacle on Center Street, others in the newly constructed store building belonging to S. S. Jones, while still others found space in rooms over the First National Bank. Joseph started teaching his classes on January 30th. Beginning the fall of 1883 and continuing until 1892, all classes were brought together and housed in the Z.C.M.I. warehouse on south University Avenue, then called J. Street.

After the death of Brigham Young in August 1877, the Board of Trustees contemplated closing the school, for it became increasingly difficult to finance the infant institution. However, through a special agreement with the faculty and local citizens the board changed its position. Of this situation Reinhard Maeser, son of Karl G. Maeser, writes:

"Through the energetic and earnest pleadings of the principal, Brother Maeser, and Joseph B. Keeler, an agreement was entered into by which the Board was relieved of the responsibility of the payment of the teachers. Some agreed to teach without pay for a while, if necessary. This arrangement was, in effect, that the faculty should appoint one of its members to receive all tuition. With the means so received he was to pay the teachers in proportion to their salaries. To this task, Joseph B. Keeler was assigned, and it proved a very successful scheme for the school and for the teachers."

As an additional means of finance it was deemed advisable to establish a school boarding house for out-of-town students. Joseph B. Keeler was appointed supervisor and Jenny Tanner matron. They were to serve without pay unless the projects income would justify a small consideration. Joseph was to employ a cook, a cook's helper, and a cleaning woman. Their pay was to be $3.00, $2.50, and $1.50 each per week. Suitable quarters were rented from David John at $400.00 per year, located in the upper part of his store building on what is now the northeast corner of Center and First West Streets in Provo. The building still stands. Joseph's records show over 100 tenants cared for during the first year of operation. During the second year Joseph's wife, Martha, became the matron. She had married J. B. on May 17, 1883.

The *Deseret News* of July 27, 1888 carries the following item: "Joseph B. Keeler, 1st Counselor to Karl G. Maeser, is head of the Academic Department: Bookkeeping, History and Civil Government." Following his appointment as counselor to Brother Maeser, Brother Keeler became rapidly involved in the administrative affairs of the school in addition to his teaching assignments. For example, *The Deseret News*, under date of July 20th of that year, quotes Principal Maeser as saying: "In compliance with instructions from the General Board of Education, it became my duty to devote a large portion of my time to visit the Church Schools in various Stakes of Zion, and to make such arrangements as would insure the usual progress here during my absence. It is, therefore, not only with satisfaction, but with a feeling of great appreciation that I report the extra labors undertaken by my fellow teachers in order to maintain the reputation and character of our institution. Professor Joseph B. Keeler assumed the executive control of the Academy, and also taught the Commercial Department. In addition to the extra responsibility already alluded to, Brother Keeler had charge of the Academic Department, conducted a Chronology class of 136 students, a Grammar and Composition class of 36 students, Commercial Arithmetic with 12 students, Physical Geography with 41, Geology with 12, Astronomy with 15, and four Bookkeeping classes containing 46 students. He also presided over the Domestic Organization. And the labors of Brother Keeler, as assistant treasurer, have been arduous and trying in many respects. All of the teachers realize that much credit is due him for the management of this branch of service."

In May, 1891, Joseph enrolled for a summer session in the Eastman Business College at Poughkeepsie, New York. Upon completion of the work, he received a diploma signifying a degree of Master of Accounts. Then, in 1894, the Church Board of Education conferred upon him the Degree of Bachelor of Didactics.

While Joseph was head of the Business Department, the school published a departmental magazine titled *The Business Journal*. The first issue appeared on October 26, 1891. In commenting on this publication a Provo newspaper, *The Dispatch*, had the following to say: "The students of the B. Y. Academy, engaged in the Business College Department of that institution, have done themselves proud by the publication of the *Business Journal*, the brightest and most meritorious journal of its kind in Utah. It outshines all other publications of the Academy and reflects great credit on the head of the Business College, Professor Joseph B. Keeler, and upon the members of the editorial staff."

In 1891, Joseph compiled a 31 page pamphlet entitled "Foundation Stones of the Earth," selected essays from his writings to *The Contributor* during a period of three years, published in volumes 9, 10 and 11.

In The *B. Y. A. Student*, dated March 24, 1891, appears this item about Joseph's writings: "Another small work from the pen of Joseph B. Keeler has just been issued from the press. It is a genealogical record of the Keeler Family which contains upwards of 800 names and 25 pages and is a very creditable work of its kind."

Of the many tributes written of him, we present the following by one of his students, Amy Brown Lyman, who later became general president of the Church Relief Society:

"Among my best loved teachers of the old Brigham Young Academy, during the years of 1888 and 1890, was Professor Joseph B. Keeler. Under his tuition I studied English Grammar, English Composition, and Theology. I remember Professor Keeler in his various capacities, among them important as an executive and department head, but I remember him especially at that time, as he stood before us, located in the southwest corner of the old Z.C.M.I. warehouse.

"It was a pleasant, sunny room, but not more pleasant or sunny than the countenance of this kind and genial teacher. Professor Keeler was a conscientious, painstaking and successful teacher. He spared no time nor pains for his students in their progress, both in and out of class."

"While he insisted on careful preparation and thoroughness on the part of his students he was considerate of those who found the work difficult, and patient with those whose study habits were faulty. He had such respect for human personality that I never knew him to embarrass or humiliate a student in class. He was generally appreciated by all those who worked under him."

"Like all teachers with lofty ideals and standards, he influenced his students as much by his splendid life and example as he did by what he taught them. He practiced what he taught and taught what he practiced. He was a noble character, a fine Christian gentleman and a faithful and devoted Latter-day Saint. He loved the youth of Zion, and to them he was a great power of faith. He was a true friend and a true neighbor, for these qualities I have had a chance to test. He loved the Lord and he loved his fellow men."

On January 4, 1892, the B. Y. Academy formally moved from its temporary quarters in the Z.C.M.I. warehouse to its new home on north Academy Avenue. Brother Karl G. Maeser retired as head of the school and Benjamin Cluff was installed as the new Superintendent, with Joseph B. Keeler as assistant. Also, at the first faculty meeting in the new building, held January 5, 1892, he was again sustained as president of the Theology Department.

Joseph was also school librarian, among his other and varied assignments, for the faculty minutes of January 15, 1892 state that "O. W. Andelin was appointed assistant librarian to Joseph B. Keeler."

It appears also that shortly before the move to the new quarters or shortly thereafter, Joseph was assigned to organize a military unit at the Academy. An article, published in *The Business Journal*, dated January (?), 1892, speaks of 120 students being organized into a battalion having three companies—A, B, and C—for military training. It also mentions that 50 ladies were attached to the outfit and composed Company D. First Lt. Wright of the 16th Infantry, U. S. Army, was appointed department head. The article describing this new organization is signed, "Joseph B. Keeler, in charge."

During the school year of 1891-92 a student loan association was organized. This was perhaps the first of its kind at the Academy. Joseph participated in its organization.

A minute book in B. Y. U. files records the organization of the first B. Y. A. Alumni Association. This took place on May 9, 1893 in Room D. Joseph B. Keeler was elected president. However, a few days after accepting this honor he received a mission call from the First Presidency of the Church. He therefore resigned his leadership of the Alumni Association and George H. Brimhall was subsequently elected president.

The balance of his story follows:

1893-5   Supt. of the Utah Stake Y.M.M.I.A.
            J.B. temporarily presided over B.Y.A. during absence of President Benjamin Cluff at Ann Arbor, Michigan, procuring a master's degree.
1894-96   Member of Board of Trustees, U.S.A.C.
1895-1901   Bishop of Provo 4th Ward
1895   J. B. Keeler appointed chairman of a Museum Com-

	mittee to make collections during the summer. Profs. Woolf and Hardy assisting.
1896	Wrote text book for use by business department at B.Y.A.
1897	Gave the first $100 for Memorial Hall (College Hall); on finance committee with Chairman Reed Smoot
1901	Jan 13—Utah Stake reorganized with David John as President and Joseph Keeler and La Fayette Holbrook as counselors
1904	Pub. *Lesser Priesthood and Notes on Church Government* 1906 second edition—book used throughout the Church
1908	Sustained President of Utah Stake with LaFayette Holbrook and J. Will Knight as counselors—released October 16, 1919. Elected Vice President of Provo Reservoir Company
	President of B.Y.U. Alumni Association—start of the Maeser Memorial
1910	With company which established pump system on Utah Lake to water Lehi and Salt Lake Valley
1912	August 1st—Company franchise granted for inter-urban rail, Payson to Salt Lake, J. B. one of trustees.
1920	Retired from school work after 37 years of University service. Devoted time to farm of 180 acres and business
1921	Patriarch of Utah Stake, until death

He was frequently mentioned in the "B. Y. U. STUDENT" and with his death, an epoch in educational struggles came to an end. He materially helped to establish a permanent foundation for a great university.

J. GOLDEN KIMBALL

Born: June 9, 1853   **Place:** Salt Lake City, Utah

Father: Heber Chase Kimball; born June 14, 1801, in Sheldon, Vermont; died June 22, 1868, at Provo, Utah caused by a buggy accident at night; a giant of physical strength; came to Utah July 24, 1847; made a member of the Twelve Apostles, Feb. 14, 1835; head of the first Mission to England, 1837; returned to England in 1840; recruited Mormon Battalion on the Missouri River, 1846; when the First Presidency re-organized, was made the first counselor to Brigham Young; built the first school house west of the Mississippi.

Mother: Christeen Golden; born Sept. 12, 1824; died January 30, 1896; married in the Nauvoo Temple, the tenth wife; tall and stately, the youngest and the only one of her family, to join the Church; her grandfather was the famous John Goldy, whose five sons were at the battle of Trenton in the American Revolution. Having only one gun between them, they left their farm barefooted to join Washington's troops; one of the boys fired upon and killed several British officers; three of the sons disappeared or were killed in the skirmish. Coming to Utah, Christeen sewed in Z.C.M.I. and took in boarders.

Brothers and Sisters: (Jonathan Golden), Elias S., Mary Margaret Mofitt.

Marriage: Jeanette "Jane" Knowlton; daughter of John Q. and Ellen Smith; married Sept. 22, 1887 in Logan, Utah; three children born in Logan.

Children: Jonathan "Jack", Quince "Jane", Elizabeth, Gladys, Richard and Max.

Death: September 2, 1938, at age 85, in an automobile accident

J. Golden was but fifteen years of age when his father died, leaving him to care for a mother, his brother Elias and a sister Mary Margaret. His father built the first school in the mountain west and all children who cared to come were welcome. Reading and writing were stressed and J. Golden learned to read early in life, especially the scriptures.

His mother sewed for the Z.C.M.I. and later took in boarders. Each wife had to help rear her own family and the family in a large sense was self supporting. Supplies from father Heber C.'s garden and orchard were distributed as equally as possible. This garden was surrounded by a six foot eight inch wall, but was little barrier to the Kimball boys. One of the big brothers could hoist a lighter and smaller boy over the wall to secure the carrot, turnip, or fruit and drag back the boy and supplies by rope. J. Golden got so he could "shinny" any tree, pole or wall. "Any wall became an invitation to me."

He liked animals and easily made friends with them, especially favoring horses and mules. He became one of the west's first M.D.'s —mule driver, of course. When his father died the railroad was on its way west and exciting tales were told of its building and what it would do for Deseret. Great opportunities would open up for young men. Mule transportation was thriving and J. Golden early secured a team of government freighter mules and set out to haul for the railroads, getting good pay. The bulk of hauling for the railroads terminated soon after the joining of Union and Central Pacific Railroads in 1869. J. Golden contracted jobs until he was 20, being known for his honesty, punctuality and fairness. He dug cellars, hauled rock and often was up at 4:00 a.m. to start his work.

In 1876, with his mother and family, he moved to Meadowville, Rich County, four miles from Bear Lake, where J. Golden and Elias bought property from Isaac and Solomon Kimball, two of the eleven sons of Heber C. in that territory. They signed for $1,000. The boys helped to cut and haul logs for the Logan Temple, often finding the temperature 40° below zero in Logan Canyon, where J. Golden said, "It was nine months winter and three months fall." The family lived in a log cabin 16 x 20 feet.

Something happened, however, in 1881, which changed his life. Dr. Karl G. Maeser went to Meadowville to speak in the interest of BYA, and spoke for an hour and half. Both J. Golden and Elias were so moved with the challenge that they immediately decided to go to the school. A life scholarship had been paid to the University of Deseret for J. Golden in 1867, but his father's death a year later terminated its value. The two boys sold washing machines for miles around. They paid cash for fifty machines to an agent who was never seen or heard of again—nor were the machines. This set back made them more determined, and on a bitter cold night they threw their small packets into the wagon bed of a friend, hugged their hopeful mother and sister, and left to go to Provo, 200 miles away. They stayed at Evanston, Wyoming, almost frozen, taking three days to reach Provo. The mother moved to Provo to board the two sons and five young men. The boys hauled vegetables to Coalville and coal on the return trip, as two happy years went by all too quickly for J. Golden; Elias remained for three years. J. Golden won several speaking contests and early revealed the dry art for which he became famous. He wore a moustache and side-burns at BYA.

Speaking of his education, he told BYA faculty and students, "I have had a testimony of the Gospel from the beginning, and the beginning was in the Brigham Young Academy under the teaching and instruction of Brother Karl G. Maeser."

On April 6, 1883, President John Taylor called J. Golden Kimball to go on a mission to the Southern States under Brigham H. Roberts, where he contracted malaria in his last year which affected him the rest of his life. In 1885 he was released and in 1891 was again called by President Wilford Woodruff to succeed William Spry as Mission President, working for three years. On the way back from this mission he got 1500 names of the Golden family; Elias, J. Golden and their mother did Temple work for all of them. He seldom referred to his mission experiences, but testimony of converts told of his frequent persecutions and miraculous healings.

J. Golden took up ranching in Bear River Valley after his first mission and married comely Jane Knowlton in 1887.

In 1892 he was ordained a Seventy by Francis M. Lyman, and in 1895 he moved back to Salt Lake City. In 1896 he was set apart on the YMMIA General Board, and from 1900 to 1922 was one of the First Presidents and secretary to the First Council of Seventies.

From 1884-86 he was sergeant-at-arms for the Territorial Legislature.

When he was asked what influence his father had on his life he rose to his full height and said, "When I stop believing in my father and mother, I will stop believing in the human race, for where they go I want to go."

Several biographies have been written of this unique leader; one in particular by his friend, co-worker and neighbor, Claude Richards. I shall glean just a few stories from his book which best reveal the man as most of his friends knew him. I took notes of the several speeches given by him at the Brigham Young University (to the students and faculty) during the Presidency of F. S. Harris. He sensed a keen responsibility on these student occasions, being careful to weigh all his words that none might offend or be misconstrued. He was a champion of truth and honesty. "I mix the wheat with the chaff and it's up to you to take your choice. In my talks you will find foolishness, maybe some wisdom, and, I hope, a lot of truth."

"I find a man can act good, talk good and look good and not be any good."

He told the BYU students to keep their thoughts clean and their bodies and tongues would be clean. "Don't ever start swearing; it is a nasty habit and can get you into a lot of trouble. I guess I ought to know. (Once he was cut off of his broadcast on air just prior to this speech.) There is only one occasion when a man should swear to keep his temper and that's when you're driving mules." He told of his many friends who were warning him about his swearing (mostly hell and damn) and saying that he might lose his membership if he swore in Church. His favorite reply was "They can't cut me off, I repent too damn fast." Once, when President Frances M. Lyman told him he upset the authorities too much by such language he replied, "Well, Brother Lyman, you talk to send them to sleep and I have to talk to wake them up."

He was advising caution in selecting a mate, to get a girl who could make good bread, sew on buttons, patch pants and chop wood when she had to; "Some select a girl because she has pretty eyes, some because she has pretty hair. I know a man who chose a girl because she could sing. He married her and the next morning, when he saw her without any paint or powder on, and saw a part of her hair on the dresser, he looked at her and said, "Sing, for hell's sake, sing!"

When he arose to speak people started to smile, not only in friendly anticipation, but just to look at him caused easy risibility. You felt good in his presence. He was a very plain man with no pretense of being anyone but himself. This is the way Claude Richards describes him:

"Seventy five inches in height; very slender, somewhat bent by the heavy physical work done in his teens and the burden of his four score years; a head unusually larger and unlike any other, with a sizeable bump at the back; his complexion sandy; a few lonely hairs on top that have triumphantly weathered the storm; keen and penetrating eyes, black and beautiful, expressive of humor and sympathy; a very long narrow perpendicular face, intensely interesting, with features regular; withal a serious countenance, expressive of sadness rather than of the humor for which he is noted. He seldom laughs, but is often seen to smile dryly as he speaks."

Wallace Stegner, in his *Mormon Country* described J. Golden Kimball in this manner: "J. Golden Kimball gave himself a good deal of trouble during his long life, and was sorry about it. He also gave the Mormon Church a good deal of trouble, and was even more sorry about that. . . . He regretted his breaks instantly and wholeheartedly, and though the Church never did more than admonish him and bar him periodically from the tabernacle platform, he grieved over it. . . . They called him the Will Rogers of the Church. That was a mistake. He should never have been compared with anyone, because J. Golden was an original . . . But like all originals, he defies transcription. He was himself, no less, no more, and nobody knew it more than he."

I first heard him in the old Third Ward in Ogden, Utah, when Brother Torgeson was Bishop, a short, dark and handsome fellow who easily could have walked under Brother Kimball's arm and looked up to the tall man as he introduced him for the evening's talk. President Kimball rubbed his long fingered hand over the Bishop's heavy head of hair, then rubbed his own sparse head, almost devoid of any covering: "Has only one use, a fly's good skating rink", he commented as he kept knocking at an obnoxious creature darting in and out from his nose and head. With no further to-do he began in a very high piping voice, (an octave higher than an average man's): "When I was first born my head was so small they could cover it with a tea cup. The bigger it got the less I knew. If this pesky fly will leave it alone I'll do the best I can with what I have." He bore an impressive intense testimony.

He loved a cup of coffee and would frequently go into his favorite cafe and with a sly wink have the waitress put coffee in his weak postum. He went into the cafe with a brother of the Apostleship, who was very strict and sincere about the Word of Wisdom. The brother ordered "postum" and J. Golden gave the new waitress his usual knowing wink. "Make mine postum, too." The smiling waitress soon returned and uncertain of the proper disposition of the two drinks, asked, "Which of you two gentlemen ordered coffee in your postum?" J. Golden said he could tell what he replied but couldn't repeat what he thought.

When he died thousands paid him tribute. He was killed in an auto accident at age 85, on Sept. 2, 1938, leaving only pleasant memories of a man who was fearlessly honest and despised hypocrisy. He had an abiding faith in the eternity of the individual man, his privilege of exaltation, and the mercy of his Heavenly Father. He conquered years of ill health by giving his life in serving his fellow men.

SAMUEL ANDREW KING

Criminal lawyer in Salt Lake City

Born: Jan. 9, 1868 in Fillmore, Utah.

Father: William King
(See biography of his son, William Henry King.)

Mother: Josephine Henry
Married in Nauvoo, Ill.
Died 1868

**Brothers
and Sisters:**   Sen. Wm. H. King
Lillian, m. Ira N. Hinckley
Josephine, m. John W. Thornley

Marriage: 1) Maynetta (Janette) Bagley of Salt Lake City on Sept. 14,
1892.
2) LaRen Watson of St. George, Utah on Sept. 22, 1929.

Children: (Maynetta)
Creighton Grant
Renan, m. W. D. Johnston
Karl Vernon, Lawyer in Salt Lake City
Margaret, m. James P. McCency of Washington, D. C.

Death: Aug. 27, 1943 at 75 years.

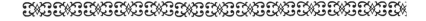

Samuel A. King, affectionately known as "Sam" possessed the talk and wit of his Irish ancestry, played and worked hard in Utah's first capital, and early cultivated the art of argument. He came to BY Academy in his teens and felt the influence of Karl G. Maeser and his devoted faculty. Nearly four years younger than his brother, Wm. H., he emulated William's leadership by enrolling in the Academy and completing his courses in 1888. As his interests turned to law he attended University of Utah for one year.

In 1890 he was called to a mission to Ireland, the ancestral home of his grandmother Creighton and the mission field of his father, serving with distinction for nearly three years at a time when Home Rule discussions were at their height. Advanced schooling took him to the University of Michigan where he received his LLB in 1893. He had married beautiful Maynetta Bagley, a BYA student, in September of 1892.

He opened a law office in Provo in 1893 and was immediately accepted into the profession and the activities of the city and county seat. He became a member of the firm King and King, brothers teaming in legal pursuits, and was elected County Attorney in Utah County, 1896-98. He also served as Provo City Attorney and Prosecuting Attorney for the 4th Judicial District, 1898-1900. It was in these later offices he decided to devote most of his practice to criminal law as he enjoyed talking to juries, winning his points when victory often was most problematical.

Sam moved to Salt Lake City for the major years of his legal life, being a partner for the most part with his talented brother, William H.

Mining and politics occupied much of his time not consumed in court. He was attorney for mines in Utah, Colorado and Nevada when great mines were in full production and litigation frequent. He boasted that he had been in every mine in Utah. Cattle rustling and railroad hold-ups were not uncommon; trials by jury were on extensive docket. Winning a jury over to his way of thinking was similar to experience in leading crowds to political choice; they were both based on group appeal in which Sam excelled. He was called to neighboring states to defend various defendants, some of them accused murderers. His fame took him to Washington, D. C., for his last years.

The *Salt Lake Tribune* in the issue of Aug. 28, 1943, in an obituary records: "Mr. King probably defended more persons charged with murder than any other lawyer in the nation. None of his murder clients was ever executed although some were sentenced to prison terms. Most of these, however, were subsequently pardoned."

Of his travels to different locales for important trials the Tribune further writes: "During this period bloody sheep and cattle wars flared in Wyoming. For 10 years Mr. King rode horseback into

111

the rangelands of that state to defend approximately 20 men accused of murder. About half of them were convicted, all eventually receiving pardons. It was largely through his mediation efforts that the battles of the rich grazing lands were brought to a close. When violent strikes involved Carbon County miners Mr. King defended 27 men accused of murder as the outgrowth of mining. All were acquitted."

Among his many celebrated clients were Jack Dempsey, Marie Dressler and Charles Chaplin. He filed suit against Chaplin for $500,-000, whom he represented in a divorce action. He collected a good portion of the amount.

Sam was a 2nd Lt. in World War I, a member of the American Bar Association and associations in Utah, Colorado, Nevada, Wyoming and Idaho. The Utah Bar Association, paid him this tribute: "With the passing of Mr. King passes an epoch. He was virtually the last of a race of legal giants who practiced in Western America. . . . Not only was he a distinguished lawyer, industrious, resourceful and loyal to the interests of his clients, but he loved his fellow men. He had a rare capacity for making and retaining friends that few men have possessed."

The news of his death at seventy-five while on a visit to Salt Lake brought a flood of telegrams from lawyers across the nation, and friends wrote letters from all over the West. He came from a period when BYU produced eminent barristers; Sam King was one of the best.

WILLIAM HENRY KING

Born: June 3, 1864, in Fillmore, Utah.

Father: William King, son of Thomas Rice King and Matilda Robison of New York State. Settled in Fillmore, Utah. A Bishop and member of the High Council. In charge of mission at Hauvern, Ireland, 5 years. Merchant, manufacturer and stock raiser.
Died: 1892 in Salt Lake City, Utah.

Mother: Josephine Henry, daughter of Andrew Henry and Margaret Creighton of Ireland.
Married: Nauvoo, Illinois. Utah pioneers of 1850.
Died: 1868.

Brothers and Sisters: (William H.)
Lillian, m. Ira N. Hinckley
Josephine, m. John W. Thornley
Samuel A., m. Nettie Bagley

Marriage: 1) Louisa Ann Lyman, Mar. 17, 1889 at Manti, Utah, daughter of Francis M. Lyman and Rhoda Taylor, pioneers of Oct. 13, 1848, Amasa M. Lyman Company.
Died: 1906
2) Vera Sjodahl of Salt Lake City, born in Manti, Utah on Oct. 10, 1892, daughter of Jan Madison Sjodahl, Associate editor of the Deseret News.

Children: (Family of Louisa Ann:)   Family resided in Provo and Salt Lake City.
Romula
Paul Browning
Josephine
Adrieinne
(of Vera:)
Kathleen, b. April 19, 1914; m. Fielding Kimball.
David S., U.S. Congressman.
Twins; John Creighton—Lt. Col. in Air Force, West Point Graduate and Eleanor.

Death: Nov. 27, 1949.

"Bill" King was born to pioneer parents, the eldest in his family. Never a large man, he knew hard farm work of a frontier town and listened to politics around the cracker barrel in the town's grocery store. He lived in Utah's most stressful days, born just after Johnston's Army had left the state and the Civil War was concluding. Debate on State's Rights vs. Federal Power and the fact that Federal power had aided in the Nauvoo expulsion and had sent an army west to quell a non-existing rebellion caused many of the Utah colonists to espouse the Democratic Party with States Rights philosophy and further strengthened their challenge of Federal influence when statehood was denied Utah Territory until 1896. Bill King was an ardent Democrat.

The King boys, William and young Sam were omniverous readers, and each revealed his personal tastes and inclinations by the books he borrowed or bought. Property rights, water problems, federal, state or individual ownership offered problems of intrigue for Will; what was a contract and the binding power of a deed or a will gave him ample challenge. Sam became more concerned with the hazards and conflicts of the person in society rather than the property he may have owned. Both read Blackstone and wore out its pages.

Wm. H. completed his BYA course when seventeen years of age, entered the U. of Utah for a year then served a two and one half year mission to Europe where he observed the various types of government with monarchy and experimental democracy. Returning home, his course was definite. He entered the University of Michigan Law School and graduated with his well-earned LLB.

He had a beautiful deep voice and was frequently called upon to sing; favorites in school and on his mission were "Rocked In the Cradle of the Deep" and "The Sword of Bunker Hill." In those days it was not so hard to get an accompanist as most of the entertainment centered in the home around an organ or in the ward church.

He began practice in Fillmore, then moved to Provo and was an immediate success. He had been a prize orator and winning debater at BYA, so his name had speaking value from the very start. He formed a partnership, King and Burton. He entered politics from the first month in the growing city, simultaneously becoming Provo City Attorney and Utah County Attorney. He held three terms in the state legislature, territorial, and was president of the Senate for one term.

In 1894 he was appointed associate judge of the State by President Grover Cleveland. Statehood for Utah in 1896 was a boon to most politicians and helped to change power in Utah when the State gained admission under William McKinley. With Woodrow Wilson and World War I the Democrats again held sway and William H. was elected to the Senate in 1917.

In passing, we should mention that he served in the 55th Congress for 2 years, declined to run but was elected to 56th Congress when Brigham H. Roberts was unseated to fill out the rest of the term, April 25, 1900 to Mar. 3, 1901. Twice he was defeated for 58th and 59th Congress. His seat in the Senate ran from 1917-1941. He gained prestige with each year, but was an unsuccessful candidate in 1940 elections.

With government ties released he remained in Washington for legal practice until April of 1947 when he returned to Salt Lake until his death. He was buried in the Salt Lake Cemetery.

Paralleling his political career was another Provo man and BYA graduate, Reed Smoot. They frequently opposed each other in Senate voting but were best of friends in civic and church activities. William H. was a Seventy in the LDS Church and one of the ablest orators in the Senate when oratory was much more cultivated than today. As one of his friends stated, "He looks like and has the bearing of a statesman."

JESSE KNIGHT

Born: September 6, 1845   **Place:** Nauvoo, Illinois—Moved to Utah when 5 years old.

Father: Newell Knight
Born November 13, 1800. Died January 11, 1847. Left Nauvoo with his family of 7 children. Son of Joseph, who gave money and aid to Jos. Smith, Jr. when translating the Book of Mormon. Gave supplies from his general store, including paper. First miracle performed in the Church on him. His marriage was the first to be solemnized in the Church. He directed the first company of 50 to leave Nauvoo. Died leaving wife and 7 children, all under the age of 13. Eighth child born after his death.

Mother: Lydia Goldthwaite
Born on June 9, 1812, in Suttry, Worcester Co. Mass., and died April 3, 1884, at St. George, Ut. Had five sisters and six brothers.

1827—At fifteen, to a boarding school for a good education.

1828—At sixteen, married Calvin Bailey, a school mate.

1829—A daughter born and died in 1833. Husband drank and left her in poverty. Parents welcomed her back home.

1833—The Freeman Nickersons took Lydia to Mt. Pleasant in Canada, crossing Lake Erie on ice. Here she first met Joseph Smith and Sidney Rigdon at meetings held in Nickerson home. In October, she was baptized. She rejoined her parents who disapproved of her joining the Mormons.

1835—Permitted to go to Kirtland to join Mormons and parents gave her ample money, fifty dollars of which was given to free Joseph Smith from prison. In the fall, Lydia went to Hyrum Smith home to help his wife and here became acquainted with Newell Knight. On November 24, she wed Newell. She was left behind in 1847 at death of Newell and others used her teams and wagons. She remained until 1850, rented oxen for the journey to Salt Lake. She paid off the debt in two years. Her first pound of butter paid as tithing. Unable to repossess her own equipment from borrowers. Older boys greatly disillusioned, affecting Jesse later. Newell Jr. remained estranged rest of life. Son of Newell Jr. named Jesse, father of Goodwin Knight, a recent governor of California.

Brothers and Sisters:	Samuel, Sally, James, Joseph, Newell Jr., Lydia, Jesse
Marriage:	Amanda McEwan Born on November 13, 1851, in Salt Lake City. Married January 18, 1869 in Salt Lake Endowment House. Died in Provo December 15, 1932. Daughter of John McEwan, b. Feb 12, 1824; d. Feb 27, 1879; and Amanda Melvina Higbee, b. May 20, 1826; d. May 24, 1882 in Provo. Amanda's parents were married by Orson Pratt, Dec. 23, 1845. Amanda was fourth child of 9 children.
Children:	Six children, all attended B.Y.U.; five born on parents' ranch in Payson. Minnie, Studied under Karl G. Maeser, died at 17. Raymond, A successful rancher, and a town in Canada named after him. J. William See chapter in this book. Inez, was dean of women at B.Y.U., m. Robt. Eugene Allen, had 5 sons, all B.Y.U. Jennie, m. W. Lester Mangum, had 7 children, all at B.Y.U., 4 got degrees. Iona, m. Knight Starr Jordan, son of Pres. David Starr Jordan of Stanford University. Two children at B.Y.U., later at Stanford.
Death:	March 14, 1921.

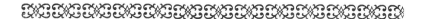

The life of a boy is often but a reflection of his parents. The lives of Newell Knight and Lydia Goldthwaite are so representative of many of the parents of the first students at B.Y.A. and B.Y.U. that I shall give more detail for these than for most other parents represented in this volume. The history of the L.D.S. Church is revealed in their lives and shows the background of faith and loyalty not uncommon with those early pioneers.

Newell Knight is interestingly written up in the "Juvenile Instructor" and briefly described in the *Jesse Knight Family* by J. Will Knight. President Jesse Knight corroborated many of the facts himself in interviews I held with him as he sat on his family porch on Center Street.

Newell was born Nov. 13, 1800, and died Jan. 11, 1847. His birthplace was Marborough, Windham Co., Vermont. He was the son of Joseph, born Nov. 3, 1772, at Oakeham, Worcester, Mass., and Polly Peck, b. Apr. 6, 1776, in Vermont and died August 7, 1831.

The family moved to a farm on the Susquehanna River for two years, then to Colesville, N.Y., for nineteen years. The father, Joseph, was a Universalist. He employed Joseph Smith, Jr., loved by Newell.

1825, June: Newell married Sally Colburn, a delicate girl to whom Joseph Smith often related events in the gospel's restoration.

1830, April 15th: The first public discourse preached by a Latter-day Saint was delivered by Oliver Cowdery at the house of Peter Whitmer in Fayette, N.Y. Newell was subject of casting out of devils by Joseph Smith, reputedly the first miracle in the new Church. Soon thereafter, Newell was baptized at Fayette.

—June 1: First Conference held with 30 converts present who were confirmed and some ordained officers in the priesthood. Knights were present.

—June 9: Oliver Cowdery baptized Joseph Knight, his wife, Joseph Knight Jr., Polly Peck, Emma Smith and others.

—Persecutions began and Joseph Smith Jr. taken to Colesville for trial; Newell a witness.

—August: Newell moved Prophet and family from Harmony, Penn., to Fayette, N.Y., to live with John Whitmer.

—Newell a missionary with Hyrum Smith and Orson Pratt.

1831—April: Colesville Branch with Newell as leader left their homes and started for Kirtland, Ohio August 6: Polly Peck, his mother, died. August 7: Joseph Smith Jr. attended her funeral. Hers was the first death to occur in the Church in this dispensation.

1832—October 14: Samuel Knight born, Saints soon thereafter driven from their homes-church in Jackson County, Missouri, fled for lives in stormy weather.

1834—September: the ailing mother, Sally, died, a baby son having died previously. Newell left son, Samuel, with an aunt and returned to build temple in Kirtland.

1835—November: wed Lydia Goldthwaite; married by Joseph Smith at Hyrum Smith's house, the first marriage ceremony performed by the Prophet. Stayed until Temple was dedicated.

1836-1844—Left Kirtland, met persecution in Clay Co., Missouri, then went on to Far West and moved with Saints to Commerce (Nauvoo, Illinois).

1844—June 27: The Prophet and Hyrum Smith martyred at Carthage jail, Illinois, changing plans of thousands of Saints.

1846—Newell was one of first to leave Illinois for the mountains. Seven children by now, Samuel by first wife and Sally, James, Joseph, Newell Jr., Lydia, and Jesse of Lydia. Newell appointed captain of first 50. Stopped on their journey by letter from Brigham Young; told to winter. Built fort and Ponca Indians were their friends.

1847—January 4: Newell taken ill and died on the 11th "in peace" with the world.

By understanding the parents, we are better able to understand their children.

Jesse was too young to remember his illustrious father; too young to understand the reasons for his moving across the country. Samuel, thirteen, was permitted to go on to the valley, but Lydia was urged to give her three oxen and two wagons to others who could go immediately. In August 1847, a son, Hyrum, was born. The mother and her family lived in a dugout for a year, while she worked with her needles and wash tub.

1850, June 1: The little family started with Bishop Hunter Company for Salt Lake City, and on October 3rd was met by Samuel. Two oxen had been rented for forty dollars, covered by a note, which Lydia paid within two years. Two cows helped to pull her wagons and furnish daily food.

Lydia soon opened a small school in Salt Lake, was happily successful, and later became a Ward school teacher which gave her a more assured income. With her first pound of butter she paid for tithing.

1858—Johnston Army came to Utah and Lydia took her family to Provo where she arranged to buy the Hook's farm. Lydia met and married a widower, James McClellan in 1860, and moved to Payson with her family and his two daughters, aged 11 and 13. When Mc-Clellan was called South he took his families to Santa Clara, Utah, leaving Jesse and Hyrum with their brother, James, in Provo. Brother McClellan died on February 10, 1880. In 1882, Lydia moved to St. George, did Temple work and lived comfortably, until she died in her sleep on April 3, 1884, one of the great pioneer mothers.

Jesse was now 24 years of age, having only the reminiscences of a mother to acquaint him with his illustrious father. He remembered being greeted in Salt Lake by his brother Samuel, of their living in a two room log cabin, of his mother teaching school and the enforced exodus to Provo as Johnston's army marched through Salt Lake.

Their moving to Provo took them away from the persons who had taken their mother's oxen and wagons (when Newell had died) with a promise to return the property when she arrived in Salt Lake. The young boys learned where the oxen and wagons were and went to reclaim them only to be told by the "owners" that Brigham Young had given the animals to them and they owed nothing. Before the matter was settled, Lydia had to purchase two more oxen and the children were told they would have to work all the harder; then the move south came. This matter of obligation—denial so affected the older boys that it was a matter of bitter conversation for several years. It so affected Newell Jr. that he strayed from the church, and it had a strong influence on young Jesse. Newell Jr's. grandson, Goodwin Knight, Utah born, became governor of California.

To relate but meager details of Jesse's life spells a tale of toil, hard work, great adjustments and the rejuvenation of a spiritual soul. At age eleven he took oxen on shares and hauled wood. When twelve years old he purchased a colt with his own hard-earned money, and enjoyed breaking it in, having it come to him by whistle command, search his clothes for a carrot or some tidbit. Watching his mother sew by the light of a burning grease rag he had but one thought, to drive a good bargain and buy her a cow. A strong affection for each other was deepened by such sacrificial deeds on Jesse's own initiation. She worked the farm, got some good books and taught her children to read and pray. At fifteen he was freighting into Nevada, days and nights alone; at sixteen he held his first regular job with Benjamin Roberts who contracted him for $30 a month. Jesse did so well that Roberts paid him $50 a month. At seventeen he drove back over the Pioneer Trail to help get some 650 Saints into Utah. Thirty of them died and he helped to bury them on the plains. He then freighted into Montana and met men of logging and freight camps, gunmen and fortune hunters. In 1867 he guarded one of the settlements in Sanpete County in the Black Hawk War. When the railroad approached Salt Lake City he worked with his teams for the Union Pacific Railroad at $20 a day, a fabulous sum for the times. He saved his money and worked towards the purchase of a good ranch.

He saw lynched men hanging from trees, some bullet ridden. On one occasion he hid his payment in gold in the hub of his wagon wheel as hooded men searched his wagon.

Most of the fellows in their early twenties thought mostly of marriage, horse back rides with the girl sitting in back of her boy friend and her arms around his waist. It took some time for Jesse to get enough courage to invite a girl he greatly admired to sit back of him on a saddle. He finally asked Amanda McEwan, vivacious and pretty, with mischief in her eyes, to be his partner. On such occasions she would tease Jesse with very pointed questions leading to marriage. The bashful fellow soon fell desperately in love and a wedding date was fixed. The opportunity to make big money on the railroad delayed the date from October, 1868, to January 1st. Starting the trip for Provo from his job, he became snowbound and unable to advise his bride-to-be. She patiently waited and set the date again for January 18, 1869, when the wedding was consummated in the Endowment House in Salt Lake City. On their return to Provo one horse died and Jesse had to borrow a replacement to complete the trip. "A most unhappy start to end so happily." They lived in a two-room adobe house on 5th West in Provo which Jesse had made and for which Amanda had sewed rags for carpets and had helped to build the kitchen furniture. She tailored the first suit he ever owned after they were married. She was not yet eighteen.

In conversations with Jesse, J. Will and Uncle Jesse's daughters, I learned considerable of the man, Jesse Knight, and of his family, which I briefly narrate:

Jesse stayed away from the Church for fifteen years, but used no profanity nor condoned any immorality. One winter the children became sick unto death, when Jennie (Mangum) was two years old; Amanda, the mother, wanted the Elders, but Jesse demurred. When the Elders came Minnie asked to give her life to save Jennie, and all the children were delirious. After administration Jennie became immediately well and Minnie died. Inez, possibly the sickest, was also spared. This incident completely changed Jesse's life. J. Will told us on different occasions that his father became sensitive to spiritual promptings. Near his home in Payson he heard a voice say, "This country belongs to the Mormons." When he located the "Humbug Mine" he was compelled to remark: "We will some day save the credit of the Church." The great ore strike was made in August of 1896 as the Humbug made good from the very start. The second shipment brought over $11,000. He bought the Irvin Blossom and Uncle Sam claims, both highly productive, and found rich ore in six different locations. His investments produced more than ten million dollars.

When Knightville sprang into existence, there were no saloons, miners were paid twenty-five cents per day more so that Sundays would be free. Miners who got drunk were fired.

He never kept large sums of money in the bank; he always found good use for it.

He payed back tithing, what he thought to be a liberal estimate, adding a good interest. President Heber J. Grant, in Conference in Provo, said that Jesse Knight had given more than $680,000 in tithing.

He built the first Church and school in Raymond, Alberta, Canada, and gave some 1500 acres to home builders, being known as the "poor man's friend in Canada."

His enterprises and benefactions further reveal his true character.

Knight Consolidated Power Co.—was registered in 1910 with a capital
    corporations in this grouping. Each of his children was given
    10,000 shares, leaving 50,000 shares for himself and his wife.
    Mining properties were extended to Colorado, Nevada, and different locations in Utah.

Knight Consolidated Power Co.—was registered in 1910 with a capitol
    stock of $2,000,000; seven plants operating. This was sold for

$1,892,083, for a profit of $300,000. He immediately wrote out a tithing check for $30,000.

Knight Woolen Mills—erected to make work for people of Provo, especially widows. Some four hundred adults worked in the mills whether times were good or bad. They received their regular pay. A fire of major proportions gutted the mills in 1918 and the business never sufficiently recovered to warrant operation.

Tintic Drain Tunnel—built to secure water for Tintic-Eureka district.

Ellison Banking Co.—officer and director, Layton, Utah.

Layton Sugar Co.—officer and director, Layton, Utah.

Spring Canyon Coal Co.—one of the large Carbon County deposits.

Springville-Mapleton Sugar Co.—capital, $1,500,000.

Blue Bench District—Uintah Valley Irrigation System; 1916 bonds worth $100,000 given to B.Y.U. By 1940 principal and accrued interest worth $217,307.82, and from these funds Allen Hall (boys) and Amanda Knight Hall (girls) were erected to be self liquidating.

Knight Trust Savings—$300,000 capital; in 1931 joined with First Security Bank of Utah and Idaho.

On several occasions Jesse Knight came to the rescue of the LDS Church itself. The Church owed over a million dollars and the Federal Government confiscated all Church property. When Jesse learned through Bishop Joseph B. Keeler that the Church desperately needed $10,000, Jesse sent Brother Keeler to Salt Lake with a check the next morning. On another occasion when Heber J. Grant told Jesse that several brethren were financially pressed and needed $5,000, Uncle Jesse sent $10,000 and Reed Smoot sent $1,000 for good measure.

When "Uncle" Jesse, as they began to call him when he moved to Provo in 1890, put his children in the B. Y. Academy a tie of friendship and interest for the school began which has never ended. He began to find and make employment for students. In 1898 after the Humbug mine started to pay and change his own life, he gave the Academy $1,000 for the College Building. Amanda and Jesse Will gave several mounts. In 1901, the Training school and the Gymnasium were erected, with $75,000 coming from Uncle Jesse. Another $5,000 was given to complete the job. Founders Day of 1909 was a banner occasion when the Maeser Memorial was presented to the school by the BYA Alumni Assn., sixty-five thousand dollars coming from the Knight family, Brother and Sister Knight giving $41,000. Scholarships were established for needy students. In 1904 he gave the money to build the blacksmith shop on 5th North. In 1907 he deeded the school 500 acres on Provo Bench, augmented later by 40 more acres. He gave land on which the great "Y" is now seen.

By 1901 he was placed on the BYU Board of Trustees and in 1911 was elected Vice President, a position he held until his death.

For many years he was chairman of the Executive Board and carefully watched the growth and needs of the University.

The Banyan of 1914 was dedicated to Uncle Jesse Knight.

He helped with finances in the building of the pavilion for a grand-stand view of the spirited athletic events won by BYA and BYU. He best enjoyed the foot races.

As he grew older he spent more of his hours on his shaded front porch, in a favorite rocking chair, using a bamboo fan. On rare occasions he would come up to College Hall and address the students for a short period, after a factual introduction by President George H. Brimhall, which always embarrassed him. Most of his speeches were about integrity, the blessing of work, respect for parents, and building of the Church. "Money has no value unless you share it wisely." A conversation with him consisted mostly of monosyllabic answers to your questions.

He was a great benefactor, noble father and husband, devout member of the Church, and ardent advocate of character education. Much of the BYU is a monument to his thrift and Church loyalty.

His noble soul passed away on a Monday, the morning of March 14th, 1921. The Tabernacle could not hold the number of friends and relatives present to pay him tribute. Authorities from the Church and state sat with miners and mill workers, townsmen and students. President Heber J. Grant and Anthony W. Ivins spoke of his spiritual qualifications; John Smith, a close friend, told us that Uncle Jesse never started a business deal until he first discussed, "Is it Right?" President Brimhall said, "President Brigham Young, Abraham O. Smoot, and Jesse Knight were the three great fathers of BYU."

The beautiful and modern College of Commerce on the new campus is named the Jesse Knight Building, and a masterly oil portrait by Emil Kosa of Hollywood welcomes you to its halls. No tribute will ever do him full justice.

J. WILLIAM KNIGHT

The second son of Jesse Knight.

Born: August 20, 1874   **Place:** Payson, Utah

Father: Jesse Knight
He became a close companion to his son, J. Will, who cooperated in most of their mining ventures and business transactions. The burden of the Knight investments were gradually turned over to J. Will who outlived his father by 35 years.

Mother: Amanda McEwan
She was the fourth child of nine children; experienced the vicissitudes and trials of the wife of a prospecting miner, rancher, and empire builder. She had great faith in the power of healing and patiently watched the conversion of her husband to a devout churchman and benevolent philanthropist. Amanda believed with him that wealth had value if wisely shared.

**Brothers
and Sisters:**   Minnie, Raymond (J. Wm.), Inez m. Robert Eugene Allen (five sons, all attended B.Y.U.); Jennie, m. W. Lester Mangum (seven children, all at B.Y.U.); Iona, m. Knight Starr Jordan, son of Pres. David Starr Jordan, famous president of Stanford University (two children, attend B.Y.U.)

Marriage: Lucy Jane Brimhall of Provo, Utah
Married January 18, 1899, in the Salt Lake Temple with John Winder officiating. Daughter of President George H. Brimhall and Alsina Wilkins who, with Inez Knight, became one of the first two women missionaries for the Church. They went to Great Britain, and a beginning courtship between J. Will and Lucy Jane began just after she was dismissed from her British mission.

Children: Richard, b. June 9, 1911, at Provo; graduated B.Y.U. 1937; m. Gale Stewart.
Philip S., b. February 28, 1915; graduated B.Y.U. 1936, Stanford U. in 1939; m. Eileen Binns Jan. 18, 1937.

Residence: 300 East and Center, and Edgemont, Canyon Road, Provo, Utah.

Death: March 11, 1956.

J. William Knight was a tall boy at an early age. He became an expert horseman, owned his own racing horses, and was jockey for his father and himself. Both ardently loved horse racing, summer and winter, and the Knights kept blooded stock until J. Will moved out on the Canyon Road.

Athletic activities were more generally participated in during pioneer days, and Wards or blocks would have their champion runner, broad jumper, Indian wrestler, tug-o-war team, rope and tree climber, steer wrestler, etc., where individual skill was paramount. J. Will excelled in the broad jump, hop-skip jump, calf-cutting, and Indian wrestling, prone or standing. He jumped fences as hurdlers do today; his lasso was accurate and strong.

Will believed implicitly in the "Word of Wisdom"; could climb mountains with speed and but little fatigue. He thrilled to a beautiful landscape and especially loved the beauty of live water in mountain streams.

He became a practical geologist and learned the indicating rock formations that hinted of ore deposits. From the days of the great mine Humbug on he was his father's constant mining companion.

When office work in Provo limited his horse and ranching activities, he took to city sports. He aided in county fairs and track meets, built his own tennis courts near his former house on 3rd East and Center Street, and became an ardent devotee, playing until he was 66.

May I share with you a tennis experience. He played in tournaments many summers and a car load of Provo tennis players would go to Salt Lake to compete for the Knight tennis cup. I suggested one day as we rode back from Salt Lake in John Smith's big Hudson that J. Will give a cup for seniors and I would give one for the juniors. The State Tennis Committee accepted the offers and the cups were put in annual competition. On a later trip to Salt Lake, I sat in the back seat and read aloud the sports news from the *Morning Tribune*. Will was driving and listened attentively. After reading of the semi-finals victories of Buck Dixon and Earle Pierce, I kept on as if actually reading from print. "In the senior tournament, the brilliant play of veteran J. Will Knight of Provo was outstanding. His accurate service, court generalship, and bewildering placements kept his team in a commanding lead until two straight sets sent them victoriously to the showers." All the fellows joined with me in congratulating him. His face beamed in delight, as he thoroughly enjoyed being a winner in anything he started. Three days later he phoned and said he had looked through all the papers, but couldn't find the tennis article I had read. What issue was it in? I said I would try and find it but didn't have the heart to tell him the facts.

Being around him was a joy; clean thoughts and ready laughter permeated his day. He met a problem square on, solved it to his best ability, and was ready for the next piece of work or assignment. As was the case with his father, his church, his country, his family, and B.Y.U. became his major projects. So much of his wealth was tied up in real estate that he lost heavily in the deficit-dealing depression. But not once did he lose his ready smile, concern for his family, and hopes for the B.Y.U.

It is a pleasure to unfold a portion of his life as reflected in a calendar of his activities:

Education:

His mother was his first and best teacher. J. Will was in school in Payson until he was sixteen when Uncle Jesse moved his family to Provo to receive the benefits of the B.Y. Academy. Karl G. Maeser and George H. Brimhall frequently visited the Knight Payson home and "sold" education and the Academy to the growing family.

J. Will took several classes under Dr. Maeser, Benjamin Cluff, and George H. Brimhall but his major professor was Joseph B. Keeler in the commercial department, from which he graduated in 1894 having the use of the new education building and a budding library. He was early used as an official in track meets and in his maturity was a member of the B.Y.U. Athletic Council for years.

His home library contained a diversified collection of information —history and religious works. He read very few novels; "Life is too short to waste on fiction when more interesting real stories are all about you." He had great respect for the educated man who used his learning wisely. J. Will gave many scholarships to needy students.

Occupational Activities:

1894-96—Farmed near Milford for two years.

1896-98—Went on a British Mission.

1899—Went to Canada and ranched with his brother Ray. Built fine ranch home 15 miles east of Cardston (Bar K2). 4,000 head of steers; 30,000 acres of land with high grass; a fish-filled lake; beautiful flowers. His wife Lucy joined him when his house was finished. Lafayett H. Holbrook and wife were with them in town of Raymond (Raymond Holbrook born and named here.)

1907—Returned to Provo to help father with mining and made vice-president of the Knight Investment Company. Developed "Humbug" and other mining properties. Lived in Provo the rest of his life except for 1933-39 (tax commissioner in Salt Lake City) and 1944-46 (with wife in presidency of Temple in Salt Lake).

Other Occupations: Officer or director in

Knight Trust and Savings Bank	*Mining Companies*
Knight Woolen Mills	Miller Hill
Provo Reservoir Company	Tintic Central

Utah Lake Irrigation Company
Layton Sugar Company
Knight Sugar Company
Ellison Ranching Company
Utah Ore Sampling Company
Pacific Life Assurance Company
Knight Ideal Coal Company
Great Western Mines Company

Ibex Gold
North Bingham
Bingham Empire
Nevada Park & Milling Company
Columbian Corporation (South America) Sugar and Rubber
Keno Mining and Milling Co.

Church Activities:

Attained a sequential progress in priesthood promotion in harmony with age advance.

1896—On mission to Great Britain in Cheltenham and Bristol; visited Europe with his brother Ray, sister Inez, and her companion, Lucy Jane Brimhall, who were dismissed from the mission at the same time as J. Will in November, 1898.

Made first bishop of Raymond Ward in Canada on October 10, 1891; 1903—became second Counselor to Taylor Stake with President Heber J. Allen; 1908-1919—second Counselor in Utah Stake to J. B. Keeler; 1919-1946—Presidency of Salt Lake Temple.

Politics:

Life time member of the Democratic party and early worker in primary and state politics; delegate to National Convention; elected to State Senate two terms, 1916-1924, worked for prohibition and women sufferage; democratic candidate for Governor, 1908—defeated by Governor William Spry; member of Utah State Tax Commission with Governor Henry H. Blood, 1933-39; member of USAC Board under Governor Simon Bumberger, resigned after two years to serve in Senate.

Civic and Scholastic Activities:

Member of Board of Trustees, B.Y.U., 1921-1937; member of Utah State Board of Panama-Pacific Exposition; life member of American Mining Congress; President and director of Provo Chamber of Commerce; President of B.Y.U. Alumni Association—two terms; B.Y.U. Alumni Association Distinguished Service Award, 1946; Vice President of Timpanogas Council Boy Scouts of America.

Most of the honors which came to him he deferred to his father, and he was one of the most unselfish and magnanimous men I ever met. He truly loved his fellow men; he thought of B.Y.U. as one of his children of whom he was boastfully proud.

RICHARD R. LYMAN

Born: November 23, 1870 in Fillmore, Utah.

Father: Francis Marion Lyman, b. January 12, 1840 on the plains of Goodhope, Illinois. Son of Amasa M. Lyman. At age 8, drove ox team across the plains. Council of Twelve Apostles 1880-1916. Five sessions in Utah Legislature, speaker of House one session. Spent 7½ years as missionary in Europe. Lived in Fillmore for 14 years. d. November 1916.

Mother: Clara Carolyn Callister, daughter of pioneers of 1847, Thomas Callister and Caroline Smith, b. April 14, 1850; m. October 4, 1869 in Salt Lake City, Utah.

Brothers and Sisters: Richard R.; George Albert, b. November 14, 1873; Lucy Smith, b. August 5, 1876; Ida, b. August 2, 1878, m. Eric H. Anderson; John Callister, b. September 24, 1880; Amy, b. December 10, 1882; Don Callister, b. June 21, 1886.

Marriage: Amy Cassandra Brown, sister of Professor James L. Brown. b. February 7, 1872. m. September 9, 1896. School Teacher of Pleasant Grove and at BY Academy. Member Relief Society General Board 36 years, president 1940-45. Member State Legislature 1923. Distinguished Service Award, BYU Alumni, 1937. d. December 5, 1959, at 87.

Children: Wendell Brown Lyman, b. December 18, 1897; Margaret, m. Alexander Schreiner, Tabernacle Organist, b. September 15, 1903.

Death: Tuesday, December 31, 1963 at 93.
Buried in Wasatch Memorial in Salt Lake City, Utah.

Education:

> Brigham Young College at Logan; Brigham Young Academy—graduated, 1891. Principal of High School and head of Mathematics, BYA, one year. First instructor employed by University of Utah School of Mines; Graduated, Engineering, U. of Michigan, Ann Arbor, 1895, B.S.; Cornell, M.S. 1903 Civil Engineering; Ph. D., Cornell, 1905. Head Civil Engineering at U. of U., 18 years; 1961, Prof. Emeritus of U. of U. Civil Engineering; Established Lyman Loan Fund at BYU, later consolidated with other loan funds. President BYU Alumni Association, 1927-28.

One of President Lyman's major enthusiasms was the Emeritus Club of his beloved BYU. He graduated in 1891 and proposed the organizing and establishment of a graduate reunion each year for those who had attended the university fifty years or more, starting with his class. Accordingly, in 1941, all former students of the Academy and University were invited to attend a charter event for June 3rd. Some 152 members responded and were inducted into the veteran organization. Each class from 1876 to 1941 was represented and Richard R. elected as president. It has remained a vital factor in Alumni life ever since.

Business and Profession:

> City Engineer, Provo, 1895; Sigma Xi, Theta Tau, Phi Kappa Phi, Tau Beta Pi; Life Member American Society of Civil Engineers, 1939; Honorary President Utah Society Professional Engineers, 1952; Surveyed and laid out U. of U. campus; Awarded James R. Croe Medal by American Society of Civil Engineers for study of the flow of streams; Member Engineering Board of Review for Sanitary District in Chicago; Member Columbia River Reclamation project; Member Metropolitan Water District of Southern California; Chief Engineer of Utah Power and Light Co., Melville Irrigation Co., Delta Land and Water Co., Deseret Irrigation Co.; President of Lyman-Callister Co., Burton Real Estate and Investment Co., Ensign Amusement Co.; Vice-President of Lyman-Traher Motor Co., Home Benefit Building Society; Director of Heber J. Grant Insurance Co., Pleasant Grove Water Co., California Western States Life Insurance Co., Southwestern Fire Insurance Co., Western States Security Corporation, Intermountain Life Insurance Co.; Consulting Engineer for three of the seven "modern civil engineering wonders of the United States." Spent most of his time from 1943-1963 on engineering and water projects.

Church:

> President of European Mission; General Superintendency, Young Men's Mutual Improvement Association; One of the Twelve Apostles, 1918-1943.

Civic:

President, Sons of Utah Pioneers Luncheon Club; Member National Council, Boy Scouts of America; Originated Lyman plan for marking streets, adopted by hundreds of cities in U.S. and Salt Lake Valley, start numbering from a central point, all directions; Board of Regents, University of Utah; Constructed and engineered waterworks systems, power plants, and irrigation systems; Vice-chairman, Utah Road Commission, 1909-1918 (laid down first modern concrete road in Utah); Member Utah Academy, Arts, Letters and Science; Vice-chairman, Utah Water Storage Commission; Member, NEA; Member, UEA; Prohibition was one of his major activities.

Richard R. Lyman was a man of great capacity and vigorous enthusiasms, with a zest for living, who loved young people and honored his pioneer parentage. He believed in the destiny of Brigham Young University.

KARL GOTTFRIED MAESER

Born:　January 16, 1828, in Vorbrucke, Meissen (Saxony) Germany; baptized in Elbe River, Dresden, with his brother-in-law, Edward Schoenfeld and Edward Martin, October 14, 1855; To Salt Lake September 1, 1860, with Schoenfelds; lived with Thomas Higgs in Salt Lake for a year rent free; started evening school for adults November 15, 1860.

Father:　Johann Gottfried Maeser; born 1804; Artisan in China Fabrik (master painter of china); from well educated and influential family.

Mother:　Christina Fredrica Zocher; born August 25, 1811; daughter of Hohann Gottfried Zocher and Anna C. Moritz; died September 25, 1861; buried in graveyard of old Church in Calen; grave visited by Karl, Gustave and father when Karl was on mission, 1870.

Brothers and Sisters:　Julius, born 1830; Herman, born 1832; Gustave, born 1835; the first two died young.

Marriage:　Anna Meith; married June 11, 1854 in Lutheran Church at Newstadt, Dresden; baptized in L.D.S. Church October 19, 1855 with mother Henriette Meith, sister Ottilie M. Schoenfeld, and brother Emil Meith; died April 2, 1896; buried in Salt Lake Cemetery.
2) Emilie Damke in 1895, with consent of Anna.

Children:　Reinhard, b. March 19, 1855, m. Mary Friels; Franklin, b. in England, died on board ship coming to America, 1857; Ottilie, b. in Philadelphia, Aug. 1, 1859; Emil, b. in Salt Lake City March 29, 1864; Nettie M., b. Salt Lake City, July 20, 1872, m. George S. McAllister; Eva Maeser b. Salt Lake City June 21, 1876, m. Myron E. Crandall, the last of his children and active B.Y.U. Emerita, d. Jan 14, 1967. Anna Camilla, daughter of second wife, died in infancy.

Death:　February 15, 1901; died peacefully in his bed at age 73; buried in Salt Lake City Cemetery.

Karl G. Maeser, the guiding spirit of the Brigham Young University, its chief educational founder and spiritual leader, walks the campus in benign influence as if he were present today. Nobility of character was his constant goal; he demanded honesty of his students and colleagues as well as integrity, perseverance of purpose, humility and reverence. He abominated hypocrisy and was severe in his denunciation of evil, but could forgive beyond the capacity of most men. He especially admired the hard worker with a purpose and he looked upon each of his students as a potential leader. A student to Karl G. Maeser, was somebody worthwhile until he proved otherwise and was urged to discover his talents and develop them for the good of his fellow men.

There are several books on the life of this great educator. I have gleaned the information for this biography chiefly from interviews with the late Reinhard Maeser, son and former teacher at Brigham Young University and a daughter, his last living child, Eva M. (Mrs. Myron) Crandall who died Jan. 14, 1967 in Salt Lake City. Several of Dr. Maeser's students have been most helpful. Two books, *Karl G. Maeser* by Reinhard Maeser (1928) and *Karl G. Maeser—Mormon Educator* by Dr. Alma P. Burton especially are recommended.

In Vol. IV, p. 327 of *History of Utah* by Orson F. Whitney, we read:

"Dr. Karl G. Maeser's name stands for the successful establishment of the educational system of the Church of Jesus Christ of Latter-day Saints; a system conceived by the Prophet Joseph Smith, and founded by President Brigham Young and his successors with this man."

Karl G. Maeser was a thorough searching student of everything written by Joseph Smith, and any word written by him pertaining to education was a guide post for all his future plans and philosophy. He was a keen scholar of the *Doctrine and Covenants* and learned the founding plan of education from Section 88 of this book. Many times Karl G. Maeser quoted from this revelation on intelligence and salvation. Verses 77-79 inclusive:

"And I give unto you a commandment that you shall teach one another the doctrine of the Kingdom. 78. Teach ye diligently and my grace shall attend you, that you may be instructed more perfectly in theory, in principle, in doctrine, in the law of the gospel, in all things that pertain unto the Kingdom of God, that are expedient for you to understand. 79. Of things both in heaven and in the earth, and under the earth; things which have been; things which are, things which must shortly come to pass; things which are at home; things which are abroad; the wars and perplexities of the nations, and the judgements which are on the land; and a knowledge also of countries and of Kingdoms."

Dr. Maeser built much of his educational program on this great revelation.

Karl G. was the eldest of four sons and often was involved in the usual school-boy pranks of the day. His father was the proud possessor of a family pew in the Lutheran Church, a man of distinction and highly respected, being an artist who excelled in painting chinaware. (Meissenware is still one of the world's most highly prized china.) Karl received private tutoring along with his elementary courses and became efficient in French, Italian and Latin, as well as fluent in German. In these activities he associated with the wealthy of the town and knew the highest culture of his times. An educated man of this period must also qualify in music; Karl learned early to play the pianoforte, the organ, and how to conduct choral and orchestral music. He was admitted to the Gymnasium, a school more concerned in education and the arts than physical culture. He spent two years at the Krenz Schule at Dresden, then graduated from the Friederich Stadt Normal School with high honors. When he was twenty years of age he taught in the Dresden schools, and was a private tutor in culture-centered Bohemia for three years. Returning to Germany he accepted a position as a professor with the First District School, as vice director of the institute. It was one of Germany's best schools, especially noted for its preparation of teachers.

Karl had early decided to devote his life to study as a recluse, more in the order of the religious devotee, but the friendly relations with Herr Meith's family gave him a broader viewpoint of life and the three lovely daughters became mealtime companions. Of the three Meith girls, Anna, Ottilie and Camilla, the eldest, Anna, soon became a constant companion and ultimately, his wife. The marriage was in the Lutheran Church where father John Gottfried held his pew. The young man of this day was not permitted to see his enamored lady alone, but had to get permission of the father to pay his respects to her, and only then in the presence of others.

Karl and Anna Meith were married on June 11, 1854, and had seven children. Their first son, Reinhard, was born March 19, 1855. This same year, they met three Mormon missionaries, Apostle Franklin D. Richards, President William Budge of Bear Lake Stake, and Elder William Kimball, son of Heber C. Kimball, which changed their lives.

Of this period, he writes in his diary: "In these dark days of my youth, when infidelity was growing strong around me, I craved for spiritual nourishment. I felt I had a right to ask God for a knowledge of the truth; from the depths of my soul I cried, 'O God, if there be a God, make Thyself known to me.'"

Karl had become curious about the Mormon people when he came into possession of a paper depicting the persecutions of the Mormons in the West—his liberal mind was aroused and began to wonder the more about these people. He writes further of his thinking: "Although filled with admiration for indomitable courage, sincere devotion and indefatigable energy of the great German reformer, Martin Luther, I could not fail to see that this work had been merely an initiatory one, and that the various Protestant sects, taking their initiative from the revolutionary stand of the heroic monk at Wittenberg and Worms, had entirely failed to comprehend the mission of the Reformation. The only strength of Protestanism seemed to be its negative position to the Catholic Church. Scepticism had undermined the religious impressions of my childhood days, and infidelity, now known by its modern name as agnosticism, was exercising its disintegrating influence upon me."

After reading a pamphlet on "Mormonism," written by a Mr. Busch, he writes further: "The author wrote in a spirit of opposition to that strange people, but his very illogical deductions and sarcastic invectives aroused my curiosity, and an irresistible desire to know more about the subject of the author's animadversions, caused me to make persistent inquiries concerning it. Pamphlets and some books were forwarded to me. The inaccuracies and the poverty of language I found in those publications were at first sources of some ironical amusement; but as I read on I became to be convinced the 'Mormonism' was a bigger thing than I had anticipated it to be. The humble but straight forward statements of testimony, the mistakes and the meagerness of the language used in the exposition of the wonderful truths that I could see back of it all, brought such uneasiness to me that I could not resist; my soul was on fire, as it were, and I therefore expressed a desire to have an Elder sent to me."

The above shows the style of Dr. Maeser's later writing as well as his search for truth. He was a lucid, clear writer in the best style of the day, though he never fully conquered his German dialect in speech. This dialect added a piquant style to his subtle humor and detracted nothing from his power to impress or entertain. He was an expert in mimicry and had a rich dramatic talent. He loved the opera and the drama; both flourished under his enthusiasm and guidance when he later came to Utah and the B. Y. Academy.

The first Latter-day Saint to come to Karl was William Budge, who stayed with the Maesers for nearly two months and invited President Richards and William Kimball to come to Dresden. Despite strenuous family and local objections, on a Sunday afternoon, October 14, 1855, Karl G. with his lifetime companion and brother-in-law, Edward Schoenfeld, and Edward Martin were baptized. These were the first baptisms for the L.D.S. Church to be performed in Germany. On October 19th, 1855, Anna Meith Maeser, her sisters, Ottilie Meith Schoenfeld and Camilla Meith, their mother Henrietta Meith, and their brother, Emil, were also made members of the Church.

From this family contact came eight ardent converts; they were baptized in the Elbe River.

So many versions of the happenings that followed have been given, that it may be helpful to quote Dr. Maeser himself: "On coming out of the water, I lifted both my hands to heaven and said, 'Father, if what I have done just now is pleasing unto Thee, give me a testimony, and I shall do even to the laying down of my life for this cause.' There seemed to be no response to my fervent appeal, and we walked home together, President Richards and Elder Budge at the right and left of me, while the other men walked some distance behind us so as not to attract attention. Our conversation was on the subject of the authority of the Priesthood. Suddenly, I stopped Elder Budge from interpreting the President's remarks to me, as I understood them perfectly. I replied to him in German and again the interpretation was not necessary, as I was also understood by the President. Thus we kept on conversing until we arrived at the point of separation, when this manifestation as suddenly ceased as it had come. It did not seem to be strange at all, while it lasted, but as soon as it stopped, I asked Brother Budge what it all meant, and received the answer that God had given me a testimony."

Soon after these baptisms, a Branch was organized in Dresden with Karl G. Maeser as presiding Elder. The group increased in size and some began to talk of going to Utah to be near the center of Church activities.

On June 6, 1856, a little company left Dresden, some never to return, and went to London, England. The Maesers remained in Britain until May, 1857, while Karl filled a mission to Scotland and the Schoenfelds continued on to America. Karl, embarking with his little family for "Zion," was in charge of the Latter-day Saint group and gravely concerned over the illness of his baby, Franklin, born in England. As the ship neared the American coastline, the infant died. In their quiet grief, the Maesers heard a hilarious Fourth of July celebration on the approaching shore.

Without sufficient means to travel further, the Maesers were obliged to remain in Philadelphia and this was during the great financial crash of 1857 when fortunes were lost over night. Amid the chaos of social life and speaking a very broken English, the devoted Karl was called on a mission to the south, most of it in Virginia. Anna, alone in a strange land, still sorrowing over a buried babe, found means of providing for herself, a child, and her youngest sister, Camilla, and courageously encouraged Karl to fill this latest assignment. With four companions, the missionaries trudged their way from town to town, sometimes singing for compensation to buy food, ultimately to hear the command, "Move on." Karl was blessed sufficiently to move his family into Virginia where he was engaged to tutor in music with some of the prominent families, including Ex-United States President Tyler. Later, many of the elite in Richmond entreated Karl to return from his Philadelphia visit.

On August 1, 1859, the Maeser's eldest daughter, Ottilie was born in Philadelphia. In June, 1860, during the great unrest due to the slave controversy, Karl and his family left for Zion, taking four months on the plains by ox team, another epoch story.

Patriarch John Smith was captain of the company and Karl was appointed Chaplain. On this trip the cultured, refined Maesers learned to value the worth of rougher and often crude companions. The company arrived in Salt Lake City on September 1, 1860, to be heartily greeted by the Edward Schoenfelds, who took their relatives into their modest home. The Maesers slept in a wagon box for a short time.

Soon thereafter, they moved into a house loaned to them by Thomas Higgs, father of B. T. Higgs, in the Fourteenth Ward, rent free. Such was the generosity of these "crude people." Professor Maeser, as he was soon called, opened a school in an old adobe meeting house in the Fifteenth Ward. An ad appeared in the *Deseret News*, in part as follows: "The undersigned begs to inform the Public that he intends opening Evening Classes, both for ladies and gentlemen, for English, German, French, Italian, Latin, Greek, Drawing, Book-keeping, Mathematics, and all the branches of a sound and practical education—Languages, including bookkeeping, will be taught by Mr. Alexander Ott."

In February, 1861, President Brigham Young placed Professor Maeser in charge of the Union Academy, just across from the present West High School. Tuition, which was $6.00 a quarter, in advance, was mostly paid in produce and the Professor had a new adjustment to make; that is, how best and where to barter his produce for cash.

The Twentieth Ward Seminary took Professor Maeser from the Academy in the fall of 1862—a school with three departments; Primary, Intermediate, and Grammar. Also, a night school was given for day workers. People came from far and near as word of the abilities of Professor Maeser had spread over the Church. He was kept busy with speaking, teaching and writing. His testimonies were soul inspiring and his illustrations most apt. This German gentleman of conscious culture was obliged to be a janitor, carpenter, painter, cobbler, clerk, auditor, and do all types of work now allotted to paid employees.

A lot was bought on the corner of First North and G. Streets and a house erected, the first owned by the Maesers in Zion. In this home, four children were born; Emil, Nettie, Anna Camilla (died in infancy) and Eva (the only living child in 1964). The mother, Henrietta Meith, came to Utah in 1863, to the joy of the Maesers and Meith sisters, who were made happy by her affiliation with the Church.

The school had more than an abundant number of pupils, but few of them paid for their education. With all of his abilities, Karl lived next door to poverty, and in this dilemma, he became ill when he received a letter from his father telling him there was plenty of money in Germany awaiting his decision to return home. A severe struggle and conflict confronted him and again he turned to his Heavenly Father, and received an assurance that caused him to rekindle his courage and look for another opportunity.

In 1864 Karl was employed as a private tutor to the children of Brigham Young and no longer had to go around with a wheelbarrow to collect his fees, no longer had to be a janitor. He also played the organ in the Old Tabernacle on Sundays.

In 1867, Karl G., while attending Conference, heard his name read for a German and Swiss Mission. Again, he did not falter. His house was built, but unpaid for. His wife and family had equal faith and courage. When Karl gave his wife, Anna, his only 50 cent piece, she said she would return it to him when he came back. This mission was filled with exciting and trying experiences, but best to be read in books devoted entirely to his life. He established a paper called, "Der Stern" (The Star), upon request of Brigham Young, in December of 1868. The L.D.S. German and Swiss Hymn book has 26 hymns by Karl G. Maeser, some original, others translations. He visited his native home twice, from November 1867 to February 1868, calling upon all the members of his family and many of his teachers and friends. He visited his father once more in February, 1870, and labored hard for his conversion. The family urged his return, with money to assist, but the convictions of each party were too strong for either to affect the other, and the sorrowful parting resulted.

On October 6, 1869, in General Conference, Edward Schoenfeld was called to the Swiss and German Mission and arrived in Zurich, Switzerland on March 28, 1870. These two brothers-in-law, Karl and Edward, made a powerful mission team and later, preparations were made for an extensive European emigration. On July 13, 1870, a company, consisting of 269 souls sailed on the S. S. "Manhattan" under the presidency of Karl G. Maeser, Lewis W. Shurtleff and Lorin Farr, first mayor of Ogden, Utah. (Lorin Farr is the grandfather of Dr. Pardoe and Edward Schoenfeld is the grandfather of Albert Schoenfeld, who married Dr. Pardoe's aunt, Florence Pardoe, a native of Stratford on Avon, England. These men have been excellent sources of intimate information of Karl G. Maeser.) Two babies died enroute and two were born—the ship arrived in New York with the same number of people who embarked.

Karl's homecoming was a most joyous one. A new "stove," carpet, lace curtains, furniture, all paid for, furnished the front room.

Anna met him at the front door as he came up the walk, and she called out to him, "Here's the fifty cents you gave me, and another one besides." As he looked about him, he said, "Thank God, it is accomplished. I have done my duty and my Heavenly Father has brought me back again. His great name be praised." Reinhard had been at work, and no serious want had been suffered by the family during Karl's absence.

His many friends persuaded Karl once more to teach school in the Twentieth Ward Meeting House. He was Principal, held hours of Pedagogy and German in the University of Deseret, and here he organized the first normal classes in Utah. He did much writing for the "Contributor", the "Juvenile Instructor" and other publications.

In 1875, following counsel and with consent of his beloved Anna, he espoused Emilie Damke, a convert from Karl's Germany and long-time neighbor. Also, in this eventful year, Karl received a call for another mission. He listened patiently to President Brigham Young as he explained, "We have been considering the establishment of a Church School, and are looking around for a man, the man to take charge of it. You are the man, Brother Maeser. We want you to go to Provo to organize and conduct an Academy to be established in the name of the Church—a Church school." The matter had been discussed for some time previous and President Abraham O. Smoot of Provo had mentioned Karl G. Maeser as eminently qualified for the position. All who heard the suggestion heartily approved. In a few days, Elders George Q. Cannon, George Reynolds and Warren N. Dusenberry waited upon Professor Maeser at his home and invited him to attend a Board Meeting at Savage's Art Gallery the next day. At the meeting, all necessary arrangements were made for the opening of the school on April 24, 1876—the principal to receive $200 a year.

To Professor Maeser's surprise, the only advice President Young gave him before he left Salt Lake was, "Teach nothing, do nothing, without the Spirit of God." On the 21st of April, Karl left for Provo, and immediately began preparing for the opening of School the next Monday morning.

At the first student assembly, it was announced that each school day would begin at 8:45 a.m., an unheard of hour for school training. The first students to sign the Monday morning roll were for the most part more mature students than those who go to high school now. The list of the original 29 students is in Appendix I. The last living member of the first day class was Hannah Stubbs Jones, residing with her daughter, Cleo Ricks, in Salt Lake City, Utah, who celebrated her 100th birthday on April 16, and died on May 1, 1964.

This experimental term closed June 30, 1876, with a vacation until August 27th. The school had caught on and was the major topic of conversation throughout the territory; there were sixty-seven pupils enrolled for the first term.

During the summer vacation, the Maesers moved to Provo and soon were in their own home on 148 North Second East. This modest home entertained men and women from all walks of life.

August 27, 1876 was the real day on which the Brigham Young Academy began its well-planned course of training. The roll for the term comprised about sixty names, twelve of whom were in the normal class including Jeanie Snow, James E. Talmage from England, J. M. Tanner, and George Sutherland, who became Justice of the Supreme Court. As the faculty grew, faculty meetings became more instructive and exacting; weekly reports, verbal and written, were held in greater importance and the checking-up of each pupil's daily standing became a prime purpose of meetings. The faculty partook of the genius and spirit of their leader and Professor Maeser more intimately learned the strength and shortcomings of each of his teaching corps.

The Lewis building on Center Street and Third West was the first building and had been used for seven and one-half years when it burned down on a Sunday night, January 27, 1884. When the large bell fell clanging into the lower flames, many present thought it rang out the death knell of the struggling Academy. As Professor Maeser stood looking at the dying embers of the Lewis block, he was heard to say, "Yes, fire has destroyed the house, but the Academy lives on." Only one day of school was lost, chiefly through the efforts of President Abraham O. Smoot, Warren N. Dusenberry, and the unswerving leader, Karl G. Maeser. The basement of the Old Tabernacle, some rooms over the First National Bank and the partly finished store rooms of the S. S. Jones Company all contributed space and the school year was finished.

In 1884-1885 the school was located in the ZCMI Warehouse at the south end of Academy (University) Avenue, where later the Tote-Gote hill-climber was manufactured. The Academy remained here until 1892. (The building was dismantled in 1967).

The first full academic year of four terms netted some 272 students, after much urgent proselyting in various parts of the state, chiefly in the southern portion. Grammar school was headed by Karl G. Maeser, intermediate by Professor Milton H. Hardy, and the primary by Teenie Smoot.

A more condensed biography of his subsequent life follows:

1877—2nd year. Polysophical Society organized—extra curricular in nature, divided into several sections where adults could come, listen to lectures in subjects of their choice; each Friday night a program was presented and the elite of Provo were present. In this year one of Karl's greatest admirers and a true friend, Brigham Young, died on August 29, 1877. He had been President of the Church for 30 years.

1878—Music was given in the third year. A piano was bought and presented to the school by Susa Young Gates.

1879—Real expansion of the school curriculum attained. A "Ladies Work Department" was organized and women were graded and put into two classes, A and B, Zina Young Card as matron. Each lady should have at least one major piece of work done by her own hand. Professor Maeser had two special organizations: "Monatorial" to give all pupils definite work to do, "Domestic" for welfare students living outside of school. Provo was divided into four Wards, and organization of students ran like a ward. Each student was personally interviewed by Professor Maeser and put on his honor to obey the rules of the school. He often visited teachers and their classes.

1880-1883—The school grew; music became more important and oratory greatly encouraged. Demand for teachers gave the Normal Division greater importance and preparing of teachers became a prime purpose of the Academy.

1884—Average number of students was now over 400, in seven departments. The demands of the students greatly determined the nature and size of a department.

January 24, 1884—The Lewis Building burned with no insurance; most of the furniture was heroically saved, with Karl G. Maeser leading the salvage.

1884-1885—ZCMI Warehouse, divided into 11 rooms; the school remained here until 1892. Would require $2,000 to rebuild the Academy; a movement was set in motion to acquire land and build a planned academy and thwart any demand that the school be closed.

1888—June 8th, Karl G. called by the First Presidency to become the first General Superintendent of all the Church Schools.

1889—May 7, the degree of Doctor of Letters and Didactics (DLD) conferred upon Karl G. Maeser, the first of such degrees given by the Church.

1890—Karl released from the Academy, working two years in dual capacity; Benjamin Cluff Jr. appointed Assistant Principal of the Academy.

1891—First Founders Day exercises were held on October 16, 1891. Work on the Academy building resumed. Dr. Maeser now travelling from Canada to Mexico in the interest of education.

1892—January 4, the new Education Hall of the Academy was dedicated, upon the square block on Academy Avenue from 5th North to 6th North. The entire student body assembled in the old warehouse to be led in prayer by their beloved Principal. (It was well known that this dedication was also to be a farewell; the great founder and leader was to give his valedictory.) The students and faculty then marched down the Avenue to the new building as students bared their heads and formed a double line, while the faculty and visitors moved between them into the long-awaited edifice. President Wilford Woodruff, George Q. Cannon, Joseph F. Smith, Franklin D. Richards, and Governor A. T. Thomas marched with them. Local authorities were President A. O. Smoot, David John, Harvey H. Cluff, Judge J. D. Jones, Bishop Myron Tanner, and many other trustees and faculty, all who were to pay tribute to a great educator who was to go to broader fields of service.

Because of poor health, President Woodruff requested President Cannon to offer the dedicatory prayer. And what a challenge to the youth of the Church it was! Dr. Maeser's address reveals the very core of his life and spiritual strength. It was biographical in outline with great spiritual power, a testimony of the Gospel, and a prayer for the school's continued success. He paid special tributes to President A. O. Smoot, Bishop John E. Booth, Professor Milton H. Hardy, James E. Talmage, Sister Zina Y. Card, Susa Y. Gates, and Teenie Smoot Taylor, with a fervent plea for support of his successor, Benjamin Cluff Jr. All knew he sincerely meant his closing words, "God bless the Brigham Young Academy."

In this year he served in the Constitutional Convention and was the chief referrent in all matters educational.

With his new commission he set out to organize schools in each stake; when some of the teachers failed to get the pay allotted, he told them to consider themselves on missions. "It would be easier that way." He established schools in Utah, Idaho, Arizona, Colorado, New Mexico, Canada, and Mexico.

1894—Made second Assistant to George Q. Cannon of the Deseret Sunday School Union. (A few years later he became first assistant.) He supervised the educational exhibits of the Church at the Mid-Winter Fair in San Francisco.

1895—His name was put up by the Democratic Party in Ogden for Superintendent of Public Schools. He did not want the position and was defeated by Republican John R. Park.

1896—April 2nd, his beloved and faithful Anna died suddenly, while Karl was in northern Utah. "One of the earth's noblest women." After her death he moved to Salt Lake City.

1898—Wrote the book, *School and Fireside* to express his philosophy of education and teaching. He urged that teachers "modify" all secular training by religious influence and asked for an intimate cooperation of school and home. "Discover and evaluate the worth of each individual . . . Teacher's plans should be varied and flexible to allow for student differences . . . Discover the sphere of action for which any given child is adapted and turn its thoughts and energies in that direction . . . Respect for authority should be taught from the time a child is born. In America the lack of reverence for parents and for the aged is a dangerous symptom. The exercise of authority without intelligence, justice, and kind consideration, is tyranny, and obedience without consent of the heart or brain is slavery . . . Teachers and parents should be living examples of what they teach . .` No student should be left too long without a recitation . . . The so-called 'college yells' are exhibitors of coarseness unworthy of educational institutions." These are but a small few of the choice bits of knowledge and teachings which came from him daily. Every teacher in any subject would profit by reading this book.

In this year, 1898, a grand party and tribute was given for him in Provo, honoring his 50th year as a teacher. These tributes constitute another book.

1899—Made a patriarch of the Church, giving him great joy and satisfaction.

1900—November 9, visited the Maeser School in Provo and wrote on the blackboard sentences kept for years.

When Dr. Maeser returned from the Academy he was the recipient of hundreds of letters of highest tribute; gifts were given to him from all over the Church. He numbered every letter he sent out and all he received.

1901—February 15, Karl G. Maeser peacefully passed away while in his bed. Editorials, even beyond the territory, praised his educational ideals and religious fervor. On February 19, 1901, his funeral was conducted by the Deseret Sunday School Union in a packed Salt Lake Tabernacle; Utah's best known educators were his pallbearers and included Apostles Anthon H. Lund, Rudger Clawson, and George H. Brimhall. Among the speakers were: William Budge, Dr. J. M. Tanner, Dr. James E. Talmage, George H. Brimhall (then President of BYU), Apostles Reed Smoot, Heber J. Grant, and Anthon H. Lund. "The Teacher's Work is Done," by Annie Pike Greenwood was read by President Brimhall. Immediately the idea of a memorial building was proposed and the beautiful white edifice, the first on the hill, was the result. The site was dedicated for the Maeser Memorial on January 16, 1908, the anniversary of Dr. Maeser's 80th birthday. On October 6, 1908, a number of Dr. Maeser's students assembled in the Salt Lake Cemetery and unveiled a beautiful grove monument with Professor Briant S. Hinckley as speaker. On May 30th, 1912, the Maeser Memorial was dedicated with Reinhard Maeser, the eldest Maeser son, as chief speaker.

A heroic statue in bronze donated by Nicholas G. Morgan Sr. stands in a teacher's attitude on the Joseph Smith Quadrangle, the name of Karl G. Maeser is heard daily on the campus of the University.

Annie Pike Greenwood, who also wrote the words for the College Song, paid this tribute:

To Karl G. Maeser

Come, lay his books and papers by,
He shall not need them more;
The ink upon his pen shall dry—
so softly close the door.
His tired head with locks of white
and like the winters' sun,
Hath lain to peaceful rest tonight—
The teacher's work is done.

His work is done; no care tonight
his tranquil rest shall break;
Sweet dreams and with the morning light
On other shores he'll wake.
His noble thoughts, his wise appeal,
His work that battles won.
But God doth know the loss we feel;
The teacher's work is done.

We feel it while we miss the hand
That made us brave to bear;
Perchance in that near-touching land
His work did wait him there.
Perchance when death its change has wrought,
And this brief race is run,
His voice again shall teach who thought
The teacher's work is done.

JOHN JASPER McCLELLAN

Born: April 20, 1874   **Place:** Payson, Utah

Father: John Jasper McClellan, born August 6, 1838. Convert to Church in Illinois. Son of James (to Utah in 1850). President of the Payson Opera House in 1882 seating 507 with latest opera chairs, beautiful drop curtain and lovely scenery. Gave "Johnny" every encouragement in music.

Mother: Eliza Barbara Walser, born in Switzerland. Joined the Church in Europe.

Marriage: Mary Estelle Douglas of Payson in Manti Temple. July 1896.

Children: 1 son and four daughters. Mary Genevia (Mrs. Henry Gordon) Jennings, Madeline Estelle, Douglas Jasper, Dorothy Maxine, Florence D., all born in Utah.

Death: August 2, 1925, at very height of his career.

John J. McClellan grew tall at a very young age, had a smiling face, large, dark friendly eyes and slender, active fingers, restless feet and always a mind persistent of purpose. The Payson hills were a constant challenge as he watched the soaring eagle, heard the chatter of the ground hog or the lonely bark of a hungry coyote. The bays of Utah Lake with cat tail and rush beckoned his youthful fancy to hear the black bird trill and watch great flocks of ducks and geese form for flight overhead, see the big billed pelican catch catfish, or answer the croak of the bullfrog. Nature and "Johnny" were friends and sounds especially intrigued him. He was soon known as an entertaining proficient mimic.

In 1886-87 "a boy named Johnny McClellan played the piano in the Abraham Done orchestra." The Payson Tabernacle choir was under the direction of William Clayson, famed Mormon hymn writer, who said, "Johnny never hit a wrong note." He played marches for his school on a small organ and kept the reeds in tune. Professor Clayson and Anthony C. Lund of BYA encouraged the young musician to go east for more expert training.

He started earnest study of music when ten; at eleven he was organist in his ward and worked with local teachers until he was 17. Printing fascinated him and while young he became a printer's devil. With youthful partners, he published Payson's first regular newspaper and was half owner of the "Enterprise" for two years.

At seventeen, the summer of 1891, a benefit concert was given to help Payson's best known musician to further his musical education. A depot crowd sent him happily to Saginaw, Michigan to become the pupil of Albert W. Platte, and immediately was made his assistant. His ability warranted more advanced study and he was sent to Ann Arbor to become the prize piano pupil of Johann Erich Schmael and to study theory and organ with Professor Stanley, director of the school. A year and a half later he was a student of Alberto Jonas, Spanish pianist, head of the university piano school. In the two and a half years spent with Jonas, J. J. was choirmaster and organist in the St. Thomas Catholic Church. He composed a Mass for orchestra and choir which was given on Easter of 1896. While at Ann Arbor he founded the University of Michigan Symphony Orchestra and gave two concerts. He was also president of the Euterpe Musical Club for two years and professor of Theory his last year at the Conservatory and assisted Jonas with his piano classes. He especially enjoyed playing the great Columbian Organ at Chicago's World Fair in 1893. Also at his last year in Michigan he was pianist for the Ann Arbor Choral Union with 300 voices.

Urgent invitations to return to Utah and the big organ in Salt Lake Tabernacle caused him to look westward and a further inducement was a beautiful young lady who had waited in his native town. In July of 1896 he married Mary Estelle Douglas in the Manti Temple. He had graduated from University of Michigan as its first musical graduate in June of this year, the first Utah man to graduate from a University Music course.

In 1896 John J. opened his studio in Salt Lake City and was director of music at the LDS College. He followed this with a year and a half at BYU, taking private students in Salt Lake and Provo. Some of Utah's best pianists were his students of this period.

In 1899 he went to Europe with his wife to spend a year in Berlin, working at the organ and piano, long hours into the night, going to numerous operas and concerts. He found time to edit a German LDS Hymn book, universally used by Germans. His return to Utah in 1900 began his fruitful years as professor of music at the University of Utah, organist for the Tabernacle and musical director of the Salt Lake Opera Co. He had the Tabernacle organ remodelled by the Kimball Company, who declared it to be the best organ in the world. He popularized the daily organ recital inaugurated by Professor Joseph J. Daynes by putting great diversity in his programs and artistic improvisations to reveal the scope of the great instrument.

When the organ was completed to his satisfaction in 1916, a grand concert was given to commemorate the event and was written up by the best music critics across the land. J. J. was prophetic when he said, "It will compel the admiration of the musical world and will attract thousands to hear it."

His teaching duties and organ programs were interrupted by frequent tours. In 1908 he was featured organist for the Ogden Tabernacle Choir when they went to the Oregon World Fair under the leadership of Joseph Ballantyne. The Tabernacle Choir of Salt Lake went to New York City with 197 voices under the baton of Evan Stephens, J. J. McClellan as organist, Edward P. Kimball as assistant organist, Willard A Weihe as violinist, David Reese and Fred C. Graham as tenors. Professor McClellan shared honors with the renowned choir. In the same year J. J. set the "Irrigation Ode" to music which was given in the New York Land and Irrigation Exposition.

In 1904 he conducted the Ogden High School Alumni Association opera "Priscilla" when I sang "Miles Standish" in the Ogden Opera House (now the Orpheum) and a week later in the Salt Lake Theatre. This experience began a friendship which lasted through the years. We were down in the old Green Room after the Salt Lake performance where we were recalling the humorous situations of the several performances. I was in costume and make up when J. J. said, "Turn around. Now walk in character. You know what? If you could sing as well as you act you would be a world-beater. You had better stick to acting. Go back east, get professional training and get into a good stock company." As with many others, his frank advice helped to determine their life's work and careers.

From 1911 to 1918 he was Dean of the Utah Conservatory and was organist of the Tabernacle for 25 years. The King of Belgium decorated him with a diploma and gold medal of the "Order of King Leopold" and the "Order of the Crown" for concert given the King and Queen in the Salt Lake Tabernacle.

Tributes were showered upon him by masters of music from over the world. John Philip Sousa, world renowned bandmaster wrote "Johnny McClellan is an ornament to his profession, both as a man and as a musician. He contributes great talent—yes, genius, with a most attractive personality . . . the promise of his life is great."

Elbert Hubbard, distinguished writer and traveler, who went down with the Lusitania, wrote in his *Fra* magazine in 1913, "What Paderewski is to the piano, McClellan is to the pipe organ. I once stopped over three days in Salt Lake just to attend one of McClellan's recitals. I thought I had heard organ playing before, but the exquisite modulation, the tone and tints of sweet sounds that this man produces cannot be described. They must be heard—and more, they must be felt. McClellan does not play with his hands and feet, he plays with his heart and head, and the keys respond to loves caress. Only high intelligence, sympathy and superb imagination can produce great music."

John J. McClellan, one of Utah's great.

WILFORD McGAVIN McKENDRICK

Born: June 12, 1870, in Tooele, Utah.
In a family of three sisters and four brothers, six half-brothers, and three half-sisters.

Father: Robert Kennedy McKendrick
Owner of only hotel in Tooele and manager of a butcher shop.

Mother: Agnes McGavin

Brothers and Sisters: Chauncey
Mathias
Orson
(Six half-brothers and three half-sisters.)

Marriage: Lydia Wilson, the eighth child of nine.

b. January 11, 1876 in Provo, Utah, daughter of Henry Woodville Wilson and Sussanah Armstrong. Her mother died when she was but two years of age. She was reared by Samuel and Sarah Liddiard, the only one of her family of seven brothers and sisters to be brought up in the Church. Obtained a BYU certificate in elocution and physical culture under Maud May Babcock and Miriam Nelke. Served in all offices of the Young Women's Mutual Improvement Association. Member of the Home Dramatic Co., and popular actress, under management of John C. Graham. President of the Ensignia Club in Salt Lake, and accomplished musician. m. 1892.

Children: Milas Kleone, b. Dec 25, 1893, in Provo, Utah; m. Jan 4, 1918
Calista Hale, b. Mar 22, 1896, in Provo, Utah; m. Robert H. Wallace Sept. 16, 1914
Norma Elaine, b. May 1, 1903, in Ogden, Utah; m. George P. Patrick June 12, 1930
Lydia Maureen, b. Jan 10, 1907, in Ogden, Utah; m. Ambrose A. Maycock April 10, 1929
Wilford Wilson, b. Dec 9, 1908, in Ogden, Utah; m. Lou Fisher Aug 19, 1931

Death: Monday, May 11, 1936 at 66 in Salt Lake City, Utah.

William McKendrick attended school in Tooele with Richard R. Lyman and Ephraim D. Gowans. He had a beautiful tenor voice and was a sound musician, soloing on flute and piccolo. With his wife, he sang many duets for church and charity. He had a smiling personality and radiated enthusiasm.

His daughters, Norma and Kleone, are authors of the quotes which follow:

"When he was fifteen years of age he left the familiar haunts of his childhood and entered school at the BYU, thus fulfilling a dream and hope of his far-sighted mother whose influence started him along this path of education which he followed all the rest of his life. Dr. Maeser was the President of the University at that time and he it was who discovered the homesick lad, in his first month away from home, planning to return with his schooling unfinished. He it was, in his brusque German way, who showed the boy the disappointment his return would be to his mother and this thought restrained father, and he always thanked Dr. Maeser for his interference. When he was sixteen, with his schooling yet unfinished, he obtained a certificate showing he was worthy to teach and was assigned a school at Lake Point. He was under the necessity to teach because his father, together with many other Latter-day Saint men, was arrested for polygamy, and father had to support his mother, brothers and sisters. He taught one year and then returned to Tooele to carry on his father's business. At the end of that year he was able to return to Provo and his interrupted pursuit of an education. Among his teachers were Dr. Maeser, James E. Talmage, Willard Done, and Pres. B. Cluff, Jr. He was a very brilliant student, receiving the highest marks in all classes. He was also active in student-body affairs, one of his chief activities being editor of the "BYA Student," the college paper, which is thought to be the first college paper to be published in Utah. At the end of one more school year when he was nineteen another break came in his schooling. He accepted the principalship of the High School at Monroe, having five teachers under his direction. He remained there for one year then returned once more to his Alma Mater. He finished his schooling at the BYU, graduating with the class of 1891, taking out his degree in Pedagogy. His strongest subjects were mathematics and psychology and the year following his graduation he was attached to the faculty of the BYU as Tutor of Mathematics. The next year, 1894, he became a Professor of Mathematics, teaching both lower and higher forms of that science. He also went to school at the University of Chicago, taking out a degree there."

"It was while he was a student at the BYU that he met his future wife Lydia Wilson, who was one of the most beautiful and popular girls of the school. Their romance flowered during the year of their acquaintance. They went sleigh riding, dancing, and spent many evenings with their friends in mother's home singing, accompanied by the organ, the popular songs of the day, such as "When You and I Were Young Maggie," and "Silver Threads Among the Gold,"—the latter song remained his favorite all his life. After a two-year engagement they were married in the Manti Temple, the ceremony being performed by Apostle Francis M. Lyman."

In 1900 Wilford was called on a mission to the Southern States, leaving a young wife and two children who went to live with her foster parents, the Lilliards. Under President Ben E. Rich, Wilford was used as a peace-maker, being sent to many of the trouble spots and frequently had to escape from being tarred and feathered. While on his mission he received a letter from David O. McKay, president of Weber Academy to take over the chair of mathematics. Upon being released from his mission he moved his family to Ogden and a lasting friendship sprang up between President McKay and Brother McKendrick. It was as though they had always known each other. Three other children were born to them here, Norma Elaine, Lydia Maureen and Wilford Wilson.

When David O. McKay was called to the Council of the Twelve Apostles, father was the man chosen to become President of the Weber Academy. Under his direction the new departments of Domestic Science and Domestic Arts were established with gas being installed, together with six ranges and twenty new sewing machines, all being done without any cost to the school, working in connection with the businessmen of Ogden, who financed the movement. He installed new equipment for the scientific laboratories and instituted the school band. During his regime the student-body increased rapidly. He brought to Ogden a famous lecture course upon which appeared such names as William Jennings Bryan, Sam Jones, Evangelist Maude Powell, Thomas Green, Russell Conway, Jerome K. Jerome and many others. Besides carrying his school work he served as Second Counselor to T. B. Evans in the Ogden Stake.

In 1911, the McKendricks moved to Boise, Idaho, where W. W. became one of the chief examiners for the Idaho Tax Commission. He was immediately placed in a church position, clerk of the newly organized Boise Stake. He was given a month recess to go to Jerome, Idaho and endeavor to pacify anti-Mormon conditions. A certain Reverend was bitter in denunciation but accepted a debate with Professor McKendrick before a record-breaking crowd. The daughters report the incident as follows:

"The Reverend's purpose throughout the debate was to prove the fallacy of Mormonism. Of course father's arguments were to prove the premise that it is the true Church of Jesus Christ established by

150

Him personally through the instrumentality of Joseph Smith. The Reverend, all through, was very vitriolic and at first very cocky. He was a brilliant fellow, and in the course of his argumentations it could be seen why he had such power over the people there. After his first talk some wondered how it would be possible for anyone to answer him. But father was just as brilliant and well educated, and he had truth and faith on his side. His powerful talks held the audience spellbound, so much so that when he accidently knocked his glass off not a sound came from the audience; not even a smile was seen, they just sat spell-bound. Father always used examples to bring home truth in his public speaking. He did all through the debate. In emphasizing the fact that Joseph Smith was the instrument of God he reached down and lifted up a boy fourteen years of age who was sitting on the stage in front of him, as many were, he held him by his clothes in one hand and challenged: 'Do you mean to tell me that a boy of this age could conceive and propound the great visitation of the Father and the Son and their message, thus bringing to the world a new dispensation?' This was one of the highlights of the debate. Father decidedly won the debate. The people flocked around him and proclaimed him the winner. A restaurant owner treated father and mother to the best dinner in his establishment, and last, but not least by any means, the Reverend had to leave Jerome instead of the Mormons. The attitude toward the Mormons changed for the better because of that debate."

Governor Bamberger asked Professor McKendrick to return to Utah as Special Tax Auditor. The family moved back to Salt Lake City. He gave a course of lectures in Ensign Stake every Monday for teacher training to a large, growing class. Similar lessons were given to Liberty Stake teachers at request of church authorities. He wrote a stimulating course of lessons for the Relief Society General Board.

Names are most interesting and often very revealing in background information: The name Henderson in Gaelic is MacEanruig, sometimes rendered in English MacKendrick, and is found in widely separated districts in Scotland. The principal family of Hendersons was the Clan Eanruig of Glencoe . . . The Hendersons (from Henry's son) were notable for their great strength and always formed the body guard of the chief. (From Rob't Bain's "The Clans and Tartans of Scotland.")

His brilliant mind and a most genial disposition were handicapped in his last few years because of ill health. He felt he had much work to conclude in his mortal career and worked to the last hours of his life. A highly honored and greatly loved man passed away May 11, 1936, at 66 years of age.

GEORGE QUAYLE MORRIS

Born: February 20, 1874 in Salt Lake City, Utah

Father: Elias Morris, son of John Morris and Barbara Thomas. b. June 30, 1825 at Llanfair, Wales. To Utah November 1, 1852. Led a company of emigrants to Utah; Constructed an iron foundry in Cedar City and first ZCMI store in Salt Lake City and Zions First National Bank Building. Also worked on reconstruction of the foundation of the Salt Lake Temple. Member Utah legislature; City Councilman, Member Constitutional Convention. d. March 17, 1898 in Salt Lake City, Utah while George was on a mission.

Mother: Mary Lois Walker of English extraction. b. May 14, 1835 in Leek, Staffordshire, England. Both her parents were pioneers. Married May, 1856.

Brothers and Sisters: Effie Walker Ashton; Marion Adelaide Cannon; Nephi Lowell, m. Harriet Young; George Q.; Katherine Vaughan. Four children died as infants. Twelve children by Mary Parry, wife of Elias who were half brothers and sisters.

Marriage: Emma Ramsay daughter of Major George W. and Amanda J. Ramsay. b. July 22, 1878 in Lawrence County, Illinois. Moved to Payson Utah when seven; later lived in Provo, attended BYU. Married June 29, 1905. Beautiful dramatic soprano in concert and opera. Made her debut at the Berlin Opera House with the Berlin Philharmonic Orchestra under the baton of Richard Strauss. She sang before many of Europe's royalty including Kaiser Wilhelm of Germany, and taught voice for years in Salt Lake City. Sang for President Theodore Roosevelt when he visited Salt Lake City. Sang in many concerts with Professor Tony Lund. Member of General Board of the Primary Association. Most generous with her talents at funerals and benefits.
d. Friday June 19, 1964 in San Fernando Valley, California at 85.

Children: Marian, devoted to the stage; Margery, m. Edward D. Woods, also a well known actress; Helen m. Roy T. Stewart.

Death: Monday April 23, 1962 after a brief illness (heart) at 88. Buried in Salt Lake family plot.

The life of George Q. Morris may well be written in one word, Service. The major portion of his mature life was devoted to a diversity of interests best serving youth. Though he reached the age of eighty-eight, he was never considered "old." When he was called to the apostleship at eighty he smiling said, "Moses was called at eighty." At 85 he said, "I am looking ahead, not behind." So many remarked that his leadership was unassuming; his service was quiet without fanfare or trumpeting.

He was a patient, judicious listener. At General Board Meetings of the Mutual Improvement Association, when a question was to be decided he invariably turned to Sister Lucy Grant Cannon, President of the Young Ladies, for her opinion, then asked all our Board members for comment. After a thorough presentation he quietly summed up what had been said, gave his personal reaction and asked for final decision. He was one of the most impartial, fair minded leaders I ever met. He permeated the spirit of love and confidence; his prayers were intimate and inspiring.

His life was chronologically summarized by the *Deseret News* in the issue of April 23, 1962, the day of his death:

"1874—February 20, George Q. Morris was born in Salt Lake City, a son of Elias and Mary Lois Walker Morris.

1899-1902—Missionary in England and Wales.

1904-1908—Salt Lake Stake Young Men's Mutual Improvement Association Superintendent.

1908-1913—Counselor in the bishopric of Fourteenth Ward, Salt Lake Stake.

1913—Salt Lake Stake MIA superintendent.

1914-1924—Bishop of the Fourteenth Ward

1924-1935—Member of the Young Men's Mutual Improvement Association General Board.

1929—Combined *Improvement Era* and *Young Woman's Journal*

1928-1935—Counselor in the Ensign Stake presidency.

1935-1937—Counselor in the YMMIA General Superintendency.

1937-1948—General Superintendent of the Young Men's Mutual Improvement Association.

1946—Toured the Mormon Pioneer Trail with President George Albert Smith.

1947—Served as executive chairman of the "This is the Place" Monument Commission. The monument was unveiled July 24, 1947, on the centennial of the arrival of the Mormon pioneers in the Salt Lake Valley, under the leadership of Brigham Young.

1948-1952—President of the Eastern States Mission.

1951, October—Named an Assistant to the Council of the Twelve.

1954, April 6—Sustained as a member of the Council of the

Twelve. (Ordained an Apostle, April 8, in the Salt Lake Temple by President David O. McKay, at the death of Mathias Cowley).

Business Activities—President and general manager of Elias Morris and Son, Salt Lake City, a monument and tile firm established by his father, with which he had been identified since he returned from his mission.

Civic Activities—Community Chest and Traveler's Aid Society; member of Sons of Utah Pioneers; Salt Lake City Chamber of Commerce, executive vice president of the Utah Pioneer Trails Association; affiliated with the American Pioneer Trails Association; Boy Scouts of America.

Awards—George Q. Morris Softball Park named for his work with youth and interest in the Church softball program; the Silver Antelope Citation of the Boy Scouts of America."

Personal gifts from admiring friends would number in the hundreds; Indians were most generous. He received the BYU Alumni Association Distinguished Service Award in 1959.

When we asked him for some of his early reminiscences, he seldom elaborated but spoke quietly in direct answer; "When I was a boy, we walked along board walks on Main Street and in wet weather the street was a sea of mud" and further, "Yes, there were hitching posts and water troughs for horses on both sides of the street." To lengthen the picture by question, "Yes, they wore long skirts that touched the ground and they were often splashed upon by the cantering horses." He was not one to spin a long tale; he was patient in company but best enjoyed pleasant work. His voice was not "big" but somehow managed to meet acoustic requirements whenever he spoke. He had faith in young people; his challenge was usually given to parents and elders. His testimony of life's eternal nature was beautiful to hear and always seemed so believable and logical. He put faith beyond knowledge and sought both. President Morris taught by example.

The *Salt Lake Tribune* eulogized him, in part, as follows:

"His interest in young people was profound. His enthusiasm was contagious. He was an exponent of the active life, a great believer in the benefits to be derived from participation in athletics. He loved the great outdoors. In recognition of such leadership, the LDS Church named its softball park in his honor while the Boy Scouts conferred upon him the Silver Antelope Award."

His visits to the Brigham Young University were frequent, not only to talk to the student body, but to enjoy athletic and artistic events. He was a devotee of clean sports and the sports competitive programs of the MIA grew fastest and were given more importance under his enthusiasm.

As a YMMIA Board member and drama chairman, I traveled

many miles with President Morris and during these opportunities to visit, I learned much of his love and hopes for the University. A portion of one of his speeches concludes this brief biography:

"The Brigham Young University is unique! Being the University of the Restored Church there can never be another University like it. In it, all known truth, secular and spiritual, may be taught. It has been a great influence for good in the lives of thousands of our people and will ever be growing in its power and influence with the rapid growth and spread of the Church. It will no doubt become the head of a vast educational system reaching into many communities, establishing integrity and faith and spirituality in the hearts of our youth, training and preparing them for valuable service to the Church and to the people of the world. Its influence must inevitably be felt in ever widening circles, drawing to its campus in ever increasing numbers, the youth from all parts of the world."

George Q. Morris was one of the nation's great youth leaders.

NELS LARS NELSON

Born: April 25, 1862 in Goshen, Utah

Father: Lars Nielson; born March 1, 1822, at Vielbyemark, Denmark; an accomplished scholar; taught Nels to read Danish; died when Nels was but eight years old, 1869, Goshen, Utah.

Mother: Martha (Marchen) Bendtsen; born January 19, 1833, at Taarnby, Copenhagen, Denmark; met her future husband after both had gone to Goshen, Utah having accepted the Gospel in Denmark. Died May 5, 1914.

Brothers and Sisters: Emma Nielsen b. November 6, 1860; Joseph Nielsen b. March 11, 1864; Anne Marie Nielsen b. May 30, 1866; Martha (Mattie) Nelson b. May 26, 1869; Ephraim Nelson b. May 26, 1869 (drowned when a young boy)

Marriage: (1) Isabel Marie ("Belle") Harris of Provo, in the Logan Temple, Aug. 1, 1887.
(2) Maud Noble, May 25, 1914, in the Salt Lake Temple.

Children: of Isabel
Stella Jean Nelson, m. Arthur A. Vance; Jessie Belle Nelson, m. Dr. L. Weston Oaks; Sterling Harris Nelson, m. Bertha Sorenson; Milo Alva Nelson, m. Melvina Hibbert.
of Maud
G. Stanley m. Armenta Deppe; Maud Calista, m. M. Ray Thomas; Nathan Lawrence, died in infancy, Dorothy Jane m. Don Candland; Elma died in childhood; Pearl Muriel m. Leland Floyd; Barbara; Helen Mar.

Death: Sunday, May 12, 1946, at his home in Downey, Idaho, at age 84.

Nels L. Nelson was the second child of his family and the oldest boy. He had the use of ponies, knew the work on a new farm, grubbed sage brush, and enjoyed the usual after-work leisure of the farm boy. When Nels was eight his hard working father died leaving a mother with twins, three girls, and Nels. This early responsibility sobered the young boy and gave him the foundation of a very serious nature.

At this time stake leaders and faculty members of the young BYA were being sent out to the various wards in the county to arouse interest and support for the school. One such an assignment was made in the Goshen Ward and is described by a son, Sterling H. Nelson, made from notes later written by his father:

The speaker made a very impressive presentation of the urgent need for this scholastic training. The boy Nels L. was not in attendance at the meeting but was out playing with companions in a game of rodeo, riding calves in a nearby field while the meeting was going on. This sport entertained them until sometime after dark and then young Nels went home and tiptoed into the darkened house, so as not to awaken his mother sleeping in her bedroom just inside from the living room. He stopped, as he could hear her voice. As he listened, he realized that it was a supplication to God that Nels, her son, might be impressed and inspired with a desire to go to the Brigham Young Academy at Provo, Utah. It was this earnest entreaty which determined the course of his life. Shortly thereafter Nels left to work in the mines at Eureka, Utah, a distance of some twenty miles from his home in Goshen. He secured a job and worked until the opening of the school at Provo in September. The need for saving his money was so necessary that he refrained from buying a seventy-five cent ticket on the train from Goshen to Provo and walked the entire distance carrying a well-packed gunny-sack.

He soon became a protege of Karl G. Maeser, whom he admired almost to reverence. Nels L. tells of the burning of Lewis Hall in this manner:

"In order to conserve my funds I found myself a job with a farmer near Lakeshore, a distance of about five miles from the school. I would leave Friday night and stay away until Monday morning doing work on the farm with the livestock. When I returned this particular Monday morning I was in consternation to see the schoolhouse burned to ashes, and a large crowd milling about the smouldering ashes. There being no telephones nor newspapers at this date, I knew nothing about the fire until I returned to school that morning. Dr. Maeser gathered the students there and explained that he had already arranged for a location for the school to be held in upstairs rooms in a Provo mercantile establishment on the main street of the town, and not to worry as school would go on as usual. After getting organized under the direction of Dr. Maeser, the assignments for the study for the day were given, and that was that each student should write a composition on the burning of the school building with complete details. I raised my hand when this assignment was given and asked, 'How can I do that when I did not see it burn nor know of its burning until I came to school today?' Dr. Maeser answered, 'You will write your composition from the information that you get and from your own imagination and the papers will be graded and marked, and a prize given for the best narrative and description of this catastrophe.' I applied myself very diligently to this writing and when the papers were edited I was given the high honor and prize for the best report on the fire which I had not seen."

The more Nels heard Dr. Maeser the greater became his desire to be a teacher and to go on a mission. He read voraciously and voluminously; books that gave new theories and expanded philosophy and religion were his favorite readings. He read the Book of Mormon when thirteen and re-read it to clarify some of its passages, most of this while herding sheep in the Tintic Valley.

His mother had married when she took the family to Mayfield, Sanpete County, to live in the United Order. The experiment failed and the family moved back to Goshen. Nels could save no money while working for the United Order; hauling ore between Tintic and Santaquin was hard work and expensive on his own outfit which lessened his profits. Attending school seemed more important each day and his mother's prayer urged him on until he started his studies at BYA, as related above.

By 1879, the year he started late for the Academy, he was seventeen years old, an excellent reader with an unusual vocabulary. He graduated second in his Normal Class of 1881-82, and in 1883 he was placed in charge of the Intermediate Department, where he stressed reading and comprehension.

In March of 1885 he went on a mission to the Southern States, chiefly in Virginia and Maryland. Without monetary assistance, he met persecution, bitterness, and mob violence, but persevered, won many friends and opened new fields for other Elders to proselyte. Leaving many new friends, he returned home and in 1887 married a Provo beauty, Isabel "Belle" Harris. He was reassigned the Intermediate Department at BYA, chiefly teaching language and literature.

In 1882-1888 he was secretary to the faculty. He was principal of the Academy high school from 1900-1904. In 1911 he was granted a leave to study in the East where he visited the larger colleges for special studies. From 1883-1920 he was an instructor in English.

The first course in journalism at BYA was taught by Nels L., in 1916-17. This was a part of the English course. He recommended a special department for the subject and had his students interview various pioneers and current leaders for the school and local papers. He rewarded his students by publishing the better short stories. One such a collection of his is indicative:

The Test—Ross Smoot Bean

Joe's Coyote—Lee Huff

The Washerwoman's Son—Evelyn Hinckley

The Greenhorn—William H. Snell

Grandpa's Courting Days—B. Y. Baird

Batching It—Lee R. Taylor

A Mexican Bull Fight—Lorin Jones

From his class notes we glean, "It is well for the young writer to stab his creations every few paragraphs and note whether blood or sawdust flows from the wound."

Articles came from his pen for more than forty years. Returning from his mission he was convinced that all missionaries should know how to preach, make progress in organization and vocabulary building. His text *Preaching and Public Speaking* could well be used today. He used as models Orson F. Whitney, Brigham H. Roberts, and James E. Talmage, by analyzing their sermons as heard in the Tabernacle and read in classes from print.

Most of his writing was serious and often religious. A little humor sufficed him. Subjects of his articles reveal his daily thinking: "Gospel Studies," "The Camel and the Eye of the Needle," "Deity, Two Aspects Contrasted," "Significance of Heaven and Hell," "Our Liberty in Danger," "Modern Study of the Resurrection," "Joseph Smith as a Translator," "Theology in Mormon School." He had very strong opinions on morals and conduct, shown in such articles as "The Veil—Its Uses and Abuses" "Loud Laughter is a Sin." His classes were led to a particular goal for the day.

Professor Nelson's books were very popular in their day: *The Mormon Point of View,* the book on public speaking, *Scientific Aspects of Mormonism.* One of the first of its kind and challenging today, the LDS Church thought enough of this book to procure an ownership of the copyright. *What is Truth?"* in 1941 and *The Second War in Heaven* were two of his last efforts and reveal broad reading in philosophy and religion.

He was divorced from his first wife, Belle Harris, because of incompatability. Later he married another fine lady, Maud Noble, and moved with her to Downey, Idaho, where a family of four girls and a son were reared on a productive farm. His last days were spent in study and writing and he died in his home at Downey where he is buried.

He is best remembered by his students for class discipline, broad comprehension of subject matter, an enthusiasm for better literature and the ability to inspire the art of writing. Lectures and scholars who came to Provo invariably praised his scholarship. He believed in the destiny of BYU.

GEORGE ALBERT SMITH

Eighth President of The Church of Jesus Christ of Latter-day Saints.

Born: April 4, 1870, in Salt Lake City, Utah, in a small house west of the Assembly Hall.

Father: John Henry Smith, born Sept. 18, 1848, Kanesville, Iowa, son of Apostle George A. Smith and Sarah Ann Libby; came to Utah with his father Oct. 27, 1849. Grandson of John Smith, an Apostle and second counselor to president of church.
d. Oct. 13, 1911 in Salt Lake City.

Mother: Sarah Farr
b. Oct. 30, 1849.
m. Oct. 20, 1866, in Salt Lake City.
The first daughter of Lorin Farr and Nancy Bailey Chase, pioneers of September, 1847.

Brothers and Sisters: John Henry, George Albert, Lorin Farr, Don Carlos, Ezra Chase, Charles Warren, Winslow Farr, Nathaniel Libby, Nancy Claribell, Tirzah Priscilla Gay, Elsie Louise.
Half-brothers and sisters: Sarah Ann Pond, Nicholas G., Joseph H., Lucy, Elizabeth S., Rex, Glenn, Arzella, and Josephine

Marriage: Lucy Emily Woodruff, in Manti Temple, May 25, 1892.
b. Jan. 10, 1869 in St. Thomas, Nevada, daughter of Wilford Woodruff, Jr. and Emily Jane Smith. (George Albert carried a picture and lock of hair of his wife in a locket worn on his watch chain from the day of his wedding.)

Children: Emily S., m. Murray Stewart, Edith S., m. George Elliott, George Albert, Jr., Dean of Harvard School of Business Administration

Death: April 4, 1951, in Salt Lake City at his home, on his birthday. Buried in the Smith family plot.

George Albert attended the Brigham Young school at the east side of the Eagle Gate corner on South Temple and there first met Karl G. Maeser. He worked at various and odd jobs to help in the home while his father was on a mission. George Albert was never a strong boy and frequently had to nurse his strength to achieve his assignments.

He lived across the street from the west side of the Tabernacle and attended the many sessions that filled the great auditorium. He was seven years of age when Brigham Young died and associated intimately with all the church authorities from boyhood to death. The completion of the great Temple was a daily topic over the table in his father's home, and young George spent much of his boyhood playing around the Temple grounds watching the oxen teams bring in huge slabs of granite and drag long poles for construction purposes. He memorized most of the songs sung by the great choir and always thrilled to their music.

One statement made by Karl G. Maeser in the Brigham Young school profoundly impressed him. He quoted it many times in his life: "Not only will you be held accountable for the things that you do, but you will also be held responsible for the thoughts you think." When he was twelve years of age, his parents helped him to go down to Provo to attend the Brigham Young Academy to study further under Professor Maeser and his associates. He lived with his grandmother Smith for one winter, helping with chores about the house and yard. He walked each day to the Lewis Building on Center Street and Third West, a building dedicated in 1876 by Daniel H. Wells, the brother who had earlier dedicated the grand Salt Lake Theatre.

It was in one of the summers while in the teens while he was working on a surveying party for the Denver & Rio Grande Railway, east of Green River, that heat and glare of the sun so impaired his sight that he never fully recovered and suffered intense headaches all too often.

So much has been written of this beloved civic and church leader that I shall present only a skeleton of his active and productive life. As he was my cousin and I was a frequent visitor in his home, I had many hours of association with him from boyhood to the last few days of his life. Grandparents were our common topic of conversation. Three chapters of my book about our grandfather, Lorin Farr, laid open on his bed when he died. Briefly, then, a great life unfolds:
1888-He attended the U. of U. for one year, to be nearer home, then
took a position as salesman with ZCMI, traveling through Southern
Utah with a wagon, making friends at every stop.
1891-Called on a mission to labor with young people in the interest

of the Mutual Improvement Association in Juab, Millard, Beaver, and Parowan Stakes.

1892-Married his boyhood sweetheart, May 25, 1892. After being married one week, went on second mission to Southern States for two years—His wife joined him and worked in the office—full-time mission with Lucy.

1894-Returned to Salt Lake City, to ZCMI as salesman.

1896-98-Active in politics; favored William McKinley. President McKinley appointed him Receiver for the Land Office of Utah in January—two terms in this office. Second term, appointed by Theodore Roosevelt, who became a good friend.

1903-October Conference—sustained as member of the Quorum of the Twelve—Set apart two days later by President Joseph F. Smith.

1904-Called to the General Board of the Young Men's Mutual Improvement Association.

1905-To Sharon, Vermont, with President Joseph F. Smith and party to dedicate the $38\frac{1}{2}$ foot granite monument, December 23, on the 100th anniversary of the birth of Joseph Smith. His father and grandfather were present.

1907-June—sent to Palmyra, N. Y., to purchase Joseph Smith farm. Ashby Snow and German Ellsworth accompanied him—succeeded in buying farm.

1913-July—with Joseph F. Smith and party to Cardston, Alberta, Canada, to dedicate site for Temple—first outside the United States.

1916-September—International Irrigation Congress at Sacramento, California. Chosen temporary and permanent chairman and elected Vice-president for the next Congress.

1918-July—at Richmond, Missouri, monument unveiled in memory of General Alexander Donniphan, who once saved the life of Joseph Smith.

1919-January—selected to preside over the European Mission (with family) for two years. Very satisfactory mission.

1920-Made General Superintendent of the Young Men's Mutual Improvement Association.

1922-First general preaching of the gospel by radio (May 6) with President Grant and others.

1922-May—Attended National Convention, Sons of American Revolution, held at Springfield, Massachussetts; elected Vice-President General for Pacific and Rocky Mountain States—He frequently urged eligible LDS member to join this patriotic society.

1927-August—Second trip in airplane—to Los Angeles in small open plane in six hours—return same way two days later.

1930- Centennial year for founding of the Church; appointed General

Chairman of the celebration and spent major part of his time for several months, an assignment he especially enjoyed.

1934-National Congress, Boy Scouts of America, held in Buffalo, N.Y. Given Silver Buffalo, highest award in Scouting. With him receiving this honor were Col. Theodore Roosevelt, Jr., and Paul Percy Harris, founder of Rotary.

1935-Released as General Superintendent of the Young Men's Mutual Improvement Association.

1937-January—member of the Pioneer Trails Association; discussed plans for proper monument at Emigration Canyon. Ten years later the project was realized.

1938-January—assigned to tour Pacific Missions; away six months, Hawaii, Fiji Islands, New Zealand, Australia, Tonga Islands and Samoan Islands. 27,000 miles of travel, of great Church importance.

1943-July 8—After the death of President Rudger Clawson, selected as President of the Twelve. Held this office two years.

1945-May 21—(death of Heber J. Grant on 18th), sustained as President of the Church.

1945-September 23, dedicated the Idaho Falls Temple.

1945-visited Pres. Harry S. Truman at Washington, D.C., to make arrangements to ship Church Welfare supplies to needy European Saints, especially the hungry of Scandinavia.

1946-July 10, Began automobile journey eastward over the Mormon trail to Nauvoo, Illinois, visiting all important places.

1947-Dedicated the "This is the Place" Monument at the mouth of Emigration Canyon. On the morning of July 24th, I drove up early to Salt Lake and by invitation went to my cousin's home on Yale Avenue. Pressing assignments of parade nature had kept George Albert down town longer than he intended. Crowds were moving toward the great monument at the foot of Emigration Canyon, soon to be dedicated and shown to the public. A car was driven to the curb and out stepped President Smith with Mahonri Young, the sculptor. They came into the front room and Professor Young was introduced and asked to sit down. The President went hurriedly into the kitchen to speak to Emily and called me out to them. With his arms on my shoulders, Cousin George said "You know that Brother Young is not active in the Church. Without embarrassment bear your testimony of the Gospel to him and engage him in a gospel conversation. I wish I were with you but I must go up to the monument to check several matters. Keep Mahonri here until I return. Don't let him get impatient, I'll be back soon as possible." With a blessing for both of us, he excused himself and wished us good luck. Emily, with her most gracious smile, brought in a pitcher of lemonade.

It was a grand opportunity and I began by asking Professor Young which he considered his greatest statue. He replied "How can a mother tell you which child she loves the most?" He volunteered that the great struggle of the pioneers was one of the world's most dramatic epochs filled with inspiration for the artist. He did not lead easily into any topic of our religion; he diverted each attempt into an avenue of history. The warm morning turned to a hotter day and, as a large man, he was very conscious of the heat. When President Smith was driven back to the curb close to the time for dedication I felt I had failed in an important assignment. Mahonri thanked me for a most pleasant interlude, and was then taken to the stand for the celebration. I followed in my sister's car wondering what else I might have done to rekindle his interest in our Church.

1948-February 8, was the last time I was on a program with my beloved cousin. We took part in the dedication of a plaque placed on the corner of the first grist mill north of Salt Lake, erected by Mayor Lorin Farr at the mouth of Ogden Canyon. The historic building with its great water-turned wheel was converted into a dance hall, The Old Mill, and operated by Mayor Harmon Peery. On this occasion President Smith extolled the leadership of our grandfather and challenged his offspring to emulate the virtues of the pioneers. He quoted his father as repeatedly saying "My son, you ought to be grateful that you have the blood of Lorin Farr in your veins."

1950-October 17, Dedicated BYU Science Building (last of his many dedications). Dec. 31, Spoke at Yale Ward (his own), Bonneville Stake (last of his speeches).

1951-April 4, Died (on his birthday), 81st year, 7:27 p.m. His funeral day was almost a state holiday with messages coming from all parts of the globe. He was eulogized as a leader in world peace and the most beloved man in Utah's history.

With his Church and civic obligations, he scheduled his time in numerous business connections as:

Director and vice-president of the Utah Savings & Trust Co.

Director Utah-Idaho Sugar Co.

Director ZCMI, Heber J. Grant Co., Mutual Creamery Co., Utah National Bank, Salt Lake Theatre, Decker Wholesale Jewelry Co., pres. of Libby Investment Co.

The University of Utah in March of 1950 conferred on him the Doctor of Humanities.

For sixteen years he was president of Aid to the Sightless Society.

He was President of the Church Board of Education and of the Board of Trustees of Brigham Young University.

Avard Fairbanks, world-renowned sculptor, had been commissioned to make a bust for presentation on his 80th birthday, unveiled before dozens of friends.

The National Society, Sons of the American Revolution memorialized his works and life on May 19, 1952, in special gratitude for his assistance with genealogical work and numerous courtesies.

Throughout the Church today his influence is felt and his life is often chosen as a subject for sermons.

A special edition of the *Improvement Era* was published, and pertinent quotes are printed from the hundreds of eulogies sent to the Church and his family.

George Albert Smith—A Prophet Goes Home. . .

By John D. Giles, of the *Improvement Era.*

To attempt to catalog all the virtues of George Albert Smith would be futile. They were too numerous.

Without guile, humble even in the highest places, always polite and gentlemanly, and striving to avoid offense in word or deed, he was an ideal exemplar. When occasion was afforded, he added to his advice substantial help. His numerous widespread charities will never be known. The number of people he has helped has never been counted and never can be.

Those who have been won to better lives by his love are legion. His practice of praising and encouraging people in order to bring out the best in them was most effective. His kindly attitude disarmed those who were inclined to dissension, and his warm and friendly approach won thousands to him as admirers.

His friend-making ability has been likened to that of his illustrious father's, John Henry Smith. He had friends in high and low places; receptionists in business offices knew him and showed him every courtesy. This was true also among railroad conductors, Pullman porters, laborers, and others whose acquaintance he had made.

President George Albert Smith came of a family that has rendered outstanding service to the nation and to the Church. His ancestors, some of them in the Mayflower company, participated in the Revolutionary War and served in many positions of honor and trust in the sections of New England in which they lived. Joseph Smith, the Prophet, was his third cousin. John Smith, his great-grandfather, was third Patriarch to the Church. Both his grandfather, George A. Smith, and his father, John Henry Smith, were Apostles, and both served in the First Presidency.

His maternal grandfather, Lorin Farr, descendant of the Winslows of Droitwich and Saher de Quincy, baron of Runnymeade and Magna Charta, was first mayor of Ogden and the first president of Weber Stake.

As a member of the Sons of the American Revolution, the beloved Churchman was elected National Vice-President General in 1926 and since then has been a national officer. In the Utah Society he served as president and many terms as director.

Under his presidency the missionary system has been expanded to its highest point in Church history. The building program inaugurated under President Heber J. Grant has been greatly accelerated. New stakes and wards have been created, church membership has increased, and the prestige of the Church in this and other nations has developed to a marked degree. Above all else, probably the spirit of love and unity within the Church has been made manifest in many ways. Spirituality, tolerance, and love for our fellow men regardless of creed or color, which he frequently urged in sermons and writings, have increased measurably. "All the people of the earth are our Father's children" was a favorite phrase.

His conviction that the correct name of the Church he loved should always be used instead of the various nicknames which have been applied caused President Smith to request of publishers and others that the correct name—The Church of Jesus Christ of Latter-day Saints—always be used in full. In requesting the cooperation of close associates in bringing this about, he pointed out that there is no Mormon Church nor L.D.S. Church, and no Church of the Latter-day Saints. His wishes have been respected generally, and the correct and full name of the Church is being used more frequently than ever before.

In civic affairs he served as president of the International Irrigation Congress and the International Dry Farm Congress. He was Federal Receiver of Public Moneys and Special Disbursing Agent for the state of Utah. In this capacity he was the first member of The Church of Jesus Christ of Latter-day Saints in Utah to be appointed to the federal office.

His wife, Lucy Emily Woodruff Smith, died November 5, 1937. During her lifetime they were devoted to each other and made many trips together to distant lands. Her death saddened the Church leader greatly, but he sought comfort in the companionship of his two daughters, Mrs. Robert Murray Stewart (Emily), and Mrs. George Elliott (Edith), both of Salt Lake City, and a son, George Albert Smith, Jr., fourth in his family to bear that name. All were at their father's bedside when the end came.

Always a friend of youth, President Smith became an active sponsor of scouting in 1911 when the M.I.A. Scouts were organized. He increased his activity in 1913 when, while he was a member of the general board, the program of the Boy Scout of America was adopted by the Young Men's Mutual Improvement Association. He became successively a member of the executive board of the Salt

Lake Council, a member of the Region Twelve executive committee, and a member of the executive board of the National Council, where he served as chairman of important committees, for many years. On many occasions he wore the complete Scout uniform. It was largely due to the impetus given to scouting while he was general superintendent of the Young Men's Mutual Improvement Association that the Church brought into the movement a higher percent of its boys of Scout age than of any other national group.

His honors in Scouting include the Silver Beaver Award by the Salt Lake Council and the Silver Buffalo by the National Council. The Silver Buffalo is the highest award in scouting at any level.

He encouraged thousands of young people to secure a good education, and his kindness helped to make this possible in many cases. He encouraged thrift, economy, and self-reliance.

At the time of his death, he was president of the board of Brigham Young University, a school he visited and addressed many times. His efforts to advance the interests of this important Church school have extended over many years.

President Smith was interested in and loved Church history. Under his direction, all whose accomplishments made history in this area were honored regardless of race or religion.

After having acted for the Church in the erection of several important monuments and markers, he was the organizer of the Utah Pioneer Trails and Landmarks Association in 1930 and became its president, serving in this capacity until his death. His many trips over the Mormon Pioneer Trail from Nauvoo to Salt Lake City and over other historic trails of the West made him familiar with western America. He became a recognized authority in its history.

President Smith was for many years a member of the board of directors of the Oregon Trail Memorial Association and was one of the organizers of the American Pioneer Trails Association. He had served on the national board since its organization. For a time he was vice-president and was awarded one of its earliest honorary life memberships.

Under his leadership well over a hundred historic monuments and markers have been erected from Nauvoo, Illinois, along pioneer trails to Arizona, Idaho, Wyoming, Nevada, and California.

The crowning achievement of his work in preserving western history is the "This is the Place" monument at the mouth of Emigration Canyon, overlooking the valley of the Great Salt Lake. His first efforts to bring this about were in 1915. When the great monument costing more than $500,000.00 with its setting and roadways was dedicated July 24, 1947, it marked the climax of more than thirty years of preparation and planning. When the "This is the Place" monument commission was organized in 1937, President Smith, the leading sponsor, became second vice-chairman. In 1945, upon the death of President Heber J. Grant, he was made chairman and served in that capacity until his death, and it was under his chairmanship that the monument was constructed and dedicated. The building of a scenic and historic highway along the Mormon Trail from Henefer to Salt Lake City represents another of his dreams, for which he saw the plans proceed far enough to assure final success.

One of the pioneers in aviation in the West, President Smith early became a director of Western Air Express, now Western Airlines. Under his direction, a history log of that airline from San Diego, California, to Lethbridge, Alberta, Canada, was prepared for the use of passengers. He participated in many of the early flights between Salt Lake City and Los Angeles. His interest in aviation and his love for flying continued as long as he was active.

The welfare of Father Lehi's children, the Indians, was a special concern of President Smith. His visits to Indian reservations in many parts of the country were frequent. In 1941 he spent a week on the Navajo and Hopi reservations in Arizona with stake missionaries, as he visited the homes of the Indians, blessed the sick and aged and spread good cheer and happiness among his many Lamanite friends, resulting in a revived and increased interest in the Indians and their welfare. In high places in Washington he pleaded their cause and through plans set up within the Church has brought about a most remarkable change in the attitude toward the Lamanite remnant.

As general superintendent of the YMMIA in 1929, he took steps which resulted in enlargement and expansion of the *Improvement Era* under a program that has made it one of the leading church magazines of the world. As its senior editor since 1945, his interest was increased. His monthly editorials were read by people in every civilized nation of the globe and copies were always available on his desk to be presented to distinguished visitors at his office. In 1947 he presented the centennial souvenir edition to the governors of each of the forty-eight states.

The teachings of this noble leader are condensed in the following lines:

My Creed

I would be a friend to the friendless and find joy in ministering to the needs of the poor.

I would visit the sick and afflicted and inspire in them a desire for faith to be healed.

I would teach the truth to the understanding and blessing of all mankind.

I would seek out the erring one and try to win him back to a righteous and a happy life.

I would not seek to force people to live up to my ideals, but rather love them into doing the thing that is right.

I would live with the masses and help to solve their problems that their earth life may be happy.

I would avoid the publicity of high positions and discourage flattery of thoughtless friends.

I would not knowingly wound the feelings of any, not even one who may have wronged me, but would seek to do him good and make him my friend.

I would overcome the tendency to selfishness and jealousy and rejoice in the successes of all the children of my Heavenly Father.

I would not be an enemy to any living soul.

Knowing that the Redeemer of mankind has offered to the world the only plan that will fully develop us and make us happy here and hereafter, I feel it not only a duty, but also a blessed privilege to disseminate the truth.

—George Albert Smith

I present here two tributes by life-time friends, each appraising their beloved leader in light of their personal associations.

President George Albert Smith

"Keep the commandments of the Lord; then carry on." That was the simple, direct life message of President George Albert Smith. The multitudes who came under his influence and who stood sadly by his bier learned the conquering power in life of this ideal.

His superb devotion to Joseph Smith, the latter-day prophet, made alive all that he said, taught, and accomplished. The labors of the Prophet were to him a more complete revelation of man's relationship and duty to God. These teachings became the measuring stick for the inspired words of his own sermons and for his judgment of his fellow men. . . .

All this did not remove him from the active affairs of life. He was an active participant in banks and other industrial enterprises —from digging a new canal to thirsting land, to erecting for progress a skyscraper. The light and truth of his country thrilled him. He became an honored and influential member of the Sons of the American Revolution.

In the midst of all his labors he looked with loving eyes upon eager youth. To them he gave much of his strength. They were the men of tomorrow. This led him into scouting where he rose high, into the superintendency of the Young Men's Mutual Improvement Association, and into other movements for the welfare of youth.

As he looked into the hearts of men (and he circled the earth), he saw the need of love among men. Therefore, in his preaching and labors he became the apostle of kindness and mutual human love. He taught the everlasting truth that men cannot approach the likeness of God except by the practice of love to their fellow men.

Only by love can peace and joy be made to cover the earth.

At length, he was called to preside over the Church as prophet, seer, and revelator. Majestically in his simple words he called men to repentance and to the practice of the divine law of love.

He blessed the Church. May we never forget his life's message. We are grateful to have known George Albert Smith. Thank the Lord for his life and service.

—John A. Widtsoe
President of two universities and member of the Twelve

Benediction

The Power of love was made manifest in the life of President George Albert Smith, and the feelings expressed from near and far since his passing have amply evidenced it.

Two days before he died, I had the privilege of a last brief visit with him. I had not seen him for more than two and a half months, and I ventured hesitantly to his home on this last visit only on invitation. He had had a discouraging day, and his frail physical frame was soon to be left behind by the great and loving spirit and personality that were his, and that were so sincerely beloved by so many men in so many places.

At the hour at which I, with others, was there, he appeared to be slightly improved, and for a moment or two before I left I held the hand with which he had so often warmly welcomed so many of his fellow men when he was well.

The last words I heard him speak were: "Continue the work, and keep the commandments of the Lord." They were spoken with difficulty, but understandably, and I felt that I had heard his benediction and his earnest wish for all his Father's children.

Richard L. Evans
Radio Commentator and member of the Twelve.

The most frequent association with my beloved kinsman came during the last ten years of his life. He urged and encouraged the writing of the history of Lorin Farr and told me to search records, diaries, use the Historian's office with President Joseph Fielding's benedictions and the help in its great library, which was generously offered. I was asked to make frequent reports on its progress which I willingly did and those brief appointments are some of my choicest moments. He challenged me to keep active in Scouting and the Sons of the American Revolution, to honor the pioneer and my heritage, to help guard the ideals and purpose of the Brigham Young University, to keep our family together; in short, to work with youth, honor the Constitution and serve my fellow men. He is an exemplary Son of Brigham.

ABRAHAM OWEN SMOOT

Born:	February 17, 1815 **Place:** Owenton, Kentucky
Father:	George Washington Smoot, physician and attorney. William Smoote (Smute) (George's grandfather, probably born in Holland), left England 1633 and settled in Virginia. 1793, George Smoot moved to Franklin County, Kentucky, and in about 1806 married Ann Rowlett.
Mother:	Ann Rowlett, of Prince Edward County, Virginia, whose uncle Abraham Owen, was aide-de-camp to Gen. Wm. Henry Harrison who became president of U.S. died in leading charge against Indians at battle of Tippecanoe in 1811.
Brothers and Sisters:	Nancy Beal, m. John Freeman; William, a physician; Reed, a farmer; Martesia, m. Samuel Smith, mother of Mrs. Emma Woodruff of Salt Lake City; Abraham Owen; Jemima Sophia; Cinderella.
Marriage:	Margaret Thompson McMeans Atkinson (a widow), November 11, 1838 in Far West. Emily Hill Harris (had two children), sealed to him January 18, 1846. Dianna Eldredge, daughter of Ira and Nancy Black of Indianapolis, Indiana. Pioneers of September 19, 1847. Born March 28, 1837, m. May 6, 1855. Anna Kirstina Morrison, of Norway, m. February, 1856.
Children:	of Margaret: her son, Charles Atkinson took name of William C. A. Smoot, a Utah pioneer; house, 192 South 1st East. of Emily: had two children when she married Abraham O. of Dianna: Abraham Owen II, m. Electa Bullock; Nancy, m. David R. Beebe; Olive, m. J. W. Bean; Elizabeth, m. Milton R. Hardy; Leanora; Joseph; Ella, m. Dr. George E. Robinson; Arthur; Vilate, m. Thomas A. Pierpont; Parley, m. Helen Covdur; Alma, m. Emma Stubbs; William, m. Florence Kimber. of Anna Kirstina: Annie Christina, m. George S. Taylor a member of the first BYA faculty; Alice Smoot Newell and Reed, two of the original 29 students of BYA; George M., m. Mary Ann Larsen; Agnes May Smoot, m. Charles Albert Glazier; Brigham, m. Margarette Nesbit, was general manager of Idaho Sugar Co., his family reared where Aird Clinic stood, First East and Second South; Ida Mauline, m. George A. Dusenberry, also a member of BYA faculty; Morrison, b. December 20, 65 East 2nd South.

172

Death: March 6, 1895, at the age of 80. Over 5000 people came to the Provo Tabernacle to view his remains and pay him honor.

    Bare statements fail to reveal the many adventures encountered by Abraham O. Smoot or the number of people he befriended with only a word to record the loan of a sum of money or of a team of horses. His word was his bond and he believed others had the same sense of honor. Once he assumed the leadership of the struggling university he felt duty bound to see it through.

    When Brigham Young died in 1877, the leadership of BYA fell heavily upon President Smoot, acting as liaison officer between a dubious but hopeful public and an ambitious driving leader in Karl G. Maeser. The Dusenberry's, who started the Academy, withdrew on the advent of Dr. Maeser and left him free to negotiate with President Smoot and a newly appointed board, chiefly representing the business and church-men from the four districts of the county.

    As father of the entire valley, as it were, President Smoot planned and worked for the development of the whole territory, expanding industry to support a growing population. He kept several business ventures alive that residents might have work to support their families. He supported with his own capital any venture he believed capable of helping the newly arrived immigrants. His great experience as a frontiersman, woodsman, missionary, campaigner, wagon train leader, all aided in building a new community and leading a people as a civic and Church counselor. His life briefly unfolds.

    Age 7—moved to South Western Kentucky.

    Age 13—parents moved to Tennessee where his father died, 1828. Mother and sons were converted to the Church, 1835 by David W. Patton and Wilford Woodruff.

    1836—Abraham O., at age 21, journeyed to Kirtland, Ohio with Wilford Woodruff and the first day he met Joseph Smith in the Temple. He had a view of the famous mummies which Joseph Smith had, and the papyrus with them—the Book of Abraham. He attended the School of the Prophets for one winter in Kirtland.

    1837—Missionary in Southern Kentucky and Tennessee.

    1838—Led group to Far West, Missouri. With Surveyor Ripley, he laid out the town of Adam-ondi-Ahman and came upon ruins of the ancient altar which Prophet Joseph declared to be a sacred ancient altar. He preached the funeral sermon of Mayor John P. Houston, brother of famed Sam Houston. This year in Far West, while a confined captive of Missouri State Militia, he married Margaret T. M. Atkinson, a widow with one child, William C. A. who became a Utah pioneer.

Among the first settlers at Nauvoo, he went stumping for Joseph Smith to become President of the United States; he went as far as Dresden, Tennessee and was expelled by the mob as "abolishonist." The Prophet's platform proposed the purchase of slaves and immediate emancipation.

1843—Presided over branch at Keokuk, Iowa.

1844—In May he served on the Nauvoo police force.

1844-46—Officiated in the Temple at Nauvoo.

1846—Followed Brigham Young to the Missouri River in the great exodus.

1847—Abraham led a company of immigrants to Salt Lake Valley, September 2, 1847 as captain of four hundred; his home there for 20 years. He was a member of the first High Council.

1849—Bishop of the 15th Ward and Justice of the Peace in Salt Lake Valley. He made several trips to the Missouri River as a freighter.

1851—Mission to England; first to use the Perpetual Emigration Fund.

1852—Had charge of immigration to Utah from Britain.

1856—Went east to purchase cattle and wagons for the Church. Upon return in February, he was elected Mayor of Salt Lake City, and brought the city script to par. Its second Mayor. He also married Anna Kristina Morrison.

1857—Trip to Missouri with mail from Utah, as the Saints had to rely on their own carriers. At Kansas City he learned that the President of the United States had ordered an army to Utah, appointing a new governor. With a fast team, he drove to Salt Lake City in twenty days, averaging fifty miles per day.

July 24, 1857—President Young and a large group were celebrating Pioneer Day at Brighton; Abraham O. drove to Brighton with Elias Smith and quietly gave President Young the news of the army's coming. Crowd was informed after the program.

He was Mayor of Salt Lake City until 1866, serving without pay.

1867—During Echo Canyon Campaign, he took his family to Pond Town (Salem) in Utah County.

1868—Was requested to move to Provo to be the Stake President. He arrived in the spring, and within a few days was named Mayor and held office for twelve years. In the same period he served as a member of Territory Legislature.

1875—Brigham Young Academy was founded; Abraham O. Smoot was made president of the Board of Trustees. He held this position for twenty years and was in Provo for twenty-seven years, becoming the city's dominant figure.

President Smoot had been in Provo as its Mayor some seven years when the Dusenberry brothers and Territorial officers interested him in making their school the Timpanogos Branch of the University of Deseret, a Church-supported University. The idea needed no prodding as the matter was immediately presented to President Brigham Young and a request was presented for Karl G. Maeser to be its first director. Abraham O. had no difficulty in making the transition and began necessary advertising to build the school, introduced the new principal in the person of Dr. Karl G. Maeser, using the Dusenberry school in the Lewis Building on Third West and Center. As the school was growing in numbers and physical expansion was imperative, a disasterous fire, in 1884, gutted the Lewis building and threw most of the community into a panic, but not Abraham O. Smoot nor Karl G. Maeser. Dr. Maeser immediately sought President Smoot to learn his desires and what plans could be made to "carry on." A meeting was called in the Provo Tabernacle which was crowded with eager parents and citizens.

"The Lewis Building had burned January 24, 1884. Presently Brother Maeser, whose white hair and dignified bearing had already made him venerable, mounted a chair and called the crowd to order. There was hope shining out in his fine, strong face, and courage in the ring of his voice. Bidding the students not to lose heart he invited them all to a meeting in the Stake Tabernacle. Here the lesson of the fire was impressed upon us, and we were told, not only that the school would go on, but that steps had already been taken to erect new and suitable quarters."

Events moved rapidly that day; President Smoot had just completed the bank building on the corner of Academy Avenue and Center Street. Although the First National Bank Corporation, the Smoot Drug Company, and various office renters, were ready and eager to move in, the grand old man moved them all off to give a free home to the homeless school. By the following morning blackboards had been made and placed in the walls and desks and benches filled all the rooms. That the institution should, in the face of so overwhelming a calamity, lose only one day of regular work was always thereafter a source of tender pride to its first great teacher.

Such was the feeling of sympathy for the institution that $2,000 were taken in subscriptions within a few days after the greatest loss, enough to buy the ground and lay the foundations. Here the work halted for six years. To President A. Smoot belongs the honor for furnishing the means. Not one man in ten thousand would have mortgaged his home and personal property, as he did, to borrow money for such a purpose. The first home of the institution stands today a monument to the man who did more than the founder himself in matter of means and self-sacrificing devotion to make Brigham Young University possible.

Orson F. Whitney, who is Utah's authoritative historian of this period and intimate friend of Abraham O. Smoot writes: "Among the stalwarts who stood shoulder to shoulder with Brigham Young and his conquerors in the founding of this commonwealth, no man made a better record than he whose honored name gives caption to this article," (from a biographical sketch of the great pioneer's life). He further eulogizes: "Colonizer, financier, civic officer, legislator, missionary, Bishop and Stake President, who frequently sat with the leaders of the Latter-day Saint Church. Large of frame, strong features, piercing black eyes, bushy beetling brows, dignity in his presence, rugged physique and striking personality stamped him as a leader. A natural impediment in his speech disappeared as he talked. Serious but easily led to mirth, he was fearless in defense of what he believed right; he denounced error wherever he saw it."

The great versatility of the man is revealed by the many important positions he held and the business he promoted.

As a young man he was a woodsman and farmer.

1848—Leader of Relief Train to assist others coming to Utah. He made many cross trips from the great river to mountains.

First Justice of Peace in Utah.

Organized the first Utah police force; especially active in Gold Rush period.

1853—Led the first Perpetual Immigration Company from Liverpool to Salt Lake City, Utah.

1854—Sugar House Ward in Salt Lake named by Margaret, Bishop Smoot's wife. He became second Mayor of Salt Lake City and held the position for ten years. Mayor of Provo for twelve years, serving without pay. Supervised the erection of the first nail factory west of the Mississippi. Established canneries and flour mills in Utah County.

1867—President of Provo Corporation institution to 1895.

1869—Promoted Provo Woolen Mills, manager and Vice-President to Brigham Young; later President.

President of the First National Bank and the Utah Savings Bank in Provo; Director of Provo Lumber Manufacturing and Building Company; Director of Provo Drug Store; Director of sheep and cattle ranches and developed farming properties; Erected buildings in Provo for new tenants and sold at cost in many instances.

City lighted by electric power in 1890, when Reed Smoot, representing A. O. Smoot and others, was granted a franchise to light the city and furnish power for the Provo Woolen Mills.

In his last days he assumed the debts of B.Y.A. amounting to more than $100,000 and mortgaged his properties and holdings to liquidate them. A wealthy man died practically penniless to save the honor of the Church and the University. "I was sent to Provo to help

176

in the building of a University. I have tried to honor that calling."

A building of beauty bears his name, but we can never repay his loyalty until we live the standards for which he sacrificed.

REED SMOOT

Born: January 10, 1862   **Place:** Salt Lake City, Utah

Father: Abraham Owen Smoot of Prince Edward County, Virginia; (see his biography)

Mother: Anna Kristina Mouritsen, born December 20, Daughter of Neils Mouritsen of Aalo, Norway (name was changed to Morrison)

Brothers and Sisters:
Annie Christina, m. George S. Taylor
Alice, m. Myron C. Newell
(Reed)
George M., m. Mary Ann Larsen
Agnes May, m. Charles Albert Glazier
Brigham, m. Margaret Nesbit
Ida Mauline, m. George A. Dusenberry

Marriage:
1. Alpha M. Eldredge on September 17, 1884, daughter of General Horace S. Elldredge, died November 4, 1928
2. Alice Taylor Sweets

Children:
Harold Reed, m. Ann Nibley
Chloe, m. Ariel Cardon
Harlow Eldredge, m. Anite Parlicuson
Annie K., m. Grover Rebentisch
Zella Esther, m. Carlyle Nibley
Ernest Winder

Death: Sunday, February 9, 1941 in St. Petersburg, Florida while on a visit. Interment in Provo City Burial Park.

The life of Reed Smoot reads like a biographical novel. From boyhood to death, he had to fight for his ideals, recognition, and the success of his efforts. His unswerving honesty cost him many "friends." His struggle to acquire his duly elected seat in the U. S. Senate filled hundreds of pages of government printed matters; his loyalty to his government and church without conflict to either was a subject of challenge and admiration across the country.

It is with difficulty that I condense the telling of this great man's life story to but a few pages. With their venerable father, Abraham O. Smoot, the Smoots became the saviors of the Brigham Young Academy—"The Smoots saved the school, the Knights endorsed and perpetuated it."

While Reed's father was mayor of Salt Lake City (he served twelve years in this office), he was called by Governor Brigham Young to go to Provo, start new industries, and bring the "Garden Spot" to a high fertility to benefit the entire state. Accordingly the Smoots moved to Provo when Reed was ten years of age.

Reed was reared in a portion of the house which I now occupy at 160 South 100 East. His father was appointed president of the Utah Stake and elected Mayor of Provo, giving the young gangling lad a prestige which he early endeavored to magnify and honor.

Young Reed attended the Timpanogos Branch of the University of Deseret under the principalship of Warren Dusenberry and was an interested student when it became the Brigham Young Academy in 1876, chiefly due to the efforts of Abraham O. Smoot and Warren Dusenberry.

One of the original twenty-nine students of the beginning of the new school's first term, Reed was an enthusiastic "salesman" in obtaining scholastic recruits and he enrolled primarily for studies in finance and commercial courses. He was a financier all his life.

During vacations, Reed worked at the Provo Woolen Mills, eventually laboring in every department and becoming its manager.

In 1879, he graduated from the Academy. At one time he was the only student in the Academic Department. His first position after graduation was in the "Provo Co-op", a general store projected by Brigham Young in 1868. Reed sorted potatoes, sacked fruit and stacked the stock. When on one occasion he overheard his father remark to Superintendent R. C. Kirkwood, "I see you have Reed here, but I guess he won't stay very long," Reed clenched his fists and said, "I'll stay here until I am superintendent of this place." He was its manager eighteen months later, staying from September, 1880 to April 1884. When he was made manager of the Provo Woolen Mills (expected as much to give employment to needy colonizers as it was to make a profit) his stay at the mills was a five year mission assignment.

He visited most states in the Union in interest of the mills and other Utah products while he was manager. In 1880, he and his father visited Hawaii to investigate sugar.

Reed's first business venture on his own was to purchase half interest in the drug department of the Provo Co-op with N. C. Larsen as partner in December 1883. A year later he owned all the business, and it became the Smoot Drug Co. He said he made most of his money in the sheep business, which is a story worthy of amplication and should be in any extended history of his life.

He invested in real estate in the "boom days" of 1888-89 which "favored so few and ruined so many."

In 1890, a mission sent him to Great Britain, chiefly as a book-keeper and immigration clerk for the LDS Church with offices in Liverpool. He soon cultivated the officials of Guion Steamship Line and directed the bulk of LDS emigration from that port. He won the confidence of the steamship manager, George Ramsden, and was appointed passage broker for the company at no salary, but pleasing prestige, as the Saints were given intermediate instead of steerage passage. Before returning to Provo, he visited much of Europe to contact commercial centers and various markets. He was summoned home by the serious illness of his father. Reed reached home on October 1, 1891, but A. O. Smoot did not die until March 6, 1895.

In the nineties, his commercial interest expanded as he took over much of his father's business interests and worked many hours each day on his own investments. He was manager of the Provo Lumber Manufacturing & Building Co., and in 1892 resumed the management of the Woolen Mills. He was the chief promoter of the Provo Commercial and Savings Bank (where the present Utah National Bank of Provo now centers) and its first president. Mining was taken up in several Utah fields. From 1894-96 he was a director of the Territorial Asylum for the Insane situated in East Provo.

He served in the presidency of Utah Stake and chairmaned the drive to pay the debt of the unfinished Tabernacle, one of the most beautiful edifices in western United States. He also directed the campaign for the erection of College Hall, as a member of the Board of Trustees and on the Executive Committee.

When Utah attained its belated statehood in 1896, Reed's attention was focused very seriously on politics and the part the new state was to play in the nation. Governor Heber M. Wells appointed him a member of the Semi-Centennial Commission to conduct the Pioneer Jubilee.

His life became more complex when he was called to the Apostleship of the LDS Church on April 6, 1900. He was urged to run for the office of Senator, that Utah might have a vigorous advocate who would represent the young state in a proper manner. Most of the states that had been colonized from Utah had already been admitted into the Union, Utah being the 45th.

Accordingly, Reed Smoot of Provo announced his candidacy for the Senate in May 1902 and was elected January, 1903, receiving forty-five of the sixty-three legislative assembly votes. On March 4th, 1903, he was sworn in by unanimous vote. Then began a four-year struggle for acceptance by the U. S. Senate itself. Eighteen citizens of Utah signed a petition and sent it to Congress soon after his election, stating that "Smoot is an apostle of the Mormon Church, an organization hostile to the government of the United States." This was followed by the Ministerial Association of Utah and Rev. Leilech accusing Senator Smoot of being a polygamist and demanding his expulsion chiefly on that account, with other accusations as untenable. Reed's friends from all parts of the state rose to his defense, proved that he had but one wife, the mother of six children, and the excessive charges boomeranged against his accusers in the state. But the crusade against him spread across the nation, and in December 1903, petitions from all over the Union poured into Washington demanding the unseating of Utah's Senator.

This resulted in a wholesale summoning to Washington of Church officials and members, and Utah citizens, Mormon and Gentile, to testify before the Senate Committee on Privileges and Elections. The fight against Reed cost him thousands of dollars, all out of his own purse. His patience, kind deportment, and truthful assertions before the committee and the press won him thousands of friends who wrote untold numbers of letters and sent them to the Committee. His command of facts and figures stamped him as a vigorous leader. During the trial one of his boyhood friends, Frank J. Cannon, a "free silver Republican" renounced his membership in the LDS Church and vigorously campaigned against Reed Smoot. The hearing lasted until June of 1906 and in February, 1907, it was "Resolved, that Reed Smoot is not entitled to a seat as a senator of the U. S. from the State of Utah." The vote was 28 yeas, 42 nays and 20 abstaining— a majority of 43 of Senate needed for passing. The resolution lost and Reed Smoot was seated. Several of those who voted against him congratulated him on his manly determination and victory.

His life in the senate is worthy of several volumes and his private papers covering this period are being edited and arranged for publication. Reed Smoot became a power in the Senate and served until the Democratic landslide of 1932. He became dean of the Senate and was often referred to as "watch dog of the Treasury." He excelled as a parliamentarian and forceful, logical thinker. He was never an orator, but an interesting speaker. He had a defect of speech which he worked to overcome all his life.

His protective tariff leadership led to the Smoot-Hawley Tariff Act of 1931, especially affecting agricultural raw materials, sugar and textiles.

On November 1, 1926, he addressed the BYU students: "I can see Temple Hill covered with the buildings of Brigham Young University and I expect to see the dream verified. Don't think that the institution has stopped its growth, for it was founded on faith and shall never cease growing." He loved the school and carefully watched its progress. Had not his fight to maintain the Senate seat been so exhausting to his finances, he often said it would have been better for the BYU.

After the election in 1932 and his defeat for office, he returned to Salt Lake and took residence in the Hotel Utah. He took his senate dismissal very hard and especially lamented the weak support given him in Provo, his home town. He loved the university so much he could not comprehend why school members cared for him so little.

Reed Smoot saw no incompatability between serving his government as a senator and serving his Church as apostle. Both were founded on truth and for the people's benefit—there should be no conflict. He honored both by faithful service.

Fearlessly truthful, loyal to a fault, proud of his heritage, enemy to graft and corruption, Reed Smoot will ever remain one of BYU's famous Sons of Brigham.

As we look back on the Senator's life, we surmise that Reed Smoot will be remembered more as a statesman and financier than a religious leader, although his religion was the guiding force of most everything he did.

When a young fellow, he went to the Brigham Young School in Salt Lake just east of the original Eagle Gate. When Reed was ten years of age, his father was directed to go to Provo to live. He established a home where I now live in First East Street. Apostle Smoot came over to our house in 1939 and related his boyhood experiences in the growing town. He first enrolled in the Timpanogos Branch of the University of Deseret under the Dusenberrys, who sold the idea of a church academy to the President of the stake, his father. The teacher who taught in the Brigham Young school in Salt Lake was hired to come to Provo and set up a Church academy. Karl G. Maeser soon set the school in operation, and of the twenty-nine original enrolling students, Reed Smoot, at fifteen, was pupil number one. He enrolled for business classes and finance was his major profession, in which he became a world authority.

During vacations of his school days he worked at the Provo Woolen Mills, founded by his father when he first came to Provo. Young Reed worked in every department and later became the firm's manager. Graduating from the Commerce Department in 1879, he was given a position in the "Provo Co-op" (Projected by Brigham Young in 1868) sacking fruit and sorting potatoes. Eighteen months after joining the Co-op, he was made Superintendent, September 1880 to April, 1884. Later he was made manager of the Provo Woolen Mills, being called on a mission for that purpose for a period of five years. He visited most states in the Union in interest of the Mills and other Utah products.

Reed accompanied his father to Hawaii in the summer of 1880 to observe sugar cane and pineapple cultivation. His first business venture on his own was to purchase the drug department of the Provo Co-op in December, 1883, with N. C. Larsen as his partner. In a year he bought out Mr. Larsen and established the Smoot Drug Company on Academy Avenue. At this time he bought interests in the sheep business, his most successful venture.

With monetary security assured, he wed Alpha M. Eldredge in September, 1884, a quiet and cultured daughter of General Horace S. Eldredge of Salt Lake City. They had six children, living in a beautiful brick home on First South and Second East. Alpha died November 7, 1928, after forty-four years of devoted motherhood and support to him during the stressful years of Senator Reed's fight for his seat in the senate.

In 1890 he began his really serious church work when he went on a L.D.S. mission as a bookkeeper and emigration clerk for the L.D.S. office in Liverpool, England. He cultivated the friendship of Guion Steamship Line officials and directed most of the L.D.S. emigration from this post. The head official of the Guion Company appointed Reed as passenger broker (no salary) and he was able to procure intermediate instead of steerage passage for converts going to Utah. He was visiting Great Britain and Europe when his father's sudden illness called him home and arrived in Provo October 1, 1891.

In 1892 he resumed his Woolen Mills management, promoted the Provo Commercial Savings Bank, and becoming its first president. Mining became another absorbing interest at this time. The B.Y.U. Academy had passed through its first growing period, and Reed was one of the guiding spirits to help finish the new Education Building on Fifth North and University Avenue and participated in its dedication. He was a member of the executive committee of the Board of Trustees and was the finance chairman to procure College Hall. He got the people to pay the debt of the unfinished Tabernacle. His desire to help the Academy grow into a University and his ability to raise finances for it is one of his proudest accomplishments. Like his father who died in debt because of his assistance to the University, Reed also involved his personal finances to a dangerous point because of his love for the school.

On April 8, 1900, at the age of thirty-eight, he was ordained an Apostle of the Church by President Lorenzo Snow.

In 1885 Reed was made second counselor to President Edward Partridge of Utah Stake which was literally all of Utah County and he was dependent upon horse and buggy, or often by horseback and saddle, for transportation.

Repeated efforts had been futilely made to have Utah admitted as a state in the Union. Both Abraham O. and Reed Smoot were devoted protagonists in the cause, and it became a burning desire upon the part of Reed to go to Washington and labor in its acceptance. His father died in 1896, the year Utah was accepted as a member state in the Union. As Reed went about the new state in church appointments, he was urged to represent Utah in the halls of Congress, and in May of 1902, he announced his candidacy for the U. S. Senate on the Republican ticket and was elected in January, 1903, receiving 45 of the 63 legislative assembly votes. On March the 4th, 1903, he was sworn in by a unanimous vote.

Immediately after, eighteen citizens of Utah sent a petition to Congress to unseat the tall Mormon "as he was an apostle of the Mormon Church, an organization hostile to the Government." Other petitions followed, some led by ministers, who accused Senator Smoot of being a polygamist. By December, petitions had been sent in from over all the Union demanding Smoot's immediate unseating. The entire Mormon Church was arraigned before the Senate Committee of Privileges and Elections. President Joseph F. Smith, and Senior Apostle Francis M. Lyman of the Twelve were among those summoned. Leading citizens, Mormon and "Gentile," were questioned; the press was increasingly inimical as "testimony" poured in. Four long years Reed fought for his rights to represent his constituents, at the cost of thousands of dollars out of his own resources which brought him almost to bankruptcy. His unimpeachable honesty, quiet polite responses to slanderous indictments, his mastery of facts and figures won him numerous friends and ultimate seating in the Senate with four years lost for service. In February of 1907 it was "Resolved, that Reed Smoot is not entitled to a seat as a senator of the U. S. from the State of Utah." There were 28 yeas, 42 nays, and 20 abstaining. A two-third majority or 60 yeas was necessary for exclusion, and Reed was accordingly seated to be challenged by thousands of editorials, magazine articles and remained a "lonesome figure" in the nation's capitol for some years.

World War I broke down much of the lingering animosity, and Senator Smoot's incisive speech, and ready facts at tongue-tip gradually brought him the power he ultimately earned in his country's service. As time went on he was given the soubriquet "watch-dog of the treasury." Volumes have been written of this famous political trial. One of Utah's gifted and brilliant sons, Frank J. Cannon, renounced his membership in the LDS Church and vigorously campaigned against Reed Smoot, editing such books as *Utah Under the Prophet* and *Brigham Young and His Mormon Empire*. The American Party carried Salt Lake City in 1905-07 on an anti-Church campaign but was decisively defeated in 1911 chiefly because of the success of Reed Smoot in Washington.

When he was defeated on the F. D. Roosevelt "land slide" in 1932, Reed Smoot was dean of the senate and one of its most powerful members, being chairman of the finance committee. One of his major efforts was passed in June of 1931, the Smoot-Hawley Tariff, to protect agricultural raw materials, with special protection on sugar and textile products. Utah's chief industry at that time was sugar, a business reduced to impotency by President F. D. Roosevelt's free or low tariff policies.

When former President Herbert Hoover learned of Reed's defeat in 1932, he said "your senator, Senator Reed Smoot, knows more about the U. S. Government than any other living man."

The Senator a subdued man, moved to Salt Lake with a suite in the Hotel Utah, filling his appointments for the Church and state. A gala reception was given to Senator and Mrs. Smoot in the B.Y.U. Women's Gymnasium on November 4, 1936 when more than a thousand friends, Church and civic workers attended, and an evening of eulogy was celebrated. On this occasion, his connection and service to the B.Y.U. was inventoried showing him to be one of the greatest contributors to the school, both with service and purse; his civic and commercial activities were itemized down to the days of the depression when his Provo bank failed and wiped out most of his life's investments. He modestly stated that his service in the nation's capitol was a significant contribution to his church and this state. He recalled his remarks to the B.Y.U. studentbody in November of 1926, "I can see Temple Hill covered with buildings of the Brigham Young University and I expect to see the dream verified. Don't think that the institution has stopped its growth for it was founded on faith and shall never cease growing."

In his final years, he wrote for various magazines and frequently was quoted by both major political party speakers. On a winter visit to Florida he died on February 9, 1941 and was brought to Provo for burial. No man fought harder to sustain principles which he believed to be right than Senator Reed Smoot, churchman, patriot, businessman, and loyal friend. He was the next in line to succeed president of the Quorum of Apostles when he died. His papers, diaries, notes and pictures have been collected by his grandson and daughter, Sam Smoot and Anita S. Haymond, and given to the B.Y.U. library. A reception in honor of Reed Smoot and his family was held in the J. Reuben Clark Library, April 8th, 1966.

In April of 1966 a memorial in the form of a seminar-reading room was established in the new George Washington University National Law Library to "honor a long-time public servant from a great state who helped so many young men who wanted to further their education."

He was one of Brigham Young University's greatest sons.

GEORGE SUTHERLAND

His name was the same as his father's, but he dropped the "Alexander" on coming of age.

Born: March 25, 1862   **Place:** Stoney Stratford, Buckinghamshire, England

Father: Alexander George Sutherland
He joined the L.D.S. Church in England in 1862. In 1863, he was aided by the Church, left England, and came to Springville, Utah. In a few years, he became indifferent towards the Church and drifted to Montana as a prospector. He came back to Utah in 1869; first to Silver City and later to Provo. He was a restless soul content with few comforts. He was mining recorder, justice of the peace, postmaster, and practicing attorney. He died in 1911.

Mother: Frances Slater
Born June 5, 1835. Married March 30, 1861, in Stoney Stratford and came to Utah in 1872. She was a cultured lady with expansive reading habits; made her first home in Springville, and later moved to Provo.

Brothers and Sisters: (George, eldest)
Fannie, b. Feb. 10, 1864, m. Ephraim Davis Sutton
Thomas, b. Oct. 1, 1865.
Henry E., b. Sept. 4, 1867, m. Sophia Sutton
James, b. Dec. 25, 1869, m. Clara Williamson
Fredrick, b. Jan. 5, 1872, m. Della Allen

Marriage: Rosamond Lee, daughter of John P. Lee and Elija Foscu, pioneer of Beaver, Utah, whom George met at the B.Y. Academy. She was born July 16, 1865 and married June 16, 1883

Children: Emma, b. Nov. 14, 1884, m. Charles Laurence
Philip, b. March 6, 1886, died of typhoid at Concord, N.H.
Edith b. Jan. 4, 1888, m. Robert Elmore

Death: July 18, 1942, at 81 years of age at Stockbridge, Massachusetts and interred at Abbey Mausoleum, Arlington, Virginia.

More has been written of the deeds of George Sutherland than of the man himself. Glen Miller wrote an appreciation of him for the *Salt Lake Herald Republican,* July 9, 1916, saying in part, "He received recognition of the biggest kind for our State. His stately bearing, attractive personality, to everyone a gentlemen, he is a big man in a big place. . . . He is a champion of the U.S. Constitution, with a broad construction of the Constitution." James Bryce described him as the "living voice of the Constitution." Joel Francis Paschol, who wrote a book about him, says "He stands as one of the major land marks in American Constitutional law." Samuel Gompers declared George Sutherland a sympathetic friend of labor in Congress as he championed the eight hour per day work bill and formed the Federal Child Labor Law. The American Bar Association declared him to be one of its most able jurists. In his court career, he wrote 320 opinions, 295 of them majority decisions.

From letters to friends and talks to B.Y.U. student body assemblies, we get our best picture of his youth. In Utah, his boyhood was very simple but very hard as compared to the present day standards. Nobody worried about child labor then as the average boy of ten worked very hard—a farm boy had plenty of chores. He and his barefoot companions knew the best fishing holes. His books were McGuffey's Readers and Webster's Spelling book and he learned to write legibly at an early age. He was forced from school at twelve years of age, taking a job as a clerk in a Salt Lake store, for the agent of Wells Fargo Express Co. In 1879, on his own industry and frugality, he came to B.Y.U. in Provo, presided over by Karl G. Maeser, who had a decisive influence on his life. As he later wrote to James E. Talmage in 1927, "Dr. Maeser's knowledge seemed to reach on every field . . . He was a man of such transparent and natural goodness that his students gained not only knowledge, but character, which is better than knowledge. He exerted an influence on my whole life which cannot be exaggerated." Judge Sutherland's idea of the Constitution being divine and inspired came from Professor Maeser, who said of Sutherland, "His essays were invariably models of excellence."

Every teacher of his at B.Y.U. encouraged him to go further in his education and in the summer of 1881 he left the Academy and became forwarding agent for building the Rio Grande Western Railway. Fifteen months later he arrived in Ann Arbor, Michigan, to study Constitutional law, enrolling under Dr. Thomas M. Conley, the greatest living American writer on Constitutional law and the most quoted. Because of finances, George stayed only one term at Ann Arbor, but returned to Utah to make law his life's career. He had been further convinced that law should protect the individual and preserve his inherent rights. He was licensed to practice law in Michigan in 1883, and in this summer he wed Rosamond Lee, a B.Y.U. friend, with whom he soon had a family of two girls and one boy.

He joined his father in a law partnership "Sutherland and Son," getting numerous clients and small fees averaging $15 each. In 1886 the partnership was dissolved and George joined Samuel R. Thurman, who later added William H. King to the firm. These men did much of the legal work for Utah County.

The young barrister became interested in politics as early as 1870 when the Liberal Party was organized and George became its secretary and active speaker. In 1890 he was a candidate for Mayor of Provo but was defeated by Warren Dusenberry. In this year the Latter-day Saints Church issued its Manifesto, and the Liberal Party was soon dissolved. George announced himself a Republican and advocated a protective tariff. With Reed Smoot he had already organized the Harrison-Morton Republican Club of Central Utah in 1888. In 1892 George Sutherland sought the Republican nomination to Congress and failed by six votes. In 1893 he moved to Salt Lake and joined the firm of Parley L. Williams and Waldemar Van Cott with good financial returns. In 1894 he was one of the organizers of the Utah Bar Association.

Eighteen-ninety-six was a turning point for Utah and George Sutherland. Utah was admitted to the Union and George was elected to the first legislature and made chairman of the Senate Judiciary Committee. One of his first interests was securing an eight hour day for miners. At thirty-eight, George became a candidate to Congress for the Republican Party and campaigned the state with Heber M. Wells, Utah's first governor. A brilliant orator, Wm. H. King, was the Democratic incumbent who lost the election to Sutherland by 241 votes out of the 90,000 cast. George took his seat after a year's wait. He served the House from 1901-1903: 1903-04 he was in private practice in Salt Lake, and in this year his son Philip died in Concord, New Hampshire of typhoid fever. In 1904 Reed Smoot and Sutherland routed the Kearns forces and in 1905 George was elected to the Senate. He became active in defense of Senator Smoot and made a forceful, factual speech in the Senate in January of 1907. Senator Smoot was seated on February 20. George convinced the majority of the senators that Smoot was not a polygamist and was loyal to the U.S.

To detail each of his many successes, both in the Senate and the Supreme Court, would fill a large book. He was appointed to the Supreme Court in September of 1922, and in January, 1938, he notified President Roosevelt of his decision to leave the bench. When Roosevelt was elected in 1932 he met for the first time the "nine old men" of the court he had publicly ridiculed. Chief Justice Holmes had resigned at age 91, and Justice Cardozo was named his successor. Most of the majority opinions thereafter were written by Justice Sutherland until he resigned.

Judge Sutherland, in many interviews, stated that his dominant political thinking was focused on the freedom of the individual, a devotion to the jury system, and adherence to the principles contained in the Bill of Rights. He often stated that liberty and authority should counter-balance. In 1936 he led editorial reaction when he stated that national survival is a supreme duty to which even the principles of the Constitution must yield should they conflict.

His resignation brought a flood of laudatory comment across the nation. The *New York Herald Tribune* wrote, in part, "The country loses a singularly able mind and a character as staunch as it is above reproach . . . his complete loyalty to the truth as he saw it was always of the highest value." When Columbia University conferred an honorary doctor's degree upon him in 1913, he was especially cited as being profoundly versed in law and policy of the Constitution. When the University of Michigan conferred its honorary degree upon the Judge in 1917, he was called "the ablest man in the U.S. Senate from Democrat, as well as Republican." In 1916 he was president of the American Bar Association.

After leaving the Bench, he lived in Washington D.C. with his wife, daughter, and grandson, often speaking, and wrote for publication occasionally. His wife outlived him by two years. B.Y.U. honored him with a degree in 1941.

A brief resume of his Congressional and Supreme Court activities best reveal his interests and character:

—Opened Uintah Reservation, chief protagonist

—Established Strawberry Reservoir project to supply water for Utah valley

—Procured a new hospital and barracks in Fort Douglas, Utah

—Was chairman of Public Land Committee during Republican reign

—Introduced bills and obtained legislation—

For Salt Lake City Post Office addition; Salt Lake Assay Office, Land for Utah University and Mt. Olivet Cemetery; Right of way for Salt Lake Water supply; Pensions for deserving Utah soldiers; Got the Safety Appliance act passed and the regulation of railroad employees' hours of labor; The establishment of the Department of Commerce and Labor, the Pure Food and Drug Act, Federal Meat Inspection, Income Tax Amendment (he was opposed to the income tax which the Supreme Court declared un-Constitutional in 1895), procured Parcel Post, Postal Savings' Banks, a Children's Bureau, direct election of U.S. Senators, publicity for campaign contributors, rural free delivery, etc., etc.

—Major voice in passing the Criminal Code

—Chief writer and advocate of the Judicial Code to make law

accessible and understandable.

—Panama Canal Act, a system of compensation.

—The Underwood Tariff Act passed which removed duty on sugar, bitterly opposed by President Woodrow Wilson.

Every important issue received his undivided attention all the years he served his country. He was the fifth naturalized citizen to sit on the Supreme Court Bench, and he proved himself to be one of the country's most loyal citizens and one of B.Y.U.'s most honored sons.

JOHN CANUTE SWENSEN

Born: Feb. 4, 1869, in Pleasant Grove, Utah.

Father: Knud Swensen of Veiby, Hjorring County, Denmark.
      Born: April 11, 1827, son of Sven Larsen (1772-1851)
         and Ane Petersen (1778-1851). Fought in the Army
         against Germany (1849-51). Heard Elder L. C.
         Geertsen in Veiby in 1855 and was baptized on
         April 28, 1856. John C. relates that his father "kept
         this date of baptism as a sacred date throughout
         his life," as a contract which he made with his
         God. He arrived in Salt Lake City just ten days
         after Johnston's Army had passed thru the city.
         Bought a farm in Pleasant Grove for $92.00. Met
         his future wife at a Danish Conference.
      Died: March 14, 1902.

Mother: Johanna Marie Hansen, convert in Denmark, came to
      Utah in 1859; walked across the plains, lived with Elder
      Clinger in Provo.
      Married Knud on June 24, 1860, two weeks after their
      first meeting.
      Both had been Lutherans.
      Died: May 2, 1880 when John C. was eleven years of age,
      leaving five children.

Brothers   Anna, m. Ezra Walker, 19 years of age when mother died.
and Sisters: Sven L., m. Susan Brown.
      Mary, m. George Kelly.
      John C.
      Eliza

Marriage: Ellen Davis of Panguitch, Utah, June 21, 1899, a talented
      musician and teacher.

Children: John Starr, b. Mar. 22, 1900 (doctor's fee $15.00), gradu-
      ated BYU 1918, m. Marva Carter, November, 1919.
      Carl Davis, b. Aug. 3, 1901, cadet to U. S. Naval Acad-
      emy 1916, graduated BYU 1922, m. Lura Tanner in 1923.
      Reed Knud, b. Feb. 16, 1903, graduated BYU 1936, Ph. D.
      from U. of U., 1951, m. Ruth Freebairn, 1929.
      Alice, b. May 14, 1905, died June 11, 1905.
      Margaret, b. May 28, 1906, graduated BYU in 1926, m.
      James L. Jacobs on Dec. 21, 1936.
      Francis McLane, b. June 29, 1908, mission to France 1930-
      33, graduated BYU in 1935, m. Willa Sowards.
      Louise, b. Mar. 24, 1910, named in honor of dear friend

Alice Louise Reynolds, graduated with her mother BYU in 1935, m. Jay Tolman, 1936.

Joseph Cadawallder, b. June 13, 1913, named after grandfather Davis, graduated BYU 1936, m. Verna Harding, 1939.

Albert D., b. 1915, graduated BYU, Ph.D. LSU 1941, m. Jennie Romney 1937.

Richard Davis, b. 1919, graduated BYU 1940, in U. S. Army 5 years, lieutenant, m. Orlean Stowell March, 1950. (All have been teachers during some time of their careers; each has reared a family.)

Died: August 30, 1953 at 84 years of age.

Four years after mother Johanna died, John C.'s father married a young Danish convert who had written from Denmark asking for immigration assistance. By her came seven children, one of whom was Lyman, John's half-brother, written up in a subsequent biography. Johanna's family lived in her home after John C's father left to live with his later wife, leaving Anna to care for the family.

Young John became known as a persistent questioner and a New Testament given to him was a constant companion to be read at the end of a long row of plowing as he rested against the flank of one of his oxen or while the slowly moving team furrowed to the marked row. All his life he could accurately quote much of the four gospels and favorite verses from St. Paul. He read all the books he could borrow or buy. Conflicts in society early attracted his analytical attention. Typical of his questions, he asked his father on a hot working day, "In the next world do we get tired?" His father, also typically, replied "You live in this world, the next will take care of itself."

In 1875 when John was six years of age, the United Order was established, which modified the Swensen family life, as members surrendered their land, cattle and other property to the central communal organization. The idea was for each individual to share equally. The first year went over with enthusiasm but by 1880 it had completely faded out and was dissolved. The redistribution of properties and the causes for its failure caused the young lad of eleven to ponder human frailties and built a foundation for his later professional career.

In 1886 John C. went away from home for his first time and entered Brigham Young Academy. The school year was divided into four terms of ten weeks each; he had grammar and theology under Joseph B. Keeler, arithmetic under Karl G. Maeser, elocution under N. L. Nelson. Tuition was $10 per term. His first year he stayed at the Academy Boarding House, a three-storied building on the corner of Center and 1st Streets. Alice Reynolds was a young girl in the same place.

A paragraph on Academy discipline is told by John of his third and final year:

"That year I was one of the supervisors in the Domestic Organization which was set up to govern out-of-school behavior of students. The community was divided into four wards with a supervisor over each. It was the duty of the supervisor to make monthly visits to the boarding houses or homes he was assigned to look after, then report to the faculty as to whether or not the students were keeping all of the rules they had set up. Some of these rules were: Keep the Word of Wisdom, especially as to the use of tobacco and liquor; Attend no public dances; Avoid appearance of evil by staying away from all such places as saloons (There were nearly a dozen in the town at the time). Violation of these standards was sometimes punished by dismissal from school. A student, however, could ask forgiveness, make a statement of good intention, and be reinstated in school. Eight o' clock was curfew on weekday nights. House arrest was the punishment for breaking curfew. House arrests, however, were rare. . . . I'm inclined to think house arrest was too formal and did little to retard the natural exuberance and instincts of normal young men. I doubt that there was a much higher moral standard then than now."

John had been in school about two weeks when he had a terrible case of homesickness, a feeling of inferiority. In one of his lowest moments he met Brother Maeser on the street who greeted him most cordially and said "How are you my boy?" and shook hands warmly. The greeting was so unexpected that John lost all sense of loneliness in the presence of this genial personality and went on his way rejoicing.

At this point, it is a real pleasure to present John C's opinion of Dr. Maeser, as few men observed others more keenly than Professor Swensen. "Karl G. Maeser was a gentleman in a very natural and real sense. His German military bearing seemed to add to his personal charm. On the street he always raised his hat to the ladies and also to students whom he knew. Male members of the faculty and many men of the Academy adopted the same custom. It was not alone that his personality was dynamic but it was strangely contagious to most people who came in intimate contact with him. Both students and teachers responded to this magnetic man. His influence was a dominant factor in my life at that time. His great force and power as a teacher was not in academic subjects but rather in his ability to help adjust the religious and personal problems of the students. While he was fundamentally very serious, nevertheless he did have a keen sense of humor, which on occasions, was mildly satirical or even explosive and could be either stimulating or distressing, depending on the degree of harshness the situation called for. He was not a great scholar, but he was a great teacher. What ideas he had he could teach effectively. His most famous rule for the teacher was: 'Never permit yourself to be at the mercy of your class,' by which he meant that the teacher was to see to it that students did not discover his inadequacies; . . . 'Never ask a question of a class that can be answered correctly with any answer except the one you want.' This day the trainer in pedagogy was giving an object lesson supposedly to a first reader class. The student teacher held up a luscious red apple and asked, 'Class, what is this I am holding in my hand?' 'An apple, teacher' was the prompt reply.' 'That is correct. Now, if I take a knife and cut it exactly through the middle, what will I find?' 'Worms' stated one of the class.

"As a disciplinarian he was excellent, not only in the classroom, but in managing larger groups also. His instructions were clear cut and effective. . . . I felt that he was never as effective as a public speaker as he was as a teacher with intimacies of school groups. . . .

"Dr. Maeser taught a wide range of subjects—German, history, grammar, arithmetic, elocution, and in fact, practically all of the subjects taught in the high school. . . . Teachers are always more effective if students idealize them. At least that is true in the earlier development. Dr. Maeser will be long remembered by students who came under the influence of his radiant personality, the soundness of his moral ideas, and the beauty of his personal life." This type of character appraisal was a part of John C's daily life; each person he knew he analyzed, and he was most apt in comparisons. He first looked at each of his teachers as a man, then awaited the proof of scholarship. John had to be shown.

He graduated from the Academy in May, 1899, after nine terms of residence. His graduation exercises were simple, and the students did not get formal diplomas. Among his graduating classmates, he recalled George Christensen (later District Judge), Enoch Jorgensen (later principal of Jordan High School) and Joseph Y. Jensen (teacher in Snow College). (Note the Scandinavian influence in his class.)

Professor Maeser called John to his office on October 9, 1889 and told him there was a teaching job at Panguitch in the Stake Academy at $65.00 a month (good pay in those days as John's brother Swen was clerking in a store at $25.00 a month). John tells of advice received; "Call on the Stake President, Jesse W. Crosley, and get advice for your future procedure. Meet with the Stake Board and arrange matters for your school. Let the principles of the Gospel be foremost in your teaching. Be obedient to those placed over you. Be exceedingly choice in your companions, and be kind yet firm in all your intercourse with the students. Be prayerful and humble, get the Spirit of God and follow its promptings. God bless you."

When John arrived at Panguitch he found President Crosley working a threshing machine. He looked J. C. over and said "Where are your whiskers?" At twenty-five the new teacher was well on his way as he replied "It doesn't take whiskers; it takes brains to teach."

For a school room, a curtain was drawn through the center of the old stake meeting house wherein to hold two classes, Intermediate and Primary. There were no age or scholastic requirements, and some of the students were thirty years of age and a few of them were married. The new teacher soon found the local habits of social life were much different than those of Provo and the mother school. A dance every five weeks was BY Academy ration but one each week was the program for Panguitch, and John said, "I learned while at Panguitch that I wasn't the final judge of human beings. It is better to let each one settle his own problems; to get along in life one must acquire a sense of insight and necessity, and an element of humor to help him over the bumps."

Punctuality was almost a fetish of John's. He started on time. Panguitch people started meeting when people came. John tells us, "As a project I undertook teaching ¹them punctuality by starting school on time. We, however, began school at nine and I locked the doors during our devotional period. One morning one of the girls who came late disturbed us during devotional by pounding and shaking the door, but I didn't open it. She went home, but a few days later she came humbly back to school."

One of Professor Swensen's students in Panguitch was a twelve-year old, R. Garn Clark (later well-known M. D. in Provo). In an interview in 1943, he said "His personal appearance was an inspiration to us kids. He was always immaculate. . . He was a great teacher. . . . John Swenson has done more to influence my ideals than any person except my father. He is so utterly human and sympathetic, never sanctimonious, always the cultural gentleman. He inspired me to go on. His personal clean living was impressive. He believes in deeds, not words. The strong influence he had in the way of cleaning up our town was remarkable." It was this ability to reach out in a community and affect the very core of the village life that made John C. Swensen a person worthy of emulation and certainly meriting a tribute as a Son of BYU.

While John was teaching at Panguitch Academy the Academy at Provo had moved in 1892 to the new Education Building and Education Hall was the scene of a summer school of significant import. The first two weeks in August saw the Provo school led by Benjamin Cluff, Jr., and George H. Brimhall. Colonel Francis W. Parker, principal of the Cook County Normal School in Chicago, and a Miss Heffron of the same Chicago school were nationally recognized teachers, "giving most excellent courses of study," this faculty was augmented by Professor William M. Stewart of the University of Deseret, Principal Wilford Moench of the Ogden Academy (later Weber College) and the regular staff of the school. New teachers had been added to the staff including Professor Walker M. Woolfe (graduate of Williams College), Dr. Whitely (who had been a minister in the Church of England and taught Greek and Latin), and Dr. George Phillips (graduate of the University of Edinburgh who taught physics and chemistry). In Dr. George H. Brimhall's class of History of Pedogogy John's companions were J. W. Booth, Henry Peterson, P. C. Evans, Weston Vernon, C. D. Ray and Collie Robison, all of whom became leaders in Utah's professional life.

In 1892-93, a complete course leading to a BYU degree was offered. The degree B. Pd. (Bachelor of Pedogogy) was conferred upon six persons, George H. Brimhall, N. L. Nelson, H. M. Warner, O. W. Andelin, Cora Groesbeck and Ida Alleman.

In the summer of 1893 John visited the Chicago World Fair and saw Utah's "very creditable exhibit" which included the bronze statue of Brigham Young by the Springville sculptor Cyrus E. Dallin, which attracted considerable attention. It was later moved to the intersection of Main Street and South Temple in Salt Lake City and dedicated by Pres. Wilford Woodruff on July 24, 1897.

September 9th, 1850, Utah was organized a territory—this date of the 9th was "Utah Day" at the Fair and the great Mormon Tabernacle Choir was present to celebrate and take part in the Welsh Eisteddfod. In the same city John attended the "World's Congress of Religions" at which the Mormon representatives were excluded from the main assembly but were permitted to speak to a restricted group. John writes "Before this group, Elder B. H. Roberts made a brilliant defense of Mormonism." Later, John had the pleasure of meeting Major William McKinley, subsequent president of the United States. John had that discriminating ability of selecting potential greatness and leadership when he saw it and made it a part of his social strength to meet such individuals. His scrapbook of world notables bespeaks that interest most highly, an ability he wisely later used in selecting talent for the BYU Lyceum Bureau.

In the Fall of 1893 John went to Fillmore, Utah, to become principal of the schools, where classes were held in the old State House built in 1855, Utah's first Capitol Building. In the town John met Ira N. Hinckley, president of the stake and father of a notable BYU family.

John's interim at Stanford University was a highlight of his life.

He majored as a freshman in English under Prof. A. G. Newcomer, one of America's great English teachers. Here was the world-renowned scientist and teacher, David Starr Jordan. As John tells us, "Among the men who most profoundly influenced my life during my stay at Stanford, I should mention first President David Starr Jordan. So far as I know he was not a member of any church, but he was deeply spiritual and was a strong advocate of temperate living. His address on 'The Strength of Being Clean' was cited by President Heber J. Grant as an ideal expression of the Word of Wisdom." The Swensen's first son was named John Starr in honor of the great ichthyologist, Dr. Jordan. The young student from Utah was accepted on his character and leadership rather than for the credits he produced from the BYU. John was given but three hours entrance credit to Stanford and had to make up the balance by special examinations. Tuition was but $20 a year and John registered as a special student. Each student was free to select his own courses. J. C. inclined toward the social sciences.

At this juncture of his life, Professor Swensen had to expand his viewpoints to meet the challenge of modern science. Evolution of species was vividly portrayed in his biology class under Dr. Lyman Wilbur (later to be president of Stanford) and President Jordan. He writes in his biography "I had been taught the theory of evolution was wrong, but the evidences presented in this course were so clear and convincing that I could not doubt them. So began the painful struggle of adjustment between traditional ideas of creation and the demonstrated idea of modern science. The origin of species of life forms may not be fully explained, but change and adjustment of environment is clearly shown. . . . The conflict between science and some forms of dogmatic religion is acute. Complete readjustment is not always easy, and occasionally completely unsuccessful. . . . At any rate, one should not have any trouble in our own church because theologically the philosophy of Mormonism holds to the idea that it embraces all truth, no matter from what source it comes, and secondly, that man himself is capable of eternal progression and evolution."

I have given considerable space to John's attitude to Stanford and his new concept on science. He belongs to that grand group of scholars who left mountain homes of single faith and met the new age of discoveries in philosophy and science, when Darwin was propounding *Emotion in Man and Animal,* and his *Origin of Species,* when Huxley was comparing anatomy of man and animals, and the significance of the hand, when the writings of Karl Marx were given world attention and challenged both God and capitalism; when the writings of Immanuel Kant had been translated from the German and were given liberal university status, dealing with such subjects as his system of religion founded upon reason, experience and moral law; when William James was affecting American thinking on introspection and emotions, when

Kant's critical philosophy was academically ascendant and Schopenhauer with his philosophy of pessimism was given more than a passing glance, when Wilhelm Wundt was giving exciting lectures on experimental psychology, and when Galton made the study of heredity important, when Tyndall, Pasteur, Roentgen, and Lister opened up new fields of science, the germ theory, X-ray utilities and antiseptic therapy. The whole world was awakened to a questioning, sceintific approach to nature and man's existence. German scholars dominated scholarly thinking and God had little or no place in their studies. Men like John C. Swensen, N. L. Nelson, Edwin S. Hinckley, George H. Brimhall, and James E. Talmage, to name a few, were shock-absorbers, as it were, and took the impetus of new knowledge, which easily led to skepticism and doubt, and harmonized the truths of new discoveries with Mormon philosophy, making applicable the import of our 13th Article of Faith, "If there is anything virtuous, lovely or of good report or praiseworthy, we seek after these things."

In John's senior year at Stanford he became active in the Euphrowin Literary Society and was elected vice-president. The secretary of the Society was Miss Lou Henry (later Mrs. Herbert Hoover). Will Irwin was a classmate, as was Ike Russell (a Latter-day Saint), both outstanding reporters and feature writers. Such famous people appeared on the lecture platform as Robert E. Peery, the great explorer, Susan B. Anthony, women suffrage pioneer, Edwin Markham, American poet, famed for his "Man With A Hoe." All of these people John personally met, and he decided that such minds should be introduced to Utah in a proper Lyceum or Chautauqua course. He graduated in May 1898, receiving his degree without cap or gown in the old Stanford Gym.

In the autumn of 1898 John was offered a position at BYU by President Benjamin Cluff as Assistant Professor of English and History at $900 a year. Before school started a tour of southern Utah was made, with Bryant S. Hinckley, to interest prospective students. Two young women, Maggie Davis and Mrs. Allie Clark, excellent vocalists, accompanied them to the meetings in all towns of the Panguitch Stake. This trip had lasting impressions upon John's life.

During his first year at BYU, the Ruskin Club was formed for faculty and the older students to study art. In this club were Professor N. L. Nelson, Professor Walter M. Woolfe, Miss Alice Reynolds, Mrs. Susa Y. Gates and other such persons who gained state-wide reputations. Also in this year Professor Swensen was a director of the Polysophical Society, founded by Dr. Maeser for lecture and discussion purposes. Maggie Davis had gone to Salt Lake to study voice under Madame Amanda Swenson and piano with Arthur Shepherd, later acclaimed as the orchestra leader of Cincinnati and a prize-winning composer. Margaret Ellen Davis and John were married on June 21, 1899. They rented the home of Professor Wilford M. McKendrick at 333 East, 4th North, in Provo, neighbor to Joseph B. Keeler. The rent was $8.00 a month. The Swensens resided in this home as long as they lived. Here their children were born.

During the first years of John's Academy work, the school held daily devotional exercises in College Hall, preceded by regular faculty prayer meeting. In the autumn of 1899 the academy held a convention on the geography of the *Book of Mormon*, attended by most of the church experts. John states "the discussions were interesting, varied and inconclusive." Significantly, the following year an expedition was organized to explore Central and South America to attempt to harmonize the geography of these lands with descriptions of a physical nature contained in the Book of Mormon. The expedition left Provo April 17, 1900, accompanied by John and others, on foot, as far as Spanish Fork. The expedition was disorganized by President Joseph F. Smith at Nogales, Arizona, on the Mexican border. President Cluff and a few others continued their course on their own responsibility. For years, the evidences of this trip were displayed in two large glass cases in the outer hall of the Education Building just off of Room D. The cases contained monkeys, reptiles, birds, and tropical plants and grasses. Each morning, under the direction of acting president George H. Brimhall, prayers were said in behalf of President Cluff and his party.

In 1899-1900, the financial situation of the state and the school was so bad that faculty members agreed to teach at half pay if necessary. It turned out better than they expected, "so we only missed two months pay during the year, but for several years were paid in cash and tithing office scrip in equal amounts."

On March 23, 1900 the first Swensen child was born, whom they named John Starr Swensen. On the 14th day of March, 1902, John's father and life-long companion died, a loss John never quite overcame. In this year of 1902, John taught physical education and American History as well as his regular classes. He received $44 for his six week summer term. With a group of neighbors, the Swensens built the first sewer in East Provo which led from Fourth North to Center St. on Third East. "This was a real innovation in our way of living, but it was some years after this that we were required by the city to get rid of our cows, horses and chickens, held in the barn in the back of our lot. These animals helped to feed us and were a great convenience, not to say necessity, to rural living."

In 1903, John relates that BYA became the BY University at the suggestion of President Cluff. Also in 1903 a regular Lyceum was inaugurated. This has now become the oldest lecture course in the

Western U. S. John names in his diary many of the celebrated artists and performers who were on the BYU Lyceum Course.

Soon after school ended in the spring, several of the faculty would spend some days fishing in Provo Canyon. In 1906 John, Professor Alfred Osmond, and Professor Ed Holt went to North Fork for several days' fishing. There they met President T. N. Taylor who owned a 160 acre tract. The teachers conceived the idea of buying the land as a resort and finally bought the place for $2200. A company called Wildwood was organized and other faculty members and Provo businessmen came in on equal terms. John C. was president, Ed H. Holt secretary, and Professor E. H. Eastmond was treasurer. They built their own log cabins near the stream, held outdoor Sunday School and made it an ideal place for family recreation. One portion was kept in pasture for horses and cows.

In 1907 a summer camp was established at Wildwood in Provo Canyon, with more than 100 university people living in the mountain resort.

In 1908, Christian Jensen was added to the BYU Department of History and Political Science. John was shifted to Economics and elementary Scoiology, carrying some twenty hours.

Nineteen hundred and seventeen was the year when Governor Simon Bamberger appointed John as a member of the State Board of Education for a period of six years. The appointment was extended by Governors Mabey, Dern, and Blood, making twenty-four years on that important committee, valued by John as one of the most outstanding assignments in his service career. This position gave him prestige in educational circles wherever he went and aided in his lyceum programs. He was on the central committee to welcome President Woodrow Wilson when the President spoke in the Salt Lake Tabernacle.

By 1920 John had been at the University for twenty-two years without a leave of absence. In this year he and Professor Alfred Osmond were given leaves to go to Columbia University. Here J. C. met some of the world's best-known social workers, such as Margaret Sanger, protagonist on birth control, especially with the poor in the East Side of New York City. He frequently visited Tammany Hall and met most of the name-democrats of the nation, including Governor Al Smith. Education and politics gave him entry into many select sessions and his native curiosity and winning smile did the rest.

Professor Swensen served for twenty-three years on the high council under three Stake Presidents, David John, Joseph B. Keeler, and Thomas N. Taylor. John supervised the Elders' Quorum for a number of years, especially enjoying the young men he met from all walks in life. For years he had served on the State Conference on social work on the executive board and in 1930 was president and attended the American Social Workers National Convention at Atlantic City in that summer. There he met former BYU sociology majors in Dr. Nels Anderson, Dr. Lowry Nelson and Dr. T. Lynn Smith. John had his wife with him for this occasion and also to witness the graduation of their daughter, Margaret, who obtained an M. A. degree at Columbia University.

John was a member of the State Board of Education when the L. D. S. Church gave its junior colleges (1931) to the State. As John was a committee member on junior colleges, the assignment required considerable administrative time for the first few years. When the State Board organized the Utah State High School Activities Committee to supervise all athletic and contest programs, John was named the State Board member to this committee, on which he functioned for ten years (1926-36.)

When the Springville Art Gallery was dedicated, Professor John C. Swensen was chosen as one of the chief speakers. He was asked to give the major address to the Utah Academy of Science in 1937 and his subject was "Conserving Intellectual Freedom." As Professor Emeritus, he was chosen to give the address on BYU Founder's Day, Oct. 16, 1951, one of the brilliant speeches of the series. His keen wit with Danish twist and a quiet sense of humor endeared him to thousands of his friends and students.

Many honors were bestowed upon John C. Swensen. In July of 1947, a group of his former students held a reunion in his honor, recounting the main events of his fifty years of teaching. Upon his obtaining emeritus status in 1941, he was the oldest faculty member at the university in point of service. Paying tribute to him at this event were Dr. Kimball Young, head of the Department of Sociology at Northwestern University; Dr. Lowry Nelson, head of rural sociology at the University of Minnesota; Dr. Arthur Beeley, chairman of the Department of Sociology at the University of Utah; Dr. William M. Wanlass, dean of College of Commerce at U. S. A. C.; Dr. Harold T. Christensen, head of the BYU Sociology Department (now head of the Sociology Department at Purdue U. and the first to receive a masters degree in sociology from the BYU in 1937); Ariel S. Ballif, professor of sociology at BYU, to name but a few. Dr. Nathan T. Whetten of the University of Connecticut, Nels Anderson, in charge of sociological research for the U. S. Government in Germany, and Dr. T. Lynn Smith, professor of Sociology at the University of Florida (the first student to graduate in sociology alone in 1928) sent letters of love and admiration.

The Alumnus magazine in its issue of January, 1955, featured the life work of the beloved teacher. A lecture hall in the Smith Family Living Center was named in his honor on June 2, 1961.

A character of solid integrity, unswerving loyalty, outspoken at all times, tempered with sincere consideration of others, John often ended a verbal give-and-take with one terse, all-inclusive sentence. He regretted the decline of country life as city ways encroached and roads opened up with new transportation. As he grew older, he drove his Ford with unconscious abandon. In his conversational interest he often would drive the direction he was looking, either right or left, although the road was straight ahead. On one occasion, we were stopped by a telephone pole—"Well, there are different methods of communication. I wasn't expecting a telephone call so soon." We got out of the car to survey the damage, "The Ford is a very sturdy car" was all he said, although the radiator was leaking. Then he looked at me, "I assume you are not hurt or you would have advised me. Sorry. I can't take you the rest of the way. Oh, yes, what were you saying?"

He was a most obliging person. As we convened for assembly in College Hall, the faculty sat in four rows in Stage Center. The seats were of heavy iron, uncovered and not too warm on winter days. John would come early from Room D and usually sit on the first end seat. After he had the seat nicely warmed I came up the back stairway from my office in the Little Theater, stood by him, and he smilingly moved over. More often than not he warmed his new seat without comment as he believed it was because I needed the seat at the row's end for any quick stage adjustments. He favored me in this manner for some dozen winters until we moved on the hill.

His courtesies were delightful. I never saw him seated in any session in College Hall if any girl or lady was standing. He was one of the first to offer his seat at the crowded devotional program or leadership session. When an argument was approaching an opinionated cul-de-sac, he was one of the first to refrain from further conversation. He would converse as long as progress in thinking was being made.

He was patient with backward students and devoted many hours to extra consultation, though he had little consideration for the procrastinator, excuse-maker, or apple-polisher. Many interviews were quickly ended because of his gift of asking the pointed question that got to the root of the dilemma or problem. He answered most student questions with a few counter questions, always concluding with a winning smile.

John C. Swensen, knowing the scriptures and good literature, was a most intelligent, considerate critic. He expected excellence from the trained and progress from the unlearned. He spoke constructively or not at all. He cherished friendships. His children's names attest to this. The first born was John Starr, named in honor of President David Starr Jordan; Carl was given the Davis name to commemorate the mother's family; Reed Knute was named after his beloved grandfather; Margaret carries her mother's name; Francis McLane was given his name to honor a very dear neighbor and friend, Fannie McLane (BYU teacher for years); Louise carries the name of a school companion and life-time friend, Alice Louise Reynolds; Joseph Cadawallder carries the appelation of his maternal grandfather; Albert and Richard both are given the Davis association. A person's name meant more than a symbol of recognition. John C. went deep: who are your parents; where were they born; what are they doing for society, their families, and the Church? A name of a friend soon had a biography in John's memory. Each individual stood on his own, though John C. used family traits as character indicators.

Never blessed with too much of this world's goods he provided adequately, shared intimately with a very loyal, talented companion and wife, saw honorable growth in each of his children and early became one of Utah's great teachers and educators, a venerable, beloved member of the Sons of Brigham.

ALBERT M. TALMAGE

Born: October, 1867   **Place:** Hungerford, Berkshire, England

Father: James Joyce Talmage, Born June 2, 1840, son of James E. Talmage and Mary Joyce. Emigrated to U.S. in 1876. Well-to-do physician. Practitioner of Medicine, made quarantine physician in Provo with small pox epidemic in 1877—served without or with pay. d. October 31, 1908, buried in family plot, Provo Cemetery.

Mother: Susannah Preater, (See James E. Talmage Biography)

Brothers and Sisters: Patience (d. about 2 yrs of age); James Edward, Martha Maud, Alice, Sara, Susa, Mary, Polly, Albert, John, George.

Marriage: Sarah Whalen, b. May 17, 1862 in New York City, New York. Educated in New York City and Rochester, New York; taught at Batavia in school for the blind; to Utah in 1905 to teach in Ogden; December 21, 1905, married Albert M. Talmage; 1906 to Provo, taught at school for feeble minded part time; Secretary to Society in Aid to Sightless, and L.D.S. institution; helped husband print "Messenger for the Sightless" for 20 years; received B.A. from B.Y.U. in 1912; prominent in Relief Society and M.I.A.; honorary member of Child Culture Club in Ogden; member of Sorosis of Provo; gave her life in helping the poor and needy; had no children; survived by husband and two nieces. d. December 23, 1932.

Death: Tuesday, January 11, 1955 at family home—345 East 4th North, Provo.

Previous to his sixth birthday, Albert Talmage was hammering some spikes, when one flew up and split his left eyeball. Treatment was given in a London hospital; the eye had to be removed, however. In 1876 he was still being treated when the family decided to go to Utah. He could distinguish between daylight and darkness until he was twenty. At nine he arrived in Provo. There were no schools for the blind in Utah. Accordingly, fifteen to twenty books were obtained from the East to obtain Line Letter, and he taught himself to read and helped about the house. In 1889 he was taken East to a specialist, after an operation could not aid him in distinguishing darkness from light. In 1897 he entered the School for the Blind, in Ogden, shortly after its opening. There he met Sarah Whalen, who had come from the East to teach at the school and later they were married.

He subsequently came to Brigham Young University for schooling, learning Braille and New York Point. He also learned how to make hammock, became expert in reed weaving, basket weaving, and chair covering, and became a proficient typist.

He was the first to use raised checker boards for the blind in Utah, a game in which he excelled. Would-be champions came to him from all over the country only to taste defeat. He designed and made a complete set of chess men for the use of the blind, up to 1908 the only one of its kind in the West.

After two years at Brigham Young University, he returned to Ogden to teach the blind for three years. By 1903 the need for literature for the blind was acute.

President David O. McKay of Weber Stake Academy gave him permission to set up a printing press in the Academy for which he laboriously collected $700.00. David Eccles gave $100.00; Brother Eccles' father was blind.

In 1904 an organization was set up for the blind, under State laws, called "The Society for the Aid of the Sightless," with four officers and three board members. Albert printed Sunday School lessons, his brother's *Articles of Faith*, missionary tracts, memory gems, and other Church work in Braille, using a hand press with a long lever. He set out to print the Book of Mormon as well. His wife would read to him as he cut Braille characters on the plates. He completed Nephi I and Nephi II when the Braille system was changed. This stopped Albert's work on the Book of Mormon, temporarily. In 1906, his mother died. Albert and his wife moved to the family home to care for Father Talmage.

Albert became concerned with the idea of publishing a monthly magazine for the blind, an adjunct for the "Society for the Aid of the Sightless." The first "The Messenger to the Sightless" was printed in

1912, with twenty-five copies containing current news. He never missed issuing a scheduled copy. He often stayed up all night so that the magazine might go out on time. There were three hundred copies by May 1931, with copies even going to foreign countries like China, Egypt, Turkey, and to nearly every state in the Union. He retired from this post in 1933.

The alphabet in Braille was finally determined, the international; this aided older readers in long spelling.

Albert invented a motor drive to run the press. This enabled it to be stopped immediately. All Braille characters were made on tough manilla paper which had to be dampened to print. It took three days to prepare the paper and six days after to dry it properly. After that Albert collected, stapled, and mailed the copies.

In 1928 Albert received his A. B. from Brigham Young University. When he came up to the stand for his diploma, the congregation applauded thunderously for both him and his devoted wife who stood proudly at his arm. They traveled through the state, encouraging the blind and teaching them in their own homes. He organized small societies in Salt Lake City to give companionship, which became the "Western Association of the Blind." These home groups were established throughout the state.

Albert kept a garden and chickens and fixed all repairs needed in the house. He had a hot bed for special plants which operated automatically to regulate the temperature of the plants so that they were ready to transplant in three weeks. By feeling leaves, he knew all his plants. He commented once, "It's easy to weed a garden."

After his wife's death, his sister came to live with him.

When he and his wife were away helping blind adults in various Utah homes, he fed his chickens with an attached feed bag and an alarm clock. When the bell rang, the feed fell out and the chickens were fed. His neighbors needed to give little attention to his lot or the chickens, except to help with a watering turn.

Albert M. Talmage was most modest and patient. He recognized hundreds of people by their voices and remembered many the second time. When he first met me, "Yes, I know you Brother Pardoe, I heard you in church." His handshake was hearty and his conversation alive with current thought and when appropriate, selective quotes from great poetry. He read no trivial matter as most Braille was then in the language and literature of highest levels. He knew the scriptures, all sixty-six books.

Sarah Whalen, a smiling matron with a brilliant mind, came from New York State School for the Blind. The School for the Blind in Ogden opened September 30, 1896, with her in charge. She taught Braille, basketry, musical instruments and managed this alone up to 1900, when Albert was hired to help her until 1904 in this work. In

June, 1904, Sarah Whalen and Albert Talmage were released as teachers. The "Society for the Aid of the Sightless" was organized by State law. James E. Talmage, Albert's brother, was appointed President. George Albert Smith was the vice-president; Sarah Whalen was Secretary, a position she held until her death; George M. Cannon was the Treasurer; Albert M. Talmage was the Manager. The Board of Directors included Nephi L. Morris, Thomas Hull, and Edward H. Anderson, who had the sight of but one eye.

A printing press was set up at Weber Stake Academy. In 1906 Albert moved to Provo, taking the machinery with them for printing Braille. This became the center for the blind for more than thirty years. The Talmages traveled the state to help the blind.

When James E. Talmage died, George Albert Smith became President of the Society.

By 1936 there were 800 blind in Utah; 500 blind in Idaho; 500 blind in Nevada and Arizona.

The history of the blind in Utah must be written around and with Albert M. and Sarah Whalen Talmage as founders and great benefactors. They were noble souls in a noble cause.

JAMES EDWARD TALMAGE

Born: September 21, 1862 **Place:** "Bell Hotel", Hungerford, Berkshire, England
Spent his first twelve years here; Eldest male, second child of eleven in third generation of church membership. Lived with Grandfather, whose name he bore. They were very close to each other until he died. James was with him when he died.

Father: James Joyce Talmage, b. June 2, 1840. Emigrated to United States in 1876; son of James E. Talmage and Mary Joyce. Practitioner of Medicine, made quarantine physician in Provo with small pox epidemic in 1877. Served with or without pay.

Mother: Susanna Preator. b. July 12, 1836 in Lambourne, Berkshire, England. Daughter of George and Sarah Marten Preator. Baptized in May 1848. m. August 14, 1859; to Utah with family in 1876; well read and very modest, with sound judgment.
d. June 2, 1906, when James E. was away not knowing of her death; Susy was at Columbia University in New York City, and George on Mission to New Zealand.

Brothers and Sisters: Patience (died about 2 years of age); James Edward, Martha Maud, Alice, Sara, Susa, Mary, Polly, Albert, John, George.

Marriage: Mary May Booth, Alpine, Utah on June 14, 1888. b. September 29, 1868 at Alpine, daughter of Richard Thornton Booth and Elsie Page, youngest of ten children. Marriage ceremony by Daniel H. Wells in Manti Temple. Tutored by parents, graduated from B. Y. U., where she met James E. as teacher. Taught school at Kaysville one year. Two years editor of **Young Ladies Journal**, charter member of Author's Club, in Salt Lake City. In 1893, delegate to World Congress of Women in Chicago; On Territorial Board of Woman's Suffrage Association; Vice-President of first free Kindergarten Association of Utah. Spent last year helping Albert with his Magazine for the blind.

Children: Sterling Booth, Honor geology student at Harvard University; Paul B. (dec.); Zella (dec.); Elsie T. Brandley, well known editor and writer (dec.); James Karl; Lucille

T. Carlisle; Helen May Perry, author of "All Faces West" of Ogden fame; John Russell, assistant to Governor George Dewey Clyde.

Death: July 27, 1933 at 71, in Salt Lake City, Utah

James E. Talmage was a short man of great dynamic power with black eyes that saw much and often held an audience spellbound. Although he was considered serious, a smile easily flitted across his face and revealed a kindly, interested nature. His handshake was a matter of acceptance rather than of his initial proffering. In any group he readily became the center of attention as most questions and comments were directed to him. Although his knowledge was unusually broad he gave reply to questions only when he had positive information or had an answer based on truth. Trivial subject matter did not last long in his presence.

He was an inspiring teacher with the ability of clarifying intellectual stumbling blocks; he used apt illustrations to match a student's experience and convinced him the subject was within his comprehension. As one of his better students said, "You don't go to his class unprepared; you feel ashamed."

He had a keen wit, a ready play on words, but never embarrassed a person with his tongue. Your acquaintance with him convinced you that he lived more on a spiritual level than the intellectual in which he seemed to excel. As he talked with well ordered facts you sensed he was impressing with a sincere testimony. He was best when he had time to unfold a subject, and he was one of this generation's greatest orators. He was so sincere in voice and delivery that most of his oratory was raised to the power of a sermon.

His talented blind brother, Albert, became a challenge to him to use all his senses to their greatest capacity. Albert was so pleasant, patient, creative and adaptive that he was an inspiration to his learned brother. He was president for many years of "The Society for Aid of the Sightless" and active in building the Utah Historical Society.

Dr. Talmage was equally skilled in writing and speaking. The best of his books is an inspiring one; several have remained as "best sellers" over the years. *The Articles of Faith*, *The Story of Mormonism*, and *Jesus the Christ* have been translated into many languages and have been used by ministers not of his faith. Each was the result of years of preparation and personal research. He traveled from Nazareth to Bethlehem better to understand the land, weather, topography, distances, locations of tradition, and points of controversy before he wrote *Jesus the Christ*, doing most of the writing in a special room of the Salt Lake Temple. Thorough preparation and sincerity of purpose motivated his every major effort.

"Sunday Night Talks By Radio" in the early days of K.S.L. enticed many to remain at home to hear the nine o'clock religious broadcasts without benefit of television, and gave James E. Talmage the satisfaction of reaching thousands as the increase of personal mail proved his talks' popularity. A knee injury he received while in the European mission steadily became more painful and caused him to remain close to home. It was during the preparation of one of these radio talks that he became ill while working at his desk. Within three days he was a victim of myocarditis. His death attracted national and international attention. Eulogies came from across the nation extolling his scholarship, speaking and writing abilities, the warmth of his personal charm and the high spiritual level of his personal life.

Elder Melvin J. Ballard said of him, "In this ministry he produced more volumes that shall be read until the end of time, because that which he has written is so clear and so impressive that it shall ever be among the cherished treasures of those who love the works of God. Yet these contributions he gave freely to the church, without any earthly reward."

James E. Talmage is one of the great Sons of Brigham.

So much has been written of Dr. Talmage that I shall give but an outline of his productive life.

Education:

1874	Oxford, England, diocesan prize scholar—had rigorous discipline with long hours June 1876, arrived in Salt Lake City with his parents who came to Provo
1876-1882	Started at Brigham Young Academy, as student of Karl G. Maeser, in August of 1876. Became secretary to faculty and academy librarian. Completed course at seventeen years of age, graduating from Normal Department in 1879, first in his class.
1881	Graduated June 17th from College Department at B.Y.A. He spent summers with Karl G. Maeser in studying and organizing schools.
1880-1882	Instructor of Science at B.Y.A.
1882-1883	student at Lehigh University, where he received his B.S., in 1891.
1883-1884	D. Sc. and Didactics Honor. (John Hopkins A. Honor).
1884-1888	Professor of Chemistry and geology at B.Y.A. Assistant to Principal Maeser and member of the Board of Trus-

tees. He went to B.Y.A. the year fire destroyed its only building. He had to devise ways to teach chemistry and geology with little or no equipment, and for very uncertain remuneration.

1888-1894	President of L.D.S. College in Salt Lake City.
1889	L.D.S. Genealogical Board of Education
	Also in 1889 he was offered Doctorate of Philosophy by the University of Chicago—but he declined.
1891	In charge of Deseret Museum
1891	Visited his birth town, in England; found it unchanged. Caught five fine perch in the canal. Called at the National School where he had received so many thrashings. Same old teacher, Mr. Newhook, who took him around the school and told of his American successes.
1894-1897	President and Professor of Geology at University of Utah.
1896	Ph.D. at Illinois Wesleyan University
	His Thesis: "The Past and Present of Great Salt Lake"
1897-1907	Resigned presidency but retained professorship at University of Utah
1907-1911	Consulting Mining Geologist
1912	D. Sc. (Honor) from Lehigh University and was Commencement Speaker. Assistant night watchman to laboratories.
1922	L.L.D. (Honor at Y) at Brigham Young University and the University of Utah
1924	He had a part of Deseret Museum transferred to Brigham Young University. He visited Europe six times. Member—Board of Directors American Association of Museums. Member—National Education Association.
Church:	
1873	Baptized, in England
1874	Ordained a Deacon
1877	Ordained a Teacher
1880	Ordained an Elder
1884	High Councilman in Utah Stake
	Counselor in Sunday School
1911	December 7, ordained an Apostle at 49 by President Joseph F. Smith and made a member of the Twelve; thereafter, he assisted most Stakes and missions of the Church
1924-1928	President of the European Mission, following David O. McKay; was a world renowned scientist
	Reopened Armenian Mission; moved from Aleppo to

Haifa; in (Palestine) made study of the Holy Land in preparation for his book, *Jesus the Christ.*

He traveled in Egypt, Greece, and Russia. From this date, he worked exclusively for the Church, as Church-man and scientist, he literally traversed the world

Occupational Activity and Honors:

1884	Director of Scientific Departments for Brigham Young Academy and Assistant to Karl G. Maeser
	Provo City councilman and Justice of the Peace
	Applied for and received American Citizenship
1888	Principal of Brigham Young Academy when Karl G. Maeser was made Superintendent of Church Schools
	Had outlined catalog material for school year when called to be Superintendent of Salt Lake Stake and later L.D.S. College and University.
1889	President of L.D.S. College
1891	In charge of Deseret Museum
1892	Released from L.D.S. College to labor with Captain (later General) Willard Young to establish a Church University, which was opposed by university and state authorities.
1894	Plans suspended to cooperate with Utah University. The Church, through the Salt Lake Literary and Scientific Association, gave Utah University $60,000 to carry on and remain in Salt Lake (not to be moved to Logan)
	In April he was elected President of University of Utah and Deseret, Professor of Geology
1897	Released from presidency to put full time on Geology
1891	Fellow in Microscopic Society of London
1894	Fellow in Royal Society of Edinburgh
1894	Fellow in Geological Society of London
1897	Fellow in Geological Society of America (each for life)
	Life member of the Victoria Institute of Philosophical Society of Great Britain.
	Life member in American Association for Advancement of Science
	Life member to Royal Scottish Geographical Society, At St. Petersburg, as delegate for the Royal Society of Edinburgh. He went over Urals to Siberia and returned by Crimea
1911	An Apostle in the L.D.S. Church

Authorship and Major Works:

The First Book of Nature, 1888; *Domestic Science,* 1891; *Table for Blowpipe Determinations of Materials,* 1899;

213

The Articles of Faith, 1899; *The Great Salt Lake; Present and Past,* 1900; *The Story of Mormonism,* 1907; *The Great Apostacy,* 1909; *The House of the Lord,* 1912; *The Philosophical Basis of Mormonism,* 1914; *The Vitality of Mormonism,* 1914; *Jesus the Christ,* 1915.

Radio talks over KSL; first radio broadcasts for the L.D.S. Church. "Sunday Night Talks"; he gave his last talk four nights before his death.

He is written up in "Who's Who in America" 1930-1931; "Pioneers and Prominent Men of Utah" 1913, by Frank Eshom; "American Men of Science" Third Edition, 1921; "L.D.S. Millennial Star" July 28, 1932 and August, 1933; "Improvement Era" September, 1933, by Melvin J. Ballard; "Life and Educational Contributions of James Edward Talmage", by Grant L. Wilson, 1958, University of Utah Master's Thesis; "The Improvement Era", November 1962.

One of the greatest scholars to come from Mormon culture.

THOMAS NICHOLLS TAYLOR

Born: July 28, 1868

Place: Provo, Utah

Father: George Taylor
Born March 25, 1838, in Birmingham, England, the son of Thomas Taylor and Anna Hill. Moved to Utah in October, 1863, walked most of the way, John W. Wooley Company. Member of Provo City Council; founded Taylor Bros. Company; director of Provo Commercial Savings Bank.

Mother: Eliza Nichols
Married July 4, 1857 at Birmingham, England, the daughter of Thomas Ashford Nicholls and Harriet Ball. Came to Utah with husband. (George married Henrietta Sawyer in 1865 and separated from Eliza in 1889).
First home was an adobe on First North between 6th and 7th West, then near the center of town.

Brothers and Sisters: Hattie C. McClellan; Emma; Parley G.; George; William; Thomas N; Arthur N.; Walter G.; Ashted.

Marriage: Maud Rogers
Born June 29, 1872 the daughter of Isaac Rogers and Eunice Stewart. Married on September 18, 1889, in the Manti Temple.

Children: Thomas Sterling Taylor; Ethel T. (Mrs. Harvey) Sessions; Lester R. (dec.); Vesta (died at ten); Alden R. (dec.); Marion R. (dec.); Victor R; Mary Maud (Mrs. Merrili) Clayson; Delenna T. (Mrs. Rex) Taylor.

Death: October 24, 1950

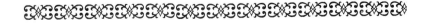

Thomas N. Taylor went to the Franklin School on 2nd South and 1st West under principalship of Anna Larson, L.A. Wilson, and George H. Brimhall. He started work in his father's store when ten years of age, September, 1878. His grandfather Taylor started a small furniture store with a photography gallery on the former site of Taylor's Inc. Young Tom had to deliver furniture on foot, often six chairs to a load. When Zina Young Williams, daughter of Brigham Young, came to teach at BYU, she had two sons, Sterling and Thomas, who became intimate pals of young Tom. When he went to BYU in Lewis Block on Center Street, one of his teachers was Aunt Zina, the late Zina Young Card. Tom was in the group which went to the impoverished school in the ZCMI warehouse at the south end of Academy (University) Avenue, taking an arithmetic class under Karl G. Maeser. He had to quit school in 1885, getting as far as our present day 8th grade when he was seventeen.

At seventeen he went into business for himself, with Julius Jensen, opening the first exclusive jewelry shop in Utah County—kept stock in a room of the Taylor Furniture Co. and sold goods from catalogues. When the father and mother separated, the furniture business was transferred to Eliza and son George. The father George kept the photo shop. In 1890, Thomas N. was made manager of Taylor Brothers Co. with Eliza Nichols Taylor, president; son George, Vice-President; John D. Dixon, Secretary-Treasurer; Thomas N., manager; and Arthur N., a director. The firm erected the county's largest building and was the biggest retail store south of Salt Lake City. T.N.T. was manager from 1890 to 1950.

His religious and business careers paralleled. For six years he was president of the YMMIA, nine years counselor to two different bishops, nineteen years as a bishop, twenty years as president of Utah L.D.S. Stake (1919-1939), twenty years as vice president and chairman of executive committee of board of trustees of B.Y.U. He was ordained a bishop by Apostle Reed Smoot and a High Priest by Francis M. Lyman. Nine ward chapels were erected while he was president of the stake.

His aggressive manner and positive thinking did not get him enough votes to win elections as he was nominated for city treasurer and city councilman and lost, the same for state senator and governor. He was elected mayor of Provo for two terms (1900-1904). The mayor was almost a figurehead as he had 10 councilmen; he did not have veto power and made city appointments. In 1900 he had erected the light poles in the middle of 5-rod streets and built a fence around the baseball park on "West Square", now known as Pioneer Park. Had a real fight to determine the location of the Union Depot, with location finally put on 3rd West. On July 12, 1901, Main Street was called Academy Avenue. In this year, street numbers were placed on Provo houses and the city purchased a right of way to construct a road to Utah Lake for $1,000. In 1902 a franchise for a street car system was granted to run up Center to University Avenue and to Utah Lake. Land was bought to add to City Cemetery. He favored public ownership of utilities and attempted to get the city to buy Telluride Power Plant in Provo Canyon. His council consisted of three Democrats and seven Republicans and government ownership was not a popular issue. In 1902 he ordered vaccinations for all public schools and was burned in effigy. He was a champion of William Jennings Bryan and introduced him in the Provo Tabernacle to give his "Prince of Peace" lecture. He was an ardent champion of Franklin D. Roosevelt and became a warm friend. He stumped for prohibition.

The Taylor Brothers, Thomas N. and Arthur, dissolved partnership and Arthur organized Dixon, Taylor, Russell with his boys as officers and directors. In 1906 T.N.T. fostered the Provo Building and Loan Society, officers to get no pay and subsequently built over 400 homes in Provo. Taylor Brothers had expanded with stores in Provo, Eureka, American and Spanish Fork. In 1906, Farmers and Merchants Bank was organized and crashed in the depression of 1932. A bank run was its undoing and loans to county farmers could not be collected but depositers were paid, the stockholders absorbed the loss.

T.N.T., as most people called him, was an original director of the Beneficial Life Insurance Company and served until 1928. He served as the director of the Home Fire Insurance Company of Utah until his death. President Heber J. Grant, president of both of these companies, was an intimate friend and frequent home visitor. T.N. was a director of the Provo Woolen Mills and the Mapleton Sugar Company, losing in both ventures. His 52 acre farm and orchard of Provo Bench was his best paying venture.

The Provo Chamber of Commerce honored him with a community testimonial at which he was eulogized by leading men of the community and state.

He was a devoted friend of BYU, a frequent visitor and Alumni president in 1912-13; he was a committee member to finish paying for the Maeser Building on the hill campus. One of the Helaman Halls bears his name. He spear-headed many financial drives to aid the fast-growing university and worked hand-in-hand with President F. S. Harris when he was chosen to lead the school. He was given the BYU Alumni Assn. Distinguished Service Award in 1948.

He loved good music, was a patron of the arts, an enthusiastic BYU sports follower, played a little tennis and more morning golf, aided many students with jobs and money. He sought new scenic sites in our mountains and travelled twice to Europe, once with his mother and daughter Ethel, and in 1913 with Dr. Horace G. and Merle Merrill; back on the Lusitania with son Sterling who joined them in Naples.

He served a useful, active life, often stormy and exciting, but mostly a happy successful citizen in a land he cherished and near a school he loved.

SAMUEL R. THURMAN

Born: May 6, 1850 in Larke County, Louisville, Kentucky.
Educated in the public schools of Kentucky, a student of
Locust Grove, Kentucky high school and in Sonora Acad-
emy
Came to Utah in 1870
Twelve years of age when Civil War soldiers marched
past his home

Father: William Thomas Thurman
b. March 1819, Washington County, Kentucky
Son of George, b. in Virginia 1787, and Nancy Musgrove
d. July 15, 1851 during infancy of Samuel R.
Discussed the Revolution and Civil War with his wife
who retold such stories to Samuel R.
Richard Thurman, direct ancestor, was soldier in the
American Revolution and with men who met Lafayette
on his arrival in America on Oct. 24, 1824

Mother: Mary Margaret Brown, b. August 10, 1825.
d. February 3, 1915
Descendant of John Yates, captain in the American
Army of the Revolution and Christina Yates, b. 1794 in
Virginia.
Her Father arrived in Utah with the Pueblo Detachment
of the Mormon Battalion
Her Mother to Nauvoo in 1844, m. 1842.

Brothers
and Sisters: George Wm., b. August 11, 1843
Mary, b. August 11, 1845
David John, b. August 11, 1847
(Samuel Richard—b. May 6, 1850)

Marriage: Isabella Karen of Lehi, Utah, May 6, 1872
dau. of Thomas and Ann Ratcliff of Liverpool, England
Pioneers of July 24, 1847 Brigham Young Co.

Children: Richard B., m. Eliz. Clayton
Mabel T., m. Moses C. Davis
Margaret, m. Dr. Ray Irvine
Lydia m., C. W. Reed
Wm., m. Pearl Taft
Samuel D., m. Henrietta Young
Victor E., m. Vaughn Christiansen
Allen G.
Death: July 12, 1941 in Salt Lake City

219

Samuel R. Thurman was one of Utah's most distinguished jurists and irrigation Lawyers.

His early schooling was in Kentucky where he heard his mother and relatives tell of the family relations to American Revolutionary conflicts and struggle for freedom. He knew, from personal experience, the tragedies of the Civil War. He never knew the guiding hand of a father and followed the teachings of a cultured mother, whose ancestors also served in the American Revolutionary Army. Her parents had accepted the Gospel and went to Nauvoo.

At twenty Samuel R. came to Salt Lake City with his mother. At a very young age he planned on being a lawyer and studied the subject at every opportunity. Arriving in Lehi, it did not take long for him to court and win Isabella Karen, a daughter of English converts who were July 24, 1847 pioneers. Young Sam was a religious man, ardent in promoting and maintaining individual rights. Constitutional law became a passion and an expense as he bought every book that gave him a new concept or stimulation. Eight children came amidst his young career and difficult times.

He studied at the University of Deseret and the BYA and taught school for eight years, principally at Lehi. He passed the Utah Bar in 1878 and was admitted to the District Court of Utah. With this background, he went to the University of Michigan and graduated in law in 1880. Returning to Utah he formed a partnership with David Evans until 1886, when he joined with George Sutherland (ardent Republican as Thurman was a Democrat) and they later invited Wm. H. King to partnership making one of Utah's strongest law firms. This lasted until 1890 when a youthful urge was consummated and Samuel R. went on an L.D.S. Mission to England

Returning to Provo in 1892, Thurman and Sutherland again formed a partnership until 1893 when the firm, became Thurman and Wedgwood who invited Senator Joseph L. Rawlins and J. H. Hurd. This firm represented the major water companies in the many litigations of the young and growing state. Genl. Wedgewood withdrew to go to the Philippines for the Spanish American War. Joined again by the General in 1902, they moved to Salt Lake City in 1906 and A. B. Irvine became a member of their firm, majoring in water rights and irrigation law.

Samuel R. was chief assistant in the legal department of the D.R.G.R.R. Co.—1893-1912.

1893-1896 he was a presidential appointment as Assistant U.S. Attorney for the Territory of Utah and was a member of the Constitutional Convention for the new state.

He was elected to the Utah Legislature five consecutive terms, 1882-1890 and chairman of the Democratic State Central Committee from 1912-1916.

In March of 1917, he was appointed a justice of the Supreme Court of Utah by Governor Simon Bamberger.

Although he was a member of the People's Party, he urged the substitution of the Democratic Party for the Peoples Party and the breakdown of the bitter religious factions.

Politics, the law and the church were the absorbing interests of his life, almost in that order. He had a great fund of stories which he used with expert ability in his speeches and won many arguments with apt illustrations. He loved a joke and told it well. He knew the power of laughter and its punitive values. Records reveal that Samuel R. was an ardent protagonist for woman suffrage.

With his interest and expansive knowledge of water rights, he was most influential in determining the pattern for farming in the west.

Because of his interest in the Constitution of the United States and its importance to the country's future, he accepted many speaking engagements at patriotic meetings and political rallys. He took his talented daughter Maybelle, who caught the spirit of his enthusiasm with him. To her we are indebted for two great monuments. She was the driving force and organizing chairman for the Mormon Battalion Monument by the Capitol in Salt Lake City and the magnificent Fort Moore Pioneer Memorial in the Civic Center in Los Angeles, California, to commemorate the raising of the flag of the U.S. on Fort Moore Hill, July 4, 1847, in which the U.S. First Dragoons, the N.Y. Volunteers and the Mormon Battalion participated. In these two monuments, a devoted daughter paid tribute to the great pioneers of the west and to her beloved mother and father.

Honoring the pioneers, teaching the principles of liberty and freedom expressed in the Constitution, the harmonizing of differences between the religious factions of the state filled the later years of Samuel R. Thurman's life. He was active to the final days of his ninety-one years.

GUY CARLTON WILSON

Born: April 10, 1864 in Fairview, Utah

Father: Lycurgus Wilson, b. February 17, 1828 in Richland County, Ohio. Son of Guy C. Wilson, b. 1805 in New York and Elizabeth Hunter, both of Richland County, Ohio. To Utah June 27, 1851, Benjamin Halladay Company. Postmaster at Fairview thirteen years, Justice of Peace 1872-74 and 1876-78. Veteran of Indian Wars.
d. March 8, 1911.

Mother: Lois Ann Stevens, b. December 15, 1835, daughter of Arnold Stevens and Lois Coon of Ontario, Canada., m. December 29, 1849 at fifteen. At fifteen she cooked for caravan freighters. Her father a member of Mormon Battalion Co. "D".
d. at Pueblo, Colorado, 1846.

Brothers and Sisters: Lycurgus Arnold, b. November 7, 1856, m. Alice Tucker; Lois Elizabeth, b. March 1, 1859, d. young; Ellen Adelia, b. October 11, 1861, m. Phillip H. Hurst; Guy C.; Justin, b. September 19, 1866, d. young; Mary Mehitable, b. May 14, 1869; Viola, b. November 27, 1871, m. Andrew Peterson; Lucy Arabella, b. October 23, 1874, m. Thos. Anderson.

Marriage: Elizabeth Hartsburg, b. October 8, 1864 in Stockholm, Sweden
Agnes Melisda Stevens, b. September 2, 1883 in Fruitland, New Mexico, d. March 21, 1965.
Anna Ivins, daughter of Anthony C. Ivins and Elizabeth Snow, b. October 20, 1882.

Children of Agnes Melissa: Elizabeth, b. December 13, 1902, m. John Leslie Reynolds, (d. November 1933), m. Gordon Sears; Guy C. Junior, b. January 3, 1905, m. Constance Quayle Cannon; David Stevens, b. June 20, 1907 m. Salonie Atwood, d. January 19, 1947; Owen Meredith, b. September 21, 1909, m. Marian Wilson, (no relation); Mabel, b. November 5, 1912, m. Oakley S. Evans; Woodrow Stevens, b. August 21, 1915, m. Orlene Boyden.

Death: January 26, 1942 in Provo at 77.

Guy C. Wilson was the fourth child in a family of eight, the son of valiant pioneers. His youth was spent in Fairview, Utah, where his father was postmaster, justice of the peace, a veteran of Indian Wars, and a successful farmer. His mother was deprived of a father's guidance when he died in an epidemic which struck many members of the Mormon Battalion at Pueblo, Colorado in 1846. The young girl helped her mother cook for freighters of the caravan.

Guy C. had a grandfather of the same name—the family frame was in the mold of tall, muscular men. Grandson Guy C. could wield the axe with any of his neighbors in a day when felling of trees and grubbing of sage brush was a necessity. On canyon trips young Guy would take works of the Church and read by flickering firelight until sleep demanded recognition.

He attended BY Academy, came directly under Karl G. Maeser and soon caught the urge to go on a mission which he filled in the Southern States from 1886 to 1888. His profession had been chosen before he went on his mission (which he filled mainly with no funds). He taught school at Fairview from 1885 to 1895, except for his mission sojourn. In 1896-97 he was a student instructor at BY Academy on a salary "too small to mention" taking the degree B.Pd. in 1900. Under martial law and duress many Mormons had gone to Northern Mexico and had established colonies needing trained educators for their children. Guy C. was chosen Principal of Juarez Academy in 1897 and also made supervisor of the Church School System, a position which he kept from 1897 to 1912, travelling thousands of miles to set up new schools for the Church while leading the Mexican School to a first class academy. He was a counselor to Anthony W. Ivins in the Juarez Stake presidency.

Guy C. Wilson lived in the colonies in the hectic times of the Mexican Rebellion. With Junius Romney they met Porferio Diaz and President Taft at the U.S.-Mexican border and plead their cause and loyalty. The resolution under Francisco Madero in 1910 had all Mexico in a turmoil and "Yankee, go home" had one of its first and most vicious enactions. The Mormon Colonies fought for their very lives, the "trial" lasting some ten years. When the Mormons finally achieved a meeting with Salazar, the rebel chief, the ultimate action had been decided. Our Church leaders had no other alternative than to ship out 2,500 women and children to the U.S., leaving everything they owned in the world. Only the able bodied men were left to salvage anything they could at the risk of nightly raids. Professor Wilson, with few other men, led their people in all manner of conveyance and on foot, to El Paso, Texas, there to be scattered over the Western states. Many sons and daughters whose parents had walked the pitiless plains from Nauvoo to the Rockies relived the hardships of a few generations ago. The patient, wise, and kind leadership of men like Guy C. Wilson buoyed a people sickened at heart for the trials they met because of their religion. Many had conquered Utah wilderness by back breaking toil and now "we begin all over again." Professor Wilson urged patience in trying to get the Mexican viewpoint of national sovereignty.

High schools were being established throughout Utah and the Church could not afford to parallel a school system to compete with the State, nor did they desire to. After months of deliberation, they established a seminary near the Granite High School in South Salt Lake and Guy C. Wilson was appointed its first director. He set the pattern for the Church and its subsequent growth, starting in 1913.

His fame as a teacher had grown so that he was known over the West and sought as a teacher and panel leader in education. His membership on the General Board of Religion Classes added to his travel responsibilities. As a speaker, he used a deliberate logical style rich with homely examples. He taught by precept, and few men lived the teachings of the gospel more than he. He kept close to the Church authorities who used him in many assignments. He believed in the separation of Church and State, although he also contended that religious principles should abet the conduct of the State. He was in the center of the conflict when Utah the State was taking over the reigns of the Church-dominated territory of Deseret. Understanding this, we get a better picture of such loyal leaders as Guy C. Wilson, who lived his American heritage as well as his Church affiliations.

In 1930 Professor Wilson moved to Provo with his growing family and became Professor of Religious Education under President Harris at B.Y.U., being department head until 1939. In 1941 he was made Professor Emeritus with a teaching career of fifty-six years. He had studied at University of Chicago in 1902 and Columbia University in 1912-13. His position as educator in Utah kept him too confined to duty to permit further degree studies. President F. S. Harris summed up a universal opinion: "In the passing of Professor Guy Carlson, BYU loses one of its best teachers and the Church one of its most valiant defenders. He was blessed by nature with the qualities that make up a great teacher and throughout his life he has used his talents for the instruction and inspiration of the thousands of students who have come under his tuition."

His funeral was held in the spacious Joseph Smith Auditorium on the BYU campus to accommodate the numbers attending. Eulogies of the highest type of appreciation were given by President F. S. Harris, Bryant S. Hinckley, Junius Romney, Wm. H. Boyle, and Bishop Wilbur Sowards. His devoted and talented family was praised for its contribution to American life and for its attainments in the educational and business world. This great teacher was a noble Son of Brigham, a man of smiles and devoted service.

Men who studied with or under

Benjamin Cluff, Jr.

(1892-1903)

Benjamin Cluff Jr. (*Jan. 4, 1892—Dec. 23, 1903*)

GOVERNOR HENRY H. BLOOD

Born: October 1, 1872   **Place:** Kaysville, Utah

Father: William Blood, son of William Senior who died three weeks after his arrival in Utah. Left three small children for wife to support, William and two others. William, Jr., grew to manhood on farm.

Mother: Jane Wilkie Hooper, daughter of John Hooper and wife. Driven from Nauvoo, settled first in Council Bluffs, Iowa. A child of eight, arrived in Utah, with parents in October, 1849, one of family of 10 children. A leading lady in the Home Dramatic Company.

Brothers
and Sisters: Annie H. Phillip
             William H.
             Mrs. George W. Underwood
             Ernest C.
             Mrs. Clyde C. Burningham
             Mrs. Mary H. Linford
             Mrs. George E. Flint
             Mrs. John E. Hill
             Mrs. Nettie J. Munsell
             Mrs. Albert E. Smith
             Dr. Wilkie H.
             Heber C.

Marriage: Minnie Ann Barnes, June 4, 1896. Born the same day as Henry H., they were childhood sweethearts and baptized the same day. Daughter of John R. and Emily Stewart Barnes of Kaysville. A student at the University of Deseret. Eight years in Governor's Mansion d. January 27, 1947.

Children: Alan B.
             Dr. Russell Henry
             Hazel Elaine, m. David J. Ellison
             Evalyne, m. Robert B. Sims

Death: June 19, 1942, at 69

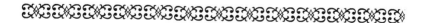

Henry H. Blood was an active boy in the growing farm community of Kaysville, Utah, working with family and merchandise work assignments. He was a graduate of the Kaysville High School and interested in athletics only as they did not interfere with his business, church, and studies. He was a student at Brigham Young Academy, class of 1897, taking business and religion subjects and working for the Kaysville Co-op until 1918. When twenty-one years of age he became interested in politics, casting his lot with the Democratic party.

Henry was treasurer of Davis County from 1898 to 1901 and was induced to teach business at the Brigham Young College in Logan, Utah, from 1903 through 1904. He was also a manager of the Kaysville Layton Milling Company. From 1911 through 1918 he was a member of the Davis County School Board and organizer of the Utah-Idaho Millers Grain Association in 1911. He received his first state political assignment when he was made Minutes Clerk for the Utah Senate. With this experience he definitely decided to enter politics whole-heartedly, as he had very positive ideas for governmental efficiency.

In 1917, Henry was appointed a member of the Public Utilities Commission of Utah and personally made a survey of Utah's water and power needs. With an insistent purpose he defined Utah's possibilities for a workable, arterial road system, looking toward government participation in road planning, building, interstate connections, and opening of the great areas of virgin territories. Where the car could not go in mountain passes or near the bays of lake waters, we saw Henry H. Blood on a spirited horse.

In 1922 he received his desired appointment as a member of the State Road Commission and become its chairman from 1925 through 1932, one of the state's greatest building periods.

With the Democratic landslide of 1932 and supporting Franklin D. Roosevelt, Henry H. Blood became Utah's seventh governor. He proved an excellent financier and was re-elected governor in 1936. During the depression he was given almost dictatorial authority to direct relief.

Under his guidance, the two percent sales tax passed into law and Utah's debt was reduced so that he could leave his office with the State holding a surplus. He was president of the Western Association of Highway officials from 1927 through 1933; in 1939 he was president of the American Association of State Highways. He also directed the Governor's Conference for the eleven western states. His financial advice was sought across the nation.

A partial list of his activities follow: Director of the Union State Bank at Bountiful, Clearfield State Bank, Kaysville Co-op, Mercantile Institution, Layton Sugar Company, Z.C.M.I. of Salt Lake, and President of the Kaysville Canning Company.

He filled an L.D.S. mission to England in 1901 through 1904 and was a bishop of the Kaysville Ward from 1907 through 1915. Later he was President of the California Mission.

The Book "Utah's Distinguished Personalities" published in 1933 was dedicated to Governor Blood. Not a large man, but erect with deep blue eyes and an engaging smile, he was one of Utah's most honored and beloved executives. At government receptions he and his gracious, queenly wife received all who came, not as loyal subjects but more as welcomed friends.

DAVID ALBERT BROADBENT

Attended B.Y.U. 1893-1897, graduating with honor. Resided most of mature life in Heber, Utah

Born: May 14, 1871   **Place:** Goshen, Utah

Father: Thomas Broadbent (son of James Wrigley and Nannie Broadbent of Oldham, England). December 29, 1833, Saddleworth, Yorkshire, England. Took his mother's name—came to Utah, September 1862. Sevier County Pioneer.
Black Hawk Indian war veteran—farmer and stockraiser d. December 14, 1901, Santaquin, Utah.

Mother: Mary Jane Nuttall
Born June 21, 1843. Daughter of Thomas Nuttall and Mary Standring of Rockdale, England
m. April 11, 1863 in Salt Lake, Utah

Brothers and Sisters: Mary Elizabeth, b. Feb. 26, 1864. m. George Gourley; m. Halbert Davis
George Heber, b. Dec. 14, 1865—died young
Annie Eliza, b. May 14, 1867—m. Lorenzo Huish
Joseph Franklin, b. May 1, 1869—m. Retta Passey
(David Albert b. May 14, 1871—m. Mima M. Murdock)
*Charles Nuttall, b. June 1873—m. Jennie Wood
Geneva Lavina, b. June 16, 1875—died
*Sylvester b. April 3, 1878—m. Josephine Murdock
*Serena, b. Nov. 4, 1880—m. Hiram Vance
Leo Moroni, b. May 7, 1883
Thomas Standring, b. August 5, 1885—m. Violet Long
*alive when David A. died.

Marriage: Mima M. Murdock b. November 26, 1879
daughter of Joseph R. Murdock and Margaret Wright of Charleston, Utah
m. May 1, 1901 in Manti Temple—Utah Mother of Year 1948 d. December 30, 1957

Children: 4 sons, 8 daughters—all children are graduates from college, 10 of the 12 attended BYU—The family has given 34 years in missionary service.
Joseph Grant, B. S. BYU
Vida B., m. Leland Wentz, BYU—MD U. of Chicago
Naomi B. Johnson, B.S. BYU (deceased)
Leah B., m. H. Wendell Jacob., B.S.—BYU

Margaret B., m. Chas. N. Merkley, B.S.—BYU. Head Home
Ec. Dept. Dixie College.
Dee A., M.S.—BYU U. of Illinois. Prof at U.S.U.
Mary B., m. Marten C. Astrig, B.S.—BYU
Mima B., m. Don L. Hicken., B.S.—BYU
Elmer E., BYU. B.S., USU
Harvey M., BYU, B.S.—U. of Minnesota
Sara M. B., m. Finn B. Paulson, B.S. U. of Utah
Helen B., m. Jens J. Jonssen—B.S. U. of Utah
(Family written up in Improvement Era, August 1946.)

Death: Died May 2, 1962 at the home of son, Dee A. Broadbent
in Logan, Utah at 90 years
Buried in Heber, Utah

David A. Broadbent stood erect whenever you met him. His
head was held as in military exactness with eyes that spoke with authority and kindness. He seemed never to hesitate in his actions but
went directly to his purpose. Eyes which burned with searching could
easily melt with smiling sympathy. He believed sincerely that life
was a series of serious moments and levity for relaxation should have
a healthy group participation. To know him was to trust him and
respect his judgment. His demeanor was that of a devoted teacher,
a leader who knew how to understand and point the way to character
growth. The transition from the home to the school room or the
pulpit was an easy one, as teaching was a life vocation. He appreciated
the teachers in his own school advancement and often quoted from
the early B.Y.U. instructors.

As soon as he finished his academic studies he accepted a two
year mission call to the Southern States and married the village
belle immediately after his return. A family of twelve followed to
enrich his life and prove his parental abilities. Four sons and eight
daughters proved to be one of the state's outstanding family groups
as each child achieved a college education, served his or her church
missions and wards, reared families and served their country with each
opportunity. Asked "What is a good measure of success," he quickly
replied, "A man's family." The obituarial tributes paid to both
Mima and David Broadbent were ample proof of their success as
parents, citizens and church leaders.

A brief of David A.'s life is shown herewith:

Education:

Early education in Provo schools, graduating from BYA in 1897
Did graduate work at B.Y.U. and U. of U.
Possessed a comprehensive library.
Much reading aloud was done in the family circle
David A. early selected school teaching as his profession and went immediately to Heber as a teacher, where he organized the first high school in Wasatch and Duchesne Counties, serving 37 years in the Wasatch schools.
1901-1923 as County Superintendent and from 1923-1937 as Wasatch Seminary teacher.
Was chief protagonist for consolidation of the Wasatch Schools
Served three years on the State Textbook Commission.
Religious Activities:
Southern States Mission 1898-1901
President of the Louisiana Conference when opposition was very bitter and meeting places denied the Elders
Bishopric Heber 2nd Ward
Pres. Wasatch Stake—8 years, when churches were built
North Central States Mission President 1937-40
Salt Lake Temple Presidency with Pres. Stephen L. Chipman and Mark Austin
Wilford Stake Patriarch at his death.
Civic:
President Wasatch County Chamber of Commerce 1916-1919
Promoted the scenic beauty of Heber Valley and urged a canning factory.
President County Farm Bureau 1915-1917
Chairman County Fair Board 1928-1931
District Chairman Boy Scout Court of Honor 1927-1934
Spent many hours in promoting and organizing scout troops
The David A. Broadbent Loan Fund at B.Y.U. was set up in his memory in June 1958.
Parent, educator, churchman and civic worker were terms used in the eulogies at the funeral of this 90 year old Son of Brigham. He is buried in the mountain valley he loved so much.

ALBERT H. CHRISTENSEN

Born: December 13, 1872
        (He used the "son" suffix in his later years.)

Father: (Lars) Lauritz Mathias Christian Christensen, Born July 22, 1847, Kobbera, Thisted, Denmark
Joined the Church and sailed to Utah May 16, 1866; his mother died enroute on the Atlantic Ocean and was buried at sea; his father a well-to-do farmer in Flaurrup, Denmark. d. November 10, 1928, at Manti, Utah; temple worker 20 years.

Mother: Else Cathrine Andersen
b. February 9, 1847 in Hvidberg, Thisted, Denmark
daughter of Anders Christian Christensen and Mette Kirstine Christensen Hvid; only one of her family to join the Church; a teacher in Denmark; became a midwife in Gunnison, one of the earliest midwives in Gunnison and its first official city physician.

Brothers and Sisters: Christian "I", b. Oct. 4, 1867, m. Caroline Larsen, d. Oct. 5, 1917.
Andrew B., b. June 6, 1869, m. Sarah Jane Bartholomew, d. Dec. 16, 1933.
Joseph, b. March 7, 1870, m. Roxie Ellen Bartholomew, d. July 23, 1926.
(Albert)
Elsie, a twin, b. March 8, 1875, m. Alma C. Bartholomew, d. June 28, 1964.
Mary, a twin, b. and d. March 8, 1875.
Emma Eliza, b. July 8, 1877, m. Charles Peterson, d. Sept. 4, 1927.
Louis D., b. March 20, 1880, m. Florence Mellor, d. Feb. 6, 1959.
Arthur Mariners, also a twin, b. July 19, 1882, m. Amelia Jane Gledhill d. Dec. 4, 1932.
Twin died same day of birth.
Elvena, b. March 27, 1887, m. George T. Clark; d. July 5, 1956.
Maren, m. Lars Myrop who converted the family.
All attended the Brigham Young Academy.

Marriage: 1. Ellen Virginia Snow, m. Sept. 26, 1900 in Manti Temple
       b. January 28, 1878 in Manti d. July 27, 1916.
       daughter of Joseph Smith Snow and Lucy VanBuren; many of her poems in Relief Society Magazine.
    2. Myrtle Farnsworth of Beaver, Utah, m. June 23, 1920 at

St. George, Utah Temple; nominated for "Mother of the Year" in 1957; teacher 14 years.

Children: (of Ellen)
Virginia, m. Daniel M. Keeler; Ellen Elaine, m. Edward W. Southwick; Albert Sherman, m. Lois Bowen; Everett Hale (dec); Phillip Van Buren, m. Gwen Johnson.
(of Myrtle)
Cullen Yates, m. Daryl Aldene Stewart; Mabel Norma, m. Reed J.; Webster E.; Kathryn, m. Albert C. Todd

Death: March 13, 1957, Provo, Utah
buried in Manti Cemetery

CRITICAL

Albert Christensen was one of Utah's most able lawyers and irrigation specialists. He spent his early boyhood in the environs of Gunnison, Utah, where he herded cattle, cut timber, and attended the local schools and was often employed as a rancher and sheepherder. He taught school at Koosharem, Utah in 1892-93.

In 1893, when a full grown young man, he registered at the Brigham Young Academy in Provo. At eighteen he carted food from home, lived with other young men under strict curfew, got better than average grades, and graduated in 1896. He worked a year as principal of the Levan School from 1896-97, and then went to the popular law school of the day, the University of Michigan at Ann Arbor, and received his L.L.B. in 1899.

With a diploma in his suit case, he looked over the hills from Gunnison to the larger town of Manti and there began his struggle and practice as barrister. He wed a pretty young girl with a beautiful voice, Ellen Virginia Snow, his companion for sixteen years. Her home was one of order, frequent family gatherings, and an ample cupboard. Family prayers were shared by all members of the family. Good books were bought and discussed with the parents. A home library grew by the week.

Albert H. passed the Utah Bar in 1899 and became a member of the Utah State Bar Association in the same year. His law practice began in 1900 in Manti, and the young lawyer threw himself into local politics as a Republican. He was appointed Deputy County Attorney of Sanpete County and two years later was elected Judge of the Seventh Judicial District Court of Utah and served two terms to 1917. Along with his Church and law activities he served as a member of the Manti City Library Board for many years and helped procure a Carnegie Grant. As a director of the Manti Commercial Club he became a prime promoter of many civic improvements and the protector of city water rights. He fought diligently for good roads into Sanpete valley and aided in getting right-of-way for the railroad to transport beets, sugar, livestock, rock salt and lime products. He owned the first garage service in Manti and helped to organize and became President of the first municipal telephone exchange South of Salt Lake City in Utah. The Judge moved to Provo in 1916 to take advantage of the University for his growing family, from which most of his children graduated with distinction. He began the practice of private law and formed some notable partnerships. In 1924 he became a partner with Arthur V. Watkins (later a US Senator), Hon. William S. Dunford (now deceased). Later, Milan B. Straw (deceased) was his partner and in 1933, his son, A. Sherman, became his partner and remained until 1954, when he was appointed to the Federal Judiciary. In 1945 the second son, Phillip, joined Christensen and Christensen, and in 1947, the youngest son, Cullen, also became a partner. A. H. Christensen resigned from the partnership in 1956.

The judge was a principal, both as judge and lawyer in some of Utah's famous water rights trials.

When he moved to Orem, Utah he became a member of the Alpine School Board and was active with his law partner, A. V. Watkins, in establishing "Scera," a community owned theatre, recreation and Church center, all net proceeds going to city recreation. Most of his life he was a member of the YMMIA Stake Board with a diversity of assignments. His hobbies were raising blooded horses and improving fruit culture.

He was fortunate in having two talented, devoted, and charming wives. The young family of the first wife, following her death, was given a mother's love and care by their foster mother in their formative and school years. At the death of the father and husband friends of the community, state, and the west praised him especially as being a capable, just judge, an able lawyer, and an ideal parent.

WILLIAM KING DRIGGS

Born: October 31, 1885   **Place:** Pleasant Grove, Utah

Father: Benjamin Woodbury Driggs; born May 13, 1837; descendant of American Revolutionary patriots; son of Shadrach Driggs and Eliza White of Vermont, neighbors to the Joseph Smith family; came to upper Nauvoo, Illinois as converts; was an expert wagoner; left Nauvoo May, 1846, making his own wagon last; went to California in 1855; returned for "Utah War" in 1856.

Mother: Olivia Pratt; his first wife, eldest daughter of Parley P. Pratt; with her husband settled in Pleasant Grove, Utah, 1852.

Brothers and Sisters:
B. W. Driggs Jr.
Ella Olivia (BYA)
Luna D. Clark (BYA)
Don Carlos (BYA)
Parley S.
Florence D. Todd
Leland (BYA)
an infant
Grace D. Smith
Alice D., m. Dr. John L. Brown
an infant
[William King Driggs]
(See Howard R. Driggs for names of half brothers and sisters.)

Marriage: Pearl Mortensen of Sanford, Colorado on August 22, 1908 Daughter of Lars Mortensen, handcart emigrant of 1852, and Cornelia Lee Decker Mortensen; served as assistant librarian at BYA; played cello in family orchestra; candidate for California's Mother of the Year.

Children: Lars Karleton Mortensen, m. Hazel Leiter; Maxine, m. LaVarn Thomas, Louise, m. Alvin McBurney (Alvino Rey), Alice, m. Robert Clarke (first husband, Azevedo, died at 36), Donna Olivia, m. James B. Conkling, Cornelia Yvonne m. Del Courtney, William King Driggs Jr. m. Phyllis Thane, Marilyn m. Howard Lloyd.

Death: April 6, 1965 at 80. Buried in Forest Lawn, Hollywood Hills.

Much of the information we glean for the subject of this biography is taken from King Driggs' own notes in answer to our questions. But he is far more interesting to talk to, as he vocally colors all his descriptions with the depictim of an artist and mimic. "Where did you get the name of King?" His answer is typical of his conversation:

"When I was born, Will King, the famous orator and later a Senator, came to see Ma Driggs and her new 10 pound baby. 'Well, Mrs. Driggs, what are you going to name him?' 'We just can't think of a name,' was the reply. 'All right, then, name him for me.' So this is how I got stuck with the odd given name of "King." It seems that the old BYA is even responsible for my name, as well as the stage name of certain daughters of mine, who have spread it upon theater foyers from Market Street to Broadway and caused it to be shouted upon the air waves." His further comment: "A lot of men are the husbands of, but I have become the father of the King Sisters. Everywhere I go I am introduced as the father of the famous King Sisters. That's all right with me as they are most worthy to be proud of."

"And while we are speaking of Will King I will tell you another fact of interest. My eldest sister, Ella Olivia, a popular young lady in Pleasant Grove and school, met Will King . . . they fell in love and became engaged. The romance was cut short by the untimely and tragic death, through typhoid fever, of the vivacious Ella. President Karl G. Maeser was the principal speaker at her funeral."

King was reared in a family of growing boys and girls, each having to adjust to the likes and dislikes of the others and all subject to the severe discipline of a serious, religious father. Education and church were accepted guides to youthful lives. The mother of the Driggs families exerted the greatest influence on their lives. Five of King's elder brothers and three sisters attended the BYA. Don Carlos was there in the fall of 1882 and "sold" the Academy to the family.

Driggs, Idaho was named for his family. When the father moved to Idaho for farming ventures some of the boys went into business and lived out their lives there. King states that Parley had a Will Rogers style of philosophy and was named for his illustrious grandfather, Parley P. Pratt.

One of King's boyhood friends was M. Wilford Poulson, also of Pleasant Grove, who went to BYA and invited King to come over and live with him in his bachelor apartment. After a hurried family consultation, King made hasty preparations. He ransacked his brother's store for a few articles of clothing, among them a pair of celluloid detachable collars. The family advised linen collars, but King was very conscious of expense and took the collars with him.

When he got to the Academy he found two boys and a faculty member equally conservative so "I took heart."

The young men of his day usually had to fend for themselves, but families played their parts; "Usually one of the parents furnished a conveyance for our return Sunday afternoon loaded with provisions, pies, cakes, fruit, staples, sausage and plenty of good home-made bread and butter. . . . We ate the sweets first and had only the plain food for the rest of the week." Wilford and King rented from Rose Brown Hays, mother of Junius J. Hayes, who became Professor of Mathematics at the University of Utah.

King early became a cartoonist, and faculty members of the Academy were prime targets of his pencil. He took math from Professor Ward, almost seven feet tall with a blonde Van Dyke beard. What a subject for a cartoon! How easy to drift from a problem to a drawing! While he learned to observe peculiarities and strong features, King also became a keen observer of character. His descriptions are worth recording:

"Dr. Maeser was a strict disciplinarian. He not only controlled the action of the students in school, but held close supervision over their homes. He was both loved and, I may say, feared by his students."

"Brother Cluff was about the kindest teacher I have ever studied under. . . . He took under his wings the Freshman class in mathematics and the backward ones at that. How many college Presidents would condescend to do that?"

"N. L. Nelson was the opposite of Benjamin Cluff. He could get down right sarcastic at times. . . . I remember that on one occasion a visiting educator from Salt Lake City addressed our student body. This short talk impressed me so much that I remember his very words. 'You have in this institution a man who is greatly underestimated and not fully appreciated in the person of Professor N. L. Nelson.' Among other things he said, 'He is a Carlyle converted to Mormonism.' "

"Under that delightful old eccentric Professor Alfred Osmond I studied Shakespeare and philosophy. The courses weren't exactly called that: one was English Rhetoric and the other Advanced Theology. You can learn theology and English construction anytime or anywhere, but I don't know how else I would have obtained my smatterings in the realm of higher knowledge had it not been for Sir Alfred and his wanderings. Blessed be the wanderer."

King was elected President of his class for three consecutive years, 1905, 1906 and 1907, and was at the Academy for four and one half years with a major in music and art. He received a Certificate from the Academy with special commendation of his Professor, Tony Lund. King was staff artist for the *White and Blue* in 1906 when Pete Peterson (from Ephraim), was editor and President of the Music Club in 1907. His class of seven was the first to throw buckets full of lime over the "Y" on the mountain. In 1909-10 he studied at conservatories in San Francisco and Los Angeles, California.

He taught for seven years in Church schools and at Snow College in Ephraim, Utah and was music supervisor in Nebo District of Utah County for another seven years.

King won the prize for the Utah State Fair Best Painting of Still Life in 1906. His opera, "The Liahona" based on the Book of Mormon was produced in the Oakland Civic Auditorium, Salt Lake Tabernacle, the Jewish Temple in Los Angeles, and in Phoenix, Arizona. His short pieces for schools, churches, and clubs are voluminous.

His most important work was to bring up a talented family, train them in music, and start his girls on their professional careers. Under his direction some 600 concerts, lyceums, etc. have been given by the group to be known as the King Sisters. The father went with them to the major centers of New England, but professional engagements became so numerous and time-consuming that a full time manager was necessary. This position was eventually taken over by his son William who has written many songs sung by his sisters. When the BYU Alumni Association and the Cougar Club presented the King Sisters on November 15, 1963, thirty-eight members of the Driggs family appeared in the George Albert Smith Fieldhouse to a capacity crowd, who gave the performance a rousing standing ovation. Father King led his group in singing its finale, with grandchildren from four years of age to the eldest daughters and husbands in the cast, a family tribute to its Church and the father's Alma Mater.

To adequately tell the exploits and reveal the talents of his family would require a large book. The four sisters became famed as the King Sisters; when the two eldest sisters dropped out the younger two took their places. Three of the young men are on missions and three girls are at BYU. Louise married a world renowned guitarist, Alvino Rey; Alice is married to talented Robert Clarke of the movies and television. Donna's husband has been President of the Columbia Records and Warner Bros. Records, but is now president of the International Educational Broadcasting Corporation for the LDS Church and its short wave station WRUL in New York. Del Courtney is the West Coast's most popular disc jockey and band leader for the San Francisco Giants. Marilyn is a talented comedienne. All the children and parents are active in the Church. (Written in 1965)

As an expression of gratitude and appreciation for the Church and its University, William King Driggs presented the Emeritus Club of the BYU Alumni Assn. a beautiful oil painting of his beloved Wasatch Mountains, now hung in the Alumni House.

Sherman Oaks, California, has been the family rendezvous.

The theme song of the King Family "Love At Home" is a tribute to their father and a noble Son of Brigham.

JOHN E. HAYES

Born: Jan. 13, 1880, Pleasant Grove, Utah

Father: John Phipps Hayes, b. Oct. 4, 1855 in England of Irish parents; after moving to London became a convert to the L.D.S. Church. Came to Utah in his teens. Settled in Pleasant Grove, Utah. Married in 1879, died 1916.

Mother: Eleanor Jane Hayes born in Lehi, Utah, July 14, 1856 of Irish parents who were converted in London, crossed the plains in wagons and came to Pleasant Grove after a Lehi residence
d. Mar. 13, 1939 in Pleasant Grove.

Brothers and Sisters: George Henry
Dr. Murray Oswald (Prof. of Geology at B.Y.U.)
Ralph Phipps,
Frances Elizabeth (died in childhood)
Rachael Eleanor, m. Walker H. Mourie
LuRena Henrietta, m. Hyrum E. Johnson

Marriage: 1.   Harriet Jeffs, Dec. 24, 1903
d. Feb. 6, 1919
2.   Harriet Lott Harris, July 14, 1920
d. Dec. 29, 1946

Children: Alton John, Wilmington, Dela.
Sheldon P., Ogden, Utah
Beth, m. Lamont Sowby, Los Angeles, California
Leith, m. Mont R. Anderson, Arlington, Va.
Emma, m. Jack Penhallegon, Wenatchee, Wash.
Maria, m. J. Legrand Forsyth, San Juan Batista, California

Death: August 22, 1962, in Los Angeles, in a hospital; was living with his daughter, Beth, at time of demise.

He was not a large man physically, but his heart and friendship spread across the globe. Fifty years of intimate contact with his keen interest in family trees and genealogical background made him an invaluable faculty official. He was the second full time registrar on the campus, starting in 1903. Before he finally registered a student (and he did most of that work alone for a number of years) he knew the person's parentage, place of birth and who his grandparents were. He asked about business and crops, health and local residents. When he had signed the admission card the student had heard two or three good jokes and a cheerful wish for academic success. In meeting the students so intimately he became an itinerant biographical dictionary. He recalled family genealogies more readily than most people remember names. He loved people; their joys and successes he cherished; their sorrows he heard and shared with others when it helped the individual. He spoke only good of people; gossip he ignored. As head doorman of all shows, athletic events and lyceum numbers for many years, he further increased his acquaintance with residents of Utah Valley and the parents of students enrolled.

Of Irish-Scotch parentage, he had an apt story for most occasions and loved dialect and homely illustrations. You told him a story; he would match it.

Life was his best school room. He came from his Pleasant Grove birthplace to BY Academy in 1900 and received a Commercial Certificate in 1903. He taught Commercial Arithmetic and Bookkeeping at B.Y.U. from 1902 to 1919, paralleling his work with registrar duties before becoming Emeritus in 1950, when he spent his spare hours on the History Committee and in the Alumni office. When he received a B.S. degree at B.Y.U. in 1924, he commented, "Well, now I must be an educated man. I can march in the faculty procession with a cap and gown."

He represented the University at many national conventions and was President of the Utah Association of Registrars in 1942-43; was clerk of Manavu Ward in Utah Stake for nineteen years and clerk of East Provo Stake for four years. His travels took him to many states in the union and for a most enjoyable summer in Europe in 1953. One of his happiest hours came when he was a recipient of the B.Y.U. Alumni Distinguished Service Award in 1955.

John's home was always cheerful and ruled by love, as attested to by his three sons and four daughters. He married Harriet Jeffs on December 21, 1908 in the Salt Lake Temple. She died on February 6, 1919, and in July of 1920 he married a beloved teacher of B.Y.U., Lottie Harris, who died on December 29, 1946. In later years he kept his Provo home but spent most of his time with his children, all of whom attended and graduated from B.Y.U. Rex preceded him in death. Surviving are Alton John, Sheldon P., Beth, Keith, Emma and Maria.

In 1957 the *Universe* paid him a beautiful tribute—"It didn't matter too much if you lost your activity card to an event because John Hayes, the gateman, knew all the students by name anyway."

Loyal friend, devoted Church worker, gentleman—we shall not forget him at B.Y.U.

EDWARD H. HOLT

Born: June 1, 1872   **Place:** South Jordan, Utah

Father: Mathew, born December 23, 1823 in Britport, Dorsetshire, England
Arrived in Utah in 1864; took up farming
Died September 25, 1901 in South Jordan, Utah within a few months of wife's death. Successful businessman of state.

Mother: Ann Harrison of St. Abbott, Dorsetshire, England
Born August 3, 1827
Married May 9, 1851
Died May 26, 1901 in South Jordan, Utah
Disowned by her family when she joined the Church and never heard from them again.

Brothers and Sisters: Nine children in the family
Three died in England; two came over on ship with parents
Rose born while parents crossing the plains
Ellen, m. Gordon S. Bills
William, m. Anna J. Hemingsen
Rose, m. Samuel H. Howard
Arthur, m. Catherine Beckstead
Samuel, m. Margaret G. Beckstead

Marriage: June 26, 1895 to Edith Holdaway, daughter of John M. of Provo
Born in Provo February 6, 1876
Died December 15, 1935
She was a happy quiet young lady called by her friends "the perfect mother". Her family and the Church filled her life.

Children: Jean M., m. R. Nels Cooper
Florence, m. Faye E. Stephens
Reed E., m. Maurine Stevenson
Afton, m. Gordon Christensen
Paul M., m. Carol Reid
Grant R.

Death: October 27, 1938 of a paralytic stroke in Provo, Utah

Most friends who think of Professor Holt think of him sitting back of a desk, pen in hand, writing. He remained concentrated on his work until you spoke and then you were greeted with an easy, pleasant smile and direct attention. Almost all his life he was a secretary—truly one who could keep a secret. He was never known to reveal any fact or statement given in confidence.

His shorthand notes looked as if they were printed,—neat, orderly and distinct in rhythmic beauty. Most professional shorthand writers could read his notes as easily as from a text book. When he had a special assignment demanding unusual care and confidential treatment, he wrote a condensed shorthand which only he could properly decipher. His memory for figures was brilliant and his ability to recall in exact words was a gift he cultivated. He enjoyed being a confidant and found strength in his talent. While he worked intimately with presidents and chairmen in many walks of life, he never yearned for or desired to be a dominant leader. He joyed in the proficiency of his records and the trust put upon him. He found pleasure in knowing that his records would outlast him as a man.

He was secretary-treasurer for the B.Y.U. for thirty-five years, clerk of Utah Stake for thirty-seven years, and paralleling these was secretary to the B.Y.U. faculty for forty-four years. Each position exacted a lifetime of service and notes always transcribed and ready for quick reference. "If I were to die tonight, I want my records to be immediately available," he said.

Nor was he without the qualities of leadership as he proved by teaching a course of dry facts and figures in a most interesting manner. He stressed accuracy, neatness, efficiency, concentration, conservation of time and the ability to go from one assignment to another without losing interest in either. He taught the value of an adequate vocabulary for any profession. Often he would pause in a dictation and ask the class what a certain word really meant—a simple word such as "libertine". The class agreed it meant someone unpleasant, such as "profligate". He would smile and tell them it came from the Latin "liberare" and meant "one made free" which led to "one free from restraint" and now a "debauchee", "free from all restraint". He often dictated words in pairs for clarification such as "exercise" and "exorcise", "which" and "witch", "sectary" and "secretary", "cutey" and "cootey", "lute" and "loot" to recognize the long u in pronunciation. "If you speak clearly you are more apt to spell accurately," he told his students. He had his classes define "pronunciation", "articulation", "ennunciation" and asked who had the best speech in the class and why. "Who wants to listen to a man with mush in his mouth." He inspired his students to seek knowledge and the means of expression.

As for his ability of leadership, when President Harris took a leave of absence for a governmental assignment to Liberia in 1929, Professor Holt was made Acting President of the University and conducted all faculty meetings and business of the institution.

Ed Holt was a man of slight build, never weighing over one hundred forty-five pounds, with dark, active eyes, and long fingers, strong and agile.

His parents were converts in England, who came to Utah and sought a good piece of farmland. The father soon became a successful merchant farmer in the Jordan district and sent his family to Salt Lake City when old enough for further education. When young, Ed came to Brigham Young Academy, and in 1893 he was given the job as "checker" in the small library. He became secretary to President Benjamin Cluff, then to George H. Brimhall and Franklin S. Harris. When President Harris arrived in 1921 he appointed no counselors, giving the secretary greater responsibility. Professor Holt had already worked on the yearly catalogs and bulletins and was given a considerable portion of work in these matters.

During World War I when times were exceedingly hard and B.Y.U. struggled for its very existence, Brother Holt, as treasurer, was put to wits end to pay the faculty their salaries or find script to substitute in lieu of cash. As treasurer he knew the finances and life secrets of all faculty families. Many times he sought help from those who had a little more to tide over those with less. The war demanded "yards of red tape," and report duties were added to the school secretary.

E. H. was a devout churchman, getting up early in the mornings to accomplish his numerous tasks for the different organizations. Nor did he neglect his family. Our family were neighbors to the Holts for several years on Second East, and we soon learned that Professor Holt was either at church, the university or home. He was never a "joiner", though invited to membership in civic organizations. "I believe in good civic groups, but I must fill my previous commitments". He belonged to the Utah State Teachers Association.

Professor Holt was called on a mission three times, but released each time because of his duties at B.Y.U. in stressful periods.

The Holt children were reared by devoted parents with laughter, love and family prayers. All went to B.Y.U. and all married but Grant. A mission and war duties took Grant away from home, and when he returned both his mother and father had passed away. Professor Holt died three years after his wife, while Grant was on his mission. Reed is one of Utah's most successful businessmen, being president of the Walker Bank in Salt Lake City, and Paul is head man for the Utah Tax Commission. Grant is a professor of business at the University of Utah and the girls are married happily to men of leadership.

E. H. Holt was a quiet man of great ability, who found real joy in being a servant of his church, university and community.

ISAAC ALBERT "BERT" SMOOT

Born: November 3, 1880, in Provo, Utah.

Father: Abraham Owen Smoot II.

Mother: Electa Bullock, daughter of Isaac Bullock and Electa Wood.

Brothers and Sisters:
A. Owen, m. Phoebe Campbell—also mayor of Provo.
Isaac Albert
Allie, m. Jacob Coleman, prominent Provo attorney.
Electa, m. LeRoy Dixon, mayor of Provo; real estate operator
Fern, m. Wells L. Brimhall, merchant.
Ethel, died in infancy.

Marriage: Nettie Parkinson of Franklin, Idaho, on March 31, 1909, daughter of Samuel R. and Charlotte Smart of Preston, Idaho, pioneers of Southern Idaho.

Children:
Ruth Parkinson, m. Russell McNitt
Albert Park, m. Julia Meacham
Richard P. m. Barbara McKean
Stephen P., m. Marilyn Holick.

Died: March 12, 1957, of a heart attack in Chicago, Ill., when President of the Northern States Mission.

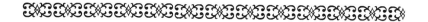

Just before Bert Smoot retired from his Salt Lake Post Office management, I walked up Main Street with him towards the Hotel Utah. Instead of having a usual walk with casual conversation, we were interrupted all along the way by a multiplicity of passing friends. A lady of distinction stopped him for final advice on a proposed investment to conclude a telephone conversation she had with Bert an hour previous, two bankers asked if he remembered a luncheon he was to attend, a jeweler stepped out of his store and invited him in to see a medal which was to be given a young man of President Smoot's Ward, a newspaper editor stopped to ask if his interest in civil service was to be continued to government workers other than postmasters. He started to converse with me, then stopped to chat with two young girls selling poppies for disabled veterans—of one he asked "Is your mother out of the hospital yet?"; of the other he learned the names of her parents, where she lived, and what school she attended and said, "Be sure to tell me 'Hello' when we meet again." So it went on down for four long blocks, a ten-minute walk extended to nearly a half hour, all with smiles, pleasure and a happy sense of living in a free country. That short trip was punctuated with questions for me about my family, Provo, the BYU, any current worthwhile drama, the Boy Scout work, and Rotary. A friendly fellow reveals his inner life in a few minutes; sincerity is felt with a firm hand clasp in the parting. Bert Smoot was a handsome fellow who attracted men and women in all walks of life.

He was reputedly a lively, mischievous lad who early knew much of Utah Valley. He got good grades in school and went to BYU Academy from 1899 to 1902, taking a business course with distinction. His father had several families and all the boys early took interest in church and politics. Aunt Diana's children were dominantly Democrats and Aunt Annie's were strongly Republican. That division was carried over to political life, but a strong family loyalty paralleled this diversity.

Bert went on an LDS Mission to England from 1903 to 1906, after a year of mining business in the Tintic District. He was hired by the Mountain States Telephone & Telegraph Company of Provo in 1906 as district manager and worked for telephone expansion until 1912, when he became Utah County Assessor. During World War I he was appointed State Land Commissioner for Idaho, 1914-1917. He was induced by the Knight interests to be a coal-mine operator from 1919 to 1933, a job which he fitted in with his politics, as did the Knights. He was speaker of the House in 1933.

Isaac Albert was a member of the Provo Board of Education for six years, 1909-1915; postmaster of Provo from 1917-1922, endeavoring to know every person who regularly came to the post office; worked hard to popularize air mail, then struggling for recognition, which he emphasized when he was made postmaster in Salt Lake City by President F. D. Roosevelt, whom he knew intimately. He was postmaster of Salt Lake for seventeen years, until he retired in 1950, and was one of the organizing leaders to form the National Association of Postmasters in 1937 and became its president. Civil Service for postmasters was the result of his leadership and many years of intense endeavor.

There were too many civic services rendered by Bert to enumerate in a short biography. He was a guide on Temple Square for 25 years. Many visitors had been told to inquire for him. The great Utah Centennial of 1947 saw him as chairman of the Arts Committee. He was chairman of the Granite district, Salt Lake Council, Boy Scouts of America. He was an active member of the Sons of Utah Pioneers, the Utah Pioneer Trails and Landmarks Association, charter member of the Knife and Fork Club, Utah Chairman of International Saving Banks Committee, State Chairman Federal Employees, 1948 Cancer Program, member B. Y. U. Alumni Board, member of six stake high councils and President of Northern States Mission for four years.

He was a member of a bishopric and the High Council in Granite Stake, President of the B. Y. U. Alumni Emeritus Club (1948), honored with the B. Y. U. Alumni Distinguished Service Award (1952), always active in Democratic party councils, interested in the preservation of pioneer and historic sites, and popular club and funeral speaker. The life of this handsome gentleman was rounded out by the companionship of a beautiful and talented wife who shared all his honors and much of his work. His family was his chief joy, his church and country his obsessions. I. A. "Bert" Smoot, a man of many friendships and talents, was one of Utah's great leaders.

IV

Men who studied with or under

George H. Brimhall

(1904-1921)

George H. Brimhall (*April 16, 1904—July 1, 1921*)

HANS ANDERSEN

Born: Feb. 15, 1860   **Place:** Odder, Denmark

Father: Anders Hansen, b. Jan. 6, 1823, son of Hans Jensen and Ane Margrethe

Mother: Maren Pedersen, b. Aug. 3, 1828,
d. Nov. 5, 1953
An expert tailor and dressmaker; owned the first sewing machine in Juab County. She sheared the sheep, washed, carded and spun yarn, wove it into cloth and dyed it. Tailored her brother Joe's first suit of clothes—his wedding garment.

Brothers and Sisters: Margrethe Jensen
Sorn Andersen
(Hans Andersen)
Christen Sornsen
Maren

Marriage: (1) Anna Katrene Jensen, b. July 31, 1859
m. 1884
d. in 1933, one year short of her Golden Wedding Anniversary. While crossing the plains at age 4, lost most of her hearing.
(2) Louisa Eastland, who cared for him the last several years, as he had become totally blind.

Children: Hattie, b. May 16, 1886, m. Thomas Lynne Wright Nov. 27, 1907
Frank, b. Nov. 17, 1887, died as a child
Mary Andersen Cozier, b. Sept. 2, 1892
Anna Andersen Markham, b. Jan. 5, 1896

Death: Nov. 6, 1948

Hans, at seven, was hired out to a farmer, Jens Hansen, to herd cows. Jens contracted to send Hans to school, but the contract was not fulfilled. This first major experience caused the young boy to question the word of most men for some time to come.

At fourteen Hans was apprenticed as a blacksmith, working for room and board in Aarhus until he was eighteen. At nineteen years of age (1879) Hans began working and travelling in Scandinavia and Europe, remaining in Berlin for a year and a half. At twenty he came to the United States hoping to find fruitful work. He stayed first in New York and then in Chicago, where he was employed as a blacksmith with good wages. The horse was king of the road and swank livery stables employed the best help obtainable. He could have remained in Chicago with wealthy employers, but did not see an opportunity for ownership. He had always wanted to own a good piece of land to cultivate and to raise high grade stock. "There is no wealth without land". A Danish friend stationed at Fort Douglas on the east bench of Salt Lake City, invited him to Utah, as the Army needed good specialists. Hans had heard much about the Mormons and was interested. With a $55.00 ticket and two dollars he set out for Utah.

Not long after arriving in Salt Lake he was told of a good dry-farm country in Central Utah which was also suitable for stock. He moved to Levan, Juab County, in the winter of 1883, put up his own blacksmith shop, and homesteaded some 164 acres of land. His first night at Levan he was staying at the home of Charlie Olsen when two government officials came looking for polygamists.

With the kindly help of his neighbors he saw ownership well within his grasp and joined the Church in 1884. "With his feet on the ground," he married Katrene Jensen, who had patiently waited with hopes that he would join the Church. Their children, Hattie, Frank, and Mary, were born in the new brick home; Frank died at two years of age for lack of medical care, as there were no doctors or nurses available in the town. Anne, the fourth child, was born in 1898.

In the early part of Hans' married life he developed stomach ulcers. His wife told him it was because he didn't keep the Word of Wisdom. One day while harnessing the horses in the stable, he became so ill he couldn't rise from the straw nor could he make any one hear him. He was quite unversed in prayer but knew there was a God who helped people. He said, "Dear God, I am very sick and unable to get up. If you heal me, I will keep the Word of Wisdom and live my religion as long as I live." He immediately felt relief, relaxed, arose and walked to the house. He was so overcome with joy that he had difficulty in telling his wife what had happened. He was completely healed. His daughter, Hattie, told us that he never knowingly broke his promise and lived until he was 88 years and 7 months old.

When he went on his mission to his native land in 1893, he sold his farm and horses with the consent and earnest urging of his wife, who "knew the Lord will bless us all." She supported the family and was able to help him as needed. She sewed for other families, traded eggs at the local store, milked cows, and raised a garden. Of such caliber was the fervor of these ardent, religious souls!

When Hans returned he was diligent in his religion and his testimony strengthened. He was often called upon to administer to the sick and saw many people healed. His own bedfast sister, Margrethe, ailing in health for months, and not a member of the Church, finally asked Hans if he thought the Lord would bless her. He told her, "If you sincerely have faith He will cure you." She requested the blessing and was completely healed and lived to be an aged lady.

Hans did well. He had taken up land given him by the state for dry farming, but he longed to be fluent in English. Professor William H. Boyle who was teaching in Levan encouraged him to go to school for that purpose. The family made it their major project. When Professor Boyle was placed in charge of the B.Y.U. Preparatory School, a way opened up. In 1904 Hans and his daughter, Hattie, went to Provo and enrolled, agreeing that he should go to school in the winter and farm in the summer. He was assured by his faithful wife, Anna, that he need have no fears for the welfare of herself or their daughters, Mary and Anna. Neither the father nor the mother lacked for money. Younger people dominated all of his classes and he was reluctant to speak with his broken speech.

When President George H. Brimhall decided to enlarge the university vocational activities, he sent for Hans and asked for a demonstration of his iron welding. Hans made a marker or brand for the school furniture out of hard steel with the letters "BYU". The steel shined as new; the edge of the letters were sharp and evenly trimmed so that one good tap of a hammer left the furniture permanently stamped. Hans was given the job with high praise. A life ambition consummated in a most unexpected manner. He was to become a teacher!

Class members increased by the week and his shop, across the street south of the Education Building, was soon too small. Students were taught to make their own tools and equipment. World War I doubled the size of the classes and the forges ran 24 hours of the day. Hans invented and made the wide section harrows later used so extensively on dry farms. Iron fences and fence posts began to adorn the yards of Provo; porches were equipped with adorning side pieces. The beautiful gates that welcomed guests and students to the lower campus were iron moulded rods shaped with pride on the busy forge of Hans and his students. When they were dismantled in the 1950's, Provo lost one of its classical beauty spots.

A son of Professor Amos N. Merrill was afflicted with polio and needed a brace for walking, one not yet on the market. Hans spent his evening hours experimenting and finally got a support that held the leg firmly and, in course of time, the boy was able to walk straight without any brace. Physicians of the state praised the mechanical skill of the modest inventor.

With the advent of the automobile the smithy had few opportunities for full time service. With the coming of President F. S. Harris, who made a survey of school services, Hans, who had taught twenty happy years at B.Y.U. returned to his farm in Levan, most grateful to his wife, family and friends for the parts they had played in his progress. His English was a delight to hear. He kept three languages culturally alive, Danish, German and English.

His prayers at Devotionals were fervent masterpieces; you felt an intimacy with a Holy Spirit. All who knew him called him honest, courageous and loyal. He was always ready to lend a helping hand. He especially gave aid to the underprivileged, widows and the poor. He lived by the Golden Rule.

Hans is buried in Levan in the hills he loved so much. A room, No. 112, in the Mechanic Arts Center on the B.Y.U. campus has been designated the "Hans Andersen Acetylene Welding Laboratory" in honor of a sincere teacher of humble birth.

MAJ. GENERAL ORVIL ARSON ANDERSON

Born: May 2, 1895, at Springville, Utah.
BYU—1914-16.
Enlisted as private, Aug. 23, 1917.

Father: Jens Anderson, son of Anders Frederickson Anderson and Marie Petersen.
Born Apr. 20, 1835.
Convert to Church; emigrated to Utah.
Died Sept. 17, 1906.

Mother: Jensene Hansen, daughter of James Hansen.
Born Jan 22., 1861.
Died Feb. 27, 1944.

Brothers and Sisters: Laura A., born Dec. 25, 1879; m. George Gordon Hoxie.
Gardena Arlesen, b. Nov. 13, 1881; m. Jos. Robert Baird.
Mary Jane, b. Apr. 1, 1884; m. Ernest Christean
Clara, b. June 11, 1886
Wilford George Nephi, b. Dec. 5, 1892; Gladys Loraine Watkins (marriage) (Orval A.)
Elmer Laurence, b. Feb. 2, 1898; m. Eva Cleo Jones. (2) Edna Lucille Davidson

Half Brothers and Sisters: (Carolina Nielson, mother)
James A., Almira, Otto, Amelia and Fred died in early youth.
Mary Caroline, m. James P. Larsen
Oscar, m. Mary Ellen Barker
Victoria, m. Timothy Leander Parmley
Dagmar, m. William C. Johnson
Jemima, m. Edward McCune
Waldemar (Walter), m. Ivy Y. Curtis

Marriage: (1) Gladys Loraine Watkins
(2) Lauretta Maud Miller of Omaha, Nebraska.
resident of Montgomery, Alabama, on May 1, 1919

Children: Susan and Nancy

Died: Maxwell AFB, Alabama, Aug. 23, 1965.
Buried in Arlington National Cemetery.

The following material was furnished by the United States Air Force, Maxwell AFB, Alabama:

Orvil Arson Anderson was born in Springville, Utah, on 2 May 1895. He attended Brigham Young University in 1914-16, and enlisted as a private in the U. S. Army on 23 August 1917. He entered the Aviation Section of the Signal Corps the same month as a flying cadet, going to the Army Balloon School at Fort Omaha, Neb. From March to May, 1918, he attended the School of Military Aeronautics at Ohio State University and then returned to Fort Omaha where he was graduated from the Balloon School. He received his commission as a temporary second lieutenant in the Air Service on 3 August 1918 and remained at Fort Omaha to become commanding officer of the 61st Balloon Company with which he moved to Langley Field, Va., in March, 1919.

He completed a navigation course at the Naval Air Station, Pensacola, Fla., in Jan., 1920, and returned to Langley where he was assigned to the 19th Airship Company as an instructor in airship navigation. He was rated an airship pilot in September, 1920; was navigator and pilot of Army Airship C-2 on the first transcontinental flight by airship; instructor in the Balloon School, Scott Field, Ill., in Dec., 1922; entered Rigid Airship Course at Naval AS, Lakehurst, N. J., in March, 1923, which he completed in Aug., 1924; graduated from Air Service Basic Flying School, Brooks Field, Texas, in 1925, and became commandant of cadets and instructor at Kelly Field, Texas; was test pilot of semi-rigid Airship RS-1, the only semi-rigid airship ever built in America, and commanding officer of the 8th Airship Company, 1926-27.

General Anderson went to the Philippine Islands in July, 1927, as Air Operations Officer with the Philippine Department, duty with the '3d Pursuit Sq., Clark Field, in April, 1929, and with the 2d Observation Sq., Nichols Field, Oct., 1930, until return to the U.S. in May, 1931. He became instructor at Air Corps Advanced Flying School, Kelly Field; assigned as test pilot for Army Dirigible TC-13, March, 1933, at Akron, Ohio. Moved to Langley Field, Va., in July, 1933, for continuing tests with the airship and made the first successful anchoring of an airship at sea in 1933, using a canvas sea anchor he had designed.

Became instructor in aerial navigation at Langley, Nov., 1933; instructor in instrument flying at Mitchel Field, N.Y., March, 1934. In May, 1934, he was assigned as operations officer for the National Geographic Society—Army Air Corps Stratosphere Flight at Wright Field, Ohio. During this assignment he was co-pilot of Explorer I balloon ascent from Rapid City, S.D., July 28, 1934. Returned to Kelly Field as bombardment instructor from August, 1934, to March, 1935.

Returned to Wright Field for further tests and stratosphere flights and, as pilot of Explorer II balloon, set altitude record of 72,395 feet on Nov. 11, 1935, a record that stood for 21 years.

In Jan., 1936 joined the 43d Pursuit Sq. at Kelly Field; entered Air Corps Tactical School at Maxwell Field, Ala., in August, 1936, graduating in June, 1937; graduated from Chemical Warfare School, Field Officers Course, 1937; graduated Command and General Staff School, 1938, after which he became a member of the Air Corps Board at Maxwell Field; became Air Corps Liaison Officer with IV Corps at Jacksonville, Fla., May, 1941.

Assigned to Air Plans Division, Hq. Army Air Forces, May, 1941; chief, Plans Division, AAF, Washington, D.C., 1942-43; chairman, Combined Operational Planning Committee, an organization composed of American and British air officers and charged with planning operations for strategic bombing offensive in the European Theater of Operations, 1943-45.

He was deputy commander for Operations, Eighth Air Force, 1944-45; on V-E Day was assigned position of senior military advisor of the United States Strategic Bombing Survey, an organization charged by the President with studying economic and military value of bombing on Germany, Japan, and all occupied territories, 1945-46.

On June 15, 1946, he was assigned as the first Commandant of the Air War College, Air University, at Maxwell Field, holding this position until retirement from active duty on 31 December 1950. In 1954 he accepted the position of executive director of the Air Force Historical Foundation, holding the post until resignation because of illness in mid-1965. (Died at Maxwell AFB, Alabama, on 23 Aug 1965. Interment in Arlington National Cemetery.

* * * * * * *

General Anderson was rated as a Command Pilot, Senior Balloon Pilot, Combat Observer, Balloon Observer, and Aerial Observer.

* * * * * * *

He held the Distinguished Service Medal with Oak Leaf Cluster; Legion of Merit; Silver Star; Distinguished Flying Cross with Oak Leaf Cluster; Air Medal; Commendation Ribbon with two Oak Leaf Clusters; Hubbard Medal of National Geographic Society for scientific achievement; World War II Medal; seven official commendations in connection with flying duty. French Legion of Honor; French Croix de Guerre with Palm; British Companion of the Bath; Belgian Croix de Guerre with Palm. For outstanding aerial achievement, received in 1935 the MacKay Trophy, Harmon International Award, Federation Aeronautique Internationale Prix Henry De Levaulx.

* * * * * * *

In 1936 he received an Honorary Doctorate of Engineering from the South Dakota School of Mines and Technology. He was an honorary member of the Rotary and Engineers Clubs of Dayton, Ohio.

His most publicized achievement is reported herewith:

Twenty years ago next Friday two Army Air Corps captains rose to record heights. In a gondola swinging from a helium-filled balloon, they soared 72,395 feet above the earth, or nearly thirteen and three-quarter miles. The voyage into the stratosphere set an altitude record that still stands. It was responsible for scientific data and aeronautical innovations that came to fruition in World War II.

On Friday a group of men, including one of the balloonists, will meet at the spot in the bleak Black Hills of South Dakota, from which the ascent was made to commemorate the event.

It was 6 degrees above zero on the ground in the bowl-shaped depression called Bonanza Bar Canyon in the early morning of Nov. 11, 1935. After six weeks of delay caused by bad weather and mechanical trouble, the balloon Explorer II was about to take off. The flight was arranged by the National Geographic Society and the Air Corps.

Dressed in heavy flying suits and football helmets, Capt. Orvil A. Anderson, the pilot, and Capt. Albert W. Stevens, the commander and scientific observer, climbed into their craft. It was nine feet in diameter and made of magnesium alloy.

The balloon, covering two acres when deflated, was made of cotton cloth with a special rubber dressing. The complete assembly weighed nine tons and was thirty-one stories high.

The flight began at 9 a.m. The balloon rose at a rate of 600 feet a minute from the bowl eleven miles from Rapid City. A crowd of 20,000 cheered the aeronauts. For eight hours and thirteen minutes the officers probed the black, dark blue and purple-tinged reaches of the sky with their instruments. For nearly all that time they talked by radio with scientists and newspaper men. Millions of listeners on regular radio sets heard the conversations. An outside temperature of more than 140 below zero, Fahrenheit, was recorded during the flight. Inside the pressurized, oxygen-supplied gondola, the temperature was 18 to 20 above. The balloon reached 72,395 feet at 1:30 p.m., four and a half hours after the take-off.

During the descent the balloonists attached the scientific instruments to parachutes and dropped them. They were taking no chances of losing the precious data in a crack-up. At 5:13 p.m. the gondola touched lightly to the ground and rolled over. The spot was a field 240 miles east of the take-off camp. Nobody realized it then, but the gondola had returned with knowledge that was to prove invaluable in a future war—information on cosmic rays, the ability of living mold spores to survive in rarified air, the intensity of solar radiation.

From the flight also were to come the pressurized systems of B-29 bombers, development of the electrical flying suit, the two-way, long-range aircraft radio, and lightweight aircraft metals.

Explorer II is still the official altitude recordholder. Unofficially, the record has been broken twice by United States military aircraft. A Navy Skyrocket recorded 79,000 feet briefly in 1951. The Air Force, in 1954, announced that the Bell X-1A had climbed to 90,000 feet. Explorer I went to 60,613 feet in 1934. At that height the hydrogen-filled bag broke and began falling swiftly. A half mile from the ground the three crew members parachuted. They were Captain Anderson, Captain Stevens, and Maj. William E. Kepner. Seconds later the balloon exploded and the gondola smashed into a cornfield.

The Air Force is planning a new balloon ascent. Capt. Edward G. Sperry and First Lieut. Henry P. Nielsen hope to take Explorer III to 90,000 feet and then parachute out. They are seeking data to help design escape equipment for high-speed, high-flying planes.

At the ceremonies Friday will be Explorer II's pilot, now Major General Anderson, retired, and Lieutenant General Kepner, also retired. Capt. Stevens, who became a lieutenant colonel, died in 1949. Also present will be Gov. Joe Foss of South Dakota, World War II Marine ace, and Gen. Curtis E. LeMay, head of the Strategic Air Command.

the NEW YORK TIMES, SUNDAY, NOV. 6, 1955

Under date of Feb. 4, 1966, we read the following from The DISPATCH, Maxwell:

Air University recently added Anderson Hall to the roll of Maxwell AFB buildings named to honor the memory of aerospace leaders. The memorialization of the home of Air War College, the Air Force's senior school, honored the memory of the late Maj. Gen. Orvil A. Anderson—early military aviator, pioneer balloonist and aerospace explorer, wartime planner, airpower effects analyst, and Air War College's first commandant from the founding of the institution in 1946 until his retirement on Dec. 31, 1950.

Maj. Gen. Arno H. Luehman, AWC commandant and vice-commander of AU, sponsored the memorialization of Bldg. 1401 at this historic base, where the Wright Brothers ran a flying school in 1910. Lt. Gen. John W. Carpenter III, AU commander, approved the action, and accepted the prestigious addition to the growing tradition of Air University's Academic Circle.

General Anderson's widow, Mrs. Maude Anderson, of Montgomery, Ala.; his daughter, Miss Susan Anderson; Mr. Thomas W. McKnew, vice-chairman of the Board of Trustees, National Geographic Society; and Lt. Gen. William S. Stone, USAF Deputy Chief of Staff/Personnel, representing Gen. John P. McConnell, Chief of Staff, also participated in the Memorialization ceremonies.

In addition to his key role at the inception of Air War College, General Anderson was linked to Maxwell AFB and Air University at other points in a military career that began in 1917. In 1937 he was graduated from the Air Corps Tactical School here, and from 1938 to 1941 was a member of the Air Corps Board.

In 1954 the forceful aerospace leader accepted the position of executive director of the USAF Historical Foundation with offices at Maxwell, and was a familiar figure at this base until shortly before his death on Aug. 23, 1965, at the Maxwell USAF Hospital.

PAUL PARRISH ASHWORTH

Born: October 4, 1887   **Place:** Beaver, Utah

Father: William Booth Ashworth, born March 10, 1845 in Craw-habooth, Lancashire, England. To Utah via Mississippi River and St. Louis, 1852. Settled in Beaver; machinist and mill operator.
Died December 22, 1934 in Provo, Utah.

Mother: Mary Elizabeth Shepherd, born March 24, 1854 in San Bernardino, California. Married, Salt Lake May 26, 1873. Moved to Provo in 1891 to educate children at BYA.
Died April 11, 1932, Salt Lake City, Utah.

Brothers and Sisters: Maria, born September 28, 1874.
Married A. L. Booth, April 12, 1900. Died October 9, 1913.
Wm. Ray, born March 18, 1877.
Married Eliza Mangum November 14, 1901. Died January 13, 1963.
Clara, died as an infant.
Elsie, born April, 1883.
Married Frank T. Bennett August 10, 1904. Died May 7, 1965.
Claude S., born June 9, 1885.
Married Ardelle Harmon May 23, 1933.
(Paul)
Claiborne, born February 9, 1890. Died 1945.
Hazel, born November 5, 1892. Died February 3, 1945.
Married Arthur Janson September 3, 1913.

Marriage: Jane Ducher Ferrin; daughter of James Clinton Ferrin and Elizabeth Ellen Edge.
Born in Provo, Utah.
Married January 14, 1916 in Salt Lake Temple. A student at BYU.

Children: Faye, born May 9, 1917, married George H. Maxwell July 29, 1936.
Don Ferrin, born January 6, 1921, married Julia Sorenson May 16, 1946.
Dell Shepherd, born July 20, 1923, married Bette Brailsford, December 21, 1946.
Gayle Claire, born January 12, 1927, married Dr. Bruce Lloyd Sept. 1, 1950.
Clinton Paul, born October 25, 1928, married Rachael Calder October 9, 1950.

Died: April 23, 1960 while visiting son, Don F., in Glendora, California.

PAUL PARRISH ASHWORTH entered Kindergarten at BYU, Provo, and continued through high school and college at BYU, class 1911. He spent one year at Telluride Institute, Olmstead, as student and faculty member; four years on Telluride Association Scholarship at Cornell University, leading to degrees of E.E. and M.E. (1914) and M.M.E. (1915). He was an instructor in Machine Design 1914-15 while attending graduate school and was a special lecturer to Electrical Engineer Seniors at University of Utah for seven years.

Professional and Business Activities: Chairman, Utah Section A.I.E.E. 1921-22. Member of the Utah Engineering Council for several years. Member of the Executive Committee, Engineering Section Northwest Electric Light and Power Association from 1919, chairman two years. He was an engineer at the Telluride Power Company, Colorado and Utah, 1907-1913; Wyoming Electric Company, Casper, Wyoming, 1914; Utah Power and Light Company, Salt Lake City, 1915-1938; Telluride Power Company, Richfield, September 1, 1938 to 1956. General Manager since 1941, Director since 1951. Vice-President, Big Springs Power Company, 1941-1953; Director, Telluride Motor Company, 1940-1950. To Salt Lake in 1956 as director and Executive Vice President. Retired 1957. Private practice as consultory engineer.

Civic and Club Activities: Boy Scouts of America: Member Executive Committee, Salt Lake Council, 1917-1938; Member National Council; Sevier District Chairman, 1938-1947; Chairman Finance Committee, Fish Lake Section, 1947-1956; Sevier Beaver, 1947-1956. American Red Cross: Vice Chairman Life Saving Committee, Salt Lake Chapter, 1930-1938; Chairman South Sevier County Chapter, 1938-1947, member Executive committee, 1947-1951. Vice President, Richfield Lions Club, 1946. President, Richfield Business Mens Alliance, 1945. Chairman Richfield Committee for Economic Development, 1944-48. Vice President, Associated Civics Club of Southern and Eastern Utah 1948-49—Director and Treasurer, 1949. Member of Selective Service Board No. 29, 1948-1956. Member, Utah Society, Sons of American Revolution, Board of Governors.

Church Activities: Served in M.I.A., Sunday School and Priesthood; High Council, Sevier Stake 1938-1946; Superintendent, Sunday School, 1947; Member Building Committee, 1940-1956.

In the words of one of his colleagues; "If you want anything done well, get Paul Ashworth. If you want a problem solved, put Paul onto it. I never knew a boy who didn't like him. He is a boy's man." He spent much of his mature life working for and with boys. His motto, "Be careful what you do; some boy is watching."

Paul looked for the good in every person he met and was keenly conscious of talented men with negative opinions. A fellow who disagreed with him became a challenge to his own thinking. "No one is always right; maybe this is my turn to be wrong. Now, let's see" and thoughtful questions often brought a common ground for agreement.

When a certain project was proposed at the Sevier Boy Scout Committee meeting, one of the members strongly urged against the amount of work involved. Chairman Ashworth replied, "Well, who's afraid of work? How else can it be achieved? Let's look at the general good and let it outweigh the individual cost. Here's an opportunity to submerge self for the good of the community and our boys." The project was carried to a useful fruition.

As a member of the local Selective Service Board, boys would ask if Mr. Ashworth were to be present. They had grown up with confidence in this youth leader and most of the inductees accepted the committee's decision with satisfaction with comments of this nature, "If Paul Ashworth thinks I should go, then that's alright with me. It's the right thing to do."

His moving around to accommodate his profession gave him no desire to avoid civic responsibility. Wherever he lived he soon became an executive officer in a Boy Scout program, in the Sevier District, on the Executive Committee for the Salt Lake Council and the National Council. He was an officer in the Lions Club, the Chamber of Commerce and the Sons of the American Revolution. Ancestry was a foundation for him to build for his posterity.

Paul Ashworth was a beloved and successful leader of boys and men.

GEORGE SMITH BALLIF

Born: June 4, 1894   **Place:** Logan, Utah

Father: John Lyman Ballif, Sr.
b. December 23, 1864, son of Serge Louis Ballif
d. December 6, 1941. Buried in Logan, Utah

Mother: Emma Smith, daughter of Bishop Thomas X. Smith and Margaret Gurney, both of England
To America and Utah in 1853
Thomas X., bishop for 45 years of Logan Fourth Ward
b. October 19, 1864; m. October 20, 1886.
d. April 6, 1942; buried in Logan, Utah
A musician and vocalist, taught her children to love music and to sing.

Brothers and Sisters: John L., Jr. (dec.), m. Cora Hansen; former Dean of Men, U. of Utah
Elise (dec.), m. Fred Barrett,
Clarmond (dec.), m. L. Roy Yearsley
Florence (dec.), m. Dr. Asael C. Lambert
(George S.)
Ariel S. b. Dec. 9, 1901, m. Artemesia Romney
Harriette, m. Theo Berrett

Marriage: Algie Eggertsen, daughter of Lars and Annie Nielsen of Provo
b. May 3, 1896
m. December 24, 1920 in Salt Lake Temple. Successful school teacher—taught at B.Y.U. 23 years service in Provo City School Board of Education "Utah's Man of Year in Education", 1958
Served term in Utah House of Representatives

Children: Algene, b. Sept. 21, 1924, m. Steven Paul Marcus
Joan, b. May 10, 1926, m. Darrell C. Jensen, D.D.S.
George E. b. June 19, 1927, m. Ruth McDonald
Anne Grethe, b. January 8, 1932, m. Chase N. Peterson, M.D.

Education: Early Logan Schools
Student At Ricks College, Rexburg, Idaho
1918-1919, World War I, U.S. Army in France, 91st Division
1921—A.B., B.Y.U.
President, ASBYU Studentbody, Valedictorian
1921-22, Student At Harvard Law School
1924, J.D., University of California at Berkeley, California
Lecturer in law at B.Y.U. 1926-32

266

Civic and Government:	General Practice of law in Provo, 1926 to date
	1924-28, Judge, City Court
	1928-30, County Attorney
	1928-30, Chairman County Democratic Party
	1931-32 State Commander American Legion
	American and Utah Bar Associations
	Member Board of Directors American Judicature Society— sole Utah member on board
	1956, City Attorney for Provo City
	1958, President of Brigham Young Chapter, Sons of Utah Pioneers
	1960, President Utah State Bar Association
Religion:	L.D.S. Mission to France and England, 1914-16
	Teacher in Sunday School and Priesthood Quorum
Affiliations:	Delta Theta Phi, Tau Kappa Alpha, Kiwanis Club of Provo, American Legion

George Smith Ballif set his professional goal early in life. As a debater and orator at Ricks College of Rexburg, Idaho and at B.Y.U. he was a winning speaker, an outstanding varsity debater in a day when debates drew capacity crowds to College Hall which breathlessly awaited the professional judges' decision. When George, Hyrum Harter, and Ernest L. Wilkinson won a very important debate against a crack, polished Princeton University team, they were hailed on the campus and in the State with as much enthusiasm as the modern football hero of today. How times have changed!

George went to France in 1918-1919 and served in the famed U.S. 91st Division, with all its thundrous bombardments and hand to hand bayonet encounters in the Argonne and Chateau Thierry. There he dropped boyhood and emerged uninjured as a very confident man when armistice was declared on that famous November 11th on the 11th hour. He had already served a mission to France in 1914-1916, learned the language which he spoke fluently. This language knowledge made him invaluable to his American buddies and officers as well.

With a foreign mission and a war back of him, he enrolled at B.Y.U. and immediately became a studentbody leader. He married Algie Eggertsen, one of the school's popular teachers of physical education and dramatic arts, whom he soon won over to his Democratic party affiliations. George was an honor scholar, was the graduating class valedictorian (1921), and served as the Studentbody President.

Both he and his brother, Ariel, are excellent singers, each a soloist of repute. Ariel has been a member of the B.Y.U. Faculty Quartette ever since he came to the University to teach. Both George and Ariel have taken leading roles in College Hall varsity plays, their resonant voices giving them power on stage and platform.

Politics and the American Legion have occupied most of George's calendar. Young George E. is his father's partner in law. While George Sr. was Provo's City Attorney, his son was city prosecutor. George is an active Kiwanian.

The Ballif's are enthusiastic supporters of the University's cultural and athletic programs.

JAMES LOUIS BARKER

Born: July 27, 1880   **Place:** North Ogden, Utah

Father: Henry Barker, the son of Frederick Barker and Ann Blygh Born October 6, 1840 at Watertown, Jefferson, New York; to Utah in 1865 with a handcart company. Marriage November 30, 1867 in the Endowment House, Salt Lake City. All three of his sons fulfilled missions, met in Italy and toured Europe.

Mother: Margaret Stalle, the daughter of Jean Pierre Stalle and Marie Jeanne Gaudin (Mary Jane Goodwin). Born October 20, 1850 at Boul Costwhich near Prarustin, Piedmont, Italy. Jean Pierre's family came to Utah in first handcart company. Died April 9, 1938.

Brothers and Sisters: James L. had nine brothers and sisters.
Mary Rosabell Barker, b. August 7, 1869, died as a child.
Margaret Emma Barker, b. January 17, 1871; m. December 28, 1889 to Calvin Wheeler.
Henry Barker, b. September 19, 1873; m. June 4, 1910 to Sadie Powell; died December 10, 1963.
Frederick Barker, b. March 26, 1876; m. April 29, 1909 to Della Ann Hickenlooper.
John Barker, b. July 26, 1878; died as a child.
(James L.)
William Nathan Barker, b. December 18, 1883; m. December 22, 1909 to Iva A. Bailey.
George Albert Barker, b. October 25, 1885; died as a child.
Ann Frances Barker, b. October 10, 1888; m. June 15, 1915 to Archibald F. Clifford; died April 28, 1920.
Lilly May Barker, b. October 15, 1892; m. June 5, 1912 to Ianthus L. Richards; died November 25, 1961.

Marriage: Kate Montgomery, daughter of Nathaniel Montgomery and Nancy Maria Clark. Born May 30, 1881 at North Ogden, Weber, Utah.

Children: Nancy (deceased)
James L., Jr. (born in Paris, France)—Attorney and judge in Salt Lake City; born 1920.
Margaret, m. Albert O. Mitchell, Ph.D., B.Y.U. speech faculty. Died Dec. 23, 1965.

Death: May 29, 1958 caused by an auto crash at Midvale, Utah. Traveling south, termed "unavoidable."

Schooling: Educated at Weber County Schools and at fourteen went to Salt Lake with brothers, Henry and Fred, and attended the University of Utah.

A.B. 1899, University of Utah.

Traveled in Europe as a student at University of Neuchatel, College de France and the Sorbonne in Paris.

1904-1911 in Europe a part of each year as a student.

1907-1914—Chairman of Language Department at B.Y.U.

1911-13—Full-time student in Paris.

1906—After marriage to Kate Montgomery, went to Europe at Neuchatel in Switzerland.

Church: From 1901-1904 filled an L.D.S. Mission in Switzerland-Austria—3 years.

1942-44—President of Argentine Mission.

1946-50—President of French Mission. With Jos. E. Evans of Ogden, translated the Book of Mormon into French. (1906) Church High Council in Liberty Stake

Member of Deseret Sunday School Union Board from November 1950 to his death; serving on the Board several times before 1950.

Author of a three-year manual "The Divine Church", a scholarly treatise of the Christian Church up to the restoration of the Gospel in 1830. Later collected into a volume book.

Educational Activities: He did considerable research for the modern Language Association in Paris and the U.S.

Chairman of the B.Y.U. Language Department, 1907-1914.

Principal of Weber Academy, 1914-1916.

1922—Professor of phonetics and lecturer at the University of Chicago, 1936-1946.

Demonstrator for corrective speech and accent with the Department of Immigration and Naturalization.

Head of Department of Languages at University of Utah He taught and spoke fluently German, French, Spanish, and Italian.

Taught at B.Y.U. as Professor Emeritus in languages and had taught for six years when the accident occurred causing his death.

Lectured in dozens of American and European universities and was honored the world over as an expert phonetician.

Degree—"License in Lettres"—University of Neuchatel.

Study with Abbe Rousselot, world famous phonetician; discovered his theory of syllable accent, revolutionary in nature.

Decorated by French Government "Palmes a' Officier d' Academie"

Lecturer and demonstrator of the U.S. Immigration and Naturalization Service.
Author of French Text and four manuals in pronunciation, English, French, Spanish, and German.

When Mrs. Barker and family gave the B.Y.U. the remarkable James L. Barker collection of books dealing with the history of the Christian Church, the 1500 volumes materially added to the wealth of gospel material in the B.Y.U. library. It reveals the great expanse of his interests and research, the care and exactness used to present his facts for "The Divine Church." Catholic and Protestant writers in English, French, Spanish, and Italian, as well as the Latin and Greek, are in the comprehensive collection. One passage in the New Testament has required a three and four months' research, exacting that patience which comes only from devoted scholars. When a book was quoted by several research authorities, James L. sought for the book until it was located. He spent hours delving in old book shops in Germany, France, Italy, and England. In these ramblings with a purpose, he would often pick up a little known book on early Mormon history and send it to the Church Historians Office or the University of Utah or B.Y.U. library. He had discriminating sense for books of value; his gracious smile and friendly approach got many books at reduced prices which students could pay.

James L. would choose a subject, get all the authoritative books available, make a list of those he needed, and, in due course of time, would go to New York or Philadelphia or across the water to Europe and begin a systematic search.

It was Dr. Barker who induced me to leave the stage and take a teaching position at Weber College for a summer school course. While there I watched him and his mission companion, G. Oscar Russell, work for hours on a syllable in English to learn of its mouth manipulations in producing such a sound. Phonetics became a passion; they conceived it as a definite means of better teaching the spoken language. Each sound was to have a phonetic symbol which would be a constant and recognized the world over. James L. first compared English with French, got all the similar sounds on a chart, then began to work on sounds not common to English. The simplicity of French speech compared to the complexity of English sounds quickly became obvious. Although they use the identical alphabet, Professor Barker was one of the first to learn that most all French consonants are "initial" in nature

271

where English is one continual running together of syllables, even from one sentence to another. This discovery attracted the attention of great French phoneticians and made the name of James L. Barker a highly honored one in French academic circles.

I was a "guinea pig" for Messers Barker and Russell, who put literally pounds of thin powdered wax in my mouth and had me go through the English consonant cycle. Barker was watching for exactness in sound as represented by the muscle adjustment. Russell was endeavoring to establish a "vowel triangle" or the relative front and back positions of the focus of the sound. The Germans and French had just previously introduced the subject as an academic challenge, and Barker and Russell were two of the first Americans to become recognized authorities.

Professor Barker could hear any foreigner speak English and immediately tell what was incorrect in his speech and how to correct it. He taught with knowledge which convinced his listener or student.

A tribute from Dr. René Belle, chairman of the French Department at University of Southern California, June 27, 1958, is indicative of the esteem in which so many linguists and phoneticians held Professor Barker. A letter to President David O. McKay in part, says, "I met Doctor Barker thirty years ago, at the University of Southern California, where he was lecturing at the time. I immediately admired one of the most distinguished professors of the French language and literature and one of the outstanding and most original masters in the science of phonetics. At the time of our first meeting, I had recently arrived from my native country, France; my heart was fast becoming Americanized but alas! not my tongue. Doctor Barker gave me then, and many times ever since, his wholehearted guidance, his help and his time . . . Everyone who knew him loved him, appreciated his understanding, and patience, enjoyed his conscience: with his wide knowledge, Doctor Barker was so generous, so simple, so kind . . .

"Justly proud to be a member of the wonderful Church over which you preside, Sir, he was a splendid representative of its high ideals. To me, who came from France, he was one of the finest Americans I ever met, one of the most admirable men I ever knew."

President McKay, in Prof. Barker's funeral sermon said, "He kept his life clean; he had knowingly wronged no man . . . he had enhanced his inherited gifts and qualifications by study and diligent application. In every walk of life he had rendered a service which will endear him to us forever . . . Death cannot touch this influence he has rendered in the lives of his students."

Tributes and expressions of highest esteem came to Mrs. Barker from all parts of the nation and even foreign countries, extolling the merits of James L. Barker, following his sudden death.

I never saw James L. without a book, usually in his hand and often in either coat pocket. He took a subject and mastered the fundamentals before he studied in any other line of thought. He would say "Sit down a minute. How does this sound to you" and then would expound a whole book in a few paragraphs. As he walked along the street, he would read from some new books in a foreign tongue—he kept five languages "alive" by frequent practice. He was as careful of his pronunciation as he was meticulous in getting thought content.

His enthusiasm was contagious. You left him with smiles, with something to cheerfully achieve. Often he would forget to eat meals, but when he ate, he invariable said, "That's the best meal I ever ate" and "That undoubtedly is the best piece of pie I ever had." His praise was genuine and frequently bestowed. He thought positively and avoided negative situations. When he played he played to win. Often a game of checkers on the back porch in his home on Jefferson Avenue in Ogden would occupy his lunch time. If a certain move led to his defeat he would say, "Let's do that over again," and he would start over many times until he solved the proper counter move.

When tired, he would say, "Got any jokes today? Let's hear a couple." Play on words and malapropisms especially pleased him. If it were a "good" joke, he would laugh, repeat it himself, laugh equally heartily and conclude "I'll have to remember that and tell it to Kate."

His family life was ideal as he had a wife who understood his absorbing interests and periods of intense concentration. I heard her say once, "Why don't you marry that book?" He replied, "She wouldn't have me" and laughed heartily.

A great teacher, a dedicated scholar with inexhaustible energy, a devout churchman, a most loveable husband and father—such was James L. Barker.

TRIBUTES TO JAMES L. BARKER
BY WORLD AUTHORITIES

Dr. C. E. Parmenter of Chicago

"We are very eager to have a report on your work in phonetics abroad at Modern Language Association. Your work is by far the most important being done by any scholar and we must have a discussion of some phase of it. Please wire title, etc."

Professor Raymond Weeks of Columbia University to Carnegie Foundation

"If your foundation is interested in the scientific advancement of speech sounds, you have in M. Barker the best man available in this country and one of the two or three strongest men in the world . . . his work lies in the very base of linguistics and philology."

L'Abbe Rousselot of Sarbonne, Paris

"The first man to do experimental work in pronunciation and to study it objectively with apparatus."

Chanoine J. M. Meunier, Catholic University of Paris

"I believe that the work in experimental phonetics of Professor Barker is destined to revolutionize the study of modern languages."

ARTHUR LAWTON BEELEY

Authority in Social Work

Born: August 28, 1890   **Place:** Manchester, England
the son of John William and Elizabeth Ann Lawton Beeley

Father: John William Beeley

Mother: Ann Lawton, came to the United States in 1908 with her son, Arthur, and daughter Maude.

Sister: Maude Beeley Jacob, born in Stockport, England 1884. Died 1960. M.A., Brigham Young University 1940.

Married: Glenn Johnson on June 6, 1916, daughter of Stephen Mary Davis Johnson, in the Salt Lake Temple.
Born March 13, 1893, in Moroni, Utah; A. B. Brigham Young University 1915; Graduate studies in the San Francisco and Chicago Art Institutes. London Central School of Arts and Crafts. Director of Pioneer Craft House in Salt Lake City, Utah.
Instructor in Art at Brigham Young University 1915-16. Member L.D.S. Primary Board 1927-31. YWMIA General Board 1932-38.

Children: Mary, married William R. Christensen, M.D.
Stephen Johnson Beeley, married Flora Sundberg.

Arthur Lawton Beeley—Sociology. A. B., Brigham Young University, 1913; A. M. University of Chicago, 1918; Ph. D., 1925, Magna Cum Laude; Post-doctoral study University of London, 1932-33.

Principal Emery Academy, Castle Dale, Utah, 1917-18; Assistant Professor Psychology, University of Utah, 1919-1921; Research Association, Ill. State criminologist, 1924-25; Assistant Professor Social Economy University of Chicago, 1925-26; Professor Sociology and Director Bureau of Student Council, University of Utah since 1927; Brigham Young University Distinguished Service Alumni Award in 1937; Dean of Graduate School of Social work; Director of Institute of World Affairs; University of Utah conferred on him an honorary Doctor of Laws in 1955. Retired from University faculty in 1956.

Criminal research in England, 1932-33, under grant from American Social Science Research Council. Member National Committee for Mental Hygiene White House conference on child health protection, 1929-30. Member A. A. A. S., American Sociological Society, American Association of Social Workers, American Association of College Professors, Utah Soc. for Mental Hygiene, President 1928-29; Phi Beta Kappa; Phi Kappa Phi; Phi Delta Kappa; President Utah State Conference of Social Work, 1929-30; member American Prison Association; Distinguished Service Award from Utah Academy of Sciences, Letters and Arts in 1954. Member American Ortho-Psychiatric Association (fellow); member board of directors English-speaking Union of United States. Lecturer National Police Academy (Federal Bureau of Investigation) 1943-45.

Church—L.D.S. European Mission. Member Young Men's Mutual Improvement Association General Board for 15 years, Executive Secretary of the Social Advisory Committee with late President Stephen L Richards.

Author, "An Experimental Study in Left Handedness"—1918; "The Bail System in Chicago,"—1927; "Boys, Girls in Salt Lake City,"—1929; "Community Health and Hygiene" with Dr. L. L. Daynes—1930; "Social Planning for Crime Control"—1935.

Arthur is an omniverous reader, looks at life with cause and effects bases. He has faith in the good in each individual and believes a person can build a character on the foundation of that good. He has become an international authority on criminological research and his work with the Institute of World Affairs for a period of sixteen years gave him an intimate association with the world's sociological leaders. His department of Graduate School of Social Work attracted scholars from the world to Utah's school rooms. He took an important part in the International Congress on Mental Health in London in 1948.

His honors have spread over a remarkable territory of scholarship and research. He was elected a Fellow and Life Member of the Ortho-Psychiatric Association. In 1965 was the recipient of the August Vollmer Award of the American Society of Criminology. He is a member of the Executive Board of the National Conference on Bail and Criminal Justice appointed by former Attorney General Robert F. Kennedy 1964 to present.

He has written numerous articles for national and church magazines, is writing the history of the Graduate School of Social Work at the University of Utah, a pioneer in the subject.

With a bit of England still left in him, he is busy with his hopes for the improvement of the world citizen and the redemption of those who err in our complex civilization.

Arthur is a director of our Brigham Young University Emeritus Club.

EZRA TAFT BENSON

Marketing specialist, U.S. Secretary of Agriculture, and L.D.S. Apostle.

Born: August 4, 1899   **Place:** Whitney, Idaho
Ordained an apostle October 7, 1943 by President Heber J. Grant

Father: George Taft Benson, Jr., son of George Taft and Louisa Ballif (father—George Taft, son of Ezra Taft I, and Adeline Brooks Andrus Louisa, the daughter of Serge Louis Ballif and Elise LeCoultre of Lausanne, Switzerland)
Born June 24, 1875
Fourth child of 13 children
Died Aug. 13, 1934

Mother: Sarah Dunkley
b. June 29, 1878 at Franklin, Idaho, oldest daughter in family of 13 children
m. October 19, 1898 in Logan Temple
Graduate Oneida Stake Academy; beautiful singer and soloist; taught all auxiliaries
7 sons filled missions all district presidents
died June 1, 1933

Brothers and Sisters: Ezra Taft, eldest of 11 children
Joseph D., b. November 12, 1900
Margaret, b. January 21, 1901
Orval D., b. August 30, 1903
George Taft and Sarah, twins, b. December 24, 1904
Louisa, b. 1905
Lera, b. May 4, 1907
Valdo D., b. May 4, 1911
Ross Dean, b. January 20, 1919
Volco, b. April 11, 1920

Marriage: Flora Smith Amussen
m. September 10, 1926
youngest child of Carl C. and Barbara Smith Amussen of Salt Lake City, Utah
Carl C. born in Kjolge, Denmark, Utah's pioneer jeweler —constructed first business block in Salt Lake City (now Richard's Candies); brought first fountain to the state
Mother a widow when Flora one year old
Flora filled mission to Hawaii

Children: Reed A., b. January 2, 1928, m. Mae Hinckley

Mark A., b. May 2, 1929, m. Lela Wing
Barbara, b. June 20, 1934, m. R. H. Walker
Beverly, b. September 20, 1937, m. James M. Parker
Bonnie, b. March 30, 1940, m. Lowell Madsen
Flora Beth, b. August 12, 1944

⁂⁂⁂⁂⁂⁂⁂⁂⁂⁂⁂⁂⁂⁂⁂⁂

Ezra Taft Benson is a roundly educated man. He was born with a love for the soil and for freedom to work it to its greatest efficiency; work, freedom and worship is his family crest.

He attended Oneida Stake Academy of Preston, Idaho; studied at Utah State Agricultural (Land Grant) College, now Utah State University; took a degree in agronomy from B.Y.U. in 1926 and an M.S. in agricultural economics from Iowa State in 1927. He was awarded a fellowship at the University of California and took graduate studies, selected for personal growth, and was elected to Gamma Sigma Delta, honorary agricultural society.

Between the time he spent at U.S.A.C. and B.Y.U., he filled a mission to England. In all his classes at B.Y.U. he was known for high scholarship, promptness with assignments, and a quiet interest in the people all about him. As I heard him give his talk in public speaking, I soon realized that he was a student with a purpose and definite goals, with experience beyond most young people's attainment. He graduated with honors at 27 and married a beautiful, talented young lady in September of that year. He was already one of the West's most experienced Scout Masters and aided in the growth of scouting on our campus.

When he took his wife to Idaho he had plans for extensive farming and ranching. He was soon put in Y.M.M.I.A. leadership in Franklin and Boise Stakes and in the Boise Stake Presidency in 1934. Scouting was an important part of his Church activities, both in Mutual and in the Stake Presidency. When he moved to Washington, D.C. to work with farm cooperatives, he was made the first president of the new Washington Stake, 1940-44.

A new Church responsibility came most unexpectedly when he was appointed an apostle to The Church of Jesus Christ of Latter-day Saints in July, 1943.

Immediately following World War II, he was called to preside over the European Mission in 1946. His special assignment was to distribute food and clothing to needy Church members and to aid in land rehabilitation.

He had been economist for the Idaho State Farm Management and the executive council of Farmer's Cooperatives in Washington, D.C. and was a natural selection to help solve the plight of the American farmer. It was right after the disastrous draught when cattle were starving on the range, farm prices were falling, and food prices had climbed beyond reason. He had proclaimed loudly and nationally against fixed food price supports which kept U.S. foods off world markets in some commodities and the tariff which had helped undersell certain other American goods. Ezra Taft Benson was particularly against subsidies and money for crops not grown. He became Secretary of Agriculture for 1952-60 and a national figure over night. He could not control the weather drought nor water nor bickering politicians plying for special district privileges, but the average American farmer saw steady improvement in his market possibilities, learned more about over-production, over-grazing, and crop rotation, heard the gospel of work for pay and information on supply and demand. One acre was often improved enough to equal the former production of two or three acres, which resulted in the problem of cooperative distribution. Secretary Benson left the farmers with a philosophy that food controls the world's progress and carries with it the responsibilities of national survival—responsibilities that demand patriotism, neighborly interests, soil rejuvenation, grange planning, willing support of judicial taxation, and continued zeal in the protection of individual rights and governmental respect. He emphasized the facts that we must build up and replace as fast as we take away; that the future is equally binding upon those who have benefited from the pioneer past.

The B.Y.U. Alumni Association gave him its Distinguished Service Award in 1950. The National Council honored him with the Boy Scout Silver Antelope, its highest award. He was cited for service to agriculture and presented a commemorative medal on the 50th anniversary of the twelve Federal land banks.

He is a member of the Salt Lake Rotary Club and a director of Zion's First National Bank in Salt Lake City, Utah.

Ezra T. Benson did not seek the secretaryship of agriculture which President Eisenhower offered him. After a modest but firm refusal, he became convinced that he should accept the position as a governmental service. His response was typical of the man all his life, "Consistent with the principles which have guided my life, I shall do my best, God being my helper."

As a college graduate and practical farmer, he specialized in agricultural economics and took with him as Secretary of Agriculture the respect and encouragement of almost all national farm groups, although he met certain Senatorial opposition from the day he took oath of office. As the fifteenth Secretary of the department, he moved into the Agricultural building, second largest U.S. Government building, housing some 8,000 employees from all parts of the country. His payroll budget covered some 56,000 workers and a budget of $2.1 billion, next in size to the Treasury department. One of the nation's biggest educational programs was his to direct, especially adult education. The great printing schedule of more than 375 different pamphlets and journals went over his desk. One of the first steps he took was to regroup the 21 agencies into four administrative units and conserve in economy and promote efficiency. Such changes obviously met individual opposition. Some problems which faced him were floods and drought; scientific experiments with all farm products; problems of distribution; the protection of the small land farmer against the oppressive competition of the great combine groups; setting parity at a most helpful level; competing with foreign markets in such commodities as sugar, cotton, beef, rice, soy beans, wood paper; obtaining tariff rates which would protect the American farmer; range disputes; and above all, lobbying for profit of sections rather than for legislation that would benefit the farmers across the land. Every problem which confronted Ezra Taft was met by the test of fairness and honesty. He was never a politician—he lived on hard work and fair play.

President Benson has a great love for this school as indicated in a speech he gave to the studentbody on December 1, 1952:

"I have great hope for the youth of Zion. I believe firmly that there's no group of young people in the whole world who have the opportunities which are yours. I believe firmly that in the days ahead this nation is going to demand and need the leadership of men and women who have been trained in the home, in the Church, in the school as you have been trained, who have your ideals, who are guided by the principles which guide your lives. You are going to be in positions of leadership."

President Eisenhower described Secretary Benson as "a man of the highest personal and intellectual honesty and courage whose services the nation could not now afford to lose." (From a statement in the *New York Times*.)

As long as Ezra Taft Benson is filling his time with service to his fellowmen, he will be happy. His Church, his country, and his family are his devotions and his hobbies. He credits his wife with much of his success and makes of her a companion in all his activities. Some of their happiest hours are found during the infrequent times they can meet with all their family.

Ezra T. is the first Latter-day Saint to hold a U.S. Cabinet assignment. When in the States he is sought as chief speaker at many of the farm cooperatives across the nation, a tribute to his leadership for their welfare and his fight for individual liberty.

We get a good character picture of Ezra T. Benson by reading the various comments made by national newsmen when he was deeply concerned with the world's agricultural problems and chosen for the second time to set them right.

Newsweek for November 30, 1953, writes in part: "Ezra Taft Benson started life as a gangling farm hand in the beet fields of Idaho, but he never had a harder row to hoe than he now faces in Washington.

"Benson became Secretary of Agriculture in a time of trouble . . . a majority of farmers believed firmly in fixed prices support. Benson didn't. He argued that it was fixed supports that had caused the surpluses to pile up and that priced American farm products off the world market . . . President Eisenhower is standing by him and will give him a chance to perform the near-miracle required to save him."

He became one of the most controversial figures in American public life, but I do not know that his character was ever impugned. He ran his office on strict principles, and honesty backed his every act. To quote further from *Newsweek:*

"At 54, Benson is a big, ruddy-faced man with thinning hair and a high forehead, whose religion is the key to all his thoughts and his acts. He begins and ends each day by leading his family in prayer, and he prays silently during the day. Mormons believe the body, purified and made whole, will be resurrected with the spirit and, therefore, should be kept undefiled on earth. As a result, Benson doesn't smoke, or touch liquor, coffee, and tea: He eats meat sparingly . . . He considers it simply immoral for a man to receive money from the government for crops he does not grow, goods he does not produce, or work he does not do . . . . Benson worked on the land, not only for his father, but also for any neighbor who needed a willing hand. He was a prodigious worker.

Politicking Democrats have called the Eisenhower cabinet a cabinet of "millionaires". The description does not fit Benson. He not only has not tried to amass great wealth; he frequently has rejected lucrative jobs because he felt they would interfere with his two great missions in life—preaching the Mormon gospel and helping the nations' farmers."

Harold Martin in the *Saturday Evening Post,* March 28, 1953, wrote several pages appraising the work of President Benson.

"His friends believe he derived (from his own boyhood experience) the philosophy to which he still clings—the stout conviction that hard work never hurt a growing boy; that the earth will reward those who toil with prayerful and unremitting vigor; that the farmers who help each other get along better than those who try to work alone; and that there is always an easier way to do a hard, mean job of farm work if a man only had the education to discover it. . . .

"During the heyday of the New Deal when it appeared that Government was seeking to convert the rugged individualistic and sometimes hungry, farmer to a stall-fed complacency, he went about preaching a message of independence to farm groups all over the country . . . that the farmer who was willing to work was foolish to trade his freedom for a government handout. To him, the Government's job, so far as agriculture was concerned, was to teach and educate, not to control, dictate or play Santa Claus . . . Producers, processors and consumers all fared best when agricultural products were sold in a market that operated as freely as possible under the old and irrevocable law of supply and demand. A farmer had a right to expect his government to protect him from disaster. He has no right to expect it to guarantee him a profit."

His latest appointment of major responsibility was to the presidency of the European Mission, with its more than 44,000 members in 420 congregations. Special films were used, such as "Mormons In Germanic Europe." How President Karl G. Maeser would have loved such a service and so many natives to give him assistance! President Benson reported at April, 1964 Conference in Salt Lake City that 27 new buildings were well under construction and 32 approved for starting the following year. Ten were ready for dedication in 1965 in the Germanic area.

President Benson, as former U.S. Secretary of Agriculture, is frequently asked to give talks to formal and government associations and he has addressed chamber of commerce groups in Frankfurt, Berlin and Bonn. Places which banned the missionaries prior to World War II all now are offering police assistance to aid in permitting Mormon literature in public and private libraries, in schools and many friendly offices.

He had served the European Mission in 1946 with authority to aid and feed needy Saints. Upon returning to the mission, again as president, he visited many of these districts, contacted former converts and has many of them working in the wards, branches, in the Temples, and as builders of chapels. Husbands and wives serve as missionaries in their communities. Farms, usually small in acreage, are visited and methods of improvement suggested, until now most of the people and the mission itself is self supporting.

Many years of vigorous hardworking service appear ahead for this devoted citizen and churchman.

OSCAR WYMAN BERG

Born: August 4, 1886, Provo, Utah.

Father: Ole H. Berg of Rod Skjeberg, Smaalenene, Fridrikshald, Norway
b. September 12, 1840, son of Hendrik Anderson;
to Utah October 8, 1866 in Andrew Scott Company
Missionary to Norway, Bishop of Provo First Ward, City Councilman
Superintendent for the interior construction of the St. George Temple;
Carpenter supervisor of Provo Tabernacle; Organized first Provo Old Folk Committee; contractor and undertaker; d. February 25, 1919

Mother: Anna Nielson, daughter of Hans Nielsen and Maren Jacobsen of Odense, Denmark, who were pioneers to Utah, November 8, 1865, b. September 11, 1847 in Odense; d. November 26, 1920

Brothers and Sisters: Olivia B. m. George A. Nuttall of Los Angeles, California
Anna B. m. Enoch Jorgenson
Mary B., m. Warren W. Beckstead of Logan, Utah
Elnora B. m. James Prestwich
Flora B. m. Walter Jenkins, Whittier, California
Christina, Henry Ward, Alma F. died in 1880's
Edna B. m. Oscar E. Groshell, New York City, New York
(Oscar Wyman)

Marriage: 1.) Josephine Thomas, m., September 11, 1911, d. April 12, 1927
2.) Veva Peters of American Fork, Utah, m., January 19, 1929

Children of Josephine: Max W. of Provo—leading mortician, President of Chamber of Commerce and active Rotarian
Marion m. Lewis Clark of Twin Falls, Idaho
Joan, m. Burke Jenkins of Salt Lake City, Utah

Death: January 9, 1955 in Mesa, Arizona, recuperating from an operation.

Wyman Berg was a mortician of national repute, who inherited the business built by his father, Norwegian immigrant, Ole H. Berg. The firm is one of the oldest in the state. Wyman took his son, Max, into partnership in the Berg Mortuary, bought the Jesse Knight mansion, and converted it into a beautiful mortuary.

He was educated in the Provo Schools, attending the Maeser and Parker Schools and graduating from B.Y.U. in 1919. He was active in dramatics and debating. He early chose his father's profession as his own and directed all of his education to that end. He became active in the business very early in his life. Being a young man when the influenza epidemic attacked the nation and became very severe in the mountain states he was obliged to aid his father and make coffins to supply the excessive demands. Wyman was a licensed mortician when eighteen years of age and aided hundreds of poorer people with their finances during the epidemic and resultant burial periods.

His community activities were numerous, including the outstanding Christmas parties given for the children of Provo for more than 32 years. He was one of the organizers of the Provo Golf Club; equipped young men's basketball clubs over the years; was an active Scouter and especially successful in raising Boy Scout funds. For twenty years he was general chairman of the Central Old Folks Committee, giving parties in the canyon, North Park, Utah Lake Resort and the Columbia (Paramount) Theatre. He was one of the first fifty members in the Provo Rotary Club and served as the president in 1940-41, leading in various Rotary projects. He was a director of the Provo Chamber of Commerce from 1935-43, and its vice-president in 1942-43. He was an active B. Y. U. alumnus and ardent sports supporter, aided in establishing the steel industry in Utah and Provo in 1923-24, and was a Red Cross worker on drives for years.

In his profession, he was the first Utahn to become a member of the National Selected Morticians and was a member and chairman of the Utah Embalmers and Funeral Directors Examining Board under Governor Herbert B. Maw. He served as president of Utah Funeral Directors association.

A lover of outdoors, he bred show horses and often displayed his five gaited pure breds in Utah shows. A good marksman, he was a member of the Bonneville Duck Hunting Club.

As a member in the L.D.S. Church, he held the office of High Priest. Few men in Utah have been more interested or done more for the advancement of Utah than Wyman Berg. His ready laugh brightened many group meetings; his kindly patience and love of beauty showed in his profession and daily life.

His establishment has an excellent collection of carefully selected oil paintings.

Wyman was one of the first to contribute to worthwhile drives and volunteered assistance for many of the B.Y.U. benefits.

ISAAC E. BROCKBANK

Born: October 17, 1882 in Spanish Fork, Utah

Father: Joshua b. May 15, 1848 at Underbarrow, Westmoreland, England
Married at 19 in Salt Lake Endowment House
To Utah September 4, 1852 with Abraham O. Smoot Co.
Policeman in Spanish Fork for ten years
City Water master many years
Broke leg below calf; limb saved but grew 2 inches shorter
Active civic and church worker

Mother: Sarah Ann Traxon—b. April, 1851, at Crostwich, Norfolk, England
To America on the ship "Windemere" with her parents Eliza Goodson
Jex and Wm. Jex, on February 22, 1854
Ship in great 10 day storm and infected by small pox
To Utah via Cuba, then New Orleans—when Johnston's Army came to Utah the family moved to Spanish Fork
d. on Isaac's birthday, October 17, 1928 at 77½ years
"A tall, slender brown eyed beauty with soft, kind voice"

Brothers and Sisters: Sarah Ann Eliza, b. January 4, 1870
Elizabeth Vilate, b. June 26, 1873, d. May 5, 1919 at 46
Wm. Ernest, b. Sept. 19, 1875
Lillian Christina, b. Nov. 10, 1877
Delbert David, b. April 8, 1880, d. October 4, 1938
(Isaac Elmer)
Albert Goodson, b. Sept 7, 1884, d. Oct. 23, 1949
Willis Mainwaring, b. Nov. 28, 1886
Heber David, b. Dec. 27, 1891, d. April 7, 1941
Eleanor Rebecca, b. July 10, 1894, d. June 30, 1915
Merrill Jex, b. Sept. 29, 1896, d. July 5, 1954
Joshua Richard, b. Jan. 21, 1872, d. Sept. 21, 1872
Henry Archibald, b. Nov. 29, 1889, d. Sept. 12, 1891

Marriage: 1. Zoe May Brimhall, m. Oct. 21, 1908, d. Sept. 3, 1913
2. Elsie Vernessa Booth, m. Sept. 1, 1916, daughter of John and Delia Winters Booth of Provo, b. April 12, 1894
Lived in Spanish Fork until 1920—then to Provo
All daughters to college and successfully married and leaders in their communities

Children:	Children of Zoe May: Alma, b. Sept. 18, 1909, d. at birth Ila, b. Aug. 2, 1911, Dale Peterson Children of Elsie: Helen, m. Merrill Welch Shirley Ann, m. Judge Monroe Paxman Elinor, m. Dr. D. Creed Brimhall Leah Patricia, m. Paul Fillmore Mary Carol, m. Dean Gray Nancy Dawn, m. Lohr Livingston Elsie Joyce, m. William Beezer Barbara Kay, m. Robert Webber
Death:	August 16, 1954 of heart attack and auto crash, buried in Spanish Fork
Education:	Spanish Fork Schools A.B.—B.Y.U.—1915 M.A.—U. of U.—1920 L.L.B.—U. of U.—1920 J.D.—U. of Chicago—1921
Activities:	District Chairman B.S.A.—member Utah National Parks Council Finance Chairman Provo M.I.A. Girls Home President Provo Chamber of Commerce President Provo Rotary Club Chairman Utah Valley Hospital Board Utah County Red Cross Chapter—7 years Practicing Attorney—35 years City Attorney—10 years Utah County attorney—6 years County Chairman Republican Party Director Jex Library Committee of Spanish Fork Director Intermountain Finance and Thrift Co. Member Provo Charter Commission Toured Europe and later took world tour Had an excellent home library and numerous paintings by local artists
Religion:	L.D.S. Mission to Germany Utah Stake High Council many years President Utah Stake Y.M.M.I.A. many years Generous donor to worthy causes Keen student of Church History His devotion to education and the Brigham Young University were universally recognized "The B.Y.U. is the soul of Utah Valley"

In whatever cause or group "Ike" joined or sponsored he soon became one of its leaders. The group had to have merit or promote civic good or he disassociated himself. His purse was generously opened for Red Cross, Boy Scouts, Rotary Park, bringing in a hospital, a book drive for the public library, B.Y.U. stadium or building funds, golf course for the city, a swimming pool for the young, or the establishment of a Canyon Home for girls.

As city and county attorney he vigorously defended the rights of citizens and fought encroachment on city or county properties and responsibilities. He respected and demanded adherence to the law of the land. He kept church and state separate but was an ardent protagonist for each and was respected by all who knew him. A tribute paid to him at death is a good character summary: *Provo Herald* editorial (8-18-1954)

"Mr. Brockbank was a man without guile. He spoke his opinions frankly. He usually had definite opinions on a subject because he fed his keen intellect by constant study and research. Whether or not you agreed with Mr. Brockbank you had to admire him because he was frank and did not hesitate to let you know exactly where he stood—Utah County will not forget Isaac E. Brockbank. His individual accomplishments and his untiring and unselfish service to his fellow men have made an indelible impression."

As a vigorous member of the Republican Party he often stated, "Federal bureaus must be abolished and individual initiative restored if we are to avoid state socialism."

On the occasion of a Rotary Club "Girls Night," Ike was the hit of the evening. He brought his nine daughters and introduced them one by one, indicating the talents of each. "I may not be able to perpepuate my name, but the man who gets any of these will get some of the best blood in the land and a darn good boss."

After his world tour with his wife, Elsie, he became even more concerned with American liberties and our great Constitution. Utah has had no more sincere defender of this precious document than I. E. Brockbank, ardent citizen, sincere churchman, able historian and scholar, generous benefactor and a bitter foe of hypocrisy. Law and principles were honored by I. E. Brockbank, a proud parent and able defender of truth.

HAROLD TAYLOR CHRISTENSEN

Residence—Lafayette, Indiana

Born: March 10, 1909, Preston, Idaho

Father: Henry Oswald Christensen son of Jens Christensen and Anna Else Larsen
(Breinholt)
Born March 21, 1881, Manti, Utah
Taught Manual Training Oneida Academy and Ricks College
Contractor and Builder
Resided in Preston, Idaho
d. June, 1960

Mother: Nettie Lavina Taylor
Daughter of Evan Taylor and Jarmelia Scott, homesteaders, of Salem
b. December 20, 1881, Salem, Utah
m. August 26, 1903, B. Y. Academy alumna
Stories in "White and Blue"
Resides in Phoenix, Arizona—Primary Association worker

Brothers and Sisters: Leland O., m. Rayola Brown
2.) Mary Parker
3.) Anna Ardith Jackson, d., June 1961
(Harold Taylor) m. Alice Spencer, of Paris, Idaho
Cornell Taylor, d. October, 1936
Arlond Taylor, b. January 14, 1914, m. Ruth Lucille Kent
Ross Taylor, b. August 28, 1918, m. Ruth Richardson Morris
Grant Taylor, b. February 27, 1920, d. 1936
Lyle Taylor b. 1922, m. Melba Bingham

Marriage: Alice Spencer
b. August 3, 1910 in Paris, Idaho
daughter of George B. Spencer and Adeline Horsley (grandson of Orson Spencer) Adeline's father Thomas, came from England
m. June 5, 1935
Talented actress, active in Little Theatre organizations

Children: Carl, b. May 4, 1936, m. Irene Masaki Aug. 8, 1963
Boyd, b. November 19, 1938, m. Betti Day June 6, 1963
Janice, b. May 9, 1942, m. Francis Hedquist, Dec. 27, 1962
Larry, b. August 22, 1945
Gayle, b. December 1, 1948
All children have attended B.Y.U.

Harold Taylor Christensen at an early age revealed a capacity for work. Never a large man, he started young on a major in the intellectual studies. In his teens he became aware of the value of good family life. He came from a close-knit family of boys with a very fair but religiously dominant father. The absence of girls in the home often became a meal time discussion and the place of marriage in world progress or stability became a matter of great interest to Harold, the second of seven sons.

Each boy realized that he would have to support himself for the most part should he go on for advanced schooling and each was encouraged by devoted and proud parents, "Our boys must amount to somebody." A mission was to take precedent over college as a foundation of character and a partial assurance against interruption in the obtaining of a degree. Harold filled a mission to New Zealand in 1929-33, being acting president his last year.

Harold was an active student in the Preston, Idaho schools. He became a leader at Ricks College, Rexburg, Idaho. At B.Y.U. where he was active in forensics and social studies, he obtained his B.S. in 1935 and M.S. in 1937.

He has been in some kind of teaching activity all his mature life, teaching in the elementary grades at Hibbard, Idaho, 1927-28. At B. Y. U. his scholarship warranted an instructorship in sociology from 1935-38. He became an assistant professor from 1938-40, professor during 1941-47, and chairman of the department from 1940-47. He was elected to Graduate Fellow in Sociology at the University of Wisconsin, 1938-39. In 1947 he was asked to head the Sociology Department at Purdue University, a position he has held ever since.

His service assignments and programs have taken him around the world. His strength in planning was shown when he was appointed chairman of the Provo Civic Welfare Committee 1941-44. He was convinced of the need for intense studies across the nation in family relations and in the problems of juvenile delinquency, early marriages, and economic insecurity. Rural and urban studies led him to definite conclusions of reform. In 1944-45 he was elected leader of Farm Population and Rural Life for the Bureau of Agricultural Economics, Northeastern Region, U.S. Department of Agriculture. He wrote numerous papers on the subject, attracting national attention. He was a member of the Utah Stake High Council.

His honors and appointments are summarized below:

Member of American and Rural Sociology Societies; National Council on Family Relations; American Institute of Family Relations (regional)

President, Utah Council on Family Relations, 1946-47, first year organized Institute on Family Relations; Indiana Council on

Family Relations, 1950-52; Ohio Sociological Society 1953-54; National Council on Family Relations 1954-56 (U.S.)

Author *Marriage Analysis,* popular college text.

Editor *Marriage and Family Living,* 1957-59 for National Council

On tour to study world family systems, summer 1964

Presided at the first section on family life at the American Sociological Association held at Montreal, Canada, late summer, 1964. Visited 33 world cities for lectures and research, including cities in New Zealand, Egypt, Israel, India, Pakistan, Burma, etc., conducting Purdue University business. Taught a semester at the University of Hawaii before returning to Purdue.

One of the nation's leading sociologists.

HERALD REY CLARK

Born: October 18, 1890 in Farmington, Utah

Father: Amasa L. Clark, son of Ezra T. Clark and Mary Stevenson Lifetime banker in Farmington; vice-president of BYU Emeritus Club.
Philanthropist, civic and church worker; Mayor Farmington (see biography)

Mother: Alice Steed, daughter of Thomas Steed and Laura Reed of Farmington. b. June 10, 1864, m. December 16, 1885 in Logan Temple.
d. August 2, 1895.

Brothers and Sisters: Alice Maude, d. as infant
A. Sterling, b. March 19, 1888
(Herald R.)
Grant S., b. July 23, 1892, d. November 8, 1940.
Half-brother and sisters (of Susie Duncan),
Julian D.
Phyllis Clark
Lewis (dec)
Nell C. Partridge
Dale G. Lewis D. (dec).

Marriage: Mabel Hone, daughter of Joshua and Susan Losser Hone. b. February 12, 1895. Graduate of BYU in 1944, accomplished vocalist, civic and church leader. Married June 9, 1915 in the Salt Lake Temple.

Children: Richard H., b. June 3, 1916, m. Beth E. Olsen
Dr. Stephen H., b. April 20, 1919, m. Margaret Ruth
Dr. Homer H., b. November 23, 1921, m. Margaret Lillian Affleck
Rand H., b. June 10, 1925, m. Marjorie Jean Hart
Dr. Philip H., b. September 17, 1929, m. Ruth Hawkins
Welsford H., b. January 21, 1932, m. Delaine Anderson

Death: May 24, 1966 at 75.

Education: BA, Business Adminstration, BYU, 1918; MBA, Business Administration, University of Washington, 1924; Studied at Rochester Business Institute, University of Utah, University of California and Ohio State University.

Occupations: 1904, Bank Clerk; 1913, Instructor in accounting at BYU; 1917, Assistant professor of finance and banking at

BYU; 1927, Associate professor of finance and banking at BYU; 1928, Professor of finance and banking at BYU; 1934, Dean of the College of Commerce to 1951 at BYU. Director and vice-president of the Davis County Bank; served in the Army Training Corps in World War I, 1918; Member of American Finance Association; of American Accounting Association; of Phi Kappa Phi; Member of the Utah State Board of Fine Arts; Member and chairman of the BYU Lyceum Bureau 1913 to present, which he has brought to world fame; President of Provo Community Concert Association (1936 until recent date); Collector of paintings bought for the university, most of which are in the galleries of BYU; Bishop of the Sixth Ward of Provo; Member of the Utah Stake Presidency; Member and chairman of many committees of the former Commercial Club of Provo and the Chamber of Commerce; Director in organizing group of Utah Valley Hospital with Common Wealth Fund; Commissary for the Alpine Summer School; Rotarian for several years.

Herald R. Clark has received more honors from his Alma Mater than any other graduate of BYU. He was bookstore manager from 1915 to 1952 and president of the BYU Alumni Assn'n twice, 1921-22, 1946-47 (a most significant honor in itself). A beautiful building, the Herald R. Clark Student Supply Center, now the Continuing Education Center, is named for him. He received the BYU Alumni Distinguished Service Award in 1953, the David O. McKay Humanities Award in 1962, and an Honorary Doctor of Art from BYU given in 1966, posthumously.

His life centered about BYU, his church, and his family. While his younger days were shared with community associations, his later life was devoted almost exclusively to BYU. When asked why he never drove a car he smilingly replied, "I have six boys growing up and one car would never do. I'll just keep peace in the family by walking. Besides, we need the exercise. Walking never hurt anybody." He thought a car in a family interfered with boys' education. His six lively and friendly boys lived with our group in the Canyon Summer School and each season was an event for all our growing families. We have had as many as five of Herald's boys on one softball or volleyball team. Rand later became a star basketball player on the varsity squad. All the boys were lovers of the outdoors and frequently went for good hikes with their father and other faculty members. Stories told around our evening campfires which brought pioneer lives to the fore were Herald's delight and he usually had an anecdote to fit the occasion. When the little party broke up for the night as the embers of glowing logs were dying out, it always brought a sense of deep admiration to watch a father and mother with six sons follow in single file, a flashlight spotting the narrow, winding mountain trail, and disappear into darkness.

Herald R. Clark was important in so many activities on our campus that his influence will be felt for many years to come.

The bookstore was his specific responsibility as soon as he registered at BYU. A modest room in the basement of College Hall was home to him for years, at a time when help was paid twenty-five cents per hour. The men trained by him advanced to responsible positions across the nation. Proceeds from the bookstore have aided in building the first Stadium and Stadium House, the George Albert Smith Field House and, recently, the magnificent Ernest L. Wilkinson Student Center.

In 1913 he was appointed instructor in accounting at BYU under President Brimhall who used Herald on most of the important school committees. His students have become economic leaders in most states of the Union and wrote to him for advice long after they graduated. He could have become cashier and executive director of his father's bank in Farmington, Utah, but he preferred the university association and the intimate relations with young people. He had associations with banks at an early age and was a director and vice-president of the Davis County Bank. He lost considerable money during the bank failures in the 1930's but paid off all his stock obligation in full, taking his losses in heroic stride. His philosophy was simple and direct—"Don't spend if you haven't got it and keep ahead for contingencies," and later, "pay the Lord a tithe and keep Him on your side. Live happily on the rest." His teaching was punctuated with trite statements, such as "Debt is a motivator if it is based on a sound investment," or "If you play the market with a sure thing be prepared to lose," and "If you buy long-term stock, walk off and forget it. It might pay you back someday."

As John C. Swenson once said, "Herald? He's an institution. There'll never be another like him."

Funeral services were held in the Joseph Smith Auditorium on the campus he so dearly loved. He is buried in Provo City Cemetery.

At the opening of the Utah Valley Symphony held in the Provo Tabernacle Oct. 26, 1966, the concert was a memorium to Herald R. Clark and the family were given life memberships in his honor.

BYRON OWEN COLTON

Born: February 15, 1882   **Place:** Provo, Utah

Father: Byron Oliver Colton
5th son and 7th child of Philander and Polly Colton
b. Nov. 29, 1848 near Council Bluffs, Iowa. d. July 27, 1930
Came with family by ox team to Utah in summer of 1850
m. (1) Sarah Jane Clark, 1870, who died in Mona Aug. 22,
1875, leaving daughter four years old.

Mother: Sarah Maria Smith
b. Jan. 1, 1856 in Provo, Utah. d. Jan. 16, 1912
Pioneered the Ashley Valley in Uintah County with Col-
tons
Attended B.Y.A. under Dr. Maeser.

**Brothers
and Sisters:** Minnie (Wilson)
Stella (Hardy), mother of 12
George Albert, died at 15
(Byron O., only living child of Byron Oliver)

Marriage: Helen Merkley
daughter of Nelson and Keturah Merkley Jr.
b. April 9, 1890. m. June 29, 1910.
d. Oct. 22, 1961
Instrumental in getting "Mill Ward" changed to "Maeser"
in the Uintah Stake

Children: Ruth*
Lula (Mrs. Dudley)*
Merrill Byron*
Margaret (Wyler), d. October 1961.
Gordon L.
Elmo S.*
Miles M.*
Sarah (Neilson)*
Grace Eleanor (Berrett)*
*Attended B.Y.A.

It is so easy to forget the deeds of the past in our absorbing interest with the present. Without men of the calibre of Byron O. Colton, who can say when Brigham Young University would have arrived?

The following is written by President Colton in response to my request of May, 1962:

It is hoped that this response to the requests made of me to add my contribution to the history of the "Upper Campus," which had its beginning in 1903-1904, will be helpful in arriving at agreement on the actual happenings.

First, I should correct the understanding which seems to exist that I was once President of the Studentbody at B.Y.A.-B.Y.U. That is not true. The facts are that I was the senior class (1904) candidate for President of the *first* studentbody organization at the school—which occurred under the initiation of the college classes during the fall semester of 1903-04—and was defeated by my cousin, Warren A. Colton, who was the 1905 class candidate. He was also a part-time teacher, and, of course, a member of the faculty.

At a meeting of the new Studentbody organization, a motion was proposed for the appointment of a committee of five student member representatives of the departmental divisions of the school to head an effort to procure a campus ready for athletic purposes and use by the next Springtime. The committee was named as follows:

College, Byron O. Colton, Chairman

Commercial School, James C. Hacking, Secretary-Treasurer

High School, Hyrum Peterson, Member

Preparatory School, George Rowsell, Member

Missionary School, Alonzo Reed, Member*

The first meeting of the committee was held just before the Christmas-New Year holidays. At the next meeting some members expressed surprise that even a second meeting was intended, but from then on, we all knew we were under challenge to make good.

To begin with, the campus idea was largely a play ground—an athletic field. However, it was soon recognized that any addition to the existing land ownership for B.Y.U. must provide room for expansion of building development also, and Temple Hill edged out all other locations under consideration. The following is a draft of a letter I recently found, together with other Campus Committee memoranda, preserved through the years, which reflects some definite facts on this bit of "Y" history:

Provo, Utah Jan. 11, 1904

To the President and Member's of the City Council, Provo City, Ut. Gentlemen:

*Later replaced by Wm. Henry Housekeeper

The students of the Brigham Young University in mass meeting assembled Dec. 21, 1903, elected a committee to inaugurate measures for the purpose of procuring a campus for the school.

Such steps have been taken and the committee has the united support of the students and faculty. It is our earnest purpose to obtain the best place to be had. Several places have been considered. Temple Hill offers advantages, in our estimation, over any other proposed.

Therefore, we wish to know if the City will sell its land there, and if so what is the lowest price you can offer. We intend to buy, and if your price is not beyond our reach, we will set our efforts in that direction.

Any favor you can show us in this matter will be fully appreciated by us as Studentbody representatives and also by the school authorities. Awaiting your action, we remain,

Yours truly,
Committee

The immediate answer of the Provo City officials was to the effect that they lacked approval of the citizens to sell the Temple Hill land which they desired before selling it. A petition was circulated by the committee to obtain the approval desired. The father of Eugene L. Roberts said, "Why son, a temple is to be built there," but "Gene" won the argument when he replied, "Yes Father, perhaps *temples* of learning." Two of us took the petition to Samuel H. King and D. D. Houtz (prominent Provo attorneys) which they signed after voicing their opposition—it appeared to be more to test the reality of our purpose than to express their own convictions.

Under the endorsement of the petitioners, sale of Temple Hill to the University was agreed to and a price tag of $2,100.00 affixed. Here President Brimhall interceded. He attended a City Council meeting with members of the committee; told the officials present the great need of the school for an enlarged campus—room for growth under the new University status—of the benefits to Provo and its people, and lastly, of the necessity of a reduction in the price set on Temple Hill to make the "Campus" effort of the Studentbody successful. In response, the City accepted $1,000.00 for its land on the hill, which together with the tract in the ownership of the Provo Fourth and Fifth wards made certain of approximately 24 acres within the new "Upper Campus" as a start toward a greater Brigham Young University.

With the location of the campus settled, collection of funds to meet the cost of the land purchased from Provo City, leveling the grounds for the Spring track and field meeting with the L.D.S. College and obtaining the materials to fence the field, and erecting a grand-stand, became the absorbing program for an enlarged and alert committee and for responsive groups of students. At this point, I can well endorse the write-up of Mervin G. Fairbanks which appeared in the June 15, 1954 issue of the Church Section of the *Deseret News*, sponsored as it was by George C. Laney, a prominent campus committee member, a B.Y.U. graduate in 1904 and one whose memories have been kept keenly alive through the years. If the Fairbanks article and a group picture of the "Noted B.Y.U. Campus Committee" are wanted, they can be made available.

In conclusion, some features which marked the "Campus" accomplishment should be noted and bear special mention. They follow:

The Studentbody organization at the 'Y' was formed in late 1903.

On December 21, a Studentbody assembly in College Hall chose a "Campus Committee" of five representatives—students of the departmental divisions of the, then, B.Y.A.

Following the Christmas holidays and as the program evolved, other members were added to carry on the work—twenty-three appearing in the picture taken of the group. Some few others assisted in various appointments, but had left school before it closed and so were not available for the picture when taken.

School housing and land were limited at the time to the "Lower Campus", as later designated. Outdoor athletics were carried on at the Fifth Ward Square (between 5th and 6th West and Center and 1st South streets); Third Ward field and Temple Hill. Temple Hill was settled on in early January, 1904, as the "Campus" location for athletic contests and school expansion—if it could be purchased.

Under the watch-care of President Brimhall and the inspiration of Edwin S. Hinckley, faculty advisor, the Committee could not fail. An appointed day and evening of fasting, prayer and testimony added greatly to the Spirit with which each was imbued and responded in service.

Responding to the approach for contributions, Emeline B. Wells, General President of the Relief Society, proudly gave the committeemen one dollar, and as proudly, accepted the receipt for it. Her son, Governor Heber M. Wells, contributed $10, praised the B.Y.U., treated the solicitors kindly, and wished them success in the present endeavor. These are but outstanding examples of the many donations freely given in response to committee contacts.

A car load of lumber was needed for fence and grandstand. Two of the Committee filled appointments with prominent lumber operators—one at Ogden, the other at Salt Lake City—and requested them to contribute the much-needed material, jointly or separately, but it remained for the Jex Lumber Company of Spanish Fork to supply the need at wholesale prices delivered at Provo.

Good cedar posts came from Sanpete County at moderate price, and when they finally arrived, the holes to receive them were dug in short order—one hole per man—by the students in mass turnout.

Land levelling and grading of the quarter mile track was accomplished by the local farmers with their teams, equipment being borrowed from Deal Brothers and Mendenhall, contractors of Springville, who voluntarily responded to that need when appraised of it. A list of the persons thus employed is available if desired.

The Fairbanks writing referred to above, provides a suitable closing: "To collect tickets, a fence had to be erected . . . When the visitors from Salt Lake City began to arrive, the last of the boards were being nailed in place. Gates had to be hung later, but the first track meet ever held on B.Y.U. premises was held there—on schedule."

Byron O. Colton, Campus Committee Chairman

An unusual tribute is paid by a graduating classmate, George C. Laney, 1904:

"REMEMBERING A FORGOTTEN MAN"

When a good egg is properly incubated there comes a time when no further growth or development can come until the shell is burst and the chick released into the great wide world. At this critical time the chick has grown to so completely fill its cramped quarters that it can scarcely move. So provisions are made for its release. A very small but very hard and sharply pointed horn is formed on the top of its beak and at this time this horn is the most important thing in the life of the chick. With it he is able by the slightest movement to cut the shell and free himself. As soon as the bird emerges into the air and light of day, this horn separates from the beak, falls off, and is lost and forgotten. In fact, few know the bird ever had such an appendage. Similar was the work and fate of the man whom this little sketch is written to tell you of. He did an all important service for the B.Y.U., yet he and what he did is all but forgotten. Fifty years ago now, in the fall of 1903, the Brigham Young University was at the state of development where it had to have more room if it was to grow. So a number of students and Professor E. S. Hinckley, having the interest of the school at heart got together and after considering conditions at length a Campus Committee was chosen. This committee, on its own time and expense set to work, exploring possibilities, seeking concessions, devising plans, soliciting funds, converting supporters, securing legal advice and whatever was found needful, with the result that by the end of the school year the shell was cracked. The lid was off. The B.Y.U. was out and on its way with room to grow.

At the beginning of 1903-1904, the B.Y.U. campus was one city block in town. At the end of the year, Temple Hill and the Fourth

Ward Park had been added and a lot of dirt moved to fill the hollow where now stands the Joseph Smith Building. A track was laid out and covered with cinders. A Grand Stand was built and a high board fence built around the track. Not the least difficult part of this accomplishment was the converting of the local church and civil authorities and even some of the school officials to believe that Temple Hill, as it is known, could best serve all interests as the site of a Temple of Learning. Logan and Manti each had a Temple on a hill and Provo, they contended, was a more important town than either of them. They were determined to see nothing but a Temple on Provo's Temple Hill.

The most important instrument in this accomplishment, the hard horn, that cut the shell and who was so soon forgotten was the chairman of this Campus Committee.

During these months when so many were giving without stint no one gave more in time and effort than did its chairman. He was Byron Owen Colton, class of 1904, going to school largely on borrowed funds. He often said wryly, "They should call me, Byron 'owin' everybody." Today little does everybody who exults in the B.Y.U.'s growth and good fortune realize how much they owe Byron Owen Colton. Thus was launched the Campus Boom of 1903-1904. It seems to be still booming. All members of the old Campus Committee who are still living including Byron O. Colton, of Roosevelt, Utah, are sure it must continue to boom. May every boom be bigger and better.

George C. Laney
Member of Campus Committee.

The following briefly outlines Pres. Colton's active life:

Education: Local elementary schools (Maeser, Uintah County, Utah); Uintah Stake Academy, B.Y.A. High School; Brigham Young University, Degree of Bachelor of Science, 1904.

Occupational Activities: Part time occupation—farming, carpentry, surveying, (1904-1930); irrigation engineering, (1904-1930); water commissioner, Uintah, Lakefork, Duchesne and Strawberry Rivers (1931 through 1961).

Church Activities: Ward President of YMMIA, Sunday School Teacher, High Council; Bishop; Counselor in Stake Presidency; Stake President; President of High Priests Quorum; Stake Patriarch.

Civic, Social, and Honorary: Chairman BYU "Campus Committee", 1904; Member Utah Commission Golden Gate Exposition, 1939; Chairman, Roosevelt District Boy Scouts of America, (1929-1937).

Governmental: County Surveyor Uintah Co., 1905 through 1908; "Trustee" School Dist. No. 5, Uintah Co., 1905-1912; Member County Board of Education, 1919-1927; Member Utah Water Storage Commission, 1929-1931; Member of Water and Power Board, October 1947-Feb. 1962;

Authorship: Annual reports of Water Commissioner years 1931 through 1961.

Following the opening of the Uintah Indian Reservation in August 1905, he was active in settlement work and irrigation development.

In 1906 he made a location survey of canal for Duchesne Irrigation Co. to lands near present Midview Reservoir, now also the feeder canal to that reservoir.

Engineer for larger irrigation companies as follows:

Whiterocks Irrigation Co.—surveys and construction of canal to lands centering around the villages of Tridell and Lapoint; and later in the development and construction of the Paradise Park and Chepeta Lake reservoirs.

Vernal Irrigation Co.—preliminary and final surveys and construction of the Highline Canal in Ashley Valley, 1912 through 1916.

Ouray Valley Irrigation Company (1917-1937) and the consolidated Ouray Valley and Colorado Park Irrigation companies (1937-1950.)

Uintah Basin Irrigation Company—enlargement of the Grey Mountain Canal and completion of the "Taylor Canal" to South Myton Bench and Pleasant Valley.

Dry Gulch Irrigation Company—plans and specifications, and construction of Montez Creek Reservoir.

The Colton family was one of more important groups in BYU. history. The Campus Committee was the spearhead of campus growth.

CLARENCE COTTAM

Born: January 1, 1899   **Place:** St. George, Utah

Father: Thomas Punter Cottam, b. September 28, 1857 in Salt Lake City, Utah
Son of Thomas Cottam (cabinet maker) and Caroline Smith
Successful merchant and farmer, 1st counselor in Stake Presidency many years; president of St. George Temple some 20 years
Worked on temple for 35¢ a day and food script
Patriarch; mayor of St. George several terms—three sessions in Utah State Legislature
d. Marcy 16, 1926 in St. George, Utah

Mother: Emmaline Jarvis, m. January 26, 1882 in St. George Temple daughter of George and Ann Pryor Jarvis
Jovial, patient, a mother to the Stake—often had to feed twenty to thirty conference visitors at one sitting;
b. March 21, 1863, at St. George, Utah
d. Sept. 21, 1944 in St. George, Utah

Brothers and Sisters: Emma Cottam, b. December 27, 1882, m. Moroni McArthur Dec., 7, 1905
Thomas Cottam, b. June 5, 1884, m. Anna Larsen, April 18, 1902
Heber Cottam, b. May 26, 1886, m. Edith Brooks Sept. 9, 1909, d. June 27, 1932
Arthur Cottam, b. August 5, 1888, m. Mary Mae Pritchard, Sept. 23, 1908
Annie Cottam, b. July 10, 1890, m. 1.) Mark Bleak, Sept. 10, 1913 2.) William Wilson, April 19, 1944
Moroni Jarvis, b. January 3, 1892, m. Ramona Farrer, Sept. 4, 1924
Walter Pace Cottam, b. March 3, 1894, m. Effie Frei, July 1, 1915, who died Aug. 28, 1964
Ivins Cottam, b. March 29, 1896, d. November 1, 1899 (Clarence)
Eva Cottam, b. August 9, 1902, m. Ellis Jones, June 2, 1926; d. Nov. 2, 1955

Marriage: Margery Brown
Daughter of A. W. and Lucinda Stewart Brown
b. January 28, 1895
m. May 20, 1920

Children:	Glenna Clair, m. Ivan L. Sanderson (Manager of B.Y.U. Bookstore)
	Margery B., m. Grant Osborn, Research expert for AMA
	Josephine, m. Douglas Day, Personnel Director of Utah Fish and Game
	Carolyn, m. Dwayne Stevenson, Administrator in Peace Corps

Clarence Cottam is the ninth child in a family of ten and was reared in the rugged environs of St. George, Utah. As a young boy he knew the problems of drought and the anxiety caused by scarcity of water. Mountains beckoned him on every side, especially the great red cliffs to the east, the towering peaks of Zion National Park when there were but few roads which were usually in disrepair. He knew the hazards of torrentuous summer floods which filled dry river beds with debris, gnarled trees and huge boulders, and the tortuous search for scattered sheep and stray cattle. Early in life he learned to know the wild animals by their calls and recognize their tracks. He heard fireside talks of the big wolves, the marauding brown bear and especially of the sly, vicious killing puma. He has seen owls and hawks swoop down upon a food searching chicken and has watched big cats as they waited for the stray calf or lamb or even a colt.

Desert flowers in brilliant colors fascinated Clarence and trees that struggled valiantly to grow from split rocks and cling to the sides of mountain cliffs caused the young boy to wonder, to learn the names of flora and fauna and be aware, when younger than most boys, that nature could be studied in different branches of classification, botany, zoology, ornithology, entomology, herpetology. He learned that rocks told the different ages of the earth, that wind and water could transform landscape into weird and indescribable beauty. Lava beds for miles around him told of a tempestuous era when volcanoes and earthquakes belched up the Dixie wonderland. He was living on land once covered by a great inland sea. Clarence Cottam was born and bred in the environment that he learned to love and has strived to preserve. His interest in wildlife was not college inspired; his interest in conservation began in boyhood days of pioneer colonization.

Education and Allied Vocations:

1919-20	Student of Dixie College, St. George, Utah
1923	Summer at University of Utah
1926	B.S. Brigham Young University—biology

1927	M.S. Brigham Young University and taught on B.Y.U. faculty 1926-29
1936	Ph.D. George Washington University—ornithology
1929-54	With U.S. Fish and Wild Life Service, Washington, D.C. as junior biologist, advanced to Assistant Biologist, Senior Biologist, Chief of Food Habits Research and Economic Biology, Assistant to Director
1945	Assistant Director of Service 1945-54
1949	To New Zealand for U.S. Government at International Science Congress
1954	Dean of College of Biology and Agriculture, B.Y.U.
1955	Head of Welder Wild Life Foundation at Sinton, Texas Services every State in the Union and most Canadian provinces, also most Mexican States

Honors and Awards:

Distinguished Service Award—Utah Academy Sciences, Arts and Letters

Distinguished Service Award—Utah State University

Distinguished Service Award—Laval University, Quebec, Canada

Distinguished Service Award—Leopold Wildlife Award and Medal

Distinguished Service Award—Sinton, Texas

Distinguished Service Award—Brigham Young University, 1964

Pooge Conservation Award

Paul Bartich Award of Natural Life Society

Wild Life Conservation Award of South Texas

Past President—National Wild Life Society

Past President—National Parks Association

Fellow—Utah Academy of Science

Fellow—Texas Academy of Science

Fellow—The American Ornithological Union

Fellow—National Academy of Science

1962 Audubon Medal for "distinguished service in conservation, as a distinguished scientist, educator, administrator, articulate exponent of the ecological approach"

Only nine of these coveted medals have been awarded

Clarence Cottam has achieved almost every major honor the field of wild life in America has to offer. He has devoted his life to research in American wild life and studies to promote preservation and proper promulgation.

His religious activities have not been neglected, as he has advanced steadily in the priesthood, being first counselor in the San

Antonio Stake Presidency, responsible for a vast territory in southern United States.

A man of national importance and stature, descendant of loyal and vigorous pioneer families, Clarence Cottam is proud of being a true Son of Brigham.

HENRY ALDOUS DIXON

Born: June 29, 1890   **Place:** Provo, Utah

Father: John DeGrey Dixon
b. July 16, 1869 in Salt Lake City, Utah
d. Oct. 4, 1923
(see his biography)

Mother: Sarah Ann Lewis
b. April 23, 1868
daughter of Bp. John William Lewis and Jane Davis of
Wales, Great Britain, pioneers of Daniel Jones Handcart
Co.
m. Sept. 18, 1889 in Manti Temple
d. Oct. 30, 1951

Brothers   (see children of father, John DeGrey Dixon)
and Sisters:

Marriage: Lucile Knowlden
b. Dec. 9, 1891
m. June 2, 1915 in Provo, Utah
graduate of B.Y.A. class of 1912

Children: Phyllis Lucile, b. Aug. 21, 1916, m. John A. Shaw
Dorothy, b. May 26, 1918, m. Verl L. Harrison
Louise, b. Sept. 18, 1920, m. E. Ferrin Larkin
John Aldous, b. June 16, 1923, m. Karma Jeppsen
Ruth Marion, b. May 19, 1927, m. Mark W. Cannon
David, b. June 24, 1931

Death: Sunday, Jan. 22, 1967 at 76 of a heart attack
Buried in Washington Heights Memorial Park, Ogden.

Aldous, as he was known to all his friends, was a cheerful, smiling "redhead", who looked for the happy side of life, but was serious as conditions demanded. He had a great ability to get things done, to get to the core of a problem with easy effort, and seldom appeared rushed. When he had a good joke to tell his eyes twinkled in preparation. His smile won friends for him upon a first acquaintance, which partially accounted for his success in business and politics. He avoided telling unpleasant news.

Honesty was the trademark of his life. As a boy he would often laugh and joke himself out of trouble, but he never compromised with truth. His companionship with his father was remarkable. His father told us on an occasion, as we sat under the shade in his beautiful orchard eating luscious peaches, "There is a wonderful boy. (as Aldous was tending irrigation at other end of the orchard). Whenever he got into some neighborhood mischief, I could always get the facts from Aldous, but he usually said, 'Yes, we did it, but don't ask me who is we'."

Fishing was a boyhood passion, but hard work on a large farm was his dominant vocation. Water turns often meant night work and Aldous became chief overseer as the family of boys grew up. Responsibility was put on his shoulders early in life, and he intimately worked side by side with his father from the farm to the bank.

He was a better than average student at school and early decided to obtain a college education. He played baseball in high school and college and was manager of the B.Y.U. team for a season, playing on the 1909 team. He was an honor man on the B.Y.U. debating team. When he completed the day's study he went directly to work for his father. There was always plenty of hard work ready. To his younger brothers he said, "It has to be done, let's do it now."

Few men did as much with their lives in a similar time as did Aldous. His lovely family with a devoted wife, Lucille, were his especial pride. All his children are college educated, active in their communities and church, and leaders with their respective talents.

The unfoldment of his major activities is ample testimony of his versatility and success.

Education:
B.A.—B.Y.U., 1914
Honor man in debating, baseball manager for one year, and on 1909 basketball team, Honorary Blue Key
M.A.—U. of Chicago, 1917
Ed.D.—U.S.C., 1937
President of Utah Conference on Higher Education, 1938
Provo City Schools Superintendent, 1920-24, 1932-37
President of Weber College, 1919-20, 1937-53

307

President of U.S.A.C., 1953-54, when he was drafted by Republicans for Representative in Congress

Honorary Ed. D. at U.S.U. in 1956

Treasurer B.Y.U. Alumni Association, and member of Alumni Council several years

Instructor at Weber Normal for four years before becoming president 1914-17

Teacher at B.Y.U. in 1918 and 1961 to 1965

Member Truman's Commission on Higher Education 1946-48

Director of Junior College Association 1900-54

Member Utah Academy of Sciences, Arts and Letters

Business:

Manager, Director, Farmers & Merchants Bank, Provo, 1924-32

Vice-President Provo Building & Loan Association

Director, Timpanogos Marketing Association, 1932

President, Timpanogos Marketing Association, 1926-30

Member Board of Directors, Salt Lake Branch of Federal Reserve Bank of San Francisco, 1945-51

Member Advisory Committee, First Security Bank of Utah

Civic and Political:

Republican all his adult life

Member of House of Representatives, First District 1954-56-58, 84th, 85th and 86th sessions.

Member of House of Representatives Agricultural Commission, to report to an Asian market development conference at New Delhi, India, Jan. 1959.

B.Y.U. Achievement Award 1955; and Distinguished Alumni Award 1955.

Praised by President Eisenhower for his work on the Upper Colorado Storage program

Inducted into Weber County "Hall of Fame", May, 1966

President of both the Provo and Ogden Chambers of Commerce

Member Ogden and Logan Rotary Clubs and Provo Kiwanis Club.

Hoffa selected him with 81 others to blacklist on elections—individual rights versus pressure politics

Favored civil rights bill, right-to-work, federal aid to libraries, and sponsored conservation and water bills

Gave his congressional files for three terms to B.Y.U.—now catalogued in the J. Reuben Clark Jr., Library, "My Six Years in U.S. House of Representatives"

Church:

L.D.S. mission to Germany 1910-12

Bishop Provo Third Ward 1924-31

General Sunday School Board 1932 to 1967, a senior member, 1966

With his wife, Lucile, he built a beautiful home in eastern Ogden near the Weber State College where he was a frequent speaker and counselor. His church, B.Y.U. teaching assignments and 25 grand-children helped to fill an active, happy life.

He gave the Education Department of B.Y.U. a $2,000 endowment for encouragement of research, on Oct. 25, 1966.

The news of his death was a state concern. All the major papers of the State wrote appreciative editorials. He was eulogized in the halls of Congress, in our own legislature and by men of national, state and church importance.

ELBERT HINDLEY EASTMOND

Born: June 1, 1876   **Place:** American Fork

Father: Thomas Jefferson Eastmond, son of Elbert Eastmond and Elizabeth Brown. Thomas Jefferson and his father, Elbert, built a steamboat and ran excursions on Utah Lake. They were responsible for establishing a very popular resort on the shores of the Lake. Grandfather Elbert joined the church and came to Utah in 1847.

Mother: Esther Hindley, daughter of John Hindley and Jane Charters Robinson of American Fork. John Hindley was a merchant.

**Brothers
and Sisters:**   Jane (Jennie) Eastmond Johnson, Elizabeth (Bessie) Eastmond Gourley (an excellent artist, dec.), Frank Eastmond, (dec.) John Eastmond, (dec.).

Marriage: Margaret Hull of Salt Lake, daughter of Thomas and Margaret Craig Swan Hull. April 2, 1913. Organized BYU Women under direction of President Brimhall. d. May 24, 1966 at 88.

Children: Thomas Hull Eastmond, commercial artist of Burbank, California. Born March 12, 1914. Died December 13, 1967. Married Clara Powelson.
Elbert John Eastmond, Professor of Physics, BYU. Born July 6, 1915 in San Francisco. Married Helen Swenson of Spanish Fork, Utah.

Died: August 17, 1936.

"Bert" was a man of many talents with a desire to bring beauty to the world. As his life unfolded he spent more time on people and less with the brush and canvas. His interest in history and especially the American Indian caused him to spend much of his time on pageantry both in the writing of script and the problems of production. Many hours of class time were spent in designing and making of costumes. Entire Relief Societies were commandeered for a Stake or civic pageant.

As a young boy he lived in Salt Lake with his grandmother, Mrs. Elizabeth Eastmond, doing art work for holidays and special occasions while going to school. When he was sixteen his father died and Bert returned to American Fork to be employed in the large Chipman Mercantile, where he was encouraged by Stephen L. Chipman to go East to study art. President Chipman offered to finance his schooling but his grandmother claimed that privilege. With eagerness to achieve young Bert enrolled in the famed Pratt Institute of Art in Brooklyn, New York. He taught art in the New York Public Schools and returned to Utah to become supervisor of art and manual training in the Utah County schools. When George H. Brimhall was appointed president of the Brigham Young University in 1904 he soon appointed E. H. Eastmond professor of art and who later was made head of the department.

At BYU he was the director in preparing parades, designing and painting stage settings for the annual operas and plays. Even the dance halls were decorated under his direction. His graduate work consisted of study of pictorial design in Columbia University, applied art and etching at Stanford University, etching and block painting under William J. Rice at Oakland. His travels in Europe gave him further prestige. He held classes in oil painting, water color, etching, block printing, charcoal, monotone and aquatint. He enjoyed experimenting.

He directed four pageants for the Salt Lake Stake, three for Granite Stake, three for Alpine Stake, two in Nevada, and numerous ones for the city of Provo and the university.

Street pageants were his speciality, "The Triumph of Democracy" and "Laurels of Victory" are examples. One of his well known indoor pageants, "The Fulfillment" was followed by a sequel "The Return of Truth Triumphant" which was presented on the front steps of the Maeser Memorial building. He personally enjoyed his "The Prayer of the Boy Prophet" produced in dozens of L.D.S. Chapels. His "Gifts of Providence" was a successful Thanksgiving pageant produced in many wards of Salt Lake City.

"A Little Child Shall Lead Thee" had wide state production. His most elaborate and impressive work, "The Kingdom of Mercy" was presented in the Provo Tabernacle with two hundred and fifty people.

For the tercentenary anniversary of the landing of the Pilgrim fathers he wrote "The Quest of Freedom" and used over 300 school children in the production. "You teach history best by having the children portray the characters they represent" was a familiar statement before adult groups.

He wrote pageants for patriotic societies across the nation. "There Is No Death" was prepared for a Massachusetts magazine. "The Kingdom of Mercy," a Christmas pageant was presented in many states of the Union.

Provo Canyon and Utah Lake gave him greatest inspiration for his brush.

The *Salt Lake Tribune* wrote of him on August 18, 1936:

"Professor Eastmond was nationally known for his ability to create and direct pageants, and his services were requested from all parts of the country. Probably his greatest work was done in the staging of the L.D.S. church centennial pageant, "Message of the Ages," in the tabernacle in 1930. At the time of his death he was planning to repeat this pageant for the 1947 centennial of the Sons of Utah Pioneers.

"He directed the pageant for the dedication ceremonies at the Hill Cumorah in Palmyra, N.Y., last year, and had been called by the church to create the church exhibit at the Texas centennial fair this year. In Provo, he took an active part in practically every celebration, being in charge of building floats for parades.

"He was the creator of the school's famous junior prom decorations for the past 30 years and also had directed the Easter sunrise rites pageant at Utah lake for the past three years."

The *Deseret News,* in part wrote:

"As a creator and director of pageants for the Church, his university, other educational institutions and cities, his fame spread wide. He satisfied requests for pageants which came from all parts of the United States. In recent years his most notable work in pageantry has been done in connection with the "Message of the Ages" pageant produced for the Church Centennial in 1930 and the pageantry at the dedication of the Hill Cumorah Monument, Palmyra, N. Y., in 1935.

"When stricken Friday, he was completing final details in connection with the L.D.S. exhibit at the Texas Centennial Exposition, Dallas. He had just finished a brochure of material to be used by the elders at the exhibit. Last spring he was called by the Church and set aside as a missionary to direct the exhibit. Another project he had been at work on was a comprehensive series of pictures to illustrate the Book of Mormon and early Church History."

He spread his talents over too great a territory, "too many irons in the fire" and all too soon a talented, patriotic soul succumbed in the zenith of his ambitions but left a legacy of imperishable value. He had a passionate love of the University, his country and his church.

In the Harris Fine Arts Center there is a well used room named the "E. H. Eastmond Art Seminar Room." His paintings and etchings adorn the office walls of many of his colleagues on the campus.

CARL FERDINAND EYRING

Born: August 30, 1899, Colonia Juarez, Chihuahua, Mexico

Father: Henry Carl Eyring, brilliant student of Latin, French, German, and an orphan at 15 years
b. March 9, 1835 in Coburg, Saxe-Coburg, Gotha, Germany
d. February 10, 1902—translated Book of Mormon into German.
His mother was daughter of Viscount George Louis von Blomberg, in the employ of King William III of Prussia —died when Henry was 8
To America in 1853 with sister, Bertha; 1855 baptized in St. Louis by Erastus Snow, 1860, August 29, to Utah; 1862, volunteer to go to Dixie; mayor of St. George 2 years; 1887, to Mexico.

Mother: Deseret Fawcett
Left St. George in 1887; two month wagon trip to Juarez, Mexico.
Lived in log cabin built by Henry while husband served mission in Mexico City.

Brothers and Sisters: Andrew Theodore m. Edith Haws
(Carl F. youngest son, born in log cabin in Mexico)
Edward
Fernanda Caroline E., m. William C. Smith
(His half brothers and sister, George A., Clara V., John E., and Wilford W. all died young, Anna Margaret m. Alonzo Taylor.)

Marriage: Fern Chipman, d. of Stephen L. Chipman of American Fork, Utah   .
(President of Alpine Stake and long time member of B. Y. U. Executive Board) and Sina Nelson
b. March 20, 1890 in Provo, Utah
m. September 9, 1914 in Salt Lake Temple, served a mission to Central States when 19, Charter member of B.Y.U. Women and Yeshara. Taught Home Economics at B. Y. U. 2 years,
President of New England Relief Society when Carl was president of the New England Mission.

Children: Robert, b. October 12, 1924
Elaine, b. January 26, 1929, m. John Rieske

Death: January 3, 1951 of leukemia contracted in 1950
Funeral in the Joseph Smith Auditorium on the BYU Campus.

Carl F. Eyring would equally be pleased to be known as a successful scientist or a devout religious man, as he excelled in each field. He believed in the harmony of the two and told his students, "To be a good scientist, the person must also be a good person, an integrated person with faith in God," and "Search for truth in the laboratory," "There should be no conflict between truth and religion; God's laws govern both."

He was as sincere and exacting in the mission office as he was at the physics laboratory. His logical mind and genial disposition made him an ideal teacher and students left his classes with a thirst for more knowledge. "Never shut the door on truth—in the class room, at a lecture or in the Church. Have your opinions, but leave the door open."

The great B. Y. U. science building was completed as his own life was ebbing away and bears his name that he might not be forgotten. His many good deeds will outlive the life of the building.

He had a rich bass voice and sang in our first faculty quartet, chiefly in College Hall. He took part in the faculty dramas during the 1920's, outstanding as Myers, the banker, in "Disrael". His bonfire chats at Summer School in Aspen Grove were attention-binding as he talked from the rich experiences of his life. Back of all his stories he seemed to challenge himself "Is it true?"

The death of his father when Carl was but twelve tended to sober an already serious child. He was twenty years of age when he arrived in Provo.
Education:

Educated in local Mexican schools and graduated from Juarez Stake Academy in 1908

1909, May, left Colonia Juarez for B. Y. U., worked hard, prepared an apartment and brought his mother and sister Fern to Provo

Assistant teacher at B. Y. U. two years

1912—graduated with A. B. degree under Harvey Fletcher, majoring in mathematics and physics; retained at B. Y. U. as instructor in physics

1914—to University of Wisconsin, assistant in physics, where both Carl and wife Fern studied

1915—M. A. summer at Wisconsin; back to Provo as Assistant Professor of Physics

1917—Professor of Physics at B. Y. U. and Stake Superintendent of Y. M. M. I. A.

1918—Assistant to Dr. Dayton C. Miller with study of sound

1919—Semester at Columbia

1922—Summer at University of Chicago

Enrolled in California Institute of Technology; Assistant in physics

1924—Received his Ph.D. under Dr. Robert A. Millikan, world famed physicist

Return to B. Y. U. as Dean of College of Arts and Sciences, a position held until his death

1929-31—Acoustical Engineer at Bell Telephone Laboratories—made study of movie sound stages and St. Patrick Cathedral in New York

1940-51—Planned and projected B. Y. U. Science Building

Church:

1917—Utah Stake Superintendent of Y. M. M. I. A.

Utah Stake Superintendent of Religion Classes

1920—Made Special Deputy Scout Commissioner of Utah Stake

First Scout Commissioner for Timpanogos Council (which evolved to Utah National Parks Council); 6 years as Scout Master; he served the Church in the New York Branch Presidency

1935—was made a member of General Board Deseret Sunday School, retained position until death

1937-39—First president of newly created New England Mission, with headquarters at Cambridge, Mass., opposite H. W. Long-fellow home.

Government Service:

1918—Enter U. S. Army, WW I as technical assistant to Robert A. Millikan at Washington, D. C. for military research; he studied sound and noise of big guns under D. C. Miller

Sgt. 1st Class, A. C.

1919—Discharged from Army

1941—With staff at San Diego in the U. S. Navy to study sound in the ocean

1944—headed group of scientists sent to Panama by U. S. Army to study jungle acoustics. He was given citations from War and Navy departments for outstanding contributions

Distinguished Service Medal presented by officers and crew of the U. S. S. Jasper, San Diego, California; he was a U. S. Naval Laboratories Chaplain—An active member in the Provo Post of the American Legion

Professional and Service Affiliations:

Member A. A. A. S.

Member Acoustical Society of America

Fellow Utah Academy Science and Arts and Letters

President Utah Academy Science and Arts and Letters

Member American Physical Society

Special Deputy Scout Commissioner for Utah Stake

Member State Planning Commission

Member Provo City Zoning Commission
Member Provo Rotary
Texts and Writings:
Essentials of Physics adapted by fifty-eight universities
Good Tidings to All People, a Sunday School text
Church manuals, co-author and editor

He could have spent his life in research for the government at a highly remunerative salary; he preferred the University where he could harmonize religion and science. He worked diligently to acquire the carillon for the Joseph Smith Building tower and good music gave him his most restful hour. When he realized that he had cancer of blood cells, he taught his scheduled classes with his usual cheerful style and especially urged his majors to make every minute of their lives a useful time in a worthwhile enterprise. Thousands of friends and former students still pay homage to his memory.

PHILO TAYLOR FARNSWORTH

Named for his grandfather who was a Pioneer of Beaver.

Born: August 19, 1906 at Indian Creek, Beaver, Utah

Father: Lewis Edwin Farnsworth
Born July 30, 1865 in Beaver the third son of Philo T. and Agnes Ann Patterson; family of seven boys and three girls.
Agnes born April 10, 1844 at Clock Manning, Scotland. Brought to Utah when four. Married Philo T. at age 14, December 16, 1858. Philo T. died three years later. She died May 1, 1909.
Lewis E. married December 28, 1904 in St. George Temple. Met wife at B. Y. U. while attending as special student. Had two daughters and two sons when he married Serena. Died January 8, 1924 in Provo.

Mother: Serena Bastian (third wife)
Born January 21, 1880, daughter of Jacob Bastian and Kirsten (Christine) Hansen, who emigrated from Denmark. Jacob was born March 14, 1835 in Sundbyvester on the island of Amager, short distance from Copenhagen. He was a ship's carpenter and well known sportsman. Married Gertrude Peterson, childhood sweetheart who converted him to Mormonism and who died three days after reaching Salt Lake. Kirsten married Jacob in 1861 and they accepted a call to settle in Southern Utah in area of Washington, St. George. Successful with fruit importations, also cotton and sugar cane (sorghum); a model farm. Kirsten born October 11, 1845 in Jutland, Denmark. Married December 28, 1904 in St. George Temple. She died May 22, 1960 in San Francisco, California.

Brothers and Sisters: (Philo T. "Phil"), the first of five children.
Agnes Ann b. October 29, 1908, m. Claude T. Lindsay
Carl Wilford, b. November 28, 1911, m. Valdis Fowler
Laura, b. December 28, 1913, m. Lawrence L. Player
Lincoln B. b. February 12, 1915, m. Iris Fowler

Marriage: Elma "Pem" Gardner of Jensen, Utah
Born February 25, 1908 daughter of Bernard Edward Gardner and Alice Maria Mecham. Student of Professor Wm. F. Hansen in Vernal. Married May 27, 1926 and went to California to work on television. A chum of Agnes Farnsworth; met "Phil" at B. Y. U. dances. Granddaughter of Johnathan O. Duke, first bishop of Provo First Ward.

Children: Philo Taylor III Farnsworth, b. September 23, 1929 in San Francisco, California.
Kenneth Gardner Farnsworth, b. January 15, 1931, died March 1932.
Russell Seymour Farnsworth, b. October 5, 1935 in Philadelphia, Pennsylvania.
Kent Morgan Farnsworth, b. September 4, 1948 in Fort Wayne, Indiana.

To write of genius is a presumption but a pleasant privilege.

Philo T. "Phil" Farnsworth comes from a very close-knit family whose father, Edwin, was self-educated, an expert astronomer, a keen observer of nature and interested in its laws. Edwin was an intimate chum to his children and especially close to Phil. His death was a severe loss to teen-age Phil.

Much could and should be written of Phil's wife, Elma Gardner, who has become his chief assistant, takes care of her husband's correspondence, and relieves him of the many small matters that absorb an inventor's time and crowd his desk. She has become an expert draftswoman who does much of Phil's drawing and early planning, thereby keeping important discoveries a family matter until time to patent them and share them with the public.

Television is the usual subject that the public credits to the Farnsworths as their greatest contribution, but right now Phil is more excited about and deeply engrossed in sustained fusion power, recently written up in magazines. Its ultimate application will greatly affect modern life in many avenues. His patent on an "Ion Transport Pump" made startling news to many nuclear physicists.

Collier's Magazine in September, 1936 had an article on Dr. Farnsworth, illuminating then and remaining an appraisal for his work of today:

"This young man, he is just 30 (September 24, 1936 D. N.), has already astounded engineers who have for years been working on a theory of television and trying to adopt it to a home set.

"The true story of this young man is one of the amazing dramas of modern times. . . . It simply doesn't make sense that this untried youth from the Wasatch ranges, skinny, blue eyed, awkward in his first pair of long pants, could have hit upon the television principle for which the entire world has been searching. He discovered the principle while a high school youth in Provo, Utah and with few of the necessities of laboratory equipment to help him over the rough spots. This 15-year old genius had only two years of high school, but he worked with such persistence and with such an unfailing zeal for enlightenment that he was admitted to Brigham Young University. . . . At 18 (1924) he had worked out the basic concept of a system of television, virtually as it stands today."

Elma has written interesting biographical material which follows:

Philo (called "Phil" by the family) can remember attending a different school every year, finishing his grade school in Ucon, Idaho. After the War, Lewis moved his family to Rigby, Idaho to help his Uncle Albert Farnsworth run his 240-acre farm.

This 240-acre farm was largely planted in hay. Philo, now thirteen, was a big help to his father. He milked the cows, cared for the stock and spent all day in the fields, then did the evening chores. He can remember one season when he spent the entire summer on a mowing machine, going from one field to another, and in those days there were no tractors; the mowers were horse drawn. It was this year that Philo was awarded first prize by the magazine "Science and Invention" for his thief-proof ignition switch for automobiles. The year before, he had wound an armature and constructed an electric motor to run his mother's washing machine which relieved him of the necessity of pushing the handle himself. The farm was powered by a Delco lighting system, Philo soon becoming the expert that kept it in operation.

In 1920 his father purchased a 140-acre farm in Bybee and Philo drove the school wagon into Rigby . . . He arose at four A.M. in order to finish his chores and get old Nap and Brownie harnessed and leave by 5:30 to pick up the other children. The temperature dropped to 40 degrees below zero and Philo heated rocks and carried quilts to keep the children warm. He was then a freshman at Rigby High School. He obtained permission to take chemistry and Mr. Justin Tolman, his chemistry teacher said this of Philo: "It was only a few days until he was sitting in on the senior class as well, 'just to listen' he said. I do not think a day ever passed that he did not come to me with from one to a dozen questions on science. While these questions covered a wide field, they mostly hinged in some way on television. Occasionally I could give him the information he wanted, often I was able to place in his hand books that gave him the information. I recall one of these books had to deal with cathode rays. This book he all but wore out. Other books dealt with the kinetic molecular theory, the electron theory, a set of twelve books by Croft that dealt with all phases of electricity. These and many others he readily devoured and came back for more." Mr. Tolman gave Philo an hour each day after school for tutoring. Philo never forgot this and often spoke to his family about the help given him by Mr. Tolman. He was unaware of the profound impression he had made on Mr. Tolman until years later when "Dissector Tube" went into interference in the patent office. Philo's Patent attorney, Donald K. Lippincott, traced Mr. Tolman to Salt Lake and asked if he remembered his talks with Phil. It seems he did and would testify in court the next day. To everyone's complete surprise he unhesitatingly drew a picture of Phil's tube just as Phil had drawn it for him fifteen years previously. Phil kept in touch with Mr. Tolman after that and always tried to see him whenever in Salt Lake. Another teacher from Rigby High who demonstrated great faith in Philo's future was Miss Frances Critchlow. She taught him music and formed a dance orchestra of her promising students (Philo included). She encouraged him when others scoffed at his "big ideas" and through the years he has valued her friendship highly.

In July, 1962, The International Telephone & Telegraph Corporation reorganized the Farnsworth Research Corporation with Philo T. Farnsworth as President and Director.

With the assistance of a small carefully chosen group of engineers and use of the shop facilities of the I.T.T. Labs, Philo Farnsworth is rapidly nearing his goal of "Power from Nuclear Fusion". As was the case with Television, it has been a long and very rough road. The conviction that he had the answer to many of the problems facing the world such as hunger, overcrowding, ambitious Dictators who were over-riding weaker peoples, and space exploration, spurred him on to pour every last ounce of his strength into getting the answers he sought. At the lab, his boys have added their strength to his and the results are very gratifying to all concerned.

Each experiment is always preceded by a thorough theoretical checking and rechecking by Phil. This makes possible a fairly accurate prediction of the outcome as well as a great time saver and has won him a reputation of creating miracles (An effective morale builder).

A source of great satisfaction to Phil Farnsworth has always been his opportunity to give an 'assist' to his men. By encouraging them to original thinking he has helped them to more nearly realize their full potential. Often referred to as "the man with a million ideas", his interests cover a broad field. His home is literally filled with scientific journals and books. In no way, however, does he slight the Arts and Humanities. He is studying soilless culture of plants because he visualizes in the future the necessity for providing additional living space for our ever increasing population. He is designing a method of building floating islands (both on sea and in space) which will necessitate some such means of producing food. He derives much pleasure from his rose culture (conventional methods) and has personally installed an underground water supply which can automatically control the moisture for each rose.

Although his work has been in the East and Mid-West, his heart is still in the West. He enjoys nothing so much as to roam the hills and valleys of his boyhood. He watches western movies on television mostly for a glimpse of his beloved mountains, although he often laments his part in producing television because of its tendency to rob our children of their initiative, because it has produced a new malady which he calls "T-Vitis" in many of us. Having once succumbed to this zombie state, the victim is easy prey for the ingenious hucksters, whether selling soap or politics. For this reason it is necessary that Johnny Q. Public must constantly police the programs fed to him, since he gets what he likes, according to the broadcasters.

Career Data:

1926-1929	Crocker Research Labs, San Francisco, California Member of the Board & Director of Research
1929-1931	Television Ltd., San Francisco Company reorganized, same position
1931-33	Fulfilled agreement for above Company to organize Philco's Television Lab in Philadelphia
1933-38	Headed Eastern Division of Farnsworth Television Inc. Philadelphia
1938-42	Farnsworth Television and Radio Corporation, Ft. Wayne—Director, Vice Pres. & Director of Research & Engineering
1942-48	On leave of absence Built his own lab in Brownfield, Maine
1948-49	Resumed active duty in Fort Wayne
1949-56	Capehart Farnsworth, Div. of Int. Tel, & Tel. Corp— Vice Pres. & Director of Res. & Eng.
1956-58	Farnsworth Electronics, Fort Wayne Vice Pres. & Director of Special Products
1958-59	Int. Tel. & Tel. Labs., Fort Wayne Technical Consultant
1959-62	I.T.T. Farnsworth Research In charge of Nuclear Research, System Cons.
1962 to present	I.T.T. Farnsworth Research, (reorganized) President, Director

(The various Companies above are really the same, the company had a new name with each new I.T.T. President)

Memberships include: Fellow I.E.E.E. (I.R.E. since 1939), American Assn. for the advancement of Science, and the Society of Motion Picture and Television Engineers. Member of the American Physical Society, and the Franklin Institute (since 1934)., and the fraternities of Eta Kappa Nu and Sigma Xi. Honors include: Eta Kappa Nu Recognition (1937), Brigham Young University Alumni Distinguished Service Award (1937), I.R.E. Morris Leibman Prize (1941); First medal awarded by the Television Broadcasting Assn., (New York 1944); Citation from the Utah Broadcasting Assn. (1953)

Doing further research for the government, he expressed a desire to return to the mountains when he "retires".

(P.S. He and family have moved to Salt Lake)

HARVEY FLETCHER

Born: Sept. 11, 1884   **Place:** Provo, Utah.

Father: Charles E. Fletcher
Born: Westford, Mass., June 26, 1843, son of Francis Fletcher and Esther B. Wright.
Died: March 9, 1922

Mother: Elizabeth Miller
Born: Sept. 16, 1856, in Lehi, Utah, daughter of Charles D. Miller and Alice Higgonbotham.
Married: in Salt Lake City, Utah, 1873.
Died: Feb. 15, 1918.

Brothers and Sisters: Sarah "Sadie" E., b. Aug. 16, 1874, m. Albert S. Jones
Charles Eugene, Jr., b. Aug. 8, 1877, m. Sarah Estella Thomas.
Francis, b. Aug. 20, 1879,
Calvin, b. June 24, 1882, m. Sarah Ann Herbert, Aug. 26, 1906, d. Feb. 14, 1909; m. Susette Ricks, Dec. 17, 1909, d. July 4, 1925; m. Clara Irene Thompson, Dec. 23, 1926 (Harvey)
Ethel, died as infant, Oct., 1887.
Milton Paul, b. June 19, 1889, m. Erma Snow.
Erma A., b. Jan. 8, 1893, m. Henry R. Atkin.
Samuel P., twin of Erma, died at birth.
Eula, b. Mar. 26, 1896, m. Charles Henry Wilkins.
Zoe, b. Sept. 9, 1899, m. John Leamon Randall.

Marriage: Lorena K. Chipman, daughter of Stephen L. Chipman and Sina (Neilsen)
Born: Aug. 22, 1888, in American Fork, Utah.
Married: Sept. 11, 1908.
Church and civic worker; elected U. S. "Mother of the Year" for 1965; active in church and university programs.
Died: Jan. 2, 1967.

Children: Phyllis, b. May 21, 1910; m. Wm. K. Firmage.
Stephen Harvey, b. Nov. 20, 1911; m. Dorothy Roberts.
James C., b. June 5, 1919; m. Fay Stanley Lee, president University of Utah.
Robert C., b. May 27, 1921; m. Rosemary Bennett.
Harvey Jr., b. April 9, 1923; m. Deah Tonks.
Paul C., b. Jan. 10, 1926; m. Norma Hunt.

Harvey grew up in the environs of the Brigham Young University. He was eight years of age when the Academy moved up to Fifth North, which was then considered "out of town." He was a better than average athlete, being a winning acrobat by the time he reached college. In a family of eleven children he was the fourth boy and mediator for the younger set, early being accepted as a leader in his school and neighborhood.

As a boy he liked to fish and took many trips with his father up the Provo River into Daniel's Canyon and over to Strawberry when the limit was much larger than allowed today. He still enjoys these trips and goes with his five sons to the places he liked best. Each trip was interesting to his inquisitive mind and observant eye. Echoes in the hills fascinated him, sounds made by tapping rocks and dry trees or limbs, the songs of the birds in the meadows and mountains, the whistles of trains which seemed to change pitch when they passed in high speed, experiments with dandelion stems and cattail reeds—all sounds of any nature were given more than passing notice.

His curiosity was rewarded by knowledge when he enrolled in physics at the B. Y. Academy. Most of the faculty were nature-lovers and had broad interests in the outdoors, being versed in fundamentals of physical laws as well as religious tenets. A course in mathematics meant more than figures; science and religion were, for the most part, harmonized and truth was sought by most of Harvey's practical-minded teachers.

A tribute paid to Harvey by Dr. Armin Hill, Dean of Physical and Engineering science at B.Y.U. follows:

"Dr. Harvey Fletcher, distinguished scientist and engineer, trail blazing investigator of the nature of speech and hearing, noted for his contributions in acoustics, electrical engineering, speech, medicine, music, atomic physics, sound pictures, and education.

"Born and raised in Provo of pioneer parents, he received his early training at the Brigham Young University, and graduated in 1907. Continuing study at the University of Chicago, he, with Robert A. Millikan, measured the charge on an electron. This fundamental research contributed greatly to the field of electronics which led to the development of the radio and television industry.

"Upon completion of his studies at the University of Chicago he was awarded a Ph.D. summa cum laude, which was the first ever granted by the Physics Department of that University. Showing his loyalty to his church and alma mater he returned to the Brigham Young University and was appointed Chairman of the Physics Department. At that time he was the only faculty member at BYU to have a Ph.D.

"After five years teaching he was advised by Joseph F. Smith to accept an offer at Western Electric Company in New York. Here he was assigned to do research in sound. His genius began to blossom and he was appointed Director of all Physical Research at Bell Telephone Laboratories. He published 51 papers, 19 patents, and two books, *Speech and Hearing,* and *Speech and Hearing in Communication* which are the accepted treatises on the subject. He guided the development of the Western Electric Hearing Aid, the first such device to use vacuum tubes. The hearing aid has given comfort and increased capacity to hundreds of thousands all over the world. He developed a group survey method using recorded sound of decreasing volume which has wide acceptance in schools throughout the nation. He aided in making the telephone a pleasant and useful tool for mankind. He was the first to demonstrate stereophonic transmission and stereophonic recording. In 1939 while working with Leopold Stokowski, he presented a concert featuring stereophonic recording to a capacity crowd in Carnegie Hall in New York. The Salt Lake City Tabernacle Choir was heard singing in three dimension to this vast audience.

"Dr. Fletcher has an enviable record of achievement and honor. He helped found the American Acoustical Society and became its first president. He was elected an honorary member of this Society—an honor which at that time was shared by only one other man—Thomas A. Edison. He was president of the American Society for Hard of Hearing, an honorary member of American Otological Society, an honorary member of the Audio Engineering Society and an honorary member of the American Speech and Hearing Society. He was awarded the Louis E. Levy Medal for physical measurements of audition by the Franklin Institute in 1924. He was president of the American Physical Society which is the leading physics society in America. He was elected vice-president of the American Association for the Advancement of Science in 1937. He is a member of the American Institute of Electrical Engineers, Phi Beta Kappa, Sigma Xi, and an honorary member of Sigma Pi Sigma. He was the first Utahn and Latter-day Saint to become a member of the National Academy of Sciences. He is also a member of the National Hearing Division Committee of Medical Sciences. He was given the Progress Medal Award by the American Academy of Motion Pictures in Hollywood. He acted as National Councilor for the Ohio State University Research Foundation eight years.

"Few men of American science have been so widely recognized. He has received honorary degrees from Columbia University, Stevens Institute, Kenyon College, Case Institute of Technology, and the University of Utah.

"Dr. Fletcher's greatness does not lie in the field of science alone. Being endowed with deep humility and faith in God, he served for ten years as president of the New York Branch of the LDS Church and in 1936 was set apart as president of the New York Stake. His guiding hand has been responsible for generating a spirit of enthusiasm, integrity, and spirituality in the lives of thousands of young students and scientists who have directly or indirectly felt the influence of his work.

"Dr. Fletcher attributes much of his success to his wife, the former Lorena Chipman. They have five boys and a girl. Stephen received his degree in Law at Columbia University. James, Robert, Harvey, and Paul have each received Ph.D.'s."

Dr. Fletcher has been honored by the larger universities across the nation as special lecturer, consultant of research in sound, hearing and stereophonic studies; elected a member and made an officer in all important institutions and societies dealing with phases of audition; has lectured in England, France and Germany; and the following institutions have presented him with doctor's degrees—ScD Columbia University, ScD Kenyon College, Case Institute of Technology, Stevens Institute of Technology, University of Utah, and Brigham Young University.

BYU has been justly proud of its illustrious graduate; B.S. Degree, 1907; Head, Dept of Physics, 1911-16; pres., Utah Academy of Science, 1915-16; BYU Alumni Distinguished Service Award, 1937; left BYU for Research in Bell Telephone Laboratories, 1916-1949; Prof. of Electrical Engineering at Columbia University, 1949-1952; First Chairman of Engineering Dept at BYU, 1953; Dean of new College of Physical and Engineering Sciences at BYU, 1954; Engineering Building at BYU named for him, 1957; Distinguished Service Award, Utah Academy of Sciences, Arts and Letters, 1958, President, BYU Emeritus Club, 1958; supervised sound equipment for theatres in Harris Fine Arts Center; designed sound equipment for Palmyra Pageant, 1961.

To name all his citations and honors would require several pages. He has received gold medals at special exercises from the Franklin Institute, Society of Motion Picture Engineers, Acoustical Society of America, and Audio Engineering Society. He has been elected a Fellow in the American Association for the Advancement of Science and various societies connected with acoustics, hearing, and physics. The U.S. Army and Navy have named him for special recognition. An international Founders Award was conferred upon him by the 150,000-member Institute of Electrical and Electronics Engineers, Inc. Mar. 1967.

His publications in scientific journals number in the dozens; his two books "Speech and Hearing", 1929, and "Speech and Hearing in Communication", 1953, have become world known and universally used. (See appended list)

One phase of his busy life is the number of patents from his fertile mind and experiments covering a period from 1924 to 1948, many of them in Testing Circuits and Systems. Twenty major patent applications were made to the Patent Office, and his patents alone would have made him a world authority in his special field of research and a benefactor for the hard of hearing.

His church activities have paralleled his busy life, from his deacon activities in the Provo First Ward to his presidency of the New York Stake, 1936-42. He was president of M.I.A. during his teaching years of his residence in Provo prior to his going to New York and served in the High Council of N.Y. Stake, 1942-52. Since his return to Provo he has been in the presidency of the High Priest's Quorum.

A patron of the arts, an enthusiastic sports spectator, a man who has shared ample hours with his family of brilliant children and appreciative wife and who devotes planned time to his church, Harvey Fletcher has brought honor to this state, church, and nation and is one of the superior Sons of Brigham.

Some publications of Harvey Fletcher

1911 Causes of Apparent Discrepancies in Recent Work on the Determination of the Elementary Electrical Charge. (with R. A. Millikan) Phys. Zeit., January

Some Contributions to the Theory of Brownian Movements, with Experimental Applications. Phys. Zeit., January

The Question of Valency in Gaseous Ionization. (with R. A. Millikan) Phil. Mag., June.

A verification of the Theory of Brownian Movements and a Direct Determination of the Value of Ne for Gaseous Ionization. Phys. Rev., August; Le Radium, July.

1914 A Determination of Avogadro's Constant N from Measurements of the Brownian Movements of Small Oil Drops Suspended in Air. Phys. Rev., November

1915 Upon the Question of Electric Charges Which Are Smaller Than the Electron. Phys. Zeit., August.

Relative Difficulty in Interpreting the English Speech Sounds. Phys. Zeit., August.

1921 The Frequency Sensitivity of Normal Ears. Proc. Nat. Acad., November; Phys. Rev., June 1922.

1922 The Nature of Speech and Its Interpretation. Jour. Franklin Inst., June.

1923 The Use of the Audiometer in Prescribing Aids to Hearing. College of Physicians, April.

Physical Measurements of Audition. Jour. Franklin Inst., September.

Audiometric Measurements and Their Uses. Trans. College of Physicians, April.

1924 Physical Properties of Speech, Music, and Noise. Bell Telephone System Monograph B-94-1, February.

Physical Criterion for Determining Musical Pitch. Phys. Rev., March.

High Quality Transmission and Reproduction of Speech and Music. (with W. H. Martin) Jour. AIEE, March; Elec. Com., April.

Loudness of a Complex Sound. Phys. Rev., September.

1925 Useful Numerical Constants of Speech and Hearing. Bell System Tech. Jour., July.

Methods and Apparatus for Testing the Acuity of Hearing. The Laryngoscope, July.

1926 Theory of the Operation of the Howling Telephone. Bell System Tech. Jour., January.

Measuring Children's Hearing. Bell Record, June.

Three Million Deafened School Children. (with E. P. Fowler) Jour. Amer. Med. Soc., December.

(Discussion of paper by C. C. Bunch) Comparison of the Results Made with Two Types of Audiometer. Arch. of Otology, July.

1927 Demonstration of Principles of Talking and Hearing with Application to Radio. Annals of Otology, Rhinology and Laryngology, March.

The Hard-of-Hearing Child. U.S. School Health Studies No. 13, July.

Hearing Aids and Deafness. Bell Record, October.

1928 Book Review. "The Theory of Sound" by Lord Rayleigh. Proc. I R E, May.

1929 Articulation Testing Methods. (with J. C. Steinberg) Bell System Tech. Jour., October.

1930 A Space-Time Pattern Theory of Hearing. Jour. Acous. Soc. of Amer., April.

1931 Physical Characteristics of Speech and Music. Rev. Mod. Phys., April; Bell System Tech. Jour., July.

1932 Can We Scientifically Advise Patients As to the Effectiveness of Hearing Aids? Annals of Otology, Rhinology, and Laryngology, September.

1933 Evaluating Hearing Aids. Bell Record, January

Loudness, Its Definition, Measurement and Calculation. Jour. Acous. Soc. of Amer., October; Bell System Tech Jour., October (with W. A. Munson).

1934 Auditory Perspective—A Symposium. Electrical Engineering, January; Bell System Tech. Jour., April.

Hopeful Trends in the Testing of Hearing and in the Prescribing of Hearing Aids. Proc. Amer. Federation of Organizations for the Hard of Hearing.

Loudness, Pitch, and Timbre of Musical Tones. Jour. Acous. Soc. of Amer., October.

1935 Newer Concepts of the Pitch, Loudness and Timbre of Musical Tones. Jour. Franklin Inst., October.
1937 Relation Between Loudness and Making (with W. A. Munson) Jour. Acous. Soc. of Amer., July.
1938 Loudness, Masking and Their Relation to Hearing and Noise Measurement. Jour. Acous. Soc. of Amer., April.
The Mechanism of Hearing. Proc. Nat. Acad., July.
1940 Auditory Patterns. Rev. of Mod. Phys., January.
1941 Stereophonic Sound-Film System. A symposium, Jour. Soc. Motion Picture Engrs., October; Jour. of Acous. Soc. of Amer., October.
1942 Hearing, the Determining Factor for High-Fidelity Transmission, Proc. I R E, June.
1944 Scientific Progress and Civic Responsibility. Univ. of Utah Press, June.
1946 The Atomic Bomb. The Improvement Era, March.
The Pitch, Loudness and Quality of Musical Tones. Amer. Jour. of Phys., July-August.
The Science of Hearing (A radio talk) October 6. Part of "The Scientists Speak," Boni & Gaer, Inc., New York, 1947.
1947 An Institute of Musical Science—A Suggestion. Jour. Acous. Soc. of Amer., July.
1950 A Mathematical Theory of the Perception of Speech in Communication. Jour. of Acous. Soc. of Amer., March.
A Method of Calculating Hearing Loss for Speech from an Audiogram. Jour. Acous. Soc. of Amer., January.
1951 On the Dynamics of the Cochlea. Jour. Acous. Soc. of Amer., November.
Acoustics. Phys. Today, December.
1952 The Dynamics of the Middle Ear and Its Relation to the Acuity of Hearing. Jour. Acous. Soc. of Amer., March.
1962 Quality of Piano Tones (with E. Donnell Blackham and Richard Stratton) Jour. Acous. Soc. of Amer., June.
1963 Quality of Organ Tones (with E. Donnell Blackham and Douglas A. Christensen) Jour. Acous. Soc. of Amer., March.
1964 Normal Vibration Frequencies of a Stiff Piano String, Jour. Acous. Soc. of Amer., March.
1965 Quality of Violin, Viola, Cello, and Bass Viol Tones I, Jour. Acous. Soc. of Amer., March.

Books

1929 *Speech and Hearing*, D. Van Nostrand & Co., New York.
1953 *Speech and Hearing in Communication*, D. Van Nostrand, New York.

He is still doing research in sound.

JAMES CHIPMAN FLETCHER

Born: June 5, 1919   **Place:** Maplewood, N. J.

Father: Dr. Harvey Fletcher, born September 11, 1884, in Provo, Utah. Son of Charles E. and Elizabeth Miller, (see his biography).

Mother: Lorena K. Chipman, born August, 1888 in American Fork, Utah. Daughter of Stephen L. and Sina Neilsen Chipman. Married September 11, 1908. Elected "Mother of the Year" for the U. S. in 1965. Died Jan. 2, 1967.

Brothers   Phyllis b. 21 May 1910. m. Wm. K. Firmage of Chatham,
and Sisters: N. J. Received M. S. Degree in Mathematics.
Stephen Harvey. b. November 20, 1911. m. Dorothy Roberts, LLB, Columbia U 1932. V.P. and general counselor for Western Electric Co. N.Y., N.Y. California Inst. of Tech. 1948. 1958 formed own Company in Missile Industry. Space Electronics Corp. Developed the able star engine and Thor Able Space Carrier.
Robert C. b. May 27, 1921. m. Rosemary Bennett. Ph.D. Physics, Mass. Inst. of Tech. 1949. V.P., Savdia Corp. (Subsidiary of Bell Telephone Co.) Albuquerque, N. M.
Harvey Jr. b. April 9, 1923. Married Deah Tonks. Professor of Math at BYU, where he got his Ph.D. Works in Apollo Moon Project.
Paul C. b. Jan. 10, m. Norma Hunt. Ph.D. physics, Columbia 1956. Dept, head and researcher for Electro-Optical Co. of Pasadena, California, (A Space firm).

Marriage: Fay Stanley Lee, daughter of William N. and Fay Lee of Brigham City. Born Feb. 1919.
Graduate of Box Elder High School and L.D.S. Business College. Attended BYU. Graduate of Columbia University.

Children: Ginger
Mary Sue
Steven
"Missy" Barbara Jo

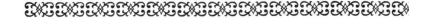

James Chipman Fletcher is a brilliant son of a brilliant father. In a family of five boys and a sister, scholastic competition was a daily exercise, with Phyllis majoring in mathematics in which she received her Master's of Science degree. The young men majored in their father's specialty, physics and mathematics, with the exception of Stephen H. who received a law degree and became vice president and general counsel for the Western Electric Co. of New York City.

Telling of his home influence, James stated: "Despite the fact that father went into industry, he was powerfully convinced of the need for education. He pushed us pretty much and if you didn't get an advanced degree, you felt you would let your parents down. Yes, the five boys were competitive. Father pitted us against each other in just about everything—chess, croquet, baseball, football. Did the boys have a laboratory in the basement? No, we had a gym!" Dr. Harvey Fletcher had been a champion gymnast at college.

James C. spent two years at BYU, 1937-39 where he met his future wife, Fay Lee and where his father met his wife. The young Fletchers have three daughters and a son.

Columbia University gave James his B.S. in 1940 and he studied at Harvard University in 1942-43. Nuclear Physics took him to California Institute of Technology, where he got his Ph.D. in 1948, summa cum laude. He was an instructor at Princeton University during 1943-45. He gained a zest for teaching and research which gave him challenge when he was research physicist for the US Navy in 1940-41. His life has been balanced between teaching and research ever since, and in his philosophy he harmonizes both.

He spent some twelve years on National Defense Research Council Programs which included bomb damage and blast wave assessment projects. He directed the analysis department of the Howard Hughes Company in California for six years, joined the Ramo-Woodbridge firm, and in 1954 became director of the electronics in the guided missile program which became the Space General Corp. of which he was chairman of the board and vice president for systems of Aerojet General Corporation.

While his research programs in California were expanding, his company earnings were increasing daily, and the Project Forecast Committee was set up by the US Air Force to study and promote the successful aims for immediate development, he was approached by the Board of Regents of the University of Utah and asked to assume the presidency of the great intermountain institution. His choice received general approbation, and to the surprise of many in the scientific and business world he accepted and assumed leadership on July 1st, 1965. His uncle, Dr. A. Ray Olpin, himself a research scientist of national repute, had been the university president for eighteen years and had responded to the arbitrary retirement age set by the university board.

At age 45, President Fletcher looks confidently to the future importance of the state university. He has retained many of his connections with government research as one of the world's authorities on space problems, but he has cast his lot in the field of academic education "as I have decided that is the direction I want to go."

Realizing the vast number of opportunities in the world, President Fletcher states that education must keep the intellectual doors open to all worthy comers; the individual is the great unit of progress.

The California Institute of Technology presented to him its Distinguished Service Award at its 75th anniversary celebration, October 1966.

He hopes to make the University of Utah one of the world's great research centers and works to build these research centers by private firms on university land and maintain close cooperation in order to better serve Utah industry.

EARL J. GLADE

Born: December 2, 1885 in Ogden, Utah

Father: James Richard Glade, b. Oct. 20, 1864 in Salt Lake City, Utah
Had eight children
Died in Provo, Utah at 46 on July 16, 1910

Mother: Annie Louise Norberg Nuttal
b. Oct. 11, 1866 in Raiisberg, Saken, Sweden
d. of Gustave and Christine Norberg
Lived with son Earl J. and wife
Died April 28, 1964 at 97½ years of age

Brothers and Sisters: James Vernon b. Mar. 9, 1888, m. Bessie Cushing
William R. b. July 21, 1890, m. Zina Larkin
Grace b. July 31, 1894
George B. b. Aug. 30, 1898, m. Velina Nuttall
Eugene H. b. June 15, 1901, m. Edda M. Snyder
Kenneth P. b. May 21, 1905, deceased Feb. 29, 1924
George F. b. Aug. 20, 1908, m. Fellma Webb

Marriage: Sarah "Sadie" Elizabeth Rasband, b. May 4, 1885 in Heber, Utah
d. of Frederick Rasband and Mary E. Hawkins
graduate of BYU—accomplished pianist and organist
active church and club woman

Children: Melba and Melva (twins) b. Jan 13, 1909. Melva m. Basil C. Hansen
Earl J. Jr., b. July 17, 1911, m. Alice L. Beardall
Dr. Frederick R., b. Oct. 25, 1914, m. Ruth Mounteer, deceased Jan. 17, 1951
Richard, b. Dec. 23, 1917, m. Marilyn Groesbeck
Keith, b. Dec. 12, 1921, m. Cleone Martin
Patricia, b. Nov. 13, 1923, m. LeGrand R. Curtis

Death: September 12, 1966 at 80

Earl J. Glade was born to promote service to his fellowmen. At an early age he revealed qualities of leadership with his boyhood companions, classroom projects, and church promotions. He was never loud or boisterous, seeming almost shy in large groups, but as one of his business friends remarked, "He knows how to get around."

A partial account of his activities is submitted herewith which shows his promotional abilities. He put himself through college by working in and building the BYA book store (later the Student Supply) and teaching classes. Each class had a project to help the young university with its growing pains. Walks had to be put down and retaining walls built on the "Temple Hill" newly acquired property. The project paramount was the connecting of the lower campus with the city sewer on Center Street. There was no indoor plumbing in Earl's early days. The Commerce division of the school was given its allotted territory on Academy Avenue where a ten foot deep trench was built. The entire school, faculty, and students did their share of digging with pick and shovel, dirt hauling, and pipe laying. The girls brought cool drinks, cookies, and sandwiches. "There were no dangerous cave-ins," Earl J. recalled, "and there was a bonfire celebration when the little cubicles, 'Ladies' and 'Men,' were sacrificed to the flames."

School days have never been the same, as pranks were as common as those of today. Two are here related with Earl J.'s permission:

"I was always in trouble when I was in school. One of my chief stunts was to put on stunts between the halves at the basketball games. I had climed on the rafters and was creating sufficient clamor to call attention to my precarious position just over the heads of the players. I was waving a banner right near the roof itself during the half, when I released a dummy and it came tumbling down with my scream, but it caught on the lowest rafter and hung dangling. Two women fainted and many were weak. I hate to think what would have happened if the dummy had gone all the way . . . how many would have. . . ."

The Rialto Debating Club was one of the active girl's clubs on the campus . . . they were giving a coed party in the Gym, strictly a girl affair and well guarded. The boys got together and wondered how they could crash the gate. . . . Mine was the only shaven face, and, after a careful examination, I was elected. . . . We had one friend to whom any could go and get proper help. . . . Kate Elliott made me up for the occasion with a wig; I was startlingly beautiful. . . . I didn't know I was really looking at me. . . . She made me practice walking until she was satisfied and my feet were nearly killing me. Kate escorted me to the stairs and I had to run the gauntlet of eight doorkeepers and passed them all; in fact, I got unusual attention. I had made a hit on my own. I had danced around the floor for about ten minutes with everybody looking at me. I had attracted too much attention when Hattie Redd let one long feminine scream and pointed at me. I was immediately surrounded by girls who began to disrobe me, but they couldn't get the clothes all off, try as they may, and they let me go unmolested but bruised. I had to go over to Elliott's to get my clothes off. This escapade was the joke of the campus for some time. When the track season came I was entered for the long distance run and went to the locker for my paraphanalia; all I could find was a pair of ladies panties."

When Earl J. married and moved to Salt Lake, the motion picture industry, "the flickers" was in its infancy. It immediately intrigued the young graduate and his fancy led him to dream of pictures with sound. "His Master's Voice" was blatant and promising—the marriage of the two was classroom and parlor conversation.

Within ten years after going to Salt Lake City, Earl J. Glade's most cherished dream became a reality; he founded the Radio Service Corporation of Utah, KSL Inc. in Salt Lake City and KLO in Ogden, Utah. That was the beginning of Utah's Salt Lake Tabernacle Choir and Organ Broadcasts. The man most honored for its inception and ultimate fruition was Earl J. Glade, whose name became known across the United States and has remained a power in radio from that memorable day in 1924 to the present. He is "Mr. Radio of the Rocky Mountains." That great program, now world renowned, has been on the air for thirty years, has received every major audio prize, and with Richard L. Evans with the Spoken Word is one of the world's great programs. It is one of the greatest missionaries for the Church which operates and cultivates it. It took years to sell the idea to the proper authorities as sound left much to be desired in its early days, but the great acoustic hall of the Tabernacle overcame most of the common acoustic problems of the day, as Earl J. was certain it would. His activities in radio alone would make the name of Earl J. Glade one of honor for any state or organization.

That he has been a most successful mayor of Salt Lake for three terms, served in the Legislature, has been honored by business, service clubs, advanced educational institutions, and his Church, makes him a worthy Son of Brigham.

Educational Activities:

    Manager Student Supply Association—1909-1912

    Head of BYU Deutche Verein—1910

    Attended University of Chicago Summer—1911

    Graduated from BYU with A.B.—1914

    Head of BYU Business Department—1911-1914

    Moved Family to Salt Lake City—1914

    Assistant Professor of Business Administration, University of Utah—1916-1936

President BYU Alumni Association—1936

Served on the University of Utah Board of Regents—1942-1949

Given B.Y.U. Alumni Distinguished Service Award—1950

Given University of Utah Alumni Distinguished Service Award —1960

Honorary Doctor of Laws Degree for leadership in Radio Industry conferred by University of Utah—1958

Designated "Man of the Year in Education" by Delta Phi Kappa—1962

Lecture Room in the Jesse Knight Commerce Building on Brigham Young University Campus named for Earl J. Glade

Church Activities:

Served as missionary to Germany and Switzerland—1904-1907

Member Highland Park Ward Bishopric—1915

Has served as a Member of the General Board of the Deseret Sunday School Union since 1935

Business and Government Activities:

Past President of the following: Salt Lake Kiwanis Club, Salt Lake Rotary Club, Salt Lake Chamber of Commerce, Salt Lake Knife and Fork Club

Was Chairman of the First Radio Code Committee of the National Association of Broadcasters.

Has been a charter member of the Peabody Radio and Television Awards Board since its founding.

Served three terms, 12 years, as Mayor of Salt Lake City, Utah —1943-1955

Served as President of the Advertising Association of the West —1956-1957

Board Member YMCA—1960-1963

Listed in Who's Who in America—1954-1955

Chairman of Local Board 21, United States Selective Service since 1941

Lieutenant Colonel Civil Air Patrol—1961

Business Achievements:

Member: Gillham Advertising Agency—1961

Founded and built KSL Inc. in 1924

Founded and built KLO, Ogden, Utah

Inaugurated The Salt Lake Tabernacle Choir, Organ and "Spoken Word" Coast-to-Coast Network Broadcasts

Now in its 36th year of continuous presentation, 1964.

Served as Salt Lake Municipal Airport Finance and Public Relations Consultant—1956-1960

Secretary and Manager of Sugar House Chamber of Commerce —1961

Vice-President, KSL Incorporated, 1964

337

His funeral was held in the Assembly Hall on Temple Square, with a capacity audience. Tributes were paid to him in many avenues; KSL gave him a television memorial, most of the state's newspapers wrote editorials praising the man and his works. The Salt Lake Tribune wrote what is universally thought; "Few men had lived a fuller and more valued life than Earl J. Glade—and few leave behind them in death so much warmth of memory and affection.

"Earl J. Glade, who died Monday at the age of 80, was teacher, missionary, churchman, business executive, radio broadcasting pioneer, promotor, civic leader, politician and public official. . . . He lent dignity to the office, and his powers of persuasion established a seldom seen era of harmony on the City Commission"

When we established KBYU radio on our campus, Earl J. was the first to congratulate us with a note "Someday, educational radio will teach more students than classrooms can hold." Practical dreamer, loyal friend, I can think of no one quite like him. There is but one Earl J. Glade.

DAVID GOURLEY

Born: December 31, 1884   **Place:** Goshen, Utah

Father: George Gourley; early convert to L.D.S. Church; born in Cornbrue, Glasgow, Scotland; came to America when three; across the plains in 1856 with the Martin hand-cart company; a sister, twelve years old, pulled baby George over the snow in winter in a washtub; he had three toes frozen off; his father died in 1887, leaving George an only son.

Mother: Mary Elizabeth Broadbent; married in the Salt Lake Temple, Jan. 16, 1882; born in Spring City, Sanpete Co., Utah; one in a family of eleven children; a Primary President for 35 years; served a rural district, summer or winter, as nurse, midwife, and helpful neighbor; married Albert Davis of Provo; seven brothers and sisters of the union; Albert died soon after Eva was born, when David was 16 and the main help to the family.

Brothers and Sisters: David the only child until mother married Albert Davis: (Half Brothers and Sisters) Flora Davis Fischer, teacher at B.Y.U.; Dr. Ray J. Davis, Professor at the U. of Southern Idaho; Boyd Davis, teacher at Orem, Utah; Blanche D. Johnson, lunch Superintendent for Sanpete schools; Eva D. Ovard, teacher in Idaho Falls, Idaho

Marriage: Dora Louise West; June 17, 1908 in the Salt Lake Temple; an accomplished musician with a lovely voice; presented a special music degree by A. C. Lund at B.Y.A.; donated the David Gourley Education Collection to the Clark Library; candidate for "Utah Mother of the Year" 1961.

Children: Eleven children, and parents, all attended BYU: Gertrude Delores, m. Alma C. Franter; Maurine, m. Philander Hatch; George A., m. Adena Nell Swenson; Lee Maughn, m. Edna Bartholomew; Rex S., m. Ruby Taylor; June, m. Lynn S. Searle; Vida Ramona, m. Frank B. Witney; Faun, m. Ben Bartholomew; David Richard, m. Pearl Warner; Ernest G ; John P., m. Jo Ann Richards. All married in the Temple, most are in education; boys were all letter athletes at B.Y.U.

Death: August 22, 1957 at age 72, in his home; buried in Pleasant Grove Cemetery.

Educational Background:
 Early education in the schools of Provo City.
 Certificate in Normal Training, Manual Training, Bachelors Degree (1915) and Masters Degree (1935) in School Administration from Brigham Young University.
 Graduate study in Education in Utah and the University of California.
 Studied Educational Methods and School Administration in several states of the United States.

Educational Experience:
 Six years as teacher—one of the first Smith-Hughes Agriculture Teachers in Utah (Utah County)—teacher in Utah County, Millard County, Washington County.
 One year working for the U.S.A.C. as County Agricultural Agent (Washington County.)
 Four years as High School Principal (Pleasant Grove).
 Fifteen years as Alpine School District Superintendent.
 Instructor Brigham Young University for two summers.
 Special Consultant on Uniform School Bus Regulations at Columbia University
 Six years as Assistant State Superintendent of Public Instruction for the State of Utah.
 Twelve years as Granite School District Superintendent.
 Chairman of the Emergency School Building Commission, State of Utah.

Six Years as:
 Secretary State Board of Education.
 Secretary State Course of Study Committee and State Textbook Commission
 Secretary State Society of Superintendents
 State Director of Intermediate Grades and Junion High School.
 Member of Committee on State Curriculum Studies
 Chairman, Survey Committee of Eight School Districts, State Board of Education.
 State Advisor of School Transportation and Director of Priorities on Bus Standards.
 Member Governor's Coordinating Committee on Safety.

Educational and Civic Organizations and Fraternities:
 Life member, National Education Association and member Utah Education Assn.
 Member Phi Delta Kappa, National Organization for Education Advancement and service.
 Charter Member of Lions Club, American Fork.

Service as Church Member:

340

Boy Scout Worker in Timpanogos Stake and life member of Y.M.M.I.A.

Served two years as a missionary in Southern States, 1905-07.

Stake Leader in St. George, Alpine, Timpanogos and Ensign Stakes.

Active High Priest.

Business Experience:

Director of National Farm Loan Association.

President of Pleasant Grove Irrigation Company.

Owned and directed the operation of a successful farm.

Experiences while attending the Brigham Young University:

1. One of twenty-one persons making the first organized hike to the top of Mount Timpanogos.
2. Member of the Brigham Young University basketball team for several years and also a member of the early track team.
3. Member of the first physical education class organized at B.Y.U. in the Training Building under John C. Swenson as Physical Education Director.
4. Manager of the dances at B.Y.U. for several years.
5. Hauled all the brick at the B.Y.U. for several years and hauled all the terra cotta, gravel and cement for the Maeser Memorial Building during its construction.

A heart attack from over work caused a slackening in Superintendent Gourley's efforts to advance education in the entire state. Thirty-five schools of the Granite District conducted a "David Gourley Day" to honor his forty-five years in teaching. They established a David Gourley Scholarship Fund and named a school the David Gourley Elementary School at Kearns, one of the state's finest. At the dedication Mrs. Gourley presented the school with an excellent portrait of her husband.

He took great pride that nine of his eleven children are educators. "A man's life is never dull when he works for the good of his family, his community and his Church." His life was one of constantly overcoming challenging difficulties, hopefully projecting the future, enjoying companionship with his family, and planning for the good of his students. David Gourley was recognized before his death as one of Utah's great educators. He was proud to be a Son of Brigham.

LEROY REUBEN HAFEN

Historian of American West

Born: December 8, 1893 **Place:** Bunkerville, Nevada

Father: John George Hafen
Born in Scherzingen, Thurgau, Switzerland on October 17, 1838; the son of John George Hafen and Mary Magdalena Hafen. Joined the L.D.S. Church in April, 1860; came to America in 1861 and Santa Clara, Utah the same year. Bishop of Santa Clara Ward for 28 years. He died May 4, 1928, in Santa Clara.

Mother: (Annie Marie) Mary Ann Stucki (Reber)
Born in Rotenbeck, near Bern, Switzerland, May 5, 1854. Arrived in New York June 16, 1860. A handcart immigrant. Cart was pulled by the father and mother with four children. Mary Ann was 6; she walked all the way. Married John Reber on August 4, 1873, was killed in a team runaway accident the day after they returned from their marriage in Salt Lake. Married John George Hafen on November 24, 1873. Died January 16, 1946, in St. George.

Brothers: Albert m. Ellen Leavitt
and Sisters: Mary H. m. D. Henry Leavitt
Bertha H. m. Edgar D. Leavitt
Selena H. m. Frank S. Leavitt
Wilford died as an infant
Lovena H. m. Parley Leavitt
Leroy m. Ann Woodbury

Marriage: Ann Woodbury married September 3, 1915 while attending BYU.
Born May 31, 1893 in Salt Lake City, Utah. Daughter of John Taylor Woodbury and Mary Elizabeth Evans. Poet, editor, schoolteacher, and noted author, co-worker with her distinguished husband receiving many honors with him and on her own recognition won first Alice Louise Reynolds Short Story Contest at BYU.

Children: Norma was born June 25, 1916 and died at age 19.
Karl LeRoy Hafen was born September 13, 1918.
Marjorie Johns—June 20, 1940
Karl LeRoy Haten was born September 13, 1918.
m. (1) Marjorie Johns—June 20, 1940
(2) Agnes "Pat" Hodgkins Murphy—November 1, 1961

EDUCATION
AB—BYU 1916
Manager of BYU debating team and one of its best debators. Won Jex Oratorical Medal 1916
MA—University of Utah 1919—Thesis "Handcart Migration to Utah"
PHD—University of California 1924—dissertation "The Overland Mail"
Honorary Litt. D.-University of Colorado 1935
Professor of History at BYU 1954 to present.
Teacher High School—Bunkerville, Nevada 1916-18
Principal High School—Bunkerville, Nevada 1918-20
Teaching Fellow—University of California 1920-23
Teacher A to Zed School, Berkeley, California 1923-24
Ex. Dir. and state historian, State Historical Soc. of Colorado 1924-1954
Professor of history—University of Denver
Visiting Professor—American History, University of Glasgow, Scotland 1947-48
Fellow of the Huntington Library 1950-51
Editor Colorado Magazine 1925-54
Had historical markers erected over state of Colorado and directed W.P.A. projects to search and write Colorado history.

MEMBER
American History Association; Mississippi Valley History Association; Newcomer Society; Authors League; Denver Westerners Club; Lions Club

EDITOR
With J. H. Baker wrote *History of Colorado* (3 vols.) 1927
The Past and the Present of Pikes Peak Gold Region (with Henry Willard) 1932
Pike's Peak Gold Rush Guide Books of 1859 (1941)

AUTHOR
The Overland Mail 1916
Broken Hand—Life of Thomas Fitzpatrick (with W. J. Ghent) 1931
Colorado—The Story of the Western Commonwealth 1933
Fort Laramie and The Pageant of the West—1834-1890 (with F. M. Young) 1938
Western America (with C. C. Rister) 1941
"Story of Colorado"—a documentary color movie used in Colorado Schools
Colorado, A Story of a State and Its People (with Ann Woodbury Hafen) 1943
Colorado And its People (2 vols.) 1948

The Colorado Gold Rush of 1859 (1941)
Diaries of the Gold Rush 1859 (1942)
Ruxton of the Rockies (1950)
> Produced more than 200 articles.
> 15-volume masterpiece *The Far West and The Rockies,* One of America's greatest contributions of historical importance (with his wife as collaborator).

CONTRIBUTOR TO
> *Mississippi Valley Historical Review*
> *Pacific History Review*
> *Dictionary of American Biography*
> *Dictionary of American History*
> *World Book Encyclopedia*
> *Atlas of American History*

AWARDS AND HONORS
> Citations from the states of California, Colorado, and Utah.
> Distinguished Service Award from Utah Academy Science Arts and Letters (1961)
> Fellow of the International Institute of Arts and Letters, Geneva and Zurich, Switzerland.
> Rockefeller Fellowship for Huntington Library research 1950-51
> Phi Alpha Theta (1954) honorary
> Distinguished Citizenship Award—City of Denver—1958
> Distinguished Service Award—BYU Alumni Association (with his wife) 1963
> David O. McKay Humanities Award to LeRoy and Ann—1964
> The Hafens gave their extensive library to the BYU 1962—written up in a brochure—"Hafen Collection of Americana"
> Third Annual Faculty Lecture, "Joys of Discovery," 1966

It is almost impossible to think of LeRoy R. Hafen without his devoted and talented companion, Ann Woodbury. They were attracted to each other while attending Dixie College, and the romance ripened to matrimony at Brigham Young University. Both knew the rigors of early pioneer life, and knew every facet of virgin farming and its attendant trials.

The first Hafens were Swiss who came to the states at the time of the Civil War, walked the plains before the coming of the railroads, accepted the call to do colonizing in southern Utah, founding Santa Clara.

Men of certain leadership and spiritual strength were urged to practice polygamy and John George Hafen was one so delegated. LeRoy was the youngest of seven children born to his Swiss parents and lived intimately with the other children of his father. Close to the

Hafens were the Leavitts, and the children grew up almost as a family. The girls of Mary Ann Stucki Reber Hafen all married Leavitt boys. The eldest Hafen brother, Albert, married Ellen Leavitt. LeRoy broke the pattern when he fell in love with his vivacious schoolmate, already developing as a writer and excellent character interpreter.

This fusing of talents found its greatest outlet in the fifteen volume set "The Far West and the Rockies," already acclaimed as an invaluable record of western history in all phases of its romantic life.

Doctor Leroy has been honored by several nations having interest in American history. Citations from the western states and several cities, historical journals and societies and fellowships from Switzerland, The great Huntington Library, honor fraternities, all speak his merits and pay him honor.

Our own university has acknowledged his worth by granting him and his wife the Distinguished Service Award from the Brigham Young University Alumni Association and the David O. McKay Humanities Award in 1964.

LeRoy has the ability to see a problem, reduce it to study avenues, and painstakingly run down each lead with results in a proved fact or date. He is a quiet detective of interesting facts which paint pictures of lasting value. His deductions are interesting, his writings are wholly reliable, his personality is one of calm and radiates credulity. His interest in history is not one of dead dates in the past, but of living life interpreted for the present. He is by nature, design and ability a factual historian who writes of events as he finds them; truth is the guide which directs the scope of his pen. He is a most worthy Son of Brigham.

345

ORVAL HAFEN

Born: November 16, 1903, Santa Clara, Utah

Father: John, born in Santa Clara, Utah, November 27, 1862, eldest child. Son of John George and Suzette Boshard Hafen who were Swiss converts. Bishop of Santa Clara Ward for 28 years, town constable, director of Bank of St. George, Utah. Married Ida and Rose Ann Gubler after deaths of previous wives.
d. November 21, 1946.

Mother: Lenora Knight, b. February 8, 1862 in Santa Clara, Utah. Daughter of Samuel and Caroline Beck Knight. m. February 10, 1887 in St. George Temple. Samuel one of first missionaries to Indians, the son of Newel Knight and grandson of Joseph Knight, Sr.

Brothers and Sisters: Two sisters and a brother died in infancy. Arthur K., b. January 14, 1888, m. Orilla M. Woods; Guy, b. November 3, 1889, m. Althea Gregerson; Jessie, b. August 3, 1893, m. Vivian J. Frei; Maxwell (Orval's twin brother) b. November 16, 1903, m. Estelle Bowler; (Orval).

Marriage: Ruth Clark, b. January 6, 1909 in Panguitch, Utah. Daughter of Joseph C. Clark and Claire Evelyn Clark. Reared in Provo, a talented interpreter and community worker. m. August 17, 1932, in Salt Lake Temple.

Children: Joseph C. Hafen, b. December 2, 1933, in Provo (dec.) March 25, 1935; Jon Michael Hafen, b. March 22, 1937 in Provo, m. Diana Brunson. Jon saved his father from drowning in December 1951 and was awarded by the National Court of Honor, Boy Scouts of America, d. February 11, 1959; Bruce Clark Hafen, b. October 30, 1940; Ruth Ann Hafen, b. January 14, 1943 in St. George, Utah; Margaret Claire, b. December 13, 1946; Michele, a grand daughter lives with the Hafens.

Death: Saturday, October 3, 1964 at 60, of a heart attack at his Snow Canyon Ranch.
The Hafen family has been written up by Leroy R. Hafen.

Orval Hafen's Life in Brief:

Education: Schools of Santa Clara, St. George; graduate from Dixie College; B. Y. U. A. B., 1925, history major; LLB, University of California

346

Varsity debater with A. C. Lambert for B. Y. U.; one of strongest teams ever to represent the University
Winner of the Provo Chamber of Commerce Efficiency Medal
Attended George Washington University at Washington, D.C.
Forensic manager at B. Y. U.

Legal:
City Attorney, St. George
Utah Legislative Council
Author of bill which created the state parks system
Author of bill creating the new Coordinative Council on Higher Education
Utah State Senate 11 years—President of Senate 1957-59
Chairman of legislative committee
President of Utah State Bar Association
Running for 4th term when he was stricken
Hafen Bill repealed law that stated epileptics couldn't wed unless they had no chance to have children. Especially repealed to help veterans who had brain injuries from war.
Washington County Attorney 10 years
Delegate to 1960 and 1964 Republican National Conventions

Religion:
St. George L.D.S. Stake High Council
10 years in the Stake Presidency

Civic:
President St. George Rotary Club
Member of St. George Chamber of Commerce

Business:
Vice president St. George Savings and Loan Association
Director—United Utah Industries
    Western States Title Insurance Company, Salt Lake City, Utah
President Sun Land Homes
Vice President and Director New Hampshire Life Insurance Company,
Salt Lake City, Utah
Owner automobile agency
Counselor to hundreds in various business lines

The State of Utah paid respects to Orval Hafen as one of its most honored sons. He was a member of the B. Y. U. Alumni Executive Board.

Tributes to Orval were printed in all the major newspapers of Utah. In part the *Salt Lake Tribune* states: "His death is a loss for the southern part of Utah, but it also deprives the entire state of a lawmaker dedicated to the larger interests of the community as a whole." He was especially concerned that the larger counties of the state would not completely dominate state privileges, representation and tax proceeds distribution. As written by M. DeMar Teuscher, "He was completely and sincerely opposed to legislative control of both the House and Senate vested in just three or four counties, no matter how populous." Steve Hale expressed what hundreds believe; "Some men are remembered by the huge monuments that are built for them, or by the number of times they are mentioned in the history books. They can't build a monument to Orval Hafen bigger than the gratitude in a lot of people's hearts."

The *Deseret News* editorial writes: "Orval Hafen never retired, and this was typical of him. Though soft-spoken and mild mannered he was a tireless fighter for causes he felt were right. He was a "senator's senator"—a man who won universal respect among his colleagues because of his capacity for hard work, his mastery of the small details that are so important in good legislation, and because of his profound respect for the dignity of the office he held,—not surprisingly he was a key figure in many of the most important pieces of legislation Utah has seen in recent years.

With all this and with a distinguished career in law and banking, he was also a highly successful husband and father and a respected citizen of his beloved St. George.

One of BYU's most distinguished Sons of Brigham.

WAYNE BROCKBANK HALES

Born: December 20, 1893   **Place:** Spanish Fork, Utah

Father: Jonathan Hyrum Hales born May 25, 1861 in Spanish Fork, son of Charles Henry Hales, Utah pioneer of 1852, one of first settlers of Spanish Fork. Married November 16, 1882. Member of Nauvoo Legion, builder and missionary. Died: January 21, 1922 in Provo, Utah

Mother: Martha Ann Brockbank
Born September 5, 1861 in Spanish Fork, Utah; daughter of Issac Brockbank; Utah pioneer of 1852. Died January 5, 1905, when Wayne was but twelve.

Brothers and Sisters: Mabel, b. December 23, 1883; m. Henry Falkner
Inez, b. May 7, 1885; m. Rasmus Neilson; d. October 3, 1937
Roy, b. September 5, 1888; m. Christine Kropt; d. March 4, 1931
Jennie, b. November 2, 1895; m. John H. Bauer
Lynn, b. April 6, 1899; m. Eleanor Peterson
Four other boys born in Spanish Fork between 1886-1904, died in infancy of children diseases.

Marriage: 1) Belle Wilson, daughter of James Brigham and Margaret Powell Wilson; sister of Judge David J. Wilson; "Utah County Mother of the Year" and alternate "Utah Mother of the Year." Born December 11, 1889 in Midway, Utah. Known to hundreds of B.Y.U. students as "A Mother Away From Home." B.Y.U. graduate in 1938 with honors. President of B.Y.U. Women and of B.Y.U. Chapter American Association of University Women; Honorary Gleaner Girl; Board Member Utah Stake Relief Society. Married September 20, 1916 in the Salt Lake Temple. Died April 1, 1963.
2) On July 2, 1965, Wayne wed a life-time friend, Vivian Parkinson Taylor, who was widowed in September 1962, the former wife of the well-known Lester R. Taylor of Provo.

Children: Dr. James Vern, b. July 21, 1917; m. Lucille Farnsworth
Dr. Dean Wilson, b. May 9, 1920; m. Ann Danvers
Isabel, b. June 1, 1922; m. George I. Cannon
Margaret, b. November 14, 1923; m. Dr. Delos E. Bown
Dr. Richard Wayne, b. February 13, 1926; m. Mary Smart; d. February 4, 1964
Dr. Robert Hyrum, b. June 2, 1930; m. Janette Callister

Born in Spanish Fork, Wayne moved with his father and family to Eureka, Utah, where the father and Wayne worked in the mines and where Wayne first was introduced to scouting.

He worked one entire summer in Spanish Fork for Bishop George Hales and received in payment one milk cow, which he led to Eureka, living on a loaf of bread and milk on the way. Wiley, the faithful cow, furnished milk for the Hales family for many years and Wayne was the only person she would let milk her, to his despair and pride.

He worked in the Tintic Mines to pay his school expenses at B.Y.U., where he enrolled in October, 1912 under Dr. Harvey Fletcher.

Education:

1916	BA—B.Y.U. in physics. A four-year letterman in track and basketball. His record for cross-country run stood for 10 years. Retired the first Horace G. Merrill Cup.
1923	MA—University of Utah—Major, physics. Thesis, "Acoustics of the Salt Lake Tabernacle."
1926	Ph.D.—California Institute of Technology underRobert A Millikan. Thesis, "Photoelectric Properties of Mercury." Graduate work at University of Chicago, University of California.
1916-21	Taught at Ricks College, Rexburg, Idaho.
1926-30	Weber College at Ogden, Utah—Head of Physics and Mathematics.
1921-24	President Snow College, Ephraim, Utah
1930	B.Y.U.—Professor of Physics in the department to date. Chairman of physics department 1954-58; Dean of General College 1958-1962; Chairman of B.Y.U. Athletic Council, 1952 to present and Dr. Horace G. Merrill Art Award
1944	Rutgers College—on research concerning jungle acoustics.

Scouting

Member of first organized troop in Utah under Dr. L. D. Pfoutz in 1910 and Scout Master of first troop in Provo. Awarded the Silver Beaver by the National Parks Council in 1942 and in 1960 was presented the fifty year veteran award. Is a member of the National Parks Executive Council.

Professional Activities

President, Utah Conference on Higher Education—1959-60; Member, National Executive Council of Sigma Pi Sigma; National Physics Honorary Society, 1958-present; Member, Council American Association for Advancement of Science—1961; Member, State Advisory Committee to Utah Coordinating Council on Higher Education.

Professional Societies Membership

Utah Teachers Association; Utah Academy of Sciences, Arts and Letters; Fellow and Past President 1931-32; American Acoustical Society; American Association Physics Teachers; American Association Advancement of Science, Fellow and Member of Council; Sigma Xi Sigma, Member and National Executive Council; American Meteorological Society; American Society for Engineering Education.

Church Positions

1937-1950, Member of YMMIA General Board; In Bishoprics of following Wards: Pasadena, Provo Fifth, Provo University Ward, and B.Y.U. Campus 6th Ward; High council—Utah Stake 1950-54; Stake President—B.Y.U. Stake 1960-1964, B.Y.U. 6th Stake, 1964 to present.

Honorary

Fellow in Utah Academy Science, Arts and Letters; Honorary Master M-Man—1950; Honorary Blue Key Member—1957; 50-year Veteran Scout Award—1960; B.Y.U. Alumni Distinguished Service Award—1959. Distinguished Achievement Award in Physical Sciences—1964 by Utah Academy Sciences, Arts and Letters.

The story of Wayne's first date with his future wife is a way of life this generation knows naught of. As Belle tells it:

"Our social group of B.Y.U. had a party and we invited all the nicest young men on campus. We went alone and met them there. We had to decide how we were going home as we had to walk a couple of miles to our homes. The hostess was very ingenious. She put a sheet upon one side of the room and we all had to stand behind this sheet and put out the toes of our shoes. Then the men came along. I think I must have put my best foot forward that night, because he selected me and, of course, we had a very nice walk home . . . How did he propose, I don't believe he ever did. But, my father said that was all right, he proposed to and was accepted by him."

The Brigham Young faculty is unique in many ways. Of its hundreds of married couples there have not been a half dozen divorces. Faculty family life is a study worthy of volumes as the companionship and loyalty of the patient wives to their teaching husbands is superbly magnificent. Almost every man in this collected biography was abetted, encouraged, and materially helped by his wife. She not only bore and reared a representative family; she worked when possible to help her husband go on a mission, acquire an advanced degree and even put food in the kitchen. Many studied for further education themselves.

Wayne B. and Belle Wilson Hales were accounted as the ideal parents and sweethearts from the day they started in serious companionship. Each complimented the other in every activity and their home was always a cultural center with good books, excellent music, a generous larder and daily family conferences. The relations between parent and child were superb. The parent was always the companion

351

to, rather than the owner of the child. Laughter and prayer were present at proper times; friends rang the doorbell frequently. What the Hales possess, they readily share.

Vivian, a successful business woman has adjusted her affairs to be a companion to Wayne on his frequent assignments for his profession, the University and the Church. Temple work further adds to their association. What was good in each previous home is now centered in one and the love of dear ones departed is further honored in the new association.

Wayne is one of Brigham's versatile, favorite Sons.

FRANKLIN STEWART HARRIS

Born: August 29, 1884   **Place:** Benjamin, Utah County, Utah

Father: Dennis Emer Harris, son of Dennison Lott Harris and
Sarah Wilson Born May 13, 1854; died July 20, 1912
Dennison L. was a brother of Martin Harris, one of the
witnesses to the Book of Mormon and Dennison L.
obtained first copy (bound) of the Book of Mormon

Mother: Eunice Polly Stewart, daughter of Benjamin Franklin
Stewart and Polly Richardson
Born in Payson, Utah, April 29th, 1860; Died Mar. 1942
Married Aug. 24, 1882, in Salt Lake Endowment House
Met her husband at B.Y.A.
Her father, Benj. Franklin Stewart has his name on the
Brigham Young Monument on Main Street in Salt Lake
City as an original pioneer
Settled in Payson and founded the town of Benjamin, Ut.

Brothers The children of the two families of Dennis Emer Harris
and Sisters: were so congenial that they grew up as one family
Children of Eunice Polly:
Dennison Emer, b. June 19, 1883
Franklin Stewart, b. Aug. 29, 1884
Leo Lott, b. April 9, 1886
Milton Hyrum, b. Jan. 1, 1888
Lula Eunice, b. Sept. 1, 1890
Marion Luther, b. Dec. 28, 1892
Karl, b. Oct. 16, 1894
Ireta, b. Feb. 23, 1897
Sterling Richard, b. July 24, 1899
Children of Annie Jane Wride (Died Dec. 1922)
Joseph Emer, b. April 5, 1887
Barry Wride, b. April 24, 1890
Jessie Martin, b. Feb. 22, 1892
Annie Asura, b. Aug. 22, 1893
George Lewis, b. Mar. 20, 1895
Jennie, b. still born
Edna, b. April 28, 1898
Nettie Jane, b. Nov. 5, 1900
Sara, b. Dec. 1, 1901
Ervin Charles, b. Sept. 29, 1903

Marriage Estella Spilsbury of Toquerville, Utah
Born Feb. 17, 1884, daughter of George Moroni and Roselia
Haight Spilsbury; she was daughter of two pioneer
families

Married June 18, 1908—met her husband at B.Y.A.
Graduated from B.Y.U. in June, 1907, Normal Diploma
Received B.Y.U. Alumni Distinguished Service Award in
1958

Children: Arlene H., m. Roscoe Grover; Franklin S. Jr., m. Maurine
Steed; Chauncey D., m. Edith Young; Helen, m. Ralph
W. Jenson; Leah Dorothy, m. Vernon D. Jensen; Mildred,
m. Ralph O. Bradley
All children graduated from B.Y.U.

Death: April 18th, 1960; he failed to fully recover from an auto
accident

సౖఖ2సౖఖ2సౖఖ2సౖఖ2సౖఖ2సౖఖ2సౖఖ2సౖఖ2సౖఖ2సౖఖ2సౖఖ2

In honoring Dr. Harris, we praise a man who has rendered invaluable service to the far reaches of the world. He has brought
honor to his state, his nation and the educational institutions which
he represented. However we look upon the life of F. S. Harris, be it
in childhood, boyhood, school, church, community, state, or foreign
lands, it tells of expansive interests, application and work, integrity
and trust. He early recognized the worth of his pioneer heritage, the
value of education, the character building precepts of his church, the
protective principles of the nation's constitution. He made farmers
feel free and at ease. He conversed with world leaders as an equal.
Scholars valued and accepted his opinions, and scientists honored him
as an authority.

It is difficult to state whether his fame rests more upon his work
as an educator or as a scientist; time may make the decision. He hired
his faculty on the basis of education and character; he expected constant
improvement in both aspects. F. S. Harris was one of the nation's
mot consistent protagonists for a liberal education, a broad foundation
to include languages, the arts, mathematics, government, history
and religion. For him, all subjects had a scientific approach, and their
worth depended upon the manner in which they affected and benefited
the individual. He made great allowance for individual differences
in faculty and students and had no inflexible mold in which to pour
a curriculum or a scholar.

He was superior in making friends; none so humble as to not
interest him. He soon learned each student's parental background,
place of birth, and personal ambitions. His office door as president of
a University was always open to any faculty member or student; he

was as much concerned with causes of failure as with attainment of success. F. S. was a faculty's champion, though he never had sufficient funds to pay the salaries he so much desired.

President Harris had Benjamin Franklin Stewart, one of Utah Valley's most colorful pioneers, as his maternal grandfather, for whom the town of Benjamin was named. Dennison Lott Harris, another rugged individualist, was his paternal grandfather. Young Frank was born in Benjamin, Utah County, on August 29, 1884 and at five years of age was taken to old Mexico by his parents, Dennison Emer and Eunice "Polly" Stewart Harris. The Harris boys knew hard work, indoors and out, Franklin working in his father's store. In this environment he acquired an excellent speaking and reading knowledge of Spanish and could easily adjust to Mexican dialects.

F. S. and brother Dennison came to Brigham Young Academy in 1903. After one year Franklin was called back to Colonia Juarez to teach science at the Juarez Stake Academy. The desert lands of Utah, southwest United States, and northern Mexico early presented a challenge to F. S., and he dreamed of conserving water and treating and fertilizing soils for a greater crop yield. Upon his return to B.Y.A. he made the acquaintance of and became the assistant to Dr. John A. Widtsoe, director of agriculture. A lasting friendship followed and soil chemistry became a driving force for each of these scholars and teachers.

F. S. Harris graduated in 1907 with distinguished colleagues, some of whom are chronicled in "Sons of Brigham". In this year he courted and won the affections of one of the more popular girls on the campus, Estella Spillsbury of Toquerville, Utah. He often repeated that this conquest was the most significant act of his life. Her vivacious personality pervaded all groups in which she mingled. His life was completely complimented by her gracious charm, friendly attitude toward faculty and students, and easy adjustments to a varying social life, whether in Mexico, Russia, Iran, or diplomatic Washington. Soon after this marriage the Harris home became a rendezvous for campus committees and student groups. His educational leadership extended from 1907 to 1950, twenty-four years at B.Y.U. and ten years at Utah State Agricultural College (Utah State).

In a biography so brief we can but touch upon the many facets of his diversified life.

Frank, with Estella, went to Ithaca, New York for graduate work to major in soils and minor in plant physiology and chemistry. He did assistant teaching in the department while maintaining "A" grades and graduating with honor. He completed his course in the four year period and in the meantime their first child, Arlene, was born, soon to be more of a companion than a daughter.

355

Upon graduation from Cornell, where he met some of the best agronomists of the world, he returned to U.S.A.C. as professor of agronomy and agronomist at the experiment station; he also became director of the school of agricultural engineering and mechanical arts, 1912. Ultimately he became director of the experiment station in 1916. His work took him throughout the state, where he established important stations in agricultural research, benefits from which still accrue to the state in better crops and more abundant species of animal foods and table edibles. Here he wrote some of his better known texts, such as *The Principles of Agronomy*, 1915, *The Young Man and His Vocation*, 1916, *Sugar Beet in America*, 1918, *Soil Alkali*, 1920. The three scientific works became national texts and *The Principles of Agronomy* was reprinted in 1929 in a revised edition. In his foreign travels his reputation as a soil scientist had preceded him and brought him a richer welcome for his visits and assignments.

With the failing health of President George H. Brimhall, President Heber J. Grant of the L.D.S. Church called the University board to name a president, and in 1921 Dr. Harris was selected for the position. His coming was notable in that he called the faculty to a special meeting, introduced himself and his wife, addressed each member present with a full knowledge of what had been done in the respective departments, asked for advice and cooperation from each faculty member, and pledged himself to work for the good of all departments for one great, liberal college. In this meeting he urged each department to increase its doctorates, get advanced degrees as fast as the school and teacher could arrange for leaves of absence, help build a great library, meet often as colleagues to discuss subject growth and each be prepared to teach some phase of our religion, as well as a full load in prepared subject courses. The faculty as a family was stressed and the feeling for friendship and professional growth was reciprocal.

When he came to B.Y.U. the faculty consisted of some seventy-eight members, ten with doctorates (as listed in the catalogue) which included James E. Talmage, Richard R. Lyman and John A. Widtsoe as lecturing professors, ten masters, twenty-five bachelors, A.B. and B.S., with six holding bachelor of pedagogy degrees. The balance were special instructors in the arts and teaching.

President Harris would be the last to say the University grew so rapidly solely because of his efforts, as he had a strong faculty about him, growing consistently each year. There were fifty-three Ph.D.'s, fifty-four Masters and fifty-four Bachelors when he left the University in 1945. The masters were working on advanced degrees.

The University, through the efforts of its Alumni officers, cleared the way for acquiring the land of "Manavu Village" or most of what was called "Temple Hill". That was in 1920. When President Harris arrived, he started to procure the one home on the brow of the hill built by Dr. Martin P. Henderson, which he ultimately acquired for the school as the president's residence. It underwent a full sized alteration before the Harris family moved in and became a social center for the school.

The first weekly faculty meetings were held in the north room, first floor of the Education Building, to discuss plans, courses in curriculum, negligent and needy students, and the needs of the respective departments and programs for the week. Each faculty member was called upon to report his program of the week, especially the visits over weekends to various parts of the state in interest of school enrollment. College Hall was rebuilt to accommodate the expanding drama programs, and by 1923 a play per school month was scheduled and presented. Scenery was built and bought and Broadway plays were introduced to intersperse with the better known classics. Encouraged by President Harris, faculty members took part in the more difficult plays.

Buildings erected during President Harris' administration:

George H. Brimhall building for applied science.

Heber J. Grant Library as part of a court connecting with the Maeser building.

Joseph Smith Building as a religious center.

Stadium House and the east side of the stadium bowl for athletics.

Allen Hall for men's residence

Amanda Knight Hall for women students

Iona Hall as a practice house

Summer School center at Aspen Grove in North Fork of Provo Canyon.

Under his regime, Leadership Week was inaugurated for adult education with emphasis upon spiritual training. The Extension Division was catalogued and became immediately popular. An infrequent lecture program was augmented into a world famous Lyceum Course with community cooperation. A few local painters had contributed some of their better works, which graced some office walls and Room "D". These were increased to a formidable collection of great paintings of local and world renown. If Dr. Harris had one especial interest it was building an adequate university library. He would walk through the stacks, thumb through the pages of a new book and note its contents, then write down the title of any he wanted to read. His interests took him to every department of the library and he took a personal interest in the packing of books from the small cubby hole library in Room "D" of the Education Building to the "spacious" quarters of the new Heber J. Grant library. A pinched budget was squeezed to a breaking point to add the much needed books of reference and research.

A briefing of his important assignments tell of his growing reputation in soil science.

1926—He was the U.S. representative to the Pan American Congress in Japan, being chairman of the agricultural section. His trip carried him into China, the Philippines, Malaya, India, Egypt and Europe. Estella joined him when he was studying at the University of Paris.

1927—His return to the campus was marked by the beginnings of a serious national depression and a movement was started to build seminaries to school church students. The Brigham Young College at Logan, Utah, was closed down, along with other church institutions, and it was a struggle to save B.Y.U. from the same fate. Superintendent Joseph Merrill of the Church School System came to Provo on several occasions to prepare the faculty for such a probability, and it was at such meetings that F. S. Harris rose to his best eloquence and most fervent defense of the importance of a church university to prepare teachers, train scholars and inculcate the Gospel in each L.D.S. student enrolled. Religion was a part of the curriculum of each college and department, as each teacher was assigned one or more classes in religion. President Harris advocated expansion, not extinction. He mustered facts and figures and spent many anxious days in procuring a budget for the following year. He rallied the necessary support to his cause and made secure the place of B.Y.U. in the church financial and religious programs. This challenge focused attention upon the B.Y.U. and the necessity for its development and growth. It gave the university a better understanding of its own obligations and church responsibilities.

1929—One of the more important appointments came to President Harris in this period. The Jews of the world long had sought a place for their people, resulting in a committee from the U.S. and Russia being formed to request assistance from the U.S. to give aid in the colonization of the Jews in the Soviet Union. President Harris was selected by our government to organize a committee and find a place to start such a colony. After an exhaustive tour of Russia and its holdings, a valley was located and recommended for further exploration in eastern Russia, the "Biro Bidjan" in Siberia in the river Amur basin. Complete reports on soil, flora and water were made to the Russian authorities and subsequently to the Jewish associations in Germany, Austria, France, and the United States. I was present with Dr. Harris when he reported to the Jewish Society in Los Angeles. They gave him so many expressions of appreciation and glowing tributes that it became embarrassing to him and he insisted that he was only a servant of the government vitally interested in his brothers in all parts of the world. Keifer B. Sauls was secretary to President Harris on this entire Russian trip.

It was in this period that he asked for the women's and men's dormitories, the Stadium House and the Joseph Smith Building.

1935—Dr. Harris was appointed chairman of agriculture of the scientific congress held in Mexico City.

1939—The Shah of Persia asked our government for agricultural help; Dr. Harris and his wife were called for this important assignment. He established a forest service and a weather bureau. The war becoming global in nature, the Harris couple were obliged to return to the U.S. which they accomplished by way of India, China, the Holy Land, Greece, and New York, arriving in September of 1940. This trip began the student ties between Iran and the B.Y.U.

The campus had grown from an enrollment of 450 students to nearly 3,000.

1946—President Harris headed a group of U.S. government men and soil scientists to six Middle East countries to plan economic and agricultural assistance. In this year he also led another group of the United Nations Food and Agricultural Organization to Greece. The Harris Report has been used as a model for other countries similar to Greece who need such support.

This brief biography cannot include all of Dr. Harris' governmental appointments. Many of his foreign acquaintances have paid him official and social visits on the campus.

To list some of the societies and honor groups in which he had membership will suffice to know the scope of his talents and activities: Fellow in the A.A.A.S.; American Society of Agronomy (he was president in 1920-21); American Geographical Society; Utah Academy of Science, Arts and Letters (past president and one of its most enthusiastic boosters, especially encouraging B.Y.U. faculty members to join); Utah Farm Bureau; American Farm Economic Association; American Association of Agricultural Legislation; American Genetic Association; Utah and National Education Associations; Utah Irrigation and Drainage Congress (president in 1923); American Oriental Society; Utah Mental Hygiene (director); Utah Council for Prevention of War; Provo Chamber of Commerce (president); Utah National Park Council; Boy Scouts of America (president).

He also belonged to many scientific and scholastic honor societies: to name a few, Sigma Xi, Phi Kappa Phi, Delta Mu, Pi Gamma Mu, Alpha Kappa Phi, Gamma Sigma Delta, Delta Phi and Tau Kappa Alpha (honorary).

He was a church worker all his life. His last assignment was to be the instructor in his ward High Priest Quorum, which he held until his last severe illness. He served on the Y.M.M.I.A. General Board for many years and had been Sunday School and M.I.A. superintendents from early manhood.

F. S. Harris was a Republican and a candidate for the U.S. Senate in 1938, being induced to run for Utah's governorship in 1938. He was an excellent, sincere speaker, but could not be classed as an orator. His style was methodical with well organized ideas. He did not break his thoughts with many anecdotes, though he knew hundreds of stories which he could have used. As one of his friendly critics said, "He was too honest to be a successful politician."

Many parties honoring Dr. and Mrs. Harris were given during the latter part of his life. The Provo Chamber of Commerce honored two of Provo's citizens at one celebration when Alex Hedquist and F. S. Harris were greeted by hundreds of friends and memorial volumes of tributes were presented to each guest. The B.Y.U. Alumni Association got out a special issue to honor the Harris couple and a grand reception was held in the Lafayette Ballroom of the Hotel Utah, where thousands of friends came to pay tribute.

As time permitted he was a member of the Rotary and Kiwanis Clubs of Provo, the Timpanogos Knife and Fork Club (a charter member), chairman of Utah County American Red Cross and was a committee member of many charitable institutions.

Often, when faculty meetings became serious or took on a sombre mood, the President would tell a good story with a joke or two. The director of a varsity comedy was often pleasantly rewarded by hearing the hearty laugh of Dr. Harris in the audience. He was probably the most frequent user and author of clever puns. If they were just a little too obvious he would be the first to challenge himself.

Somewhere around his desk he had an article or treatise just beginning or almost ready for publication. The number of scientific articles he wrote runs into the hundreds. L.D.S. Church lessons and articles frequently were seen in the *Era, The Instructor,* or *Relief Society Magazine.* Most of his colleagues looked to him as an authority in scientific matters and honored his judgment in matters of art. His travels gave him a personal power of accuracy because of his acute observation and memory for details.

Conscious of the small salaries of his faculty, Dr. Harris could encourage and advocate saving in the Provo Building & Loan Company, even with five dollars a month. He made an early contract with the Teacher's Insurance and Annuity Association to protect the teacher for retirement. This plan had the institution pay half of the monthly dues. Group insurance was another early benefit association for faculty and spouse. President Harris was a director in the Farmers and Merchants Bank (Walker Bank of today) in Provo and always had a good piece of land for farming and "emergency" purposes.

He loved good breed stock and was a critical attendant at state fairs. When he took his morning walk his black and white spaniel

"Jan" trailed closely at his heels, flushing the quail from bushes or waited for the stick to be thrown that he might retrieve. The Harris cabin in Aspen Grove was center for many family parties and summer picnics. Jan would chase the noisy squirrels and scampering chipmunks as Doctor Harris strolled under the conifers, examined the plants and flowers, mentally cataloging the numerous species of solomon seal, gentian, rudibeckia and grasses. His knowledge of plant life helped him to read the soil as a book; weeds revealed the possibility of probable plant life.

Though his interests were myriad, his greatest affection was for his family. No couple more completely complimented each other than Frank and his life companion Estella. She was companion for most of his trips, wrote many letters to save time for him, often was his secretary. They both enjoyed drama, opera and orchestral concerts; great art galleries added to their pleasure and culture. They shared their travels with many friends and especially faculty members by descriptive letters and art post cards. Their Christmas cards were beautiful and inspiring.

The family presents a full story in itself. His mother lived with or near the family most of her later years, enjoying family and university life until her demise. Surviving Dr. Harris are his wife Estella, two sons and four daughters: Mrs. Roscoe A. (Arlene) Grover, Dr. Franklin S. Harris Jr., and Mrs. Ralph O. (Mildred) Bradley, all of Salt Lake City; Dr. Chauncey D. Harris, Chicago, Illinois; Mrs. Ralph W. (Helen) Jenson, Berkeley, California; and Mrs. Vernon D. (Leah) Jensen, Pocatello, Idaho. A niece Mrs. C. Robin (Nance Becroft) Burt of Salt Lake City was reared in the Harris family from early childhood. Most people did not know that she was not a Harris child unless the matter came up for conversation. Six brothers and a sister survived Dr. Harris: M. Hyrum of Salt Lake City; Karl O. and Leo of Phoenix, Arizona; Supt. Sterling R. of Tooele, Utah; J. Emer of Boise, Idaho; Lewis of Chinn, Alberta, Canada; and Mrs. John W. (Sara) Payne of Provo, Utah. Thirty-eight grandchildren and four great-grandchildren enriched the Harris home with frequent visits.

At the funeral of Dr. Harris held in the historic Assembly Hall on Temple Square, President J. Reuben Clark Jr. said, in part, "It must be a source of deepest, grateful satisfaction that your father and husband rendered the great service, made the great achievements that brought him the honors and the unusual recognition that came to him from governments, our own and foreign governments. Probably Brother John A. Widtsoe came near to this, but he was called into the service of the Church which took him out of his availability for the things which your husband carried on . . . . I repeat, I recall none other than those two who in our modern day have had the recognition that was given to them, and particularly to your husband, who remained in the same field for so many years. They were great scholars and so recognized . . . . He was a great teacher. He had the ability of inspiring others with the same enthusiasm and with the same spirit of devotion that he had. No one, so far as I know, in the entire history of the Brigham Young University has exceeded him in inspiring the spirit of service into the faculty, a spirit without which that institution cannot prosper as the Lord intended."

Editorials, encomiums, tributes from hundreds of state, national and church friends covered the desk of Sister Harris. The *Provo Herald* said what so many others expressed, "He was an able administrator, an efficient teacher, an outstanding public speaker and a true scientist who applied his knowledge and know-how for the betterment of people throughout the world."

The *Deseret News* further summarizes, "A man devoted to many good causes, he was generous of impulse, magnanimous in overlooking the frailties of others, and always quick to take the trouble to pass on a compliment when occasion offered. He had a way of seeing through insincerities and hypocrisies without vindictively denouncing the persons involved, of honestly speaking his mind with tact and humor. He was the rare kind of man of whom it can be said that he was thoughtful of others without having to think about it."

He was a great man equal to the problems of a great age, Franklin Stewart Harris, August 29, 1884—April 18, 1960.

BRIGHAM THOMAS HIGGS

Born: March 10, 1858, Salt Lake City.

Father: Thomas Higgs, born in Utica, New York.

Mother: Elizabeth Stowe born in Stratford upon Avon, England, who came across the plains on crutches.

Brothers and Sisters: Wallace J., Alpha J., Jesse Brenthal Higgs, Susannah Higgs Slater, Annie Higgs Jensen, Zina Higgs Washburn.

Marriage: 1) Susannah Summers, who died March 5, 1929.
2) Alice M. Reid, 1930.

Children: Emma Susannah Higgs m. J. Fleming Wakefield, Brigham Thomas Higgs Junior, (deceased), George Henry, Delilah Higgs Speierman (deceased).

Death: July 12, 1939, killed in an automobile accident in Daniels Canyon, above Heber, Utah, in company with Wm. H. Snell, who was injured.

Brigham Thomas Higgs was born in Salt Lake City, near Eagle Gate, and was early apprenticed to his father, who was President Brigham Young's personal carpenter for a decade and from whom he learned precision work, accuracy, and the nature of all kinds of building materials. He was taught to get the best tools possible, to keep his tools sharp, and to do work on his own time. He worked in his Uncle James' foundry and machine shop and learned welding and repair of iron work. He followed his father to Payson and later had a joyous assignment, working on the temple in Manti, where his parents ultimately settled.

He was a member of the Emery County Board of Education for several terms and the first M. I. A. President in Orangeville.

Because he wished to give his children scholastic advantages, which were not at that time available where he lived in Emery County, B. T. Higgs made a trip to Provo to attempt to get work where he could provide a home for his family. At this time his oldest child was ready for high school. He finally secured a job in 1895 taking care of the heating plant at the old Academy building, which later became part of the Lower Campus on University Avenue, between 5th and 6th North Streets. For this service he received thirty dollars per month, and one-half of this was in Tithing Script. This heating plant was very inadequate for what it was supposed to do. Unless it was started three or four hours after midnight, the rooms would not be warm enough to conduct classes. As a result B. T. Higgs had to leave home any time after two in the morning in the winters if he was to get the fires started under the boilers in time to properly heat the building, and a lone figure with a lantern would walk the snowy streets to liven a fire in the boiler room.

B. T. Higgs soon found that the heating plant, while it required long hours of his attention, did not take his entire time. He began repairing chairs, furniture, doors, windows, and other unmended objects, unobserved; at least no comment was made by the principal. Professor Joseph L. Horne, one of the faculty, however, did notice. Professor Horne was, among other things, conducting a class in sloyd. Thomas became very interested and visited these classes from time to time. During a conversation, B. T. Higgs brought up the idea of teaching the boys to use other tools than those required for sloyd. Why not teach them to use a saw and a plane and other carpenter and cabinet tools to make something more useful than was possible with sloyd tools. He then proceeded to do some sawing and made a glue joint. Professor Horne was greatly impressed and called attention of what was told him to other members of the faculty. The next year B. T. Higgs began instructing boys and young men in the fundamentals of cabinet making and building. It was not long until his name appeared in the school catalog as Professor

Higgs. He was very much embarrassed by this. As his son, George H. Higgs says: "He refused to recognize that he was a professor in his line. Throughout his entire life he was very modest, and while he appreciated recognition, he shyed away from publicity."

After eight years with the Academy, which had become the Brigham Young University, B. T. Higgs went to Canada. He had spent his winters teaching woodwork and his summers in overseeing, overhauling and tending the buildings. By this time there were the College building, the gymnasium, and the preparatory building, in addition to the Education Building. After Brother Higgs had spent a year in Alberta, Canada, acting President George H. Brimhall, sent Brothers E. H. Holt and John C. Swenson, members of the faculty, to request his return. He came back and was put in charge of buildings and grounds. He had the satisfaction of knowing that many of his students had made good in practical building, as from time to time he received reports of them and from them. One of his greatest joys was when he took a course at the L. D. S. college under Asa Kinkey, who had started his work with Brother Higgs years before. B. T. took a course in wood polishing.

"Brigham T. Higgs glorified what might be to some a job as janitor and custodian and made it a very important educational part of the school." This is what was said of him. "He took young men who needed work to be able to stay in school and he taught them not only how to work but instilled into them principles of honesty, clean living, high ideals, and the satisfaction and glory of giving their all to their jobs." Many former students testify to this.

B. T. Higgs has been credited with starting the practice of providing part-time work for students, thus enabling many of them ,to continue and finish their school work at Brigham Young University. He would get his working crew together before their scheduled assignments and give them talks on honesty, integrity, department organization of their time for study, and cleanliness, "How To Enjoy Yourself When Alone," "Work with a Purpose," and other stimulating topics. One occasion I particularly remember. He had the boys sit on the steps leading down to the basement in College Hall whom he addressed upon the subject, "Keep Company With God." Fellows with brooms in their hands, dressed in overalls, listened intently to his sincere thoughts on character and devotion. Then he passed out copies of his talk for future reference.

For the fellow whom he knew to be inadequately fed, he would bring an extra apple, share a piece of cake or a sandwich. He would go around to the rooming or boarding house of all his "boys," learning of their money status from the landlady, looking at the condition of their sleeping and studying rooms, asking about their parents if he didn't know them. He told his boys it was no disgrace to keep clean or help others to be clean. "Be clean in your thoughts and your house will be clean." "A dirty corner reveals the character of a sluffer." "Learn to do the most in the least amount of time." "A blister reveals how soft you are, or how hard you worked; which is yours?" "If you can keep this room clean, you'll never burden your wife with extra housework."

The new Industrial Education Building of the Brigham Young University campus has a room, Number 115, designated "Brigham T. Higgs Woodworking Laboratory."

He was a custodian of buildings, but more, a builder of men. Hundreds of Brigham Young University students remember with pride and joy the man who could work with tools and keep his thoughts near the heavens.

GEORGE HENRY HIGGS

Real Estate Operator
Residence—Los Angeles, California

Born: September 2, 1885 in Orangeville, Emery County, Utah

Father: Brigham T. Higgs, b. March 10, 1858 in Salt Lake City, Utah
Contractor, builder, Educator, Building Supervisor
d. July 12, 1939, in auto accident

Mother: Susannah Summers b. March 15, d. March 5, 1929; daughter of George and Emma Hodges Summers.

Brothers and Sisters: Emma Susannah, b. December 22, 1878; m. John Fleming Wakefield
Brigham Thos. Jr.
(George Henry)
Delilah H. Speierman

Marriage: Sarah Walton b. October 4, 1883 in Schofield, Utah
Daughter of Andrew Jackson Walton and Harriet Noble
m. October 5, 1904—met at BYA and in Canada, where they took part in plays. d. March 28, 1966

Children: G. Brentanal, b. 27 Nov. 1905; m. Phyllis Hoopes
Evelyn, b. 28 Nov. 1907; m. James B. Watherspoon
Anona, b. 25 Feb. 1911; m. W. B. Irvin

George H. Higgs partakes of the many characteristics of his talented father, a hard and faithful worker deeply concerned with the welfare of his friends and neighbors and a promoter of activities which have honorable purpose and assurance of a fair profit or benefit.

The Higgs family came to Provo to give the children opportunity for an advanced education. It was on the campus of BYU where George H. met his bride-to-be, a young lady of evident culture and charm from a well known pioneer family. After he graduated from the BYU Commercial College, the young married couple went to Canada as a part of the colonizing promoted by the Knights and Holbrooks. Salesmanship was George's forte and California was the growing country for real estate owners and operators. The Higgs have called southern California their home for the last sixty years, with residence in Rosemead and winter vacation in Palm Springs country where George has substantial holdings.

His importance to Brigham Young University was first signally realized when he was put on the Emeritus Club roster as a director and made project chairman. Though his residence was in California, he made all necessary trips to fulfill officer meetings and conduct his project campaign. He organized the first successful approach to members of the Emeritus Club, in which he qualified by his registration at BYA in 1897 and his graduation in 1906.

Some 1450 members were eligible for his appeals and he launched a vigorous campaign to acquire diaries, books of early Mormon vintage, school and historical pictures and any significant item of BYU history. The program was a success from the very start as hundreds of books came in, were processed, and name plates were posted on covers to show donor's gift. As a promotion impetus, George H. offered to buy a book for any widow or former BYU student who wished to donate in honor of some friend now deceased. This memory list has grown to a formidable number. A gift of $5.00 would buy a book selected by the Librarian to honor the donor or any person designated. This project was started in 1961 and is still in effect. Brother Higgs has added hundreds of dollars to the fund. To strengthen the ties of the past with today, George H. wrote in his letter of April 2, 1963, "An arrangement has been made to place in a book to go into the library the name of every person now living who attended Brigham Young University or Academy fifty years or more ago."

His business interests are numerous, including vice-president of Desert Dunes Improvement Association, chairman of management committee of the Greater Bermuda Dunes Property Owners Association, member Aspen Grove Associates, and of Karl G. Maeser Associates.

He has been a member or chairman of the Emeritus Project Committee for eight years and President for three terms of the Emeritus Club which gave him association with the Alumni executive committee.

Since the demise of his helpful and companionable wife, Sara, he has spent most of his time promoting his interest in California.

GEORGE RICHARD HILL JR.

Born: April 10, 1884   **Place:** Ogden, Utah

Father: George Richard Hill, son of George Washington Hill and Cynthia Utley Stewart.
Born: August 22, 1846 at Mt. Pisgah, Iowa; To Utah September 10, 1847; Served mission to Southern States
Married: December 18, 1871
Hauled rock for Salt Lake Temple, moved to Springville 1889; Bishop of Springville 3rd Ward and County Commissioner 1901 for 23 years.

Mother: Elizabeth Nancy Burch, daughter of Daniel Burch and Ann W. McClellan
Born, January 31, 1849, Ogden, Utah; youngest of six children.
Died, April 8, 1911, while George R. was at Cornell University, Ithaca, N. Y.

Brothers and Sisters: Children of Elizabeth:
(George R.)
Daniel B., b. December 4, 1885, d. age 10
Reuben Lorenzo, b. March 4, 1888; m. Theresa Marie Snow
Ann Elizabeth, b. April 11; m. James R. Hindley
2) Children of Charity J. Shelton:
John S., Mary D., Cynthia J., William Richard

Marriage: ELizabeth Odette McKay, daughter of David and Jeannette Evans McKay of Huntsville, Utah, sister of President David O. McKay. Born Oct. 30, 1884. Married April 10, 1914. Well known teacher and dean of home economics at Utah State Agricultural College (USU) vice Captain Yale Camp Daughter of Utah Pioneers.

Children: Elizabeth, m. Eugene Boswell
George R., m. Melba Parker; member of YMMIA General Board presidency
David McKay, m. Fern Jensen
All children are BYU graduates

If we were to endeavor to classify the life of George R. Hill Jr. in fewest terms, it could well be, school, Boy Scouts, and Church, as he has excelled with all three and had supreme joy in each.

He graduated from the Brigham Young High School in 1904, went on to college for a BYU BS degree in botany in 1907, a BSA degree from the USAC in Logan in 1908, and his PhD from Cornell University in 1912. He returned to the Agricultural College in 1913 as Professor of Botany and Plant Pathology until 1925 and dean of Agriculture from 1916 to 1925.

We quote from a tribute paid to Dr. Hill by his nephew, David Lawrence McKay. "He was asked in 1925 to direct the Department of Agricultural Research of the American Smelting and Refining Company in Salt Lake City. Before that time, this company had been plagued with frequent law suits from farmers who had found litigation more profitable than agriculture. Dr. Hill devised a simple and effective plan. As a result, from the time of his appointment in 1925 until his retirement in 1950, not one law suit was filed by a farmer against this company claiming damages for crop injury."

A similar tribute of efficiency could be paid him in Boy Scout work. He was elected president of the Salt Lake Council in 1943; in six years of this tenure the number of Eagle Scouts jumped from 59 to 100 per year. He stressed the campaign to reach the boy "hard to get", "make a leader of a troublemaker." His reputation in boys' work is national.

When he was appointed to the Sunday School General Superintendency in 1934, he set a goal of enlistment of chronic absentees designed to get them back into an active program of character building and acceptance of individual responsibilities. His personal visits numbered into thousands—no boy or girl was too unimportant to escape his attention and interest. While records made steady advance under his leadership, so did general character growth with this advancement program. His "talks" in *The Instructor,* Sunday School magazine, are inspiring.

Recently a Logan Boy Scout Troop organized by President Hill in 1915 held a 50-year reunion to honor their first Scout Master, presented him with a book of testimonials and hung his picture in their troop room. Such honors have been frequent for the Superintendent during recent years.

George R. is a big man, physically as well as intellectually and spiritually. His interests in youth formed his career, a life time of service with boys on the farm, in Scout work and Sunday School leadership. His programs have never become static. He has met the change and stress of times with vigorous adjustments based on sound principles. His smile lights up his audience and reveals his optimistic approach to life.

He resigned from his Sunday School Superintendency in November of 1966 after thirty-one years of service.

ROBERT HENRY HINCKLEY

Business and Government Executive.
Eden, Utah

Born: June 8, 1891 at Fillmore, Utah

Father: Edwin Smith Hinckley (see his biography)

Mother: Adeline Henry
Born: Fillmore, Utah, Jan. 12, 1868
Died: July 24, 1945

Brothers and Sisters:
(Robert H.)
Leonore Adelaide
Edwin Carlyle
Norma Elizabeth
Claudius Warren
Paul Bryant
Frederick Russell
John Noble
Evelyn Marguerite   (See Children of E. S.
Gordon Holbrook   Hinckley Biography.)
Muriel Eileen
G. Marion
Angela Ruth

Marriage: Abrelia Seely, daughter of John H. Seely and Margaret Peel.
John Seely was born in the Mormon Colony of San Bernardino, California, April 24, 1855. Brought back to Mt. Pleasant, Utah in 1859. President of the American Rambouillet Sheep Breeders Association and one of the West's most successful livestock breeders—internationally recognized.
Born: Sept. 19, 1892 in Mt. Pleasant, Utah.
Married: June 23, 1915 in Salt Lake Temple.
Graduate student of LDS High Schools and attended University of Utah. Lived in Provo last year at Brigham Young Academy for Robert's graduation. Ran the auto business from 1932-1946 while Bob was director of WPA.

Children: Robert Henry, Jr., b. Jan. 12, 1917; m. Janice Scowcroft
Elizabeth, b. April 18, 1921; m. Preston P. Nibley
John Seely, b. May 9, 1923; m. Ann Holman
Paul Ray, b. Mar. 11, 1925; m. 1) Jeanne Ficteau, (died-1952) 2) Ann Thatcher (married in 1956)
(All three sons were in World War II.)

Robert H. Hinckley received all of his formal education in Provo, Utah, where he attended kindergarten, elementary and secondary grades, high school and university at Brigham Young University, graduating with an A. B. in 1916. Schooling was interrupted by a mission to Germany in 1910-1913 and abetted by marriage during his senior college year. Some of his graduating classmates were David J. Wilson, Wayne B. Hales, Fayette Stevens, Ed Johnson.

His father, E. S. Hinckley, was a member of the BYU presidency and one of Robert's teachers.

He is by his ability one of Utah's most honored governmental executives. He came naturally as a political leader following his father's example. He was a member of the Utah State House of Representatives 1918-20, Mayor of Mt. Pleasant 1924-25, President of the Utah State Municipal League 1925-26, Member of the Governor's Voluntary State Relief Committee 1932, when Depression was striking hardest, director of Utah State Emergency Relief Administration, 1933; director of Federal Emergency Relief Administration for Utah, Idaho, Washington, Oregon, Nevada, Arizona and California under Pres. F. D. Roosevelt. He became ass't administrator of the Federal Emergency Relief Administration 1934; ass't administrator for WPA program in 11 Western States, Hawaii, Alaska, 1935-38; chairman 1939-40; ass't Sec'y of Commerce 1940-42; member board of directors, American Public Welfare Association, 1934-36; director, Office of Contract Settlement, 1944-46.

In business, it was the inner urge of the man that took him from teaching school to automobiles and aviation. He saw the promise of the automobile while in Mt. Pleasant which he promoted further in Ogden. Political appointments kept him out of his flourishing business which he relinquished to his wife and later his sons when they were released from military service. He organized the Utah-Pacific Airways in Ogden in 1928 and was vice-president and treasurer, 1928-1938. In 1938-40 he was a member of the Civil Aeronautics Authority and was highly praised by President Roosevelt, who relied on Bob's judgment and business sagacity.

When Robert deemed he had served the government as long as was necessary he accepted other assignments such as vice-president and director of American Broadcasting—Paramount Theatre Inc. from 1953. He was a member of the Board of Regents, University of Utah, 1928-41, and executive of Sperry Corp., New York City, 1942-44.

Living more closely at home, he became a director of the First Security Corporation, a member of the public advisory board E. C. A. and M. S. A.; national member advisory to Arthritis and Metabolic Diseases Council; a director of Rob't H. Hinckley, Inc. in Ogden and Salt Lake; a director of his brother Frederick's company, the American Paper and Supply Co.; a member of the Board of Directors, vice-president and president of Welsh Pony Society of America, and of the Financial Industrial Fund, Inc. and the Financial Industrial Income Fund, Inc. of Denver, Colorado. One of the most significant associations affecting the BYU is the Edward John Noble Foundation of which he is a trustee, and with their co-operation the E. S. Hinckley Scholarship Fund has aided dozens of BYU students in acquiring an education.

Robert received the BYU Alumni Distinguished Service Award in 1959. He is a direct descendant of Thomas Hinckley, Puritan governor of the Plymouth Colony from 1681-1692. Bob's beautiful Garden of Eden, a home he and his artistic wife have built in the Huntsville valley, suggests the serenity of lives well lived. They act as gracious hosts to welcome friends.

On March 1, 1967, Robert was selected for the distinguished honor, the B'nai Brith Citizen of Achievement Award, one of the highest given by the Jewish organization. "It is not given every year, only when we find a person we feel is truly worthy of public recognition."

Robert and the Noble Foundation presented $250,000 to the University of Utah to finance an institute of practical politics. His interests in education is not confined to any group. His great desire is to understand and support the Constitution of the United States. Each time he visits our campus he poses some phase of this question, "What can I do to foster intelligent citizenship?" He is much like his illustrious father, and feels that man should prove his life by his works.

HARRISON VAL HOYT

Born: Feb. 14, 1885 at Nephi, Utah.
But thirteen years of age when his mother died.

Father: Henry Harrison Hoyt
Born: Nov. 27, 1851. The village of Hoytsville, near Coalville, Utah, named from the Hoyt family colonizing. Death: Sept. 30, 1926.

Mother: Alice Jenkins, daughter of Richard J. and Mercy Pitchforth
Born: April 21, 1864.
Died: June 28, 1898.

Brothers and Sisters: Richard Ralph Hoyt, b. Oct. 28, 1886.
Ray Hoyt, (deceased).
Maud Hoyt Fowkes, b. Dec. 12, 1887; (deceased).
Helen Hoyt Chadwick, b. Jan. 5, 1895.

Marriage: Helen Grace of Nephi, dau. of Isaac H. Grace and Helen Hudson desc. of Henrik Hudson.
Born: April 22, 1884.
Married: Sept. 9, 1915.
She relates: "Our first date—1906 at B. Y. U. Val invited me to a track meet on Temple Hill. A footpath led to the bleachers. Aside from that path and the track the entire Hill was a weed patch. In the evening we attended the Matinee in the Training School dance hall. It was my first and last romance."

Children: No children.

Death: Saturday, Jan. 20, 1962. Buried in Nephi Cemetery.

Education: Attended B. Y. U., 1902-06.
B. S., Purdue Univ., 1913.
M. B. A., Harvard Grad. School of Bus. Admin., 1917.
Ph. D., Stanford Univ., 1931.

B. Y. U. Positions:
Prof. of Accounting and Bus. Admin., and Dean of College of Commerce, 1921-31.
Prof. of Accounting and Bus. Admin., 1937-54.
Emeritus, 1954—
Chairman, Dept. of Accounting, 1921-31, 1937-51.

Teaching and other positions: Ass't. Engineer, Idaho Power   Light Co., Boise, 1913-15.
Production manager, J. G. McDonald Chocolate Co., Salt Lake, 1920-21.
Production manager, J. S. Ivins Co., Philadelphia.
Member and one-time director of Telluride Ass'n. Endowment Committee.
Dean, School of Commerce, Oregon State College, 1934-1936.
N. Y. Industrial Engineer, 7 summers.
Auditor for Provo Building   Loan Society.
President, Utah Civil Service Commission, 1965.

Society Memberships: Affiliated with American Accounting Ass'n.; National Cost Accounting Ass'n.; President Provo Kiwanis; Rotary, at Eugene, Oregon; Beta Gamma Sigma; Alpha Kappa Psi; Alpha Delta Sigma; Beta Alpha Psi.
Listed in Who's Who in America, Vol. 27. "Who Knows-and What."
Published "Business Conditions of the Northwest".
Service in the U. S. Navy, World War I.

Church Activities: Member of Bishopric, 1929-31, Provo Fifth Ward.
Branch president while at Harvard University.

Travel: He visited every country in Europe including Russia and satellites.
Several trips to Central America where he studied the Mayan civilization.

H. Val Hoyt was a nervous, slender man with the ability to concentrate on any given problem as conditions demanded. Alone, he wore a serious, knit-brow attitude; in company he had a ready smile and most affable manner. He said "I am a nomad at heart but have learned to travel with a purpose." That purpose became an intense interest in Egyptian art and Mayan civilization.

He traveled in every country in Europe to study mores, business methods and governmental objectives. His interest in the cost and manufacture of all man-made articles led him to many out-of-the-way factories and around-the-table discussions. As he became more adept in travel he loved to visit the seldom-seen places, and it is a great loss to our campus that he did not write up many of his unique experiences. For his last major trips he made exploratory sorties to Central America for studies in Mayan civilization and found challenging studies at Palenque in Mexico and the Temple of the Cross, so called because of the carvings at the center of the stone-cut monument. Later explorations than 1840 proved the "cross" to be the Tree of Life, the principle art symbol used by citizens of ancient Middle America. Dr. Hoyt had a plastic cast made of this tablet and crated to B.Y.U. as a gift to our archeological museum.

Wherever he went he became an investor as a means of gaining the confidence of local business men. The calibre of his students gained ready recognition wherever he taught. When he became dean of the School of Business at Oregon State College, a plan was worked out wherein he became cross-campus dean of both Oregon State College and the University of Oregon. When he left a position for more remunerative work he was invited to return at the first opportunity. While in Oregon he edited a monthly magazine, "Business Conditions of the Pacific Northwest," and at Philadelphia he bought a half-interest in a broadcasting station.

One of his most notable activities was his search for proper jobs for his graduates. His frequent surveys and work-followup left him aware of all probable local positions and many across the continent. A get-together was arranged after his retirement and some fifty former majors paid him homage, many of whom held high responsible positions. All of BYU's successive deans of business administration were his students.

His own investments were unusually sound; his stock market judgment was sought daily by his investing friends. The fund investing programs at BYU were chairmanned by Val Hoyt, or he was a member of the committees until his retirement.

The many facets of his character and success in his profession warrants his inclusion among the worthy Sons of Brigham.

CHRISTEN JENSEN

Born: February 4, 1881 in Salt Lake City, Utah

Father: Christen Jensen, Sr. of Denmark
Convert to LDS Church in Denmark
Born December 11, 1855
Died November 20, 1929

Mother: Nel Sina Johansen, born July 23, 1856. To Utah with two sisters, Elizabeth Christensen and Sophia (Andrew) Jensen
m. 1879 in Salt Lake
d. February 12, 1934

Brothers and Sisters: (Christen)
Marie—a teacher in Salt Lake Schools
Mary (died young)

Marriage: Juliaetta Bateman of West Jordan, Utah
Born: December 31, 1878
Marriage: August 17, 1904 in Salt Lake Temple by President Joseph F. Smith
Died: January 21, 1952
Brilliant literary scholar. Browning expert. Urged married women to further their cultural education

Children: Ardis—died two days after birth
Lorna—b. April 17, 1912, m. Dr. Bertrand F. Harrison, Professor of Botany

Death: August 17, 1961, on his 57th wedding anniversary of a heart attack

To pay tribute to Dr. Christen Jensen is to honor a scholar, churchman and gentleman. His quiet, reserved manner added strength to all he did. He was never given to self praise, and we had to question him to learn of his patrimony, early boyhood and struggles for an education.

Fortunately, he left a brief but inclusive record of events he considered important in his life. His devoted companion, Julia, wrote many paragraphs about Christen and wrote of him in more detail in her *Little Gold Pieces*. President Ernest L. Wilkinson got out a five-page memorial tribute in February of 1962. The B. Y. U. *Alumnus,* the *Banyan, Deseret News,* and *Salt Lake Tribune* gave him special attention, and he was one of the first Utahn's to be included in "Who's Who In America." A book of personal tributes was presented to him at the time of his retirement in June of 1949 by the Department of History and Political Science at a social at which former Salt Lake Mayor Earl J. Glade presided. At this time a beautiful oil painting of him, painted by Alvin Gittins, was formally presented. In May of 1959, I wrote "Dr. Christen Jensen, one of our most talented and efficient scholars, whose modesty has deprived him of greater recognition than he now has. From the days of President Brimhall to the present, when the university has needed an executive of reserved strength and pronounced ability he has been called upon. Gentleman, scholar and careful historian—to know him well is to admire and love him."

The struggles of his devoted immigrant parents to give him an education, the cooperation and work by his loyal and talented wife to further that education are chapters of loving sacrifice and family pride. That he repaid their assistance would be a foregone conclusion.

His education consistently progressed. He was a leading student at the Salt Lake High School (but one High School in town then). He took a normal course at the University of Utah, followed by four years of teaching. During one year at Midvale, Utah, he met another teacher who loved the arts, especially music, and their meeting resulted in courtship and marriage. He attained a bachelor's degree at University of Utah in 1907, then went to Cambridge, Massachusetts, for an eventful year at Harvard, obtaining a master's degree and a $500 debt in one year.

Application to the three universities in Utah resulted in his acceptance at B. Y. U. in 1908 as assistant professor of history and political science. He soon was achieving full professorship and remained there for some thirty-eight years. He was dean of the Graduate School for twenty years, and acting dean for three colleges on campus. He was selected as Acting President of the University, in 1939-40 while President Harris went to Iran. He became acting President again, being called from Salt Lake to assume presidential duties in the interim of Presidents Howard S. McDonald and Ernest L. Wilkinson, 1949-1951. President Wilkinson writes; "During the interval existing between the time I was appointed President in July of 1950 and September of that year, when the announcement was made, I corresponded continuously with him. . . . When I came to the campus he opened up his desk and had two massive drawers of letters and correspondence, all requiring decisions which he had felt that it was improper for him as acting president to make. In his modesty, he never wanted to trespass upon the prerogative of another even though he had much more wisdom to make these decisions than I. . . . May I finally add that when, without experience, I took over my present office, I found no one more helpful or loyal to me in the administration of my office. . . . I am happy to inform you that the conference room in the new administration building has been named in his honor." He had been given the Distinguished Service Award by the B. Y. U. Alumni Association (1951).

Christen played the piano, knew the great concertos, never missed a B. Y. U. Lyceum when he was in town. He was a better than average volleyball player when the faculty chose sides and played in the women's gym.

His doctorate dissertation was "The Pardoning Power in the American States." For this and his scholarship, he was awarded the Doctor of Philosophy degree at the University of Chicago, magna cum laude. His thesis was published (1922) and became a basic text in political science across the nation.

When we were applying for a chapter in the national forensic society, Tau Kappa Alpha, some eight former debators gathered and elected Christen as chairman. He immediately wrote to Chief Justice George Sutherland, Senators Reed Smoot and William King, Congressman Don Colton and others. National President was Governor Charles Brough of Arkansas, a personal friend of T. Earl Pardoe. Reed Smoot contacted one of his closest friends, Senator Albert Beveridge, immediate past president of Tau Kappa Alpha. With the help of these men and the exhaustive report on B. Y. U. forensic activities prepared by Dr. Jensen, the school's first chapter in an honor fraternity was formed. This was a real victory for the University, as several attempts by friendly schools to enlist B. Y. U. as a member in a national honor fraternity had failed; "the University is not a Christian institution," they claimed. Our honor chapters today cover the gamut of university subjects.

Christen was elected to Utah State Historical Society, American Historical Association, American Society of International Law, American Political Science Association, National Municipal League, Tau Kappa Alpha, Phi Kappa Phi, The American Academy of Political and Social Science, and posthumously, August 25, 1961, he was awarded the Doctor of Laws degree by the B. Y. U. Board of Trustees.

He served his Church in almost every capacity possible, being president and teacher in the respective priesthood quorums, Sunday School and YMMIA; a member of three different High Councils; first counselor in the Utah Stake; patriarch for East Sharon and East Provo Stakes; and chairman of the Church Reading Committee to sift scores of writings for the First Presidency. As confidential counselor to students, he reached hundreds.

His life was devoted to his church, his school and his profession, activities in which his talented wife intimately shared.

J. EDWARD JOHNSON

Attorney-Historian, Berkeley, California

Born: October 2, 1890, in Little Cottonwood, Murray, Utah.

Father: John Johnson, son of John Erson and Christina Person. b. April 20, 1864, at Karbenning, Vastmanland, Sweden. First of his family to join the Church, came to America in 1888. Moved family to Benjamin, Utah County, Utah, in 1891. Bishop for some 20 years. d. March 5, 1943— Buried in Benjamin Cemetery.

Mother: Edla Lundell, daughter of Anders Gustav Lundell and Gustava Caroline Erickson. b. December 5, 1865. m. November 20, 1889 in Manti Temple. Relief Society presidency for 28 years. d. June 8, 1941.

Brothers and Sisters: J. Edward, only child not born in Benjamin, Utah; Edna (Mrs. Clarency E. Smith) b. Jan. 30, 1892; George, b. March 21, 1894, died in infancy; Elinor, b. March 20, 1895, d. March 28, 1926; Elsie, b. December 28, 1896, m. Lawrence Wortley; Lawrence, b. Jan. 17, 1899; Vera, b. April 1, 1902; m. Taylor Parkinson; Halvor, b. Jan. 13, 1905; Wilma, b. November 9, 1906, m. Clinton Harvey, d. Sept. 28, 1950; Darwin, b. November 9, 1906, d. Sept. 1, 1952.

Marriage: Mamie Huish, in Salt Lake Temple, June 22, 1916, daughter of James W. and Marry Elizabeth Fillmore. Born November 2, 1886 in Payson, Utah. To Colonia Dublan, Mexico, 1900. Out at time of Revolution, 1912. Educated at BYU and U. of California. Taught in BYU Training School. Died June 13, 1933, Buried in Sunset Cemetery, Berkeley.

LaVon Ethel Brockbank, daughter of Taylor Park and Sarah H. LeCheminant Brockbank. Born August 25, 1903, in Holladay, Utah. Married August 31, 1934.

Children: of Mamie
Robert H., b. Oct. 30, 1918, m. Betty June Cummings; Marion H., b. December 18, 1922, m. Eunice Henson; Carolyn H., b. July 13, 1928, m. Harold E. DeLaMare; Thomas H., b. February 7, 1931, m. Margaret Akers.

of LaVon
Cheryl B., b. June 7, 1935, m. Earl E. Smith; Yvonne B., b. June 12, 1937, m. Gene L. Fox; Richard B. b. June 12, 1938, m. Betty Borg (Yvonne and Richard born one year apart to the hour and minute.); Harry B., b. July 20, 1943; unmarried.

J. Ed is one of the most popular of BYU's Emeritus group. His acrobatic abilities, good sense of humor, and genuine friendliness have gained him many friends. From childhood to the present he has enjoyed practical jokes and harmless fun. When he was inducted into the Emeritus Club (1914-1964 graduation tenure), he challenged any other Alumnus to do as he was about to demonstrate. He took off his coat, smoothed down his graying locks and proceeded to stand on his head on the bare, polished floor, body erect and feet together. He lowered and raised his feet (shoes size 12) several times, gently let himself down and smilingly put on his coat and waited for the challenge—with no takers. When asked why he did such a "stunt" he replied, "It is good to get some blood into your head once in a while. It helps your thinking, and it keeps you young." He has that rare ability of laughing his troubles away without minimizing their importance.

He was a tall gangling lad of great strength which was early used to good advantage on his father's farm. He entered the high school department of the BYU and was soon a welcome guest at socials, graduating in 1911 after four years' attendance. He took education courses in 1911-1912 and accepted a position to teach in Hinckley, Utah in 1912-1913. Discipline caused little trouble for him as he used laughter with his teaching and persuasion only when necessary. This experience convinced him he wanted to be a teacher and accordingly he returned to BYU and graduated in 1915 with an A.B. J. Ed was a trusted student and highly esteemed friend of President Brimhall and his counselors, E. S. Hinckley and Joseph B. Keeler, who encouraged him to go on to college. When requested to give some anecdotes recalling his residence at BYU, he submitted the following:

"First year at the "Y" I boarded—board $4 per week; 2nd year, batched with one other—Room rent $6 a month—$3 each; 3rd year batched with two others, room rent $4 a month, i.e., $1.33 each. Took out life membership tuition first year I entered BYU, at cost of $26.50. Thereafter my tuition cost for a number of years was $6.50 a year. I believe the last year of my seven at the "Y" (high school and college) the tuition was $15 or $20.

"The year before I entered the "Y" I took a load of grain to the Hoover Grist Mill in Provo. My little brother Lawrence was with me. As we entered Provo I looked for what I thought might be the BYU. I saw only the buildings on the hill at the head of Center Street, that looked like it might be it, and pointing to them said to my brother: "That's where I am going next year." It was a sort of letdown to find the BYU Campus on North Academy Avenue, and something quite different to the State Mental Hospital.

"My last year at the "Y" I took President Brimhall's theology class. One morning he walked into the class a little late, all business, and started things by reading from a slip of paper. He did not look up to note reactions from the class, and ignoring the uplifted hands, I blurted out, "President Brimhall, I don't believe that." His very prompt response in a real gruff voice was "I don't care what you believe, Brother Johnson, that is what the Lord said."

"My third year at the Y there was an SOS call late one spring afternoon for all the boys to meet at once in College Hall. In no time the hall was full and the larger part of the Faculty on the stand. President Brimhall was in charge. He was very serious and solemn. He stated word had come that a killing frost was coming that night, and the fruit growers on the Bench needed help desperately in smudging. Would we help them? Of course there was only one answer. The adventure angle no doubt contributed to the interest. Farmers in wagons, hayracks, etc., picked up students and dropped them on the windswept Bench at different points. The matter was not well organized, or organized at all. No one came to the fellows who'd been dropped off to direct them. It got dark. The old adage worked. Where there is no direction things take their natural course. I stood around in the dark and cold for hours, with no signs of life from farmers in trouble. If I had seen a single fire I am sure I would have gone to it. In due course I made my way back to Provo; I hiked. When I got to our batching quarters no one was home. The room was warm. A fire was burning in the cookstove. Two large fry pans were full of fried chicken. I had a piece, and was it good! Then I began to wonder. With the feathers, chicken heads, legs, insides in the entrance leanto I knew there had been chicken stealing from the *distressed fruit growers.* The fellows had had a feed and gone to a late movie. At once I gathered the evidence and took it a block west and threw it in the mill-race (accessory after the crime). I even had a notion to throw the fried chicken in too, but I don't recall that I did. But how often I have been amused over this. There in the assembly President Brimhall remarked that we were not going to fight the battle against the elements alone. Then he got one of the best prayers on the Faculty to implore the Lord to do His part in tempering the freezing blast. And what did us cusses do? Swiped the farmer's chickens and had a glorious feast!"

And he tells us further that he entered School of Jurisprudence, University of California at Berkeley, fall of 1917. He received the Juris. Doctor (J.D.) degree spring of 1920. He came to Utah summer of 1920 where he was admitted to the bar and commenced practice in Provo, at first alone, and then in association with Isaac E. Brockbank and Alfred L. Booth, two well-known lawyers and BYU graduates. He taught two courses at BYU school year 1920-21 then returned to Berkeley in December 1921 to become examiner of land titles in Federal Land Bank of Berkeley. In 1922 Ed became attorney for the Land Bank and in 1923 attorney also for Federal Intermediate Credit Bank, a new Federal agency. In 1926 he left these positions and became attorney for Pacific Coast Joint Stock Land Bank of San Francisco, and Mercantile Mortgage Company. In 1931 he entered private practice with W. Glenn Harmon, another BYU graduate, and Henry Ruggeri in San Francisco. He has continued to reside in Berkeley all the years to the present.

When the Berkeley Branch of Church was organized in 1925, he became president. When San Francisco Stake was organized (including all of Bay Area) in 1927, he became first Counselor to W. Aird MacDonald, President. When the stake was devided in 1935 and the Oakland Stake organized he continued in same position until 1937.

Through the years he has had various law partners and has been associated continuously with W. Glenn Harmon (since 1931). (He says that this latter fact accounts largely for such success as I have attained at the bar.)

Principal hobbies—ranching on a small sort of dude ranch scale at Orinda, over the hill east of Berkeley, where I have been maintaining a small herd of registered Herefords, a few horses, etc. and writing biographical sketches of California Supreme Court judges —some published in California State Bar Journal—and a two volume history of the Court for the hundred years from 1849 to 1950. Vol. I came out in 1963 and Vol. II appeared on the market in 1966. The Bancroft-Whitney Co. put the price of each book at $17.50 and said of it, "the story about men, the product of research and honest appraisal." It is a magnificent work reflecting Ed's sparkling abilities.

The esteem his profession and his church have for him is revealed by the positions he has held and the commissions he has honored. Writing the history of the California Supreme Court Justices was a monumental task gaining for him unstinted praise.

The world could use many more men of the stature of J. Ed Johnson.

OSCAR AMMON KIRKHAM

Born: January 22, 1880   **Place:** Lehi, Utah

Father: James Kirkham, a musician who taught all his children to play an instrument, and had a family orchestra which further aided in complete harmony between two families; a farmer who planted with purpose and tilled for perfection; born in London, England; musician, farmer, but primarily a Churchman.

Mother: Martha Mercer; born in American Fork, Utah; from distinguished Pioneer stock.
2) Emma Wooten; her children: Albert W., Richard A, Arthur Jesse, Rose Winifred, Wanda Emma, Florence Luella.
3) Miriam Eakle; married Dec. 26, 1926, after death of Martha and Emma.

Brothers and Sisters: (Children of Martha Mercer) James Mercer, Mary Ann, Francis W., (Oscar A.), Eva, Ebenezer John, Myrtle Jamima, m. Alvah Fitzgerald, Elizabeth Jane (died as infant). Only Francis W. is now living, early 1968.

Marriage: Ida Murdock of Heber, Utah; daughter of Moroni Murdock and Josephine Maria Nicol; born July 10, 1880; married May 25, 1904 in the S. L. Temple; graduate of Brigham Young Academy; board member Daughter of the Utah Pioneers; committee member for founding of the Brighton Home; a successful teacher and excellent manager.

Children: (8) all graduated from college, 5 filled missions.
Rose Carol, born 15 Dec., 1905, m. George Y. Jarvis; Elva Grace, born 24 April, 1907; m. Leslie Burbage; Rock M., born 2 January, 1911; m. Leonora Burrett; Norman Cree, born 1 July, 1913, m. Brigitte McKeinharst; Mark Mercer, born 31 May, 1915, m. Emma Jean Palmer; Oscar Ned, born 11 March 1919, m. Renee Shepart; Martha Kathryn, born 30 Aug., 1922, m. Wade H. Andrews; Jane Josephine, born 8 Oct., 1924, m. Douds S. Bassler.

Death: March 10, 1958

Oscar A. Kirkham, world renowned Scouter, had his early training in Lehi schools, inspired by Superintendent George N. Child to get an adequate education and be a leader of men. He worked on his father's farm and "hired out" after school. At seventeen he entered BYA to immediately succeed in music and drama. The school and community encouraged him to major in music and cultivate his beautiful tenor voice.

During the first winter in Provo he lived in a loft of a granary with another Lehi boy, James T. Worlton. A sack of potatoes (fifty cents), a hundred pounds of flour (three dollars), and a little home cured bacon lasted them most of the quarter. He sold vegetables in Salt Lake and "My voice easily covered a block when I called out." His friendly smile and cheery word helped to sell his cart of choice vegetables. Often he and his brother had to walk from Salt Lake to Lehi. If they had an occasional dull day, the boys slept on the steps of the old Tithing Office. He cleared oak brush and sage, hoed rows of potatoes, tomatoes and corn, herded milk cows, dragged logs from the mountains, cleaned stables—any honest work to get his education.

While at BYA from 1896-1899, he earned enough credits to graduate. He was President of his class twice. He did concert work over the state with Arvilla Clark (Andelin) and sang in Professor Lund's operas, usually the romantic leads. He went to Germany to study voice and piano for three years (in 1900). He over-trained his voice and it never completely recovered its musical brilliance, but gave him a husky resonance, both distinctive and intimate in quality, and helped to bring his audience close to him. In 1903 he received a scholarship to the Royal Academy in London for the year. He studied education at Columbia University for a year (1906) and was an assistant teacher to Dr. Farnsworth; he also became a member of the New York Oratorio Society and assistant director of the singing classes of Walter Damrosch.

Occupational Activities:

1905-1906—taught music at Ricks Academy in Rexburg.
1908-1913—Head of music department, LDS College in Salt Lake City, taking a season of training at Columbia in 1909.
1913—Field Secretary of the YMMIA to help organize the Boy Scouts of America.
1919—Scout Executive to the Salt Lake Council until 1925.
1925-1941—Was Executive Secretary of the YMMIA and Associate Executive of BSA in Region 12, comprising Utah, Arizona, Nevada, California, and Hawaii; attended 6 world jamborees as Chief Morale Officer from the U.S.A.; he was first to suggest the organization of a

Boy Scout Council for Utah County, to be fostered by Provo Rotary, which was done under the Chairmanship of Rotarian T. Earl Pardoe in 1920. Scouting was his major profession, music was his joyous avocation.

Civic, Social, and Honorary Affiliations:

President of BYU Alumni Assn., 1925-26, 1926-27. Vice President of BYU Emeritus Club, 1957-58. Silver Beaver, a Boy Scout of America Council Honor, 1953. Silver Antelope, BSA, District Honor. Dean of the General Board of the YMMIA in 1948. Member of the National Staff at six world Jamborees. Honorary member of Boy Scouts of Greece, France, and Austria. He was made Chief "Elk" of the Blackfoot Indian tribes in 1947. Awarded the Cross of Jerusalem by chief religious leaders of France in 1947. Personal recognition by Lord Baden-Powell, founder of Scouting. Citation for excellent service given by American Camping Association. BYU citation and degree, Master of Arts, for youth service in 1956. Sons of Utah Pioneers, bust by Avard Fairbanks, placed in Hall of Fame for contributions to youth in 1953. BYU Alumni Distinguished Service Award in 1957. Provo Kiwanis Club awarded him a Norman Rockwell Boy Scout Poster and beautiful painting, Feb. 1956.

Religious Activities:

He was well versed in scripture and advanced in the LDS Priesthood as the years unfolded, being held to a Seventy until death.

Aug. 1912 to Oct. 1948—Member of the General Board of the YMMIA.

1919—Field Executive YMMIA—then Executive Secretary (General Board of YMMIA was given charter to National Boy Scouts of America May 2, 1913).

1919—Scout Executive of Salt Lake Council of BSA.

1925—Associate Executive Region 12 (Utah, Nevada, Arizona, California, & Hawaii)

1941—Member of the First Council of Seventy until death.

Spent $16^{1}/_{2}$ years as a missionary.

As a Mutual Board member he covered the North American continent and had friends in most of the towns and cities in the United States. Scouting was tied up to most all of his work; his advice on youth problems was sought across the nation. As a member of the Salt Lake Rotary he was invariably placed on Scout and Youth committees.

In 1954 he was a special speaker in the "Cathedral of the Pines" in New Hampshire.

His office was a depository of citations, plaques, Indian bonnets, Scout medals and tie rings, outdoor pictures—all of which he seldom saw, as his assignments took him most of the time away from home.

He repeatedly paid tribute to his beautiful wife, Ida, for her patience with his absence. He often said, "The wife is the real missionary. She bears the burden of my trips."

His book *Say the Good Word,* gaining in popularity, was published posthumously in 1958.

No Alumnus was ever more loyal to his Alma Mater than Oscar A. Kirkham to BYU. His lecture appearances were frequent and always well attended. A Son of Brigham, he loved and was a moulder of men.

FRANCIS WASHINGTON KIRKHAM

Born: January 8, 1877 in Lehi, Utah

Father: James Kirkham; b. August 28, 1849 in London; with brothers George, Joseph, and Hyrum, came to Salt Lake and settled in Sugar House area; later moved to Lehi; married Martha Mercer and Emma Wooten; married Miriam Eakle Dec. 26, 1926, after deaths of Martha and Emma.

Mother: Martha (Mattie) Mercer; married Dec. 18, 1871; endowed her children with a love of learning, early coached them in reading good books and taught the value of time.

Brothers and Sisters: (Children of Martha)
James; Mary Ann, m. Mons Anderson; Francis W.; Oscar A.; Eva (died at 15 years of age); Ebenezer John; Myrtle Jamima, m. Alvah Fitzgerald; Elizabeth Jane (died as an infant).
(Children of Emma Wooton)
Albert Wooten, Richard Astington, Esther Ruth, Arthur Jesse, Rose Winnifed, Wanda Emma, Milo Franklin, Florence Luella.

Marriage: Zina Robinson; married January 2, 1901; died October 3, 1941; seven children, Preston, a boy, died as a baby.
Marguerite Burnhope Harris; married November 18, 1942; musician and teacher of piano.

Children: of Zina
Eulalia K. Tillotson, b. June 25, 1902; Francis R., b. August 23, 1904, m. Ellis Musser, Lawyer in San Francisco; Dr. Don, Internationally famed soil physicist, m. Betty Erwin, b. Feb. 11, 1908; Dr. Grant, b. June 12, 1912, Dentist in Washington, D.C., m. June Hodge; Rose m. Don C. Kimball, b. Oct. 28, 1914, teacher of physical education in Rock Springs, Wyoming; Geraldine m. Dr. Keyne P. Monson, b. July 4, 1922.
of Marguerite
Marguerite had two children when she married Francis W: Joyce Harris, m. Robert Stanton, b. April 24, 1924; Myrna Mae Harris m. Greeley Nebeker, b. October 20, 1930.

Residence: 436 South 12th East, Salt Lake City, Utah.

A few ancestral facts add interest in appreciating the fibre of the Kirkhams. George William Kirkham was born in London, England, March 18, 1822, the son of James and Ann Jeatt. James was a mariner in the English Navy for more than 21 years, a man 5 feet 3 inches tall. He was also a tailor and measured Tom Thumb for his clothes. At 51 he selected Ann for his wife, a spinster whom he wed on February 2, 1813. George W. was sent to school at Greenwich and pledged to the Navy of authority so directed. He married Mary Astington on December 14, 1844, at Trinity Church, Bourough, London, England. Her father was a sharpshooter under the Duke of Wellington and fought at the Battle of Waterloo; he was also a band man, playing the French horn and the violin in the orchestra, and bugle for the army, being both versatile and popular. Mary had a dream of her mother that her desire to go to Utah to be with the Church would be realized. When her elder brother died and left her $800, she had enough to take herself and family to Zion. George W. and Mary left England on the ship "Tapscot" April 7, 1859 with children James, 9, George, 6, Joseph, 3, and Hyrum, 3. Arriving in Salt Lake City September 18, 1859, they moved to a small house on the present City and County Building site. In spring the family moved to Lehi, near the Jordan Bridge. Then they moved back to Salt Lake City to 11th East, stayed there for four years, and returned to Lehi. The four sons of George had a ballroom orchestra, one of the first in the state, and travelled throughout Utah and southern Idaho.

After half a century of unsettled residence and many financial struggles, the Kirkhams finally found a resting place to rear a family in religious and civil freedom, where opportunity depended upon the initiative of each individual. Those sons rose to prominence and won national fame.

Francis W. Kirkham's life has been so orderly in the organization that it is readily chronicled:
Education:

Elementary Schooling, Lehi, Utah, completed 1892; Secondary, BYA, Provo, completed 1896; Higher Education, BYA, 1899-1904, University of Michigan, 1904-1906 with a B.A. in Economics and History, Leland Stanford University, graduate studies in education, University of Utah, 1911-1913, LLB, University of California, 1921-1923, Ph.D Degree awarded 1930, Education and Jurisprudence.
Occupational Activities:

Manager of Raymond Mercantile Company, Alberta, Canada; Assistant Professor of Education, BYU, Provo, 1906-1908, 1902-1904, 1909-1911, 1917-1924; LDS Business College principal, one year; Superintendent of Schools, Granite School District, 1924-1935; Director, National Child Welfare Association, New York City, N.Y.,

1929-1935; Director, National Youth Administration, 1935-1938; Founder and manager, Country Mutual Life of America, 1938-1959 (Retired at age 82, July, 1959; retained as a consultant); National Youth Fitness Coordinator; Honored by Salt Lake Trade Institute as "Utah's first director of Vocational Education" April 1966.

Church Activities:

Mission to New Zealand, 1896-1899; mission again to New Zealand, 1915, six months, Kirkham's "Maori Grammer" printed this year; he is a recognized authority on Maori language; returned to New Zealand a third time, for four months with his wife, Marguerite; Stake President of MIA in Canada 1902-1904; Member of High Council of New York Stake, 1929-1935; Sunday School teacher in Salt Lake 8th Ward and 33rd Ward; One of the most popular speakers in the Church, his speaking dates are limited only by time possible to accept them; A High Priest.

Civic, Social and Honorary Affiliations:

Member of Utah Academy of Sciences, Arts, and Letters; the Sons of Utah Pioneers; the Utah Historical Society; the Utah Aging Committee; Member of the National Youth Fitness Commission, doing most of the work in Wasatch County; Past President of BYU Emeritus Club, 1953-54.

Authorship:

"Character Education" booklet for National Child Welfare Association in New York City, 1929-35; Youth Education pamphlets, 1935-38; *Source Material Concerning the origin of the Book of Mormon,* 1937; *New Witness for Christ in America,* Vols. I, II, and III; "Why Cooperative Insurance", 1943; "Maori Grammar" as noted above; "Educating All the Children of All the People", his doctoral thesis published by the U.S. Office of Education.

His hobby is to play the organ or piano which he learned to do at Brigham Young Academy under Professor Lund. The better concerts and musicals in Northern Utah find the Kirkham's in the best reserved seats.

Francis and Marguerite have taken summer trips with BYU Travel Bureau to Europe, Mexico, and Hawaii.

Dr. Kirkham established a fund to aid students preparing for missions and copyrights to two volumes of *New Witness for Christ in America* have been given to Brigham Young University to be used to best advantage.

Kirkham is a name of highest repute at Brigham Young University.

VERN OLIVER KNUDSEN

Born: December 27, 1893   **Place:** Provo, Utah

Father: Andrew Knudsen; son of Hans and Bergite (Larsen) Knudsen of Loiten Hedemarken, Norway; born in Loiten Hedemarken, Norway July 13, 1854; migrated with his family when nine years old to Utah (1864) with a handcart company from Council Bluffs to Salt Lake City; buried youngest daughter near Echo, Utah (died of measles); settled west of Provo; successful farmer, director of Farmers and Merchants Bank; city councilman; Bishop of Provo First Ward; died December 15, 1891.

Mother: Chersty Sward; daughter of August and Ellen Johnson Sward; born in Malmo, Sweden, 1853; came to Utah in 1873, to Provo when seventeen years of age; married June 9, 1877; active in Relief Society and charitable organizations; her droll stories were listened to by hundreds of friends.

Brother and Sisters: Albert, Karl, Heber (all on missions in Norway), Lydia m. W. D. Rawson; Nettie m. Miles E. Miller, Vilate m. H. D. Reynolds.

Marriage: Florence Telford of Ogden, Utah; married December 19, 1919; she met her future husband while both were on a mission in Chicago, Illinois; he courted her by correspondence soon after.

Children: Marilyn, Robert, Morris and Margaret (twins); a family of musicians, Robert at the piano, Morris the cello, and Margaret the violin.

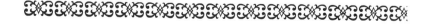

Vern was born on a farm where he and his three brothers and three sisters each had prescribed year round daily chores, schooling, farm and dairy work, and music lessons to fill their young lives. A beautiful fresh water lake nearby furnished fishing, swimming and boating, with shore skating in the winter. Ducks, geese, pelicans and gulls swam the lake's waters and hatched on a not-too-distant island. Frogs, toads, and water snakes were numerous, bees swarmed in season, jack rabbits were abundant, crows, meadow larks, robins and blackbirds mingled within and combed the grain fields. All the sounds from the meadow, the bull-rushes, the lake inlets, interested young Vern from the very beginning.

The father was a musician as well as a good teacher and farmer. The family early had a trio or a small orchestra, as the father played the violin and clarinet. Most of the children played the piano and organ. Father Knudsen led the First Ward Choir for eight years and played in orchestras and bands for some twenty-five years. "You'll always hear music when you go down to the Knudsens." The father gave a year in 1874-75 to work the Temple at St. George, Utah and filled a mission to Norway in 1887-89. Religion was a vital part of the family life. Vern's older brothers all went on missions to Norway and Vern filled a mission to the Chicago area, where he was mission secretary and Branch President, and where he met his future wife whom he married soon after their return from their assignments.

Wherever Vern went he was sensitive to sound and its basic principles. His imitations were expert and his ear keen. When he went to college he chose the University in his own home town and BYU was the gainer thereby. There he came under the influence of Harvey Fletcher who became his chief guide and inspiration. Physics, and mathematics early became his absorbing interests. When he graduated from BYU in 1915 he was the class valedictorian, speaking on the subject "Reflections of the Human and Divine in Physics." In Chicago the city noises intrigued his interest and often annoyed him.

After his mission he went to the Bell Laboratories in New York to work under Dr. Fletcher for a year, and then to Chicago University where he studied with world famed physicists Michelson and Millikan, Nobel prize winners. He took his PhD in 1922 with a dissertation, "The Sensitivity of the Ear to Frequency and Intensity." The course of his major interests in his research was now well established and before many years he was acknowledged as the world's outstanding authority in architectural acoustics.

His professional life unfolds in the following:

In 1923 at a small Junior College, a branch of the University of California, in Los Angeles, he became professor of physics and was near the motion picture world, feverishly working on the problems of synchronizing light and sound. This college, UCLA, soon became a four-year University and by 1928 was moving into new, magnificent quarters in West Wood Village, where Vern was allotted a building spot on a new laid street for his home.

His study of eight auditoriums with bad acoustics led to his work in the science of architectural acoustics. He publicly lamented the building of beautiful halls and auditoriums with no concern for acoustical quality. He convinced the Hollywood producers that their problems were tied up with absorption and reflection of sound and soon was consultant for Hollywood's first sound studies. His designs became world standards.

When Columbia Broadcasting Company on Sunset Boulevard sent to London for expert sound advice, they were informed that the best authority lived in their own city.

Dr. Vern directed the remodelling of Aime Semple McPherson's Four Square Gospel Church and engineered the acoustics installation of the B'Nai B'Rith Temple on Wilshire Boulevard. Whittier High School was one of the first schools in the nation to seek acoustic help. When he built his own home it was treated acoustically and started a trend influencing modern home construction.

He designed the internationally famous Hollywood Bowl, reputedly the finest outdoor auditorium in the world.

In 1929 he called a group of acoustical engineers to convention, resulting in the organization of the Acoustical Society of America, with Dr. Harvey Fletcher as President and Vern O. Knudsen as Vice President, later its President.

1932-38—He became chairman of Department of Physics, U.C.L.A.

1934—Dean of their Graduate Division. $1,000 prize by American Association for Advancement of Science for his studies of the absorbing of sound in gases.

1937—Received the BYU Alumni Distinguished Service Award.

1941-45—War Research; research against submarines; he worked in England and San Diego, California; studied sound in relationship to all sub-surface warfare.

1950—Dean Knudsen appointed Chairman of a three-man administration commission to run UCLA Campus until the arrival of Dr. Allen in 1952.

1956—Vice Chancellor to 1959.

"He is admirably qualified by character, ability, and experience for the performance of the duties assigned the new vice-chancellor including representing the chancellor at official functions, acting for him when he is away from the campus, serving as chief liaison between the administration and the faculty, aiding in recruitment of personnel, educational planning and the administration of sponsored research" stated President Robert G. Sproul of Berkeley, California.

1959—Chancellor of UCLA—he says "a one year chancellor, as 67 is age for compulsory retirement."

1961—James E. Talmage Scientific Achievement Award at BYU Commencement exercises.

Articles by Dr. Vern have appeared in various scientific and weekly magazines, and aroused national interest. *Time* featured him in the January 2, 1961, issue, under the title "The Noise Haters", with such statements as "Noise costs the U.S. industry $2,000,000 a day", "Noise is a hazard to physical health", "Noise of too great intensity can cause permanent deafness, nausea, and mental illness," etc. Vern is a great advocate of earplugs ("Ear defenders" are his invention) and abatement of noise in traffic, airplanes, automobiles, auditoriums and at home. He has tested major noise centers throughout the world and visited the world's famed buildings. He has been seen in world capitals with his professional companion, the sound level meter.

His Books: *Architectural Acoustics*
           Audiometry, used as a text
           Acoustical Designing in Architecture, co-authored with
             Cyril Harris; have a world market.

He is working on another study in sound research.

He wrote "I shall always be greatly indebted to BYU for the training I received in religion, ethics, and character building. Nothing in my entire educational life has been of greater value to me."

BENT F. LARSEN

Professor of Art Emeritus

Born: May 10, 1882   **Place:** Monroe, Utah

Father: Bent Rolf Larsen
Born at Riesor, Norway, September 24, 1845. Sailor as a boy, saw the world, once shipwrecked. His parents accepted Gospel in Norway, converted children and came to U.S. His father and two sisters died of cholera at Mississippi. Mother came to Utah before railroad.

Mother: Lorena Eugenia Washburn
Born at Manti, Utah, January 10, 1860. First settled in Fountain Green—then Monroe.

Brothers and Sisters: Bent F., first child
Ida L., m.' Wm. Bartholemew
Lottie L. m. Archie Robinson
Parents of BYU coach Clarence Robinson
Enoch, m. Mabel Christiansen
Floy L., m. Heber Turner
Parents of Professor Glen Turner, Utah Artist, BYU
Pearl L., m. Floyd Bartholomew
Ella L., m. Taylor Turner
Clarence L., m. Marjorie McComb
Fern L., m. Guy Mellor

Marriage: Geneva Day, September 25, 1907 in the Manti Temple.
Born at Mt. Pleasant, Utah, April 14, 1885
Past president BYU Alumni Emeritus Club.

Children: Rex Bent, b. May 8, 1909; married Mary Barton, June 7, 1934; Eugene Clarence, b. August 12, 1911; married LaPreal Winterton; Celia Geneva, b. December 3, 1914; m. Willard Luce; Ronald Franklin, b. December 8, 1916; married Helen Brown; Grant Alvin, b. October 7, 1923.

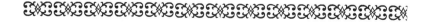

Education: "B. F." as he is familiarly known, graduated from the Monroe public schools in 1899, being the oldest boy in a large family whose father was weakened with poor health. Responsibilities of farm work delayed Bent's educational progress. Urged by a devoted mother, he entered Snow Academy at Ephraim, Utah, and completed a three-year normal course in two years, graduating as class president in May of 1901. He became principal of Monroe Schools.

In Fall of 1906, Bent entered BYU, receiving an Art diploma in one year. He became instructor of art at Springville High School and supervisor of the Training Schools in 1908. He received an AB degree from BYU in June, 1912, being class president of the first class of BYU to graduate with a four year course requirement. He served the "White and Blue" and the yearbook.

He took a Master of Arts degree at U. of Utah in 1922. By now his art talents were fully entrenched in school associations. He studied with masters at every opportunity, extensively in Paris, France, and Provincetown.

His exhibits have gone halfway around the world, being honored in Paris and more than two dozen major cities in the U.S. His pictures have been selected for the circulating exhibit of the American Federation of Arts, the American Artists' Professional League in New York and New York's World Fair. His membership in professional art societies runs into more than a dozen and his biographies run into another dozen Who's Who categories. Many art journals and magazines have reproduced his pictures, chiefly landscapes.

Most of his "free" time has been devoted to his church, where he has been teacher in priesthood quorums and auxiliary associations, being a counselor in a bishopric, a member of Utah Stake High Council, and president of his High Priests Quorum.

When presented the David O. McKay Humanity Award by BYU in 1960, his citation read in part:

"But Brother Larsen's true strength lies in his generous and open-minded attitude toward all types and styles of sincere creative expression. While his own work exhibits personal integrity and constancy of basic artistic values, he has been willing to experiment, to study, and to search with those of the *avant-garde*. In his tolerance and breadth of understanding, he has been an inspiration to hundreds of students and painters in the intermountain region. The BYU Art Department under his leadership became known for all that was good in art expression and was never identified as being committed to one style over another.

"Through his teaching, writing, and example he has promoted beauty and order in home, community, and Church. He has awakened aesthetic awareness and made thousands conscious of the artistic qualities in architecture, landscaping, public parks, and city streets, knowing that full appreciation of these things makes for better citizenship, community morale, and brotherly love and understanding."

Artist and teacher; a worthy Son of Brigham who recently gave a magnificent collection of his paintings, sketches and drawings to the University.

ANTHONY C. LUND

Professor of Music; Salt Lake Tabernacle Choir Director

Born: February 25, 1871, at Ephraim, Utah

Father: Anthon Henrik Lund of Ephraim, son of Henry Lund, and Anna Christina Anderson.
Born: May 5, 1844, in Aalbarg, Denmark.
Mother died when he was 3½ years old; lived with grandmother.
Father a brilliant linguist; taught English to converts; to Utah Sept. 23, 1862.
Ordained an apostle Oct. 7, 1889; Second Counselor Oct. 7, 1901; First Counselor April 7, 1910.
Died: March 2, 1921 in Salt Lake City, Utah.

Mother: Sarah Ann Petersen
Born: Jan. 4, 1852, in Lehi, Utah; Daughter of Knute Peterson.
Married: May 2, 1870.

Brothers and Sisters: Anthony C.
Henry C., m. Julia Farnsworth.
Sarah H.
Herbert Z, m. Emma Jensen.
Canute L.
Athnial R., m. Mabel Hall.
August William, m. Josephine Brown.
George C.
Eva A.

Marriage: 1) Laura Graves, Aug. 14, 1895.
Children: Weber Anthony and Grant.
2) Emma Cornelia Sorensen, daughter of Niels Sorensen and Sarah Capson.
Born: March 8, 1882, in Gunnison, Utah.
Marriage: Dec. 24, 1902. Civic leader and State club officer
Died: June 26, 1959.

Children (of Emma Cornelia) Anthon Henrik, b. Dec. 11, 1903.
Herschel S., b. Feb. 11, 1905.
Cornelia (Utter), b. Sept. 20, 1907.
Max Welton, b. July 31, 1910.
Irene (Flygare), b. Sept. 8, 1913.
Phyllis (Beaulieu), b. Feb. 14, 1920.

Death: June 11, 1935 of a heart attack.

Tony Lund, as he was affectionately called by hundreds of his students and colleagues, grew heavier as he grew older and laughter dominated his social life. He loved good jokes and knew how to tell them. His Danish stories were often hilarious and always characteristic. He frequently would stop a choir rehearsal to share a pleasant anecdote, inheriting the ear and ability of mimicry from his paternal grandfather, who gleaned good stories wherever he found them. Tony's father was devoutly religious and had one of the kindest voices I ever heard, being aspirate with pleasant resonance. When Anthony H. Lund became an apostle, Tony was eighteen years of age and well versed in religious music.

His aunt, Hilda Peterson, gave Tony music lessons on the organ when he was but eight years old and he soon was playing for the ward choirs. At eighteen he was a well-known choir leader of Ephraim. He attended Brigham Young Academy from 1888 to 1891, obtaining a B. D., bachelor of didactics, and had the counsel of Dr. Maeser who was a better than average musician himself. When Tony later came to BYA, Dr. Maeser turned over to him the leading of all congregation singing, and Tony was director of music at BYA from 1893-1900, 1902-1915. He left the school of his affection to take the leadership of the Salt Lake Tabernacle choir which had been so long under famed Evan Stephens.

In the interim of 1891-1894 he studied voice and piano in the Royal Conservatory of Leipzig, Germany, graduating with distinction. He also spent a year in Paris and a year in London with world-famed leaders and teachers.

His marriage to Cornelia Sorenson was one of the most fortunate events in his life. She was a student of great promise, a good musician with a zest for life. They were married on Christmas Eve with hundreds of friends wishing them every happiness and choral groups singing them "bon voyage." When needed, she could play his accompaniment and cook a big meal for unexpected guests whom an impulsive husband so often "invited in."

"When a husband spends so much of his time in civic and church duties, a wife should advance with her own respective abilities. Yes, indeed, my family came first." In a few words she gave a brief outline of her life. In the late hours, as the family grew up, Tony and Cornelia would discuss their days' activities and she would have a "snack" ready which he many times extended to a hearty meal. "He used to say, 'I've got some money—let's go to the drugstore.' He surely liked the sweets." (He weighed 285 pounds when he died.) That was her polite way of saying that Tony was overweight. He would remark "I'm only plump and confortable. Who wants wrinkles?" Cornelia was president in her Relief Society, president of the Lafayette Parent-Teachers' Association, chairman of the state Red Cross during World War I; Captain of Camp 2, Daughters of Utah Pioneers and president of the State organization for four years; for two decades she was president of the Salt Lake City Women's Chamber of Commerce; served on the Utah State Historical Association during administrations of Governors Henry H. Blood and Herbert B. Maw. One of her greatest honors was to serve as a member of the executive committee for "This Is The Place Monument." To be vice-president of the State Association of County Officials, treasurer of the Central Civic and Beautification League and a director of the Utah Chemical and Carbon Company would be honor enough for most women. To be elected to the Utah Hall of Fame and runner-up in the Utah Mother of the Year in 1947 was further recognition. No wonder a tired husband would come home and ask "What new job did you take on today?" and her smiling retort "Where is the choir going next?" At her last public speech which was given before the Brigham Young University Emeritus Club on June 5th, 1959, she said "I became very active in politics and embarrassed my husband no end. I worked very hard for Woman's Suffrage and he opposed my efforts almost as bitterly. He voted against everything I voted for, especially about women in politics." She added "With it all, he remained so much a boy. He loved to fish in his spare time and he somehow found spare time very often." You could best know Tony Lund through his wife's eyes. She called him a great man, a talented, inspired musician and a grand companion.

The music of Tony Lund was heard by hundreds of Utahns as he took his expertly drilled voices to the respective communities to give concerts to aid some building cause, or "sell" Brigham Young University, a school he served some twenty-one years. His annual operas were acclaimed for their all-around excellence, musically sound with only the best voices. He was unexcelled as a vocal teacher. He had a baritone voice highly praised by Giovanni Sbriglia in 1902 and again in 1909 by William Shakespeare, his teacher in London. His "placement of tone" was superb. He put his very soul in each lesson he taught and could scold as bitterly as he so often praised. He taught from talents rather than faults. For a student who worked and made progress he had "all the time in the world—never mind the clock." Some students would wait long periods of time for him to finish a lesson with a budding artist in his studio. They waited, as they knew the same courtesy would be extended to them when occasion arose. He was offered a flattering position by Dr. Chadwick of the New England Conservatory because of the training given his students who later attended eastern schools of music. He taught such talented people as Florence Jepperson Madsen, David Reece, Willard Andelin, Arvilla Clark Andelin, Clarence Hawkins,

Mabel Borg Jenkins, Lida Edmunds, Constance Reese, Hazel Taylor Peery, Oscar Kirkham, Emma Ramsay Morris, Arthur Overlade, King Driggs, Jessie Evans Smith, Mark Robinson, to name but a few. Students had to take aptitude tests before being assigned to classes.

I interpolate an interesting bit at this point. Sam Jepperson, the self-taught artist, would paint scenery for Prof. Lund's operas to pay for the lessons given to Florence and Sam, Jr., who became a famed band leader. Florence was so adept that she was assigned to teach Tony's classes of missionaries. Also in passing, Tony took his first music classes at the academy under Prof. Henry E. Giles and was a frequent consultant of Dr. Maeser's. While he was in Leipzig, 1898-99, his position was filled by John J. McClellan who became the great Tabernacle organist.

There is a chapter of Tony's life not too well remembered. When he returned from Europe in August of 1894, he was elected to the First Constitutional Convention of Utah, held in Salt Lake City, in March of 1895. He was reputedly the youngest member present—he voted against women suffrage and prohibition. But politics was not his forte.

The popularity of Prof. Lund is revealed by university figures of 1902; over 200 of the enrolled list of 575 students were in the music school.

William F. Hanson's "Sun Dance" was a favorite of Professor Lund; and he considered it one of his most popular operas. He produced it more times than any other opera of his repertoire. Most of the Academy's and early Brigham Young University's operas were staged in the old Opera House on First West between Center and First North on East Side, which is now a parking lot. Prof. Lund had two opera seats made into one seat on the aisle which was considered his private property, as it was the only seat to accommodate him. He sang the lead in "Bohemian Girl" with Professor Clare W. Reid conducting. Needless to say it was a smash hit as many testified to his glorious voice. He preferred teaching and conducting to any other activity in the arts.

When Tony went to Salt Lake he knew he had to compete with a great conductor in Evan Stephens, whose reputation was international. He also knew he left many better voices at BYU than were found in the Choir. By special agreement all Tabernacle Choir members were released with a grateful vote of thanks so that a new group could be organized. Each singer had to submit to a check-up and vocal trial. When a voice showed promise, though untrained, Prof. Lund gave the person eight special lessons to build him for key choir positions, resulting in a gradual quality improvement and a greater choir balance. His former student and friend, John J. McClellan sat at the great organ and together they soon had a national reputation with invitations to perform across the nation.

Appearances at the Hollywood Bowl in July of 1926 and an extended tour to California music centers with a group of 206 voices was a step further in extending the great choir's reputation. Radio was making rapid strides, and with the initiative and drive of Earl J. Glade, the Choir was booked for weekly broadcasts over the NBC, starting on July 15, 1929 with Edward O. Kimball at the organ. This program of one hour was carried by him within three weeks of his death. In 1932, the American Choral Alliance of Boston selected Tony for the board of directors. With George D. Pyper as tour manager a trip to the Century of Progress for the Ford Motor Company was made by the choir in Sept., 1934.

The professor was commissioned by G. Schirmer Company to translate the music theory works of S. Judassohn into English, a contribution of importance for musicians in England and America. When Tony brought the great pianist Emil Bauer, to Provo and personally lost $600.00, he did not berate the absent public but said "Whatever the cost, it was worth it for the school."

Prof. Lund was an avid reader of poetry. In an article he wrote for the "BYU Student" of April 1891, he said "Poetry is an art that has every charm to attract and every motive to please."

He begrudged the insistence of the clock to tick off the hours and demand a cessation of his practice or teaching. "Had the day 28 hours it would give me 4 more hours with the melodies I crave." His love of melody is revealed by his choice of operas he staged, as he said "somewhat limited by talent I need." "Maritana," "The Beggar Student," "Priscilla," "Daughter of the Regiment," "Princess Ida," "Erminie," "Boccaccio," "Bohemian Girl," "Carmen," "Il Travatore," were a few of his annual operas.

A book easily could be written about this talented, fun-loving man. His children adored him, but never knew quite what to expect. One anecdote I enjoyed; At the table, he would look around at the children. "You can't eat any of my prunes. So, I'm hiding them." They spent hours trying to find them and ate until they were all gone. To his wife, "That is one way of keeping them regular. Hide the prunes."

Tributes of gratitude and good wishes were expressed by Utah County residents for many weeks when the final time came for Tony's leaving for Salt Lake, leaving a choir in Provo that rivaled the Salt Lake in every way. President Brimhall, usually very conservative, said in part; "The school will be weakened by the absence of Professor Lund more than by the absence of any other member of the faculty . . . the President not excepted. . . . Professor Lund is a great musician but as a teacher he is wonderful. He has made our school an institution to which the educational authorities of a group of states are looking for music directors and teachers. We have no one in sight who can fill his place."

To be a student in any of his classes was a real experience, as gems of wisdom were intermixed with quotes from the Bible or sayings from the latest paper cartoon. Lives of the great musical masters were compared with stories of the Danish pioneers or the deeds of the aborigines. He would look at a young lady whose progress was slower than some of the others, "You need company. You look as lonesome as C at the top of the keyboard. Get out and make friends, meet people, loosen up so your music has some feeling. Throw out a bunch of notes and bring them together in a harmonious family. Here are three soprano notes (using the blackboard); see if you can introduce them to some fine-looking tenor notes on this scale. And tomorrow, have these get acquainted with three pairs of altos and basses." Such a conversation would often be a conclusion to a class in composition. While you were learning harmony and composition you were being introduced to the world's great music masters, some as real to Tony's students seated before him in a class. There were very few classes that did not get choice Bible bits, usually most appropos.

The impetus given the music department by Anthony C. Lund has been carried over to this date. And he once said, "You who learn to sing in our choirs have prepared yourselves to sing with the Angels of heaven. What could be more wonderful than that?"

Those who knew Tony Lund saw a huge body with a most refined soul or an unshaved fisherman quote beautiful poetry, a Danish story-teller reciting the Biblical beauty of the desert psalms, a sincere student upholding the principles of American democracy and the Gospel restored by a lad of the Vermont mountains. He loved the beauties of his mountain valleys and let his thoughts wander in the glories of vales beyond.

A master musician who loved BYU is an honored Son of Brigham.

ARCH LEONARD MADSEN

Born: December 4, 1913   **Place:** Lake View (Provo), Utah

Father: Parley W. Madsen
Born October 22, 1879 in Provo, son of Peter and Lena Johnson
Married September 18, 1912, Salt Lake Temple
Member, High Council of Sharon Stake, patriarch of West Sharon Stake, superintendent of Sunday School over 34 years
Connected with Utah-Idaho Sugar Company and Taylor Brothers Dept. Store from 1921 to retirement.
Died January 22, 1966

Mother: Christina Nuttall, daughter of L. John Nuttall and Christina Little of Lake View, Utah County, Utah.
Born November 21, 1888
B.Y.U. student for three years. Taught school and all L.D.S. auxiliaries; a dynamic leader.

Brothers and Sisters:
Viola, m. May 20, 1938, Earl Sabey (dec.).
Velma, m. Sept. 18, Aaron "Bus" Williams.
Dr. Parley W., Jr. m. June 27, 1945, Romania Christenson
Dr. Carlos N., m. March 21, 1949, Margaret Young
Kenneth R., m. July 15, 1955, Sandra Lucy Snow
Ronald E., m. March 9, 1951, Katheryn Eliz. Heacock
Lowell L., m. June 7, 1961, Bonnie Amussen Benson

Marriage: Margaret Peggy Higginbotham, March 30, 1938, Salt Lake Temple
Born June 4, 1919, Ogden, Utah daughter of Francis E. Higginbotham and Margaret Dent Dee

Children: Erik H.
Margaret Frances
Alan Leonard
Maren Christine
Anita Maude

Arch attended Lake View and Provo schools; went to B.Y.U. for two years; attended University of Utah for a season, and studied at University of Montana. All of his brothers are doctors or lawyers, with the guidance and urging of their parents.

He taught radio and television classes in B.Y.U. as a member of their communications faculty, and received the Distinguished Service Award from Brigham Young University Alumni Association in 1962. He was a member of the B.Y.U. Alumni Executive Committee; President Alumni Association, 1963-64.

Arch started in the radio business in 1933, building and operating a point-to-point radio station for the U.S. Army Signal Corps. He has been manager of KSUB in Cedar City, Utah; KOVO at Provo; KID, Idaho Falls; Commercial Manager at KUTA in Salt Lake City; was a director of the Utah Broadcasters Association and also served a term as President.

In 1951 he was selected a member of the Board of Directors of the Radio Advertising Bureau of New York, and in 1953 left Utah to join that organization as Director of Member Services. Later he was General Manager of *Sponsor Magazine* in New York City, then joined the Association of Maximum Service Telecasters in Washington, D. C. as Assistant Executive Director.

In 1961 he was asked by the L.D.S. First Presidency to become President of KSL, Inc.

At present, he serves as President of the Bonneville International Corporation, the Church operating company, holding interest in KSL Radio and Television; KIRO Radio and Television, Seattle, Washington; KID Radio and Television, Idaho Falls, Idaho; KBOI Radio and Television, Boise, Idaho; and WRUL (Radio New York Worldwide), the five international broadcasting stations with studios in New York City and transmitters at Scituate, Massachusetts.

Bonneville International recently completed arrangements to buy a powerful FM broadcasting station in New York City, which will be broadcasting from atop the Empire State Building. If the Federal Communications Commission approves, it will be housed with the new WRUL studios and offices on the third floor of the communications center at 485 Madison Avenue, New York City.

In attempting to fulfill the responsibilities of Church electronic communications given to him by President McKay, he has guided the expansion of the coverage of the semi-annual General Conference of the Church from some 20 television stations to a coast-to-coast and international television coverage of some 175 stations.

In the last several years radio and television programming to international areas has started to expand, particularly in South America. At the present time, excerpts of General Conference are being prepared sound-on-film with special language lip-sync in five languages, including Spanish, Portuguese, French, German and Mandarin-Chinese.

Arch comes from a deeply religious family. Since young manhood, he has been active in Church assignments. He served a mission as Temple Square guide in Salt Lake City for five years, which he counts as one of the most satisfying experiences in his life.

He was the building Bishop of the beautiful Oak Hills Ward and Stake House in the expanding east area of Provo and served on the High Council of East Provo and East Sharon Stakes. When he went East to establish residence, he was chosen Bishop of the Chevy Chase Ward in Washington, D. C.

President Arch has traveled more than a million miles by air to appear before industrial, civic and patriotic organizations. The Provo Chamber of Commerce elected him as its President; Utah Valley Hospital of Provo appointed him a Board Member. He is a member of the Rotary Club of Salt Lake City, having been a Rotarian in Provo; he is also a member of the Board of Directors of the Deseret News Publishing Company.

Arch has one major ambition which exceeds all others: to have the message of the Church heard and seen around the world via radio, television and film with over half the world now being served.

FRED L. MARKHAM

Born: July 3, 1902   **Place:** Spanish Fork, Utah

Father: Joseph Markham, b. August 27, 1868 in Spanish Fork, Utah, son of Stephen Markham and Mary Curtis. Stephen Markham was bodyguard and companion to the Prophet Joseph Smith and one of the leaders of the 1847 pioneer company. Missionary to New Zealand 1892-1896. Attended Brigham Young Academy in the late 1880's. Died at Provo, Utah, April, 1932.

Mother: Mary C. Lewis born March 21, 1874, Spanish Fork, Utah. Daughter of Fredrick Lewis Sr. and Agnes R. Ferguson. Married to Joseph Markham, January 25, 1899, Salt Lake Temple. Attended Brigham Young Academy. Received teaching certificate. Taught school in Sanpete and south Utah County. Latter, following her marriage, taught in Provo City Schools for a number of years, active in civic and church affairs in all auxiliary organizations. In 1966, was 92 years of age, active and very much interested in life.

Brothers and Sisters: Joseph Aldus Markham, b. March 23, 1900, Spanish Fork, Utah, m. Gladys Seamount. Graduated Brigham Young University 1925; Lucille b. October 31, 1908, Spanish Fork, Utah m. Harold Thorne (dec.). Currently on Library Staff at Brigham Young University.

Marriage: Maude Dixon, daughter of John DeGrey and Sarah Lewis Dixon. b. February 28, 1901 in Provo, Utah. Married in the Salt Lake Temple, June 25, 1924.

Children: John Frederick, b. September 5, 1928, Provo, Utah m. Reeda Bjarnson; Dixon Joseph, b. September 18, 1931, Provo, Utah m. Junece Jex; Barbara, b. May 29, 1936, Provo, Utah m. Weldon Daines; Diana, b. June 28, 1940, Provo, Utah m. Gary L. Stewart.
All four have graduated from BYU and the boys have served on missions.

409

Fred is good company, always ready with a generous smile, eager to hear your news and accept helpful ideas. He cannot be hurried; has a deliberate, logical mind and a very observant eye. He lives one idea at a time and enjoys its progress. He was a top athlete in college and was an excellent actor and continues both of these activities today as a means of enjoyment and relaxation. A brief of his life follows:

Entered Brigham Young University Training School in the Fourth Grade in the fall of 1911. Brigham Young University High School in the fall of 1915. Graduated from Brigham Young University with a major in mathematics, minor in chemistry in 1923. During college years, participated on staff of White and Blue, on staff and as editor of the Banyan, 1921. Member of the track team 1921-22; participated in varsity plays 1920, 1921, 1922; president of Junior Class in 1922. Served two years, 1924-26 in the Eastern States Mission. Studied at the School of Architecture, Massachusetts Institute of Technology 1927-30. Taught intermittently at the Provo High School and Granite High School in Salt Lake City, 1922-35.

Began practice as an Architect in 1930 with Claude S. Ashworth. Opened office for personal practice 1939. Design work on the Brigham Young University Campus includes the following: Joseph Smith Building, 1940; Knight Mangum Halls, 1946; Temporary buildings to house the School immediately following the war, 1946; Carl F. Eyring Science Building, 1949; Heritage Halls Units, 1952-55; In collaboration with Richard Jackson, the George Albert Smith Fieldhouse, 1951; Herald R. Clark Service Center, 1953; David O. McKay Classroom Building, 1954; Joseph F. Smith Family Living Center, 1955; Alumni Building, 1960; In collaboration with Pittsburgh, Des Moines Steel Company, the Stadium, 1964; Ernest L. Wilkinson Student Center, 1964; In collaboration with offices of Willard Nelson and Dixon & Long Architects, the Stephen L Richards Physical Education Building, 1965; Addition to the Central Heating Plant, 1966. In addition to the design of individual buildings, participated in the overall campus design working closely in later years with Mr. Sam F. Brewster of Physical Plant.

Other buildings in the state include: Provo High School; Provo Barbizon Manufacturing Plant; Provo City Library; Scera Theatre; Student Union Building, University of Utah; Monument Park Ward Chapel, Salt Lake City, Utah, Ogden Stakes Tabernacle, Ogden, Utah; Student Union Building and its recent addition, Utah State University; Engineering & Physical Science Building, Utah State University; Student Union Building, Snow College, Ephraim, Utah.

Served on Provo City Planning Commission; On original Utah County Planning Commission, serving four years as chairman. Served 16 years as member of the Architect's Licensing Board for the State of Utah, 1941-57; Nationally, served as an officer for the National Council of Architectural Registration Boards and as President from 1954-1956. Subsequent to that as chairman of the Examination Committee which has developed a procedure for the preparation of national examinations for licensing in the field of architecture. 1949-1954 as a member of the Survey Commission for Architectural Education and Registration, which Commission, as a report on its work, published two volumes, *The Architect at Mid-Century.* Member of national committees of the American Institute of Architects covering Urban Planning and Education. In 1958 at the invitation of the West German Government, served as a member of a ten man Architects-City Planners Team to review the post war architecture and city rehabilitation in West Germany. From 1958-1965, served as member of the National Architectural Accrediting Board, a six man body which has the responsibility for accreditation of the schools of architecture of the nation. Acted as its President 1963-1964. Made a Fellow of the American Institute of Architects 1957 for meritorious work in Architectural Design and Service to the Profession.

Served in various capacities in the Church in Utah Stake including: President of 34th Quorum of Seventy; First President of the Utah Stake Mission; Counselor in the Third Ward Bishopric; Member of the Utah Stake High Council; Counselor to Stake President, Victor J. Bird, 1946-60; President of Utah Stake 1960 to present.

Fred's love of BYU is well expressed in his comments: "Having attended elementary school, high school and college there and having been closely associated with the University through my entire adult life, it has become very much a part of our family. It has been a great privilege to have worked with the many fine board members, administrators, faculty and staff members who have served on the campus over the many years in which I have had close association with the School."

Near the end of World War II, Elder Harold B. Lee commented to me as we walked across the campus between the Brimhall and Joseph Smith Memorial Buildings, "The Church must not stop until the Brigham Young University becomes the greatest educational institution in the world. We are well advanced toward that goal. It is our desire to assist in every way possible to help BYU to live up to its potential." Fred Markham has been one of its greatest builders.

411

MILTON MARSHALL

Born: May 10, 1895   **Place:** Vernal, Utah

Father: James Marshall of Wilsden, Yorkshire, England
Born April 3, 1864
Died May 22, 1945 in Vernal, Utah

Mother: Mary Robinson Marshall born in England

Brothers   Calvin born March 19, 1897 in Vernal Utah and died
and Sisters: December 2, 1931
Victor Ewart born November 25, 1898 in Vernal, Utah
and died March 14, 1954

Half Brothers James and Earl
and Sisters: Ethel, m. Bud Connor
Frances, m. Reuben Hartle
Merle, m. Newell Knight Merrill
Ellen, m. Larvin Atwood
Vera, m. Burnell Hatch

Marriage: Julia Richards Taylor
Daughter of Dr. Fred Taylor, granddaughter of President
John Taylor, great-granddaughter of Willard Richards
Church and civic worker
Married September 7, 1918—resides in Provo

Children: John T. Marshall, D.D.S., b. August 28, 1920, m. Mary
Miner
Robert T. Marshall, M.D., Ph. D. b. June 8, 1922, m. Norene
Hess
Marie Marshall, b. June 7, 1925, m. E. M. Miner, M.D.
Paul T. Marshall, D.D.S., b. January 28, 1928, m. Carol
Dawn Larsen
Mark T. Marshall, Atomic Scientist, b. March 22, 1930,
m. Beth Wessel

Death: Saturday, Sept. 16, 1961

Citation read for the Karl G. Maeser distinguished Teaching Award, with notes added by the editor.

Milton Marshall was a teacher and scientist who worked conscientiously and gave many years of devoted, efficient service to science and the Brigham Young University. He received his elementary and high school education from the Vernal schools, Uintah High School and Brigham Young High School. He came to BYU as a teacher in 1919, after receiving the Bachelor of Arts degree here in 1918. He obtained the Ph.D. degree at the University of Chicago in 1924 under the directorship of the scientific laureate, Dr. Michelson.

He served as Flying Cadet in World War I, having his ground work at the University of California at Berkeley and his flying at Mather Field near Sacramento, California.

When World War II came along, he was called upon to teach the men of the Army Specialized Training Program at BYU courses in electronics and engineering. He taught one course in instrumentation for Geneva Steel. For many years he was a consultant for the Pacific States Cast Iron Pipe Company of Provo, Utah, and has also done inspection work for Bureau Veritas of New York City, Pierce Testing Laboratories of Denver, and the Underwriter's Laboratory of Chicago.

In 1956-57 he was chairman of the American Society for Metals. He has served as chairman of both the Physics and Mathematics Departments at BYU, and has taught heavy loads at all levels of physics and mathematics, giving countless hours of individual instruction and assistance to graduate students in research projects. He was on the Athletic Council, the Campus Planning Committee, and chairman of the BYU Employees' Credit Union.

He laboriously worked out the schematic chart to evaluate points for the All-Round Track Championship with a computed point scale as distance was increased in field events or time was shortened for track; a chart used to this day.

Dr. Marshall loved children, and was very proud to have served on the Provo City School Board for twenty-five years and was given a special award of honor as the state's most effective school board member by the Utah School Board Association, the first person to be so honored.

He enjoyed church activities and served as superintendent of Sunday School in which he also taught several classes. Milt has been president of the Young Mens Mutual and taught Priesthood Quorum classes.

He belonged to the American Physical Society, American Mathematical Society, American Association for the Advancement of Science, American Foundry Society, was the first secretary of BYU chapter of Sigma XI.

He was devoted to his wife, having married Julia Richards Taylor, daughter of the late Fred Taylor. Together they reared four sons, John, Robert, Paul, Mark, all professional men and college graduates, and a daughter Mrs. Ernest M. (Marie) Miner. The Marshalls spent many happy hours in their most interesting hobby of "rock hunting" and lapidary, a means for keeping the family together until school separated them in search of advanced degrees.

Milt's friends knew him to be an expert mathematician and a keen student and counselor in education, one of B.Y.U.'s outstanding teachers.

THOMAS LYSONS MARTIN

The first of six children in his family to live beyond infancy; emigrated to Utah when fifteen years of age; worked and sent for parents four years later.

Born: November 21, 1885   **Place:** Pendlebury, Lancashire, England

Father: James Martin, born April 29, 1866, Manchester, Lancashire, England
Worked in an English coal mine; taught himself to be a first class jeweler, a trade he followed in the United States when he came over in April, 1902.

Mother: Mary Ann Lysons; born July 5, 1865, Pendlebury, Lancashire, England

Brothers and Sisters: John, Charles, Walker, Martha Alice, and Ray died as infants.
7) Minnie, m. Chester C. Pulley (2) Julius Christensen
8) James Hyrum, m. Margaret Zenger
9) William Martin, died of influenza in World War I.
10) Mary Ann, m. Edmund R. Hansen
11) Sarah Ellen, m. Melvin Devey (2) Gerald Muzzell
12) Edward Lysons
13) Henry Lysons, m. Lola Manwaring
14) David Lysons, m. Aila Marsyla

Marriage: Hattie Paxman, of American Fork, Utah; born August 4, 1891 in Hatch, Idaho; married June 7, 1911; daughter of William Paxman, leader in the free school education movement, and one of the founders of American Fork band; she died December 16, 1950.
2) Irma McKeever Patch; married July 3, 1952; a widow with 5 children; graduate at BYU as a practical nurse.

Children: William P., m. Harriet Hammond; Helen, m. Dr. Willard J. Draper; James P., m. Cleo Long; Irene, died early; Thomas P., m. Elaine Erickson; Ruth, m. Howard Duncan; Beth, m. Robert F. Warnick, grandson of F. G. Warnick

Death: June 16, 1958, in Provo after extended illness.

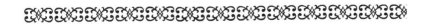

"Tommy" Martin, as he was affectionately called, was an enthusiastic dynamo. He overcame the bonds of poverty in England and worked with many handicaps in the States.

He was a very short fellow, just over five feet, and was often sensitive of his size, yet could stand beside Harrison R. Merrill (6'5" tall, weight around 300 lbs.) and thoroughly enjoy the contrast. And while we are telling of these two we'll share a bit of fun caused by their presence on the College Hall stage. I produced Van Dyke's "The House of Rimmon," a story of Naaman the Leper and when we held the two dress rehearsals Tommy, for reasons all his own, would not put on his costume, but insisted he was all right and would appear properly attired for the play. (He had the role of the enemy's emissary) Harrison, dressed in royal purple, seated on an elevated throne and wearing a towering head gear looked more of a giant than he really was, both arrogant and demanding. The servant announced the enemy's messenger who insisted on a royal audience. The script had prepared a very dramatic, tense situation. In marched the impatient messenger in soldier uniform with bared legs nearly to his crotch and a small skirt around his hips, the costume he had been given to wear, but the large circular shield he carried covered his body from neck to hips and all the audience saw was the pristine white flesh of legs and moorish darkened arms and face, appearing to them as if he were nude in two colors, and slightly bow-legged! The gasp of the audience quickly burst into loud laughter, so disconcerting Tommy that his natural high tenor voice raised even higher to a soprano command "Surrender! In the name of the King, surrender!" The entire situation was so incongruous to the mammoth King on his throne that he burst into uncontrolled laughter. With such a cue the audience outdid itself in unbridled hilarity, holding up the play for a good ten minutes with bursts of laughter punctuating the rest of the performance. Several weeks later the Faculty Quartet sang for a devotional with Tommy, T. Earl Pardoe, Franklyn Madsen and Carl F. Eyring, and as the audience more than smiled at the receding line of height, T. E. couldn't refrain from saying, "which proves the shorter the column the higher the tone," and Tommy in a good tenor responded, "Yes," looking up to them, "I'm as tall as these two, anyway," as he pointed to Frank and T. Earl. Carl the bass was nearly six feet tall. Tommy never really knew that the laughter on the night of Rimmon was not entirely because of his size, and I never told him all the real reasons. It was he himself who said, "I have a pint sized body with a million dollar ambition."

He loved to sing and would start a group song with the least provocation or invitation. His favorite song was "The Sweetest Story Ever Told," which we sang many times for personal enjoyment.

He is best remembered as a teacher. Each lesson was well prepared, logically presented, and he put it over as if it were the most important bit of truth in the world. Many days he would lecture himself into a state of fatigue, and his enthusiasm too often became emotional. Soil science was to him the most important subject in the entire curriculum. "If you don't prepare and build the soil, you can't grow good crops and if your crops fail, where are you? You have to eat to live, so, q. e. d."

He developed a mold that cured infection years before Dr. Fleming gave the world penicillin. He knew its curative power but didn't realize its commercial value.

Tommy was a vigorous debater for the BYU, keeping a stream of ideas in constant flow always surprised at the quick passing of time. This experience on the campus qualified him for charter membership in Tau Kappa Alpha, the University's first National Honor Fraternity. He also won medals in school oratory and often regretted his size as it robbed him of being a leading man in the opera. "If they won't let me sing, they'll have to hear me talk."

He was known across the United States as a leader in soil science and one of the country's most successful agronomists. Conventions featured him as a chief speaker and expert panelist. His students were sought over the nation and hold key positions to this day.

When he was appointed to the Deseret Sunday School General Board it fulfilled one of the great ambitions of his life—to teach the Gospel over the Church and bear his testimony of gratitude for his coming to America and rearing a family in a land of opportunity. For him, the harmony of science and religion was a major theme. He served the Sunday School Board for seventeen years until his health became a serious problem.

His boyhood and family life is like a story from Dickens, reserved for another's telling. A frail mother in coal country had severe difficulty in rearing her family and Thomas L. was the first of six to live beyond infancy and was six years of age before he was able to walk, the year his family joined the Church. At twelve he passed the British labor examination so he could get a job. For two years he worked in a damp coal mine and went to school at nights. The Gospel opened new vistas of life and at fourteen he came to Utah, forsook all pleasures and earned enough money to send for his parents and family. He graduated from American Fork High School, came to BYU and lived mostly on a diet of potatoes, rejoicing each day in his progress.

When he was a Junior at BYU he met and wed Hattie Paxman, daughter of two pioneer families: William Paxman, her father, was one of the founders of the free school system in Utah, and a good musician, as was her mother, Emily Abel.

Hattie was his faithful and hard working wife, helping him

417

through his University struggles, rearing their excellent family of three boys and four girls, all successful BYU graduates, except Irene who died early.

For the graduating class of 1912 at BYU T. L. was valedictorian and the proud father of his first son, William, who is now head of the Soils Department at the University of Minnesota. In this year he went to the Big Horn Academy and remained there for three years. James, who now conducts the Salinity Laboratories of the Citrus Experiment Station at Riverside, California was born there. Cornell University had long beckoned Tommy and in 1915 with a wife, two sons, and $800 he landed in Ithaca, N. Y., which ultimately honored him with a PhD. in 1919 and offered a position on the faculty. Son Thomas was born and is now agronomist as specialist with the Milk Products Company at Sunnyside, Wash. All of the Martin boys honored their father's profession and enthusiasm. The three girls took their B.S. degrees at BYU, with bio-chemistry a dominant subject.

I first met T. L. when he was principal of the Millard Academy in Hinckley, Utah, when we took a play down to their school. There I learned of his doctorate studies at Cornell, the problems of soil in Millard County, and his burning desire to return to BYU.

When President F. S. Harris came to BYU, himself an expert in Soils Science, he wished for a strong leader in agronomy and wrote his Alma Mater, Cornell, for recommendations. They unqualifiedly endorsed Thomas Lysons Martin as one of their most outstanding students. In 1921 a happy Alumnus of BYU came to the school and headed his department for thirty-seven years, becoming Dean of Applied Science, and encouraged more than a hundred men to obtain their PhD's in soils. At his death some seventy-five of these students were on the faculties of thirty-two universities.

In 1949 his students began a Thomas L. Martin Scholarship fund to assist soils students and the total has been steadily increasing, with Ezra Taft Benson as one of its most active boosters.

In 1950 the American Society of Agronomy paid Thomas L. a national tribute. He was soils expert for the Utah-Idaho Sugar Co., an active member of Sigma Xi, director in the Western Society of Soil Science, became President of the Utah Academy Science, Arts & Letters, member of the American Society of Agronomy, and the International Society of Soil Science, and wrote numerous articles for his society magazines. He was co-author of Sunday School manuals and was a popular speaker for church and community programs. He was most happy with a test tube in front of him or when he was behind the pulpit.

His wife, Hattie, was ill the last years of her life and confined to her home, dying just before Christmas of 1950. In 1952 he married a beautiful widow, Irma Patch, who was a most amiable companion, and already the mother of five children. She had graduated from BYU as a practical nurse and was again obliged to practice her profession before the death of Thomas L. on June 16, 1958.

BYU honored T. L. Martin by presenting him with the first Karl G. Maeser Distinguished Award for outstanding teaching in 1958, just ten days before his death, "a mighty mite of great ability, and unlimited enthusiasm."

The class room building of the huge new Life Science Laboratory complex is to be named as an additional honor to the world famed agronomist.

CHARLES E. MAW

Maw families for 350 years as free holders in the Isle of Axholme, Lincolnshire, and Epworth, England

Born: November 21, 1875, Plain City, Utah

Father: Abraham (Abram) b. April 10, 1837. Second Son of Edward Maw, who came to Utah in 1862; four years old when his mother, Dinah Gledhill, died. Civil War at height when Maws came to U.S. His first home in Utah was a clay dug-out in Plain City. Worked on Union Pacific Railroad (1869). Grew cotton enough to make a dress. First man in Utah known to grow sweet peas. d. January 5, 1927, at 91 years of age.

Mother: Eliza Tripp, b. March 24, 1837 in Faraby, Lincolnshire, England. Daughter of Thomas and Sarah Jane Snell Tripp. Left England with husband and two babies. Nursed both babies from breast and walked every step from Florence, Nebraska, to Salt Lake City. Her baby Mary Jane died soon after they reached Utah and was the first to be buried in Plain City Cemetery. d. November 22, 1909 at 72 of a stroke while singing in a concert given for benefit of a meeting house in Plain City.

Brothers and Sisters: Robert and Mary Jane (born in England); Dinah; Abram; John; Henry Thomas; Joseph; (Charles Edward); Florence S.; Abraham 14 and Joseph 3 died of diphtheria at the same time.

Marriage: Margaret Peterson of Deseret, Utah, June 28, 1899. b. August 9, 1874. Daughter of N. C. and Grethe Peterson. Immigrated to Utah 1877 with parents and sister Mary. To B.Y.U. at 16, graduated Normal Course. Taught five years; member of Utah's Teacher Examining Board; first woman member of Provo City Board of Education 1924-28; In "Who's Who" and International Blue Book; Became well-known author, business woman and civic worker; Organized Provo's Women's Council and B.Y.U.'s Girls' Loan Fund; President of Western Federation of Women's Clubs (12 states); Successful in having eliminated the rule which prohibited Negroes and Mormons from holding National Women's Federated Club offices at Swampscot, Mass., July, 1929. d. April 12, 1966.

Children: Carlyle E. Maw, former Editor Harvard Law Review, Attorney in New York City, residence Bronxville, New York; Marilyn M., m. B. B. Smith, Scarsdale, New York; Jean M. m. H. B. Woodman New York City, New York; Margaret M. m. E. F. Blettner, Winvetka, Ill.

Death: May 26, 1950

Charles E. Maw went to Stanford and met the great teacher, Chas. Cubberly who advised him to go into chemistry because Charles wanted less opinion and more facts.

"Pedagogy taught me how to put a lesson over."

"Can't fill students up, you have to draw them out."

1903—at B.Y.U. under Pres. Benj. Cluff, but mostly with President George Brimhall

"They gave me a small room, a bench, a few seats, some alcohol burners, a few pounds of chemicals and said 'There you are. Now teach them all you know about chemistry.' "

F. S. Harris, a chemistry student under Professor Maw, who was first to recommend Harris to Dr. Widtsoe at U.S.A.C. in Logan.

1910—M.S. at Columbia

1924—Ph.D. at Leland Stanford University, an honor student.

Students in his B.Y.U. class had insufficient number of seats and desks and had to stand through classes until a long delayed Board action gave assistance. (Got benches by donation from President A. O. Smoot of the Board who owned a lumber mill.)

On one occasion when "Tony" Lund had failed to report for the morning's assembly, President Brimhall called over to Charles E. Maw and faced the students; "It seems that a large part of our music department (Brother Lund was a huge fellow) has other duties to perform. I'm calling on one of your members to emulate the example of his illustrious father. This man's father was one of the greatest choir leaders in the Church. Let's see if his son learned any of his art. Prof. Maw will lead us."

Such was the informality of this faculty and the readiness of preparation shown by Charles Maw who surprised his audience with his musical precision. He was taught the scales and musical notations in the sand near his father's barn—"It was easy to print and cost nothing to erase and start anew."

When young Ernest Carroll told Professor Maw he wanted to teach, he was asked "Just how much? Do you know what I get per year? Eleven hundred dollars! And half of that in script, good only in American Fork. Now, do you want to teach?" (Professor Carroll became one of the leading teachers at the University of Illinois)

More than two hundred students of C. E. Maw went to all of the states in the union and some to foreign lands. Carl J. Christensen, Dean of Metallurgical Research, U. of U.; John R. Lewis, Chairman of Metallurgical Dept., U. of U.; Esmond Snell, Professor of Biochemistry; University of Wisconsin; George R. Hill, Director of Research, American Smelting and Ref.; Smith Broadbent, Professor of Chem., B.Y.U.; "Name an important college, and I'll venture a Maw trained chemist is at the head or soon will be," said one of his colleagues. Universities in California, Missouri, Pennsylvania, New York, Nebraska, Minnesota, New Mexico, Indiana, Kentucky, Illinois, to name but a few, have or had Maw trained chemists. He taught from his own texts and notes.

A scholarship to B.Y.U. known as the "Charles E. Maw Chemistry Award" was given by his family after his death as an expression of love his kin have for him.

As his life unfolded, Charles E. first thought that music would be his life's work, but a request from President Cluff changed his school plans and he took up chemistry, a subject yet to be developed. His logical and retentive mind and the ability to quote easily from the greatest books and great passages gave spice and interest to his classes, not so commonly heard today. A theorem would evoke a couplet from Shakespeare or a scene from Dickens. As Charles went to Stanford for his A.B., he received a call to go on a mission for the L.D.S. Church. He asked that the call be to California and the request was granted.

As a missionary, he organized a choir for the San Francisco L.D.S. branch and led a study group which became the Palo Alto Branch.

In 1903 at B.Y.U. one room was given Prof. Maw in which to organize a chemistry department. He and his students, with the help of B. T. Higgs, built the shelves. There was but one room for classes, laboratory and supplies, with fumes of various nature to confront a recitation in company with an experiment. A balance! What an extravagance! All majors had to be assistants to get the work done and what a training in exacting they received. The experience of running a stock supply on an impoverished budget was theirs—they built their own gas plant! "It seems each day we have to teach with less and less."

As occasion permitted, Dr. Maw went to selected men of chemical repute in the U.S., at Western Reserve, Columbia, N.Y.U., Stanford, and the University of California and was known by his colleagues as Utah's best trained chemical analyst.

When he was twenty-four he married a brilliant young teacher, Margaret Peterson, who took his principalship in Plain City while Charles studied at Stanford University. This marriage proved a blessing to each. She joined him in Palo Alto in his third year. His keen mind enabled him to pass off German, French and Latin and shorten the time of his procuring a doctor's degree, which he acquired in 1924.

The great war had opened up chemical vistas undreamed of before, and the subject became a popular academic choice. With the advent of Pres. F. S. Harris at B.Y.U. in 1921 a greater impetus was given to chemistry and B.Y.U. students were sent over the land on scholarships. It is of record that no Maw trained chemist ever failed an advanced class.

Charles was a member of Sigma Xi, the American Chemical Society, the American Academy of Advancement of Science and held numerous honors from various local and national associations. His trade journals and writings were numerous and learned, with impeccable English.

When I enrolled at Stanford University in 1903, at first I lived at the home of Dr. Swain, Prof. of Chemistry. When he learned that I was a native Utahn, he said, "I had a Utah boy in my department, a Senior of last year. One of the better graduates and one of the keenest minds I have ever met. We had hopes he would stay with us." Each of his Stanford teachers held similar opinions of him.

Charlie Maw put chemistry on a solid foundation at B.Y.U. which has been maintained through the years, a department with a national reputation. Dr. Maw was a successful, patient, exacting teacher versed in many subjects and expert in the sciences. He was one of the west's better scholars.

AMOS N. MERRILL

Born: March 15, 1875 in Richmond, Utah

Father: Marriner Wood Merrill of Sackville, New Brunswick Canada b. September 25, 1832, Sackville. Son of Nathan Merrill and Sarah Ann Reynolds. Came to Utah, September, 1853 with William Atkinson Company. Educator, traveller, legislator, contractor, apostle. Progenitor of one of the largest families in Utah, reputedly with more doctor degrees than any other American Family.
d. Feb. 6, 1906 in Richmond, Utah.

Mother: Sarah Ann Atkinson, b. September 28, 1834. Daughter of William Atkinson and Phoebe Campbell of Sackville.
m. November 11, 1853 in Salt Lake City, Utah
d. October 16, 1915.

Brothers and Sisters: Phoebe Ann, m. James R. McNeil; Marriner Wood Jr., m. Mary M. Cardon and Lucian Shephard; Thomas Hazen, m. Emma B. Olsen and Margaret W. Thompson; Alma, m. Almira E. Hendricks and Rebecca Hendricks; Rhoda Louise, m. William S. Hendricks; Clarissa; William, m. Lucy Cardon; Louis Edgar, m. Clara Hendricks; Carrie Jane; Amos Newlove, m. Eliza Drysdale.

Marriage: Eliza Lewis Drysdale of Logan, Utah. m. April 25, 1900 in Logan Temple. An accomplished oil painter, protagonist of beauty.
d. February 2, 1951 in Provo.
Josephine Coltrin Paramore, widow, April 28, 1952 in Manti Temple. She has two children, Pauline and Mary Paramore.

Children of Eliza: Amos Lyman, b. May 10, 1902; Vernon Newlove, b. October 24, 1904, m. Zella Moody; Erma Jenette, b. May 27, 1906, m. Dacosta Clark; Sarah Lucille, b. June 27, 1909, m. A. Melvin McDonald; David Marriner, b. August 12, 1912, m. Leola Green; Alton Drysdale, b. June 13, 1915, m. Dora E. Quist.

Death: July 4, 1953 in Provo, following major surgery.

Schools Attended

Public schools of Richmond, Utah; Brigham Young College in Logan, Utah; Utah Agricultural College, B.S. 1896, attended U.S.A.C. one year after graduation; University of Illinois, 1906-08, M.S., 1908; University of Chicago, 1922-23, studied in education; Stanford University, 1925-26, Ph.D. degree, Thesis "Objective Basis for Materials for course of Botany in Secondary Schools"; Cultural trips with family during summers of 1930-35, U.S. and Canada.

Church Positions and Missions

Mission to England, 1897-1900, 30 months; President of Liverpool Conference for about 15 months; Presidency of Sunday School in Benson Stake; In bishopric, Logan Second Ward, 1906-09; Bishopric Provo Fifth Ward, 1911-1918; Presidency of Utah Stake, 1911-1919; High Councilman Utah Stake 1919-1938; Patriarch of Utah Stake, 1938-1953.

Positions Held

With Cache Valley Dairy Co., 1900-1901; Taught grade schools Richmond, Utah, 1900-1902; Mechanic arts instructor, B.Y. College, 1902-1907. One of the first mechanic arts departments in Utah; Agriculture and Biology instructor 1908-1909 (B.Y. College).

At Brigham Young University

Head of Dept. of Agriculture 1909-1922; professor; Principal of B.Y.U. High School, 1912-1915; Professor of Vocational Education or Secondary Education, 1922- ; Dean of Church Teachers College, 1914-1922; Professor of Secondary Education and Supervisor of Secondary training school, 1924-29; Acting Dean of the College of Education, 1929-1931; Dean 1939-1945; Second Councilor in Presidency of B.Y.U. 1915-1921; Professor emeritus of secondary education, 1945-1953; Petition Committee, 1923-30, Also aiding graduate employment, 1930-37; Organized Farmers and Housekeepers Conference in Provo; Organized Agriculture and livestock exhibits at fairs in Provo; Chairman of faculty Y Day activity, Also administrative council, 1919-20.

Other Educational Activities

Taught Summer School in Mexico, 1927; Visiting professor at U. of Maine, 1940; On Logan City Board of Education (about 1909); On Provo Board of Education, elected first in 1926. President in 1931, 1941, 1946, 1951. On the Board 1926-31, 1936-53.

Miscellaneous Activities

Owned and built homes in Logan and Provo. Had Orchard on Provo Bench which he worked during the summer. Belonged to Utah Academy of Arts and Letter, Phi Delta Kappa, U.E.A. President 1929. Author of articles on Botany and agriculture: books, *Balance Wheels, Mormon Way of Life,* and *Improved Teaching* (German translation made in 1936)

Amos Newlove Merrill gave his life to his church and education. The youngest child of ten children, reared in a virgin territory with pioneer problems, he early learned the rigors of the farm, gathering of winter wood, working early and late until he went to Logan and college. His devotion to soil products fashioned his early life. He was self taught in agricultural science.

His father was dynamic, hard working, alert, and exacting in all his duties. Work was laid out for all his children of several wives and each day's assignments were critically checked, praised or condemned as merit or lack of it demanded. Amos was usually in the acceptable column and often given extra work as proficiency increased. When Amos came to Utah Valley and bought a farm on the "East Bench," nor Orem, his rows were straight and weeded, ditches cleaned, with well built head-gates. Berries, fruits and grains supplied a growing family and amplified the resources of an underpaid school teacher. His fruits won prizes and graced many choice tables. He was generous with his produce, giving away to the less fortunate as much as he sold or took home to his table. "You can keep boys close to you when you have a good farm. And you learn habits of conduct that carry over in all walks of life." Amos never wore overalls at work, carried a brush to keep his clothes clean. Tools were kept in planned locations, covered to protect them from weather and always ready for use.

These habits in work reflected in his teaching and in his speaking. Each lesson was methodically planned with time for class elaboration. His speech was precise without being pedantic and his voice revealed a man of sincerity, conviction and audience awareness. It was always a pleasure to hear him unfold an idea with a most apt and select vocabulary; he was understood in a small faculty room in the Education Building or in the greater expanse of the Provo Tabernacle.

He presided with quiet authority, put others around him at ease and was especially considerate of beginners. As president of the Provo Board of Education, of the Utah Educational Association, in the Utah Stake Presidency, as a counselor to President George H. Brimhall at BYU or in a farm group session or a home economics gathering, his smile radiated interest and personal efficiency; he was prepared with his subject, he knew the abilities of his associates.

Amos N. Merrill was an educator's teacher, having those qualities which inspire trust and confidence. His students seldom failed his classes as he spent untold hours in bringing them to a desire to study or find the errors of their failures. His advice was frequently sought and honored.

An example of his concern for students is shown when he observed some of the girls graduating from High School wore dresses of most elaborate design and beauty, costing over a hundred dollars while others were obliged to wear simple frocks of inexpensive materials, often hand made. As president of the Board of Education, he advocated a uniform gown to wear over school clothing, giving the group a beautiful appearance with no inequality. The practice caught on and soon went over the state.

Professor Merrill was a patron of the arts, enthusiastic for clean sports, honored authority and shared his own leadership. In his spare time he wrote three interesting books, counseled hundreds of students, generously shared his farm produce, was active in community, education, soil science, church and politics, and was an admired citizen and educational leader; a loyal Son of Brigham.

ALBERT MILLER

Correct name—Ernst Ludwig Adelbert Müller or Moeller

Born: July 13, 1875 **Place:** Grossvargula, bei Erfurt, Thruing, Pruessen, Germany

Father: Carl Friedrich Müller, tradesman
b. September 30, 1823; d. April 8, 1894

Mother: Johanna Louise Henrietta Wald
b. April 25, 1835; d. May 22, 1890

Brothers and Sisters: Carl Ernst, Christina Bertha, (Albert)

Marriage: Emma Elsa Miller (same family name as husband)
Jan. 2, 1901 in Salt Lake Temple by President John R. Winder. Nine other couples were married that day, among them President David O. McKay and Emma Ray Riggs and Francis W. Kirkham and Martha Alzina Robison

Children: Hilda Elsa Miller, b. Jan. 21, 1902, Provo, m. James B. Harvey
Karl Albert, b. Oct. 3, 1903, Provo, m. Frances Augusta Crocheron, B.Y.U. employee for over 30 years
Alberta Miller, b. May 6, 1906, Provo, m. Peter Edwards

Death: Jan. 31, 1906 in Provo, Utah at age of 30

When music was at its German ascendant and every town had its orchestra and opera house young Albert Miller followed the trend of the day, was tested for ear accuracy and rhythmic sense and found capable. He studied piano, violin and the horn and much of his time was devoted to practice. The town of Vargula had an exceptional band and Albert early planned to march down the Strasse in a bright uniform. His strict parents kept him at practice until he was fourteen. He helped his father until he was eighteen when he joined the German Army to advance his music and take a formal education. For three years he was in the music division as a trumpeter and violinist, stationed at Erlangen, Bavaria. Summer concerts took him to many famous spas and beach resorts, and the strict military discipline became a part of his daily life for the years to come.

At twenty-one, he procured a position with the court band and orchestra in Dresden, Saxony, where none but the best musicians were employed and lived in sumptuous barracks. He met and became acquainted with some of the world's best music leaders. While in Dresden he heard the Mormon missionaries and on April 26, 1898, was baptized in the River Elbe by Elder Francis Salzner, the same place where Karl G. Maeser and Edward Schoenfeld had been immersed forty-three years previous.

In December of 1899, Albert emigrated from Hamburg, Germany to Utah and Lehi, where he stayed in the home of George and Mary Ann Ward, the parents of Mrs. Francis Salzner, the wife of the baptizing Elder. His musicianship was soon made apparent in Lehi both in Church and community, as he soon organized the "Silver Band" of some twenty-five men and their excellence became known over the territory. Prof. Anthony C. Lund of B.Y.U. and Sam Jepperson of the Provo Band went over to Lehi to hear Professor Miller play the violin and the trumpet. They were amazed and immediately offered work for him should he come to Provo. A formal invitation followed within a week. A concert was billed for College Hall and was a decided "hit," in fact it received an ovation. After the concert, eleven students asked for private lessons. He was also invited to remain and assist in teaching at the Academy.

This made it possible for his marriage and in January 1901, he wed Elsa Miller (no previous relation). His title at B.Y.U. was assistant Professor of Music, conductor of band and orchestra. Five pupils constituted his first class. By 1905-06 it became necessary to organize and add a fourth band, which he called "The Concert Band." This gave him four bands, an orchestra, a class in religion, a weekly trip to Salt Lake City to play in the Salt Lake Symphony Orchestra, under the direction of the late Arthur Shepherd, and private students to teach. Like most well trained German music teachers, his admonition was "There is no clock in music; practice until you get the results you wish."

Professor Miller, a well-trained solidly based musician, was beginning to compose at the time of his death. An earnest and strict teacher, he tolerated no laziness or procrastination—his rebukes were always followed by smiles and sympathy. His sudden death at age thirty was felt as a community disaster. The school flag hung at half mast and tributes came from musicians throughout the West.

His students who achieved numbered in the many dozens, among them Sam Jepperson, one of the great band leaders of the West, John Sonderegger, first clarinetist in the Boston Symphony, Clarence J. Hawkins, director of bands in Salt Lake City and the University of Utah, Kenneth J. Bird, teacher and music supervisor in the Alpine School District, Ralph Booth, concert violinist at B.Y.U., Utah and California, William McAllister, Chairman of the Dixie College Music Department and David Gourley, leader in music and later well-known educator in Utah's public schools to name but a few. The B.Y.U. band has maintained the excellence given it in its founding years by a talented German immigrant and convert, Albert Miller. A thesis on the life of Albert Miller by Richard W. Robison was accepted by the B.Y.U. Music Department on June 1, 1942. It revealed the affection of the faculty and studentbody for its musical leader cut off by untimely death from a most promising career as composer and director.

JOSEPH KELLY NICHOLES

Born: October 10, 1887   **Place:** American Fork, Utah
                                                    born in a log cabin

Father: Joseph Nicholes, son of Josiah and Ann Marsh of Isle of
Jersey
b. April 23, 1861 in American Fork
d. October 8, 1941, well known banjo player

Mother: Eleanor Kelly, daughter of William and Kirsten Brudahl
Kelly; b. May 31, 1866—had five brothers and four sisters; Dr. P. M. Kelly, Walter, Nora S. Stubbs survived her
m. May 7, 1886 in American Fork
Well-known primary teacher and D.U.P. organizer; expert seamstress; d. December 23, 1959 at 93 in American
Fork, Utah

Brothers
and Sisters: (Joseph K.)
Ray D., m. Fern Scott
Elmarian H., m. Eldocia Brown
Victor W., m. Norma Jones
F. Rulon, m. 1.) Ethel Parker and 2.) June Fjeld

Marriage: Olive Maiben
daughter of Henry Joseph and Louise Evelyn Harrison,
both from England (father of Olive was the son of Henry
Maiben—a McBain in Scotland)
m. June 25, 1912, poetess and gifted artist

Children: Dr. Henry J., m. Hildegarde Polster of Vienna, Austria
Dr. Eleanor Louise
Max M., m. Mary Kane
Ruth, m. Prof. Martin L. Miller of B.Y.U.
Virginia Kirsten, m. Virgil H. Stucki
Elizabeth Jeane, m. G. Carlos Blain
Margaret Ann, m. Glenn Otterstrom
Mary Joyce, m. H. Hugh Woodbury
Dr. Karl Ray Kelly, m. Velyn Washburn
(all children attended B.Y.U.)

Death: Sunday, October 4, 1964 at the age of 77

Joseph Kelly Nicholes will long be remembered as a teacher and parent; his three centers of activity were his home, his classroom, and his Church. He successfully met the struggle of saving Dixie College and was the chief salesman of the transfer to the state when the L.D.S. Church could no longer operate the school. He was a director in the St. George Chamber of Commerce, president of the Stake and president of the college at the same time and spent most of his time and whole efforts in keeping the college alive, putting it on a foundation for future growth that bespeaks his ability as a business man and organizer.

As his family of brilliant children grew he saw the necessity of a larger college environment and moved to Provo. There he lived less in civic and commercial activities and devoted his life to the classroom, the Church and home. Many faculty members and colleagues over the years have repeated what most of us at B.Y.U. know, that "Joe" was one of the most devoted and respected teachers the great institution ever had. His children were leaders in student body life, excelled in their various majors and added stature to his family name. His talented wife, Olive, many times was given public recognition for paintings and writings.

Chemistry, usually a challenging subject to most pupils, was made understandable by this master teacher and most generous friend. He had the time for any anxious or inquiring student; "I'm never too busy." B.Y.U. has been blessed with outstanding leaders and teachers; Joseph K. Nicholes must be remembered as one of the best.

A brief of his activities follows:

Education:

    1904-08—Commercial Diploma, B.Y.U.

    1914-16—A.B.—B.Y.U.

    1923-24—M.A., Stanford University

    1933, 34, and 36—summers at University of Utah and Stanford University

    1961—Honorary D.Sc., B.Y.U.

Occupational:

    Teacher, Dixie College, St. George, 1912-33

    President Dixie College, 1919-23, 27-33

    Teacher—B.Y.A. Chemistry 1933-61; chairman of department 1945-55

    Distinguished Service Award, B.Y.U. Alumni Association, 1956

    Karl G. Maeser Distinguished Teaching Award, 1959

Church:

    Officer in all L.D.S. Auxiliary organizations

    Priesthood—Advanced in sequential rank to High Priest

    Mission to Denmark 1909-12; he earned the money for same by working in the mines in Eureka, Utah

Secretary in charge of emigration to U.S. and Canada, 1910-12
Member of the General Sunday School Board for 8 years 1938-46
President St. George Stake 1925-31
Utah Stake Superintendent of Sunday School
Civic and Social—Honorary Affiliations:
President St. George Building Society—12 years
Chairman of Dixie Chamber of Commerce
American Chemical Society
Annual "Utah Award" American Chemical Society, 1960
Sigma Xi member; member Utah Academy Science, Arts and Letters
Government B.Y.U. Liaison officer with ASROTC on campus, World War II
Inspector for the San Francisco ordnance in Utah County, World War II
Author—two freshman chemistry journals

Joseph K. was a most deliberate thinker and speaker. He was not bothered by time; "We have all there is but the present is the most precious. Yesterday I've had but tomorrow may never come for me. So, let's understand this problem now." He had a sweet patience for every student and acquaintance and his expressed conclusions were built on facts as he understood them.

I always felt a spirit of peace in his presence.

LEONARD JOHN NUTTALL II

Born: July 6, 1887 in Salt Lake City, Utah

Father: L. John Nuttall Jr., son of L. John and T. Elizabeth Clarkson. b. December 5, 1859 in Provo; m. March 11, 1880 in St. George Temple. Leader of Provo Tabernacle Choir several years. Served two missions and last years in St. George and Salt Lake Temples.

Mother: Christina Little second daughter of James A. and Annie M. Baldwin Little of Kanab, Utah. b. January 12, 1863. At B.Y.A. 1884-1885. d. March 7, 1918 on her 38th wedding anniversary.

Brothers and Sisters: Elizabeth Annie, b. Oct. 19, 1822 m. John D. Baker
Josephine, d. as infant
(Leonard John)
Christina, b. Nov. 21, 1888, m. Parley W. Madsen (father of Archie)
Ethel, b. May 19, 1890, m. Oro H. Moore
James A., b. Aug. 4, 1892, m. Leona Bunnell
Vernon Malcolm, b. Nov. 28, 1893, m. Minnie Dowling
Velma, b. Dec. 12, 1894, m. George B. Glade
William B.
Rulon, b. Dec. 20, 1900, m. Bernice Hayles
Clarissa, b. July 28, 1902, m. Howard Cordaer
Maurice, b. Dec. 19, 1904, m. Margaret Lyons
Hazel, b. Oct. 12, 1907, m. John West

Marriage: Fanny Burns of Pima, Arizona. m. November 1, 1911. Instructor in Domestic Science at BYU 1911-12.

Children: Drayton B., Education Director, Professor of Education Administration, BYU 1960-62, d. Dec. 13, 1962, Lyal; Ralph Leslie, Captain in Italy when father died (1944); Doris; Herbert Vernon, Capt. at time of father's death; H. Wendell, Corporal in Army; Leonard John III; Richard; Jerry A.; Ned A.; Barbara; Janet; Eleven alive—all with degrees.

Death: April 18, 1944 at 57. Heart attack at his home.

L. John Nuttall II had a reverent respect for his illustrious grandfather, for whom he was named, a man who was private secretary for President John Taylor and with him during his last days of self "exile" and at the time of his death and who also served Wilford Woodruff as his private secretary. He was property agent for the Church and many valuable parcels of land were transferred to his name, revealing the trust church officials had in him. Served a mission to Great Britain with John Henry Smith. In Provo, President Nuttall was a city councilman, recorder and auditor. He was probate and county clerk in Utah County for ten years, moving to Provo to educate his larger family. He did the first printing done in Provo or Utah County on his own printing press. Served as regent for the University of Deseret. Young John's life was greatly affected by his grandfather and parents who lived closely to President Nuttall and honored his example.

Young John had his early schooling and High School work at Pleasant Grove. He took a BS and MA at Columbia University, 1911 and 1912, a Ph.D. from Columbia in 1929. He was critic teacher at the Brigham Young Training School from 1908-12, a High School teacher at Payson 1912-1915, principal at Spanish Fork for a year and was elected Superintendant of Schools for Iron County 1916-19. The Nebo School District hired him as their superintendent, 1919-1922.

One of his major ambitions was consummated when he was appointed Dean of the College of Education at Brigham Young University in 1922 and served until 1930, also with the title of Professor of Educational Administration. The department was re-organized under his direction. In the absence of President Harris, L. John was appointed acting President of Brigham Young University for 1926-1927.

With his doctorate back of him, he accepted a bid for his services from the University of Utah and was given the title of Professor of Elementary Education and Director of the Stewart Training School connected with the University. His stay at the University lasted but two years, 1930-32, when he achieved the goal of his teaching career, to become Superintendent of the Salt Lake City Schools which he directed from 1932 until his untimely death in 1944.

Education was the dominant motivation of his life. As Superintendent he was a frequent visitor to each of the schools in his jurisdiction, asked advice from the respective principals and had periodic interchanges of ideas for stopping delinquency before it gained too strong a foothold in the student. Interviews with parents consumed much of his time. He was a strong protagonist for the Parent Teachers Association.

Superintendent Nuttall was president of the Utah Education

Association, 1922-1923, and seldom missed an opportunity to encourage membership and participation. He was the State director of the National Education Association and an active member of National Study for Study of Education. He was chairman of the Appraisal Committee of American Association of School Administrators, a division of N.E.A. in 1937. From 1940-44 he was vice chairman of the Salt Lake Youth Council and interested service clubs in its purpose and functions.

The eulogies at his funeral accounted him one of the West's outstanding educators.

ALFRED OSMOND

Born: Oct. 5, 1862   **Place:** Willard, Utah

Father: George Osmond, born May 23, 1836 in London, England Heard Gospel at fifteen, came to New Orleans at eighteen. Early colonizer of Bear Lake country. Stayed with Anson Call at Bountiful. Later moved to Willard. Taught in Logan in winters. Bishopric of Bloomington, Idaho, for a number of years. Counselor to President Budge; two missions to England. 1892 called to Star Valley as Stake President. Died in Afton, Wyoming, March 25, 1913.

Mother: Georgiana Huckvale, married in St. Louis, 1855.
Born in Oxford, England.
Died March 14, 1922 in Bloomington, Idaho. They crossed the plains together.

Brothers and Sisters: Anson (fell from barn to death, 1905).
(Alfred)
Rosabelle, m. William J. Starkey
Ira (remained single)
Ida, m. Oliver C. Dunford
Ella, m. Louis Newman
Nellie, m. Eugene Hart
Alice, m. Forest Reed

Marriage: 1) Frances Nelson, married 1887. She died one week after daughter, Pearl (who died four months later), was born.
2) Annie Lloyd
Born September 8, 1869
Married June 16, 1897 after a 6-year engagement.
Taught school 34 years to help her children with their education.

Died Aug. 2, 1961 at 92.

Children: Wendell, m. Erma Christensen
Harvard, m. Melba Condie, d. October, 1967
Marcia, m. John R. Bourne
Nan, m. Harry Grass (on B.Y.U. faculty)
Waldo, m. Miriam Lillywhite
Constance, m. Merrill J. Bunnell (deceased)
Irene, m. William E. Spears (on B.Y.U. faculty)

All attended B.Y.U. and five graduated

Death: April 1, 1938 in Logan, Utah of a heart attack at age of 76.

Alfred Osmond was a large man with laughing blue eyes which roguishly danced when he was telling a good story or a personal joke. He almost talked with his fluent hands. Especially were his body and arms active when he interpreted Shakespeare, as he had studied with some of the nation's best dramatic teachers who taught "systems" in mimetic action and believed gesture to be the important phase of any character portrayal. "Conspicuous gesture" it was named by its critics. He was highly commended by his teachers, Trueblood of Michigan, Blanchard of Chicago, Kittredge of Harvard, and Brander Mathews of Columbia. The latter two were "book" interpreters, doing most of their work with the voice. With this background, Alfred harmonized principles and became a very popular interpreter of classic literature. His classes often were entertained by his renditions. Who will ever forget "The Cataract of Ladore" once they had heard him recite it? He gave more than a hundred Shakespeare recitals in Utah schools.

As he grew older he turned more to rustic verse and nature stories, enthusiastically reading James Whitcomb Riley, Mark Twain, and Artemis Ward. Just before he retired from B.Y.U. he stated that he could still recall most of *Hamlet, Julius Caeser, Othello* and *Macbeth* but he would rather write rural rhymes for farm folk. "Anybody can understand Will Rogers."

Always a nature lover, he was fascinated by the woods, the lake and our great mountains. He was an expert fisherman and had a camp on the Strawberry Reservoir, owning his own motor boat. Summer was a real vacation for him, a time to fish, read and write. For this time of the year, he would have his hair shaved off to the great disapproval of his meticulous wife and lovely daughters. He was a perfect gentleman in society and school and entirely relaxed in a camping outfit. Enlivened by examples from great literature and exciting experiences from his travelled life, his classes were never dull nor lacking in apt illustration. He inspired students "to travel the roads which lead to great thoughts and great events."

He had a very amusing eccentricity which delighted me; when he met an Eastern visitor on the campus he slipped into a definite Harvard (Hahvad) dialect, a polite way of sharing his eastern education.

When trouble arose involving a student he was usually on the side of the fellow in school. "After all, he's only a boy." His own boyhood pranks must have been legion, as he could invariably pull an example out of his experience hat. As one of his majors remarked, "He is so well read and so human."

His philosophy of life could be summed up, "It is better to smile than to frown." His wife, Annie, whom he adored, was often tested to a breaking point of patience when he failed to return from a fishing

438

trip per schedule. "He's the hardest man to get mad at of anybody I ever knew," she said. If he were unusually tardy, say for a few days, he would come to the doorstep, throw his hat into the kitchen and await the response. "Silence is the worst punishment."

I could relate dozens of stories which reveal the almost pixy character of Alf Osmond. In many ways he really never grew up. As his wife related, "I never could tell what he would do next. But whatever it was, he never meant to hurt anybody." His imagination was almost boundless which gave him the ability of making scenes in plays "come to life."

He was an opportunist. A story will point just how. One spring when we held all of our classes on the lower campus, the rain often came in torrential volume. I had a very large expensive umbrella and hung it just outside the door of the Little Theatre, where I taught and held many of my classes. There were other umbrellas and coats hung along the hall racks. Near noon, I looked out the window and saw it was again raining heavily. I put on my rubbers, went out to the door and reached for my umbrella. It was gone! I had heard men's voices near the doorway just before the bell rang and I made a mental accusation of the possible pilferer. At faculty meeting that afternoon, I asked President Brimhall if I could make an announcement. Granted. I arose and half in earnest, said, "This morning I hung my umbrella on the hook just outside the Little Theatre and by noontime it had disappeared. I have reason to believe it was taken by a faculty member. I'll leave the door ajar and whoever you are you may leave the umbrella just inside the door. I'll say 'Thanks' now as I'd rather not know who the person is." President Brimhall flipped his glasses over his eyes, looked over the faculty and said, "I'm sure no faculty member has taken your umbrella. But, if he has, he will have it back, with apologies, by tomorrow." The next morning I went down early, left the door ajar and went up to my desk back of the plush curtains on the stage. I heard someone step through the door, remain a second and leave. A few minutes later, I heard a similar visitation but refrained from opening the curtains. It was getting close to class time when I arose and gave vent to a vigorous sneeze. The door flew open and an umbrella fell into the room. I opened the curtains and there was Professor Osmond frozen like a statue. He tried to say something, sputtering, but could only point to the umbrella on the floor. Then, I began laughing. Slowly, he unfroze and began laughing with me. "You see, my umbrella was gone and I—well I took the first one I saw, and I, well, . . . " He was babbling broken ideas when I pointed to the corner close to the door. There were *three* other umbrellas leaning against the wall. We became close pals after this.

A brief summary of a most interesting fellow is given herewith:

At thirteen he had read all of Shakespeare's plays and began memorizing major selections. He was seldom seen without a book in his hand.

He graduated from the University of Deseret in the Normal Department and went to Bloomington, Idaho, to teach an ungraded school in a meeting house.

In 1887 he married a comely lass, Frances Nelson, and a year later went to Ann Arbor, Michigan with Charles Hart to study law. In December of this year his daughter Pearl was born, and in a week's time his wife had died. The frail little baby followed the mother within four months. With this experience and conditions attending therewith, he lost interest in law and decided to become a teacher of English with emphasis in dramatic arts. There were no speech departments in his day.

In 1893 he accepted a call to an L.D.S. mission to Canada. He loved people of all classes and overcame much prejudice in his contacts.

Returning from the mission he devoted his winters to arduous study of the classics. Part of each day he devoted to memorization. His greatest ambition was to play Macbeth and Hamlet. He would enact a scene with the slightest invitation.

He married a beautiful young lady, Annie Lloyd, after six years of courting. She doubted his ability to be serious long enough for marriage but he convinced her that he had his many sober moments. Returning to Bloomington he became probate judge and county superintendent of schools. By 1903 he acquired an A.B. degree from Harvard University, one of the first mountaineers to receive this English major diploma. His guiding professor was famed Dr. Lyman Kittredge. With this credential he came to B.Y.U. and motivated a growing department. He was head of the English Department at B.Y.U. from 1905 to 1933 and was as much an actor as a teacher in his classes, entertaining as much as he taught. His mind was restless and ever searching.

The first few times we met, he asked me what I got out of this or that selection; how I would interpret the character of Malvolio or Puck, etc.? He had good reasons for all of his own interpretations and was very consistent in his enactments. He prized his M.A. from Columbia received in 1920, a year which helped him to see some of the world's great performers on the New York stage.

From his cabin in "Wildwood" in the North Fork of the Provo Canyon (which he named) he would make sorties to distant canyons and fishing holes. On Sunday afternoons he would entertain other campers with a Shakespeare, Tennyson or Bible program. From the quiet canyon retreat of his camp on the Strawberry Reservoir, he would write his poetry or articles. His best known books are *The Exiles* (1926), *My Philosophy of Life* (1927), *Happy Humorist* (1932), and *Married Sweethearts*. *Lyrics of Life of Love*, a posthumous book, was edited by his daughter, Irene.

He not only excelled in fishing, but was a state champion in pitching horsehoes and won medals at the Utah State Fair. He learned to drive a car and type after he was 65 years of age. He often walked from his Wildwood cabin to Aspen Grove for his 7:00 A. M. summer school class and was back in time for breakfast—truly a task for the best athlete.

When some friends apologized for not calling to see him when he was ill, he remarked "I wasn't on exhibition."

He was an unusual teacher and an enthusiastic actor. His students learned about Shakespeare and English but better, they carried away a strong love of the best literature and a desire to learn more. He taught application as well as appreciation. He was a unique character in B.Y.U. history.

ERNEST DeALTON PARTRIDGE

Born: November 1906 in Provo, Utah.

Father: Ernest DeAlton Partridge
born June 13, 1869 in Fillmore, Utah
died May 28, 1923, in a train wreck east of Price, Utah.
Valedictorian of his college senior class—BYU professor.
Bishop of Fourth Ward in Provo many years.
Laid out "Block Y" on east mountain.
Paternal grandfather, Edward, first Presiding Bishop of the Church
Maternal grandfather, Wm. Clayton, author, "Come, Come Ye Saints"

Mother: Elizabeth Truman, daughter of Abram Kordite and Gertrude Harrison Truman.
Born January 23, 1872, in Lansing, Michigan.
Attended Michigan Agricultural College (Michigan State)
Married August 16, 1896 in Lansing; later solemnized in Salt Lake Temple.
Died Mar. 19, 1966 at 94

Brothers and Sisters: Ruth Louise—BYU graduate 1930—Author of prize novel. Registered nurse.
Truman—married Louise Engar, BYU graduate 1926. (De Alton)
Gertrude—married Joseph F. Deane, M.A. Columbia Univ.
Lyman Maurice BYU (1935) married Louise Richards, BYU, 1938.

Marriage: Nell Clark. daughter of Amasa L. and Susie Duncan Clark.
Graduate BYU 1924; Camp leader for New Jersey schools.

Children: Robert Truman, Ernest De Alton Jr., Lyman Clark.

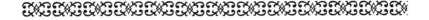

Dr. E. DeAlton Partridge became President of Montclair State College in 1951. A member of the faculty of the college since 1937, he served as Dean of Instruction for four years prior to his appointment as President.

During the administration of Dr. Partridge, Montclair State College has more than doubled the undergraduate enrollment and expanded the physical plant greatly. Today there are ten new buildings on campus which have been planned and erected since 1951.

Majoring in psychology for his doctorate, Dr. Partridge has written extensively in the field of adolescent psychology and child guidance.

During recent years, Dr. Partridge has been active in the field of audiovisual teaching aids. He inaugurated the extensive visual education program of the Boy Scouts of America and was director of a number of successful motion pictures produced by this organization. More recently, he has been active in educational television. As chairman of the Committee on Television for the American Association of Colleges for Teacher Education, he was instrumental in launching Continental Classroom, the first network course for college credit. This series of courses has proved to be unusually successful. At present he is vice chairman of Learning Resources Institute, an organization which produces network courses for college credit.

Dr. Partridge received his A.B. degree from Brigham Young University in Provo, Utah, and his Ph.D. from Columbia University Teachers College. He has been a trustee of the Montclair Art Museum. Currently he is a member of the National Personnel Committee and of the National Council of the Boy Scouts of America. In addition, he has been vice chairman of the National Board of the Camp Fire Girls and for a number of years was on the National Boy Scouts' staff as Director of Research and Program Development. He is educational consultant to Coronet Films.

During World War II, Dr. Patridge served with the U.S. Navy as a lieutenant commander in the Aviation Psychology Branch of the Bureau of Medicine and Surgery. Included among his publications are *Time Out For Living,* which he co-authored with Catherine Mooney, *Social Psychology of Adolescence, Leadership Among Adolescent Boys,* and several sections of *Encyclopedia of Child Guidance.*

Dr. Partridge has three sons. He resides in Upper Montclair, N.J.

A son of illustrious pioneer parents; whose father was a descendant of the first bishop of the Church, an eminent athlete and scholar and a professor at B.Y.U., and whose mother was a Presbyterian who went to Michigan State College, met the handsome athlete and school valedictorian, was converted and married him. They came to Provo and reared a family of three sons and two daughters.

Ernest DeAlton Partridge was named for his father, was

educated under the old bell tower and knew the plays of College Hall. He married a schoolmate, Nell Clark, daughter of Emeritus officer, Amasa L. Clark. The Partridges have been a teaching-recreation team since marriage, both nationally known for their out-door camping leadership.

DeAlton is an author, popular lecturer, Boy Scout Executive, audio-visual techniques expert, educator, and innovator in education.

His books, *Time Out For Living, Social Psychology of Adolescence*, and *Leadership Among Adolescent Boys* have national accrediting and usage. He has written for the *Encyclopedia of Child Guidance* and was director of research for the National Boy Scouts of America and a member of the National Council.

As former president of the Montclair (N.J.) State College, he is billed for many speaking engagements in the more important educational centers. The New Jersey college recently bestowed two honors on their immediate past president, the naming of the new classroom building for him and granted him the position of President Emeritus. Presently, he is president of the Near East Foundation, with educational programs in Iran, Jordan, Lebanon, Iraq, Kuwait, Egypt and other countries.

The Partridges have a summer home in Heber Valley, Utah.

ANDREW THEODORE RASMUSSEN

Born: August 10, 1883 in Spring City, Utah

Father: Andreas Thustrup Rasmussen, descendant of long line of Danish blacksmiths. Born July 23, 1849 in Viby, Lolaand, Denmark. Married Hanne Jensen in 1875; came to Utah in 1877.
d. September 3, 1915 at Spring City, Utah

Mother: Hanne Jensen, b. May 1, 1852 in Skovhuse, Denmark. d. September 9, 1912 in Spring City, Utah.

Brothers and Sisters: Christian Waldemar Rasmussen, b. March 8, 1876 in Natskov, Lolaand, Denmark. Married Sorine Sorensen in Spring City, Utah. Died August 6, 1933, they had 12 children; Thora Magrete Rasmussen, b. March 21, 1878 in Spring City, Utah, d. March, 1882; Olga Matilda Rasmussen, b. February 6, 1887, m. Peter Frandsen June 16, 1909, d. cir. 1914.

Marriage: Gertrude Brown, b. February 2, 1886, daughter of Prof. James Lehi Brown and Ella Larson. Married 1911, while husband was head of Department of Biology at B.Y.U. d. February 9, 1967.

Children: Theodore Brown Rasmussen, b. April 28, 1910 in Provo, Utah, m. Catherine Cora Archibald, December 18, 1947 at Moncton, New Brunswick, Canada. Chief of the Department of Neurosurgery in the Medical School of McGill University at Montreal, Canada; Waldemar Curtis Rasmussen, b. February 5, 1912 in Provo, Utah, married Jean Domke on September 12, 1942 at Colorado Springs, Colorado, Staff member of the Mayo Clinic, Rochester, Minn., d. June 11, 1958 at Colorado Springs, Colorado; Richard Carl Rasmussen, b. May 17, 1918 at Minneapolis, Minnesota, m. Marilyn Hise February 9, 1942 at San Francisco, California; Charlotte Rasmussen, b. February 18, 1922 at Minneapolis, Minnesota, m. Dr. Walter Lusk Roberts on January 24, 1945 at Los Angeles, California.

Death: October 15, 1955 at LaCanada, California of coronary thrombosis.

Worked way through school and college—BYU. Student Body president two terms. Member of debating team and starred on the track. AB—BYU in 1909; Instructor of biology BYU 1909-1911; Assistant Professor two years; Head Department Biology 1911-1913; 1913-1916, Instructor and graduate student of Physiology, Cornell University; Ph.D, Physiology and anatomy 1916; 1916, University of Minnesota, Instructor in neurology and anatomy under Dr. C. M. Jackson; 1918, Assistant Professor at University of Minnesota; Associate Professor 1919; 1925, Full Professor at University of Minnesota.

He would often go to the lab at four a.m. and work fifteen hours; Chief examiner Medical School of Minnesota; wrote popular texts, *Laboratory Directions in Neuro-Anatomy, Outlines of Neuro-Anatomy,* 8th printing of 3rd edition 1931; *The Principal Nervous Pathways,* 4th edition 1932, also 100 articles on scientific and medical journals. He was a medical artist—many illustrations; ". . . as a teacher, he was unsurpassed." His teaching demonstrations collected consisted of some 500 specimens, the finest and most constructive ever produced.

Distinguished Service Award, 78th Annual Commencement BYU 1935; Retired June, 1952, demanded by other universities; was visiting professor at University of Southern California, to whom he donated all his drawings; Visiting Professor, Department of Investigation of Medicine, UCLA, held position until death. Expert in brain dissections; lauded for this the world over. Later books, *Atlas of Cross Section of the Brain* 1951; *Handbook of Neurology* 1952, used internationally.

Member: A.A.A.S.: American Association of Anatomists; Member executive committee 1934-38; Vice President 1948-50; American Physiology Society; Association for the Study Internal Secretions v.p., 1923-36; Society for Experimental Biology and Medicine; Sigma Xi.

Written up in *The National Cyclopedia of American Biography; Who's Who in American Education,* 1932-38; *Who's Who in America,* 1897-1947; *American Men of Science* with asterisk in 6th edition.

The resolution adopted by the University of Minnesota is a biographical tribute, which merits sharing with you:

The following resolution was unanimously adopted by a rising vote of the University Senate at its meeting February 2, 1956.

ANDREW T. RASMUSSEN
1883-1955

Andrew T. Rasmussen died at his home, 4636 Indianola Way, LaCanada, California, on the evening of October 15, 1955. He was born in Spring City, Utah, August 10, 1883, from a long line of Danish blacksmiths. He worked to earn his way through high school and college.

After receiving the degree of bachelor of arts from Brigham Young University in 1909, he became assistant professor and two years later, head of the Department of Biology. From 1913 to 1916, he was instructor, and graduate student in the Department of Physiology, Cornell University, receiving the degree of doctor of philosophy in physiology and anatomy in 1916. His professors at Cornell considered him the best student they had ever taught.

In the fall of 1916, he became an instructor in anatomy at the University of Minnesota under the headship of C. M. Jackson, one of America's leading anatomists of all time. Two years later, he was advanced to the rank of assistant professor, one year later to associate professor, and to the rank of professor in 1925.

Andrew Rasmussen's acceptance of the Minnesota post in 1916 was the beginning of one of the finest teaching and research programs in neuro-anatomy that the world has seen.

He was a prodigious worker, never working by the clock but until the job was done. Over the years, it was not unusual for him to arrive at his office and laboratory at four o'clock in the morning and work continuously for 15 hours or longer.

His *Laboratory Directions in Neuro-Anatomy* was in the third edition when he left Minnesota, while his *Outlines of Neuro-Anatomy* had gone through the eighth printing of the third edition. *The Principle Nervous Pathways* was in the fourth edition and was one of the most extensively used textbooks in neuro-anatomy in this country. He also published approximately 100 articles in scientific and medical journals.

Dr. Rasmussen was a medical artist in his own right and produced large numbers of drawings and illustrations for his books, scientific articles, and demonstrations.

He taught neuro-anatomy to more than 4,000 regular medical students and about 200 postgraduates. One graduate student said, "Of all medical courses I have taken anywhere, his was the best remembered and the one most actively participated in by the students. Perhaps there are other neuro-anatomists who are as well known as Dr. Rasmussen, but as a teacher, he was unsurpassed."

Dr. Rasmussen's teaching demonstration collection consisted of some 500 specimens assembled over a period of nearly a third of a century. This collection has been designated by neuro-anatomists in this country and abroad as the finest and most instructive ever produced.

He held membership in many of the learned societies in anatomy and closely allied fields and had been vice-president of the Association for Study of Internal Secretions and of the American Association of Anatomists, of which he was also a member of the executive committee. At the 78th annual commencement of Brigham Young University on June 8, 1953, he was presented with the distinguished service award.

447

Having reached retirement age in June, 1952, Dr. Rasmussen was immediately in demand in other schools and promptly became visiting professor at the University of Southern California where he taught neurology for a semester. He made some 200 colored drawings of slides, many from his own private collection, and from dissections he made to facilitate his teaching—just as he did at Minnesota. At the end of the course, he donated all of this to the Department of Anatomy of the California institution.

He then accepted a visiting professorship within the Department of Investigative Medicine, University of California at Los Angeles, which position he held until his death. There he made over 60 fine dissections of the brain that are being embedded in plastic. This is to be known as the Rasmussen Collection and will be used for teaching, both at Westwood Campus of the University of California at Los Angeles and their laboratories at the Veterans' Hospital, Long Beach.

In 1954, Dr. Rasmussen took leave to accept a visiting professorship for a few months at the Montreal Neurological Institute, where he gave an advanced course in neurology for the fellows and staff members. While there, he also did a series of brain dissections to be imbedded in plastic. He had accepted a visiting professorship for a few months at Yale University during part of the school year of 1955 and 1956, where his work would have been the same as that at Montreal the year before.

During the day of the evening when he suddenly died from coronary thrombosis, he received a letter from Dr. Allen D. Keller, head of the Physiology Department of the Army Medical Research Laboratory at Fort Knox, Kentucky, asking him to become chief of an anatomy section in that department. He was giving this position serious consideration when he died.

In 1911, while head of the Department of Biology at Brigham Young University, he married Gertrude Brown, daughter of Professor Brown, then Dean of the School of Education. From that time on, in all of his work, Mrs. Rasmussen constantly encouraged and assisted him. Their four children are all university graduates. Theodore B. is now professor and head of Neurology and Neurosurgery at the Montreal Neurological Institute, McGill University, after having served as chief of the Department of Neuro-surgery, University of Chicago. Waldemar C. is instructor in neurology, Mayo Foundation, Rochester, Minnesota. Richard C. holds a high position in the securities field in Chicago, and Charlotte is the wife of Dr. W. L. Roberts, an opthalmologist in Los Angeles.

President

Andrew T. Rasmussen, one of America's greatest medical scientists.

ALMA WILFORD RICHARDS

Born: Feb. 20, 1890, in Parowan, Utah.

Father: Morgan Richards

Mother: Margaret Adams

Brothers   Mrs. Mary Isabelle Tanner of Ogden, Utah.
and Sisters: Mrs. C. E. Tanner of Layton, Utah.
                       Catherine Richards of Salt Lake City, Utah.
                           survived Alma

Marriage: 1) Marian Gardner (divorced)
                       2) Gertrude Huntimer (divorced)
                       3) Lenore Griffith of Orange, California.

Children: Joanne, m. R. Youngberg.
                       Mary, m. R. Shrager.
                       Paul Morgan Richards.

Death: Wednesday, April 3, 1963 at 73, of pneumonia in Long
                       Beach Veterans Administration Hospital.

Alma W. Richards grew tall with great leg power. He had fair success as an athlete in high school but it took the genius of Eugene L. Roberts, his college coach, to discover his great jumping ability, give him timing on the spring, and encourage his competitive spirit. Gene tried very hard to get Alma to lean more over the bar on his jumps and thereby get a higher distance; but Alma jumped with his body erect and his legs scissored or crossed under him, a marvelous leap for so large a frame. His style startled the jumping world, but Alma's technique remained quite his own. When Gene had another champion jumper in his training, he was able to get Clint Larsen to put the body almost horizontal over the bar with his feet advancing first and become another Olympic champion.

Alma, by nature, was a smiling, recessive fellow, at his best when competing in a track suit. He said he got his running and jumping from chasing jackrabbits near the Parowan hills and fields. He jumped the barbed wire fences other young men had to crawl under.

After a sub-college graduation (1913) from BYU, World War I claimed his major attention, and he attained a lieutenancy in the U.S. Army. He had gained an international reputation with his Olympic high jump record (6'4") at Stockholm, Sweden in 1912. He was high jump champion in the National A.A.U. meet in 1913 and decathlon champion for the National A.A.U. in 1915, competing in the ten events in one day.

He was enlisted by the University of Southern California for athletics and later admitted to the California bar. He had more time for training by taking a teacher's job; he taught in California secondary school for 31 years, retiring in 1953.

His athletic powers took him, by scholarship, to Cornell University, and some dozen major colleges and universities offered him flattering invitations to study at their institutions. His triumph at Stockholm was written up by his coach and admirer, Gene Roberts (Timpanogos Roberts, as some called him) in the 1913 "BYUtah."

"The world's greatest athletes were assembled in that stadium. The royalty of Europe with thirty thousand enthusiasts packed the stands; Englishmen praying for the English, the Swedes for the Swedes, and the Americans for the bearers of the Stars and Stripes.

"Into this glorious assemblage a Utah boy found his way. His bearing, while not haughty, was erect. Utah's valley tan and his splendid physique caused him to appear to advantage in his jumping togs. He was pitted against fifty of the world's best; the champion, himself, was among them. One by one, as the jumping grew upward, these worthies fell out, leaving, finally, the great Horine, Lieske, the German, and Richards of the BYU. Horine had noticed the naturalness of Richards' spring, and all of a sudden developed a peculiar longing for San Francisco. It was at this juncture that this great jumper had to fall out, leaving the BYU to battle for the Stars and Stripes. Lieske cleared, and twice Richards knocked the bar down; a third trial, however, saw him over, with inches to spare. The bar was raised and the German failed to clear. It was at this point that the young Utahn was under his greatest strain. The honor of his country, his state, and his Alma Mater were in his custody and visions of this responsibility for a moment numbed him.

"Then, after warming up slightly, he summoned his powers and reinforcing them with a liberal portion of that old, determined BYU spirit, he jumped. The official photographs show a margin of over two inches, and a grimace that would shade Roosevelt's. When the talented Lieske saw Richards' spring he suddenly remembered some pressing business that was pending in Berlin. After this event, the great German jumper could not even get his knees up to the bar.

"Throughout the entire journey our jumper was treated royally, shaking hands with monarchs and being given the freedom of European cities were among the every-day occurrences. In New York and Boston, there were demonstrations of the American sort. Governors and mayors vied with one another in their efforts to extend a rousing welcome.

"Richards' real calibre was indicated all along the line. Money offers of all kinds were made him in an effort to secure his services. A tobacco company wanted his picture for advertising purposes, and some schools offered him special privileges with mercenary advantages, but he turned the whole bunch down."

Al Warden, Ogden sports reporter and good booster for Alma writes "before he passed away a year ago had won more than 245 medals and trophies in track and field in all parts of the world. All of these are in Helms Hall in Los Angeles—they should all be in a room at BYU. He was Utah's first Olympic champion in any sport."

As a matter of record, almost all of Alma's medals were displayed in a case in Room D. of the Education Building and photographed for the "BYUtah" school journal of 1913, page 187. When Alma was approached for the Helms Hall of Fame, he returned to the BYU Campus and took his medals back to Los Angeles—our great loss and their gain.

John Mooney, Salt Lake Tribune Sports editor, reports Alma's records viz., 1910-32:
"High jump 6'5" Penn. Relays
Broad jump 23'4½", Penn. vs. Cornell
16 lb. shot put—45' 11¾", NCAA, 1916
12 lb. shot put—53'8", 1916
Pole Vault, 11'6", USAC vs. BYU, 1913
Discus throw—144'11" Southern Pacific AAU, 1922

56 lb. weight—36'9", Southern Pacific AAU, 1932
100 Meters—11.6 sec., Nat'l AAU, 1915
400 Meters—53.8 sec., Nat'l AAU, 1915

"Jim Thorpe and Richards competed against each other in numerous meets and the great Carlisle Indian never finished ahead of the Parowan star in any individual event."

Most veteran sports writers of Utah voted Alma Richards as the greatest athlete ever to represent Utah, with his twenty-one years of competition in major track and field to testify and prove their selection. In the great Centennial Celebration for the State of Utah in 1947, a brochure was presented and Alma was nominated "The Mountain West Athlete of the Century" first choice over all others and was feted significantly during the celebration. He was the high scorer in the A.E.F. championships in Paris in 1918. Gen'l John J. Pershing in complimenting Alma on his championships said, "Lieut. Richards, you are the greatest athlete in the armed forces."

He won 55 championships in 63 events. His decathlon points in 1915 at San Francisco's World Fair topped Jim Thorpe's Olympic record by 1000 points.

If he had had the publicity given Jesse Owens or Jim Thorpe, he would be more frequently recalled as one of the world's great athletes.

EUGENE LUSK ROBERTS

Born: May 13, 1880   **Place:** Provo, Utah

Father: William D. Roberts, b. Sept. 4, 1835 in Winchester, Illinois; d. March 8, 1912
"Every phase of pioneer life was experienced by William D. Roberts"—freighter, Indian interpreter, guide, captured by the Crow Indians and rescued; came to New York by way of the Isthmus; introduced eighteen colonies of bees from California; captured a herd of wild horses and sold them in Utah; captured a murderer, Webb, five miles west of Camp Floyd—a mob interceded and hung the prisoner; member of the posse to capture Indian Chief Tintic; imported blooded horses, cattle, pigs and chickens to Central Utah; trip from Salt Lake City to Sacramento in ten days and eleven hours; first and only man who kept up with mail without laying over on the road; member of the first dramatic company in Provo; served missions to Britain and California; member of the first brass band in Utah County; member of Provo City Council for five years; first postmaster of Provo after Utah became a state; a successful miner; helped to bring the first steam power brick-machine to Utah. A handsome man with magnetic personality.

Mother: Julia Maria Lusk, b. July 24, 1837 in Indiana, reared in Missouri; daughter of John Nicholson Lusk and Cynthia Ann Beeler; talented musician and vocalist; m. in Missouri, Feb. 6, 1862; soon came to Utah with wagon train. Learned to type after she was 75. Died in Glendale, California, Jan. 29, 1936 at 99 years.

Brothers
and Sisters: Family of 11—6 of whom died in infancy
Lillian Aldula, b. Dec. 16, 1864, m. Volney deLory
William DeWitt, b. Jan. 6, 1867; popular proprietor of Hotel Roberts
Homer Dermont
Orpha Zulema, b. April 21, 1873, m. James M. Walker
Eugene, the youngest to reach maturity
Lillian, reputedly the first Utah girl to graduate from Eastern Conservatory of Music; taught Emma Lucy Gates, Emma Ramsey Morris and others

Marriage: Sytha Brown of Provo, daughter of Professor James L. Brown and Selena Charlotte Curtis; m. June 20, 1906 in Salt Lake Temple; teacher at B.Y.U.; b. May 13, 1884 in Pleasant Grove, Utah; resides in Los Angeles, California

Children:	Selena R., m. F. M. Adams
	Ruth Marie, m. Edward N. Lusk
	Dr. Walter Lusk Roberts
	Dr. William D. Roberts
	Dorothy L., m. Stephen H. Fletcher
	Dr. James Eugene Roberts
	Gertrude, m. Laynard Cash (nickname "Dickie")
	Sytha Jean, m. Harvey Berkey (died Dec. 6, 1964)
	All children attended college
Death:	July 9, 1953 in Provo, while teaching in Provo B.Y.U. Summer School

Gene Roberts conceived of healthful and happy living as possible for every adult person. Athletics to him meant group participation. His program in the University was to get every faculty member and every student in health and physical education classes. He yearned for a gymnasium that would accommodate this group and strenuously objected to an elaborate football field until an adequate gymnasium had been provided for all the faculty and student body.

When the Stadium House and the hillside seats were installed for the football field, it became a personal challenge to Gene, who felt the sport for a few men had been made a dominant interest over the health of the large student and faculty groups. Not that he disliked competitive sports, as he fostered and successfully coached them all his B.Y.U. days, but he believed that exercise and health for all were more important and merited first attention. This enthusiasm almost developed into a passion, causing him to worry and he ultimately became so dissatisfied that he sought another territory for his talents and training. I took him to Los Angeles when he left the B.Y.U. for the University of Southern California. We have to know this about him when we try to understand why he left the school he loved so much and for which he never lost admiration. He taught in California, but his heart was mostly in Provo and his beloved Wasatch mountains. On the road going to California when his mind was filled with anticipation of his new position and its challenge to make good, he frequently recalled the many good days he had experienced in Provo and at the University. He expressed these thoughts in different ways, "Some day, they will think more of the faculty's and studentbody's health than of playing football on a field used but a dozen days a year. A gymnasium would be used sixteen hours

454

a day throughout the year; a football field is used half a year a few hours a day by fifty boys with an occasional audience."

With this in mind, we learn more of the man by following a calendar pattern of his life. As a young boy he had considerable companionship with his versatile, talented father, who related pioneer and Indian stories as long as time permitted. His father was a pattern for his life.

Gene was the tenth of eleven children, six having died in infancy. The mountains east of his Provo home invited numerous hikes and the many canyons were frequently explored by Gene and his chums. A train took him down to the resort on the lake where fishing and boating, as well as swimming, delighted his boyish heart and picnics were spread out on the lush grass for an evening party.

As he matured, he sold papers on the streets, was a popular bell hop at the Roberts Hotel famed for its beaf steak dinners and travelling salesmen's parties, worked in the Eureka mines, and worked three and one-half years in the old Provo Post office. He was a fairly successful jockey for amateur races and early watched the physical habits of Provo's athletes such as Bean, a well-known bicycle rider, popular at the old Salt Lake Salt Palace. He gave instruction to a boot black who became famous as a world champion, Jack Dempsey. Wrestling and its training techniques also gained his attention, and Henry Jones was glad of his "pointers." He studied anatomy on the hoof, as he said, watched muscle movements, their reflexes, causes of sprains and stiffness, the value of hot towels and rest. In short, he directed athletes early in his teens and became one of the West's greatest trainers. Before college he was captain of a football team and a basketball group, and had tried every event in a track meet.

He enrolled at B.Y.A. in 1898 under President Cluff who agreeably encouraged all kinds of athletics and competitive teams and urged the erection of gymnasiums. Gene was a frequent contributor to the school's early papers and year books, being managing editor of the "White and Blue." As captain of the B.Y.A. track team, he won Utah's first intercollegiate track and field championship and was sub-quarter for the last football team to represent B.Y.A. before the school abandoned the game after the death of one of its members. He then became captain and quarterback on the "outlaw" eleven which was called the Provo team. Gene was president of the class of 1903, but took an A.B. from B.Y.U. in 1916 and an M.A. from U.S.C. in 1936.

Much of his writing was done under a penname, and in his later B.Y.U. years he used the name of "Harry Kemp," a person supposed to live in the East who wrote articles for the Provo papers. Gene played many practical jokes on his friends by asking them if they had heard of or knew Harry Kemp. When I told him I had heard of Mr. Kemp and he was a good writer, he told the boys at the

455

newspaper office to kid me along which one of them proceeded to do at our first meeting. "You don't know any Harry Kemp as he is Gene Roberts." I got a magazine with a poem by Harry Kemp and took it down to the newspaper. For some reason the next article in the paper was signed "Henry Davidson Kemp," but there was not a word for me from Gene. The title of President Rowland Sill's recent book *The Upward Reach* comes from a verse written by Harry Kemp.

While writing for a sports column, Gene is credited as being the first to designate the B.Y.U.'s athletic teams as "Cougars." He also was the first to author the Timpanogos legend, "Utahna and the Red Eagle," and the meaning of the great bleeding heart in Timpanogos Cave. He worked long on the history of the Mormon Battalion, a story no one ever surpassed in its telling. Gene was the master of interesting tales around the bonfire. All he had to do was to relate some incident in his own father's life to hold a crowd spellbound.

E. L. took a group of professors up to Aspen Grove in 1905 as pioneer path finders when there was no cut or graded path and the mountain was heavily wooded up to the glacier. In 1906 he married a popular, vivacious B.Y.U. student, Sytha Brown; daughter of Prof. James L. Brown of the University. They accepted a call to go on a German-Swiss mission. At the end of a year and a half Sytha returned to Provo with her baby, Selena, while Gene finished his mission. He came home most enthusiastic for mountain climbing and organized hikes. The first hike Gene had with faculty members was the result of stories told by John C. Swenson of the trips he had made from Pleasant Grove when he was a boy. John, urged by young Gene, led John L. Brown, J. E. Hickman, former B.Y.U. professors, and a Dr. Scott of Michigan up the Pleasant Grove side to Timpanogos, a more difficult and dangerous hike than the Aspen Grove-glacier side. Gene's first organized Timp Hike in 1912 consisted of twenty members.

E. L. was on the B.Y.U. faculty for eighteen years and was head of the athletic department. In 1911 he organized the Invitational Track Meet and soon added the famed posture parade with dynamic Wilma Jeppson as director. He produced some of the best track and basketball teams in the country. Such world renowned track stars as Alma Richards and Clint Larsen, both Olympic high jump champions, Dale Schofield, hurdler and runner were his proteges; he won second place in the National Invitation Tournament for Basketball in Chicago in 1917 and re-introduced football at B.Y.U. after twenty years absence and was its first coach.

In 1920, as President of the B.Y.U. Alumni Association the

456

first official "Homecoming" was introduced, a three day celebration. The new term gave greater choice of dates and program than was offered by Founder's Day, though the time was approximately the same. In 1949 the B.Y.U. Alumni Association gave him its coveted Distinguished Service Award.

An opportunity for acquiring advanced degrees and projecting his theories in general physical and health education came to him from the University of Southern California, a school that knew of Gene's ability in coaching and group techniques. In August of 1928, Gene went to Southern California with Dr. T. Earl Pardoe. Both enrolled at U.S.C. and taught. In a short time, Gene was given complete freedom with his class projects and was soon assisting the track coach in the high and broad jumps and pole vault, producing champions in all three events. He was elected grand national president of Pi Sigma Epsilon fraternities, physical education honor association, and was an active leader in Skull and Dagger, a U.S.C. honor society.

His eight children married into happy and successful families, living across the continent. Some of his summers he spent in Utah teaching classes for B.Y.U. and visiting his numerous friends. The Roberts home in California was always interesting and had "things happening" as Gene often said. His mother, living with them for her last thirty years, was learning German at age ninety. Family discussions were numerous and instructive as both Gene and Sytha joined in the topics and helped to clarify the more difficult subjects. The young men courting mingled freely with the family, part in fun and part in learning. When E. L. died he had twenty grandchildren. His three sons had their doctorates; his five daughters married college men.

While vacationing and teaching in Provo, Gene succumbed to a heart attack on July 9, 1953. His picture hangs over the door of the George Albert Smith Fieldhouse facing the majestic Timpanogos he loved so much. He had a good start on the history of the athletic department of B.Y.A. when his sudden death left the work unfinished. He left it to a colleague, Dr. Charles J. Hart, for proper conclusion.

Tributes were sent to Sytha Brown Roberts by the hundreds, memorializing the broad scope of E. L.'s life. She keeps their Baldwin Hills home in Los Angeles open for the Roberts' children's frequent visits.

The Invitational Track meets and the world renowned Timpanogos Hike will ever recall the fiery enthusiasm of their founder. As one of his friends remarked at his funeral, "He was not only a great teacher and a great coach; he was warm, witty, and an understanding friend. He was an artist, a poet, a journalist, a philosopher . . . Athletic programs were only a means to comprehensive educational ends."

LEROY JASPER ROBERTSON

Born: December 21, 1896, Fountain Green, Utah

Father: Jasper Heber Robertson. B. 1870 in Fountain Green, Utah, son of Edwin Robertson. d., 1937.

Mother: Alice Adams, daughter of W. H. Adams. Born 1872 in Fountain Green, Utah; m. June 28, 1893 in Manti Temple. d. 1923.

Brothers and Sisters: (Leroy); Floyd, deceased; Ora R., m. Cal Draper, Salt Lake City, Utah; Dr. Wanda Robertson; Marcel, m. Arthur Anderson; Joseph; Doyle.

Marriage: Naomi Nelson, m. September 1, 1925. Daughter of Waldemar Nelson and Marie Jenson Nelson.

Children: Dr. Alice Marian Robertson (U.S.U. faculty); Renee R., m. Stephen E. Whitesides of Kaysville, Utah; Karen R., m. Gary Post of Salt Lake City, Utah; James.

Leroy Robertson shared in most of the arduous work for boys around a farm and early revealed his love for music. He herded cows and especially desired the companionship of his grandfather, a practical farmer given to contemplation and philosophy, who was especially efficient in relating tales from the Bible to life about them.

His grandfather was an excellent actor and was used as "Uncle Sam" in many of the valley's patriotic parades and programs. Roy was also used in some of these community shows and especially coveted a place in the band. On the Fourth of July grandpa would be "Uncle Sam" and Roy would beat the drums. He had a truer sense of rhythm than many of the men. He cultivated his ear accuity until he had an almost absolute pitch so useful later in life when conducting orchestras. Often he has stopped an orchestra and pointing his baton to a certain player, "You are sharp," and to the drummer "Tighten the base."

Instruments of high quality were beyond the purchase power of most farm boys. Roy tried to carve a violin out of a thrashing machine box and with better tools would have succeeded. Much of his exercise led to strengthening his long fingers, wrist and upper arm. His tenacity of purpose was native, and singleness of attention was early evident. He started composing simple melodies for the violin in his early teens and worked on the note sequence until he was satisfied or felt he could go no further for the time. After he had graduated from the New England Conservatory he took a composition done in his early youth out of his trunk and found it to be correct in every detail. Many of his early musical phrases now appear in some of his best compositions.

Roy has always had a type of fearless courage which disregards personal safety. It is told that he stopped a runaway team hitched to a buggy with a small girl in the seat. The swerving carriage twice righted itself as the horses gained speed. The slender lad ran with the horses, gained a few feet in front, jumped to the single tree, frantically grabbed the loose reins, and with sheer strength brought the lathered team and carriage to a halt. As the crowd quickly gathered around, solicitous for the endangered, screaming child, Roy quietly slipped away, went home to lie down and rested for hours to recuperate his spent strength. When asked by his parents if he were the boy who had saved the little girl's life, he replied "Aw, that was nothing; just fun." He didn't show them a bleeding palm.

His extracurricular hours at college were spent with orchestras, bands and string ensembles. He was concert master for the University symphony, played violin for Student Body programs and was sought for funerals.

He graduated from B.Y. High School in 1916, even then a well-known violinist. George Fitzroy, teacher of piano and harmony, and

Florence Jepperson Madsen, vocalist and composer had recently come from the New England Conservatory and with others, encouraged Roy's enrollment at the Boston Music Center, where he came under the personal aegis of the great director, Professor George W. Chadwick.

In Boston he was featured in Conservatory programs and graduated with distinction in 1923. With the advent of Dr. Harris and his desire to build an outstanding music department, Roy was engaged as professor of music at BYU in 1925, a position that he held until 1948, when he was invited to head the music department for the University of Utah in Salt Lake City and assist in building the Utah Symphony. He honored his position until retirement in 1964.

He taught a full teacher assignment at BYU in 1923. He worked with Carl Busch in 1925 and Ernest Bloch in San Francisco in 1930 and in Switzerland in 1932. In Berlin in 1933 he was a student of Hugo Lichtentritt. On his grand piano you may find a piece he is working on as time permits, often late into the night.

LeRoy received his A.B. and M.A. in music from BYU (1932) and a Ph.D. from the University of Southern California in 1954.

Some of the more important compositions are listed below:

An *Overture* submitted in Boston by invitation won first prize in 1923

Quintet for Piano and String Quartet—1932; *Fantasia for Organ,* 1934; *Quintet for Piano and String* won first place in contest conducted for publication of American Music, New York, 1936.

Trilogy, completed in 1939, won the Riechhold award of $25,000 in 1947, the largest music prize to date won by a Utahn

American Serenade for String Quartet, 1943

Rhapsody for Piano and Orchestra, written for Ander Foldes, 1944

Punch and Judy, for Orchestra, 1945

Oratorio, text from *Book of Mormon* 1946-46-52
acclaimed by noted musicians across the land

Chamber music played by string quartets in Chicago, Walden, New York, NBC, Hart House, Lever, San Francisco and by Roth, Paganinni and others. Orchestral works performed by BYU, Utah Symphonies, Houston, CBS, Detroit, Toronto, Los Angeles, NBC.

Professor Robertson is completing a concerto for cello and orchestra and a concerto for piano and orchestra; he is a Fellow in the Utah Academy of Sciences, Arts, and Letters, and a member of American Society of Composers, Authors and Publishers (ASCAP); chairman of the Executive Music Committee of the LDS Church; recipient of the BYU Alumni Distinguished Service Award, 1953.

He tells us; "With Ernest Bloch in Switzerland I learned of the spiritual strength of Bach; Hugo Lichtentritt in Berlin gave me the secret of the 16th Century composers; Arnold Schoenberg of Austria gave me the moving simplicity of Beethoven; Ernest Toch unfolded the melodies of Mozart."

A critic wrote of him:

"The American Serenade" a musical tale of rough, spiritual men of the West told with a broad sweep and environmental accuracy, cowboys and Indians. The horse drawn thrasher and the roar of melting snow, even the meadowlark once so numerous—these were tonal pictures to fire his imagination, nor was the Indian forgotten.

"The Lord's Prayer" has gone around the musical world; was so good that the publishers broke their agreement not to publish any music set to the Prayer. "One who really understands the words has given us the most appropriate music"—"When we read yours we decided that it was so excellent, so devotional, so finely executed and so genuine an expression of these great words that the committee threw its rule away and made the kind of an exception that every committee should make when it meets the real thing, rule or no rule." Excerpts from review of LeRoy Robertson's works:

Detroit News, December 12, 1947:

"Trilogy" is a pure adventure in the realms of tone, with no attempt at "program" or picture-painting. The first over-all impression which a listener receives is that its composer is full of invention, in the matter of themes, and a natural-born craftsman with orchestra instruments. Time after time he fashions a beguiling little melody, states it emphatically, and, with what amounts to boldness, employes as enrichment every resource available. "Trilogy" . . . constant blooming, forever bursting with surprise. It is fresh and free and altogether American, original and engrossing in almost every page."

Detroit Free Press, December 12, 1947:

". . . The heart and soul of the composition is, nevertheless, all-Robertson, and therefore all-American. There are climaxes that are as moving as the snowy peaks of the West that gave it birth; there is a gusty sort of humor that springs only from the American soil. There is also a dignity that is incomparable, as in the slow movement when the virile drive of the tempo changes to a march of funeral grandeur. The exciting use of counterpoint in the finale is one of the most gripping experiences of the three movements."

LeRoy Robertson has become a power in American music, known to all reputable orchestras and symphonies, nor is his reputation confined to this continent.

He has become Utah's best known musician in this day of keen competition, writing only for the highest level of musical composition in the tradition of the great masters. His "Passacaglia" has already won a firm position in foreign orchestral programs. His reverential "Lord's Prayer" and the great expanse of his moving American

461

Trilogy reveal the scope of his imagination and artistic temperament. Each month adds further recognition of his talents and compositional abilities. Carl Fischer, Inc., one of the nation's largest music publishers recently produced six volumes for Leroy, titled *Hymns From the Crossroads*, each volume containing thirty hymns.

JAMES WILLIAM ROBINSON

Resident of Salt Lake City, Utah

Born: January 19, 1878   **Place:** Coalville, Utah

Father: John Robinson
Born July 14, 1832 at Wheatty, Northumberland, England
Died May 1908

Mother: Jane Rust (Ruff)
Died November 10, 1908

Brothers and Sisters: Thomas George Robinson
Jennie Ann Robinson
Lynda R. Price
John Robert Robinson
Emma
Isabel R. Watson
Margaret Ethel Robinson

Marriage: Birda Billings
Daughter of George Pierce Billings and Lydia Anna Young
Married August 16, 1908 in the Salt Lake Temple.
Died January 27, 1962
Attended BY Academy
Member of Stake Relief Society Board
Member of Alice Louise Reynolds Club
Member of Utah Sorosis

Children: Tom Junius, m. Ione Hickman
Ruth R., m. Robert Franklin Harris
George Billings, m. Florence Ellertsen
Maree R., m. Wade M. Fleischer

Death: Wednesday, December 2, 1964 in Escondido, California

J. Will, as his friends knew him, early selected his career and all his mature life was devoted to politics. He was an excellent speaker and debator at BYU, taking an A.B. from this university in 1908, the year of his marriage.

He taught school and was principal of the Uintah Stake Academy at Vernal, Utah in 1905-06 and principal of the Wasatch High School in 1909-1910. He went to the University of Chicago and received his Doctor of Jurisprudence, with honors, in 1912. He immediately began the practice of law in Provo, Utah, soon forming a strong partnership with George Parker. He also taught pre-legal classes at BYU from 1922 to 1925.

His fortunes fluctuated with the success of the Democratic party, as he was an ardent protagonist of party politics. His success in business proved he also had good economics practices, as he became attorney for the Farmers and Merchants Bank of Provo, for the People's State Bank of American Fork, and the Delta Exchange and Savings Bank.

J. Will was Utah County Attorney in 1918-20, the war period, and was Utah County Food Administrator for World War I, a most exacting position of trust when food was rationed by coupons. He played no favorites and proved most impartial.

He served as vice-president of the Springville-Mapleton Sugar Company and was a long-time director of the Provo Building and Loan.

His greatest state service came in the U.S. Congress when he served from 1933-1947, heading or being a member of many committees affecting western land, water, and rights. He had "the friendly ear" of President Franklin D. Roosevelt, being chairman of the House Roads Commission and chairman and ranking member of the Public Lands and Irrigation Committee. He became the recognized spokesman for the Hill Air Force Base at Ogden, Utah.

Bill also was a member of the University of Utah Board of Regents for ten years, 1925-1935.

After his unsuccessful run for Congress in 1946, he was appointed Director of Grazing in the office of Land Management, Interior Department, 1947-1950.

With his competent and helpful wife, Birdie, he moved back to Utah, where he entered into local and social activities in the growth of Salt Lake.

For four years he was Superintendent of the Utah Stake Sunday School and was active in priesthood duties most of his life. State and National Bar Associations claimed much of his spare time and while at Provo, he had one of the most enjoyable periods of his life playing tennis on the Knight Woolen Mills Courts and casting a line from the banks of Provo River. When he left Provo for Washington, D.C. he said "My sporting days are over," which proved all too true. He became a devoted public servant.

His family burial plot is in the Provo City Cemetery.

EDWARD MORRIS ROWE

Born: December 9, 1874, at Spanish Fork, Utah

Father: Owen (J.) Rowe (he used the J. for designation only) Son of Edward and Elizabeth Thomas Rowe who had four sons. Elizabeth worked in coal pits to support family when husband died. b. May 12, 1850, Merthyr Tydfil, Glamorganshire, South Wales; Baptized May 18, 1866 in Wales; to Salt Lake City, 1870 in Karl G. Maeser Company.
d. September 29, 1915.

Mother: Ann Creer, b. March 31, 1857, in Salt Lake City, Utah. Daughter of Edward Creer; (b. November 3, 1813, in Bolton, Lancashire, England), and Ann Morris, (b. December 27, 1814 at Chorley, Lancashire, England, the youngest of 15 children). Parents to Utah, 1854. m. June 20, 1835.
d. February 9, 1938.

Brothers and Sisters: Ann Rowe, m. Morgan Beck; Elinor, m. John T. Morgan; (Edward M; Owen Jr. (infant death); John William, m. Barbara Christensen; Mary Alice (died at 17); Lenora, m. Hyrum Robertson; Grace Elizabeth, m. Mark Johnson; Genevieve, m. Vern Thomas; Lily Dale Rowe; Lewis Ephriam, m. Mae Williams; Ross Thomas, m. Hazel Webb; Roy Orson a twin to Ross Thomas (died at birth); Glen Archibald, m. Maggie Barton; Leah (infant death)

Marriage: Minnie Berry, daughter of William Shanks and Rebecca Beck Berry. b. February 21, 1884, at Spanish Fork, Utah; m. June 3, 1908. Taught school in over twelve schools; resides in her home in Provo, Utah.

Children: Helen Ann, m. Frank S. Gragun; Grant Browning, m. Virginia Feerlink (Major, U.S. Army); Owen B., m. Dorothy Hedquist; Lewis Marion, m. Kathleen Johnson; Capt. Glen M., U.S. Air Force; Hazel Blanch, m. Douglas Busterud.

Death: November 13, 1951 of heart attack

Ed M. Rowe had the national characteristics of a jolly Welsh-man, short and stocky, with blue eyes, a good singing voice and a love for scenic and mountain beauty. One of his great joys was to have a book of pastoral poetry near a running brook, a "soft rock" to lean upon, and an hour or so to read and meditate. He saw and felt rhythm in nearly everything about him. Wordsworth, Keates, Shelley were his "boyhood companions," and their presence in print warmed his mature life. Most of the classes he taught had poetic flavor and for him, romantic fervor. Nature, with its boundless expanse, at times held him as one transfixed. I have seen him pick up a perfectly formed leaf, turn his head admiringly to the tree and slowly catalogue the forest. "All these leaves look alike, yet no two are ever the same. There is no limit to generic diversification but all things are subject to universal laws. (turning away) How many men are as useful as a tree?" If he stayed long enough at any given place he would endeavor to quote an appropriate line or two from one or more of his literary friends. His memory for apt quotes was remarkable.

After his mission in Ireland and a visit to Wales, he developed a fervent interest in Welsh history and folklore of Britain. His year's study at Aberystwith, the university capital of Wales, further enhanced his enthusiasm and he became an ardent protagonist of Welsh culture in America, especially for the Welsh immigrants who settled in Spanish Fork. He worked hard to arouse state participation in Gymanfa Ganu and in the great Eistedfod we once fostered with Evan Stephens in Salt Lake City. He became the leading force in establishing the National Welsh Library at BYU and had strong backing from the central national committee. Books began to come in to the Grant Library for the National Welsh collection and a Utah committee consisting of Professor Elbert and Mrs. Ann Thomas, Irene Staples, Ed M. Rowe and T. Earl Pardoe began a systematic program of building the library. Professor Pardoe got Emlyn Williams, the most successful contemporary Welsh playwright, to donate a full collection of his plays autographed, to present to the collection and his play "The Corn is Green" was staged in College Hall to capacity crowds for one week with Kathryn Bassett Pardoe in the leading role. Proceeds went to the Welsh Library Fund for new books. When Dr. Pardoe visited Aberystwith and the Welsh University he arranged for BYU to receive many of the duplicate copies of Welsh books in exchange for duplicates of American books in our library. Just before the exchange and at the height of the campaign, Professor Rowe died and left the work to be finished by the Thomases and Dr. Pardoe.

At this time the national directors of the North American Welsh Association held a series of meetings and two of its members asked that the library be established in the East, preferably at Yale

University, nearer the nation's population center. Our University and library executives preferred not to establish the national North American Welsh Library on our campus unless it had unanimous approval of its national directors. Accordingly, all the work that had been done, the space proposed for such a collection in the new J. Reuben Clark Library and the many years' dream of Professor Rowe came to naught. The books and artifacts acquired are kept in Provo, and it has been proposed that we consistently add to the Celtic culture section of our library and call it "The Edward M. Rowe Welsh Collection." Many of his friends wish for this consummation.

Students of Prof. Rowe came from his classes with a deeper love of nature and its beauty and meaning, and poetry had appeal hitherto unappreciated. He spoke with very clear diction, loved to read aloud to his classes, and inwardly yearned for the time that he might write. One of his songs is in the L.D.S. Hymn Book, (1948 ed.). It is often sung and popular with choral leaders—"Oh, Sons of Zion" music by Robert Manookin.

Here is a bit of history which Ed M. delighted to tell. In 1899 the University of Utah held a Field Day in Salt Lake City, with sports on their field on the west side of Salt Lake and the culture contest in the old Salt Lake Theatre in the afternoon. The baseball game ended 12-11 for University of Utah and they won the major number of track events, although Lewis N. Ellsworth of the Y won the half mile race. The B.Y. Academy won both the debate and oral story telling—Leo Bird and Ed M. Rowe in debate and Annie Pike the story telling. The Salt Lake City papers came out with the heading: "U of U for Bunions and B.Y.A. for Brains."

Ed had three major avocations; Church, politics and Welsh. He debated national issues while at school and early took a leading part in the Republican party becoming county chairman and delegate to the National Convention. He chairmanned the Lincoln Day Dinners.

While principal of the Spanish Fork High School he was a member of the City Council. He was patrol officer for the State Industrial School in Ogden from 1912-15.

He first came to B.Y.A. in 1897, staying to 1900, taking a State H.S. diploma in Literature in 1911 and an A.B. from BYU in 1923. He did graduate work at U.S.A.C., University of Chicago, Cornell and University of Wales, becoming assistant professor of English at BYU from 1928 to 1935, and professor from 1935 to 1949, when he retired to Emeritus rank; he edited the White and Blue at B.Y.A., 1898-1899.

Along with his Welsh Library project and politics, he spent considerable time organizing the Sons of Utah Pioneers. He wrote an ode for the Utah Centennial 1947, "Sons and Daughters Pioneers in

Utah Valley." He loved sports and was a devotee of football and tennis and an active member of the Down Town Coaches Club. He made an effort to know each varsity athlete and proferred teaching assistance to many. As a High Priest he led a balanced choir and much of his ward singing.

Coming from a large, active family, he especially joyed in his own family of six, and with his devoted wife anxiously lived through war days and was grateful for the return of all four sons.

Yearning for time for leisure, he was seldom at rest and made many appointments outside his school and Church schedule. A teacher, book-lover, politician and spokesman, he had friends in many walks of life. As his children left, one by one, his greatest joy came when sitting at home by an open fireplace to read poetry and scriptures to his attentive and devoted wife. One of his last remarks, "My sweetest dream is for a great BYU."

ROBERT HERMAN SAUER

Composer and Band Master

Born: October 3, 1872   **Place:** Rommeneau, Saxony
Germany

Father: Friederick Wilhelm Sauer
Born March 27, 1837, in Rommeneau, Saxony, Germany
Farmer and Musician; played bass viol

Mother: Charlotte Amalie Anders
Born March 11, 1839, in Bretnig, Saxony, Germany.
Married May 13, 1860, in Hauswalde, Bautsen, Saxony.

Brothers and Sisters: Robert Herman, fifth of six children.

Wife: Augusta Trabert, m. Erfurt, Germany on October 27, 1896.
Born December 6, 1875 in Erfurt, the daughter of George Trabert and Marie Johanna Brand.
Married in Salt Lake Temple on March 3, 1907.
She was Relief Society worker in Provo Third and Fourth Wards for 25 years.
Knit for Red Cross many years.
Died 2 March, 1947, in Provo, Utah.

Children: Annie, born in Germany, m. Arvil Clayton of Salt Lake City, Utah.
Elsie, born in Germany, m. C. J. Perry
Eric Leroy, born in U. S. Died of influenza at 14.
Paul, m. Grace Baker; lives in Hayward, California.
Gertrude, m. Glen L. Humphries, Maywood, California; graduate of Brigham Young University in 1933.
Mabel, m. Gus A. Welsch of La Habra, California.

Died: January 5, 1944, of cerebral hemorrhage.

Robert Sauer was a very even tempered man, easily made to smile. He looked kindly on all people and stood more in the background until he took the baton. Then his eyes glistened, covered an entire orchestra at a glance, detected the least inaccuracy in pitch from any instrument wherever located. It did not take him long to become known as one of the best band masters in the West. His students were eagerly sought and assigned positions of importance, becoming the outstanding school band leaders wherever they went.

Band music was his obsession—each instrument necessary for a well balanced organization caused him to seek willing students, players to fill a gap to become expert with the oboe, piccolo, bassoon, flute, French and English horn, the bass horn, the tuba and even the glockenspiel. He spent extra hours with his tympani, the slide trombones and the instruments which more easily got "out of time." "Any body can blow a clarinet, a saxaphone or a trumpet—but only a moosician can get a moosical tone. Any body can oom pah wid an alto but it takes a moosician to blow sveet moosic. Correct breathing is first to be learned before the lips or tongue can control the vay it comes out. Vhen you blow on a mouth piece vhile I count a hundred you are beginning to get a foundation for tones vhich have to be held, maybe eight or ten measures. Learn to follow the beat and vatch when I come down wid da stick—dat keeps us together."

Professor Sauer had a good vocabulary but never entirely overcame his German speech. His *th* was either *t* or *d*, as tin for *th*in, dem for *th*em, etc. His w's and v's were interchanged as in German. *Ve* for we, *w*owel for vowel, etc. My first meeting with him will indicate his interesting dialect.

I went to the Alex Hedquist Drugstore near the corner of Center Street and University Avenue. Several ladies and two men were in the store and the ladies were browsing. Alex called to me and said, "Do you two men know each other? Professor Pardoe is the new head of the drama department and this is the band leader, Professor Sauer." We shook hands and exchanged compliments. "Now, what can I do for you, Professor Sauer? You were first." "Dat's alright; vait on him first." "Come on, you're next." The professor looked around not wishing to be seen purchasing goods usually bought by the lady of the house, especially in his native land. "Vell, I don't do dis often, but I vish some talcum powder." "That's fine" said Alex, "Mennen's?" Looking around again, Brother Sauer almost whispered, "No, vimins."

That was in 1919. His dialect almost disappeared before he passed away.

One of Robert's good friends in Germany was Albert Miller, who joined the Church, came to Provo and became the head of the music department at B.Y.U. and its highly praised band and orchestra leader. Through him, Robert was induced to come to Provo and after Professor Miller's death was named the new band leader.

Professor Sauer was trained with famous teachers of music in Rodeburg, Germany, and played with the Erfurt Infantry Band. He was sent to Dresden to play with the Grade Twelfth Engineer's Corps and studied under some of Germany's best teachers, including Professor Kretshman, well known opera composer.

On October 27, 1896, the twenty-four-year-old promising musician married Augusta Trabert, herself a well grounded musician. They joined the Church in Germany in 1899 and in 1905 came to Provo, eager to teach and conduct a military band. Robert found that a good foundation had already been laid and needed only further training and money for expansion. Sacred concerts were played by the Academic band in the special stand erected in Pioneer Park on West Center Street, attracting crowds numbered in the hundreds.

In 1920 Professor Sauer was made assistant professor of music and he asked for help in promoting the wind instrument section. Accordingly, the Pardoe Gold Medal was offered to a BYU student who excelled in a contest with some wind instrument. Clair Johnson of Springville, long time band leader for Weber College, was the first winner and Mac Haycock was the second year winner (now a retired Sear's manager).

Professor Sauer's study was a downstairs room in the College Building and his students watched for a chance to practice in some empty room. Those who taught in the College Hall heard various tones, good and bad, the day through and the full band practiced at noon. His studio was next to my "office" for several years and he would bring a new composition to me to hear and give comment. I did this for over a year with his "Spring Time In The Rockies"; a poem by Mrs. Mary Hale Woolsey of Salt Lake City being his inspiration. He strove for classical composition and sold several of his band numbers to New York Music Publishers. One of his compositions was played by the U.S. Navy Band when they came to Provo in 1943.

His "Spring Time In The Rockies," once introduced, quickly caught on, was played and sung across the nation and may still be heard. Elva Chipman Olpin, wife of President Ray Olpin, and myself sang a duet for the Columbia Faculty Club in New York in 1924. On one occasion in College Hall, Professor Sauer was asked to play his success and he proudly announced, "By special request, ve vill now play the national anthem 'Spring Time In The Rockies.' "

He was honored on many occasions. Norman G. Berndt, well known jeweler of Salt Lake City made up a most beautiful medal and made the presentation at a capacity honor concert to "Utah's Outstanding Musician." The 1944 Banyan was dedicated to his honor with a special music edition.

He was a national band adjudicator for some of the nation's greatest contests.

Robert Sauer was loyal. He couldn't understand why the United States and Germany should go to war. World War I became a most bitter trial to his soul; he wanted to be loyal to his fatherland and he had to be loyal to his beloved adopted land. His relatives were in Germany; his friends and family were in the States. He was so confused for a while that he denied himself any conversation on the subject, often reading the paper headlines with tears rolling down his cheeks. Once, when he started to play a Wagnerian Overture, some enthusiast stood up and shouted, "That's German. Who are you for anyway?" The piece was stopped and a hurried substitution made. In his studio, with eyes that looked hundred of miles ahead, "Moosic is for de vorld; it belongs to all of us."

It took some time for him to bill a German master in his programs. World War II was even a greater trial and brought on a withdrawal from civic music participation. He was made Professor of Music in 1938 and Emeritus in 1943. He responded to calls from the Utah Symphony and the Salt Lake Opera Orchestra when bassoon or oboe solos were to be played, but he did more of adjudicating than playing during World War II.

He arranged his own funeral a year in advance. Robert Sauer was always the gentleman, a well educated musician who deeply frowned upon mediocrity, a man who was admired and loved by hundreds. Despite the meager salary paid him as a teacher the royalties from "Spring Time In The Rockies" cleared the mortgage on his Provo home and gave him a new car. With a most devoted wife and loving family he felt the world had been good to him. "I hope I have done good to somebody." He blessed his generation.

WILLIAM JAMES SNOW

Born: April 16, 1869   **Place:** Lehi, Utah

Father: William Snow, a native of St. Johnsbury, Vermont. One of four brothers who joined the Church, one being Apostle Erastus Snow. Early Utah pioneer. Moved to Pine Valley in 1871. Zerubbabel, a brother, became Associate Justice for State of Utah. Died in 1879.

Mother: Sally Adams of Stanstead, Lower Canada. Married in Nauvoo where she met William.

Brothers and Sisters: Julia Maria, m. Joseph Cox
Sarah Saphronia, m. George Forsyth
Lucy Almira, m. Reuben Gardner
Chloe Louisa, m. Royal J. Gardner
Emma Lucretia, m. H. Joseph Burgess
Maryetta, m. Osro Gardner
(Wm. J.) only son in family of seven children

Marriage: Hattie Maria Thornton, May 10, 1899, St. George Temple. Born Dec. 2, 1875 in Pinto, Washington County, Utah, daughter of Amos G. Thornton, first lady missionary in the Eastern States. Died November 10, 1963

Children: William J., Jr., m. Dixie Mangum
Emma, m. Paul B. Pearson
Ronald, m. Naomi Seamount
Gordon W., m. Beth Todd
Claude W.,—killed in Italy during World War II. Interpreter of Indian cultures and promising artist. Buried in American Cemetery beyond Fiesole, Italy, outskirts of Florence. All were B.Y.U. graduates.

Death: October 16, 1947 at his home in Provo, 487 N. 300 E.— cerebral hemorrhage at 78.

William J. Snow was a tall and slender man with a restless body, an ever searching mind, always asking why? What are the facts in the case? Where is your authority? Where do we go from here? Why are dates so important? When you come to know the man, all these questions were logical steps in satisfying a truth loving fellow. He honored tradition only when it had a good purpose or was founded on folk facts. He had all the qualifications of a great history teacher.

On the preceding page, we have indicated that he came from excellent, early American stock. His great great-grandfather, Zerubbabel Snow was a colonel in the American Revolutionary forces. His father, William, was one of four brothers who joined the Church. Orson Pratt and Lyman Johnson converted the Snows and Farrs when they preached at St. Johnsbury and Waterford, Vermont. The miraculous healing of Olive Hovey Freeman Farr by Orson Pratt was a stimulating factor in arousing interest in the Farr's cousins, the Snows. A brother of William, Erastus Snow, became an LDS apostle and Zerubbabel was the first Mormon to be appointed to a Territorial office. William Snow met, wooed and wed Sally Adams in the busy water town of Nauvoo, Illinois.

When William J. was but a year and half old, the last child of his pioneer parents, he was taken to Pine Valley in southern Utah on a call by Brigham Young. In this western wilderness, six sisters helped to bring up their only brother. Early chores, garden and field farming, pasturing stock, gathering wood, making furniture, carding wool were the duties of this fast growing son. He made friends with the frequently visiting Indians and early pondered their origins, tribal customs and asked what could be learned from each other.

McGuffey Readers, a large family illustrated Bible, some borrowed magazines became his nightly companions. He early learned to read, mostly self taught, writing down each new word until he almost had a dictionary of his own making.

One day, while plowing, he puzzled over some new words he had encountered and could reason no proper meaning of them. He stopped his heavy horses, leaned against the plough, looked toward the north and said aloud, "Yes, sir, I'm going to go." Just like that, he had determined to go to school! When the team suddenly broke and ran toward the barn, he was convinced that he should go. After a family conference, sisters wondering what they would do without their little brother (he had grown to six feet), he bid them all farewell. Bundles of clothing, bedding and food supplies were packed in a light wagon and over the hill the anxious young man drove out of sight. He was twenty-two years of age, the owner of a small piece of land and a dozen head of cattle. After eight months at B.Y. Academy, he returned to Pine Valley, his home and his cattle. He knew then he was going to be a teacher.

He taught school at Pine Valley for six years, learning more himself than he taught, so he said. He was hired as Superintendent of Washington County schools and, for good measure, managed the Pine Valley Co-op. He married Hattie Thornton in May, 1899, just before going on his mission. In 1899 to 1901 he was an active missionary in New York City and environs, with Brooklyn his headquarters.

In 1903 he returned to Provo for college study and was given an assistant teaching assignment. His wife helped in many ways, not only to rear a family but to help fill the pantry. Each day he returned home and told his wife how fortunate he was to be a teacher, to learn something new each day, meet such wonderful students filled with hope and promise. Every student became a challenge to his abilities and pride.

His educational growth made progress as time and finances permitted. In 1910 he received his A.B. degree from B.Y.U. Summer school at U. of Chicago, U. of Utah and California helped him to an M.A. at Berkeley in 1922, doing much of his work with Professor Bolton, and a Ph.D. from California in 1923. "Now, I can do many of the things I have long wanted to do," he said, among them research in many of the unsettled problems of western history.

His teaching is summed up viz:

1904-05 Instructor in mathematics at B.Y.U.
1905-06 Instructor in history at B.Y.U.
1906-08 Principal of Uintah Stake Academy
1908-10 Instructor in English at B.Y.U.
1913-17 Assistant professor of history
1917-41 Professor of History
1941-47 Professor Emeritus

He taught until 1945 when his health made it advisable to retire from active teaching, although he had a desk at the University until his death, where students could get advice and research assistance.

His committee assignments indicate his worth to the university: Library, 1916-1941; Petitions 1910-1911; Publicity 1917-18; Debating 1920-1935; Graduation 1923-24; Personnel 1928-37.

His doctorate research showed his prime interest, "The Great Basin Before the Coming of the Mormons," a scholarly study, highly prized by members of his profession. In the Utah County's Sesquicentennial he wrote *Escalante's Vision of Utah Valley*. The book was illustrated by an artist friend, E. H. Eastmond (1926). Another brochure of interest was his "Who and What Is Timpanogos?"

Long active in the Utah State Historical Society, he was its contributing president for eight years and was a consulting member of the National Oregon Trails Association, a member of the Pioneer Trails and Landmarks Association, and wrote articles for state newspapers, historical and religious journals.

Nor was his Church neglected, as he held some kind of administrative office from early boyhood being both teacher and officer in Primary, Ward and Stake Sunday School and YMMIA. All his teaching was on a high, spiritual tone and he encouraged challenging questions in his classes. "If you never doubt, you never learn."

His addresses were always well planned, carefully thought out, self-challenged and interesting. He had a high, husky voice which soon faded into the strength of his thinking. One interesting gesture habit was his shifting from one foot to another. When he made two or three shifts, you knew he was coming to the core of his thought, and when he pinched his nose, he was done with that particular point. His stories were limitless as he drew from world history, mythology and simple, local happenings. This device made his presentation very lucid and worthwhile.

You had no doubt where he stood on any question. In politics, he was an ardent, almost vehement Democrat. He seldom missed a convention. What he did he did enthusiastically. His religion did not conflict with his science; to each he gave honorable credit and harmonized their basic principles. I never heard of one of his students whom he left in confusion. He made special appointments to help a person clear his own thinking to an amicable conclusion. "Don't kill a doubt-get at its roots and let truth find your answer."

His home life was ideally harmonious; his classroom was a rendevouz of progressive thinking. William J. Snow was a great teacher and a loyal American.

LYMAN KNUT SWENSON

U.S. Navy Captain

Born:	November, 1892 **Place:** Pleasant Grove, Utah
Father:	Knud Swenson (see writeup with John C. Swenson) Bishop of the Manila, Utah Ward
Mother:	Anne Maria Hansen, eldest of five children. Born Aug. 10, 1856 at Orslev Kloster, Viborg, Denmark. Joined L.D.S. Church July 3, 1876. To Utah 1883. Married Jan. 31, 1884; mother of seven. Died May 27, 1930.
Brothers and Sisters:	Ezra J. Swenson of Pleasant Grove, Utah, m. Elsie Walker Wilford Swenson of San Francisco, California Georgia, m. M. Edward ANderson. Attended B.Y.U. (1908) Children of Johanna m. June 24, 1860—died May 7, 1880 —mother of eight Anna, b. 1861, m. Ezra Walker Swen L., b. 1865, m. Susan Brown Mary, b. 1867, m. George Kelly of Ogden John C., m. Ellen Davis of Emery Eliza, b. 1871, d. 1917
Marriage:	1) Milo Abercombie of San Francisco, California in 1917 (div) 2) Laretta Brunner of New York and Washington, D.C. (no children).
Children:	of Milo: after a divorce, Captain Lyman was awarded the custody of his two children: Robert Celia
Death:	Nov. 13, 1942, going down on the "Juneau", sunk by the enemy in battle.

One of the great war heroes of World War II was a middle-aged man born in Pleasant Grove on a farm in a large family of brothers and sisters and half-brothers and sisters living as one harmonious community group.

For ten years Lyman K. Swenson had the guidance of a very spiritual father who died at a mature age of 75 years.

Books of travel were sought and read at every opportunity and young Lyman acquired a strong urge for world travel. Automobiles were getting more common and the picture-show (flickers) further whetted his desire to see the world. He saved enough money to pay his tuition to the nearby Brigham Young Academy. It was the thing to do for each young man to acquire a college education, as Lyman heard the sincere appeal of Karl G. Maeser, the challenging eloquence of James E. Talmage and Ed. S. Hinckley. Almost every Sunday he heard of the growing academy and expanding faculty. His brother, John C. Swenson, had pointed the way and proved education's worth. Lyman had two years at BYA, completing a normal course in 1912.

In that year he was appointed a cadet to the Annapolis Naval Academy and graduated with honors in 1916; this act determined his life career. He taught two years at Annapolis, two years in the naval research laboratory in Washington, D.C., was an Ensign aboard a submarine in the first World War, and subsequently served the navy around the world, assigned to various divisions.

In 1917 he married a beautiful girl in San Francisco, Miss Milo Abercombie, and they had two children, Robert, who attended BYU, and Cecelia. When the parents were divorced, the children lived with their mother in San Francisco. Later, Lyman wed Laretta Brunner of New York, N. Y., who later moved to Washington, D.C.

Son Robert also went to the Naval Academy at Annapolis and followed a navy career for some time.

Between the two World Wars, Lyman added yearly to his rank and ship assignments. He was Provo visitor in 1940 in interest of the Navy and spoke to the student body.

Captain Swenson was in command of the destroyer which took President F. D. Roosevelt to his mid-Atlantic meeting with Prime Minister Churchill in August, 1941. He counted this association as one of the highlights of his life.

When the $12,000,000, 6,000-ton light cruiser Juneau was added to the Navy at the Brooklyn Yard in 1942, Captain Lyman K. Swenson was put in charge of the 30 officers and crew of 600. Five Sullivan brothers of Waterloo, Iowa, and four Roger brothers were in the Juneau crew. The Sullivan brothers were memorialized in a stirring movie soon after the conclusion of the war.

His life was entirely tied up with naval matters to the day of his death. World attention was given to the Captain and his gallant crew when the cruiser Juneau was sunk in the great sea battle off Guadalcanal on November 13, 1942, the cause of the ship's explosion never being accurately determined. President Roosevelt awarded him the Navy Cross for extraordinary heroism in the line of duty, stating "in the line of his profession during action with enemy forces on which occasion the force in which he was attached engaged at close quarters and defeated a superior enemy force. His daring and determination contributed materially to the victory which prevented the enemy from accomplishing their purpose." It was reputed that the Captain was the last man seen alive as the fast-coming waters engulfed the sinking ship.

In Feb. 1944, a destroyer from the Bath Iron Works, Bath, Maine, was launched with the name "Swenson" to commemorate Lyman's heroic death near the Solomon Islands, his daughter Cecelia being sponsor.

The spirit of the Vikings lived in Lyman K. Swenson and he sank with his ship which was his burial vault. He had a deep reverence for nature, admiring most the mountains and the sea. The American flag was his constant companion and a beacon to challenge daily conduct.

"The Story of the Juneau, 'A Survivor's Tale of Fate' " by Jos. P. F. Hartney is given, briefly, herewith:

Dec., 1943

It was not premonition that I felt at that moment that sent a shudder across my spine. The Juneau had been through some hard-fought battles before, and I had no fear that she would not go through others. For I am alive. And over seven hundred of my shipmates are not, 700 men with whom I had worked and laughed and fought, my friends and my officers. The Juneau was a happy ship. There could be no better. She was commanded by *Captain Lyman K. Swenson,* and you can judge for yourself what kind of a man he was by the remark I overhead him make to the commissary Steward on the bridge one day:

"If the ship ration isn't adequate to give good chow—I'll supplement it out of my own pocket."

Do you wonder the Juneau's crew swore by him?

And not only for that. He'd brought us through many a tight place. We'd been in on the initial invasion of Guadalcanal, supporting the landing operations, and we'd been with the Wasp when she went down, and the Juneau had been in the thick of the battle of Santa Cruz. Captain Swenson had returned the compliments of his crew, and many a times at quarters he had expressed in blunt and salty phrases his appreciation of the men who backed him up."

An excerpt from the Navy Department, Division of Naval History (OPO9B9) History of Ship Named Juneau

About one minute past eleven o'clock 13 November 1942, horrified watchmen abroad SAN FRANCISCO observed two torpedo wakes pass ahead of their ship, headed for JUNEAU. With all means of communication gone as the result of battle damage, SAN FRANCISCO was unable to warn JUNEAU who was about 1000 yards on her starboard beam. The JUNEAU literally disintegrated in one mighty column of smoke and flames which rose easily a thousand feet into the air. JUNEAU was the victim of torpedoes fired by Japanese submarine I-26. Only ten of her men aboard at the time, survived the loss of the JUNEAU. Among her 700 casualties was her commanding officer, Captain Lyman K. Swenson in whose honor destroyer LYMAN K. SWENSON (DD 729) is named, and the five Sullivan brothers in whose honor the destroyer THE SULLIVANS (DD 527) is named.

JUNEAU (CL 52) earned five battle stars for her participation in the Solomon Islands-Buin-Faisi-Tonolai Raid, 5 October 1942; the Battle of Santa Cruz Islands, 26 October 1942; and the Naval Battle of Guadalcanal, 12-13 November 1942.

Captain Swenson is honored in our Memorial Hall in the E. L. Wilkinson Student Center.

VASCO MYRON TANNER

Born: October 29, 1892   **Place:** Payson, Utah

Father: John Myron Tanner, b. August 20, 1866. Son of David Dan Tanner and Rebecca Moore. David Dan b. February 8, 1838. d. July, 1948.

Mother: Lois Ann Stevens, b. April 2, 1872 in Fairview, Utah. Daughter of Ransom and Tranquilla Brady Stevens. m. December 21, 1891 (later in Manti Temple). Married Willis A. Brady after death of John M.

Brothers and Sisters: Vasco M,; Geneva, d. at 3 years; Ray S., m. Fay Miner; Lora, m. Carl Swenson; LeRoy, d. in infancy; D. Wilmer, m. Helen Brown; Ransom Rulon, d. in infancy; Jeanette, m. Lee Mower.

Marriage: Annie Atkin, b. December 14, 1891, m. June 5, 1917. Prize winner in poetry and short stories.

Children: Carol, m. Leo Evan Smith; Gloria, m. Maurice Edward Smith; Marilyn, m. Edward Smith Murphy; Carmela Dawn, m. David Pond Forsyth; Vasco Jordan, m. Patricia Nowell. All children college graduates and community workers. Jordan leads a cultural program in Indonesia.

Vasco M. Tanner is one of the outstanding scientists of the Western United States and one of the world's great authorities on beetles. His entomological research has taken him over most of the United States and many foreign lands. His ichtyhological studies were enhanced by personal study with President David Starr Jordan of Stanford University, world authority on fish.

A need for scientific editorial talent and the popularizing of scientific knowledge led Vasco into the editorial field until he became one of the better known science writers of the continent. He has edited several professional journals concurrently; was founder and editor of *The Great Basin Naturalist*, secretary, editor and president of the Utah Academy, especially active in its formative period being a fellow and life member, a fellow in the American Association for the Advancement of Science, and the Entomological Society of America. In 1957 he conferred for several months with some of Europe's best acknowleged authorities by visiting them in their own university centers. He maintains an exchange of research with many of these men.

Nor is Dr. Vasco confined to the laboratory of insect world. He enjoys research in pioneer history, being a descendant of one of Utah's great leaders, John Tanner. His grandmother, Rebecca Moore, was an omniverous reader of history and travel, especially of exploratory ventures. Drake, Magellan, Cook, Vasco da Gama and the like were the heroes written up in her day whose adventures she shared with her grandchildren. She too, was an inquisitive naturalist.

Vasco is a heavy set, blue-eyed man, (growing in weight as long trips become less frequent), with remaining evidences of fading red hair. He is deliberate in action and speech, using an extensive apt vocabulary. His style of speech and writing is logical and seldom, if ever, flowery or verbose. His conducting of meetings whether for the Provo City Power Board, a science session or as president of the Sons of Utah Pioneers, was always carefully planned, time conscious and selective with importance of program material. "Give it to Vasco; it will get done." He honored the importance of time in scheduled meetings.

Conservation and adequate use sums up most of his philosophy on natural resources. He believes in an intelligent cooperation of private business and government, with government owning and operating the utilities. He is an active Democrat and served his State in the legislature, worked for a city charter, and serves the U.S. Forest Department in advisory capacity by making frequent examinations of the flora for harmful insects. Polution of the storage waters receives his especial indictment; the cleaning up of the Great Salt Lake and Utah Lake have received hours of his attention and study.

Dr. Tanner has a restless mind with a free manner of bodily operation; he is not easily hurried. His teaching is thorough and his students have achieved across the continent. For thirty-eight years he has been one of B.Y.U.'s leading professors and the West's best known scientist. A brief of his activities follows:

Education: Head Department Biological Sciences Dixie College —1916-24

Graduated B.Y.U.—A.B. 1915

U. of U., M.A. 1920; Stanford U., Ph.D. 1925; To B. Y.U. 1925, Professor of Zoology and Entomology;

Activities and Honors:

Editor and Founder, *The Great Basin Naturalist,* started 1939 to date; Editor, *Weevils of the Western United States*; Secretary, Utah Academy Sciences Arts and Letters 1928-38; President Utah Academy Sciences Arts and Letters 1945-46; Distinguished Service Award, Utah Academy Science, Arts, and Letters 1959; Fellow—A.A.A. Science, Royal Entomological Society of London, Entomological Society of America; Fellow and life member—Utah Academy Sciences, Arts, and Letters; Member—California Academy of Sciences, Cooper Ornithological Club, American Microscopal Society, Entomological Society of Washington, American Society of Ichthyologists and Herpetologists, American Society of Sigma Xi Stanford University, 1925, Beta Beta Beta Biological Fraternity, 1930, Royal Entomological Society of London; Charter member American Society of Mammologists and member Society of Systematic Zoologists; President National Society of Sons of Utah Pioneers 1962-63; Vice President three years; President Brigham Young Chapter of Provo, 1959; Chairman Provo City Power Board; Provo Chamber of Commerce Forest and Conservation Committee, Uintah National Forest Advisory Council 1961; Utah State Legislature 1962.

HARVEY L. TAYLOR

Born: August 28, 1894   **Place:** Harrisville, Utah

Father: Harvey Daniel Taylor, son of Harvey Green Taylor, grandson of Pleasant Green Taylor, one of Utah's valiant and most loved pioneers. d. in May, 1895, when Harvey L. was ten months of age.

Mother: Lettie May Saunders. After death of Harvey D., she married Samuel Ferrin.

Brothers and Sisters: Oles Mae Taylor and ten half brothers and sisters.

Marriage: Lucelle Rhees of Pleasant View, Utah. Born July 26, 1896, daughter of Bishop Reuben Rhees and Mary Rebecca Tucker. Married May 18, 1916 in Salt Lake Temple. Author, pageanteer, teacher, member L.D.S. Primary Board, and Golden Gleaner.

Children: H. Darrell, m. Barbara Brossard of Rigby, Idaho, killed in auto accident on Scout trip, leaving five children. Ph.D. in modern languages. Mollie May, m. Harvey Johnson; Janyce Lucelle, Ph.D., teaches at University of Utah in Education. Honored by the faculty and students as year's outstanding teacher; Betty, m. Reed Rosenberg.

When Harvey L. Taylor is introduced to an audience, it is not uncommon for the speaker to say, "Civic Leader, author and educator." No Utah man in public today better deserves such an introduction.

He began his civic work before he graduated from College in 1921. His record of some fifty years in the Boy Scout program which led to his Silver Beaver is but one of the activities in which he excelled. Much of his civic work has been tied in with young people, both in his native state and his adopted state of Arizona, where his leadership was early recognized and honored. He served on Arizona governor's Youth Council, Safety Council, Mesa City Health Council, and Mesa Planning Board. He located a natural outdoor amphitheatre near Mesa and wrote and staged patriotic pageants for the thousands in enthusiastic audiences. He was chairman of the Mesa Parks and Playground Board for sixteen years, and one of the best recreational areas is named, "Taylor Field." He is also the recipient of Mesa's first most valuable Citizen Award. Arizona further honored him by giving him the Arizona State Farmer Award and The Phoenix (Ariz.) Rotary "Orchid Award" for outstanding service to youth.

Youth may have been his favored avocation; education is his life time vocation. He was a boy leader and a school leader in high school and college. At Weber College in Ogden, Utah, he was one of my students in public speaking. At a James L. Barker oration contest, he chose as his subject, "Don't Kill the Flowers," and earnestly pleaded for the preservation of our state flower, the Sego Lily (now almost extinct) and the Indian Top, Johnny Jump-ups, stream side buttercups, wild daisies, and mallow—these too have vanished from our mountain sides and rolling hills. Beauty and order have been the expressions of his life. His thoughts are organized in his speeches; his yard is a show place of beautiful flowers and trimmed lawns; his desk is neat and his office expresses taste and sincerity.

Education has been his motivating force, at home, in church, and in the schools. He has a practice of learning something each day. "A teacher must keep ahead of his subject, eternally vigilant for truth, progress and change."

His school experiences seem to indicate that his time has been occupied only with the class room. He believes school and education are as much or more out of the classroom than in it. Some of his best teaching has been done on a street corner, on the gym steps, or by a campfire. He lets example teach when words may fail.

He worked his way through school, accepting jobs of hard labor and little pay to clothe himself and prepare for tuition and books. At Weber College, he met another student, Ernest L. Wilkinson, who also worked his way to honor graduation, formed a friendship which has lasted through the years and led to scholastic associations at B.Y.U.

Harvey was first principal in the rural village of Pleasant View in Weber County, was principal at Hoytsville up Weber Canyon and Weber Seminary in Ogden. He was an instructor at Weber Academy, Weber College, and a teacher at B.Y.U. Harvey spent part of his college days at B.Y.U. under Doctor Brimhall, took an AB from the University of Utah in Sociology, and his masters at Columbia University in New York City, 1925. It was at the latter place, where we lived as room-mates in 1924-25 opposite Saint John the Divine, that I best became acquainted with Harvey. Evening and morning prayers, regular hours for meals and study, a fresh shirt and shined shoes each morning, a ready smile for children on the crowded streets, even a peanut for the little monkey as the hurdy-gurdy played "On The Side-Walks of New York"—all became part of his life. He allotted his evening time only to the best in shows, concerts, and the university lectures when they did not interfere with thesis concentration.

In Arizona, he came to full educational stature. The *Deseret News* wrote of him in 1952, "Mr. Taylor is recognized as a national leader in professional education and has served officerships in the Arizona Education Assn., Arizona North Central Accrediting Committee, and the National Sponsors Student Councils." He has taught at BYU, Arizona State College, and the University of Arizona being educational consultant for the two Arizona Universities. He was credited with bringing to Mesa one of the most modern school systems in the country as superintendent of its schools. He had been president of Gila Junior College at Thatcher, Arizona before going to Mesa. Harvey did post graduate work at Stanford University and State Teachers College of Colorado. The Arizona State College at Tempe further honored him by conferring upon him an honorary doctor of laws degree in May 1956.

It was at the peak of his Arizona leadership when the Board of Directors of the B.Y.U. accepted the nomination of Harvey by President E. L. Wilkinson to be assistant to the president at the church university. He has fulfilled this appointment in the highest degree, honoring each new assignment given him by the president. He became vice president with full responsibilities in all student relations and in addition the vice administrator of the L.D.S. Unified Church School System.

His many talks in educational sessions, his part in panel discussions, his ability to focus attention on proper student needs and trends in social pressures have made Dr. Taylor invaluable to this University and the Church. An edition of the school paper wrote in appreciation of Vice-president Taylor in 1953, "If the facts of personal history mean anything, they indicate that Harvey L. Taylor will undoubtedly become one of Brigham Young University's greatest men." It may have happened, but I have never heard one student speak disparagingly of Harvey L. Taylor; he elicits universal confidence and admiration.

When President Wilkinson was induced to seek nomination and election for the U.S. Senate, it became necessary for him to resign his presidency and executive responsibility; accordingly, Harvey was appointed acting chancellor of the Unified Church School System and Dr. Earl C. Crockett was named acting president of B.Y.U. The campus became more extensive than ever to Harvey and travel became a major part of his executive commitments. New Zealand, Hawaii, Mexico, and Canada welcome his smiles and great experience. At the return of Dr. Wilkinson to again assume the presidency, Dr. Taylor became chancellor of the Unified Church School System with the world as his campus and B.Y.U. as his operating base. The great increase in conversions and corresponding desires of the converts to attend B.Y.U. as the church university makes cooperation between the university and the church school system more necessary than ever.

A Distinguished Service Citation presented to Dr. Taylor by the American Association for Health, Physical Education and Recreation for "his leadership and vision of the values in activities and education for American youth," was made at the Las Vegas convention, March 1967, with our Dr. Leona Holbrook as president.

Harvey Taylor, a noble Son of Brigham, measures up to every challenge.

HENRY D. TAYLOR

Born: November 22, 1903   **Place:** Provo, Utah

Father: Arthur Nicholls Taylor, the son of George Taylor and Eliza Nichols. Parents came from Birmingham, England, started first furniture store south of Salt Lake with photo shop and undertaking.
Born November 2, 1870. Graduated from B.Y.A. Business College 1891. Manager Taylor Bros. Furniture Department for 20 years. Organized the Dixon Taylor Russell Company October 2, 1921. Employed 125 persons in 10 retail furniture stores. Died September 10, 1935.

Mother: Maria Louise Dixon, daughter of Henry Aldous and Sarah DeGrey Dixon.
Born January 5, 1872, married May 9, 1894 in Salt Lake Temple. Served an L.D.S. Mission in England September 4, 1902 to March 1, 1903.
Died February 17, 1947.

Brothers and Sisters: Arthur D., born October 4, 1895 in Provo, m. Maurine Goodridge.
Lynn D., born May 6, 1898 in Provo, m. Celestia Johnson.
Eldon LeRoy, born June 22, 1900 in Provo, m. Ethel Scott.
Henry D., born Nov. 22, 1903 in Provo, m. Alta Hansen.
Alice Louise, born Nov. 18, 1906 in Provo, m. G. ElRoy Nelson.
Clarence D., born May 11, 1909 in Provo.
Orson Kenneth, born Nov. 3, 1913 in Provo, m. Ethelyn Peterson.
Ruth Elaine, born March 20, 1917 in Provo, m. Dr. Fred D. Kartchner.

Marriage: Alta Hansen of Richfield, Utah, on December 26, 1929 in Salt Lake Temple. Daughter of Anders K. and Amelia Hepler Hansen.
Born December 17, 1905.
President of P.T.A. at B.Y.U. Elementary School, graduate of B.Y.U. 1929. Member of Board of Trustees of the B.Y.U. Alumni Association.
Died July 6, 1967.

Children: Henry D. Junior, Anthony H., Stephen K., David A.
All attended B.Y.U.

Henry D. Taylor was one born to leadership. In early life his ready smile and understanding heart drew the rest of the fellows around him and he was invariably chosen as a school class officer and quorum president. His fair play was spontaneous and became expected.

He graduated from B.Y.U. in 1929 and received a Masters Degree from New York University School of Retailing in 1937. Working on various civic communities he was voted president of Provo Chamber of Commerce in 1952, and of the Provo Kiwanis in 1953. He also was Vice-President and Chairman of the Executive Committee of the Utah Valley Hospital for the Church. Much of his daytime activity was absorbed as Secretary-Treasurer and Assistant General Manager of Dixon Taylor Russell Company in Provo.

Religious Activities

His advancement in the church were the results of his earnest efforts and devotion. Mission to Eastern States 1924-1926 under President B. H. Roberts. He served as president of Connecticut District and as Mission Secretary. Returning home, he was appointed President of 123rd Quorum of Seventy—1927-1929. His work with young people was awarded when he became a Master "M" Man in 1939. His quiet efficient service made him a High Councilor and Stake Clerk for Sharon Stake 1933 to February 20, 1944 when he became the Bishop of Pleasant View Ward—February 20, 1944 to January 20, 1946, then becoming the President of Sharon Stake (succeeding Arthur V. Watkins, former U. S. Senator) from January 20, 1946 to time of stake division on November 23, 1952. President of East Sharon Stake November 23, 1952 to August 28, 1955, when he was appointed President of the California Mission—September 10, 1955 to August 20, 1958. While president of the stake he was chairman of welfare work from 1951 to 1955. Sustained assistant of Council of the Twelve on April 6, 1958. Set apart on April 10, 1958.

He was appointed Managing Director of General Church Welfare Committee July 2, 1959, and elected Grand President of Delta Phi Fraternity (Returned Missionaries) on May 21, 1960. In this year he also received the B.Y.U. Alumni Distinguished Service Award. His most gracious and helpful companion, Alta, passed away after a long period of illness. She was a mother to hundreds of young people in the California Mission field and a complete compliment to Henry's church duties.

President Taylor would not be classed as an orator but is one of the most popular speakers in the Church. He inspires confidence and is accepted as a leader in constructive ideas and he is at ease before a business group as he is conducting welfare session. His principles are the same for all walks of life. He lives the ideals which were advocated by founders of Brigham Young University.

HENRY ROLAND TIETJEN

Born: May 21, 1891   **Place:** Santaquin, Utah

Father: Ephraim Henry Tietjen, b. August 10, 1861 at Goshen, Utah. Son of Johann August Heinrich Tietjen and Edna Fredericka Krueger, both of Prussia, Germany. Graduated from German University. Married and moved to Sweden where they heard the gospel. Sold their property for keg of gold; helped twenty-six converts with passage to America. Settled in Santaquin and bought first hay mower in the district. Johann died May 23, 1894.
d. June 15, 1936.

Mother: Elizabeth Euzella Holladay, b. October 28, 1864 in Santaquin. Daughter of David Holladay of Alabama and Henrietta Taylor of Ohio. Living in Nauvoo when Prophet and Hyrum Smith were martyred. The district in Salt Lake known as Holladay is named for the David H. Holladay family before they were sent by President Brigham Young to settle Santaquin, where David H. was bishop until he died. Married December 21, 1882. d. June 20, 1921.

Brothers and Sisters: Jennie Elizabeth, b. July 27, 1884, d. July 30, 1884; Ida T., b. January 8, 1886, m. Arthur Hone; Nettie Chloa T., b. October 7, 1887, m. Albert Greenhalgh; H. Roland; Charles Martin T., b. September 2, 1893, m. Ina Gillette; Eliza Dottie T., b. September 2, 1893, m. R. Floyd Openshaw; David Mayrell T., b. September 23, 1895, m. Emma Jane Johnson; Zelda Druce T., b. July 30, 1902, m. Halbert Jakle; Norman Clifton T., b. January 8, 1909, d. as a child.

Marriage: Sarah Genevieve Willardson, b. April 28, 1891 at Ephraim, Utah; daughter of Erastus Christian Willardson and Caroline Brunhneild Thurston. Married August 18, 1915 in Salt Lake Temple. Attended Snow College and U. of Utah; brief time school teacher. "Mother of Year" from Sanpete and Sevier Counties. Filled mission at Hawaii; Hawaiian Temple Matron.

Children: Elizabeth Bernell T., b. February 24, 1917, m. Reece Dell Cloward; Barbara T., b. May 16, 1919, m. Briant Jacobs, Ph. D.; Henry Willardson T., b. March 19, 1921, d. March 27, 1921; Edward Roland T., b. May 18, 1926, d. May 22, 1926; Melvin E. T., b. November 15, 1927, m. N. Dolores Christensen.

H. Roland Tietjen is a man whom you immediately recognize as a courteous gentleman, a person keenly interested in his fellowmen, a leader of ability with keen insight.

His early home was one of order, neatness, and family devotion. The spirit of his grandfather, whom he never saw, lingered in his father's home—that of a man who put religion above money and service above worldly honors.

Roland was an active debater on the B.Y.U. campus, being president of the Debating Society 1914-15 and vice-president of the Student Body, 1914-15, and taking his AB in 1915. He taught school at the Uintah Academy for two years, then he became assistant cashier of the Payson Exchange Savings Bank for four years (1917-1921). He was executive vice president and cashier of the Monroe State Bank (1923-1956) which was one of eight banks in the state not requiring Federal Funds to put in its capital structure during the great depression 1930-33. Roland became manager of the First Security Bank when his company merged with the Security group. He served as vice president for Utah in American Banking Association 1953-54 and president of the Utah Bankers Association 1951-52. For four years he was a member of the Executive Council of the American Bankers Association. He spent much of his time developing farms and securing industry for Sevier and Richfield valleys, with good personal holdings scattered in this territory. He operated the Tietjen Insurance Agency, representing ten of the nation's largest companies.

Roland was Charter President of the Monroe Lions Club (1927) and president of the South Central Utah Knife and Fork Club. Youth interests early led him to Boy Scout activities as Chairman of Troop No. 626 of Monroe and vice president of the Utah National Parks Council 1939-40, being a Director at Large of the Boy Scouts Council in 1957.

His governmental appointments have been varied and many. He was a member of the War Finance Commission at Payson, Utah, in World War I as well as on a similar committee for World War II. He served in the Utah State Legislature for two terms (1948-52) and was a Republication State Senator (1952-56), and a member of the Legislative Council for 1948-1956.

Paralleling his financial and civic activities have been his church duties. He has been active in all his priesthood quorums, Stake Clerk for three years, missionary to California, counselor and teacher in all the auxiliary organizations, President of the South Sevier Stake 1938-47; patriarch of this stake for 1947-58; director of the Bureau of Information for Hawaiian Temple and the Temple's president from 1959-1963. He was appointed Patriarch for Oahu Stake, 1961-63.

He semi-retired in 1963, which has given the Tietjens time for study travel, as President Tietjen is chairman of a committee on Religion of Book of Mormon Lands. Tours of Mexico, Yucatan, South America, and the Holy Land have been part of his studies.

President Tietjen was elected second vice-president of the B.Y.U. Emeritus Club in 1965 and accepted the chairmanship of its Project Committee, to which he devotes much of his time. He was elected president for 1966-67. His talented wife is companion to most of his interests, as both are keenly interested in the destiny of B.Y.U.

He was sustained as Patriarch for B.Y.U. Sixth Stake and the Language Training Mission on Sunday, November 16, 1966.

JOHN T. WAHLQUIST

Born: September 10, 1899 **Place:** Heber, Utah

Father: Charles John Walquist, b. February 5, 1866 in Ostra Ryd. Ostergotland, near Stockholm, Sweden, son of Anders Frederic and Arma Cathrina Olofson. To America with mother and sister Esther; arrived Heber, Utah July 18, 1877. Helped complete Strawberry Canal. Bishop of Buysville Ward, County Attorney of Wasatch County at thirty-six. d. April 22, 1923.

Mother: Elizabeth Campbell, b. March 11, 1867 in Heber, youngest of 10 children, daughter of Thomas and Elizabeth Davis Campbell. m. August 28, 1895; well-known vocalist. d. August, 1935.

Brothers and Sisters: Keith Campbell, Superintendent of Heber County Schools, d. 1941; Charles Frederick, Mission to Gallup, New Mexico at 68; John Thomas; LeRoy, Associate Superintendent of Ogden City Schools; Mabel, Buyer for Allied Stores, Ogden, Utah; Ruth, died in infancy.

Marriage: Grace Dorius of Ephraim, Utah, b. March 23, 1901, daughter of Lewis O. Dorius and Violet Mellor. m. August 30, 1923. Graduate of Snow College, 1920; Graduate of University of Utah, with honors, 1936; Past President, Salt Lake City, Council of Women; Member General Board of L.D.S. Primary 7 years, and Pioneer Monument Committee; Organizer Utah Minute Women, World War II.

Children: Don Dorius, b. January 27, 1925, Journalist, novelist; Carl Dorius, b. January 14, 1927, architect.

John T. Wahlquist is a tall, well proportioned man of Swedish-Scotch descent and has a light complexion. He appeared to be in his forties when retired from the Presidency of San Jose College at sixty-five.

As a young man he left his beautiful Heber Valley, came to B. Y. High School to graduate as valedictorian and complete a freshman year.

His accomplishments bear record of his life's vocation and professional career. His college companion, Grace Dorius, is one of Utah's leading women citizens and has been a helpful companion in his educational activities, listed below:

Education:

B.Y.U. 1919; B.S., 1924, University of Utah, High Honors, Philosophy; M.S., 1926, University of Utah, Educational Administration; Ph.D., 1930 University of Cincinnati, Secondary Education; Teachers College, University of Columbia, 1939.

Experience:

Principal and teacher in Uintah and Weber Counties, 1918-24; Critic teacher and instructor, University of Utah, 1924-28; Chairman, Home Study Department, University of Utah, 1930-32; Director of Training, William M. Stewart Training School, University of Utah, 1932-41; Visiting Professor at University of Cincinnati, Washington University of Washington (Seattle), San Francisco State College, University of California at Los Angeles, University of Southern California, 1931-47; Dean, College of Education, Professor and Head Department of Education Administration, University of Utah, 1941-52; President San Jose State College, 1952-64.

Affiliations and Activities:

National Council of Education, 1940-47; Utah Education Council Secretary-Teasurer, 1920-42; N.E.A., Committee on Individual Guidance 1937-41; Board of Directors, Utah, 1941-48; Philosophy of Education Society, Fellow 1947; Horace Mann League, National Director 1948-51; American Association of Colleges for Teacher Education, Utah, Representative 1948-51; Rotary Club, President of Salt Lake Club, 1945; Member San Jose Club, 1952; Utah State Text book Committee, 1941-52; Utah Conference on Higher Education, President 1946; Utah Commission on Higher Education, Chairman, 1946-48; Utah Education Association, President college and high school section, 1932-46; Taxation Committee, 1925-28; Legislative Committee, 1940-41; Committee on Teacher Education 1948-52; Utah Academy Sciences, Arts and Letters, Fellow, 1939; Future Teachers of America, Utah State Organizer, 1938-41; Phi Kappa Phi, Phi Delta Kappa, National Delegate, 1935; Kappa Delta Pi, 1953;

495

Intermountain Radio Council, 1942-45; White House Conference on Rural Education, 1944; National Clinic on Teacher Education, 1946; University of Utah, Faculty Council, 1947-52; Chairman, Graduate Committee of Education, 1932-52; Graduate Council, 1932-52; Graduation Committee, 1936-41; Chairman of University Reorganization Committee, 1947-48.

Dr. Wahlquist has professionally appeared in most states of the Union on educational assignments.

Publications:

Reveal forty years of professional print in the *Utah Education Review, School and Society, Journal of Education, Junior College Journal, Salt Lake Tribune, Education Administration and Supervision, Educational Forum, Deseret News, Colliers Encyclopedia, California Schools* and various other journals, including *State Colleges and Universities,* 1964 for Library Education.

Retired on September 10, 1964, on his 65th birthday as President emeritus. Serving as consultant to Dr. Owen J. Cook, acting president of College of Hawaii, Laie, Oahu.

ARTHUR VIVIEN WATKINS

1433 North Inglewood Street, Arlington, Virginia
Grandson of Utah handcart and covered wagon pioneers

Born: December 18, 1886 at Midway, Wasatch County, Utah.

Father: Arthur, Uintah basin pioneer
Born October 22, 1864 in Provo, Utah
Son of John Watkins and Harriet Steel, natives of England
and handcart pioneers
Architect and builder of Coleman Home in Midway

Mother: Emily Adelia Gerber
Born October 12, 1864 in Mound City, Wasatch County,
Utah
Daughter of Johannes Gerber and Anna Maria Ackeret,
native of Switzerland
Johannes an M.D.—doctor in Africa
m. March 19, 1886 in Midway, Utah
Taught school and worked in general store—milliner shop
in Vernal

**Brothers
and Sisters:** (Arthur V.)
John Franklyn, b. August 25, 1888, m., Joanna Todd
Ethel, b. December 17, 1890, m., Dr. Homer Rich (dec.)
(m. Foster)
Nora Adelia, b. September 26, 1892, m., Joseph Cook
Harriet Steel, b., October 22, 1894, d. infancy
Sterling Ackerdt, b. January 8, 1897, died at 16
Fern LaPreel, b., February 11, 1899, d. at birth
Lyle Dewey, b. May 6, 1902, m., Alfreda Myers
Avis, b., April 19, 1900, m. Eugene Chisam

Marriage: Andrea Rich, b. Jan. 18, 1894, daughter of Ben E. Rich
and "Nina" Diana Farr, daughter of Lorin Farr, Ogden's
first mayor and first president of Weber Stake—m. June
18, 1913

Children: Nedra, m. Thomas Reese, Orem
Arthur Rich, Ph. D., m., Ruth Hansen
Don Rich, deceased
Venna R., m. Carl Swalberg, S.L.C.
Jeanene, m. Richard Scott, with General Rickover
Nina, m. Dr. Martin Palmer

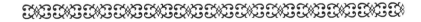

"Art" Watkins, as he is affectionately known, is one of the most respected U. S. Senators of this generation.

His life has always been active and promotional. He was a leader in his grade and high schools and an outstanding college student. He entered B.Y.U. at sixteen, participated in forensics and drama and was a star forward on B.Y.U.'s first championship basketball team. He served a three year mission in the Eastern States, chiefly in Newark, New Jersey and New York City.

After graduating from B.Y.U. in 1906, he attended New York University and in 1912 was awarded an LLB degree by Columbia University, being admitted soon after to practice of law in the State of Utah and beginning his practice in Vernal, Utah. While on his three year mission he had met the youngest daughter of President Ben E. Rich, Andrea, and they were married in the Spring of 1913. The marriage was a happy one for both families as they all were ardent Republicans.

Politics soon played an important part in the young lawyer's life and he was chosen Assistant County Attorney of Salt Lake in 1914, the year of World War I. Moving to Orem, Utah, he answered the call for food production from 1919 to 1925 and was leader in establishing Orem's famous "Scera," a center for community, spiritual, social, athletic and educational needs—a beautiful motion picture palace on week days, used for worship on Sundays, with net proceeds going to city's recreational needs.

In 1929, Arthur was made President of the growing L.D.S. Sharon Stake, a position he held for sixteen years, until he was elected to the U.S. Senate in 1946. He was district judge of the 4th Judicial District of Utah, 1928-33. In 1934 he was chosen chairman of water user's group and became general counsel of the association, successfully sponsoring the Provo River Project.

A few of his many accomplishments in Congress:

Sponsored, won approval and support of President Eisenhower for $760 million Colorado River Storage Act; was recognized as leading Reclamation lawyer and advocate in the Senate.

Author of $70 million Weber Basin Project Act; an organizer of Provo River (Deer Creek) Project.

Author of Bear River Compact legislation; supporter of the proposed Virgin River (Dixie) Project.

Leader in opposition to wasteful Federal expenditures of funds for "pork-barrel" and otherwise unjustifiable projects.

Sponsor of successful Senate action to finance Vernal Unit and Davis County water projects.

Constant supporter of Eisenhower-Benson flexible price-support program on basic commodities.

Advocate of farm production-and-marketing research programs.

Co-sponsor of the National Wool Act of 1954; supporter of the Sugar Act increasing U. S. Allotments.

Sponsored legislation passed to extend farm-credit and drought-relief aids.

Co-sponsor of legislation to return jurisdiction over meat-packer wholesaling practices to Federal Trade Commission.

Champion of Bear River Wild Life Refuge and of the Federal fisheries program.

Proponent of public-lands management legislation, including protection for Utah's school lands.

Sponsor of bills for tariff protection of lead, zinc, and other minerals.

Specialist's knowledge, gained as former member of public Roads Subcommittee, aided in legislation dealing with primary-secondary, forest-access, State-Federal cooperative and other such projects.

Proponent of Federal interstate defense "pay-as-you-go" super highways system.

Hoover Commission economy-in-Government recommendations.

Member of Joint Economic Committee; worked urging national full employment.

Proponent of measures leading to establishment of Small Business Administration.

Active supporter of bills permitting wider membership in Social Security program, to aid local school districts in federally impacted areas, consistent voter for funds to support National Institutes of Health, medical research, and National Science Foundation scientific research programs.

Successful in forwarding selection of record number of Utah jurists to federal-bench authority.

Chosen chairman of the unpopular duty to conduct the Senator McCarthy Censure Committee which gave him national acclaim.

Long-time member of Subcommittee on Internal Security, organized to expose Communist and other subversive activities in U.S.

Specialist through study, here and abroad, in immigration, alien orphan and refugee problems.

Supporter of Veterans' educational, farm-and-home purchase, and medical-aid programs.

Proponent of legislation to assure to Congress more hand in foreign trade policies.

Civil Rights and Indian Affairs

Administration spokesman for Civil Rights legislation, 84th and 85th Congresses.

Leading Senate figure in promotion of "freedom" policy for Indians, better educational opportunities as at Watkins-sponsored Intermountain School, Brigham City, better health and self-support programs. Active supporter of Indian Claims Commission.

1960—appointed chief commissioner of the Indian Claims Commission by President Eisenhower and to adjust and assist Indian tribes in their claims against the U.S. Government to see that original treaties were honored.

His Senate and legal training have enhanced his worth to government and Indian groups.

The government has consumed most of his time since 1946. But he has not been forgotten by his Utah friends, as he was the recipient of the B.Y.U. Distinguished Service Award in 1951 and was given an Honorary Membership to the National Service Fraternity, Blue Key, by the B.Y.U. Chapter in 1957. He has been honored by membership in Lions, Kiwanis, and Rotary Clubs. In 1965, he was given the Abraham O. Smoot Public Service Award by our University.

Retiring from government duties in 1967, he will spend much of his time writing his memoirs of Congress and Washington life.

JOHN ANDREAS WIDTSOE

Born: January 31, 1872   **Place:** Island of Froyen, Norway in tiny hamlet of Dalöe, Norway.

Father: John A., b. in Trondheim, capital of Norway. Died when John Andreas was six years old. A school teacher; devout member of Lutheran Church, had a well stocked library.

Mother: Anna C. Gaarden, b. June 14, 1849. To New York with her two sons, November 17, 1883.
d. July 11, 1919.

Brother: Osborne, six years younger than John, b. 1878; well-known professor of English at University of Utah. d. 1921.

Marriage: Leah Eudora Dunford, b. February 24, 1874 in Salt Lake City; married June 1, 1898. Daughter of Dr. A. B. Dunford, Utah's first dentist and Susa Young Gates, daughter of Brigham Young. Head of Home Economics Department at B.Y.U. 1897-98, one of first in U.S. if not the first. B. Pd. at B.Y. Academy, 1898; Matron, 1906-07; Author, teacher, and lecturer; Honorary Doctor of Humanities, BYU, 1960; Founded the Utah Women's League of Voters and became its first president; President B.Y.U. Emeritus Club 1954; Elected to Utah Hall of Fame in 1958.

Children: Anna G. Wallace; Karl M. (dec); Leah Eudora, m. T. Homer Durham; Mary (dec); John A. (dec); Mark Adriel (dec); Helen (dec).

Death: November 29, 1952

501

From the island of Froyen, the Widtsoes moved to the city of Trondheim to a two room apartment. Widow Widtsoe took her boy's shoes to a shoemaker and asked to have them done quickly as possible. As she left, the cobbler told her he knew of something of greater value than a pair of shoes, the Lord's plan of salvation. She was told he was a Mormon and Mrs. Widtsoe left immediately. When she called for and got the shoes, son John found some paper in the toe of each shoe. They were tracts which the mother ultimately read, called on Cobbler Johnson and went, out of curiosity, to one of his meetings. Two years later, she was baptized in an icy Norwegian fjord (April 1881). By 1883, widow Widtsoe and her two boys John (11) and Osborne (5) landed in New York November 7, 1883.

They soon settled in Logan, Utah in a one room house, their mansion. Six weeks after they arrived, John was attacked by a mad dog and his legs and arms were so badly torn that he remained in bed for six weeks unable to work until following Spring. The mother toiled as a dressmaker while the boys assisted as best they could. At her insistance, they went to B.Y. College in Logan and John graduated in 1891. From there he went to Harvard, where he graduated with highest honors, a stamp of approval he merited all his days.

He was offered a job at U.S.A.C. which he gladly accepted, as professor of chemistry. In 1898, he married Leah Dunford, a beautiful and talented girl and had a "miraculous" honeymoon. John was offered the Parker Traveling Scholarship and the young married couple went to Europe. In 1899, John A. Widtsoe was awarded the Master of Arts and Dr. of Philosophy, with high honors at the University of Gottingen, Germany.

In 1902 he became director of Utah Agriculture Experiment Station and started the non-farmers "Farmers" Roundup and the "Housekeeper's Conference," where husband and wife met for an exchange of news of farm and home progress. A new life was opened up for the farmers and the latest crop soil and table discoveries were passed on to them. To Dr. Widtsoe goes the honor of inaugurating irrigation science.

The direction of his life once established, his progress was constant, and the rest is a record of a busy, brilliant career. In 1905 the Widtsoe family moved to Provo for two years to direct the School of Agriculture and meet some brilliant students. In 1907 he went back to Logan as president of U.S.A.C. In 1917 the Board of Regents appointed him president of the University of Utah, and he brought the school to a full University status. During World War II he was a member of Utah State Council of Defense, and also Food Production Chairman for Salt Lake City.

In 1919, Ann Gaarden Widtsoe died, a precious soul proud of

her two sons' achievements and her testimony of the Gospel. And in 1921, a beloved only brother, Osborne, also passed away. In this year John A. was elected to the Victoria Institute in England, an honor received by only one other L.D.S. scholar, James E. Talmage—this society fosters the ideals of the Christian faith.

The first soil survey of Utah was made under his supervision. He became the forerunner in the world to make irrigation a science and dry farming revolutionized many semi-arid districts. There is a township of Utah named in his honor.

In 1921 he was made an Apostle of the L.D.S. Church, the epitome of his life of service and the avenue of his greatest joy and satisfaction.

Such books as *Who's Who In America, Who's Who in American Education,* and many others attest to his fame as a scholar, a scientist, a public servant and a man of God.

In one of his last letters to the compiler of this book, he wrote, "To help the common man has always been my consuming desire. Hence have come teaching young people, taking the problems of the toiler, notably the farmer, and lifting all into a spiritual realm, hence my devotion to the spread of Gospel knowledge. . . . And I must confess that all my life I would have preferred the quiet, unobtrusive life, especially in the field of experimentation. That drove me into the desert to establish dry-farming as a safe practice." John A. Widtsoe, who's stimulating autobiography *In a Sunlit Land,* says of the B. Y.U. faculty in chapter ten: "The faculty was composed of men and women who had sufficient education for the work to be done, and in the main they were good teachers, better far than the average. Geo. H. Brimhall, N. L. Nelson, J. B. Keeler, and others, younger men who in teaching ability stood high above the average. . . .

"Let it not be forgotten that the B.Y.U. has kept pace educationally with the other institutions of higher learning in the State. Notably under the Presidency of Dr. F. S. Harris, the academic standing of the faculty has become comparable with the best in the land.

"There has been a tendency to over value high learning as a means of good teaching. Out of profound scholarship comes the material used in teaching. It does not follow, however, that the man who discovers truth is a good teacher. Frequently a man of lesser learning, if what he knows is sound, is better able to teach discovered truth than the discoverer himself. A university must possess the research spirit and teach man's knowledge effectively, else it fails in its purposes. It is one of the most difficult problems for university administration to find men who combine good research and teaching ability. Many a young life has been marred by the vain efforts of a learned man to impart his knowledge to others.

"Within the last few decades a vicious practice has grown up in academic circles. Every beginning student is looked upon as a possible candidate for an advanced academic degree. Consequently, the beginning courses of a subject are crowded with difficult, remote problems. For example, the first course in chemistry gives endless time to the mathematics of the laws of Boyle and Avogadro, until the freshman loses interest in the whole subject. Were the fascinating descriptive parts of the science taught first, with laboratory work, a successful return to the laws now heavily stressed might be made. If students are thought fit to enter a class, it should be so taught as to be within the easy understanding of the students. A professor who boasts of failing many of his students should, were education held in right esteem, be quickly dismissed from service. By his own testimony he is a poor teacher, out of sympathy with human life."

He went to Logan in 1907 and I called on him when we took the comic opera "Ermine" from Ogden. This first meeting started a life-time friendship.

Of George H. Brimhall—"As a teacher he was successful, beloved by his students; as a university president he was under severe limitations, small appropriations and narrow acquaintanceship with other and larger universities. His five-minute addresses at the morning assemblies of the students were genius of thought and inspiration. All in all, he was a remarkable man, an example of the majority of the teachers trained in the B.Y. University.

"And it may be added, the B.Y.U. had and has no other reason for existence than to make Latter-day Saints."

"The majority of the patrons of B.Y.U. were farmers—so a department of agriculture was organized with Professors Lewis A. Merrill and William H. Homer, Jr. on part time to assist."

At the conclusion of this chapter he wrote:

"If the B.Y.U. fulfills its destiny it will more and more draw students from the whole world to seek revealed truth and worthwhile practical knowledge . . . It is to be fervently hoped that as the Lord blesses his faithful children with funds beyond their needs, they will make endowments, small or great, as may be possible, to this worthy cause. The largest universities of our country, Harvard for instance, are supported entirely by gifts and grants-in-aid from their many alumni and admirers. We, the students and beneficiaries of this great school, the B.Y.U., must help financially in her growth as well as to be proud of her achievements . . .

"The B.Y.U. must become earth's greatest university."

Some writings of John A. Widtsoe

In Search of Truth; Evidences and Reconciliations; Gospel Interpretation; Rational Theology; Early Discourses of Brigham Young; Priesthood and Church Government; Concordance to the Book of Mormon and Doctrine and Covenants of the Mormon Church; "An Understanding Religion," series of 13 radio talks over KSL; *The Successful Missionary; Gospel Doctrine of President Joseph F. Smith*, by Widtsoe et. al; *Word of Wisdom*, with his wife Leah; *Seven Claims of the Book of Mormon*, with Franklin S. Harris; *Dry Farming*, Translated into several languages; *Principles of Irrigation Practices; Western Agriculture; Education for Necessary Pursuits; Success on Irrigation Projects; Arid Farming in Utah*, with Lewis A. Merrill; *How the Desert was Tamed; Joseph Smith as a Scientist; Lead Ore in Sugar Beet Pulp*, with Lewis A. Merrill; *Man and the Dragon* and other essays; *The Movement of Water in Irrigated Soils; In a Sunlit Land*, autobiography; *In the Gospel Net*, biography of his mother, etc. etc.

One of the West's great scientists was recently honored by the university in "naming the huge new Life Sciences Laboratory Building for the late John A. Widtsoe." The importance of his contributions grow in value with the passing of time.

ERNEST LEROY WILKINSON

Born: May 4, 1899 in Ogden, Utah

Father: Robert Brown Wilkinson, from a family of ten brothers and sisters. Born October 17, 1865 in Salton, East Lothian, Scotland, a suburb of Edinburgh. To Utah in 1875, age of ten, with his father and two brothers, Andrew and Alexander. Worked for John Browning, famed gun inventor, as a farm hand. At fifteen worked for David Eccles in lumber yard. Worked two years in Colorado. To Promontory Point with Southern Pacific. There met and married Cecilia of Bear River City. Worked twenty-five years for Southern Pacific Railroad Company as fireman and locomotive engineer. U.S. Mail contractor for twelve years, working between Ogden Post Office and Ogden Union Station. He and his wife moved to Redondo Beach, California in 1935. After death of wife, lived with his son, Ernest L. until his death at 94, one month lacking 95 years.
d. September 18, 1960.

Mother: Annie Cecilia Anderson of Bear River City, Utah. Daughter of Rasmus Peter Anderson and Ann Marie Jensen. Born October 5, 1874; Married June 12, 1895. Began painting after moving to California, achieving exceptional artistry with more than 100 large canvasses; sales across the country.
d. July 25, 1945.

Brothers and Sisters: Alexander, (died in infancy); Ernest L.; Claude, an engineer, d. in 1942; Robert A., journalist, Massapequa, New York; Elva A. Bell, of Washington D.C.; Glen A., lawyer in Washington D.C.; Woodrow A., vice president Valley State Bank, Salt Lake City, Utah.

Marriage: Alice Valera Ludlow of Spanish Fork, Utah, daughter of Nathaniel and Alice Margaret Jones Ludlow. Born March 7, 1902; married August 15, 1923. Chairman of Cultural Refinement; General Board Relief Society. First lady of a scholastic empire, active in campus programs.

Children: Ernest Ludlow Wilkinson, M.D., Captain U.S. Navy Reserve; Marian, m. Gordon Farr Jensen; Alice Ann, m. John Knight Mangum; David Lawrence, graduate of University of California Law School, student of Oxford University in England for two years; Douglas Dwight.

Education:

Weber College, Ogden, Utah, 1917-1918. Editor of school paper, twice president of the studentbody; member state championship debating team, valedictorian and given efficiency medal for best all-around student. Taught English and public speaking 1921-1923.

Brigham Young University, Provo, Utah, A.B. 1921; Honorary L.L.D. 1957. President of his class, winner of Rocky Mountain extemporaneous speaking contest, member several victorious debating teams, editor of school paper; founder and president of Public Service Bureau; one of recognized leaders in the country.

George Washington University, Washington D.C., LL.B 1926, summa cum laude. Awarded scholarship to Harvard Law School.

Harvard University, Cambridge, Mass., S.J.D. 1927.

A member of faculty, Weber College 1921-1923; of the Business High School, Washington D.C. 1923-1926; Superintendent Camp Good Will, Washington D.C. 1925; appointed assistant professor of law, University of California 1927, resigned to become professor of law, New Jersey Law School, 1927-1933; member of Governor's Committee representing Utah to White House Conference on Education, 1955; President of Brigham Young University 1951 to 1964, reappointed, 1965 to present. Chancellor of Unified School System of Church of Jesus Christ of Latter-day Saints, comprised of one university, one junior college, 130 institutes of religion serving 130 universities and colleges, and 158 released time and 1,075 non-released time seminaries of religion, 1953-1964; member Accreditation Commission for Business Schools, 1961-1964.

The second great period of his life further reveals his ability as a superior educational executive. No facet of the great university has gone unobserved nor neglected. Faculty intellectual growth and departmental expansion, student body needs in scholarship, housing, avenues for research in libraries and laboratories, individual growth, care for health, diet and opportunities for work to meet necessary needs are daily concerns; campus expansion, utility, and beautification are constantly praised, approved and improved. The foundation of the university as a center for religious study and application has been stressed in every day of a crowded calendar. From a student body of some 5,000 to a resounding 20,000 speaks volumes of evident growth, but reveals little of the number of challenging problems to meet such phenomenal expansion and promise of population pressure.

President Wilkinson has built his faculty in number and quality in each department of the university. The art of teaching, the humanities, religion, the sciences, the arts, health and physical education, agriculture, all have had improved physical surroundings and many have acquired the most modern equipment. The great student center, the magnificent F. S. Harris Fine Arts Center with its numerous theatres, music, art, and speech aids, the superb J. Reuben Clark Library to accommodate a million books, the spacious Stadium and sports center, the Richards Olympic swimming pools, dance and game center, the commodious dormitories for men and women, a village for married families, several High Rises for more students, restaurants and cafeterias to feed the thousands—these best reveal the real Ernest Wilkinson. He asks that his works be his advocate. We will never know E. L. Wilkinson by sitting with him in the parlor. We have to see him at work. He finds a problem, studies it's source and needs, calls his best advisers on the subject, gets their answers and suggestions, then sits alone at his desk, perhaps for hours or even days, and comes up with a well worked out plan for presentation and fulfillment. His ability to present a problem in a concise, well documented manner, having all foreseeable challenges answered beforehand, the use of statistical proof to fortify his major premise, these have been time saving techniques that have greatly pleased his colleagues, the Church authorities, and various boards of which he is a member. When a certain friend of his and mine saw Ernest coming in the doorway of the Church office building, with a bulging brief case and a very serious face, he turned and said, "We'd better give it to him now and save time for all of us." When ever E.L.W. presents a case or makes a request, he is prepared.

Nor is the "Little Man", as some of his colleagues refer to him, always so serious. He loves a joke and can tell some of them. He may appear as the unmasked "Cosmo", the school mascot, or you'll see him chase and catch a greased pig before the student body and to the surprise and delight of thousands of students in the field house, he pulled off his coat and did more than a half hundred "push-ups" as they unitedly counted. And that not so long after a heart attack! Some of them almost had attacks of their own watching him.

His Alma Mater has honored him in many ways. The Alumni Association presented him its Distinguished Service Award in 1963. In June, 1957, his Board of Trustees conferred upon him the honorary degree of Doctor of Laws for being "an able scholar, outstanding lawyer, dynamic leader, distinguished administrator, prodigious worker, man of simple faith and multiple deeds." He is a "Friend of the BYU Library", an honorary Cougar Club member, also an honorary Blue Key. By popular demand of the students, the beautiful student building (one of America's most beautiful edifices) was officially named "The Ernest L. Wilkinson Student Center."

His honors are national in scope as he was awarded the George Washington Medal by Freedom Foundation for Speech on Free Enterprise, 1961; and the award of American Coalition of Patriotic Societies, 1963.

508

It is quite natural that a man of executive ability, wealth and speaking power would be elected to various boards of business and service. He was a member of the U.S. Chamber of Commerce Committees on Government Expenditures, 1952-1958; on National Defense, 1959 to 1962. He is a member of the Board of Directors, Deseret News Publishing Co., 1954 to date; Beneficial Life Insurance Co., 1957 to present; KSL Incorporated, Radio Service Corp. of Utah, 1960 to date; Ellison Ranching Co., 1962 to date; Rolling Hills Orchard, 1961 to date; member Board of Trustees of Utah Foundation, 1960 to date; Foundation for Economic Education, Inc., 1960 to date; member National Committee to evaluate United Service Organization, 1962; Committee Member International Council for the Hall of Free Enterprise for World's Fair in New York in 1964; member National Speakers Bureau of American Medical Association, 1962; member Board of Visitors, Freedom Foundation at Valley Forge, Penn., 1964 to present; Board of Directors, the Right to Work Committee Inc., Washington D.C., 1964 to date; member of Provo and Salt Lake City Chambers of Commerce; Honorary Rotarian.

At the solicitation of friends and party leaders, he consented to become the Republican candidate from the State of Utah for the United States Senate in 1964. Like many a good Republican, he succumbed to the Democratic landslide and was immediately reinstated as president of the Brigham Young University. He lists himself as a Jeffersonian Republican and encourages students to earnestly study government and politics and have a sound business education.

GOVERNMENT AND PROFESSIONAL:

Short enlistment in U.S. Army as private, 1918. Admitted to Washington D.C. Bar, 1926, Utah Bar, 1927, New York Bar, 1928. Associate in law firm of Hughes (Chief Justice), Schurman and Dwight, New York 1928-1935; deputy superintendent of insurance for New York State to investigate insurance companies, 1931; member Moyle (Walter Gladstone) and Wilkinson, Washington D.C., 1935-1940; head of E. L. Wilkinson firm, Washington D.C., 1940-1951; member Wilkinson, Cragun and Barker, Washington D.C., 1951 to date remaining as senior partner. Represented Ute Indians in obtaining largest judgment ever obtained against the United States (see comments in later paragraph).

At various times engaged by Standard Oil Co. of New Jersey, Standard Oil of California, Fox Film Corporation, Ford Motor Co., Chicago Title and Trust Co., Atlas Powder Company, and Rose Packing Co. For a time general counsel for the National Council of Farmers Cooperatives and also the National Grange. Prosecuted and defended anti-trust suits; appeared before government agencies in the field of taxation and communications. Member of National Committee of Army and Navy Chaplains, 1947-50. Member Order of Coif, Fellow of American Bar Foundation, 1965 to present.

That we may more fully judge the legal ability of our present president I have asked permission to present a few paragraphs from his legal colleagues to aid in this evaluation. Possibly no other set of cases before the United States Court of Claims ever attracted such professional attention and praise as his prosecution of the Claims of the Ute Indians. In part it follows:

Illustrative of his legal acumen and industry was his representation of the Ute Indians, in which he succeeded Judge Hughes, when the latter was appointed Chief Justice of the United State Supreme Court. Engaged by them to prosecute claims having a value of not to exceed two million dollars, which on investigation proved to be lacking in merit, he undertook a detailed study of the century old relationship between the Ute Indians and the United States. This investigation and the succeeding prosecution of claims against the government, which became *causes celebre* in American Jurisprudence, was so carefully and painstakingly planned and executed that before it was over some 13 years later, he and his assistants had been successful in obtaining judgments of nearly $32 million and the restoration of some 429,000 acres of land. One of the judgments for $25 million, the trial of which lasted for 16 weeks and was conducted personally by Mr. Wilkinson, was the largest judgment ever obtained against the United States.

The Court then proceeded in accordance with the provisions of his attorney's contract with the Ute Indians to determine the value of the services of Mr. Wilkinson and his assistants. Since it is rare for an attorney's ability and services to be evaluated by a full court in contested litigation of this nature, a summary of the appraisal of Mr. Wilkinson's services given by distinguished witnesses and the court in a printed opinion of 73 pages (120 Court of Claims, 699) is unusually pertinent. Testifying for Mr. Wilkinson were the late Owen J. Roberts, who had resigned as an Associate Justice of the Supreme Court of the United States in 1945, Homer Cummings, former Attorney General of the United States, and Seth Richardson, who had been Assistant Attorney General of the United States in charge of defending Indian tribal suits during the Hoover Administration and who at the time of the hearing was chairman of the Subversive Activities Board of the United States.

Roberts testified to the "high measure" of "fidelity" of Mr. Wilkinson; further that "at every stage of the proceedings* * * the right course to bring the results seems to have been chosen" by Wilkinson and his associates despite "amazing difficulties" which they had to meet constantly. He paid Mr. Wilkinson the compliment of having handled the claims "with all the skill of a great advocate and a great trial lawyer," further stating "As I cast the horoscope of these cases, thinking of what I would have done had I been the lawyer * * * I would not have known how to proceed."

Mr. Cummings testified that in his opinion Mr. Wilkinson and his associates were "men of eminence, reputation and un-doubted ability" and that the main case which they handled "ought not to be called a case. It is a lifelong adventure." He stated that it was a "tribute to their public spirit" that men of such eminence would take the Indian claims on a contingent fee basis, and he paid tribute to the "tenacity, optimism and never-say-die spirit of counsel." As to their performance, he testified: "I don't think any disinterested person can trace the history of this case without doffing his cap to counsel who prevailed against such odds. It is an amazing performance."

Mr. Richardson testified that although he had actively and strenuously practiced law for nearly half a century and had tried al-most every known kind of a case, including Indian cases, the amount of service rendered by Wilkinson and his associates "almost staggers our imagaination * * * I never saw anything like this in my life. I never expect to again. I don't think you will ever see anything like it * * * To me the amount of services rendered here is almost impossible for the ordinary mind to grasp." He stated that the amount and char-acter of service rendered by counsel could "almost be written as a text book to give to young lawyers to show what men can do if they have got sufficient courage and industry and brain. * * * There have been no sponges left in the wound of this operation, it has been almost a classic job." The most extraordinary feature in the case, he testified, was the "detailed faithfulness with which the interests of these In-dians have been preserved." He opined that "three-quarters of this case, speaking in rough fractions, was dug up and found, mined out and discovered" by counsel for the Indians.

Pointing out that at one time Mr. Wilkinson set himself a goal of recovering $30 million, Mr. Richardson testified: "* * * it is an extraordinary thing to look at $30 million as a goal over the rough pathway that this suit had to go, and then come out with $32 million. * * * That is two million above perfection." Stating he was testifying without any monetary compensation, he concluded: "I will tell you what I did. I got a copy of it (Wilkinson's affidavit of services) and took it to the two attorneys in our office that are now working on Indian cases and said, 'Boys, the time you spend reading this is the most valuable time you can spend in the next two years. You nor I never had an opportunity to contact human work in the profession of law that compares with this case. It is the most extraordinary thing I ever saw."

The Court, in its findings of fact (120 C. of Cls, 609) found that "Mr. Wilkinson's rating by Martindale Hubbell law directory is the highest given for legal ability and character. He is a man of complete integrity with high principles of duty and performance, and is a prodigious worker."[1] The Court also found that "the nature of the understanding was such as to require of the Attorney more than the prosecution of normal litigation in which the claims are known and defined and the forum exists when counsel are engaged. It required virtually the full range of services known to the legal profession. * * * professional experience and skill of a high and versatile order." (p. 668). "His professional responsibility approached the ultimate." (p. 668).

In more detail, the court, in exhaustive findings, made the following conclusions as to the legal ability and professional conduct of Mr. Wilkinson and his assistants (the phrase "the Attorney" refers to Mr. Wilkinson personally): "Novel and difficult questions of law were involved in the cases. Counsel had to chart new paths * * * . (p. 669) "Counsel exhibited high skill and unusual industry in their discovery, investigation, analysis, and presentation of the claims." (p. 670). "The administrative services of counsel were conducted with constancy and persuasive skill." (p. 670). "The acumen and finesse devoted by counsel, principally by the Attorney, to legislative work * * * the ability of the Attorney to anticipate the questions of Congressional committees, to assemble the facts and present them to the committees as an orderly and convincing case on the merits, met the highest professional standards." (pp. 670-671). "The record of these cases is one of complete fidelity on the part of the Attorney to the interests of his clients. * * * When he was offered an over-all settlement of $20,000,000, he declined it and insisted upon securing the full measure of compensation to which he felt his clients were entitled, although such action on his part was, at the time, fraught with the prospect of indefinite delay in realization by him of remuneration for his services." (pp. 671-672).

As to the accomplishments of Mr. Wilkinson, the court found: "This proceeding marks the culmination of 16 years of successful advocacy by the Attorney in behalf of his clients. The Attorney has presented an impressive record of industry, skill, tenacity, and fidelity, all directed into the channels of artful persuasion." (p. 657). "The results accomplished were outstanding." (p. 669). "The recovery was

---

[1] In a footnote to its findings, the court noted that during the 16 year period from 1935 to 1950 his professional working hours exceeded 10 per day, Saturdays and legal holidays included, with only two short vacations. "The hours he has worked in 16 years would be the equivalent of 26 years" for persons who work 8 hours per day, 5 days per week, the court observed.

larger than the goal that had been set." (p. 670)

The broad range of Mr. Wilkinson's clients from large corporations to penniless Indians, some of whom he served without compensation, shows his dedication to the ideal that both the rich and the poor are entitled to justice and that attorneys have an obligation to make this ideal a reality even though it means no compensation.

I have known Ernest L. Wilkinson since his school days at Weber Academy, when he and Harvey L. Taylor were enrolled in my public speaking classes. It was there I first became acquainted with his alert mind and systematic approach to all his problems. With his own transportation company he moved my household belongings from Ogden to Provo and roomed with us for a short spell while at school. I had him in one of our first varsity plays but learned he was a better speaker.

In many of our plays we had a lovely, vivacious young lady, pretty, punctual, dependable and an excellent actress. Alice Ludlow of Spanish Fork responded to Ernest's attentions and a popular marriage was consumated in 1923. Both Alice and Ernest are deeply religious. The burden of the upbringing of a family of five has been left chiefly to the efficient mother. She has been an officer in the YWMIA and is an active member of the LDS Relief Society General Board, filling many speaking assignments. The Wilkinsons' or President's Home is the scene of numerous receptions, faculty and student gatherings, presided over by a queenly hostess.

The nine leaders of the University have each in their own peculiar and sincere way left a record of devotion, progress and expansion to fit the special needs of the times and have left that image imperishably stamped on the institution. President Wilkinson has built on the foundation left by each of the previous presidents, magnified their dreams and brought the school to its place of importance which President John A. Widtsoe predicted, a School of Destiny.

If you knew his father you could expect honest effort and hard work from his sons; if you knew his mother you would look for gentility, affection and artistic appreciations. There are no half way efforts with either of them. Ernest L. has been written up in "Life" as a "Mormon Dynamo", colleagues have referred to him as a "Little Napoleon"; all admit he is an indefatigable worker, often absorbed in concentration to such an extent he will pass a loyal friend without recognition. He thinks big, plans big, achieves big. He is a courageous patriot, sincerely religious and shares his blessings with hundreds of needy students. He is one of America's great educational leaders.

DAVID J. WILSON

Judge of the United States Customs Court

Born: October 27, 1887   **Place:** Midway, Utah

Father: James B. Wilson was born August 22, 1856 in Carson City, Nevada. He was the son of James T. and Isabel Ross Wilson. Long time member of the Utah State Legislature (25 years). Was a member of the first class to be graduated from the University of Utah (Deseret). President of Midway Town Board for many years and in the bishopric for 15 years.

Mother: Margaret Powell, daughter of Reese Powell and Margaret Morgan, born September 2, 1858 in Llansawel, Cavarthenshire, South Wales. Mormon convert; came to Utah with her parents. Married on September 29, 1881 in the old Salt Lake Endowment House. Homesteaded with husband in Midway.

Brothers and Sisters: J. Brigham, b. July 12, 1882, m. Lota Huffaker
Edna, b. April 4, 1884, m. Wm. G. Young
Belle, b. Dec. 11, 1889, m. Dr. Wayne B. Hales
R. Arthur, b. Jan. 13, 1896, m. Eva Huber
Edith, b. May 22, 1898, m. Grant Y. Anderson

Marriage: Mary Jacobs of Ogden, Utah; daughter of Henry C. and Emma Rigby Jacobs. Born February 17, 1896; married, May 31, 1916. Former member of the L. D. S. Relief Society Board; eight years Corresponding Secretary and member of the Board of Directors of the American Mothers Association of New York.

Children: Marion, m. Dr. O. Meredith Wilson; President of University of Minnesota
Margaret, m. L. C. Barlow, M. D.; Eugene, Oregon.
D. Jay, m. Blanche Peterson; Ogden Attorney
L. Keith, m. Margaret West; Professor at University of Utah
Don B., m. Lorraine White; Ford sales manager
All five children were born in Ogden, Utah and the first four graduated from the B.Y.U.

Educational Activities:

David J. was born to be a leader. All through his schooling he was selected to lead his class in various celebrations and school activities, all the while working on a farm with its fence, food, gardening, planting, and haying activities.

He went to Brigham Young Academy in the days when it was emerging to a university. There were no formal leagues or athletic conferences, but David encouraged inter-mural competitions and was the first student body president to set rules governing debate, drama, athletics, student honors, etc. As manager, he arranged debates with Southern California and the University of Nevada and with Hawaiian student, Charles Schwenke, won both contests.

While Student Body President, he led in procuring funds to send Alma Richards to the Stockholm Olympics in 1912. Richards won first in the high jump.

He contributed various articles affecting student government to the "White and Blue" for two years while on the editorial staff. When he was S. B. President in 1911-12, the responsibility of publishing a yearbook was taken over by the student body instead of an uncertain publication by various classes as previously done.

In 1914 he was president of the Senior class and was its valedictorian. He sponsored the student body fee to enable all students to attend school functions and provide a fund and budget concerning all student activities.

David is a very handsome man looking every inch a judge, as he is. His black eyes demand and keep attention; his fearless honesty is his great strength. He is serious but never dull and smiles easily brighten his face while the number of friends has increased as his territory of activity expands. One of his better students called him a man's man, to which he easily answers.

He added stature to his reputation as editor of the *California Law Review*; was awarded the Willard D. Thompson Scholarship for two years and elected to Phi Alpha Delta, legal fraternity.

Teacher:

Head of the English Department Weber Academy 1914-16. Taught college English and Commercial Law Weber College in 1919-21. Teaching Fellow, Political Science, University of California 1916-17.

Professional Career:

Admitted Utah State Bar 1919; engaged in general practice of law Ogden, Utah, until 1954. Member Utah State Bar Commission 1953-54; presently member of Utah State Bar and of Federal Bar Association. Served as Weber County Attorney 1921-25; District Attorney, Second District Utah 1929-33. Appointed United States

Judge in July 1954, serving on United States Customs Court in New York City for twelve years. Moved to Salt Lake as a Senior Judge of the court, holding sessions in the western United States.

Civic Affairs:

President Lake Bonneville Council Boy Scouts of America 1947-48-49; Chairman, Advisory Board, Salvation Army, Ogden, Utah, several years; Secretary and President Ogden Kiwanis Club, and Secretary Utah-Idaho Kiwanis District. Now Honorary member of Ogden Club. Helped organize United Fund (Community Chest) Ogden. Presently member of Advisory Committee, American Mothers Committee, Inc., New York, and of Lochinvar Club, an organization composed of about twenty-five former western men now serving in prominent positions in New York. Awarded honorary degree, Doctor of Law, 1963, Brigham Young University, where he delivered Baccalaureate Address.

Business:

One of organizers of Federal Building and Loan Association and of Associated Investment Corporation. Served as Director, Vice President, and General Counsel of former company 1922-54, and of latter corporation 1930-54.

Political:

Weber County Republican Chairman, 1924-30; Chairman, First Congressional District, Utah, 1922-32; Utah State Republican Chairman 1936-44; Delegate Republican National Conventions 1932 and 1940; Party's candidate for Congress 1946 and 1948.

Church:

Served as Ward and Stake Sunday School Superintendent; Stake Y.M.M.I.A. Superintendent; member of Mt. Ogden and New York Stake High Councils; Bishop Ogden 12th Ward September 1924 to December 1935; Mt. Ogden Stake Presidency, 1935-39. Taught Investigators' Class, Westchester Ward, New York Stake, for past several years.

Residence in New York:

He has now spent approximately eleven years as a United States Judge serving on the United States Customs Court and has conducted court in all the principal cities of the United States, including Honolulu. He has also held court in San Juan and Ponce, Puerto Rico. During their residence in New York his wife, Mary, has served continuously as a member of the General Committee of the American Mothers, Inc. She has been Vice President for several years and is serving as a member of the Executive Committee of the National Council of Women.

The Wilsons have given the world a notable family, each having achieved in his or her own rights. Retirement brings them back to their mountain home where David continues to be an active Son of Brigham. He is Project Chairman of the B.Y.U. Emeritus Club 1966.

V

Men who studied with or under

Franklin S. Harris

(1921-1945)

Franklin S. Harris (*July 1, 1921—Jan. 30, 1945*)

ARIEL SMITH BALLIF, SR.

Born: December 9, 1901   **Place:** Logan, Utah

Father: John Lyman Ballif, Sr.
b. December 23, 1864
m. October 20, 1886
d. December 6, 1941
Successful merchant and devoted churchman.
He was especially active in serving the poor.

Mother: Emma Smith, daughter of Bishop Thomas X. Smith and Margaret Gurney of Logan, Utah.
b. October 19, 1864 m. October 20, 1886 d. April 6, 1942
An accomplished musician with a beautiful voice which she generously shared. Reputed for the beauty of her surroundings and the love she radiated.

Brothers and Sisters: John L., Jr. (dec), m. Cora Hansen
Elise (dec).
Clarmond (dec), m. Roy Yearsley
Florence (dec), m. Dr. Asael C. Lambert
George Smith, m. Algie Eggertsen
(Ariel S.)
Harriette, m. Theo Berrett

Marriage: Artemesia Romney, daughter of George Samuel and Teressa Artemesia Redd Romney. b. August 27, 1904, Chihuahua, Colonia Juarez, Mexico m. August 28, 1925 Two missions to New Zealand. Organized Primaries in 1927-30. Excellent actress and dramatic reader.

Children: Ariel S., Jr. b. May 29, 1926, expert stage designer for U. of Utah
Moana B., b. June 4, 1928, m. John Harper Bennett, member YWMIA General Board
Merilyn B., b. December 1, 1930, m. James Oman Lavenstein
Jae R., b. July 5, 1932, m. Carma Fillmore, on B.Y.U. faculty.
Bonnie Laurie, b. February 15, 1940, professor of psychology.

Education:
Ricks College—Teacher's Certificate
1925—BYU—B.S.
1937—USC—M.A.
1945—USC—Ph. D.
Major in sociology
BYU Varsity football, basketball, and track
Won the Gold Medal for Vocal Music in Contest, 1924
1922-23 Taught at Parker High School, Rexburg, Idaho
1925-26 Taught at Madison High School, Rexburg, Idaho
1926-27 Taught at Ricks College
1927-30 Principal Maori Agriculture College, Hastings, New Zealand
1930-36 Principal Seminary, Midway, Idaho
1938- Teacher at B.Y.U. to date
1928-39 Instructor
1939-43 Assistant Professor of Sociology
1943-44 Associate Professor of Sociology
1944- Professor
1952-54 Acting Dean of Summer School
Advisor to Foreign Students
Specialist in family and race relations and social welfare.
Chairman of Foreign Student Activities at BYU
Acting Dean of Students 1954
Religion
L.D.S. Mission to New Zealand—1927-30
L.D.S. Mission to New Zealand—1955-58; President
Went with his wife, Arta and daughters, Marilyn and Bonnie
High Priest, High Council, Bishop, East Provo Stake President, President of Y.M.M.I.A., Patriarch.
Affiliations
UEA
American Sociology Association; A.A.A.S., Phi Kappa Phi
Alpha Kappa Delta
National Council on Family Relations
Civic and Government
Relocation Adjustment Advisor War Relocation Authority
Commissioner one term for seven Western States
Mayor of Provo, Utah until Charter revoked 1961
A six-week interim mayor of Provo.

Ariel Smith Ballif is a large man, with broad shoulders which have known hard farm work and the crash of padded opponents on the football field. His smile is readily used and his frown is infrequent. He has a happy disposition and always looks for the more pleasant situations in life.

Reared in a fervently religious family with most congenial parents, he early learned to avoid trouble, but not to shirk an honest task. The fellow on the next block was as interesting to him as the boy next door; peoples of the world challenged his boyhood interest, while books of history and countries occupied much of his early reading. The success and downfall of a nation proved as interesting to his inquisitive mind as the reason for success or failure of a cause or person. Family and government easily became his major concern and shaped his college career. Had not the Church consumed so much of his time, he would have been an officer in national sociological circles.

His mission to New Zealand in his twenties opened to him the Polynesian doors of culture and ethnic importances. His return to New Zealand in years later to establish schools and a temple further broadened his knowledge and developed an understanding of the common brotherhood of man. As chairman of the foreign students at our Church University, his scope of interest is world-wide, and students from all over the earth count him as friend and wise advisor.

His counsel on social matters, family relations, governmental trends and reform is sought by his colleagues as well as by his numerous students. In his maiden and only effort in politics he was successful and became mayor of Provo, a term shortened by a change in city government. He was relocation adjustment advisor for the War Relocation Authority for seven Western States.

With the strong emphasis put upon religious training at B.Y.U., Ariel is one of Brigham's leading sons. His talented and cooperative wife has further added to his university and educational strength.

RAYMOND EARL BECKHAM

Born: February 18, 1927   **Place:** Chandler, Arizona

Father: Charles Marvin Beckham

Mother: Quintilla Spurlock

Brothers and Sisters: Rodric Charles, Anna Laree, Lorraine

Marriage: Ida Lee Jackson, daughter of Leland and Ida Walser Jackson of El Paso, Texas. m. June 17, 1947 in the Arizona Temple

Children: Raymond, Eric (Rick), Randall, Renae.

Ray Beckham is one of the present university's outstanding campus leaders. The university has been the chief cause for his coming to Provo and the sole reason for his remaining.

He was educated in Arizona elementary schools, a graduate of Safford High School, where he was a student body officer and a star athlete, being tall and wiry and adept in basketball, softball, football and tennis. Usually he was the captain in M.I.A. activities. At B.Y.U. he was responsible for athletic publicity in 1949-50 and was a member of the important Athletic Council. He helped to organize the B.Y.U. Cougar Clubs, both on and off the Campus.

Ray registered at the University of Utah after high school graduation. He had completed one quarter when Uncle Sam appointed him a member of the United States Navy. Soon after entering the Navy, he was converted to the Church in Oakland, California, which directly gave him the course which has affected his life. After an honorable discharge in May, 1946, he entered BYU and immediately became an active leader in student affairs by being elected a member of the Intercollegiate Knights and Blue Key organizations, service groups on the campus. He was elected vice-president of the growing BYU Student Body, became associate editor and business manager of the "Y News" (Universe). Graduating in 1949 in marketing and journalism, he was employed by the University as assistant director of the Extension Division (1949-52) and organized the first BYU Evening School and the Department of Travel-Studies. As chairman of Public Services (1950-52) he was responsible for many of the new school-city relations and expansion of the student Program Bureau. He edited the expanded Alumni Magazine in 1951 and 1954.

On September 17, 1954, Ray was appointed Secretary of the BYU Alumni Association, succeeding W. Cleon Skousen. With this new responsibility and challenge Ray's executive ability was given greater scope and opportunities. The full membership of the great Alumni had never been contacted and the Alumnus Magazine previously was sent only to those who paid a membership fee. Ray set about getting an up-to-date mailing list and started a biographical file for every former student of record. Because of the great number enrolled in the first two decades of the school who were mature and older, the Alumni records were set up to include students whether they were taking a full course or not. With the Alumni officers approval, Ray set 1920 as the year to start including only those students in the Alumni Association who had passed a quarter or more of registered college work. When he set up programs to acquire funds through Alumni participation, the Magazine started to go to all Alumni. Alumni dues were abolished and all Alumni were made to feel a part of the organization. The B.Y.U. Alumni Association was the first in the nation to place its records on IBM cards.

As fast as machinery could be set up to inaugurate fund raising campaigns, Ray added proper personnel and began the systematic organizations for Alumni Fund raising. His experience with the American Alumni Council was invaluable. He is the original planner of the Destiny Fund, one of the most successful in the school's history, and is probably responsible for raising more money for B.Y.U. than any man in the history of the school. The Alumni Fund was first promoted in 1956. Ray was a key member in the Central Committee for the B.Y.U. Field House Drive, 1949-51, named for President George Albert Smith. As the momentum of the drives increased, he was the Acting Director of University Development 1964-66 and was appointed Director of University Development on January 19, 1966. This marked the beginning of the first permanent long-range development and fund raising program for the school, and national committees were set up to direct the work. Such activities and pronounced successes led to his appointment to membership on the B.Y.U. Administrative Council.

He was the Senior Class Advisor until 1964 and was the designer and original promoter of the magnificent B.Y.U. Alumni Association Aspen Grove Family Camp, growing in popularity each year. He has been faculty advisor to many student organizations, serving with the Intercollegiate Knights since 1949.

For the Church, he has been chairman of the ward building fund, a member of the East Provo Stake High Council, the Bishop of the 9th Ward in the B.Y.U. Stake 1956-62, member of the B.Y.U. Stake Presidency 1962-64, and Stake President B.Y.U. First Stake 1964. Nor are his activities confined entirely to Church and Alumni. He is one of the four major persons to secure the bell from the battleship "Utah" for the State of Utah and present this bell to the Utah State Historical Society in Salt Lake City. He arranged the first Armed Forces Radio Service broadcast from this area of a B.Y.U.-University of Utah basketball game in February of 1956.

Ray is an active Rotarian, has been a Red Cross District Chairman, advertising director for Taylor Brothers for six years, member of Board of Directors for Taylor's Inc. and secretary of the board, and vice-chairman of Utah County E. L. Wilkinson Senate Candidacy.

His promotion of the most extensive Explorer program on the campus has attracted church and national attention. He participates in all major student body activities, usually as a committee member and a chairman of some group, such as a work party on "Y Day". It was on one of these days he caught the greased pig (1956) to the delight of thousands of onlookers.

The Beckham family pools their interests in getting out an annual Christmas letter, gems of family information and Yuletide cheer.

Brigham Young University is the richer in many ways for the coming of Raymond E. Beckham.

WAYNE CLAYSON BOOTH JR.

Born: February 22, 1921

Father: Wayne Chipman Booth, son of Robert Ebenezer Booth and Lovenia Jane Chipman. b. April 16, 1892. Graduate B.Y.U. 1924. d. 27 April 1927.

Mother: Lillian Clayson Booth (Davis), daughter of Eli J. Clayson and Ann E. Hawkins. m. (1) Wayne Chipman Booth, (2) Dr. Ray J. Davis of Pocatello, Dec. 29, 1958. A.B., B.Y.U. 1940; Dean of B.Y.U. Women; Stake MIA President; Organist for ward and stake; M.S., B.Y.U. 1950. d. Mar. 30, 1967

Brothers and Sisters: (Wayne C.)
Lucille B., m. J. Merrill Bushnell

Marriage: Phyllis Barnes of Long Beach, California, daughter of C. Douglas Barnes and Louella Strong. b. March 15, 1926. m. June 19, 1946. She is a clinical psychologist.

Children: Katherine, born 1948.
Richard, born 1951.
Alison, born 1954.

Former Provoan and Brigham Young University Graduate—Bachelor of Arts Degree, 1944; Master of Arts, University of Chicago, 1947; Ph.D., U. of Chicago, 1950.

Brigham Young University visiting faculty member, Summer 1950.

Wayne taught at Haverford College, Pa. in the English Department, where he directed an experimental freshman English course financed by the Carnegie Corporation. He went to Earlham College in Richmond, Indiana, in 1953, as head of the English Department (Chairman).

In 1952, he was awarded a Ford Foundation Fellowship and for a year did research in the philosophy of value. He was awarded the John Simon Guggenheim Memorial Foundation Award and spent the year of 1957 abroad working on *The Rhetoric of Fiction*. He returned to Europe in 1961 to complete the book. Both times he was accompanied by his wife, the former Phyllis Barnes, also a BYU graduate (1947) and their three children.

Wayne has had various papers published, some of which are: "Knowledge and Opinion: An Address to College Seniors", published in the Journal of General Education; and "Did Sterne Complete Tristram Shandy?", published in Modern Philology. He was editor of the Banyan (BYU) 1943 and served U.S. Army Infantry, 1944-46. Wayne was recipient of the Ford Foundation fund to develop a reading program in philosophy, spending much of the research time in Provo. His research book *The Rhetoric of Fiction*, 1962, has attained international acclaim, receiving the Christion Gauss award of the Phi Beta Kappa Society for the most distinguished work of literary scholarship in 1962. He has been on the National College Accreditation Board. He received his most significant honor in Dec. 9, 1964, when he was made dean of the College of University of Chicago, with some 2,100 students in the College, and a faculty of 300 full-time teachers. He continues to teach both undergraduate and graduate courses in English and is a popular lecturer. He is reputedly the youngest dean of a major college or university.

REED HOWARD BRADFORD

Born: April 10, 1912 at Spanish Fork, Utah, the youngest child of seven

Father: Pleasant Jones Bradford
Born December 27, 1866 in Spanish Fork, Utah
son of Pleasant S. Bradford and Jane Jones
Successful farmer and operator of flour mill

Mother: Jane R. Howard
Born November 8, 1869 in Murray, Utah
daughter of George Howard and Christine Christensen
m. December 23, 1892
Expert with flowers and prize exhibitor
Devoted teacher and especially served the sick

Brothers and Sisters: Pleasant Howard, b. September 20, 1895, m. Dora Taylor
Wendell Howard, b. August 28, 1898, m. Margaret Dixon (dec.)
Jennie, b. January 4, 1894, m. Oscar Terry
Lola, b. May 17, 1897, m. Milne Wall
Irma, b. July 11, 1902 m. Jan Bantjes
LaReta, b. March 13, 1906, d. June 13, 1906

Marriage: 1. Nora Tait, m. August 16, 1941, dec. February 11, 1947
born September 12, 1900 in Darlington, Durham County, England, well-known musician
2. Shirley Constance Aamodt, m. June 5, 1947
b. July 30, 1925, a practical nurse

Children: Mary Constance, b. December 21, 1948 in Provo, Utah
Sharon Ruth, b. June 30, 1950, Lansing, Michigan
Ralph Daniel, b. August 11, 1954, Boston, Mass.
Marleen Ann, b. November 7, 1956, Provo, Utah
Ray Nathan, b. March 5, 1958, Provo, Utah
Randall James, b. August 29, 1961, Provo, Utah

Education:
    B.A. Sociology, BYU, 1937
    M.A. Sociology, L.S.U., 1939
    Research Asst., L.S.U., Baton Rouge, 1938-39
    Tutoring and teaching fellow, Harvard, 1939-42
    M.A., Harvard University, Sociology, 1941
    Assoc. Prof. Rural Soc. W. Va. University, 1942-43, 45-56
    Ph.D. Harvard University, Sociology, 1946
    Assistant Prof., Assoc. Prof., Prof. BYU 1946-61
    Visiting Prof., Sociology, Michigan State University, 1950
    Chairman, Department Sociology, BYU, 1954-61
    Acting Dean of College of Humanities and Soc. Sciences, 1959-.
Government Service:
    U.S. Air Force, Pvt. to Sgt. 1943-45
    Regional Director Point 4 Program in Iran, 1951-54
    Director, Utah State Council on Social Welfare, 1960-
    Utah Coordinating Council, 1958-
Professional:
    Member:
    American Sociology Association
    Utah Academy Sciences, Arts and Letters
    Rural Sociology Society
    American Academy, Political and Social Sciences
    Society on Racial Problems
    National Council and Family Relations
    Professor of the Year Award at BYU
Authorship:
    Co-author, "Marriage and the Latter-day Saint", 1951
    with Ballif and Canning
    Co-author, "Introductory Sociology", 1960
    "Iran; an Investment in People, 1960"
    Contributor to *The Instructor* and professional journals
Religion:
    LDS Mission to Germany, 1932-35 during Hitler regime
    Sunday School General Board, 11 years
    Executive Secretary of the Adult Committee of the Church Co-
    ordinating Council

Reed H. Bradford was an active leader in the Spanish Fork
High School, one of the schools' better debators and orators, winner
of the Palmyra Stake M. Men public speaking contest and a successful speaker on the BYU campus.

His life is an unfoldment in education and youth group associations, as his major interests have been centered on the family and
the part religion may have upon its harmony and individual incentives.
His life on the farm enured him to hard work, helped him to make
his way through college, gave him experience and an ample supply
of apt stories. His mission contacts provided him with opportunities
for observing a people in national unrest and the supplanting of

home life for state enthusiasm. His three years in Iran as regional director of the Point 4 Program for the U.S. Government gave him the challenge of observing and understanding a Moslem home and an old civilization emerging into a changing world.

Keen on perception, excellent in observation with a facility for coordinating facts and recording them, Reed has developed into one of our outstanding teachers and discussion leaders. The early death of his first wife made him the more appreciative of the meaning of home, a growing family, and the dependence of democracy upon a harmonious group of well-educated, cooperating individuals.

NEWBERN ISAAC BUTT

Born: November 2, 1890   **Place:** Lehi, Utah

Father: William Francis Butt
Born Nov. 30, 1857, Malvern, Carroll Co., Ohio; son of Henry Butt and Elizabeth Calloway; worked as a miner, carpenter, and merchant; died June 11, 1940; buried in Lehi, Utah.

Mother: Laura Ellen Bushman
Born Oct. 9, 1865 in Lehi, Utah; daughter of Martin Benjamin and Lucinda Goodwin; married November 10, 1885 in Logan Temple; praised for her art work and as florist; died May 3, 1899.

Brothers and Sisters: Jesse Edith, born Feb. 1, 1887, m. Albert A. Bahr.
William Francis, born Oct. 1888, died Dec. 25, 1906. (Newbern)
Iris Alice, born Dec. 1892, died June 4, 1912.
Laura Louisa, born Dec. 25, 1895, died Sept. 9, 1942.
Rhoda Esther, born Aug. 24, 1898, died Feb. 28, 1919.

Marriage: Ethel Cutler, married March 1, 1923 in the Salt Lake Temple.
Born June 20, 1889 at Mound Valley, daughter of Orson P. Cutler and Jane McGregor, a USAC graduate. B.S. Prof. of Home Economics Brigham Young University. Cutler family genealogist.
Died Oct. 21, 1945 in Provo.

Children: Newbern Cutler Butt
Rhoda Carol Westenskow

To understand Newbern best we must realize that he has made a physical liability a personal asset, as he became acutely deaf following high school days; he used the resultant quiet as a help to concentration. When he wishes to work unmolested he turns off his hearing aid and disturbance or conversation fails to bother him. Library work was an easy and natural choice for him. He travelled in the Western States to study libraries in Oregon, California, and Idaho. He also took an eastern trip for the same purpose and made special studies at the University of Chicago, Columbia University in New York, and the Library of Congress at Washington D.C.

He collects Latter-day Saint history from original sources. Diaries are microfilmed or copied and given tables of contents and name indices. He indexed Dr. F. S. Harris' voluminous writing, the *History of Salt Lake* by Tullidge, and the complete volumes of the *Contributor, Improvement Era, Journal of Discourses*, Conference reports to 1909, Brigham Young University Board of Trustees Minutes, 1875-1945, BYU Faculty Minutes, 1876 to present, and learned enough Welsh to catalog the National Welsh Library in the Clark Library. He created a faculty file of biographies (brief), collected obituaries on many of the faculty, and is obtaining histories of separate departments of the BYU.

He attended school at Lehi High School, obtained his BS at USAC in 1915 and his MS at BYU in 1939. He did graduate work at Columbia University and the University of Chicago.

He was given a citation by Mountain Plains Library Association at Logan in 1956 for excellence in library science and as a lexicographer. His education early led to a definite goal, library work, which is most often neglected. He specialized in the making of valuable indices.

His indices have saved thousands of hours of research for university and church scholars. His occupations and positions have helped develop his present efficiency. Some of his positions were as follows: Assistant at Agricultural Experiment Station, Logan, Utah, at USAC; Editing publications and making indeces, 1914-1921; Library Associate, BYU, 1926 to date, and chairman of its history committee. He is the Bushman family genealogist and associate editor for the Cutler family records.

He is author of: *Soil Alkali*, F. S. Harris and N. I. Butt; *Scientific Research and Human Welfare* with F. S. Harris, Macmillan, 1924; *Fruits of Mormonism* with Dr. Harris; "A Family of Slaves that Help You" *Relief Society Magazine*, Feb. 1925; "Enemies of Friendship," *Relief Society Magazine*, Nov. 1925; "Education and Size of Family," *Journal of Heredity*, 1928; "Pioneer Spirit in Irrigation", *Irrigation Farmer*, 1943; *Bushman Family History*, BYU Press, 1956, and many additional papers. He will best be remembered as a research expert, collector of original papers and index specialist.

He was presented the Brigham Young University Award for distinguished service and for being an index expert in 1965. Newbern is one of the most accommodating gentlemen on the BYU campus.

ALBERT SHERMAN CHRISTENSEN

U.S. District Court Judge

Born: June 9, 1905 in Manti, Utah

Father: Albert H. Christensen, the son of (Lars) Lauritz Mathias Christensen, and Else Catherine Andersen Christensen, both of Denmark.
Born December 13, 1872
Died March 13, 1957 in Provo, Utah

Mother: Ellen Virginia Snow, the daughter of Joseph Smith and Lucy Van Buren Snow.
Born January 28, 1878 in Manti.
Died July 27, 1916

Brothers and Sisters: Virginia married Daniel M. Keeler
Ellen Elaine married Edward W. Southwick
(Albert Sherman)
Everett Hale - (deceased)
Phillip Van Buren married Gwen Johnson
(Half brothers and sisters)
Callen Yates married Daryl Aldene Stewart
Mabel Norma married Reed J. Webster
Kathryn married Albert C. Todd 2) married Brigham Delworth Gardner
      Children reared by second wife of Albert H. after the death of Ellen Virginia Snow Christensen, when he married Myrtle Farnsworth of Beaver on June 20, 1920.

Marriage: Lois Bowen of Spanish Fork on April 4, 1927.
G.O.P. State Committee woman from Utah County.
Member of the Utah legislature; Brigham Young University graduate
Born August 10, 1905.
Daughter of William Jones and Judrun Dena Bjarnason Bowen.

Children: A. Kent married Elizabeth Ann Reynolds (Sears)
Karen married Roger Childs
Krege married Judith Lynne Brown

When A. Sherman was nominated Utah's second federal district judge, considerable data was accumulated to be sent to President Dwight D. Eisenhower to submit to the Senate. A life time appointment requiring Senate confirmation was a prize sought by more than fifty prominent attorneys over the nation. Sherman was recommended by Utah's senior senator Arthur V. Watkins, a family friend of many years standing. He was the state's first native son federal district court nominee from outside of Salt Lake City and the first to be a member of The Church of Jesus Christ of Latter-day Saints.

Senator Watkins, in part, stated, "Because of the usually high calibre of candidates, selection was extremely difficult. Efforts were made to select a nominee of the highest qualifications. In addition to sound legal training the nominee was expected to have wide experience as a trial lawyer, because the federal court is a trial court. Furthermore, he was expected to be a man of integrity, possessed of judicial temperament and of an age to permit good service on the bench for years to come.

"A. Sherman Christensen met all those requirements. I have known him and his family for many years and have watched his performance as an outstanding lawyer and citizen. In all circumstances, he has stamped himself as a man of competence and ability, with an excellent reputation for honesty and integrity. He will make a fine reputation for himself and for Utah as a member of the federal judiciary system."

He has abundantly proved worthy of the appointment.

A brief summary of his professional life follows: Reared in Manti during childhood he knew the chores of the farm and the requirements of a small school. The family was moved to Provo to procure the advantages of the Brigham Young University.

At Brigham Young University Sherman was a varsity debator and took part in major drama each year of attendance. He had leading parts in such shows as "State of the Union," "Bill of Divorcement," "The Music Master," "The Winslow Boy," "Lady Windermere's Fan," "If I Were King," "The Man Who Came To Dinner," "Peter Ibetsen" and "Julius Caesar." Few will ever forget the quarrel scene between Brutus (Sherman) and Casius (Parley A. Christensen). It smacked of highest professional power. This appreciation of the dramatic carried over to the court room and disturbed several of Sherman's legal antagonists who lacked that ability. Also at Brigham Young University Sherman was praised for his debating power and was elected to student body offices.

An ardent Republican, he early became interested in politics, led discussion groups all through high school and college. He desired to emulate his able father. He went to Washington D.C., and became an assistant business specialist of the U.S. Department of Commerce, 1930-32, who was admitted to the District of Columbia Bar in 1932, the Utah Bar in 1933. He practiced law with his father in Provo 1933-1942, 1945-54. He was a member of the American, Federal, District of Columbia, Utah, Utah Junior; and Utah County Bar associations, being president of all three Utah associations. He was named a member of the American Bar Association's Subcommittee on Post-conviction Remedies in 1960.

Sherman was past president of the Provo Chamber of Commerce and received their Distinguished Service Award in 1939. In 1957 he and President F. S. Harris were given honorary achievement awards for service to government by Pi Sigma Alpha, national honorary political science fraternity.

His appointment as U. S. Judge Second Federal District Court for Utah has determined his life's course. He keeps a consistent schedule of exercise to partially balance as arduous legal schedule for court held in the legal chambers of Salt Lake City.

His charming and talented wife, whom he met and courted on the thespian boards of old College Hall, is his efficient helpmate and ablest critic. Herself a trained speaker and law maker, she follows her husband's course with keen interest and intelligent cooperation. Their three children have added lustre to their names. The Christensen's have been Brigham Young University Alumni executive officers and are loyal supporters of its fund and aesthetic programs.

GERRIT de JONG JR.

Born: March 20, 1892 in Amsterdam, Holland
Naturalized U.S. Citizen 1913
To U.S. in 1906 direct to Salt Lake City, Utah

Father: Gerrit de Jong—b. April 22, 1869 in Amsterdam, Holland
Merchant in dry goods in Amsterdam
To the U.S. in 1895, Salt Lake July 28th.
Joined L.D.S. Church in 1907 in Salt Lake
Merchant in Salt Lake City
d. March, 1949

Mother: Lijda Marianna Kuiper
b. April 28, 1870 in Apeldoorn, Holland
Daughter of Teunis Kuiper and Maria van Mossel
(Parents of first Mormon converts in district)
Expert seamstress and cultured mother
d. August, 1940

Brothers and Sisters: Trijntje (Catherine or Katie)
b. February 10, 1894 in Amsterdam, m. Frank Pia at Salt Lake City (born in Vienna). Resides in Salt Lake City.

Marriage: Rosabelle Winegar on Sept. 14, 1911
b. May 12, 1889 in Salt Lake City
Talented Artist—daughter of William Winegar and Rosa Shaw
In auto accident—Dec. 26, 1939
d. January 12, 1940
Thelma Bonham on Sept. 14, 1951
Author and teacher—Principal Aberdeen High School, Idaho
Missionary to Southern States. Member L.D.S. Primary General Board.

Children of Rosabelle: William Gerrit, b. July 3, 1906—d. Jan. 10, 1913
Belle Felice, m. Dean E. Van Wagenen
Nola Eloise, m. Clyde E. Sullivan
Carma Rose, m. Richard L. Anderson

I first met Gerrit in Salt Lake in Prof. Tracy Y. Cannon's studio. Tracy and I exchanged studios, mine on Kiesel Avenue in Ogden and his on East South Temple in Salt Lake. Gerrit then had long golden hair reaching to his shoulders, wore a loose shirt and long bow tie, and frequently came to town with wooden shoes. At lunch time, we occasionally ate together and exchanged ideas on the arts, especially music and painting.

His recent conversion to the L.D.S. Church and his impending citizenship papers were engrossing subjects for conversation from which I learned he was already a keen scholar in U.S. history, that he had a very excellent foundation in world literature, and that he was proud of his Dutch heritage. He was fluent in German and the Netherland language. He had two special inherent gifts, adaptability in languages and a keen judgment in art forms and principals. None of his family was talented in music, yet Gerrit worked daily in acquiring piano and organ techniques. If he were to become a composer he must learn the wind instruments. Accordingly, the French Horn intrigued him and soon he mastered the intricate lip control and beauty of tone. The Glockenspiel came naturally, nor were the drums too difficult. His restless mind led him to the piano or bits of orchestration, a study of Bach, Mozart, or Beethoven, the simplicity and fervor of Mormon hymns or a coveted practice session on the Great Salt Lake Tabernacle Organ. In his pockets we often found copies of Heine, Goethe or Lessing in German, or a volume on Phonetics in Italian. He was surprised that many of his new friends had never heard of Van Goyen, Brueghel, van Ruisdael, or Vermeer, nor could they name the masterpieces of Rubens, Rembrandt, Hals or Van Dyke. I was impressed by this young Mormon convert and felt that I had met a most artistic soul with a gift for languages, a keen talent for music and the breadth of a world citizen. Neither of us then knew that we would soon be employed by the same university.

After he came to Provo to organize the Fine Arts Department under Pres. F. S. Harris, I always knew when he had visited his family in Salt Lake as the cadence of his native speech was strongly emphasized for several days. Family influence was strong.

Dean de Jong was blessed with a keen sense of humor, and he found many apt illustrations for play on words from the same seven languages he has studied over much of his life.

In faculty parties he has entertained his colleagues with comic piano bits, improvisations to suit the occasion, or he would delight his audience in a faculty performance in such a play "You Can't Take It With You" or as a musician in "The Music Master." Many Sunday School sacramental interludes have been composed by Gerrit. We frequently sing one of his compositions from the hymn book, such as "Come Sing To The Lord." The Utah Symphony has played several of his orchestral compositions.

His studies in world gospel and Mormon writings have been of great service to the Deseret Sunday School Union, in which he is a Senior member, and for them he has authored several study manuals, such as the current popular book *The Living Gospel.*

His proficiency in world phonetics and his organizing ability along with his language fluency, warranted the U.S. State Department to assign him as director of the Cultural Center in Santos, Brazil. Upon request, he has written text books in all Romance languages and German. As world Lyceum artists came to the campus he would be appointed official greeter and faculty welcome chief. The great French orchestra leader, Monteaux, and his players found little reason to use faltering English when Dr. de Jong was present; opera stars and foreign lecturers were greeted with friendly phrases in their native tongue. Dean de Jong has long been one of the key men on the BYU faculty and wrote the impressive overture for the dedication of the grand F. S. Harris Fine Arts Center on campus.

He is dean emeritus of the first university Fine Arts College in the West.

Education:

A.B. - U. of U. 1920
M.A. - U. of U. 1925
Grad. work - U. of Mexico - Summer 1921
    U. of Munich (Germany) 1926-27
Ph.D. - Stanford U. - 1933
Began private practices of piano and organ 1910
Instructor of Music - Murdock Academy, Beaver, Utah 1916-1918
Instructor of modern languages - LDS University, Salt Lake City, 1919-25; Associate professor modern languages, BYU, Provo, Utah 1925-27; Professor Modern Languages, BYU, 1927; Dean of College of Fine Arts, 1925-59; Dean Emeritus of Fine Arts, BYU, 1959

Activities:

Director Centro Cultural Brasil - Estados Unidos, Santos, Brasil 1947-48; University Fellow - Stanford U. - 1931-32; Fellow Utah Academy of Science, Arts and Letters;
Member: Modern Language Association; American Guild of Organists; American Association Teachers of Spanish and Portuguese; American Musical Society; General Church Music Comm., LDS; General Board Deseret Sunday School Union; National Association Latin-American Studies; President Utah Coordinating Council on Higher Education 1963-64
Editor - O Nosso Proprio Livro de Leitura (a Portugese reader)

Author:

> *Gospel Standards* 1943; *Greater Dividends From Religion* 1950; *Living the Gospel,* 1956; *The Gospel Plan,* 1951. All the above for use by the Deseret Sunday School Union.
>
> Articles in the Proceedings, Utah Academy Science Arts and Letters "German Culture and the New Government," 1943; Literature of Germany Since 1933; "Liberal Arts of the War Time College Curriculum," 1941-42; "Portugese among the Modern Languages of Today," 1946-47; "Brazilian Music and Musicians," 1948-49; "An Approach to Modernity in Art." Articles for the *Instructor* and *Improvement Era,* also in the Latin American studies and journals.

Compositions:

> Dean de Jong has written some 18 major musical compositions, 4 hymns, among them "Come, Sing to The Lord" in LDS hymns; 5 choral compositions with orchestra including "I Will Praise The Lord" used to dedicate the Heber J. Grant Library; 2 solos with orchestra; 2 instrumental ensembles, one for wood-wind quintet and another for English Horn and orchestra. His "We Bring Thee Offerings" for full chorus, soprano solo and symphony orchestra was written for and played at the dedication of the F. S. Harris Fine Arts Center.

He has been called the ideal teacher for a liberal college, expert in languages, all the arts, English literature, and versed in Church doctrine; he composes for the orchestra, string quintet, the choir and solo instruments, is a professional pianist and organist, and conducts with authority. Dean de Jong pioneered in establishing a superb fine arts college, one of the first in the nation.

OAKLEY SPENCER EVANS

Vice-president of J. C. Penney Co.
Residence—Darien, Conn.

Born:	May 14, 1913, in Springville, Utah
Father:	Shirl Osborne Evans b. Parowan, Utah, Dec. 10, 1890
Mother:	Blanch Oakley b. Springville, Utah, Oct. 26, 1892, daughter of Ami and Amanda Wing Oakley m. (2) Corwin R. Graves of Salt Lake City
Brothers and Sisters:	Dr. Shirl O. Evans, specialized surgeon, Pasadena, California. Mrs. Viola E. Patrick—Salt Lake City, Utah. (Both attended BYU.)
Marriage:	Mabel Wilson, daughter of Prof. Guy C. Wilson and Agnes Melissa Stevens. b. Nov. 5, 1912 m. Sept. 13, 1935
Children:	Antoinette, b. Aug. 20, 1936, m. Dr. John R. Clark Wendy Melissa, b. June 24, 1938, m. John R. Ruppel Christine, b. Dec. 24, 1944 Julie Ann, b. May 14, 1946 Elizabeth, b. Sept. II, 1951

Oakley Spencer Evans is a tall, slender man of many talents who looks very much like a successful executive. He is an excellent speaker with quiet power. In debate, he was persuasive with abundant facts to prove his thesis. Oakley was a college favorite. He graduated summa cum laude in 1935 from Brigham Young University, Provo, with an A.B. in business administration.

College Activities:

President of Blue Key, scholastic fraternity; president of debating society and its manager; president and winner of scholastic award of Alpha Kappa Psi, business fraternity; played in school orchestra three years; was Junior Class President; served on Banyan staff three years, was manager in senior year.

Professional Background:

Started with J. C. Penney Company, department store chain, as part-time salesman in 1935 at Butte, Mont.; became assistant manager there and went in same capacity to the Salt Lake City, Utah store in 1942; from there, was promoted to manager of the Kansas City, Kan., store in 1947; from 1951-53 was a district manager in the Rocky Mountain area; came to the New York Central Office in 1953, setting up first store planning division in the executive department; promoted in 1958 to assistant to the director of the district management (now store) department; appointed director of planning and research 1960; assistant director of real estate and store planning department in 1962; advanced to vice-president and director of real estate and store planning January 30, 1966.

Professional Activities:

Member of the Council of Urban America, New York, national citizens' organization dealing with urban renewal; member, International Council of Shopping Centers (ICSC); member of the board of Directors of the Shopping Center Research Foundation of ICSC; member Advisory Council to Management Conference, Brigham Young University.

Clubs:

New York Athletic Club; Woodway Country Club, Darien, Conn.

Hobbies:

Golf, reading, bowling.

Church Activities:

Member of The Church of Jesus Christ of Latter-day Saints; Sunday School Teacher (Scarsdale, N.Y.); Superintendent of Sunday Schools (Salt Lake City Yale Ward), Kansas City, Kansas, Denver, Colorado; Branch President, Kansas City, Kansas.

Oakley is a frequent campus visitor and business department speaker.

541

JOSEPH EARL GARRETT

Born: May 22, 1907 in Nephi, Utah

Father: Louis Garrett, Nephi, Utah Juab Co.
Born January 29, 1874
Deputy Sheriff of Juab County and Sheepman.
Died September 11, 1930

Mother: Estella Boswell Garrett, Nephi, Juab Co., Utah
Born July 19, 1879
Married July 8, 1896 in Manti Temple
Died Sept. 9, 1961

Brothers and Sisters: Hortense E. Garrett, b. September 4, 1897, m. Albert B. Allen
Eleda P. Garrett, b. November 26, 1900, m. Howard P. Matthews
L. Glen Garrett, b. December 30, 1902, m. Winnifred Cranney
J. Earl Garrett, b. May 22, 1907, m. Eugenia V. Buchanan
Rex B. Garrett, b. December 22, 1909, m. Edith Sells
Ralph L. Garrett, b. January 21, 1912, m. Mildred Meldrum
Dean R. Garrett, b. March 18, 1914, m. Amy E. Buchanan
Paul M. Garrett, b. December 8, 1915, m. Lola B. Bowman
Bernice L. Garrett, b. June 25, 1918, m. Joseph H. Clayson Jr.

Marriage: Eugenia V. Buchanan, Born September 7, 1907, Venice, Sevier Co. Utah. Marriage: May 31, 1927. B.Y.U. student. Daughter of Eugene Delos Buchanan and Elizabeth Watson Buchanan. B.Y.U. alumna.

Children: Joseph Earl Garrett, Jr., b. February 12, 1929. m. 1) Dorothy J. Johnson. 2) Betty J. Lucas—they have eight children.
Eugene B. Garrett, b. July 28, 1931. m. Norine Peterson (also B.Y.U.)
Patricia Vee Garrett. b. May 18, 1943, single.
All children have been students at B.Y.U.

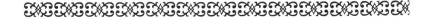

Among the native sons of Utah who have risen to prominence in the business world is J. Earl Garrett, recently retired, president of Arden-Mayfair Markets, second largest supermarket chain in the West with headquarters in Los Angeles, California.

After attending grammar and high school in Nephi, Utah, he enrolled in the Brigham Young University and graduated as an honor student with a B.S. Degree in 1929, majoring in accounting and business administration.

In 1930, J. Earl moved to California and took a position as an accountant with a large dairy products company in Los Angeles, advancing to company auditor with that firm. Later he was appointed Treasurer of Van's Markets in 1937. This company was merged in 1948 with Mayfair Markets, at which time Earl Garrett became Treasurer of the combined operation. Five years later, in 1953, he was elected President of Mayfair, then operating 32 markets with 1,500 employees in Southern California with an annual volume of $60,577,000 —now operating 220 units in 6 states with 7,300 employees and sales volume in 1963 of $325,000,000. (By the end of 1964, Mayfair was operating approximately 225 markets with anticipated sales volume of $360,000,000.) This company is one of the hundred largest companies in the United States, due primarily to Earl Garrett's strong leadership.

He was a member of the Stake presidency in the Glendale Stake for nine years and was also a former member of a bishopric and High Council. The B.Y.U. Alumni Association presented him with its Distinguished Service Award in 1964. He is presently honoring three assignments for B.Y.U.; member of the National Advisory Council for the School of Business, Trustee for the Research and Development Foundation, Southern California Chairman for the National Development Council.

As president of Mayfair, Grand American and El Rancho Markets who use Green Stamps, he procured educational gifts from the Sperry and Hutchinson Company of San Francisco of $165,000 for B.Y.U.'s Destiny Fund.

He has three successful obsessions: his church, his family, and his business.

Imri Joseph Hutchings

Born: April 5, 1909   **Place:** South Jordan, Utah

Father: Joseph Nephi Hutchings
Born April 8, 1880 in Salt Lake City, Utah. Filled a Mission to Great Britain 1902-1904. There met his future wife and converted her to the Church.
Married January 1905.

Mother: Elizabeth Ann Bird
Born Beccles, England, September 13, 1882
Died October 12, 1959. An ardent church worker all of her life.
Active in community and political affairs.

Brothers and Sisters:
Theodore N. b. October 14, 1905 m. Joyce Page
Mary Alice, b. June 21, 1907; Died at birth
Ethel Louise, b. June 21, 1907; Died at birth
(Imri J.)
Theron B., b. January 5, 1912; m. Vida Palmer
Brian L., b. June 11, 1915; m. Ellen Anderson
Stanley A., b. Nov. 23, 1918; m. Velma Steadman
Calvin B., b. Sept. 12, 1923; m. Margaret Clark
Theron, Brian, and Imri all obtained Ph.D. degrees in Soils, Chemistry, and Microbiology; Stanley and Calvin are D.D.S.'s practicing dentistry in Midvale, Utah.

Marriage: Bernice Page August 28, 1933
Born August 5, 1912, Riverton, Utah; daughter of Gwyne and Mary Jensen. Gwynne Page owned and operated the Riverton Motor Co., Riverton, Utah. Served as a County Commissioner of Salt Lake County. Died 1962.

Children: Paul Norman, b. June 17, 1937. m. Joan Millard. Graduate of BYU 1960, presently Systems Engineer IBM. Three children Sharon, Todd, and Scott.
Janet Elizabeth, b. March 5, 1941. Graduated BYU 1963, presently assistant administrative dietician Butler County Memorial Hospital, Butler, Pa.
Alan Page, b. April 8, 1944
Mary Elaine, b. July 1, 1945

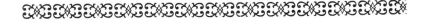

Imri J. Hutchings is a dedicated scientist. All his life he has asked the questions, Why? and How? Results led him to investigate causes well before his teens. Small life intrigued him, "What is smaller than this?" Chemistry and the test tube were interesting introductions to microbiology; experimenting with chemicals led him to food processing, germination and preservation. He early saw the field of food chemistry as both interesting and remunerative.

He was an honor scholar at BYU, taking his bachelor's and master degrees in chemistry and biology. His doctorate was achieved at Rutgers University in 1936. In mid-career, he enrolled in the Management Executive Training University in 1956.

From 1936-47 he was Technical Director of Store Products Co. and in 1949 began his career with the great H. J. Heinz Co. of Pittsburgh, where he has since made his home. From 1947-50, he was Head of the Bacteriological Research, spent a year as Head of Packaging, and in 1951 assumed direction of the work he most desired, Food Research, which office he filled until 1962. From 1964 to date Imri has been General Manager of Research, promoting expansion of the pickle, mustard, and packaging industry.

Nor has he lacked identity in civic and church work. He is a member of the University Club; the Pittsburgh Chemists Club; Sigma Xi; Phi Tau Sigma. He is a Fellow in the American Assn. for the Advancement of Science; member in The American Chemical Society; The Institute of Food Technologists (its president in 1960-61); American Assn. of Cereal Chemists; Society of American Microbiologists. The Government commandeered his services for food work in World War II.

His Church work has been constant since boyhood. He has been YMMIA president; Branch Chorister; first Counselor in the Branch Presidency of Philadelphia 1944-47; District President West Pennsylvania 1949-60; 1st Counselor of Eastern Atlantic States Mission 1960-to date.

Dr. Hutchings is a busy business executive who finds time for business, home, civic, and church activities.

BEN ELDEN LEWIS

Business man - Educator - Churchman

Born: November 6, 1913   **Place:** Mesa, Arizona

Father: George William Lewis, the son of John Moss Lewis
Born Oct. 29, 1864 in Paris, Idaho
Married Sept. 21, 1899 at St. Johns, Arizona
Rancher and dairy farmer. To Salt Lake City, 1921, missionary on Temple Square.
Died Oct. 24, 1933.

Mother: Olena Dorthea Kemte, daughter of Christopher Jensen Kemte and Ann Dorthea Johnson.
Born July 31, 1874 at Richfield, Utah
Student at BY Academy, excelled in art, poetry, enthusiast for education.
Died Nov. 17, 1951 in Salt Lake City.

Brothers and Sisters: Anna Martha, m. Ralph W. Evans; George K. Lewis; Ora m. Clifford S. Wilson; William Chrisman Lewis; Ruth m. Parlell G. Peterson; (Ben Elden); Walter Malin Lewis.

Marriage: Barbara Rae Wootton, on Oct. 4, 1944.
Daughter of Lorenzo A. Wootton and Thelma Ohlweiler of Heber, Utah. Worked for the FBI for 3 years, Washington, D.C., 2 years at BYU, met Ben at BYU.
Home—1840 N., 1840 E., overlooking the Valley.

Children: 1) Linda Gean, b. Dec. 30, 1946.
2) Stephen W., b. Feb. 15, 1951.
3) James W., b. Dec. 30, 1952.
4) Mary Ann, b. Oct. 27, 1954.
5) John W., b. Oct. 3, 1959.
Reared 3 children of Ora, Ben's sister, Clifford L. Wilson, Anita Louise Wilson, Gregory L. Wilson.

Ben E. Lewis stands tall and handsome, wears a ready smile, and looks for the best characteristics in every person he meets. His boundless energy and capacity for work make him a man of many interests and numerous assignments, with a zest for achievement and a desire to complete a task that he might accept another. His various positions of trust and importance augment his opportunities for multiple acquaintances and friendships.

His father was not a strong man as his life unfolded which gave Ben's dynamic mother the obligation of much of the family leadership. She was the spearhead of education for all the family, attended the BY Academy which she instilled into her family of seven children when religion dominated or was prevalent in the teaching of every class. Each proved himself capable of leadership; Georky (George K) becoming a successful photographer and inventor.

Ben went to the LDS High School in Salt Lake, graduating at fifteen. The family moved to Provo for its educational advantages where Ben soon established himself as a leader, becoming president of the BYU Junior class and Student Body President the following year. While here he became secretary to the Pacific Student President's Association. He graduated from BYU in 1940 with Honors and a major in government and banking, being one of the first Alfred P. Sloan Scholarship recipients. A master's degree from the Denver University followed in 1942.

When the newly appointed president of BYU started to expand his faculty, Ben was one of the first acquired and immediately fell heir to a multiple occupation as Director of BYU Auxiliary Services in 1952. Housing, demanding daily, almost hourly attention; food services requiring expansion techniques by the hour; the University press bursting for room and increasing work load every month; sitting in committee sessions by the hour to cope with services of student and faculty growth are part of his activities. A key member of the Universities' executive council, he sees the problems of the University from the students' requirements and viewpoints and is known as The Students' Friend.

His business accuity reflects the success of his early training as bank messenger and bookkeeper for the Utah Savings and Trust Co., budget director for the U.S. National Housing Agency; budget director and director of merchandizing for Marriott's Hot Shoppes, Inc., Washington, D. C. All were recommendations for his being a Board Director of Hotel Utah, of the Utah Valley Hospital; being a member of the Advisory Board of Farmers and Merchants Bank (branch of the Walker Bank and Trust Co.), and a member of the Board of Directors for Taylor's, Inc.

He is also active in Provo City's Planning Commission and the Provo Kiwanis Club.

Part of his great strength lies in his religious fervor. He served a Northern States mission in 1934-36; served a stake mission in Washington, D.C., and in the bishopric of the Washington Ward, 1947-1951. He was a member of the Washington Stake High Council 1951-52. Here in Utah he has been a member of the High Council in the Sharon Stake and president of the East Sharon Stake. It was a project of his while in this position to have some 1,500 members read the Book of Mormon in entirety.

One of his close friends said of him, "President Lewis has the unusual ability to work on common grounds with youth of the Stake." And with him in every venture is his talented wife, Barbara, whose home is a place of welcome to hundreds of students and friends throughout the year. The Lewis Christmas letters with family pictures are beautiful, informative, often inspiring and reveal a great family love. Their spacious home on the eastern slope of the Y mountain overlooks the verdant Utah Valley and gives them a broadening view of life itself.

Ben E. would fit into any period of history as a leader of men.

WESLEY PARKINSON LLOYD

Born: June 16, 1904 Ogden, Utah

Father: Charles Edward Lloyd—son of Thomas Lloyd and Susanna Stone who crossed the plains with hand cart companies
b. January 19, 1865, in Wellsville, Utah
Moved to St. Anthony, Idaho—became a member of Yellowstone Stake Presidency
Businessman, rancher and real estate agent; one of founders Utah Woolen Mills
d. October 12, 1926

Mother: Lucy Parkinson
b. September 27th, 1869, in Franklin, Idaho
daughter of Samuel Rose and Charlotte Smart Parkinson, leaders in Cache Valley pioneering; To Utah with early pioneers
Married December 23, 1897
Lifetime Church worker and teacher, protagonist against corporal punishment in schools. After death of husband, became Dean of Women at Ricks' College for 11 years; Temple worker in Salt Lake Temple
Inspired good study habits in her own family
d. Wed. Oct. 28, 1964 in Palo Alto, Calif.

Brother and Sisters: Charles P., b. Oct. 29, 1898, d. 9-2-1927
"Lucille" Lucy Vesta b. 5-22-1900 m. John Morgan (Wesley P.)
Donald P., b. Sept. 21, 1905, m. Helen Carroll, BYU graduate, leading manufacturer's executive
Sherman P., b. Jan. 11, 1914, m. Edith Ann Gunn. U.S. Congressional Representative
Erma b. Dec. 15, 1927 m. M. Boyd Smith

Marriage: Lillie Murdock, December 30, 1926
Born October 24, 1905, at Midway, Utah
Daughter of David S. Murdock and Emily Van Wagenen
Met her husband when a student at BYU.
Active in civic and Church affairs

Children: Kent M. b. Mar. 5, 1931, m. Eleanor Forstl, Ph.D, Stanford
Gary M. b. Sept. 17, 1934, m. Carolyn Provan, BYU grad.

Wesley P. Lloyd revealed many facets of a promising student and scholar when very young. It was not unusual for him to be "head of his class." He has been a leader ever since he enrolled in school.

He attended elementary and secondary schools in St. Anthony, Idaho and Salt Lake City, was a star athlete at BYU in football, basketball and track, and a successful debater and public speaker. His speech is deliberate with precise diction and his full voice carries without being raucous. B.S. (1927) and M.S. (1934) were achieved at BYU and a Ph.D. with distinction, at the University of Chicago in 1937.

Wes was an athletic coach and social science instructor during 1927-28 at the Midway High School at Rexburg, Idaho, and principal of the Edmunds High School in the same town the following year. In 1930 he became principal of the LDS Seminary in Grace, Idaho, then was assigned the same position in Oakley, Idaho. By now his direction in career was fixed, to teach in the social sciences and become expert in religious education. A scholarship aided his two years study at Chicago where he wrote his doctoral dissertation, "The Rise and Development of Lay Leadership in the Latter-day Saints Movement."

At BYU he started in a dual capacity as Dean of Men and Assistant Professor of Philosophy of Education. By 1939 he was a full professor and chairman of the Department of Philosophy of Education. In 1940 he brought out his *Learning to Live* and was appointed to the General Board of the YMMIA. In the war years he was a member of the Defense Council of Utah County and served as bishop of the Seventh Ward.

In 1945-46 Wesley was appointed Dean of Students with all its attendant duties, and also published his study *Administration of Student Personnel Service,* which was publicized. In 1946-47 he served as president of Utah Conference on Higher Education. His other activities include National Association of Deans and Advisers to Men, Academic Council of the Western Personnel Institute, National Association of Student Personnel Administrators (President 1949-1950), Utah Academy of Science, Arts and Letters, and member of most of the key committees of the BYU faculty.

His later interests have taken him over the world, representing the U.S. State Department and foreign governments. In 1951 he was offered and accepted the appointment as director of the Japanese Universities Guidance and Welfare Institute, an organization sponsored by the Allied Powers Supreme Command. He has been called back to Japan to further develop the significant beginnings made during the next twelve years. In 1955 he directed a team of specialists in higher education in Japan. Also in 1955 he was a member of a team who held conferences with ministries of education and university officials in seventy university centers in Europe, Africa, and Asia. In 1958 he was special consultant on educational reorganization for Burma and countries of Europe, Near East and Far East. The American Red Cross made him a member of the Advisory Committee on Higher Education. In 1961 the U.S. State Department selected him as a consultant on State Department Projects for Universities in Colombia, South America. His position on world education in international committees has materially added to the stature of BYU in international importance and credit acceptance.

Dean Lloyd has been active in the Timpanogos Knife and Fork Club, Provo Rotary Club, N.E.A., U.E.A., Phi Eta Sigma, Phi Delta Kappa, and as lecturer to Senior Citizens and women's culture clubs. As dean of the B.Y.U. graduate school with rapidly increasing numbers of doctorate candidates and their dissertations, his time is being more confined to the premises of the campus. It has been remarked that he is BYU's best known consultant on higher education, whose reputation is internationally recognized. He is written up in *Who's Who in America, Who's Who in American Education, Who's Who in the West* and *Current Biography* and received the BYU Alumni Distinguished Service Award in 1964.

His latest appointment: president of the Western Association of Graduate Schools comprising fifty-three universities in western United States and western Canada.

HARRISON REUBEN MERRILL

Born: November 13, 1884 in Smithfield, Utah.
H. R. was born in Smithfield, but he was reared in Oxford, Idaho, moving later to a farm in Cub River valley by Preston, Idaho.

Father: Orrin Jackson Merrill
Born in Little Cottonwood, Utah (near Salt Lake City), June 22, 1855; a farmer; kindly soft spoken man.
Died in April, 1933 in Franklin, Idaho.

Mother: Elizabeth White
Born Feb. 7, 1853 in Lehi, Utah.
Married Feb. 14, 1875 in the Salt Lake Endowment House.
A devoted mother, encouraging music and singing in the home. All of the children were talented.
Died Sept. 22, 1932 in Preston, Idaho.

Brothers and Sisters: Orrin Preston Merrill, b. Aug. 5, 1876 (deceased).
Elmer Sam Merrill, b. Mar. 12, 1878 (deceased).
Franklin Thomas Merrill, b. Feb. 11, 1880 (deceased).
Jessie Elizabeth Merrill, b. Sept. 11, 1881. m. Peter G. Whitehead.
(Harrison R.)
Ralph Douglas Merrill, b. Apr. 23, 1888 (deceased).
Myrtle Merrill, b. Nov. 5, 1891 (deceased).
Dr. Madison W. Merrill, b. Jan. 22, 1896, outstanding dentist and civic worker.
Margaret Merrill, b. Jan. 22, 1896, m. Jacob I. Smith

Marriage: Edna Johnson
Born May 19, 1886 in Hyde Park, Utah, daughter of James Johnson and Harriett Emeline Lamb.
Married on Jan. 27, 1909 in the Logan Temple.
Graduated from Oneida Stake Academy in 1905. Taught school three years. Attended BYU two years.
President, BYU Women, 1928-29.
Died May 3, 1966 at 79 in Spanish Fork.

Children: Harrison J. Merrill, b. August 4, 1912; m. Lotta June Miller, Paul J. Merrill, b. Jan. 24, 1917; m. Camilla Spillman. Ruby Merrill, b. Oct. 12, 1919, m. George J. Amstad.
All three graduated from BYU.

Death: August 20, 1938 at the age of 53.

Harrison R. Merrill grew to be a giant-sized man, so well proportioned that you had to stand near to him to realize his bigness. And his heart was as big as his body as a young student spoke of him. When he approached you it was a welcome of happiness and good cheer. He would joke about a person but would never belittle him or speak any evil. I presume he could frown but I never saw him do so. "A smile spreads so easily over your face while a frown takes work," was one of his observations.

He got his early schooling from a reading, musical mother, the schools of Smithfield and Oneida Stake Academy, being valedictorian for the latter. He early showed interest in words and their shades of meaning and kept books of antonyms and synonyms near him, looked up all new words as they crossed his reading path. It was natural for him to major in English literature, become editor of school papers and a young contributor to farm journals and society magazines.

His genial nature and huge frame set him apart in any crowd and he had stories equal to any occasion. He received a B.S. from Utah State Agricultural College in Logan in 1920, studied in the summers 1921-23, choosing teaching as a profession, instructing in Oneida Stake Academy, 1912-1920. He came to BYU with President Harris in 1921 as instructor of English, 1921-23; assistant Professor of English and Journalism 1930-31; and professor of Journalism 1931 to his death.

He became chairman of publicity and advisor to all BYU student publications. His greatest task and opportunity in writing came when he was appointed Managing Editor of the "New Improvement Era" in 1931-1935. He changed the format of the "Era" which pointed the way for the excellent magazine it has become today.

For him, religion was a code of good will, interest in one's neighbors, doing good without praise, giving without publicity, a personal interest in one's own progress and church service without pulpit prodding—it meant establishing an intimate relationship with his Heavenly Father "as though you were on talking terms." He was bishop of the Third Ward in Preston, Idaho; was an active and popular General Board Member of the Young Men's Mutual Improvement Association from 1908-11, and served a mission to Ireland when the whole island was one country and from this center, travelled in Great Britain, France, and Canada.

H. R. was a perfectionist in many matters. When he went away for advanced degrees he chose teachers rather than the institution. He was at Northwestern University in 1927 and at Columbia University 1929-30 to receive his Masters in journalism. His students have spread over the west in journalistic work.

Even with a heavy teaching and supervisory load, he was able to write more than six books and dozens of articles for church and farm journals. His works include *Poems of the West,* 1925, *Bart of Kane County,* 1925; *Dust of the Desert,* 1938; *Utah Sings,* co-editor of anthology of Contemporaneous Verse, 1934; *Rimes of the Rockies* and the Reading Manual for the Mutual Improvement Association, 1935-36.

All too soon a promising life of great talent was snuffed out by ambitious action following appendectomy. This poem became his epitaph:

LET THIS BE HEAVEN
—H. R. Merrill

Oh, God, let this be heaven—
I do not ask for golden streets
  Or long for jasper walls,
Nor do I sigh for pearly shores
  Where twilight never falls;
Just leave me here beside these peaks,
  In this rough western land,
I love this dear old world of Thine—
  Dear God, You understand.

Oh, God, let this be heaven—
I do not crave white, stainless robes,
  I'll keep these marked by toil;
Instead of straight and narrow walks
  I love trails soft with soil;
I have been healed by crystal streams,
  But these from snow-crowned peaks
Where dawn burns incense to the day
  And paints the sky in streaks.

Dear God, let this be heaven—
I do not ask for angel wings—
  Just leave that old peak there
And let me climb 'til comes the night—
  I want no golden stair.
Then, when I say my last adieu
  And all farewells are given
Just leave my spirit here somewhere—
  Oh, God, let this be heaven!

JOHN CLIFTON MOFFITT

Born: June 10, 1896, in Manti, Utah

Father: John W. Moffitt, son of Bishop Andrew Moffitt; b. September 27, 1866 in Manti, Utah; Took family to Boneta, Duchesne County, Utah, an Indian rendezvous with frequent difficulties, when Cliff was 11 years old. d. December 17, 1926.

Mother: Evelyn Cox daughter of Frederic Walter and Cordelia Morley Cox. b. December 8, 1866 in Manti, Utah; m. December 11, 1899 in Manti Temple; 98 years of age on December 8, 1964.
d. Friday February 12, 1965.

Brothers and Sisters: Margaret, b. March 12, 1891, m. Harvey A. Pace; Lillis b. August 28, 1890, m. Rueben R. Wilkins, husband deceased; Oleta, b. July 25, 1899, m. Jowett A. Fortie; (J Clifton); Howard b. February 12, 1905, m. Fern Titcomb, d. 1931.

Marriage: Elsie Erickson of Fairview, Utah. Daughter of Carl August and Eliz. Mower Erickson b. August 11, 1897 in Fairview, m. October 4, 1916.

Children: Mayna, m. (1) Don Conover (killed) 6 children (2) m. Harold J. Campbell; Maurine, m. Bill Coltrin, had son and daughter; sports writer for Salt Lake Tribune; Barbara, m. Max G. Broadhead, 2 sons; Dr. J. Weldon Moffitt, b. Oct. 1927, m. Helen Snonberger, 6 children, Professor at BYU.

John Clifton Moffitt is a native of Manti, Utah. He attended the public schools in Manti and in Boneta, Duchesne County, where his parents moved when he was eleven years of age. It was in Duchesne County where he began coming to BYU to complete his work for his B.S. Degree.

He graduated from BYU in 1926 and was a successful debator, taking his Master's Degree at BYU in 1929 in Psychology. He then did graduate study at Stanford, Southern California and Northwestern Universities, before entering the University of Chicago. He completed his graduate work at Chicago and took his Ph.D. Degree at that institution in 1940. The title of his dissertation at Chicago was *The Development of Centralizing Tendencies in Educational Organization and Administration in Utah.*

Following his graduation from BYU in 1926, he was appointed principal of the Timpanogos Elementary School in Provo and in 1928, was appointed Director of Research for Provo City Schools. He became principal of Provo High School in 1930, serving in this capacity until 1937 when he was appointed Superintendent of Provo City Schools, June 30, 1964.

Dr. Moffitt has been active in local, state, and national Parent-Teacher Associations. In 1957, he was elected as second vice president of the National Congress of Parents and Teachers, after serving in a similar capacity in Utah. He served in this latter capacity for three years. During these years, he was on both the executive board and the board of managers of the National Congress. In 1961, he was elected as chairman of the standing committee of Parent and Family Life Education and to the Board of Managers of the National Congress, serving for three years, and in May of 1964 was elected as Treasurer of the National Congress of Parents and Teachers and again elected to the Executive Board and the Board of Managers for a three-year term.

He is past president of the Utah Education Association and has been active in the American Association of School Administrators, serving on the committee to adopt its first code of ethics. He received the associations award for distinguished service in the field of education, 1965.

For twenty years, he has been teaching a class as part-time professor at BYU and regularly teaches one term of summer school at this institution. He has similarly taught at the University of Utah, Utah State University, University of Colorado, and Arizona State University.

His community service includes being President of the Chamber of Commerce, and for twenty-three years he was on the Public Library Board. He is past president of the Provo Rotary Club and a Past

District Governor of Rotary International, District 542, Utah and Idaho, and was one of the organizers of Provo Youth Service.

His Church service includes two-years in the mission field, bishop of the Boneta Ward, and superintendent of Sunday School.

He has written for most of the professional journals in education of nationwide circulation and has written the following books: *The History of Public Education in Utah, John R. Park in Utah Culture,* and *A Century of Change: the History of the Utah Education Association.* He is a member of the National Society for the Study of Education and is a contributor to this society's yearbooks. His most recent book, published in 1963 by Prentice-Hall is titled *In-Service Education of Teachers.*

Dr. Moffitt has studied education first hand in the Latin American countries of Central and South America, in most of the countries of Asia, in countries of Europe, and in the U.S.S.R.

Since his retirement as Superintendent of Provo Schools in June, 1964, he is engaged in research for the State of Utah concerned with individual differences in learning. He is a well-known authority on education in America. The American Association of School Administrators at a recent Atlantic City Convention honored "J.C." for "distinguished service in school administration."

George Harding Mortimer

Patent Attorney

Born: Nov. 18, 1903   **Place:** Provo, Utah

Father: William John Mortimer, son of Wm. Mortimer and Dorcas Chislett.
Born July 3, 1870, Trowbridge, Wiltshire, England. Emigrated in 1881 to live with uncle and aunt in Provo. Carpenter, contractor, school teacher.
Died July 11, 1928, struck by two high school boys in auto while riding his bicycle.

Mother: Mary Maria Harding, daughter of John Harding and Jane Evans.
Born Sept. 24, 1876, Sugar House, Salt Lake City.
Marriage Sept. 26, 1900, Salt Lake Temple.
Was devoted teacher in all LDS Auxiliaries.
Died March, 1957.

Brothers and Sisters: Dorcas Mary b. Oct. 5, 1901, m. Arthur Lewis
(George H.)
William Earl b. Oct. 22, 1906, m. Margaret Johnson
Lillian Myrl b. Oct. 22, 1906; m. Andrew Hardee Young
Ireta b. June 29, 1909, m. Jesse Baker

Marriage: Veda Jane Porter, daughter of Hyrum Kilburn Porter and Adrea Rich.
Born Aug. 20, 1902, Porterville, Utah.
Married July 1, 1931, Salt Lake Temple.
Teacher in elementary grades and high school, President of auxiliary organizations in wards and stakes. Genealogist and author of "Instructor" articles; student at BYU.

Children: George Allen, b. April 9, 1932, m. Grace Swan
Jean Louise, b. Oct. 26, 1935, m. Walter Lewis Williamson
William John b. Dec. 30, 1939 m. Margaret Henry
Celia Ann b. May 30, 1943, m. Devon Etsel Hokanson

George Harding Mortimer lived in the environs of the Brigham Young University all his boyhood days. His father was an expert carpenter and young George became a willing helper, expert enough to put himself through high school and college. His carpentry skill has never left him as evidenced by the beautiful cabinet work he executed for the new ward church built in Montclair when president of the Stake.

He was always a quiet-spoken person, walking away from a quarrel but enjoying the contest of a good debate. Graduating from Brigham Young University in 1925, he accepted a call from the Church to serve a mission (Swiss German), with headquarters in Basel, Switzerland. In a short time he was branch president with some fifty missionaries under his direction, using the money he had saved from carpentry to further his education to pay his mission expenses. He toured Europe and visited art and cultural centers.

In 1928 he returned to Utah and taught school at Kaysville until he received a Civil Service appointment which took him and his wife to the U.S. Patent Office and Washington, D. C. His wife, Veda, was a graduate of 1929 and taught school before her marriage. In the Capitol City, George worked in the Patent Office by day and attended night classes in law at George Washington University. At the University he was appointed editor of the University Law Review, a position held only by top grade students. He also achieved the Order of the Coif and graduated with distinctive honors, receiving degrees in both the law and electrical engineering and was awarded a prize for excellence in patent law. His law degree was J.D.

He accepted a position as patent attorney for a Wall Street firm and in seven years was sought by Colgate-Palmolive Co. They have recently made him assistant General Counsel—Patents. He is a member of the New York State Bar, the District of Columbia Bar, and the United States Supreme Court.

His Church positions reveal religious loyalty, as he believes law and religion compliment each other. He has advanced in priesthood quorum office from counselor in the Bishopric of East Orange Ward of the New York Stake to Bishop, from counselor to president in the growing New York Stake. As population enlarged, this Stake was divided and the New Jersey Stake was instituted with headquarters at Montclair, New Jersey, and George as the new president took on added responsibilities.

His family of four children all attended BYU; George A. received his B.S. at BYU and his Ph.D. in chemistry at M.I.T.; Jean Louise took a B.S. in education and is the wife of a patent attorney; Bill attended BYU and is a Captain in the U.S. Air Force; Celia Ann attends BYU and is the wife of a BYU student.

George and Veda make frequent trips to Utah and have been campus visitors, George giving talks to BYU students in the professional series. Wherever the Mortimers go there is a healthy BYU atmosphere of loyal support.

LOWRY NELSON

Born: April 16, 1893 in Ferron, Emery County, Utah

Father: Hyrum Alonzo Nelson b. December 28, 1860 at Manti, Utah. Homesteaded on Ferron Creek in 1879; State legislature 1908-10; farmer and stock raiser. d. August 19, 1949.

Mother: Mary Artemesia Lowry, b. March 30, 1860 in Manti, Utah. Married January 18, 1884 in Endowment House, Salt Lake. Met her future husband while cooking on a homestead for her brother Dan at Ferron's Creek. d. April 18, 1914

Brothers and Sisters: Clyde (81) in Salt Lake; Selma (79) Bromley in Salt Lake; Victor D. (76) in Salt Lake; Lowry in St. Paul, Minn.; Lloyd (70) in Logan, Utah; Hazelton John (68) Price, Utah; Orson (65) Price, Utah; Aleda N. Simmonds (62) Apache Jet, Ariz. All living December 1965.

Marriage: Florence Newell, b. April 7, 1902 in Salt Lake City, Utah. Daughter of Clark Newell and Jennie Buckley (deceased 1963). Married on February 13, 1924 in Salt Lake Temple. Attended BYU 1921-23. Secretary to President George H. Brimhall when she married Lowry and first secretary of Extension Division.

Children: Florence Ann Lowry, b. December 23, 1924, m. Louis Diamant; Lowry Jr., b. March 1, 1926, Prof. at Yale University; Ph.D. Yale; Janet, b. March 2, 1930, m. G. H. Fridell, M.D.

Lowry Nelson was born in a small town in the Rocky Mountains, early knew the rigors of reclaiming sage brush land and pioneer farming. He knew what it meant to search for a lost sheep on the mountain side, to herd cattle for grazing in the highlands and watch for hungry coyotes ready to stalk an unsuspecting calf. He learned the proper use of a gun to bag game for winter's food.

He lived in a town built around a "square" on which was built a church and a school with a few stores and houses facing all sides of the town square. Back of most of the houses was a little garden for spring and table vegetables with a ditch to convey water for seasonal irrigation. A pump for the culinary water was placed by the sink in the board floor kitchen. There were chores for young boys, morning, noon, and night. Lowry was a sturdy boy who came in the middle of his family; two brothers were older and three were younger. This gave him the responsibility of following and leading.

This family cooperation and town organization intrigued Lowry, who was a lad who frequently asked "why"? People and their actions became an absorbing study as Lowry early learned to observe much and speak little. He greatly admired strong, virile leaders and sought their company. In this category he was fortunate to meet Franklin S. Harris when he started to study at the Utah State Agriculture College and became secretary to the president. He was encouraged to study the sources of harmony found in the Mormon village made up of people of so many differing strata of life, nationalities, economic levels and linguistic foundations.

He came to the conclusion that to know people you should live with them, study them over a period of time, be acquainted with their sources, mores, race characteristics and educational inclinations. In short, he decided to enroll in a young but fast growing subject, sociology.

Lowry Nelson has become one of the world's acknowledged leaders in rural sociology. He is an average sized man, stands erect, speaks easily in the quiet manner, is never stampeded or emotionally overactive. His ready smile brightens his studious countenance. His vocabulary is expansive and most apt as he has a facility of expression with voice or pen. He has been highly successful as editor, author, and speaker.

His life at BYU, when he came to Provo with Doctor Harris, was one of leadership in organization, launching of new activities, increasing enrollment of scholars at the University, counseling and being chairman of various faculty and student activities and acting as assistant to the president without the title. He was one of our most efficient actors, being especially remembered for his portrayals in "The House of Rimmon" and "The Fires of St. John."

He was married in the Salt Lake Temple to a beautiful and also quiet young lady, secretary to the president, Florence Newell, daughter of a union of two pioneer families. Their three oldest children are university scholars, Lowry Jr. teaching at Yale University.

While BYU lost a superior leader when Lowry left, he gained a world reputation for his going. His professional career is briefly tabulated by the University of Minnesota in May of 1958:

"LEADING RURAL SOCIOLOGIST TO RETIRE

"*Lowry Nelson*, one of the world's foremost rural sociologists, will retire June 30 after 21 years on the University of Minnesota staff.

Nelson is a professor of sociology and head of a section of rural sociologists on the St. Paul campus. He is internationally known as a specialist and researcher in rural community organization and population trends and problems. In recent years, he has been particularly concerned with sociological studies in the northern Minnesota forested area.

"Born in 1893 at Ferron, Utah, Nelson graduated from Utah State Agricultural college in 1916. He later attended the University of Wisconsin, where he earned an M.S. in 1924 and his Ph.D. in 1929.

"He was secretary to the president at Utah State in 1916-17 and was assistant state county agent leader there from 1917-18. He then was agricultural agent in Utah's Sanpete County until 1921, was editor of the *UTAH FARMER* from 1921-23, director of the extension division at Brigham Young University, Provo, Utah, 1923-34, and was dean of the College of Applied Sciences at Brigham Young from 1929-34.

In 1934, Nelson organized the social welfare division of the Utah Emergency Relief Administration. During the next year, he was regional advisor for the rural rehabilitation division of the Federal Emergency Relief Administration in Utah, Nevada, California and Arizona. He was assistant director of the Rural Rehabilitation division in Washington, D.C. in 1935-36, then returned to Utah State college where he was director of the Agricultural Experiment station until coming to the University of Minnesota in 1937.

"He was a member of President Roosevelt's Farm Tenancy committee in 1936, which drafted the recommendation that Congress create the Farm Security Administration.

Nelson has had many overseas assignments while at the University. He was U.S. representative to the first meeting, in Geneva, Switzerland, of the Permanent Agricultural committee of the International Labor Organization (ILO) and attended conferences of this committee again in 1947 and 1949.

"As rural sociologist for the U.S. State Department, Nelson in 1946 made a study of Caribbean rural life. In 1954 and 1955, he studied Italian rural life under a Fulbright Research award.

"In 1952, he was a consultant for the Ford Foundation, to study the problem of evaluating technical assistance in Latin America.

"Nelson has led a number of sociological research projects in Minnesota, has been a widely-known teacher and is author of nine books, 54 articles and 23 monographs. *Rural Sociology,* a textbook first published in 1948, revised in 1955; *Rural Cuba,* 1950; *The Mormon Village,* 1952; and *American Farm Life,* 1954 are unusual favorites. He also published *The Birth and Growth of a Science & History of Rural Sociology* in 1966.

"He is a member of several honorary and professional groups. These include: Rural Sociological society (former president); American Association for the Advancement of Science (fellow and former vice president); American Sociological society; Utah Academy of Science, Literature and the Arts (former president); the Minnesota Academy of Science; the Population Association of America and the Midwest Sociological society.

"In March, 1957, Nelson received a distinguished Service award from Utah State Agricultural college."

To the above report by Minnesota, the following is appended:

Field man for the People's Sugar Co. Moroni, Utah 1920

Original chairman of "Leadership Week" at BYU.

President of Timpanogos Council Boy Scouts of America 1930-33

Fellow and president (1934-35) Utah Academy Science, Arts and Letters.

Received their Distinguished Service award in 1956.

Director in Provo Chamber of Commerce

Member of Alpha Kappa Delta, Phi Kappa Phi, Gamma Sigma Delta

Co-author *Poems of the West,* 1923

Fostered the first volume of *Utah Sings* with the late H. R. Merrill and Carleton Culmsee.

Author—"Some Social and Economic Aspects of American Fork, Utah" 1936

Fellow in A.A.A.S.

Editor of "Rural Sociology" 1936-41

Taught at Brazil 1956, Cornell University 1960, University of Florida 1961; Summer School U. of Puerto Rico, Consultant to Pan American Union 1963, U. of Miami, Research Prof. of Latin America Studies, 1967

Rural Minnesota, published by University of Minnesota

The Community published by Macmillan Co.

Rural Cuba is used by Fidel Castro for many of his reform movements (Saturday Review 6-20-59)

Teacher of "Gospel Doctrine" Sunday School class at Minneapolis branch.

His vast experience, world travel and international assignments have given him stature as an educator, sociologist, and author. His "Mormon Village" pioneered a field of sociological importance and introduced him to the world as a true Son of Brigham. His retirement has been filled with semester assignments of some of the larger universities across the nation.

HUGH W. NIBLEY

Born: March 27, 1910 at Portland, Oregon

Father: Alexander (Alex) Nibley, son of President Charles W. and Rebecca Neibaur, born in Logan, Utah, May 7, 1876. (Charles W. in LDS Church presidency with Heber J. Grant). Business and lumber man. Lost a fortune in Glendale real estate in the 1930 crash.
Died September 1, 1959.

Mother: Agnes Sloan, daughter of Hugh R. and Margaret Reid Sloan, born October 17, 1885 in Manti, Utah. Married June 27, 1907 in Salt Lake Temple. Her home in Glendale, California, the center for artists of Southern California for years. On Board of Directors for Glendale Symphony. Died May 28, 1959.

Brothers and Sisters: Connie (daughter of first wife, Constance Thatcher, d. 1905), m. Tom Edwards; Sloan, m. Linda Sterling; (Hugh W.); Richard, m. Nadine Monson; Reid, m. Marjorie McBride; Barbara, m. Lynn Richards.
Sloan is well known scenarist of Hollywood, Richard is concert master for BYU, Salt Lake Symphonies; Reid is nationally known, concert pianist performing with the great symphonies of the U.S., taught at BYU, U. of U. and now head of piano Dept. at U. of Michigan.

Marriage: Phyllis Ann Draper, daughter of Frederick Pratt Hawks. Reared by Otto Draper (d. 1935) and Edla Peterson Draper.

Children: Paul; Christina; Thomas; Michael; Charles; Rebecca; Martha; Zina.

Hugh Nibley, according to many of his students, "looks and acts like a college professor." When I repeated this remark to him he said, "A rather dubious compliment, don't you think?" His wide knowledge of languages gives him many opportunities to play on words, clarify expressions, put words in their proper category or meaning, and frequently relate the circumstance when a word came into usage or was first used in print. He would be embarrassed if he didn't know the source of a word found in our modern college dictionary. In brief, Hugh W. Nibley is one of America's best known linguistic scholars.

In his early teens, he was proficient in Romance languages, deeply interested in word origins which led him to study Greek, Hebrew, Egyptian, Babylonian, Coptic, and later Sanskrit and Arabic.

Early in his life, religion, and specifically the Mormon doctrine motivated his language studies. "How can I harmonize or even challenge the similarities, differences, language and mores of the Hebrew on the Asiatic and American continents if I don't know the history and languages as revealed by translation in the Old Testament and the Book of Mormon?" In trying to answer the many questions presented by the early Hebrew and Nephite prophets, he became an authority on scriptural studies and history in the days of Jesus. The debate of succession in the Christian priesthood and its restoration by Joseph Smith further motivated his religious studies and subsequent writings. He was prepared to put the value of the recent Dead Sea Scrolls in their calendar importance. A brief sketch is given here, although his printed works best reveal the man.

He was born in Portland, Oregon, of parents who loved the arts and who promoted young artists of promise. Moving to Glendale, California when Hugh was but a lad, the Nibleys grew up in a beautiful mansion in Rossmoyne district of Glendale, fraternized with the best musicians and many of Hollywood's more serious players. Hugh would talk with the different foreigners who were guests at his mother's musicals, often imitating their speech sounds until the visitor complimented him on his accuracy.

Hugh's grandfather was Charles W. Nibley, in the presidency of the Mormon Church, and all the Nibley children were imbued with a desire to serve their Church and their country. Hugh majored in history with a minor in the classics at UCLA, receiving his BS in 1934, was a research fellow at the University of California, 1936-37, obtaining a Ph.D. in 1938, as one of their distinguished scholars.

He served an LDS Swiss-German and Northwestern States mission, being transferred because of war. From 1942 to 1945, he served in the US Army as intelligence officer and on D Day of 1944, parachuted behind enemy lines and worked many months with the underground. His near captures were frequent and escapes often very clever. His German was almost detection-proof. Once he and a companion walked into a German artillery headquarters, believing it to be Yankee holdings, kept his German harangue going and calmly walked out with no one giving them any attention. For his war efforts, he received several citations of high order.

One could follow him around and fill a notebook with wise sayings and witty responses. One of his major faults is talking faster than his audience can assimilate or getting through with a thought before his listeners have gotten an adequate base of comprehension. On one occasion, as he was giving one of his television programs, so rapt was Hugh in his subject that he ignored the guiding clock in front of him and Owen Rich, program director, could see a 30 minute program dwindle to 15 minutes. While the camera switched for a station break, Owen wrote a hurried note. "Slow down, you are going too fast." Professor Nibley turned the paper over and scribbled, "That's alright; it's Fast Sunday".

Hugh joined the BYU faculty in 1946 and advanced to Professor of History and Philosophy from 1960 to the present. He is called upon over the state for lecture time; his Firesides bring large Sabbath crowds. He was selected to give the second annual Faculty Lecture in March of 1965, to present the Changing Images of Christianity and Judiasm in light of recent documentary discoveries—which attracted a majority of his faculty colleagues. His restless mind keeps several subjects alive as he writes over several desks. A listing of some of his major works follows:

1. "New Light on Scaliger," *The CLASSICAL JOURNAL* xxxvll, No. 5, Feb. 1942, pp. 291-5.
2. "Sparisones," *The CLASSICAL JOURNAL* XL, No. 9, June 1945, pp. 515-543.
3. "The Arrow, the Hunter, and the State," *The WESTERN POLITICAL QUARTERLY*, Vol. 11 (1949) pp. 329-345.
4. "The Hieroncentric State," *The WESTERN POLITICAL QUARTERLY*, Vol. III June 1951, pp. 226-253. (Pi Sigma Alpha and Centennial Lecture at U. of U., Feb. 15, 1950).
5. "Review of J. W. Swain," *The Ancient World* (Harpers, 1950, 2 vols.)., in *THE HISTORIAN*, vol. XIII (Autumn, 1950), pp.
6. "The Unsolved Loyalty Problem: Our Western Heritage," *WESTERN POLITICAL QUARTERLY* Vol. VI, No. 4, December 1953, pp. 631-657.
7. "Do History and Religion Conflict?" Great Issues Forum, U. of U., Ext. Div. Pamphlet (U. of Utah, 1956).
8. "*Victoriosa Loquacitas*, the Rise of Rhetoric and the Decline of Everything Else," *WESTERN SPEECH* XX (March, 1956)

9. Review of Edward A. Shils, *The Torment of Secrecy* (Free Press: Glencoe, Ill., 1956) in *American Political Science Review,* 1, 3 (Sept. 1956) pp. 886-8.
10. "Christian Envy of the Temple," *The Jewish Quarterly Review,* Vol. 50, Oct. 1959, No. 2, pp. 97-123, No. 3, Jan. 1960, pp. 220-240.
11. "The Passing of the Church: Forty Variations on a Forbidden Theme," In publication, U. of Chicago Press. *Church History* XXX (1961), pp. 131-154.

LDS

1. *No Ma'am, that's Not History!* Bookcraft, Salt Lake, 1946.
2. "Baptism for the Dead in Ancient Times," The IMPROVEMENT ERA, Vol. 50 (Dec. 1948), pp. 78ff to June, inclusive, 1949 (7 articles) (Cf. B. M. Poschini, "Those Who are Baptized for the Dead," in CATHOLIC BIBLICAL QUARTERLY XIII
3. "Lehi in Desert," IMPROVEMENT ERA, Vol. 53, (1950) Jan. to Oct. inclusive. (10 articles.)
4. "The World of the Jaredites," IMPROVEMENT ERA No. 1951-July 1952 inclusive (nine articles).
5. *Lehi in the Desert and the World of the Jaredites,* 272 pp. $1.25 Bookcraft: S. L. C., 1952 (Appeared in German in *Der Stern.*)
6. "The Stick of Judah and the Stick of Joseph," IMPROVEMENT ERA, Vol. 56 Jan 1953 to May 1953. (5 articles.)
7. "Columbus and Revelation," THE INSTRUCTOR, Vol. 88, No 10, Oct. 1953, pp. 319f.
8. "New Approaches to Book of Mormon Study," IMPROVEMENT ERA, Vol. 56 Nov. 1953 (pp. 830ff.), to July 1954 (9 articles)
9. *Time Vindicates the Prophets,* Radio Series over Radio Station KSL weekly from March 7 to Oct. 17, 1954. Published leaflets (30 items.)
10. *The World and The Prophets* (Salt Lake City: Deseret Book Company 1954) 242 pp.
11. *The Way of the Church,* Part 1: "Controlling the Past," IMPROVEMENT ERA Vol. 58, Jan. 1955-Oct. 1955.
Part II: "The Apocalyptic Background," Nov-Dec. 1955.
12. "There were Jaredites," IMPROVEMENT ERA, Vol. 59, Jan. 1956-Feb. 1957.
13. "More Voices From the Dust," THE INSTRUCTOR, Vol. 91, March 1956, pp. 71-2.
14. "Acclamatio," paper read at annual meeting of American Arch. Association San Diego, 1941.
15. *An Approach to the Book of Mormon.* (Salt Lake: Deseret News Press, 1957) Course of Study for the Melchizedek Priesthood Quorums of The Church of Jesus Christ of Latter-day Saints. pp. 416)
16. "The Idea of the Temple in History," MILLENNIAL STAR, Vol. 120, No. 8 August 1958, pp. 228-237, 247-249.

17. "Strange Ships and Shining Stones" in *A BOOK OF MORMON TREASURY,* Salt Lake, Bookcraft, 1959, pp. 133-151.
18. *The Myth-Makers.* (Salt Lake City: Bookcraft, 1961). 293 pp.
19. "Censoring Joseph Smith's Story," *IMPROVEMENT ERA,* Vol. 64 (1961), July, pp. 490 ff.
20. *The World and the Prophets,* enlarged ed., (30 pp. added), 1962.
21. "The Book of Mormon: True or False?" *Millennial Star,* Nov. 1962, 274-7, Feb. 1963, pp. 28-34.
22. "The DSS Some Questions and Answers," INSTRUCTOR 98 (July, 1963) 233-5.
23. *Sounding Brass.* (Salt Lake City: Bookcraft, 1963), 286 pp. reviewed by anti Mormon writers.

Recent Honors and Publications of Hugh Nibley—January 1965

1. Article on "Jerusalem and the Christian Church" (about 30 pages) in the forthcoming *Encyclopedia Judaica.*
2. Forthcoming article on Christian traditions of the 40 days after the resurrection, in the *Vigiliae Christianae.*
3. Forthcoming article on the Arabic traditions of the Dead Sea Community in the *Revue de Quamran.*
4. Pi Sigma Alpha National Political Science Honor Society Lecture at the University of Utah on May 21, 1964, "Tenting, Tolling, and Taxin," to be printed in the forthcoming issue of the *Western Political Quarterly.*
5. An *Instructor* article (December or January) on Jesus' youth in the Apocryphal traditions.
6. An *Improvement Era* series, currently running, on recent developments in the fields of Biblical Archaeology.
7. A recent edition, moderately revised, of *An Approach to the Book of Mormon,* published by the Deseret Book Co.

One of the best tributes heard of his teaching is, "You'll never go to sleep in any of his classes" and he is one of the teachers at BYU whose classes are among the first to be filled at registration.

ALBERT RAY OLPIN

Born: June 1, 1898, Pleasant Grove, Utah

Father: Albert Henry Olpin, son of Joseph and Ann Dee Olpin
b. August 11, 1870, in Gloucestershire, England
To Pleasant Grove, became carpenter and millwright
Served mission to Southern States without purse or script
d. August 13, 1923

Mother: Alvira Smith
b. May 22, 1876 in Pleasant Grove, Utah,
daughter of Daniel Miley, Sr., born in Quincey, Pennsylvania and Emma H. Sinfield Smith born Bedfordshire, England
m. July 31, 1895 in Salt Lake Temple
d. January 17, 1958
One year to Weber Academy and graduate from Normal Course, B.Y.A. Widow 35 years—raised chickens and sold eggs to support and educate her children, seven of eight children reached maturity.

Brothers and Sisters: Cora, m. Matthew Bezzant, U. S. Steel official, retired (A. Ray)
J. Lloyd, m. Ivy Stowell, Assoc. Prof. of Math, B.Y.U.
Pearl, m. Owen Whitehead, d. 1950
Lawrence D., m. Cynthia Larsen, architect in Ogden, Utah
Ralph S., m. Lucille Harmon, C.P.A., San Francisco, California
Ruth, m., Lee B. Christiansen, Oil operator, Provo, Utah

Marriage: Elva Chipman of American Fork, Utah
m. April 12, 1922
daughter of Stephen L. Chipman on Board of Directors, B.Y.U. (see his biography)
Honorary Member of University of Utah Mothers Club and civic worker

Children: Helen Rae, m., Rulon Ellsworth Snow (dec. June 4, 1955) Callahan
Barbara Ann, m., William Russell Hooks
Virginia m., Neal Harris Adams
Howard Ray, m., Marilyn Johnson

Education:
    Graduate of Pleasant Grove High School
    A.B.—B.Y.U. 1923—Varsity debator, President of the Student Body
    Ph.D.—Columbia U.—1930
    Instructor in Physics B.Y.U.—1922-24
    Asst. in Physics, Columbia U.—1924-25
    Prof. Industrial Research Ohio State University 1939-1945
    President University of Utah, 1946-July 1964
    Consultant at U. of U. on development and intercultural programs, 1954
    Fellow American Physical Society
    Member U.E.A. and N.E.A.
    Associate Editor Journal of Applied Physics, 1937-38
    President of National Association of Utah State Universities 1961-
    Editor of New material section, "Review of Scientific Instruments," 1941-42
    Managing editor "Science and Appliance," 1939-
    Author many treatises on education and technical papers on scientific subjects relating to photo-electricity
    Built an outstanding faculty at U. of U., obtained millions for research, added 26 departments. Three colleges, extended university land by Fort Douglas Government gifts.
    "Changed a liberal Arts College into a University."
    B.Y.U. Alumni Distinguished Service Award 1955
    Retired as President of U. of U. June 30, 1964
Church:
    L.D.S. Missionary to Japan 1916-1920
    Japanese consultant for the L.D.S. Church
Civic and Government:
    Member Executive Board, Great Salt Lake Council, Boy Scouts of America
    Judge, Miss America Contest 1952
    Acoustic research for Army and Navy—World War II
    Member Board of Directors Utah Symphony Orchestra
    Member Executive Board of Directors Utah Symphony Orchestra
    Member Advisory Council National Fund for Medical Education
    Member Research Advisory Comm. National Assn. Manufacturers
    Member Army Ordnance Association.
    Assoc. Member Comm. on Economic Development
    Member A.A.A. Science, Tau Kappa Alpha, Sigma Xi Phi Kappa Phi, Alpha Phi Omega, Simga Phi Sigma, Phi Betta Kappa
    Member American Chemical Society
    Member National Geographic Society

Rotary, Alta, Aztec, Bonneville, Knife and Fork
Chamber of Commerce—Timpanogos Club
Fort Douglas Club
Member of the Leaders and Specialist Branch of the Educational
Information Administration of the State Department—summer
tour major cities of the world to exchange ideas—1953

Occupation Activities:
Member technical staff Bell Telephone Labs, N.Y.C., 1925-33
Lecturer—Brooklyn Poly. Tech. Inst. 1931-33
Research—Kendall Mills, Charlotte, N.C.—1933-39
Director Industrial Research Experiment Station, Ohio State
University, 1939-42
Director Research Ohio State Research Foundation, 1939-42
Executive Director Ohio State Research Foundation, 1942-45
Consultant Anthony Wayne Research, Toledo, Ohio, 1944-45
Advisor to the president of Seoul National University in Korea,
under direction of the Asia Foundation, on six months leave
of absence from the U. of U.

A. Ray Olpin is easy to meet and encourages friendly association. In the mountain town of Pleasant Grove he knew the chores of a farm boy in a rural community. His birthplace is a town of cultural activities and early challenges its young people to look to education as an outlet of ability and promise of a future. Here, entertainment comes from the Church and school and Ray was active in each, also excelling as a scholar. Although he was a better than average athlete, he chose books and the laboratory for his "leisure time" activities. He was born with "why" on his mind and to this day seeks for the new and for answers to problems which challenge progress. The question "What makes an object work" early inspired his curiosity and made of him a leader in research. His friends have admired his interest in taking a complicated problem and reducing it to elemental units. In college debates we found him equally facile with induction as deduction. He cultivated simple statements in preference to ornate expressions, and this training aided in his becoming an excellent executive and a patient research scholar.

One of his colleagues described him as "a serious man with a smiling face". When he officially retired from the presidency of the University of Utah, the board of regents, faculty and studentbody gave him an outstanding tribute of appreciation and admiration. The faculty club paid him further honor by presenting him a gold medallion set in native green onyx, thanking him for superior leadership interest in all branches, departments and phases of education affecting an expanding state. The arts and sciences held his equal attention; law and medicine grew with gratifying strength to achieve national reputation. His love of books and their importance to scholarship impelled his efforts toward a national and international search for volumes of exceptional worth. The Japanese section of the University of Utah Library is fast becoming of national import under his personal efforts.

His post-university life is aptly expressed, "I am retiring to activity. He and Elva have moved into a commodious new home on the slopes of the Wasatch Mountains where they can survey the beautiful Salt Lake Valley and the expanding campus of a great historic university.

CHESLEY GORDON PETERSON

Born: Aug. 10, 1920

Father: Brigham Peterson, son of Solomon Peterson and Albertina Erickson. Graduate of BYU, 1913; active as studentbody officer.
Died May 12, 1952.

Mother: Ethel Pugh, daughter of John Pugh and Ellen Fanny Holbrook. Married June 8, 1918 in Butte, Montana; later solemnized in the Salt Lake Temple.
Resides in Ogden, Utah.

Sister: "Jean," Emogene, m. Wayne L. Clayson.
Jean was a BYU student.

Marriage: Audrey Boyes of South Africa, actress from Capetown. When war broke out, was unable to return to Africa. Two brothers in British Army at the time.
Married June 26, 1944, in London.

Children: Michael Gordon
Karen Audrey

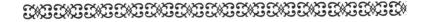

"One of the outstanding young men of the year 1942", U.S. Jr. Chamber of Commerce.

First American to be named commander leader of famed R.A.F. Eagle Squadron.

Enlisted, U.S. Army Air Corps, 1939—began flight training at San Diego, California. At Randolph A.F.B., Texas, he resigned in August, 1940 to go overseas. August 10, 1940, his twentieth birthday, he left Ottawa, Canada, to sail for England as a member of the R.A.F.

Record with the R.A.F.—110 flights across the English Channel into enemy territory.

Credited with shooting down seven Nazi planes, with many more "probables."

At twenty-one, while a flight lieutenant, awarded the D. F. C. Citation, "This American pilot has led his flight during the past three months. He has taken part in 42 operational sorties and has destroyed two, probably destroyed two others, and damaged one enemy aircraft."

The British King, George VI, personally conferred the Distinguished Service order upon him in March, 1942. He became commander leader of the Eagles in November, 1941. He was the first commander to lead the unit and the youngest squadron commander in the R.A.F. at the time.

When the Eagle squadron was transferred to the U. S. Army Air Forces, Colonel Peterson was commissioned a major and was made operational officer with the Fourth Air Group in England. He was advanced to Lieutenant Colonel early in November of 1942, the youngest so commissioned.

Salt Lake had a "Major Chesley Gordon Peterson day", Oct. 30, 1942, with the state paying him exuberant homage.

Holds the British Distinguished Service Cross, American Air Medal and Purple Heart (October, 1943).

Survived two immersions in the English Channel.

"Whenever they make nominations for the premier fighting pilot—Peterson's name is mentioned. Certainly he is one of the most illustrious and best-known among the Americans, at 23!" Press comment of the day.

Chesley's story of how it all began.

"I was just a button about nine. A couple of barnstormers sat an old crate down in dad's alfalfa patch and asked if they could use it for a while as a landing field.

Next day, my father talked them into taking me and my kid sister up for a ride. They did. When I came down I said to myself 'This is a darn good thing!' "

"In high school the infection took sovereign domination whereupon I began cutting my life to be an army pilot. Dismissed the commercial pilot work as I heard the army frowned them down.

"At the end of the sophomore year at Brigham Young University, I asked myself what I was doing there still—the air corps only required two years of college. I quit."

In my speech classes at BYU, Chesley proved to be a good, methodical speaker with well-organized ideas. Many of the speeches of his choice were on flying and aircraft. When I was asked to be chairman of the Provo Freedom program for July 4th, 1956 celebration in Provo, I immediately started to acquire Chesley as our featured speaker. With the aid of Senator Arthur V. Watkins and the Air Corps, the Colonel flew into Ogden, motored to Provo, gave a stirring speech and was given a notable reception.

After quitting college, he enlisted in the Air Corps and was washed out for "inherent lack of ability." An officer had learned that Pete was too young for enlistment and kindly dismissed him to avoid serious trouble.

When Chesley slipped away to Canada in 1940 the F.B.I. followed and brought him back to the U.S.

A second try to join the R.A.F. in Canada was successful, and in a short time the tow-headed young man was in England. On one occasion his billet was bombed by the Germans as he slept; he escaped injury.

As one of the original Eagles squadron fliers he met Colonel James S. Childers, who held many interviews (for the Birmingham News) and wrote one of the war's best books, *War Eagles*, using Chesley as a featured hero.

While based in England, Chesley met a pretty black-haired South African lass, Audrey Boyes. A popular actress and a war hero—such a combination led to but one conclusion, marriage.

The *Deseret News* writer in 1943 describes Chesley, "Peterson, though very young, gradually emerged not only as a superb flier, but as a leader and a hard student of tactics. He was revealed as a natural-born military man . . . . He is tall and approximately knock-kneed (I never observed this of him). He is sinewy, has flaxen hair and deep-socketed, blue eyes. He is self-possessed and uncommonly well-poised. His obvious precocity serves in the stead of maturity. There is an affable exterior from which winsome boyishness escapes now and then, but the salient characteristic is combativeness. . . . He became an archetype of fighter pilots."

When he was shot down during the Dieppe raid, he maneuvered his parachute to land in the English Channel. Riding a Thunderbolt, he went down in the channel again—this time less than a thousand feet, when his parachute almost failed to open. A black eye was his major injury.   After this he was grounded for a spell by a close-observing command.   In such absence from the battle line, he made his visits to his home in the mountains and his boyhood environs.

At the BYU Home Coming Parade in October, 1942, the Major was the honor guest to ride with Queen Lucy Bluth and received an ovation at the BYU—USAC football game.

Another incident in his boyhood activities and its aftermath:

Chesley was an active Boy Scout in Santaquin.   He earned enough merit badges to qualify for an Eagle rating, but his troop failed to re-register in time for him before he had to leave for college. When he visited his home in October of 1942, Chief A. A. Anderson of the Utah National Parks Council and Dr. T. Earl Pardoe, chairman of scout advancement, presented Major Peterson with his Eagle badge.   A miniature Eagle badge was presented to the Major's mother. Ches said regulation forbid his wearing any insignia while in uniform, but he would cherish the Eagle Boy Scout Award as being as choice as any he may ever achieve.

His assignments take him around the world.   He has been based at Headquarters U. S. Strike Command (J5), MacDill A. F. B., Florida.   In March of 1967, Major General Peterson and his beautiful wife Audrey paid the B.Y.U. campus a day's visit on their way to Hickam Field, Hawaii, from which base he will pay more frequent visits to VietNam environs.   He was deeply grateful for the honor paid him in our Memorial Hall and praised the University as one of the most beautiful in the world.   He was the featured speaker at the Hall's dedication, Dec. 8, 1967, flying from Taiwan for the occasion. A portion of his medals and citations are displayed in the Memorial Hall in the Wilkinson Student Center as a part of its permanent collection.

LYNN STEPHEN RICHARDS

Born: February 3, 1901

Father: Stephen L. Richards, b. June 18, 1879 in Mendon, Cache Co., Utah. Son of Stephen Longstrath Richards and Emma Louise Staynor. Grandson of Willard Richards, who was private secretary of the Prophet Joseph Smith and with him at his martyrdom. Outstanding lawyer, apostle, and member of presidency of Church of Jesus Christ of Latter-day Saints.
d. May 19, 1959.

Mother: Irene Smith Merrill, b. June 4, 1874 in Fillmore, Utah, daughter of Clarence and Bathsheba Smith Merrill. Bathsheba Smith was the daughter of George A. Smith, nephew of Joseph Smith Sr. Married February 2, 1900. Resides in Kenwood Ward of Wilford Stake in Salt Lake City.

Brothers and Sisters: Lynn; Irene Louise, m. Stephen G. Covey; Lois Bathsheba, m. Frederick R. Hinckley; Alice Leila, m. Jesse Knight Allen; Georgia Gill, m. Ralph Harvard Olson; Phillip Longstroth, m. Elma Smith; Richard Merrill, m. Mary Guernsey; Helen Murle, died as infant; Joseph Albert, died at fourteen in accident.

Marriage: Lucille Jeanette Covey, b. September 25, 1901 in Salt Lake City, Utah, daughter of Stephen Mack Covey and Hannah Saunders. Married December 11, 1924.

Children: Lynn Stephen, b. September 10, 1926 at Palo Alto, California, m. Annette Nibley; Joseph Covey, b. January 1, 1929 in Salt Lake City, Utah, m. Joanne Timpson; Rosalie Lucille, b. September 25, 1931 in Salt Lake City, Utah, m. Clarence J. Frost; Victoria Janett, b. April 12, 1934, in Salt Lake City, Utah m. Stanley A. Taylor; Joyce Louise, b. May 5, 1940 in Salt Lake City, Utah, m. Verl Dee Shell; James Mack, b. December 1, 1942 in Salt Lake City, Utah, at BYU as Engineer Major.

Lynn S. Richards was born to lead. His distinguished ancestry gave him a background of prestige and character pride. His talented father, Stephen L, pointed the way in the legal profession and the first son in a family of nine awaited the day when he could head his own law firm.

Lynn is an enthusiast of clean, competitive sports and a good critic of art. He gave the BYU Art Department a painting by Adolf Shreyer (1828-1899) a German painter of international repute noted for his paintings of peasant life and horses.

The importance and expansion of the BYU Alumni Association has been a major concern of his since his graduation. Almost a lifetime ambition was consumated when the Alumni House was erected and supreme happiness came to him and his family when the superb BYU gymnasium was named in honor of his father.

His pride in ancestry is evidenced by his interest in beautification of the nation's and state's burial grounds. Lynn is nationally known for his ideas and leadership in this matter and was chosen president by the national society of cemeteries which gave him the opportunity to activate his plans and program.

A family man of great drive and interested in the advancement and progress of his many friends, Lynn early caught the "Spirit of the 'Y' " and has become one of the illustrious Sons of Brigham.

Educational Activities:

Latter-day Saints University, Utah State U., BYU (AB-1925), Stanford University Law School (J.D. 1929); Principal, Oneida Stake Seminary, 1923-25; President, BYU Alumni Association, 1937 and 1956. Under his Alumni presidency, Cornelius R. Peterson was hired as first full time Alumni Secretary. Also, under his presidency, all of the Quorum of the twelve were inducted as Honorary Life Members of the Alumni Association and at that time were made the Board of Trustees. In his last term, the Association organized the Alumni House Committee with Grant Thorn as chairman and President E. L. Wilkinson secured the consent for the building of the Alumni House. Received the Alumni Distinguished Service Award in 1959.

Professional:

A practicing lawyer and senior member of Richards, Bird and Hard in Salt Lake City. Associate member of the advisory board for registrants for the State of Utah. Special Assistant to the Attorney General Hearings Officer, Universal Military Training and Service Act, 1954. Member Utah State Bar, Salt Lake City and County Bar Association, president 1939-40; American Bar Association. Member Motor Carrier's Lawyers Association. Phi Delta Delta, legal fraternity. Co-author,

"Principles of Legislative Drafting for Utah".

Civic and Governmental:

Member, Salt Lake City Chamber of Commerce; Distinguished Service, War Finance program; Elected Utah State Senator, 1943; Member, Utah Society Sons of the American Revolution; Salt Lake Knife and Fork Club, director 1954; State Chairman Cancer Society of Utah; Member Board of Directors, Utah Foundation; Fort Douglas Club member; Editor Utah Senate Journal 1933.

Business:

President Wasatch Lawn Cemetery Association; Vice President and Treasurer Wasatch Land and Improvement Co.; Director Collett Investment Co.; Terminal Service Co.; President Western Cemetery Alliance, 1944-48; President Utah State Cemetery Memorial Park Association; Director and President American Cemetery Association; Secretary and General Counsel, Utah Self Insurer's Association; Director Granite Furniture Co.; Covey Oil Co.; President Investors and Insurance Co.

Church:

Missionary for LDS Church, Eastern States 1919-21; Bishop University Ward 1945-49; Bishop Federal Heights Ward, 1949-52; 2nd Assistant General Superintendent Deseret Sunday School Union 1952-1967; 1st Assistant General Superintendent Deseret Sunday School Union 1967-; Contributor to *The Instructor.*

OLIVER PRESTON ROBINSON

Resident of Salt Lake City, Utah, the seventh child of a family of nine; the sixth son of six sons.

Born: June 25, 1903, Farmington, Utah

Father: James Henry Robinson, the son of Oliver Lee and Lucy Miller Robinson—Oliver born at Bennington, Vermont, Feb. 18, 1811
Born in Farmington, Utah, Nov. 8, 1865
The seventh child of a family of eleven, the fifth son of five sons
Merchant 40 years—mayor of Farmington two terms
First city marshal—charter member Chamber of Commerce
President South Davis Stake, 1915-1937
d. January 18, 1954

Mother: Romina Chaffin
(Blessed by the name of Rhuemenia)
daughter of Darwin E. Chaffin and Victoria Elizabeth Wilson; b. Nov. 3, 1866, the second child
m. Dec 18, 1889
d. July 10, 1943 at 76

Brothers and Sisters: Harold Henry, b. Feb 3, 1891
Edward Chaffin, b. Aug. 30, 1892
Alta Barber, b. Feb 22, 1894
Sherman Chaffin, b. April 29, 1896
Gilbert Milton, b. Jan 24, 1898
Darwin Glen, b. Oct. 7, 1899
(O. Preston)
Afton Charlotte Riches, b. Jan 31, 1907
Naomi Ruth Lewis, b. Mar. 29, 1909

Marriage: Christine Hinckley September 16, 1929, daughter of Bryant S. Hinckley. Member Relief Society General Board and the L.D.S. Church Correlation Committee Adult Planning Group

Children: Miriam, b. June 29, 1930, m. Richard P. Rebholz
Dr. Bruce Hinckley, b. July 14, 1934, m. Jane Romney
Christine Carol, b. Mar. 16, 1941, m. Thomas M. Burton

Preston studied in the Farmington schools, going to the University of Utah in 1922-24; University of Grenoble, France; University of Munich, Germany; B.Y.U., 1927-28, A.B.; New York University 1928-35, M.S. and Doctor of Commercial Science, (D.C.S.)

While advancing in his major studies he was a professor in the School of Retailing at N.Y.U., 1929-46; Co-director of personnel specialist program at N.Y.U.1922-42; in charge of retailing of Hofstra College in Hampstead, New York, 1934-37; instructor at University of Newark, 1935; and in charge of Marketing Instruction, National Institute of Credit, 1935-46. Meeting the World War II needs, he was assistant director of N.Y.U. War Training Center.

The War gave him a natural break in his teaching career and he accepted the chairmanship of the department of Marketing and Director, Bureau of Merchandising Services, University of Utah, 1947-50.

The Deseret News Publishing Company made him assistant general manager when they reorganized their news and publishing setup in 1950-52, and he became the general manager and editor of the *Deseret News* and *Salt Lake Telegram* from 1952 until he was called to the presidency of the British Mission in 1964. With his advent as editor, Salt Lake had but one evening newspaper, thereby strengthening the afternoon news outlet for Salt Lake and the intermountain area. He became a member of the Board of Directors for the Deseret Book Company and Director and Secretary of the Board for the Newspaper Agency Corporation.

With such background he became author and co-author of twelve books relating to his field, which also included merchandising courses for the International Correspondence Schools and section on chain stores in the *Encyclopaedia Brittanica.*

His major works are: *Store Salesmanship* (co-author) has had 33 printings, written in 1932, with 5th edition in 1959, one of the nation's best known sales books; *Store Organization and Operation* (co-author) 1938; *Retail Personnel Relations,* author, 1940; *Successful Retail Salesmanship* (co-author) 1946; *Retail Business Operations,* 1947; *The Dead Sea Scrolls and Original Christianity,* 1958; *The Challenge of the Scrolls—How Old Is The Gospel?* 1958; *Biblical Sites in the Holy Land* (co-author) 1963. Spanish editions have been printed for most of his business books. *Must We Lose the Middle East?* is a publication of interviews he had with world leaders such as President Nasser, President Rene Coty, President Ben Zvi, many prime ministers, heads of state and numerous ambassadors. Many interviews have brought him significant importance to our Department of State, as he has toured the Middle East three times, 1954, 1957, and 1962, visiting seventeen major countries. He was appointed civilian aide to the Secretary of the Army for the State of Utah, 1956.

His community activities reveal the remarkable energy of the man and his ability to organize his own time. He is a board member for the following: Utah Association for the United Nations, Utah Association for Mental Health, Utah Manufacturers Association (chairman of public relations), Association for the Gifted Children, Utah Safety Council (also president), National Association on Alcoholism, First International Congress on Smoking and Health (also chairman of the publicity committee); Chamber of Commerce Advisory Council, Salt Lake Rotary vice-president; has been president of the Utah Symphony Board. The *Deseret News* has received most of its many National Honors while O. Preston was editor and manager.

Nor has his Church been neglected in this busy career as he has served a French mission, been a branch president, member of bishoprics, superintendent of Sunday School and M.I.A., member of a High Priest's quorum presidency and the High Council. He has been an active member of the Deseret Sunday School Union Board and president of the British Mission with headquarters in London. His three years as a missionary in France gave him a solid foundation in a foreign language and further encouraged his native ability to learn other languages, better understand the world we live in and developed his use of English both in print and the platform. He is one of Utah's better speakers and is popular in service clubs and educational centers.

O. Preston is an outstanding Son of Brigham and was given the B.Y.U. Alumni Distinguished Service Award in 1961.

MARION GEORGE ROMNEY

Born: September 19, 1897 in Colonia Juarez, Chihuahua, Mexico

Father: George Samuel Romney, son of Miles Park Romney and Hanna Hill. b. November 12, 1874, in St. George, Utah. At seven, moved with family to Old Mexico. Worked his way through high school as carpenter and teacher. When Mormons were expelled from Mexico in 1912 because of the Revolution, family of husband, wife, and eight children were left penniless. Attended BYU, class of 1912. Taught school at Cassia Stake Academy, Idaho three years, then went to U. of Utah for final two years for his degree. He was assigned to Ricks College during its rapid growth period. Appointed President of Fremont Stake; took Masters degree by summer study at Stanford University. d. December 19, 1935 in Rockford, Illinois, while President of Illinois Mission.

Mother: Terressa Artemesia Redd, daughter of Lemuel H. and Jane Spillsbury Redd. b. August 14, 1874 New Harmony, Utah. Married December 5, 1894 at Colonia Juarez, Mexico by Apostle Teasdale. Attended BYU, class of 1941; received BYU Alumni Distinguished Service Award 1956.
d. October 11, 1964 at age 90.

Brothers and Sisters: Tessa R. b. October 6, 1895, m. Chas. S. Clark; (Marion G., the eldest son); Lurlene R. b. September 24, 1900, m. Rulon Cheney; Antone Kimball, b. September 20, 1902, m. Gretta Parkinson; Artemesia R. b. August 27, 1904, m. Ariel S. Ballif; Jasmine R. b. September 7, 1906, m. John K. Edmunds; Leona R. b. May 21, 1910, m. George Miles Montierth; Maurine R. b. December 2, 1912, m. Kent Johnson; Jennie R. b. September 24, 1914, m. Albert Swensen; Merlyn R. b. April 13, 1917, m. Fred Walters Jr. First seven children born in Colonia Juarez, Mexico.

Marriage: Ida Olivia Jensen, b. Oct., 1890 in Levan, Utah. Married September 12, 1924 in Salt Lake Temple, daughter of Charles Jensen (of Levan, Utah) and Lettie Christensen. Taught English at Ricks College, met Marion G. and resumed courtship at BYU. Taught in Idaho and Utah, Ricks and BYU before marriage. Expert in Mexican history. Talented musician. Received Golden Gleaner Award for YWMIA. A constant companion to a very busy church and public servant.

Children: A son and daughter died in early infancy.
Richard J. Romney, b. December 13, 1927, m. Joanne
Ware; George J. Romney, b. July 5, 1934, m. Joane
Jensen. Both sons attended BYU.

Marion G. Romney

1912-July, Mexican Revolution broke out. The family fled to
the States, in turn to El Paso, Los Angeles, California, Oakley
and Rexburg, Idaho. Marion, a football and basketball star for
Ricks Normal College (two years) Captain and star player of
the champion basketball team 1919. 1918—Stationed at Fort
Douglas; 1920—Graduate from Ricks (a two year college); put
himself through school as a carpenter; 1920-23-Mission to
Australia; 1924-Attend BYU, furthered his courtship and
married Ida Jensen; 1926—Graduated from University of Utah;
1932—LLB at U. of Utah; Practiced law in Salt Lake City for
eleven years; Partner with Delbert M. Draper and John S.
Boyden. Elected to Utah House of Representatives; Chairman
of Judiciary Committee from Salt Lake, member of banking,
corporations, education, University of Utah, and USAC Committees. Assistant County Attorney; Assistant City Attorney;
Assistant District Attorney.

Religious Activities:

President Quorum of Seventy; Bishop 33rd Ward of Liberty
Stake, Salt Lake City for 3 years; President of Bonneville Stake
for three years; Assistant to Twelve, 1941-51; Assistant Manager
Director, Church Welfare 1941-51; Appointed Apostle in the
Quorum of the Twelve, October 1951-to date; Director of
Church Welfare, General Chairman 1959 to date; Regional
Mission President to supervise work the Central American,
Spanish American, West Spanish American and all Mexican
Missions; Chairman of the Adult Coordination Commission of
Church Coordinating Council; Chairman of the Education
Commission of the General Priesthood Commission; Chairman
of the Executive Commission of the Board of Directors of Zions
Securities Corporation; Member, Board of Trustees of BYU; The
Church Board of Education, Advisor to General Board of Prim-
ary Association Advisor.

Additional Activities:

1952-Executive Council BYU Alumni Association; 1957-
Baccalaureate Speaker for BYU; 1962-BYU Alumni Distinguished

Service Award; The Board of directors of Beneficial Life Insurance Co., Board of directors of Heber J. Grant and Co.

A tribute from Elder Harold B. Lee in the October, 1962 *Improvement Era* is quoted in brief, "Few men in our day have come into the council with a broader background than he or with more varied experience and distinguished church and public service in preparation for the lifetime calling of an apostle. . . . In his mature years, as he occupies an important role in the church welfare program, where thrift, honesty, and work are to be enthroned in the lives of this people, one could well believe that his early training served to lay the foundation for the service he was to give as the directing head of this great church welfare program today."

A frequent and popular speaker before the larger BYU student body, he is a valiant son of a great pioneer family whose influence has spread over the mountain west. Good music and clean sports afford him much of his infrequent recreation. As chairman of the Church welfare committee he is vitally interested in world affairs, is informed of each major disaster and knows the financial status of all the missions and branches of the Church throughout the world. A man of a most varied experience he has proved equal to the tasks which daily confront him.

KIEFER B. SAULS

Born: Aug. 14, 1896 at Grays, South Carolina.

Father: John Wilson Sauls, son of John Sauls and Mary Collins Bowers
Born Aug. 17, 1872 in South Carolina.
Ancestral Background—His ancestors fought for the American Revolution of 1776.
Died Dec. 10, 1934.

Mother: Mary Terry, daughter of James Michael Terry and Phoebe Rebecca Tuten
Born Feb. 28, 1876.
Married April 22, 1894.
Died May 9, 1956.

Brothers and Sisters: Phoebe Sauls, b. Oct. 20, 1903; m. Valentine Ivins Bentley.

Marriage: Elizabeth Cannon, daughter of Lewis M. and Mary Alice Cannon.
Born Mar. 2, 1894 in Salt Lake City, Utah.
Married Aug. 19, 1932.
Member of Domestic Science Dept., BYU; Pres. BYU Women; State pres. and state historian A.A.U.W., pres. Manavu Ward Relief Society; Gamma Phi Alumnae.
Died July 20, 1962.

Children: Mary Alice b. Jan. 24, 1934 in Provo, Utah, m. Stan Collins.

Kiefer B. Sauls is one of the quietest men on our campus,
a profound knowledge of students and events. As secretary
President for a decade, purchasing agent for two decade
treasurer of the university since 1939, he knows the very heart
school's financial struggles, the lowest depths of most of the stu
pockets, and the extreme limits of the faculty's solvency. As
our punsters remarked, "There's a man who knows what cer
faculty has." He is a keen observer, a thinking man who listen
honors confidence, an expert counselor, a faithful churchman
tended experience. "When he speaks it is wisdom," said one
closest friends.

His trip to Siberia as Secretary of an American Comm
in search of territory for Jewish Colonization was a highlight i
busy life.

When Kiefer was given the Alumni Distinguished Se
Award on Oct. 24, 1959, a life-time friend, Christen Jensen,
this:

"It is a distinct honor to have the privilege of presenting Ki
B. Sauls to receive the Alumni Distinguished Service Award. He
man who is modest, retiring, and somewhat backward in his disp
tion. Because of these traits, he is not as well known as some ot
members of this association. But his career has been one of continu
service to Brigham Young University.

"He has been treasurer of the University for many years, sec
tary of the Board of Trustees, and assistant to the President.
addition, in times past he has been in charge of many of the auxilia
services of the institution such as housing, the dairy, the laundry, t
post office, etc.

"In religious matters he has also been active. He has served in
ward bishopric. At the present time he is a member of a High Cou
cil in one of the Provo stakes.

"But in spite of his modesty, he is venturesome. Recently h
has invaded the field of politics. I saw him two or three days befor
the recent municipal primary election. 'Kiefer,' I asked, 'how is th
politician?' 'Well,' he replied, 'I am not much of a politician, but
am learning.' Then he added, 'I am getting my eyes opened,'—and
I suspect that they were opened still wider after the election.

"I should like to be personal for a few moments. During the two
periods that I was acting-president of the University Kiefer Sauls was
my right-hand man. He knew more about the details of university
administration than any other man on the campus. I leaned on him
heavily. His office was just across the hall from mine, and there was
a beaten path between the two offices caused by frequent conferences
and consultations between us. Kiefer was a very much appreciated
member of the Brigham Young University staff.

"It is, therefore, a very great honor and pleasure that I now have in presenting Kiefer B. Sauls to receive the Alumni Distinguished Service Award." He received a standing ovation.

Some of the wittiest bits in the various faculty programs have come from the lips of Kiefer; spontaneous responses to a situation which often silenced his colleagues or brought subdued reaction from the more vocal. When two of his friends left each other in strong disagreement, he turned to us and said "Anger is transitory; love is much more durable." His life is one of service and patient understanding.

GRANT S. THORN

Born: November 8, 1910 in Springville, Utah

Father: Ashel O. Thorn of Springville, Utah. b. November 28, 1884 in Springville, son of Joseph A. and Eliza Hall Johnson Thorn.
d. November 28, 1955 in Provo, Utah

Mother: Annette Sanford, b. December 3, 1883 in Springville, Utah, daughter of Cyrus N. and Mary Jane Hunt Sanford. Her grandfather was Jefferson Hunt, Captain of Mormon Battalion. Cyrus was Springville's first school teacher. Married February 4, 1904.

Brothers and Sisters: Paul A. (See biography); Bryce L., b. February 17, 1918, m. Mary George, October 10, 1945. Veteran of World War II. Owns and operates Sage Motel and Restaurant, Springville.

Marriage: Naomi Dalton, b. January 22, 1912. Daughter of Alonzo and Sarah Clements Dalton. Married July 20, 1932.

Children: Jerry G., b. December 18, 1935 in Provo, BYU graduate 1960, LLB., Duke University 1963, m. Carol Jean Straw December 30, 1955; Neil D., b. March 26, 1940 in Provo, BYU and North British Mission; Linda b. August 23, 1943 in Provo, BYU graduate 1965, studying law m. Clyde C. Pearce; Diane, b. November 7, 1951 in Provo.

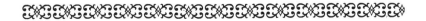

Grant Thorn is a big man in many ways. He was a star in football and basketball at the Springville High School and came to Brigham Young University as a highly touted athlete. He was a Frosh quarterback for Coach G. Ott Romney, during one of the school's most successful sport years.

Nor did Grant confine his talents to athletics, as he was a popular leading man in the High School Senior play (1929) "The 13th Chair". He refrained from trying out for parts in BYU's drama program as studies, commuting, and football took all his time. Always deeply religious, he accepted a call to honor an Eastern States Mission, returned in 1932, and in July of that year married his childhood sweetheart, Naomi Dalton.

When his father got the contract for the grading of the Farmington cut-off, in the fall of 1933, Grant was a key man in the project and "I never went back to school." Contracts for road building and road building materials increased, and the Thorn family expanded with each new opportunity. The need of gravel, sand, and ready mixed concrete became a major business and big equipment became more necessary for digging, excavating, cartage and laying of road-bed. Utah County is one of the nation's greatest and most economic gravel centers; deposits in the alluvial fans of the majestic Lake Bonneville stretch along the valley within easy access. The Thorn's have capitalized on this provision of nature.

Grant is president of Thorn Construction Co., of the Thorn Rock Products Co., and of Superior Asphalt Paving Co. with contracts covering the inter-mountain west.

He is a member of the New Projects Committee of the Provo Rotary Club; chairman of Central Utah Cancer Crusade; member Board of Directors, Utah Division American Cancer Society; BYU Alumni President 1956-57; recipient of BYU Alumni Distinguished Service Award 1961; President of Associated General Contractors; President New Hampshire Life Insurance Company of Salt Lake City; Director of Utah Manufacturers Association; Chairman BYU Alumni House Committee six years; member Aspen Grove Associates; Honorary Master M-Man; recent president of British Mission; former Bishop of Springville Fifth Ward; a Counselor in BYU First Stake. He was named Utah's "Young Man of the Year" for 1944 by Junior Chamber of Commerce. He served as an active Republican in the Utah State Senate for two terms, was praised by both parties.

Grant is a tireless worker, ready to help in promotion of better business, education and church service. As president of UVIDA, an organization to promote industry in the Utah Valley, he meets with the prominent manufacturing leaders of the nation.

PAUL A. THORN

Born: March 7, 1905, Springville, Utah

Father: Ashel O. Thorn
Son of Joseph Ashel Thorn and Eliza Johnson
Born November 28, 1884
Died November 28, 1955—Provo, Utah (On his birthday)

Mother: Annette "Nettie" Sanford
Born December 3, 1883, Springville, Utah
Daughter of Cyrus N. Sanford and Mary Jane Hunt

Brothers: Grant S. Thorn
Born November 8, 1910—Springville, Utah—President of
British Mission and B.Y.U. Alumni Assn.
Married July 20, 1932 to Naomi Dalton in New York
Bryce L. Thorn
Born February 17, 1918, Springville, Utah
Married October 10, 1945 to Mary George in Texas

Marriage: Madge Johnson
Born April 9, 1906—Mapleton, Utah
Daughter of J. William Johnson and Henrietta Hales—
Johnsons were converts from Iceland
Married April 8, 1925 in Salt Lake Temple

Children: Robert Paul Thorn (Son)
Born March 5, 1929, Springville, Utah
Married Norma Brockbank June 4, 1952 in Salt Lake
Temple
Four Children
James A. Thorn (Son)
Born September 18, 1931, Springville, Utah
Married Karen White, May 8, 1953 in Spanish Fork—
Civil Ceremony
Four Children
June Thorn (Arbon) (Daughter)
Born January 19, 1935, Provo, Utah
Married Robert Arbon, September 5, 1955 in Salt Lake
Temple
Four Children
Louis W. Thorn (Son)
Born May 24, 1936 in Springville, Utah
Married Donna Sanford—September 11, 1959 in Spring-
ville, Utah   Divorced 1963
Two Children

Paul A. Thorn was reared in Springville, Utah and attended the Springville schools. He was best known as an excellent athlete. At ten he drove a team for his father with a plow or scraper, working on construction jobs. His grandfather, Joseph, started construction work in Springville chiefly laying down railroad track beds and bought the second automobile sold in Springville that he might get around more easily and quickly. His boys were two of the youngest drivers of autos in the state; drivers' licenses were easier to procure in those days.

Paul came to B.Y.U. in 1924 a strong fellow of nineteen. He was not long on the football field until one of the boys dubbed him "Simba", inspired by a lion motion picture of the time. And Simba he has remained up to the present. He attained All-Conference first team honors as fullback in football and starred in basketball and track. One of his opponents said of him "When Thorn hits we go with him." He married his high school sweetheart in 1925 and soon thereafter served a mission in South Africa for three years. In the early 30's he was a coach and teacher in the Springville High School, working for $1,500 a year. He was very conscious of this fact when wages were discussed and he became chairman of the Board in the Nebo School District.

In 1934 the father asked Paul and Grant, his two sons, to come in with him as partners in the growing construction business. It is in this business that the two boys have showed their caliber of leadership. The business grew and it became necessary to expand, until today the combined contracts amount to two and a half million dollars yearly. Paul is president of the Thorn Construction Co., secretary-treasurer of the Thorn Rock Product Co., president of the Superior Asphalt Paving Co., of Thorn Inc., and has a national reputation in his profession. In 1944 the Thorns purchased 100 acres of land in Provo to build a plant for ready mix and concrete, the first south of Salt Lake.

When the first stadium was built for B.Y.U. on the hillside, five Springville contractors donated heavy equipment to put the hill and field in shape for seats and gridiron in the space abutting and occupied by the present-day Richards Gymnasium.

Civic activities have filled much of Paul's non-business time as a member of the Springville Art Board, of the Springville Art Gallery, and the Springville School Board. He was obliged to change residence to Orem, Utah, for work convenience and was elected a member of the executive committee of Provo, Utah, Inc. and became active in the Provo Chamber of Commerce. He is past president of the Associated General Contractors Association, Utah Chapter, President of the Utah Manufacturers Association, and on the state and national legislature committee for the association.

It is the desire of the Thorns that the construction business be carried into the fourth generation. Paul's son Robert O. is a vice-president, Jim a superintendent and Louis W., heavy equipment operator.

When *Sports Illustrated* magazine celebrated its Silver Anniversary, it called for candidates from eighty-one universities and colleges across the land. Chosen from Utah to honor this select group of twenty-five athletes was Paul A. Thorn. Always interested and a loyal supporter of B.Y.U. growth, he has been a member of the B.Y.U. Alumni Board and for years an off-campus member of the Athletic Council. "In whatever manner I can serve B.Y.U. I am ready and willing."

OWEN MEREDITH WILSON

Born: September 21, 1909, Colonia Juarez, Chihuahua, Mexico

Father: Guy Carlton Wilson
(see his biography)

Mother: Agnes Melissa Stevens, b. September 2, 1883 in Fruitland, New Mexico, daughter of David Alma Stevens and Sariah Agnes Johnson, descendant of Deggory Priest of "Mayflower" through lineage of Abigail Elizabeth Holman, wife of Walter Stevens.
Died: March 21, 1965

Brother and Sisters: Elizabeth, b. December 13, 1902, m. John Leslie Reynolds (d. Nov. 1933) m. Gordon Sears
Guy C. Jr., b. January 3, 1905, m. Constance Quayle Cannon
David Stevens, b. June 20, 1907, m. Salonie Atwood, d. January 19, 1947
(Owen M.)
Mabel, b. Nov. 5, 1912, m. Oakley S. Evans (Vice Pres. J. C. Penney Co.)
Woodrow Stevens, b. August 21, 1915, m. Orlene Boyden

Marriage: Marian Wilson, daughter of Judge David J. Wilson of Ogden, Utah (Now Judge of U. S. Customs Court) and Mary Jacobs (also of Ogden)
In New York City (Related to her husband only by marriage)

Children: Meredith Jr.
Connie
Mary Ann
John
David
Margaret

Education:

Educated in Salt Lake schools

AB—B.Y.U. 1934; Student Body President

Graduate work at Universities of Heidelberg, London and California

Faculty, B.Y.U. 1934-42 (studied in Europe two years)

Ph.D.—University of California—History 1943—Phi Beta Kappa

University of Utah faculty, January 1943-June 1945

Associate Dean of University of Chicago, 1944-47

President of University of Oregon at Eugene, Oregon, 9th President 1953-1960

Chairman—Western Interstate Comm. for Higher Education— 8 states

Ninth President of University of Minnesota—1960-1967 the nation's fourth largest University, founded in 1817

Director of the Center for Advanced Study in Behavioral Sciences on Stanford University campus, July 1967

Civic and Government:

Secretary of the Fund for Advancement in Education 1952

Authority on American Colonial History

Delivered Milton Bennion Memorial Foundation Annual Lecture for 1961, University of Utah

Trustee—Teachers Insurance and Annuity Association and the Carnegie Foundation for the Advancement of Teaching

Chairman Association Advisory Committee of College of University Presidents

President Institute of International Education

Chairman American Council on Educators

Trustee of the Committee for the Economic Development

Serves in advisory capacity to the Business Ethics Advisory Council on the U.S. Department of Commerce, the Defense Advisory Committee on Education in the Armed Forces, U.S. Department of Defense

On U. S. National Committee for UNESCO and President's Science Advisory Committee

National Council—Boy Scouts of America

Consultant and chief lecturer on Utah Conference on Higher Education—summer 1964

Committee on White House Fellows, Pres. Johnson appointment 1964

Complimentary doctorates from:

Lewis and Clark College; Reed College; Carleton College, Macalester College; University of Utah, University of Notre Dame, University of North Dakota, College of Saint Thomas

597

National Advisory Council on Education of Disadvantaged Children, chairman, President L. B. Johnson appointment

Business:

Director Northwestern National Bank of Minneapolis
Chairman Northstar Research and Development Institute
Director Northern States Power Co.

The University of Minnesota Alumni News in October 1960 issue prints a good summary of "Met's" educational abilities:

"O. Meredith Wilson, ninth president of the University of Minnesota has been called an 'educational statesman' by one contemporary, 'the greatest thing to hit the University of Oregon campus' by an Oregon alumnus, and 'the most irreplaceable man in the entire Oregon educational systems' by a long-time member of the Oregon Board of Education. Loved and respected by Oregon faculty, students and alumni during his nearly six years as president here, he already has made his indelible mark on the University of Minnesota. Educator, administrator, historian and indefatigable speaker before any and all public and civic groups as well as gatherings of his official family, President Wilson has made his presence known in no uncertain terms— and the people love him for it."

He served an L.D.S. mission to Great Britain in 1929-31 and became interested in the British system of education.

A popular speaker before Rotary, P.T.A., educational or business groups, he never fails to advance the importance of education as a builder of men more than being the expositor of a subject or a study. Dean Charles Duncan of Minnesota states: "He is one of the top administrators who is also a scholar—he can talk knowledge with scientists, humanists and social scientists."

Always an athlete, he played varsity tennis, intramural basketball and even semi-pro baseball (as a catcher). The press of duties, frequent faculty and committee sessions have led him to golf, where he can be free of the telephone and appointments for a few hours. He plays an excellent game of golf and exercises daily. The Wilsons keep a constant "home night" for their family congeniality and Marion's tribute to her husband is noteworthy. "My husband is the most objective person I've ever met. He works completely on principle and is above personal action—and he's completely kind. Dad still helps his children yet living at home."

His spoken word, impromptu or studied is learnedly correct but not pedantic. A well turned phrase often will express a thought which other speakers take several sentences to achieve, and he has the rare ability of keeping an audience within his subject atmosphere at the exclusion of local surroundings. His mother stated that early in life he achieved what he wanted; his wants were basic and to him very important. Although he has been the chairman of funds in the millions, his own life is frugal without waste in any discernable manner. His wit is keen, often with gentle satire more common to the British speaker than the American. He is one of the most cultured gentlemen I have ever known.

Howard S. McDonald (*1945-1949*)

HOWARD S. McDONALD

Sixth President Brigham Young University and
Tenth President of Salt Lake Temple.

Born: July 18, 1894, in Holladay, Utah.

Father: Francis McDonald
Born September 17, 1851, Middleton Lintrathen, Angus, Scotland

Mother: Rosella Stevenson
Born March 31, 1865, Salt Lake City, Utah

Brothers and Sisters: Emily S. McDonald Carlisle, born September 6, 1886, Holladay, Utah, marriek to Harvey C. Carlisle

Grace S. McDonald Fillerup, born August 30, 1888, Holladay, Utah married to Albert F. Fillerup

Leona S. McDonald Smith, born February 7, 1891, Holladay, Utah. married to John Henry Smith.

Melvina S. McDonald Jeppson, born August 4, 1892, Holladay, Utah, married to Orville Jeppson*.

Howard S. McDonald, born July 18, 1894, Holladay, Utah, married to Ella Gibbs.

Louisa S. McDonald Wilson, born May 15, 1898, Holladay, Utah, married to Marion Wilson.

Helen S. McDonald Livingston, born January 24, 1900, Holladay, Utah, married to Leland V. Livingston (deceased).

Joseph S. McDonald, born June 12, 1902, Holladay, Utah, married to Evelyn May Douglas.

Stevenson McDonald, born August 15, 1904, Holladay, Utah, married to 1) Elizabeth E. Andrus (died) 2) Sylvia E. Robinson.

Ervin S. McDonald, born February 10, 1906, Holladay, Utah, Married to Ruby Zondervon.

Clara S. McDonald Duffin, born October 13, 1908, Holladay, Utah, married to Spancer Duffin.

Marriage: Ella Gibbs on September 27, 1917, of Brigham City, Utah. The daughter of Joseph and Hulda Korth Gibbs and married in the Salt Lake Temple.
Born July 5, 1894.
Died December 18, 1966.
Served an LDS Mission to the Eastern States.
Matron of the Salt Lake Temple, May 1, 1964 to death.

---

*Note: Orville Jeppson and wife Melvina M. Jeppson have given several hundred acres of land, equipment, buildings, dairy, about 600 head of dairy stock and well furnished dairy to the Brigham Young University. The land and dairy is near Rexburg, Idaho.

| Children: | Erma Ruth, married Louis B. Boyer, M.D. Born October 16, 1918, at Brigham City, Utah. |
| | Melva Fay, married Douglas H. Orgill, Ph.D. Born November 5, 1923, in Logan, Utah. |

Education:

President McDonald is one of the most successful teachers in the West. His reputation for sound leadership has taken him to California's educational centers as teacher, superintendent, executive and college president. Whether in a city school room or before a class in religion for his Church, he has a definite plan for every hour of instruction. In an interview printed in the 1954 *Instructor*, he stated: "I never go to a class unprepared, I wouldn't think of waiting until Saturday night to prepare my lesson (for a Sunday School class). I begin preparing my lessons the first time I have the class manuals in my hands. At the first of the year I read the entire course of study. By doing this I can get some perspective of the material to be used in the coming weeks and months. I can then begin preparing my lessons weeks in advance. Even so, I seldom spend less than three hours a week in getting my lesson ready for Sunday, and that is a bare minimum." As he stands before his audience you know he is prepared.

He attended Holladay Schools and graduated from the Granite High School and received his Bachelor of Science degree from Utah State Agricultural College in 1921, and remaining as an instructor in mathematics until 1924. California offered him a good position in the San Francisco schools where he continued his education and received his Master of Arts degree from the University of California in 1925. Also from this institution he obtained a Doctor of Education and in 1952 a Doctor of Humanities.

His progress in the Bay Area was rapid, going from the deanship of boys at Balboa High School in San Francisco to the directorship of teaching personnel in the San Francisco schools and in 1935 he was appointed superintendent of San Francisco public schools. At the frequent school functions his Grecian like figure stood tall and imposing in the group and teachers crowded about him to shake his friendly hand and receive his gracious smile. A call to his beloved Utah to become superintendent of the Salt Lake public schools answered a long repressed desire, a position he accepted and held from July 1, 1944 to November 14, 1945. The vigor of his program in Salt Lake again proved his leadership and made him a most popular choice for the presidency at Brigham Young University. He was inaugurated on the November date above.

War problems confronted him on every side and his extensive experience with government officials in the Bay Area pointed the way to numerous avenues of school expansion. As the veterans returned on government subsidy class rooms "bulged at the seams." Temporary buildings rose on the campus over night, class rooms, faculty officers, quarters for married students, Quonset and Butler Huts formed rows of temporary accommodating quarters. Wymount Village was erected to house 200 married veterans and 350 single veterans, Knight-Mangum Hall, a woman's dormitory, was completed, with Social Hall to follow. The superb Eyring Science Center was begun and almost completed. The original plans for the Field House were changed chiefly by President McDonald to double the first proposed capacity. The Speech Department with its Little Theatre and two rooms in College Hall was transferred onto the hill into four connecting Butler Huts with sloped floors and KBYU had its first adequate quarters. New tennis courts were built and the stadium enlarged. A modern heating plant was installed.

California authorities continued to seek the services of President McDonald and a great challenge was offered to him to return. On October 30, 1949, he left Brigham Young University and accepted the position as President of Los Angeles City College and Los Angeles State College of Applied Arts and Sciences, with millions of dollars to let for contracts to plan and build a new campus and reshape another. Hours of work with committees, politicians, civic workers, state and local school authorities almost broke his health. But he joyed in the daily progress of the important educational center. Also started the San Fernando State College. Three colleges with over 20,000 enrollments in each built by Pres. McDonald.

When he retired in 1962, he accepted the appointment as regional representative of the U.S. Office of Education for the Pacific Region, a position he filled with distinction until his appointment as president of the Salt Lake Temple by the First Presidency of the LDS Church on May 1st 1964.

Paralleling his life of 44 years in education in his church devotion. His advancement in the priesthood has been consistent with his age and he honored a mission call to the Eastern States from October 28, 1914 to November 20, 1916 being president of the West Pennsylvania Conference from November 22, 1915 to November 20, 1916. He was an officer in Young Men Mutual Improvement Association in Logan, Utah, and president of the San Francisco Stake YMMIA. Sunday School Superintendent in Berkeley, California. He was made president of the San Francisco Stake from 1941-43 and an alternate member of the East Provo Stake High Council 1947-1949.

603

His record in Scouting is equally impressive. He was Scout Master for Troop 7 in Berkeley, California, a member of the Executive Board Boy Scouts of America, San Francisco, Area Council 1940-44, of the Salt Lake Council 1944-45 and of the Utah National Parks Council, Provo, Utah, 1945-49. Scout commissioner in Cache Valley Council.

He served in the U.S. Army in World War I, was active in the Provo Chamber of Commerce, a member of the American Association of School Administrations, vice president of the Utah Society for Physical Handicapped Children, president of the California School Masters, an active Rotarian and a member of the Knife and Fork Club.

His beloved wife, Ella has been his intimate companion from the day of his marriage in 1917 to her death in December of 1966. Many Temple workers often have commented "What a handsome couple." They were beloved by all who ever knew them.

President McDonald has spent his life in service to others, makes new friends each day as president of the great Temple, finds time to aid in civic causes, writes for church magazines and looks confidently to the future of our government and the spread of Christian principles throughout the world.

Ernest L. Wilkinson (*Jan. 1, 1951—Jan. 9, 1964*)

The faculty and administrative officers working with President Wilkinson are one of the strongest academic groups in the educational world. His abbreviated biography has been written on pages 506-513. Many of the present faculty, added since his coming, have achieved national reputations in their respective fields; buildings have been erected which set a world pattern for utility, excellence, and beauty.

The outstanding gifts received during his presidency attest further to his administrative abilities. A report on his tenure and faculty achievements should follow this volume at the first appropriate time.

Principal:

Warren N. Dusenberry	November 22, 1875	April 15, 1876
Karl G. Maeser	April 24, 1876	January 4, 1892

Presidents:

Benjamin Cluff Jr.	January 4, 1892	December 23, 1903
Geoge H. Brimhall	April 16, 1904	July 1, 1921
Franklin S. Harris	July 1, 1921	January 30, 1945
Howard S. McDonald	July 1, 1945	October 30, 1949
Ernest L. Wilkinson	January 1, 1951	January 9, 1964
Ernest L. Wilkinson	Reappointed January 4, 1965	

Acting Presidents:

L. John Nuttall	1926-1927
E. H. Holt	1929
Christen Jensen	1939-1940 and 1949-1951
Earl C. Crockett	1964

INDEX